The Ethiopian Borderlands

Essays in
Regional History from
Ancient Times to
The End of the 18th Century

The Ethiopian Borderlands

Essays in Regional History from Ancient Times to The End of the 18th Century

Richard Pankhurst

The Red Sea Press, Inc.
Publishers & Distributors of Third World Books

11-D Princess Road   P. O. Box 48
Lawrenceville, NJ 08648   Asmara, ERITREA

The Red Sea Press, Inc.
Publishers & Distributors of Third World Books

11-D Princess Road   P. O. Box 48
Lawrenceville, NJ 08648   Asmara, ERITREA

Copyright © 1997 Richard Pankhurst

All rights reserved. No part of this publication may be reproduced, stored in a retrieval system or transmitted in any form or by any means electronic, mechanical, photocopying, recording or otherwise without the prior permission of the publisher.

Book design: Ghetahun Seyoum
Cover design: Linda Nickens
Cover illustration: King Motalämé presenting Saint Täklä Haymanot with gold, in thanks for allowing him to use his baptismal name: a much later Ethiopian painting of Gondarine time.

Library of Congress Cataloging-in-Publication Data
Pankhurst, Richard.
    The Ethiopian borderlands : essays in regional history from ancient times to the end of the 18th century / Richard Pankhurst.
        p. cm.
    Includes bibliographical references.
    ISBN 0-932415-18-0 (cloth : alk. paper). -- ISBN 0-932415-19-9 (pbk. : alk. paper)
    1. Ethiopia--History--To 1490. 2. Ethiopia--History--1490-1889. I. Title.
DT383.P35   1997
963--dc21   97-10205
                                                   CIP

Contents

INTRODUCTION ix

Part I. ANCIENT TIMES (c.3500 BC - 523 AD) 1

1. THE NORTH: The Land of Punt, Ophir, and the Red Sea Coast 3
2. THE NORTH and NORTH-EAST: The Aksumite Kingdom and the Afar Depression 18
3. THE WEST and SOUTH-WEST: The Béja, the Bareya Country and Sasu 26
4. THE BORDERLANDS and THE INTERIOR 31

Part II. THE EARLY MEDIEVAL PERIOD (c.890 -1454) 35

5. THE NORTH: The Land of the Bahr Nägash 37
6. THE EAST: Ifat and Adäl. 39
7. THE NORTH-EAST: The Afar Country 61
8. THE SOUTH-EAST and SOUTH: Fätägar, Däwaro, Aräbabni, Bali, Shärkha, Darha and Harär 68
9. THE SOUTH-WEST and WEST: Guragé, Wäj, Kämbata and Wälamo, Gämo, Hadeya, Gänz, Enarya, Bosha, Damot, Gafat, Janjero, Käfa, and the Countries of the Bareyas and "Shanqellas" 75
10. THE BORDERLANDS and THE INTERIOR 93

Part III. THE ERA OF ZAR'A YAQ'OB AND
LEBNA DENGEL (1433-1540) 99

11. THE NORTH and NORTH-EAST: The Land of
    the Bahr Nägash, the Afar Country, and
    the Country of the Dobe'as...........................101
12. THE EAST: Ifat and Adäl................................113
13. THE SOUTH-EAST and SOUTH: Fätägar,
    the Country of the Mayas, Däwaro, Bali,
    and "Galla"..130
14. THE SOUTH-WEST and WEST: Guragé,
    Wäj, Gänz, Gämo, Hadeya, Damot, Enarya,
    Gafat, Bizamo, the Country of the Gämbos,
    Käfa, and the Country of the Bareyas 138
15. THE BORDERLANDS and THE INTERIOR.........156

Part IV. THE ERA OF IMAM AHMAD (1526-1545)....163

16. THE SOUTH-EAST and SOUTH: Adäl, Däwaro,
    Fätägar, the Countries of the Mayas and
    Dobe'as, Ifat, Bali, Shärka, and Därha 165
17. THE SOUTH-WEST and WEST: Wäj, Guragé,
    Hadeya, Gämo, Gänz, Wälamo (or Wolaita),
    Kämbata, Enarya, Damot, Gafat, Käfa,
    Mazäga, and the Country of the Hamajs
    and Bareyas..204
18. THE NORTH: The Country of the Bahr Nägash.....218
19. THE BORDERLANDS and THE INTERIOR. 221

Part V. THE ERA OF GALAWDEWOS and
SARSA DENGEL (1540-1606) 231
20. THE NORTH and NORTH-EAST: The
Country of the Bahr Nägash, and the Land
of the Afars 233
21. THE SOUTH-EAST and SOUTH: Däwaro and
Fätägar, Wäj, Adäl, Harar, and Bali. 241
22. THE SOUTH-WEST and WEST: Guragé,
Enarya, Wägäm, Gumär and Bosha, Damot,
Gafat, Hadeya, Bizamo, the Country of the
Gämbos, Käfa, Konch or Konta, and the
Countries of the Dobe'as, Shinashas and Bäläyas. ... 250
23. THE BORDERLANDS and THE INTERIOR 269

Part VI. THE OROMO MIGRATION and
THE GONDARINE MONARCHY (1522-1800) 277

24. THE GREAT OROMO MIGRATION 279
25. THE SOUTH: Bali, Däwaro, Fätägar, Wäj, Ifat,
and the Country of the Mayas 324
26. THE SOUTH-WEST and WEST: Gämo, Guragé
and Wäj, Hadeya, Kämbata, Enarya, Damot,
Gafat, Bizamo, the Country of the Gämbos,
Janjero, Käfa, the Countries of the "Shanqellas",
Gongas and Dobe'as, and the Senaar frontier 327
27. THE EAST: Adäl, Harär, and Awssa 373
28. THE NORTH: The Land of the Afars, the
Country of the Bahr Nägash, and Massawa 383
29. THE BORDERLANDS and THE INTERIOR 418
30. CONCLUSIONS 431

HISTORICAL TABLES 445
BIBLIOGRAPHY 451
INDEX 469

INTRODUCTION

Historical studies of Ethiopia, like those of other countries, often tend to concentrate on events at or near the centre of political power, and devote far too little attention to other areas. Concentration on the interior is intensified in the Ethiopian case by the imbalance of archaeological and literary sources, which are infinitely richer for the centre of the country than for the borderlands, particularly those to the south and west.

The present very tentative account attempts at least in part to redress the balance by shifting attention to the "peripheral" regions, which, though of central importance to their own inhabitants, tend to receive relatively little attention in studies of the Ethiopian region as a whole. The coverage of such areas in these pages is, however, also unbalanced, for it reflects the geographically very unequal availability of sources. The attention accorded to different places at different times is thus based less on their actual importance than on the historical records at our disposal. It seemed more useful to present such data as is available for each area more or less as it stands rather than to compress or expand it in accordance with any imposed schema which would doubtless also be fairly arbitrary.

The nature of the sources has also greatly influenced the subject matter covered. Most Ethiopian chronicles and other historical documents, both Christian and Muslim, are largely preoccupied with war. The story they tell, and which thus finds its way into these pages, thus often focuses on bloodshed and rapine rather than on the more significant events of everyday life for which data is often sadly lacking. Where information on such matters is available it has, however, been presented in detail.

***

There can, however, be no denying the importance, and destructiveness, of war in the period under discussion, which extends to the end of the eighteenth century. The battles of this time, irrespective of their rights and wrongs as seen by their protagonists, were often most debilitating. Religious conflicts, though ostensibly fought for the highest motives, were no exception. The great migrations, though later a source of pride or nostalgia for the survivors' descendants, were often accompanied by much fighting and numerous casualties.

THE ETHIOPIAN BOARDERLANDS

The picture of warfare here presented is inevitably often one-sided, for we have been obliged to rely on the historical records available from one side or another. Seldom are sources available simultaneously from both sides. A one-sided account, we may argue, is, nevertheless, better than no account at all.

Traditional Ethiopian armies in the period under review differed from those of modern times, in that they had neither pay nor rations, let alone any commissariat system of supply. Such armies, irrespective of their origin, and whether composed of highlanders or lowlanders, Christians, Muslims, or animists, lived in large measure on the lands through which they passed. This resulted willy nilly in extensive looting, which took place in the soldiers' own homeland and the lands through which they passed, no less than in those with which they were at war. Some of the fiercest fighting of this period was between territories of the borderlands and those in the central highlands, but no less violent conflicts were waged among the states on the periphery themselves, as well as by rival contenders for control of the interior. This unsatisfactory, and often tragic, situation was brought to an end only by military reforms, based on the principle of a paid army, first conceived in the second half of the nineteenth century by Emperor Téwodros II, and haltingly introduced a generation later by Emperor Menilek. Peace in the last analysis was made possible only by the eventual unification of the whole area.

The movement, and above all the quartering, of troops throughout much of the country over the centuries was, on the other hand, also an integrating factor. It led in various areas, perhaps most noticeably in Ifat in the east as well as in the Oromo-occupied territories of the south, to considerable ethnic intermarriage, and hence to the extensive cultural assimilation of peoples.

Fighting in the period under review was almost invariably accompanied not only by killing and destruction, but also by the extensive capture of slaves, which led to no small loss of lives and property. Slaves, if not exported, were for the most part assimilated by the victors, and thus led to a great further inter-blending of peoples and cultures.

***

The historical picture, though at times overshadowed by conflict, is at the same time, as we shall see, one of considerable regional interdependence. The great migration movements of our period, from

Introduction

Aksum southwards in ancient times, from Shäwa eastwards in the medieval period, from Adäl westwards during the time of Imam Ahmäd ibn Ibrahim, today better known as Grañ, in the sixteenth century, and the subsequent northward Oromo migration, all involved the periphery virtually as much as the central provinces. The most important struggles of the period, notably those between Sultan Sabr ad-Din II of Ifat and Emperor 'Amdä Seyon, and later between Imam Ahmäd and Emperors Lebnä Dengel and Gälawdéwos, were likewise fought for the domination of the entire Ethiopian region, including the borderlands, no less than the interior. Several locally based rebellions, among them that of Bahr Nägash Yeshaq, in the far north of the country, were likewise undertaken not for separation, but for control of central political power.

***

The region, though consisting at first sight of innumerable largely self-sufficient communities, was at the same time a single economic and in a general sense also a cultural unit inter-linked by many important trade routes upon which the economy and welfare of the whole area depended. These routes embraced the borderlands just as much as the interior. The south-western periphery was thus a major source of gold, ivory, civet - and slaves. The north-east provided rock-salt, which served as "primitive money" throughout much of the region. The eastern lowlands yielded valuable incense of all kinds. The northern and eastern borderlands moreover possessed the Red Sea and Gulf of Aden ports through which the products of the interior were exported, and manufactured goods were imported, while the western borderlands were traversed by trade-routes which likewise handled a sizable export-import trade.

Such inter-regional trade was important not only commercially, but also politically, for it was very largely from the exports of the borderlands of the south-west that the states of the interior paid for their fire-arms, which were imported through the borderlands to the north and east, as well as to a limited extent through those to the west. These latter borderlands in their turn were heavily dependent on the trade of the interior.

Inter-dependency found expression in the movement of caravans and itinerant traders upon whom virtually all long-distance commerce was based. Merchants thus traversed virtually the entire region, linking the periphery with the interior. There were likewise countless markets, great and small, where goods from one area were sold in another, and where peoples of two or more areas met, and exchanged their wares.

The historic inter-connection of the region was further strengthened by other movements of population, which involved the borderlands no less than the interior. Early Syrian Christian missionaries arriving in the northern periphery made their way southwards to establish monasteries further inland, while Ethiopian monks from the Christian highlands later proceeded southwards, eastwards and westwards to evangelise other areas. Christian pilgrims from the interior also travelled to the northern and western borderlands on the way to Jerusalem. Innumerable Muslim religious leaders moved inland from the coast to convert the interior to Islam, while many others from the interior made their way through the eastern periphery as pilgrims to Mecca.

Governmental links, as emphasised in these pages, were also often widely embracing. Chiefs and officials on the periphery were frequently appointed by the emperors of the interior, while many rulers or governors of the borderlands travelled inland to have their status confirmed. There were moreover numerous dynastic and other marriages, many of which transcended ethnic and linguistic and others even religious differences. Emissaries from the periphery also brought to the capital inland tribute of all kinds, while others travelled there in search of appointment or justice. Many persons from the borderlands were furthermore recruited by the rulers of the interior, whose inter-ethnic armies frequently fought in the periphery as well as in the central parts of the region.

***

Grateful thanks are due to friends and colleagues without whom this volume could not have been prepared. One of my greatest debts is to my friend Denis Gérard, an expert photographer in Addis Ababa, who generously provided virtually all the photographs here reproduced. Photographs of Awash caves were kindly supplied by Professor Georges Fonteret, and of a Harari coin by Ahmed Zacharia, of the Institute of Ethiopian Studies museum. The photograph of the popular Ethiopian painting of Imam Ahmad ibn Ibraham al-Ghazi (Grañ) in the museum was taken by another skilled photographer in Addis Ababa, Marie Chordi.

PART I

ANCIENT TIMES

(c. 3500 BC-523 AD)

Chapter 1

THE NORTH: THE LAND OF PUNT, OPHIR, AND THE RED SEA COAST

THE LAND OF PUNT

Early Commercial Contacts with Egypt

The Red Sea and Gulf of Aden coast of Africa was situated beside one of the world's earliest maritime trade routes, which linked Egypt and subsequently the countries of the Mediterranean with Arabia, India, and the Far East. The coastal areas of Ethiopia in Pharaonic times formed part of what the ancient Egyptians termed the Land of Punt, and sometimes God's Land. This territory has sometimes been considered an undelineated stretch of territory along the Red Sea and Gulf of Aden shores of both Africa and Arabia. Careful scrutiny of the articles obtained from Punt, would, however, "appear to speak clearly", as the modern British Egyptologist K.A. Kitchen says, for an African Punt, and to exclude an Asian one.[1]

The Land of Punt was commercially important for the goods it provided to Egypt, and, more generally, to the outside world. The bulk of these exports originated in the interior of what later became known as Ethiopia and the Horn of Africa. Such articles were brought to the coast by ancient trade routes linking the Red Sea and Gulf of Aden coast with the economically more productive hinterland.

Egyptian inscriptions and pictorial reliefs dating from early times indicate the objects which the Land of Punt supplied to the Pharaohs. Such goods included gold, doubtless from the Ethiopian interior, ivory and panther and other skins, which could have come from almost anywhere in the region, and myrrh, myrrh-trees, and ostrich feathers, probably originating in the African coastal belt. In return for these and other similar goods the Egyptians sent hatchets, daggers and necklaces, known later to have been in great demand among the local population in the Afar country and elsewhere.

Most Egyptian inscriptions and reliefs concentrate on the activities of the Pharaonic state. They have little to say about ordinary

---

[1] Kitchen (1971), p. 185.

commercial transactions, and do little to set them in their Puntite perspective. Relations between the two countries, or regions, are thus depicted as a series of heroic achievements by Egyptian rulers - though these were in fact part of a two-way process involving trade on both sides. Egyptian evidence, though one-sided, is nevertheless of major importance, for it affords us our first brief, but valuable, glimpses of foreign trade in this part of the ancient world.

In considering the location of the Land of Punt it may be argued that though the term may have been used by the Egyptians to cover a vast extent of territory on both sides of the Red Sea and Gulf of Aden, the area on the African side was the more important. It was there that large quantities of gold, ivory and myrrh could most easily be obtained. It may further be urged that the northernmost area, what is now the Eritrean coast, probably constituted the most frequently visited African section of Punt. The area's northerly location, and consequent relative proximity to Egypt, would have given its trade a significant edge over that of more distant areas, such as the Somali country.

Time, it should be emphasised, was of the essence. The Trade Winds dictated that ships from Egypt, sailing at perhaps 30 miles a day,[2] had to travel during the three or so summer months, June to August, when the wind blew southwards, and had to complete their trading enterprise, doubtless no rapid affair, by November, when the winter winds began to blow in the opposite direction. Southbound vessels probably needed about a month to reach the northern Eritrean area, about the same time again to arrive at the coast opposite Aden, and a further month to reach Cape Guardafui. The southerly winds would by then be abating. It would therefore appear doubtful whether Egyptian commercial navigators could have easily sailed much further in the time permitted to them by nature.

The northern area, because of its location, would likewise have been the most convenient part of the Puntite region for Egyptians travelling by land to reach.

Earliest Contacts

The first known contacts between Egypt and Punt date back almost to the cradle of Egyptian civilisation. Pharaonic records reveal that as early as the First or Second Dynasties (3407-2888 BC) the Egyptians

---

[2] Kitchen (1971), pp. 196-202

were in possession of myrrh, one of the most prized products of the Ethiopian or Horn of African region. This area, as J.H. Breasted, the American historian of ancient Egypt, observed, soon became the source of fragrant gums and incense "indispensable in the life of the oriental". Slaves from Punt were probably also obtained at around the same period, for during the Fourth Egyptian dynasty (2789-2767 BC) a Puntite slave is mentioned as having been in the service of a son of Cheops, the builder of the Great Pyramid.

Supplies from Punt, Breasted assumes, probably first reached Egypt by an overland route which would doubtless have taken them down the Blue Nile and Atbara rivers, to the Upper Nile. This long land route was, however, far from satisfactory, for the Egyptians, to judge from later evidence, probably had difficulties with intermediary peoples, who would have attempted to levy their own, possibly exorbitant, taxes on the trade.[3]

Such obstacles to commerce were in all probability a major consideration causing King Sahure (2708-2697 BC) of the Fifth Dynasty to attempt direct sailings to Punt. An inscription of his reign records that his fleet returned with 80,00 undefined measures of myrrh, 6,000 of "electrum" and 2,600 staves of some costly local wood. The term "electrum" poses a problem. The word was usually employed for an alloy of gold and silver, but in the context of imports from Ethiopia and/or the Red Sea area probably referred to pure gold, which alone was widely available there, or else to a natural mixture of gold and silver as found in some colloidal amalgams in the region.[4]

Further expeditions by land and sea followed. After one of the former King Pepy II (2573-2554 BC) of the Sixth Dynasty noted that he had received a Tenq, or small-boned slave, from the Land of Punt, whom he said that he liked better than all "the tribute of Punt". The term "tribute" must not be taken literally, for it was merely a Pharaonic way of referring to goods imported for barter or exchange.

Expeditions to Punt were largely based on the town of Elephantine on the Nile in Upper Egypt. Since this settlement had no direct access to the Red Sea its inhabitants travelled by land to one of the Red Sea harbours, such as Koseir or Leucos Limen, from which they sailed southwards to Punt.[5]

---

[3] Breasted (1905), p. 127.
[4] Maspero (1889), p. 304; Jelenc (1966). p. 137.
[5] Breasted (1905), p. 142.

The rise of ancient Egypt coincided, it may be noted, with a great expansion of Red Sea and Gulf of Aden trade. The subsequent Hykos invasion of Egypt, and the resultant disturbances, led to a decline in Egyptian trade with Punt, and the silting up of the canal between the Red Sea and the Nile. Puntite-Egyptian contacts were, however, soon to rise to unexpected levels.[7]

Queen Hatshepsut's Reliefs and Inscriptions

The founding of the new Egyptian Kingdom, around 1600 BC, was followed by the resumption of sailings from Egypt to Punt. By far the best known, though not necessarily the largest, of these expeditions was dispatched by Queen Hatshepsut (1501-1479 BC), probably around 1495 BC. It travelled down the Nile, through a canal passing by way of Wadi Tumilat to the Red Sea, as recorded in inscriptions and reliefs on the walls of the queen's famous temple of Dar el-Bahri at Thebes. These reliefs, which Breasted considered "as beautiful in execution as they are important in content", constitute veritable archives in stone, and provide the most detailed account of Puntite foreign trade ever produced.

The temple contains ten major reliefs, each accompanied by important hieroglyphic inscriptions.

The first relief illustrates the expedition's departure from Egypt. The fleet consists of five vessels, three of which are seen under sail, and two still moored. An inscription notes that the ships are "sailing in the sea" towards the Land of Punt, which is also referred to as "God's-Land". A further caption makes the official Pharaonic claim that the expedition had been commanded by the lord of the gods, Amon, lord of Thebes, in order to bring him the "marvels" of Punt.

The second relief depicts the expedition's safe arrival at Punt. On the right the king's messenger advances at the head of a group of soldiers, who are described as an "army" - an indication that the Egyptian party was at least well guarded. Piles of necklaces, hatchets and daggers - presumably articles of trade or gifts from Egypt - lie in front of the envoy. The name of the chief, or ruler, of Punt is given as "Perehu", which in view of the vagaries of transliteration need not be taken too precisely. He is seen advancing from the left, followed by a corpulent wife, called "Eti". She is accompanied by their children, two sons and a daughter, and three other individuals, who are driving

---

[7] Breasted (1905), pp. 183-4, 256, 276. See also Vycichl (1957), pp. 71-2.

a donkey, which is said to have carried the wife. In the background we see the Puntite landscape, in which there are a number of conical houses apparently set on poles, surrounded by trees. Behind is a strip of water, suggesting that the scene is near the sea or by some river in which the Pharoanic vessels have anchored.

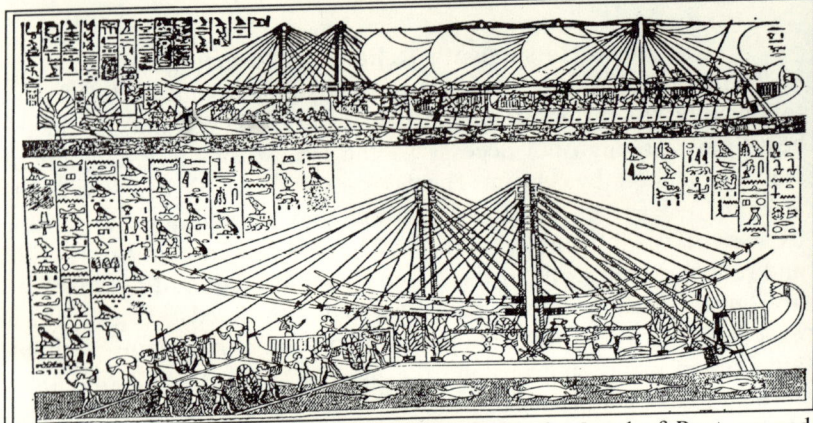

Egyptian Queen Hatshepsut's boats trading with the Land of Punt, around 1495 BC., from a series of reliefs at the temple of Thebes in Upper Egypt. The upper picture depicts the departure of the vessels from Egypt; the lower, vessels being loaded at the Land of Punt with myrrh trees and other goods bound for Egypt.
From J.H. Breasted, <u>A History of Egypt</u>.

The Egyptian articles depicted undoubtably represent trade goods or gifts, but the inscriptions, designed to glorify the Egyptian queen, seek to present them very differently. They are described as "every good thing", sent by the Egyptian court for the goddess Hathor, "mistress of Punt, for the sake of the life, prosperity, and health of her majesty". The Puntites welcoming the Egyptians are likewise said to be "doing obeisance, with bowed head, to receive this army of the King", and to "give praise" to the Egyptian lord of lords Amon-Re".

Another block of hieroglyphics, over the Puntites, attempts to flatter Hatshepsut by suggesting that no previous Egyptian expedition had been seen, at least in that area, within living memory. The inhabitants are thus made to declare, "Why have ye come thither to this land, which the people [i.e. the Egyptians] know not? Did ye come down upon the ways of heaven, or did ye sail upon the waters, upon the seas of God's Land?"

The third relief provides a glimpse of the trade, which, we are told, had been conducted "in the myrrh-terraces of Punt on the side of the sea". To the right is a tent described as belonging to the "king's messenger", who stands in front of it. Beside him are the products of Punt, and, approaching from the left, is the chief of Punt with his wife. A long line of Puntites behind them can be seen carrying goods.

Nearby inscriptions again attempt to describe events not in terms of two-way commerce, but as one-way tax-collection. A text in front of the Puntites declares that their chief has come "bearing tribute at the side of the sea", while another by the Egyptians claims that the scene depicts the "reception of the tribute of Punt, by the King's messenger". That the relationship was based on mutual hospitality is, however, evident from a further passage. It states that the Egyptian tent had been pitched "in order to receive the chiefs of the country", who were provided with "bread, beer, wine, meat, fruit, everything found in Egypt", as "commanded in the court".

The fourth relief is devoted to the loading of the vessels for the return journey. Two boats are heavily laden with myrrh trees, sacks, probably of myrrh, elephant tusks, and large apes, while men carry further sacks and trees on gang-planks from the mainland. A solicitous passage above the porters exclaims, "[Look to] your feet, ye people! Behold! The load is heavy", and adds, "Prosperity [be] with [us], for the sake of the myrrh trees in the midst of God's Land, for the house of Amon".

An inscription over the vessels reading, "the loading of the ships very heavily with marvels of the country of Punt", provides an informative account of the articles obtained. They are listed as comprising "all goodly fragrant woods of God's-Land, heaps of myrrh-resin, with fresh myrrh-trees, with ebony and pure ivory, with green gold of Emu, with cinnamon wood, *khesyt* wood, with *ihmut*-incense, *sonter*-incense, eye-cosmetic, with apes, monkeys, dogs, and with skins of the southern panther, with natives and their children." A final sentence, once again designed to praise the queen, concludes: "Never was brought the like of this for any king who was since the beginning".

The fifth relief depicts the return of the Egyptian ships, three of them under full sail. An inscription states that they were "journeying to Thebes with joy in their heart", and were accompanied by chiefs of

Punt. It is further claimed, once again to honour Hatshepsut, that because of the greatness of the fame of the revered god, Amon-Re, lord of Thebes, the expedition had carried back "marvels of Punt", the like of which had not been brought for any previous monarch.

The sixth relief, designed to further demonstrate Hatshepsut's power and benevolence, portrays the presentation in Egypt of the supplies from Punt. The queen, on the right, is approached by two lines of men bearing the goods, four rows of kneeling chiefs, and behind them Egyptians and Puntites with myrrh-trees and other articles from the latter's country. An inscription asserts that the chiefs from Punt, as well as others from Nubia are "doing obeisance with bowed head, bearing their tribute". (This was the first mention of Nubia, some of whose gold may in fact have come from what is now Ethiopia's western borderlands). A passage over the Puntite chiefs declares, "They say as they pray for the peace from her majesty, 'Hail to thee, King of Egypt, Re, who shines like the sun, your sovereign, mistress of heaven.... Thy name reaches as far as the circuit of heaven'".

The seventh relief, which also has much to say about Puntite trade, shows the queen offering gifts to Amon. She stands on the left with products of Punt and Nubia before her. An inscription states that this is a "presentation of the marvels of Punt, the treasures of God's-Land", and "gifts of the countries of the South", to Amon, lord of Thebes, that the queen "may live" and her heart "be joyful". Several captions provide additional information on the articles presented, though which originated in Punt and which in Nubia is not always specified. Beside a group of gifts there is a note stating that they comprised "electrum; eye-cosmetic; throw sticks of the Puntites; ebony; ivory; and shells". A picture of a large creature is labelled "a southern panther, alive, captured for her majesty". A final passage refers to the arrival of "electrum, many panther-skins, and 3,000 [small cattle]". The latter were apparently too numerous to have come by boat, and were therefore probably part of the "tribute" from Nubia.

The eighth relief, a continuation of the preceding, is devoted to the weighing and measuring of the above imports. A triumphant inscription describes the scene as "taking the measure" of the "electrum" and the "measuring of the fresh myrrh-trees", for Amon. The text describes this as "the first of the harvest" of the "marvels of Punt", and states that the god Thoth was recording the information in writing, and Sefkhet, God of Letters, was counting in numbers.

Hatshepsut, it is claimed, took an active part in the proceedings. An ecstatic passage observes: "Her majesty herself is acting with both hands, the best of myrrh is upon all her limbs, her fragrance is divine dew, her odour is mingled with Punt, her skin is gilded with electrum, shining as do the stars in the midst of the festive-hall, before the whole land". The entire people are said to have praised the queen "in her divine qualities, because of the greatness of the marvels which have happened to her. Never", the text concludes, "did the like happen under any gods who were here before, since the beginning. May she be given life, like Re, forever".

Elsewhere on the picture two huge piles, one of them higher than a man, and captioned "heaps of myrrh in great quantities", are being scooped into measures by four men. This is explained by a note, which says, "measuring the fresh myrrh, in great quantities, for Amon, lord of Thebes; marvels of the countries of Punt, treasures of God's-Land". A fifth man, referred to as the scribe and steward Thutiy, is keeping records for the queen, while the god Thoth, extreme left, performs a similar office for Amon. An enthusiastic nearby caption exclaims, with numerical sophistication, that the deity is "reckoning the numbers, summing up in millions, hundreds of thousands, tens of thousands, thousands, and hundreds".

The relief also depicts a huge pair of scales, one side of which contains gold in large rings, and the other weights in the form of cows. Beside the scales are piles of the precious metal in bars and rings, with a caption reading, "weighing the gold and electrum, the impost of the southern countries for Amon-Re". The reference to "southern countries" rather than to Punt would suggest that these supplies had come from Nubia, probably by land, rather than from the latter area by sea. The weighing operation is presided over by the god Horus, and another deity, Dedun of Nubia, whose presence seems to confirm the metal's Sudanese origin.

The ninth relief, which throws further light on contacts between Egypt and the Land of Punt, reports the queen's announcement to Amon of the success of her expedition. She stands at the extreme left, staff in hand, before the god who is enthroned on the right. A long inscription enunciates the official claim that Amon had been responsible for the expedition, and adds: "A command was heard from the great throne, an oracle of the god himself, that the ways of Punt should be searched out, that the highways to the myrrh terraces should be penetrated". It was done, we are told, "according to all that the majesty of this revered god commanded, according to the desire of her majesty, in order that she may be given life, stability, and satisfaction, like Re, forever". Amon is quoted as speaking to the queen affectionately as her "sweet daughter", and "favourite", and saying to her, "I have given to thee all Punt as far as the land of God's-Land". Elaborating on this statement the god declares that the area visited by the expedition was "a glorious region of God's-Land", and adds, "it is indeed my place of delight. I have made it for myself, in order to [divert] my heart... They took myrrh as they wished, they loaded the vessels to their hearts' content, with fresh myrrh trees, every good gift of this country, Puntites whom the people know not, Southerners of God's-Land... They have brought all the marvels, every beautiful thing of God's-Land, for which thy majesty sent them: heaps of gum and myrrh, and enduring trees bearing fresh myrrh... May thy majesty cause them to grow!".

The tenth, and final, relief depicts Hatshepsut reporting to her court on the successful outcome of the expedition. She is enthroned on the left of a splendid kiosk, with three nobles before her. The foremost courtier is described as "the hereditary prince, count, wearer of the royal seal, sole companion, chief treasurer, Nehsi", who had been commanded "to dispatch the army [to] Punt". An inscription which states that the expedition was undertaken in the ninth year of the reign, reproduces a speech by the queen to the grandees and companions of the court, in which she once more asserts that Amon had commanded her "to send to the myrrh-terraces, to explore his ways [for him], to learn his circuit, to open the highways", and states that the myrrh-trees had accordingly "been taken up in God's-Land, and set in the ground [of Egypt]... for the king of the gods".[8]

The above ten reliefs and inscriptions all in all provide revealing evidence on the scope of "Puntite" trade, and the importance the Egyptian queen attached to it. Most of the articles depicted or referred to, most notably the gold, as well as two animals, the giraffe and the rhinoceros, were of undoubted African origin, and must almost certainly have come from the Ethiopian region.[9] The exception was cinnamon, which did not grow in the area, and then, as in later millennia, probably constituted a coastal re-export from the East,

---

[8] Neville (1894); Breasted (1962), II, 102-26. See also Maspero (1879), pp. 10-26; Budge (1902) IV, 6-10.

[9] See especially the discussion in Kitchen (1971). pp.185-9.

perhaps India, Ceylon or Java. The inscriptions are also interesting in that they indicate not insignificant "Puntite" involvement - as manifested by the Puntite chiefs' reception of the Egyptians; the erection by the latter of a tent in which to provide hospitality for the Puntites; and, even more important, the voyage of the latter all the way to Thebes.

Hatshepsut's claims as to the uniqueness of the enterprise cannot, however, be accepted uncritically, for the enterprise was probably no more than the best recorded of a series of such operations, not a few of which may indeed have passed unrecorded. It is well to remember the warning of the Swedish historian Torgny Säve-Söderberg, that "many, or even perhaps most" of the Pharaohs dispatched expeditions to Punt, and that almost each of them tried to claim that he was the first to do so. Hatshepsut's expedition, he argues, was therefore perhaps "hardly to be regarded as of especial importance".[10]

Support for this view is found in the fact that Hatshepsut's brother, Thutmose III (1479-1447 BC), dispatched yet another expedition to Punt. It returned, according to an inscription, in the thirty-third year of the reign, i.e. around 1446 BC, with various "marvels" of the country. They included a large quantity of "dried myrrh", as well as 1,685 *heket* (or over 223 bushels) of gold, 134 slaves, male and female, 114 oxen and cattle, and 305 bulls, beside an undefined quantity of ivory, ebony, panther skins, and "every good thing of this country".[11]

All this points to the conclusion that the Land of Punt was confronted not by a single expedition dispatched by Hatshepsut, but by a series of sailings, which must have had an important on-going influence on the commerce of the entire region.

Later Pharaonic Inscriptions - and the Arrival of Puntite Boats in Egypt

Though the Egyptian inscriptions were almost exclusively concerned with Pharaonic participation in the trade of Punt there are indications that the Puntites, within at least half a century of Hatshepsut's great Red Sea enterprise, were engaged in commercial voyages on their own account. Testimony to this is found in an unknown Egyptian official's tomb at Thebes believed to date from the reign of King Amenhotep II (1447-1420 BC).

---

[10] Säve-Söderberg (1942), p. 29.

[11] Breasted (1905), p. 305.

This tomb contains several interesting reliefs. One depicts the presentation to an unidentified Pharaoh of various articles from Punt, including gold, incense, ebony trees, ostrich feathers and eggs, skins, oxen, and antelopes(?). These goods were reportedly brought by "chiefs of Punt", two of whom are seen kneeling in front of the Egyptian monarch.

Perhaps the most interesting feature of the relief, however, is the representation of two small Puntite sailing vessels. Their presence, as the archaeologist N. de Garis Davies has argued, reveals for the first time that the people of Punt were themselves making long sea journeys. Discussing these voyages he comments that the commerce revealed in Hatshepsut's inscriptions seems to have been continued, in part at least, by Puntite vessels which brought their freight to an Egyptian port, probably near Koseir, where the Egyptians met them and bartered their manufactures for such produce as the Puntites had been able to transport.

The precise character of the Puntite vessels cannot unfortunately be established from the relief. Their hulls, Davies remarks, are depicted as "bolster-like shapes, rounded at both ends", and, like the background, coloured pink. Their shape, colour and absence of marking seem to preclude their constituting a heavy wooden structure, such as would be needed, not only to weather the storms and defy coral reefs, but also to hold the high mast and steering gear presumably required by such a vessel. The boat's personnel was small, and comprised a captain, a steersman, a crew of one, perhaps also a stevedore, and a cook with a small pot, as well as apparently a woman and child as passengers.

The tomb also bears a representation of the arrival of an Egyptian official to receive the Puntite goods, which include incense, ebony, a monkey, skin sacks, and an incense tree.

Beneath this relief is represented the departure of the official and his men, with an inscription which states that they are "carrying thousands [?] of products of Punt", including most notably myrrh and incense trees. Many articles can be seen carried by donkeys, while a tree is being dragged along by two men with yokes. The Puntite party includes two small children, possibly slaves.

The arrival of goods from Punt is also shown in another tomb of the period. The principal commodity depicted was fragrant gum, brought in sacks or stuffed into skins, and some of it emptied for better inspection or pressed into pyramidal shape. There were, according to Davies, two cheetah skins and two live animals of that species, "the happier in that they brought their own skins to market". The gum was tipped out into a heap and was being measured in bushel measures, which the "receiving" scribes duly checked and jotted down. The relief also depicts two individuals captioned "chiefs of Punt". Their presence provides further visual testimony that the Puntites were by now travelling on their own account to Egypt.[12]

Though this is passed over in silence in the reliefs and inscriptions it may be assumed the Puntites returned home in the vessels in which they had come, and took with them manufactured goods such as those referred to in the earlier Pharaonic records. This trade, like that based on the large state-owned vessels of the Pharaohs, linked Egypt with the Puntite coast and, through the latter, with the Ethiopian interior.

Later Puntite Trade with Egypt

Commercial contact between Egypt and Punt continued for several further centuries. An inscription of the reign of King Harmhab (1350-1325 BC) of the Nineteenth Dynasty contains a relief showing him receiving "chiefs" from Punt. They are bearing sacks of gold and ostrich feathers. One caption states that the Puntites are "bringing tribute", a Pharoanic claim which must once more be taken with "a pinch of salt". Another quotes them as saluting the king with the fulsome words "Hail to thee, King of Egypt... We know not Egypt; our fathers had not trodden it" - a memorable phrase, but not, after so many years of Puntite travel to Egypt, one to be taken very seriously.

One last, by no means inconsiderable, expedition to Punt was dispatched by the latter-day Pharaoh, Ramses III (1198-1167 BC) of the Twentieth Dynasty. The canal through the Wadi Tumilat was by then apparently out of use, so the imports from Punt were transported across Egypt by land. An inscription tells of galleys and barges returning from Punt, "laden with the products of God's-Land", including many "strange" articles, besides "plentiful myrrh.... laden by ten-thousands, without number". The "children of God's-Land" who brought these artefacts are, significantly, also depicted.[13]

---

[12] Säve-Söderberg (1942), p. 25.

[13] Breasted (1905), p. 485-6.

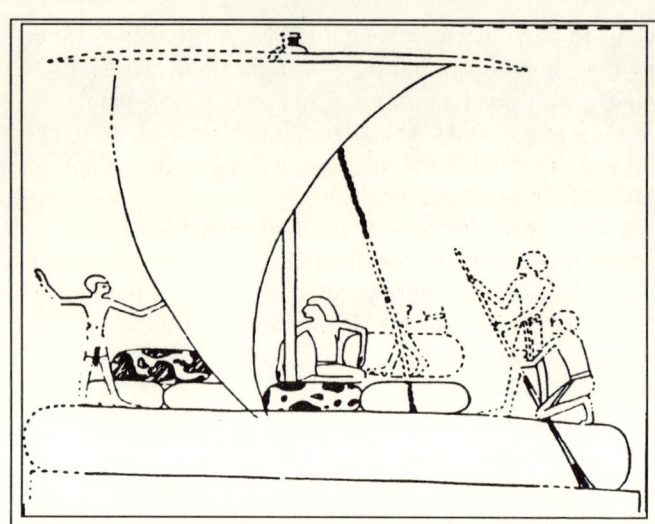

A Puntite boat, from the time of King Amenhotep of Egypt, 1447- 1420 BC. Note the use of sail and oar.
From N. de G. Davies, "The Egyptian Expedition of 1934-1935. Trading with the Land of Punt".

OPHIR
Commercial Contacts with Palestine

Trade such as that described in the ancient Egyptian inscriptions continued into the post-Pharaonic period, and may have found expression in Biblical references to the commerce of the Land of Ophir. To it ships of King Solomon (c.973-930 BC) are said to have sailed in search of gold, *algum*, or incense, trees (conceivably myrrh or similar trees), and precious stones.[14]

Some historians have suggested that the word Ophir is related to Afar, the people and country of that name in north-eastern Ethiopia. This identification, which is by no means implausible, would tend to confirm the long-established character of the Ethiopian region's foreign trade. If Ophir was in fact situated in the area, it would indicate that gold, presumably from the Ethiopian interior, and incense trees, from the coastal stretch of the Horn of Africa, were still

---

[14] 1 Kings, 9: 28, 10: 11, 2 Chronicles, 8: 18, 9: 10. See also I Kings, 22: 48, Job, 22: 24, 28: 16, Psalms, 45: 9, Isaiah, 13: 12.

being exported a millennium and a half after the earliest Pharaonic inscriptions - and indeed a thousand years before the birth of Christ.[15]

THE RED SEA COAST
The Ptolemaic Quest for Elephants

The Red Sea coast of Africa attracted outside attention again over half a millennium later when the Ptolemaic rulers of Egypt saw the area as an important source of elephants. The military importance of these animals was so great that they have aptly been termed the "tanks of the ancient world". Egyptian elephant-acquiring expeditions to the southern Red Sea coast of Africa were dispatched during the reign of Ptolemy Soter (305-285 BC), and more especially that of Ptolemy III Eurgetes I (246-221 BC). One of the harbours visited at this latter time was Adulé or Adulis, soon to become the principal port of the Aksumite state. Evidence of this is found in a Greek inscription, erected there, in the name of "Ptolemy, son of Ptolemy and Queen Arsinoe, twin gods".

This trade in its day was so important that special elephant-carrying vessels, known as *elephantegoi*, were constructed. The inhabitants of the Ethiopian interior apparently participated in operations, and had the reputation of being so skilled that the Greek historian Diodorus of Sicily wrote of the Ethiopians as a people of "elephant-hunters".

Elephant-hunting continued until as late as the time of Ptolemy IV Philopator (221-204 BC).[16]

---

[15] Franchetti (1930), p. 226; Sergew Hable Sellassie (1972), p. 39.
[16] Oldfather (1935). p. 157; McCrindle (1929), p. 57-9; Pankhurst (1976), pp. 119-29.

Chapter 2

THE NORTH AND NORTH-EAST; THE AKSUMITE KINGDOM AND THE AFAR DEPRESSION

Aksumite Foreign Trade and the Port of Adulis

Historical evidence from the early Christian era indicates that the Red Sea port of Adulé, better known as Adulis, handled the bulk of the foreign trade of the Aksumite kingdom, which was situated in what is now northern Ethiopia. According to the *Periplus of the Erythraean Sea*, an account of commercial conditions written in Greek around the first century A.D., articles shipped from the port consisted primarily of ivory, tortoise-shell and rhinoceros-horn, as well as some obsidian. The latter was used in the manufacture of jewellery and votive offerings. The Roman author Pliny (d.79AD) mentions the export in addition of three other items: "hippopotamus-hides, apes and slaves". Five of these seven exports almost certainly originated in the Ethiopian interior. The exceptions were the obsidian, which came from a coastal area east of Adulis (probably at Hawakil bay), and the tortoise-shell from waters in the vicinity of the Dahlak islands. Much of the export trade passed by way of the town of Coloe (the Kohaitu of modern times) which the *Periplus* describes as "the first market for ivory".

The imports of Adulis, which were bound mainly for the great capital city of Aksum and its environs, came for the most part from Egypt, India and Arabia. These goods, which were more varied than the exports, consisted, according to the *Periplus*, of "undressed cloth"[1] made in Egypt for the Berbers; robes from Arsinoe;[2] cloaks of poor quality dyed in colours; double-fringed linen mantles; many articles of glass, and others of *murrhine*,[3] made in Diaspolis;[4] and brass which was used for ornament and - cut in pieces - as money; sheets of soft copper, used for making cooking utensils and bracelets and anklets for the women; and iron which was made into spears used against the elephants and other wild beasts, as well as in wars.

---

[1] Probably made of linen, according to Schoff.
[2] Arsinoe, situated in the neighbourhood of modern Suez.
[3] Probably a cheap coloured glass made by the Phoenicians or Egyptians.
[4] Diaspolis, literally the City of God, probably Thebes.

The North and North East

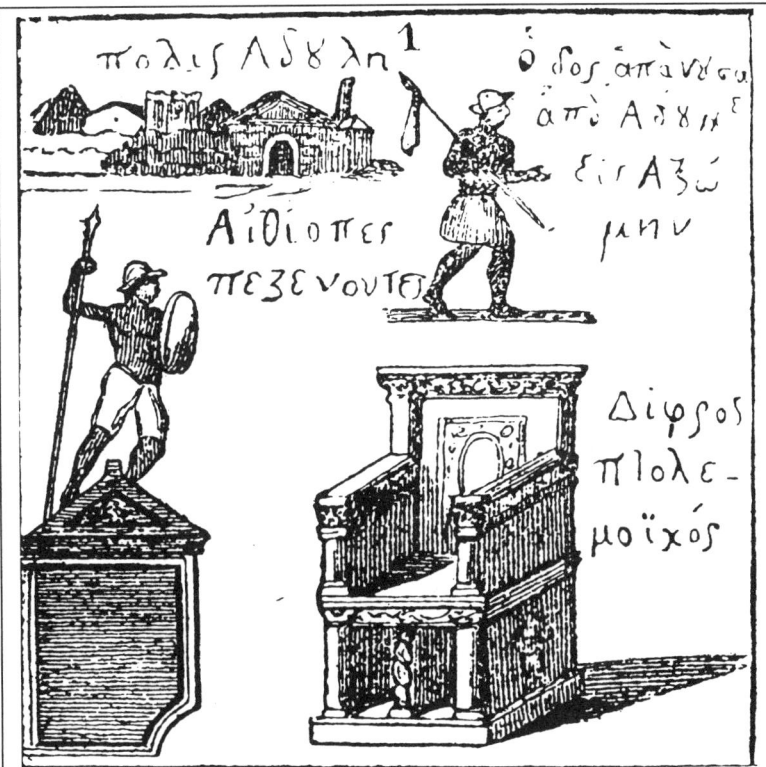

Picture 1: Adulis, top left, and an Ethiopian of ancient times travelling between that port and the then capital, Aksum. See also statue of Ptolemy Euergetes, lower left, and an Aksumite throne, lower right.
From J.W. McCrindle, *The Christian Topography of Cosmas, an Egyptian Monk*.

In addition to these, the text continues, axes were imported, and adzes and swords; copper drinking cups, round and large; a little money for foreigners in the area; wine of Laodicea [Latakia in Syria] and Italy, but not much; olive oil, not much; for the king [of Aksum] gold and silver plate made after the design of the country; and for clothing, cloaks, and unlined coats, of no great value. Likewise from the district of Ariaké [north-west India] across this sea, there were imported Indian iron and steel, and Indian cotton cloth, the broad cloth called *monache* [?] and that called *sagmatogene* [?], and mallow cloth, a little muslin, skin cloaks, and coloured lac.

Much of this trade probably passed through the commercial town of Coloe, the Kohaitu of later times, and the site of an ancient dam. The settlement was situated only three days' journey inland from Adulis, and is described in the *Periplus* as "the first market for ivory".[5]

A detail of the Aksumite dam at Coloe, a location now known as Kohaitu, a few miles north-east of Addi Qayeh.
From E. Littmann et al., *Deutsche Aksum-Expedition*.

Though the bulk of Aksumite trade passed by way of Adulis a number of other ports further to the east, on the Gulf of Aden coast, also served as a link between the interior and the outside world. They doubtless then as later handled the commerce of the more easterly,

---

5   Schoff (1912), pp. 23-4; Pliny, VI, 34. See also Huntingford (1980), pp. 20-1; Pankhurst (1961), pp. 18-19; Dombrowski (1985), pp. 3-6.

and southerly, areas of the Horn of Africa. Such ports, as explained in the *Periplus*, included Avalites, situated at or in the vicinity of the modern port of Zäylä', and Malao, the Berbera of later times.[6]

Trade between the coast and the Ethiopian interior seems to have run into difficulties from time to time. One such occasion is recorded in an inscription of the great fourth century Aksumite ruler King Ezana. It reports that the Tsarane, an unidentified people living in what is described as Afar, possibly the Saho area, had "attacked and massacred a merchant caravan". They thereby incurred the wrath of the monarch, who accordingly sent an expedition against them.[7]

The Aksumite realm, though centered on the city of Aksum, extended north-eastwards to the coast at Adulis. The kingdom thus included the highlands north of the Märäb river (which were subsequently to constitute the Country of the Bahr Nägash, and much later present-day Eritrea). Confirmation of the Aksumite presence in the northern periphery is likewise apparent from another of Ezana's inscriptions. It tells of its author visiting HMS - probably a consonantal form of the name Hamasén, one of the principal districts in the area.[8] Evidence of the extent of the Aksumite presence is likewise to be seen in the considerable distribution of archeological sites in that area.[9]

The Conversion to Christianity of the Aksumite State

The conversion of the Aksumite State to Christianity in the early fourth century, during the reign of Ezana, was a direct result of contacts with the coast, and had a major impact on the entire Aksumite kingdom. Hamasén and Säraye, important highland districts north of the Märäb river, both adopted Ethiopian Christianity at an early period. They recognized the paramountcy of the church of Maryam Seyon at Aksum, which they, as others, regarded as the religious capital of the realm.

---

[6] Schoff (1912), pp. 24-5; Huntingford (1980), pp.21-2..
[7] Munro-Hay, (1991), p. 227; Huntingford (1989), p. 55.
[8] Littmann (1912), IV, 20; Huntingford (1989), p. 52.
[9] On such archaeological sites see Drewes (1962), and map in Sergew Hable Sellassie (1972), p.32.

One of the great ancient obelisks of Aksum, as seen in an early nineteenth century engraving.
From G. Valentia, *Voyages and Travels.*

Evidence of contacts between the northern highlands and the interior is also found in several Aksumite land grants. They include a grant of the sixth century Aksumite emperor Gäbrä Mäsqäl, preserved in the monastery of Däbrä Libanos south-west of Sänafé, and another near Kesad Da'ro in Särayé.[10]

---

10   Conti Rossini (1901), pp. 182, 184.

Coin of the fourth century Aksumite ruler King Ezana, issued before his conversion to Christianity. Note representation of the sun and moon, top. His later coins bear the representation of the Cross of Christ, the first such emblem to appear on a coin anywhere in the world.

The coming of Syrian missionaries, notably the so-called Nine Saints, who established the first monasteries in Ethiopia around the fifth century, also had an important impact throughout the region. Probably for the most part travelling inland from the Red Sea coast, these holy men influenced the Aksumite periphery no less than the interior. They, and others, were responsible at this time for introducing the monastic system, which rapidly spread over an extensive area of what is now northern Ethiopia. The most important of them, in the north, was Abba Mätä'a, also known as Abba Libanos, who reportedly lived for seven years in the Bäqla area inland from Massawa.[11]

This period also witnessed the erection of a number of fine Aksumite style churches, among them one at the village of Asmära in Hamasén, and others at Gunaguna, Aramo and Baraknaha in Scimezana.[12]

---

[11] Conti Rossini (1928), p. 157. See also Balaynesh Michael and others (1975), p. 103.
[12] Littmann (1912), II, 195; Mordini (1940), 105-107; (1961), pp 131-8..

Adulis, the Country of "Barbaria", and the Dahlak Islands

Adulis throughout this time maintained its importance as the principal port of the north. This was noted by the early sixth century

The old Aksumite church at Asmära
From E. Littmann et al., *Deutsche Aksum-Expedition*.

Egyptian merchant-cum-monk Kosmas Indikopleustes, who visited it in 523 AD. In his geographical treatise, the *Christian Topography*, he described its trade, and that of the Ethiopian and Nubian interior, with India, Ceylon and elsewhere.

The Aksumites at this time reportedly obliged all vessels passing through that part of the Red Sea to pay for the right of passage, and call at Adulis. A visiting Byzantine embassy of 531 AD, revealing the prevalence of elephants just inland from the sea, also reported that at Aue, midway between Aksum and the port, they had seen "a large group of them, about five hundred in number", and adds: "None of the natives found it easy to approach them or turn them away".

Considerable trade was also carried out through the eastern Horn of African coast, referred to by Kosmas as the country of Barbaria. Its inhabitants, went up into the interior, he says, and brought down frankincense "and many other articles of merchandise".

Commerce, at least later, also seems to have passed by way of the Dahlak islands, which the ninth century Arab historian and geographer al-Yaqubi considered the main trade outlet for the Ethiopian region.[13]

THE AFAR DEPRESSION
Commercial Relations with the Highlands

Commercial relations between the Afar lowlands and the Ethiopian interior date back at least to the early Christian era. Such contacts were then, we may assume, already of no small antiquity, as well as of considerable importance. Since time immemorial the Dankali depression provided the inhabitants of the highlands with the bulk of their supplies of salt. This mineral, which was carried into the interior in the form of *amolés*, or bars of rock salt, was particularly important. It was used as an article of consumption, by humans and perhaps then as later also by cattle, and likewise served as "primitive money" throughout most of the Ethiopian empire for at least a millennium and a half.[14]

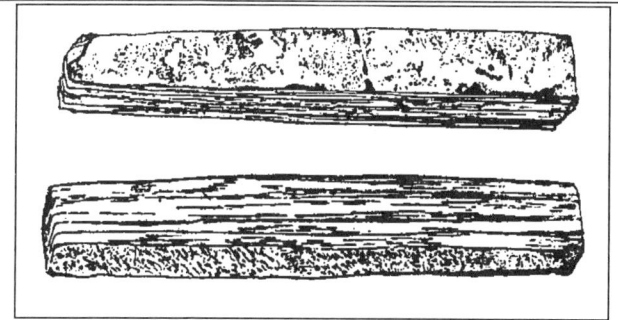

Amolés, or bars of salt, mined in the Afar country, and used as "primitive money" throughout much of the interior. From A.H. Quggin, *A Survey of Primitive Money.*

Evidence of the use of salt bars as a medium of exchange in the Ethiopian interior is provided by Kosmos, who tells, as we shall see, of the mineral being taken inland to exchange for gold from the west or south-west of the country.[15]

---

13 McCrindle (1929), pp. 51, 365-71; Houtsma (1883), p. 219; Wilson (1994); Ostrogorsgy (1968), pp. 74-5.
14 Pankhurst (1961), pp. 261-5.
15 McCrindle (1929), pp. 52-4.

Chapter 3

THE WEST and SOUTH-WEST: THE BEJA, the BAREYA COUNTRY and SASU

THE BEJA

Forced Resettlement

Interesting evidence on the Aksumite kingdom's relations with the Béja people on its western borders is afforded in three fourth century inscriptions of King Ezana, written in Greek, Ge'ez and Sabaean. They report that the Béjas had rebelled, whereupon the monarch dispatched his two brothers, Saizana and Adefan, against them. They captured the rebels, and brought them to Aksum, together with 3,112 head of cattle, 6,224 sheep, and many beasts of burden. During the journey, which took four months, the rebels were given meat and wheat to eat, and beer, wine and water to drink. Six rebel chiefs, with 4,400 followers, were provided with 22,000 loaves of bread a day. On reaching the capital they were fed and clothed, after which they were forcibly settled at a place called Matlia, where each chief was accorded supplies, including 25,140 head of cattle.[1]

Ezana, and his sixth century successor King Kaléb, in their inscriptions both claimed to be rulers *inter alia* of Béga, as well as of Kasu, another westerly territory often equated with Kush.[2]

THE BAREYA COUNTRY

The Aksumite state seems to have been at times in conflict with the people or peoples on its western borders, from which its soldiers captured many slaves. Some of the earliest of these battles are referred to in an undated inscription copied by Kosmas at Adulis. Its author, an unidentified ruler probably of Aksum, who lived in one of the first centuries of the Christian era, tells of an expedition he had undertaken against two peoples, the Béga and the Tangaitae, on "the borders of Egypt". After its successful conclusion, he claims: "I took

---

[1] Munro-Hay (1991), pp. 224-5.
[2] Huntingford (1889), pp. 45-8, 50-2, 54, 56-9, 63-5; Munro-Hay (1991), pp. 226-31.

what I wished of their young men and young women, and of their youths and possessions".[3]

A later campaign is recorded in two inscriptions of King Ezana. One tells of a punitive expedition allegedly carried out because the Noba, breaking their oaths, had attacked their neighbours, among them the Bareya, the Sälim, or Blacks, and the Säba Qäyh, or Red People. After this the victorious monarch proceeded against the Kasu people at the confluence of the Nile and Täkkäzé Rivers. In the course of this operation he captured 629 *séwa*, or captives.

The second inscription, referring to this or another campaign against the Noba, asserts that the latter had overrun the Bareyas who had appealed to the Aksumite king for help.[4]

Such early references to the Bareyas add weight to the tradition that they were one of the earliest peoples to be established in Ethiopia. This view is found for example in an anonymous traditional history of Särayé, the *Mäshaf Nay 'Alitat*, or History of Peoples, which claims that they had inhabited the country since "the beginning of Creation". An echo of this view was later provided by the nineteenth century British traveller James Bent, who described the Bareyas as the "aborigines of Abyssinia".[5]

Apparent confirmation of the Bareyas' antiquity is provided by Greek and Roman classical writers. Stabo shortly before the Birth of Christ stated that a tributary of the Nile near Meroe was called the Astaboras, presumably the river later known as the Atbära, a name which seems signify the Asta, or river, of the Bora, i.e. Bareya. This was almost certainly the group which Diodorus of Sicily at about the same time referred to as the Megabari, and which the Roman author Pliny called the Megabarri or Adiabari, all three words based on the term *bari*. Diodorus states that they carried round shields covered with raw-hide and clubs with iron knobs, and Pliny that they lived "over against Meroe", and included nomads who ate the flesh of elephants.[6]

---

[3] McCrindle (1929), pp.62-3.
[4] Littmann (1912), IV, 32-42; Anfray, Caquot and Nautin (1970), p. 266; Munro-Hay (1991), pp. 227-9.
[5] Conti Rossini (1942), pp, 176, 179; Bent (1894), p. 296.
[6] Strabo, Geography, XVI, iv, 8; Diodorus Siculus, III, 33; Pliny, Natural History, VI, xxx, 189. See also Conti Rossini (1914-15) pp. 302-3.

An indication that Bareyas, probably captured in war, were serving as slaves is found in a fourth century land charter of Kings Ella Abraha and Asbeha, i.e. Ezana and one of his brothers. It states that the great Church of Seyon at Aksum had been given "the Bareya of Demah", the latter being a territory north of the Märäb River.[7] The phrase seems to suggest that the said Bareyas were of servile status.

Evidence of fighting against the Bareyas, and of raids on them, is provided a few centuries later in an inscription by another Aksumite ruler, Hasani Danél. He claims to have come to Käsäla, near what is now the Sudan frontier, after which he "plundered the Bareya".[8]

One final early glimpse of the Bareyas is provided by the late tenth century Arab geographer Ibn Hawqal. He states that they, and neighbouring peoples, among them the Bazin, i.e. the Bazén or Baza now better known as the Kunama, lived in the Baraka Valley, and fought with bows, poisoned arrows and spears, but did not use shields. The Bareyas had the custom, he adds, of "pulling out their fore teeth and of slitting their ears". They lived in mountains and valleys, where they cultivated the land and raised "large and small cattle".[9]

SASU
A Gold-Producing Area and Its Silent Commerce

The Aksumite state, at least after its defeat of the Noba, was in commercial relations with a gold-producing region to the south-west, which Kosmas referred to as Sasu. Much intrigued by the unusual manner in which the gold was obtained he described the trade in some detail. He states that the King of Aksum, under the auspices of a functionary whom he terms the Governor of the Agäw, sent officers to the area every other year. They were accompanied by as many as five hundred private traders, who took advantage of the greater security afforded by the expedition to travel, and do business, on their own account.

Describing this trade in a notable passage the early Egyptian author wrote:

---

[7] Huntingford (1965b), p. 29.
[8] Littmann (1912), IV, 43.
[9] Ibn Hauqal (1954), 53.

"They take along with them to the mining district oxen, and lumps of salt and iron, and when they reach its neighbourhood they make a halt at a certain spot and form an encampment which they fence round with a great hedge of thorns. Within this they live, and having slaughtered the oxen, cut them in pieces, and lay the pieces on the top of the thorns, along with the lumps of salt and iron. Then come the natives bringing gold in nuggets like peas, called *tancharas*, and lay one or two or more of these on what pleases them - the pieces of flesh or the salt or the iron, and then they retire to some distance off. Then the owner of the meat approaches, and if he is satisfied he takes the gold away, and upon seeing this its owner comes and takes the flesh or the salt or the iron. If, however, he is not satisfied he leaves the gold, when the native, seeing that he has not taken it, comes and either puts down more gold or takes up what he has laid down and goes away. Such is the mode in which business is transacted with the people of that country because the language is different and interpreters are hardly to be found.

"The time they stay in that country is five days more or less, according as the natives more or less readily come forward to buy up all their wares. On the journey homeward they all agree to travel well-armed, since some of the tribes through whose country they may pass might threaten to attack them from a desire to rob them of their gold. The space of six months is taken up with this trading expedition, including both the going and the returning. In going they march very slowly, chiefly because of the cattle, but in returning they quicken their pace lest on the way they should be overtaken by winter and its rains".

Kosmas went on to state that "the sources of the River Nile", i.e. the Blue Nile, or perhaps one of its tributaries, lay "somewhere" in those parts, and that the country's seasonal "heavy rains" created "numerous rivers", which obstructed the path of the traveller.[10]

The above references to the "Governor of the Agäw" and to the "Sources of the River Nile" suggest that Sasu must have been in western Ethiopia, probably in the Wämbärya area, south-west of Gojjam, or, a little further afield, in Bäni Shangul. Wämbärya, which the modern historical geographer G.W.B. Huntingford refers to as a "somewhat vague district of Agäwmedr", i.e. the country of the Agäw. This area has sizable gold deposits, and would have been the gold-

---

[10] McCrindle (1929), pp. 52-4.

producing area nearest to Aksum. Bäni Shangul on the other hand had far larger deposits for which it has long been renowned.

The term *tancharas* mentioned by Kosmas in the early sixth century, had a long history. It was still current in the twentieth century, among the so-called Shanqellas in the west of the country, who collected the metal for sale, and used the word to refer to their arm-rings.[11]

Gold from the area, it may be assumed, met the Aksumite realm's needs of the precious metal. It was used in the manufacture of jewellery and coins, which were struck at Aksum for hundreds of years, and was also a major export item.

---

[11] Huntingford (1989), p. 211; Usoni (n.d.), pp. 185-94; Weld Blundell (1906), pp.544-9; Crawford (1958), p. 80.

Chapter 4
THE BORDERLANDS and THE INTERIOR

Though information on the Ethiopian borderlands in ancient times is scarce such data as is available, and discussed in the previous three chapters, indicates that the commerce of the region, and of its periphery, was of great antiquity.

The Coastal Areas

As noted in Chapter 1 the coastal areas, known in Pharaonic times for several millennia as the Land of Punt, were of major commercial importance. They linked the Ethiopian and East African interior with the Red Sea and Gulf of Aden coast. Contacts between the coast and the hinterland facilitated the export of myrrh, gold, animal skins, ostrich feathers and other articles. Some of these commodities came from the coastal belt, but others must have originated far in the interior. In return for such goods the region as a whole received a wide range of imports from Egypt and elsewhere. These included hatchets, daggers, necklaces and other manufactured goods. The coastal area known as the Land of Punt thus since time immemorial played a major role in the economic life of what we now know as the Ethiopian region.

This pattern of Horn of African export-import trade may well have continued into Biblical times, when the country of Ophir, possibly situated in or near the region, dispatched gold, incense and other valuables to ancient Israel.

The Red Sea coast of Africa was once again economically important in Ptolemaic times. It was regarded by the Egyptians as a major source of elephants, which were then in great demand for military purposes. The Ptolemies dispatched many naval expeditions in quest of these animals, and the Ethiopians of the period enjoyed a notable reputation as elephant-hunters.

In the ensuing Aksumite period the Red Sea and Gulf of Aden coast likewise handled the greater part of the region's foreign trade. This was based on the Red Sea port of Adulis, and two Gulf of Aden ports, Avalites, or Zäylä', and Malao, or Berbera. Adulis was the principal port of the Aksumite empire, while Avalites and Malao served the more southerly and easterly regions of the Horn of Africa.

Aksumite exports, of ivory, rhinoceros horn, gold, slaves and other commodities originating in the interior, were transported across the coastal area, largely by way of Coloe, later known as Kohaitu, before being shipped from the port of Adulis. Most of the region's imports, of textiles, raw metals, manufactured goods and luxury articles, from Egypt, India and elsewhere, similarly entered through that port, and were then taken to many destinations inland. The export-import trade of Avalites and Malao was broadly similar to that of Adulis.

The highlands bordering the coast, beside being economically linked to the hinterland, constituted an integral part of the Aksumite empire, and shared the main features of its civilisation. Christianity, which entered the country by way of the coast, affected the coastal areas no less than the interior. The Nine Saints, missionaries from Syria, passed through the coastal area, and one of them, Abba Mätä'a, or Abba Libanos, spent seven years in Bäqla. The northern monastery of Däbrä Libanos held important Aksumite and later other royal land grants.

The Afar Country, the Béga People, the Land of the Bareyas, the Noba and Kasu, and Sasu

The Afar country, since ancient times, was economically also of immense importance for the interior. The Dankali depression supplied a large stretch of the highlands with rock salt. This commodity was well-nigh invaluable. It was used for human consumption and probably also in the feeding of cattle, as well as an article of "primitive money". Bars of salt from the far north thus contributed significantly not only to the diet of the entire region, but also to its trade. This included the acquisition of gold in Sasu, situated in the far west of the region.

Fighting meanwhile was taking place against the Béja and various "black" peoples to the west of the Aksumite kingdom. Around the first century an Aksumite ruler undertook an expedition against the Béga and Tangaitae on the "borders of Egypt". Later, in the fourth century, King Ezana dispatched his brothers Saiazana and Adefan on a campaign against the Bégas, led by six chiefs, who were captured together with their followers, after which they were fed and clothed, and forcibly settled in a place called Matlia.

Ezana was also in conflict with the Nobas, who had attacked the Bareyas and the neighbouring Sälim, or "black", and Säba Qäyh, or "red" people. He also carried out a campaign against the Kasu people at the confluence of the Nile and Täkkäzé Rivers. Such warfare led to the capture of many male and female slaves, particularly, it would seem, among the Bareyas, some of whom appear to have been attached to the church at Aksum.

Sasu, which was mentioned by Kosmas in the early sixth century, was apparently the region's principal source of gold. The precious metal was of major significance in the commerce of the region as a whole. It was used in the local production of jewellery, and currency, which was struck for hundreds of years. The rare metal however also served as one of the Aksumite empire's principal export articles, and thus paid for much of the wide range of imports.

Conclusion

The products of three peripheral areas, the salt-producing Afar depression in the north-east, the gold-producing country of Sasu in the south-west, and the slave-yielding lands of the Bareyas in the north-west, contributed significantly to the empire's economy. Goods from all three areas were of major importance in the region's foreign trade, which passed through a fourth border area, namely the coastal belt. All four peripheral areas were thus to a greater or lesser extent part of an inter-locking economy.

PART II

THE EARLY MEDIEVAL PERIOD

(c. 890-1454 AD)

Chapter 5
THE NORTH: THE LAND OF THE BAHR NAGASH
The Port of Massawa

Massawa, or more properly Metsewwa, was the principal Red Sea port handling the foreign trade of northern Ethiopia in early medieval times. The port was situated on the western side of the offshore island of that name, and was known to early Arab geographers. Al-Ya'qubi referred to it in his *Kitab al-Buldan*, or Book of Countries, written about 891-2, as Badi, a corruption of its local Tegré name Basé, while al-Mas'udi wrote of it in 935 as Nasé.[1]

Since the port was an island, traders doing business there also made use, it may be presumed, of the neighbouring coast, where the mainland port of Arkiko, or Hergigo, also called Dehono, is known to have existed somewhat later.

The Zagwé Dynasty and later Founding of Monasteries

The decline of the Aksumite kingdom around the seventh century AD was followed by the rise in the tenth century of the Zagwé kingdom based on Lasta. Not long after this the northerly districts of Hamasén and Säraye both passed, like much of the northern highlands, under Zagwé suzerainty, as the modern Ethiopian historian Taddesse Tamrat has noted. Confirmation of this statement can be seen in a land grant by the great Zagwé king Lalibala preserved in the already mentioned Däbrä Libanos monastery of the north.[2]

Two notable monasteries were soon afterwards established in the far north: Däbrä Bizän in Hamasén, founded by Abba Felepos (c.1323-1406), and Däbrä Maryam in Säraye. They were important centres of religion and church learning fully comparable in status and organization to the major monasteries of Tegray, and later Christian lands further south.[3] From the religious point of view the northern districts nevertheless continued to be dependent, like the Christian empire as a whole, on the old spiritual capital, Aksum.

---

[1] Wiet (1937) p. 159; Meynard and de Courteille (1861-1877), III, 34, 157; Trimingham (1952), p. 50

[2] Taddesse Tamrat (1972a), p. 80; Conti Rossini (1901), pp. 182, 184-7.

[3] Taddesse Tamrat (1972), p. 210.

Expedition of 'Amdä Seyon; Land Grants of Säyfä Ar'ad, Dawit and Yeshaq

The subsequent establishment of the "Solomonic" dynasty further south in Shäwa around 1270 likewise had its impact on the northern periphery, which within only a few decades came under the effective control of the new rulers. A hagiography of this time claims that Emperor 'Amdä Seyon (1312-1342), the greatest of the early "Solomonic" monarchs, travelled to the Red Sea, where he mounted an elephant and entered the water. Contact with the north is likewise apparent in another medieval text which indicates that the courtiers of Emperor Dawit I (1380-1409) included men from Hamasén, Särayé and neighbouring districts.[4]

At least four Ethiopian monarchs of this period granted land to monasteries in the far north. Emperor 'Amdä Seyon gave a land charter to the monastery of Däbrä Libanos. Säyfä Ar'ad (1342-1370) allocated two areas in Särayé to the convent of Abba Mädhanina Egzi'e of Bankwal. Emperor Dawit presented an estate at Karneshim in Hamasén to the monastery of Däbrä Bizän. Emperor Yeshaq (1412-1427) gave a stretch of land in Särayé to that of Däbrä Abbay.[5]

Yeshaq, conscious of the importance of the coast, went even further, and, to judge from a soldiers' song of his reign, established a garrison at the port of Massawa.[6]

The northern periphery, like regions to the south, throughout this time remained spiritually affiliated to Aksum. The district of Särayé was nevertheless much influenced by the teachings of Saint Ewostatéwos, a holy man from the more southerly Tegray district of Gär'alta, who favoured the celebration of the Saturday Sabbath. He established his monastic community in Särayé, before travelling to the Middle East, and to Armenia, where he died around 1352.[7]

A *Gädl*, or Acts, of Ewostatéwos was later composed at Däbrä Bizän. One of its miracles tells of a monk who while fetching water was captured by slave raiders. Captures such as that, it may be supposed, were in times of disorder far from rare.[8]

---

[4] Taddesse Tamrat (1972a), p. 77; Conti Rossini (1900), p. 65.
[5] Conti Rossini (1901), pp. 1812, 201-10, 216-17; Huntingford (1965b), pp. 32, 34. See also Huntingford (1989), p. 82.
[6] Guidi (1889), pp. 55-7.
[7] Taddesse Tamrat (1972a), pp. 107, 207-13.
[8] Getatchew and Macomber (1981), p.131.

Chapter 6
THE EAST: IFAT and ADAL

IFAT

Ifat, known to the early Arab geographers as Wifat or Awfat, was situated to the north-east of Shäwa, and had become part of the Ethiopian Christian empire in early medieval times. The province was the most northerly, and for a time also the richest, of the country's central Muslim territories. Its importance owed more to its strategic position than to its size or resources, for, though small, it controlled much of the trade between the central Ethiopian interior and the sea. Ifat also had considerable political influence, as the modern Ethiopian historian Merid Wolde Aregay has observed, over nomads and pastoralists migrating through its passes into the highlands.[1]

Mountains to the east of Shäwa, identified by Huntingford in his *Glorious Victories* as being in Ifat: an early nineteenth century engraving.
From Rochet d'Héricourt, *Second Voyage sur la cote orientale de la Mer Roughe.*

Because of its proximity to Shäwa, then the heartland of the Christian empire, and to the Muslim port of Zäyla', Ifat was, as we shall see, frequently embroiled in commercial and religious struggles between the coast and the interior. These seemingly intermidable conflicts were the main preoccupation of the chroniclers, both Christian and Muslim, whose writings constitute our principal source of information for this period.

---

[1] Cerulli (1936), pp. 5-6; Merid Wolde Aregay (1974), pp. 622-3.

Founding of the Wälashma' Dynasty

The first known ruler of Ifat was Sultan 'Umar ibn Dunya-huz. He was appointed, according to the Arab historian Maqrizi, a sympathetic and pro-Muslim commentator, by a "Hati", i.e. Hazé, or Emperor, of Ethiopia, almost certainly Emperor Yekuno Amlak (1270-1285). 'Umar, "dear to all through the excellence of his manners", died around 1275, and was succeeded by "four or five sons", who ruled successively. Most of their successors, who included a woman, Mä'ät-läylä, had only short reigns, but one of them, Bäzitu, ruled for no less than thirty years (c.1279-1299). The last of these rulers was Sultan Säbr ad-Din Nahwi ibn Mänsur ibn 'Umar Wälashma', or Säbr ad-Din I, who reportedly died of extreme old age around the turn of the century.

Säbr ad-Din was succeeded by his son Sultan 'Ali, whose fame, according to Maqrizi, "flourished throughout the whole region". He was "the first to revolt against the customary allegiance" to the Ethiopian emperor, but later returned to it. He did so, according to Maqrizi, because "the people of the country not only disagreed with his action, but rebelled against it".[2] Imperial Ethiopian power was thus re-established. This enabled Emperor Yagbe'a Seyon (1283-1292), as we shall see, to mount a campaign much nearer the coast, in the vicinity of Zäylä'.

'Amdä Seyon and the Rebellion of Haqq ad-Din I

The Ethiopian empire's control over Ifat was again challenged by its Muslim rulers during the reign of the renowned Christian warrior Emperor 'Amdä Seyon (1312-1342). A conflict between the monarch and the Ifat leaders began around 1320. It was precipitated by the Mamluk sultan of Egypt, An-Nasir Muhammäd ibn Qala'un, who was then persecuting the Egyptian Copts and destroying their churches. 'Amdä Seyon responded by dispatching a mission to Cairo, in 1321-2. Its brief was to warn the Egyptians that if they continued with their persecution he would retaliate against the Muslims under his rule, and would divert the course of the Nile to stop it reaching Egypt. The latter was an idle threat, for the diversion of the river was almost certainly far beyond his technological ability. The Egyptian sultan, who may have realised this, rejected the Emperor's arguments, and dismissed the Ethiopian envoys. Fear that the Ethiopians might

---

[2] Rinck (1790), pp. 17-18; Cerulli (1931), pp. 42-5..

tamper with the Nile was nevertheless to remain with the Egyptians for many centuries.

The dispute between 'Amdä Seyon and the Mamluk sultan had immediate repercussions in Ifat. Its ruler, Sultan Haqq ad-Din ibn Muhammäd ibn 'Ali, or Haqq ad-Din I, seized one of the Emperor's servants, a young man called Te'eyentäy.

According to 'Amdä Seyon's chronicler, who naturally presents the story from his master's standpoint - and is almost exclusively interested in the monarch's military exploits, the irate Emperor responded by riding into Ifat. He was accompanied, it is claimed, by only seven other horsemen, but managed to kill a large number of Haqq ad-Din's men. A part of the monarch's army later followed him down to Ifat, and is said to have "utterly destroyed" its capital of that name. 'Amdä Seyon then confiscated much of its wealth, including a considerable amount of gold, silver, bronze and lead, as well as innumerable garments.

The Emperor followed up this victory by sending his army further, into "all the lands" of the Muslims. These included Kuelgorä and Bequlzar, which according to Huntingford, were probably situated near Aleyu Amba and north of the Kässäm river respectively. 'Amdä Seyon's troops also advanced to five unidentified localities, Gedayä, Kubät, Fädsé, Qädsé and Hargayä, as well as to "all the land" of Shäwa. It is clear from this account that much of the latter province was then inhabited by Muslims. The Emperor's soldiers made war on all these areas. They killed many of the inhabitants, burnt "great and strong" towns, and took "countless" prisoners, who, as so often in Ethiopian history, were doubtless assimilated by the victors. The latter also seized much livestock.

While this fighting was in progress other Muslims, seeing that the Emperor had only a few troops, endeavoured to attack him. His assailants included the people of Gäbäl or Wärjeh. They were reportedly "very skilled in warfare". As a result "the land of the Christians", according to the chronicle, was in its turn "laid waste". The inhabitants of both Medra Zega (south of modern Märabété), and Manzeh (i.e. Menz), who were then Muslims, surrounded the Emperor. He nevertheless succeeded in defeating them, and killed their commander Dädader, a son of Haqq ad-Din.[3]

---

3   Huntingford (1965a), pp. 56-7; Taddesse Tamrat (1972a), pp. 65-6, 132-4; Trimingham (1952), pp. 70-1. On identifications of localities in this chapter see

'Amdä Seyon and the Ambitions of Säbr ad-Din II

A few years later, in 1332, Haqq ad-Din's brother and successor Sultan Säbr ad-Din, or Säbr ad-Din II, emulated his predecessor by confiscating some of 'Amdä Seyon's goods which were being taken through the empire in the course of trade with the coast. 'Amdä Seyon, furious at this action, complained to the chief: "You took away the commodities belonging to me obtained in exchange for the large quantity of gold and silver I had entrusted to the merchants... you imprisoned the traders who did business for me".

A little other information on the people of Ifat is provided by the chronicle, admittedly a biased source, which claims that they foretold the future by means of sand, and took omens from the sun, moon and stars.

Säbr ad-Din, it appears, had decided on a major insurrection. His ambition, 'Amdä Seyon's chronicler claims in a significant passage, was to make himself "king over all the land of Ethiopia", to "rule over the Christians", and "destroy their churches". He reportedly spoke of his intention to rule, and appoint governors, over the entire empire, as 'Amdä Seyon had done before him. The objective of Säbr ad-Din was thus to maintain the traditional Ethiopian state, but on a Muslim basis. He accordingly nominated some two dozen functionaries for various provinces and districts. These included not only nearby places, such as Fätägar and Alamalé (i.e. Aymälläl, part of the Guragé country), but also provinces of the north, including Damot, Amhara, Angot, Endärta, Bägémder and Gojjam.

Säbr ad-Din is quoted as making several other threats: 1) to turn Ethiopia's Christian churches into mosques. 2) to convert the Emperor to Islam, and to reduce him to the rank of a provincial governor, or, if he refused conversion, to hand him over to the Wärjeh herdsmen to look after their herds. 3) to make his consort, Queen Jan Mängäsha, work at the grinding mill. 4) to turn 'Amdä Seyon's capital, Tägulät (which he referred to by its Muslim name, Mär'adé) into his own residence, and 5) to plant there the stimulant *chat* (*Catha edulis*). He proposed the latter on the interesting grounds that the plant was much loved by the Muslims, and was an article, possibly of tribute, which he had formerly sent to his overlord, the Emperor.[4]

Huntingford (1989), pp. 89-92, and, on Ethiopian threats to block or divert the Nile, Hecht (1988), pp. 1-10.

[4] On the use of *chat* see Cerulli (1936), pp. 20-1.

The Ifat rebellion, according to the chronicler, was thus conceived as a *jihad*, or Holy War. It had significant repercussions in several neighbouring Muslim territories, for Säbr ad-Din, as we shall see in Chapters 8 and 9, was immediately joined by two other Muslim rulers: Haydära, the governor of Däwaro, to the south, and the Amäno, or local ruler, of Hadeya, far to the west.

Säbr ad-Din divided his troops in Ifat into three divisions. One, travelling north-westwards, set forth for Amhara. The second, advancing northwards, made for Angot. The third, which he commanded in person, pushed westwards to invade Shäwa.

'Amdä Seyon responded to this triple challenge by mobilising his soldiers. To encourage them to the utmost exertion, he presented them with gold and silver as well as fine clothing. He made so many gifts, his chronicler maintains, that lumps of the precious metal became as numerous as ordinary stones, and costly raiments "as common as the leaves of the trees or the grass of the field". Having adorned his warriors in beautiful clothing he dispatched them against the Ifat army. However, because of the "badness of the country", and the "roughness and even absence of roads", most of his troops failed to appear. One detachment nevertheless managed to find, and attack, Säbr ad-Din, who was obliged to flee from his residence. 'Amdä Seyon's men pursued him, but he escaped. Not long afterwards the remainder of the Emperor's army arrived in Ifat. They ravaged its capital, killed a "very large number" of its soldiers, and once more pursued Säbr ad-Din, who nevertheless made good his escape.

The Emperor's forces then rallied for a decisive onslaught on Säbr ad-Din. They attacked one of his camps, and looted its treasure houses, where they found a vast amount of gold and silver, as well as "fine clothes and jewels without number". In the course of the fighting they also killed many men, women and children. Those who survived were seized as prisoners. The victorious monarch, as we shall see in Chapter 8, then marched on to attack Haydära, the ruler of Däwaro.

Säbr ad-Din, realising the hopelessness of his position, thereupon sued for peace. He sent a message to Queen Jan Mängäsha, declaring his willingness to surrender. She replied, on the instructions of her husband, that he did not care whether Säbr ad-Din came or not, for he was determined to search him out, and would not return to his capital until he had done so. The Ifat ruler, seeing that further resistance was impossible, then came to apologise for his rebellion. Many of 'Amdä

Seyon's courtiers demanded that he should be executed, but the Emperor was "merciful". Not wishing to kill his enemy, he had him placed in chains. [5]

After Säbr ad-Din's arrest, 'Amdä Seyon, wishing to re-establish control over Ifat, appointed the deposed chief's brother Jämal ad-Din, whom Säbr ad-Din has earlier detained, as its ruler. The new appointee Jämal ad-Din I, was made king, the chronicler says, of "all Muslim lands". The Emperor then decorated him, in accordance with traditional Ethiopian practice, with "many splendid ornaments".

The people of neighbouring Adäl and Mora, who probably lived to the north of Ifat in the neighbourhood of Awssa, chose this moment, however, to rebel. Their plan was to attack 'Amdä Seyon before he could reach their country. This resulted in further bitter fighting out of which the Emperor emerged victorious.

'Amdä Seyon's troops, exhausted by these campaigns, then came to their master, begging him to let them return home. They declared that the enemy had been defeated, and that the rainy season was approaching. The monarch, however, obstinately refused to listen. He declared that he would not leave Ifat as long as the rebels continued to resist. He was, he proudly affirmed, king of "all the Muslims of the land of Ethiopia", and put his trust in God.

Jämal ad-Din, his recently appointed governor, also approached him, and, bearing many gifts, begged him to return to his capital. The Ifat ruler sorrowfully declared that the country of the Muslims was ruined, and appealed to the monarch not to "ravage it again". If the latter spared the country, he promised, its inhabitants would serve him with their trade, for he, and all the Muslims of Ethiopia, considered themselves the Emperor's slaves.

The relentless 'Amdä Seyon, however, again refused to abandon his march. On camping for the night, he was at once attacked by an army made up of soldiers from what the chronicle terms the seven "great towns", or districts, of Adäl, Mora, Tiqo, Paguma, Läbäkäla, Wärgar and Gäbäla.

At around this time Jämal ad-Din, though 'Amdä Seyon's appointee, also joined the rebellion. He urged the ruler of Adäl to collaborate with him in surrounding the Emperor's forces. The chief accordingly mobilised his men, after which the armies of Ifat and

---

5   Taddesse Tamrat (1972a), p. 85; Huntingford (1965a), pp. 53- 64.

Adäl encircled 'Amdä Seyon's army, but, as we shall see in the next chapter, were eventually defeated.[6]

At the end of the Adäl campaign 'Amdä Seyon, on his way home, made his way once more to Ifat. On reaching Bequlzar he called upon Jämal ad-Din to deliver all the province's Christians who had abjured their faith. The chief began by handing over the apostate priests, deacons and soldiers. The Emperor commanded that they should each receive thirty lashes, after which he had them turned into slaves, and placed in chains. He then demanded the other turn-coats. This led to a dispute, as a result of which he deposed and imprisoned Jämal ad-Din, and again ravaged Ifat, after which he replaced the chief by another brother, Näsir ad-Din. The principle of maintaining the ruling family in power was thus continued.

The Emperor then proceeded to the town of Guét, and in the course of the fighting killed many men, and captured a large number of women and livestock. He later repulsed the people of Harla, somewhere in Somaliland, who had attacked his camp. He then made his way to the town of Delhoya, whose inhabitants had burnt to death the governor whom he had appointed, together with many other Christian men and women. In retaliation he looted the town, killed many of its inhabitants, and seized their livestock. He then attacked the town of Dägwe, and killed many of the nearby Wärjeh pastoralists, whom the chronicle describes as "very wicked", for they "neither knew God nor feared men".[7]

The Reports of Ibn Fadl Allah al-'Umäri and Taki ed-Din Ahmäd Maqrizi

A detailed account of Ifat in the aftermath of all this fighting was written shortly after 'Amdä Seyon's death by an Egyptian courtier, Ibn Fadl Allah al-'Umäri. He learnt about the territory from 'Abd Allah, a learned citizen of Zäylä', who was then visiting Egypt. Al-'Umäri's account differs from the chronicles in that it is refreshingly unconcerned with warfare, and gives a very plausible picture of the territory's economic, political and social life.

Ifat, according to al-'Umäri, was the largest, as well as the richest, of Ethiopia's Muslim provinces. He states that its inhabitants spoke

---

[6] Huntingford (1965a), pp. 66-95. See also Taddesse Tamrat (1972a), pp. 106, 137-45.

[7] Huntingford (1965a), pp. 95-107; Taddesse Tamrat (1972a), p. 106.

"Abyssinian", by which he probably meant Amharic. The territory extended, he says, no less than twenty days' journey in one direction by fifteen in the other. (Assuming a speed of four kilometres per hour and five or six hours travel per day, i.e. a little over twenty kilometres per day, this would suggest that the territory may have measured around 400 kilometres by 300, which is perhaps an exaggeration).[8] It comprised, seven "towns", or districts: Bequlzar and Kuljura (or Kuelgorä), both mentioned in 'Amdä Seyon's chronicle, and five other places: Shimi, Shäwa, 'Adäl, Jämma and Läo.

The entire province was watered, al-'Umäri says, by a "large river", in fact the Awash. The area was well cultivated, and densely populated, with numerous villages almost adjoining each other. Agricultural produce included three main cereals, wheat, sorghum and *téff* (*Eragrostis tef*), as well as beans, aubergines, melons, cucumbers, marrows, cauliflowers, and mustard. Many different types of fruit were grown, among them bananas, lemons, limes, pomegranates, apricots, peaches, citrons, mulberries and grapes. Other plants included the sycamore tree, sugar cane, from which *kandi*, or sugar, was extracted, and inedible wild figs. There were also several local fruit trees, which al-'Umäri could not identify.

Another plant grown was the stimulant *chat*, already mentioned in 'Amdä Seyon's chronicle. Its leaves, when chewed, increased perception, gave pleasure, and enabled people to survive for long periods without food, drink, or sexual activity. *Chat*-chewing was much favoured by the inhabitants, particularly those who wished to study, work, travel or keep awake for long hours. The plant was so popular that it had by then been introduced into Yämän.

Ifat abounded in "large numbers" of cattle and sheep, and some goats. There were also chickens, which were however considered dirty because they were said to eat filth. Both buffaloes and wild fowl were hunted. The latter reputedly made good eating. There were likewise many wild animals, among them antelope, gazelle, wild ass, ostrich, ibex, rhinoceros, leopard, lion and hyena. The province was reputed to yield butter and honey.

---

[8] For this calculation see Pankhurst (1958), p. 283.

The Awash River, forded by a camel caravan, a nineteenth century engraving.
From J.M. Bernatz, *Scenes in Ethiopia*

Imports from abroad, consisting mainly, we may assume, of manufactured goods, were extensive. This was partly because the province was within easy reach of Yämän and other parts of Arabia; and partly because it controlled the port of Zäylä' which was frequented by most merchants active in the area.

Trade from the interior was also important, and included gold from the Ethiopian territories to the west, including Damot and an unidentified district called Siham. The rare metal, depending on its quality, sold for 80 to 120 Egyptian *dirhems* per ounce.

Though the province had no money of its own, use was made of Egyptian *dinar*s and *dirhem*s, which were brought into the area by travelling merchants.

As for dress al-'Umäri reports that the sultan customarily wore a silk headband round his head, while *amir*s and soldiers had ones of cotton. Shirts and sown clothes were rare, for most people covered themselves only with a loin-cloth. Soldiers, on the other hand, wore trousers. Some scholars and the well-to-do also had shirts, but most people wore nothing but two simple pieces of cloth, one round the shoulders, the other round the waist. Scholars wore turbans; the rest of the population, *kuffiyas*, or white Muslim caps.

The status of the sultan was emphasised in different ways. At court he would be seated on a tall iron throne four cubits high (i.e. four arms' lengths), encrusted with coloured stones, with two servants bearing arms behind him. The principal *amir*s would be seated around him, on less elevated chairs, while the lesser chiefs remained standing. When riding the ruler had a silk parasol carried over his head: If he was on muleback it would be held by a servant seated behind him; if on horseback, by one walking alongside and holding the reins. When walking on foot the sultan, or even an *amir*, would be supported by two servants. He was also usually surrounded by *qadi*s and lawyers, but reserved the exercise of justice for himself. This was perhaps just as well, for none of the lawyers, al-'Umäri claims, were renowned for their legal knowledge.

On leaving his palace the sultan would be preceded by chamberlains and sergeants, who would scatter the populace before him. He would also be preceded by musicians, blowing oboes and trumpets made out of bamboo with cow-horns fitted at their upper end. Some musicians beat drums slung around their necks. Those at the head of the procession blew a massive three cubit long trumpet made of antelope horn. It produced a loud sound that could be heard half a day's journey, i.e. perhaps almost ten kilometres, away, and thus informed the entire neighbourhood that the ruler was on the march. Those accustomed to travel with him would at once hasten to join him, while those wishing to flee would do so.

The Ifat sultan, unlike many eastern potentates, did not keep a common table, but ate alone with only a few courtiers. On certain occasions he would, however, give cattle to his *amir*s, but the largest number distributed, even to a great lord, would be no more than two.

Ifat possessed a large army. It consisted of twenty thousand or more infantry, and fifteen thousand horsemen. Most fought with spears, but there were also a few archers. Neither soldiers nor chiefs received any payment, or even landed estates. They were nevertheless self-supporting, for they possessed large herds of cattle, and cultivated the land. The cavalrymen made use of Arab horses, which they rode without saddles, but covered their steeds with fine-haired goat-skins. Even the sultan rode in this manner. Most of the time, however, he and his people used mules.[9]

This remarkable description of Ifat was paraphrased almost a century later by the Arab historian Maqrizi, who wrote around 1434-5. His account contains a few additional passages gleaned from a North African traveller, Sheikh Shihab ad-Din Ahmäd al-Mujasi.

---

[9] Gaudefroy-Demombynes (1927), pp. 5-14.

They indicate that agricultural and other produce in Ifat was cheap. Thirty pounds of meat sold for only half a *dirhem*, while four *dirhem*s would purchase a bunch of about 100 Damascus grapes.[10]

Säyfä Ar'ad and Ahmäd 'Ali

The period after the composition of al-Omari's report witnessed a further struggle for Ifat. 'Amdä Seyon's son Emperor Säyfä Ar'ad strove hard to exert imperial control. He was, however, confronted by a series of problems, which are recorded by Maqrizi, who, it will be recalled, looks at events from the Muslim side.

Säyfä Ar'ad began, we are told, by appointing a new governor of Ifat, whom he selected, as was customary, from within the local ruling dynasty. His choice fell on Ahmäd, also known as Harb Arad ibn 'Ali. He was the son of Säbr ad-Din's son Ali, who had been the first to revolt against the empire. 'Ali, and most of the other members of the ruling family, were then imprisoned. He was kept in detention for eight years, but later regained the Emperor's favour, and returned to his old governorship, in place of his son. Ahmäd had meanwhile been summoned to the imperial court, where he remained under the Emperor's patronage, and begot three sons.

Säyfä Ar'ad reportedly embraced Ahmäd with love. He subsequently wrote to the latter's father 'Ali, instructing him to appoint Ahmäd as a district governor. 'The young man accordingly held district office for some time, but was later killed in an uprising.

Haqq ad-Din II and Säyfä Ar'ad

Ahmäd's son, Sultan Haqq ad-Din II, subsequently rose to prominence. He devoted himself to learning, but incurred the displeasure of his grandfather 'Ali, and of the latter's son Mola Asfah. These two, both functionaries of the Ethiopian Christian state, reportedly regarded Haqq ad-Din with hatred. He was accordingly driven from the capital of Ifat, and wandered around the province for some time, before eventually winning the protection of another local chief, for whom he collected tribute. He proved such a successful administrator that he gained a large band of followers. He later rebelled, and killed the governor who had appointed him, after which he gathered his soldiers, presented them with rich presents, and launched an insurrection against his uncle.

---

10 Rinck (1790), p. 11.

Confronted with this threat Mola Asfah appealed for help from his liege, Sayfä Ar'ad, who dispatched a large force of 30,000 soldiers against the rebel. A fierce battle followed, in which Haqq ad-Din inflicted many casualties on the imperial army, and emerged victorious. Mola Asfah was put to flight, and sought refuge with the Emperor, who sent him back with another considerable army, which Haqq ad-Din again annihilated. His uncle was among the many killed. The victorious rebel then besieged the town of Ifat, where his grandfather 'Ali was still in residence, grieving at the death of his favourite son.

'Ali, though incensed against his grandson, was in too weak a position to seek revenge. Haqq ad-Din, for his part, behaved well to his grandfather. He confirmed the old man in his position, and gave him much wealth. Later withdrawing his troops from the town, he took many of its inhabitants with him to Shäwa, where he built a new town called Wahal. This settlement, according to Taddesse Tamrat, was probably further to the south-east. There Haqq ad-Din made his capital. The old town of Ifat then began to decline, and was soon deserted. 'Ali later once more lost imperial favour. He was imprisoned by the Emperor, and kept a captive for the next thirty years.

Haqq ad-Din was described by Maqrizi as a "warlike, bold, and magnanimous" leader, "swift in action and terrible" to his enemies. He reportedly fought no less than twenty battles with the imperial army in a single year. He was "ceaselessly" involved in fighting with the Emperor, from whose army he took "many captives". This warfare continued until Säyfä Ar'ad's death in 1370, after which Haqq ad-Din "continuously" assailed the monarch's son. Maqrizi refers to the latter as Emperor Dawit, but he was more probably the latter's brother and predecessor Wedem Asfäré (1370-1380).[11]

Sä'd ad-Din, Dawit and the Defeat of Ifat

Haqq ad-Din eventually died in battle around 1376. He was succeeded by his brother Sultan Sä'd ad-Din Abdul Muhammäd, the last great ruler of Ifat. He began his career, Maqrizi relates, by waging "continual war" on the Emperor's forces. He was at first so successful that his army rapidly grew in numbers, his onslaughts on the empire became "more frequent", and the area under his control steadily expanded.

---

[11] Rinck (1790), pp. 18-22. See also Taddesse Tamrat (1972a), p. 150.

Sä'd ad-Din did battle over the years not only with the Emperor, but also with chiefs loyal to the latter. He thus fought against the Amano, or local ruler, of Hadeya, and put him to flight. Not long afterwards the victorious Ifat ruler attacked the Zälän, a neighbouring pastoral people, from whom he seized so much booty that his personal share was said to amount to 40,000 cattle. These he distributed among the poor and needy, as well as to his soldiers, "leaving nothing but what might suffice for one of his wives". He then laid siege to a place called Zamdu, which was inhabited by "many infidels", probably Christians. Severe fighting ensued, in the course of which he took numerous prisoners.

The tide of war at this point, however, began to turn. The then Emperor, presumably Dawit, collected a large army, and dispatched it against "the land of the Muslims" - an apparent reference to Ifat. The Christian force was resisted by a certain Amir Muhammäd, who fell in battle with almost all his men. Allegedly only one of them, a horseman, survived to tell the tale.

The Emperor later dispatched a second army, under a chief called Barwa. Sä'd ad-Din set forth against him, taking with him preachers and peasants who had vowed to fight until death. A "terrible battle" ensued, in which the Ifat army was seriously defeated. It suffered many casualties, among them no less than 400 elders, each of whom carried an iron bar as his insignia of office, and was in charge of a specific number of preachers. Those who survived the engagement thereupon fled, and were vigorously pursued by the Emperor's army. Sä'd ad-Din himself was chased as far as Zäylä', whither he took refuge, but was soon discovered. He was killed in 1415 after which his ten sons escaped to Arabia, and found asylum with its ruler Näsir Ahmäd ibn Ashraf Ismail.

Dawit and the Restoration of Imperial Rule

Sä'd ad-Din's death was a major turning-point in the history of Ifat, for it was followed by the restoration of full imperial control. Emperor Dawit and his soldiers settled in the territory, where, Maqrizi claims, they "ravaged mosques" and "built churches out of them". The Muslims were then "harassed" for twenty years, as a result of which their power "abated". This judgement was accepted by the British historian of Ethiopian Islam, Spencer Trimingham, who claims that the Emperor's occupation put an end to the Ifat kingdom, which was "permanently occupied", and "heard of no more". The land where Sä'd ad-Din fought and died was, however, to be called after him for at least a century.[12]

Dawit, the victor of this long drawn out struggle, then made his abode in Ifat. He resided, according to a royal chronicle, at a place called Tobeya, where he planted many trees.[13]

The Adäl desert as seen from the mountains of Ifat, an early nineteenth century engraving.
From T. Lefebvre et al., *Voyage en Abyssinie*.

ADAL

Adäl, which lay to the east of Ifat, and was at times nominally included within it, has been described by Huntingford as a vague, and indeed changing, term used to refer to "all the Muslim lowlands" in the strategically and commercially important area east of the Shäwa-based Christian state.[14] In this chapter the term is used more specifically for the lowlands east of Ifat. The area here defined as Adäl thus included much of the Awash basin, and stretched northwards to Lake Abbé, and eastward to the lowlands between Shäwa and the port of Zäylä'. Awssa and several small neighbouring amirates were also sometimes tributaries of Adäl.

Because of its large area, and varied geographical conditions, the Adäl population practiced different occupations. Those near the

---

[12] Rinck (1790), pp. 22-7; Trimingham (1952), p. 74.
[13] Perruchon (1893), pp. 152-3; Basset (1897), p.7; Taddesse Tamrat (1972a), p. 152.
[14] Cerulli (1936), pp. 15-16; Huntingford (1989) p. 91.

Awash River and Lake Abbé probably combined some agriculture with cattle rearing, while those in the arid lands to the east were primarily nomads, herding camels and goats.[15]

Zäylä' and the Arab Geographers

Zäylä', which was situated at or near the site of the ancient port of Avalites, had handled Horn of Africa trade since time immemorial. The port was known to early Arab geographers, several of whom refer to it in passing. It was thus mentioned in the ninth century by al-Ya'qubi, and in the tenth by al-Mäs'udi. The latter described it as an "Abyssinian" coastal town, inhabited by Muslims, but under the protection of the "Abyssinian" state. Later in the century Ibn Hawqal noted that the settlement served as the place of embarkation of Abyssinian Christians travelling to Hijaz and Yämän.

In the early twelfth century Zäylä' received the attention of al-Idrisi, who reports that it was visited by "many foreigners", as well as by ships bringing supplies for Abyssinia. Exports included gold and slaves, both of which probably came from the Ethiopian interior. The port was also the place through which many Muslims passed on their way to and from the great Hajj pilgrimage to Mecca.[16]

Early in the thirteenth century another Arab writer, Ibn al-Wardi, called the port "the emporium of Habash", i.e. Abyssinia, while Shams ad-Din Abu 'Abdallah Muhammäd claimed, with obvious exaggeration, that gold, presumably from the interior, was so plentiful there that it was worth no more than iron.[17]

Later, in the fourteenth century, Ibn Sa'id described Zäylä' as a major centre for the export of slaves and horses from Abyssinia. Ibn Batuta at about the same time stated that the port was "a large city with a great bazaar", albeit "the dirtiest, most abominable, and most stinking town in the world", on account of the great quantity of fish and the blood of camels slaughtered in its streets. Another contemporary, Abu'l Fida, likewise referred to Zäylä' as a prosperous port serving Habash.[18]

---

[15] Merid Wold Aregay (1974), p. 23.
[16] Wiet (1937), 159; Meynard and de Courteille (1861-77), III, 34, 157; Kramers and Wiet (1964), 54; Dozy and de Goeje (1866), pp. 27, 55. On pilgrimage see also Cerulli (1943a), p. 288.
[17] Guillain (1856), I, Part I, 236-7; Devic (1892), pp. 54-5.
[18] Gibb (1929), p. 110.

Proselytisation

Ethiopian tradition, embodied in the medieval Ethiopian *Gädl*, or Acts, of Abunä Zéna Marqos, suggests that Adäl was the site in the Middle Ages of much Christian proselytisation. Zéna Marqos was himself one of those involved in this movement. He was a cousin of Mädhaninä Egzi, the grandfather of the notable Shäwan monk Saint Täklä Haymanot (c.1215-1313), and a sometime governor of Fätägar. Zéna Marqos reportedly proceeded to Adäl, where he succeeded in converting the provincial governor.[19]

Marco Polo's Account

One of the earliest Western references to Adäl is found in the *Travels* of the Venetian explorer Marco Polo (1298). He told the "fine", albeit confused, story of a Christian "King of Abash", or Abyssinia, in all probability Emperor Yagbe'a Seyon (1283-1292). This monarch wanted, he says, to go on a pilgrimage to Jerusalem, but, because of the risks of the journey, was deterred by his nobles, and instead sent a bishop (or more likely, some lesser cleric). The latter duly reached the Holy Land, after which he returned by way of "Aden". Described as accessible by land from Abyssinia, this place could not have been the Arabian port of that name, but was presumably somewhere on the Ethiopian side of the Red Sea, and most probably Adäl. Its inhabitants, according to Marco Polo, regarded Christians as their "mortal enemies". Their sultan attempted to convert the bishop, but, failing to do so, allegedly released him after having had him forcibly circumcised as a Muslim.

On learning of this insult the Emperor mustered "an immense force", and marched on the "kingdom of Aden", i.e. Adäl. Its ruler, hearing of the monarch's approach, summoned to his aid two great, but unidentified, nearby "Saracen", or Muslim, kings. Accompanied by a "vast multitude of infantry and cavalry he then went to await the King of Abash at the fortified frontier passes, to defend his land, and prevent the Christian monarch from entering it. The latter and his army duly reached these passes, where they found the enemy in great numbers.

The "cruelest and most terrible battle" then began. The three Saracen rulers could not, however, hold out against the King of Abash, and his "many and excellent troops". The Saracens were

---

[19] Getatchew Haile (1987), IX, 268.

obliged to retreat, after which the Christian monarch and his men entered the territory. The Muslims "barred the way at certain fortified places"; but sought to defend them in vain, and were killed "in great numbers".

The Christian occupation, according to Marco Polo, lasted only "about a month", during which the Emperor harried the land, and killed a "great multitude" of Saracens. He then declared that the prelate's "ignominy" had been "avenged", and that he could honourably return home. He and his companions accordingly left, and did not rest until they had reached "Abash".[20]

The Venetian author wrote as though the struggle had come to an end, but it apparently soon flared up again. Arab traditions record that Muhammäd Abu 'Abd Allah, a Muslim shaikh, collected an army to attack the Christian empire in 1298-9. His expedition, however, collapsed. A peace treaty was then concluded, whereby the Emperor ceded certain frontier districts in return for Muslim recognition of his sovereignty.[21]

Yämäni Attempts to Gain Influence at Zäylä'

Zäylä', though loosely part of Adäl, was at this time virtually independent. The port and its environs were inhabited, according to the fourteenth century Coptic historian Al-Mufäddäl ibn Abi-'l-fada'il, by seven different tribes, each of whom recited the *hutbäh*, or prayer of allegiance, in the name of their own separate chief.

The ruler of Yämän, wishing to profit from this disunity, and acquire paramountcy over the coast facing his own country, dispatched building materials and equipment for the construction of a mosque at the port. He did so in the hope that the people would recite the *hutbäh* in his name. The idea, however, did not appeal to the citizens, some of whom took the stones, and threw them into the sea. The Yämäni ruler was so angered that he detained several Zäylä' boats for a year.[22]

Säbr ad-Din III, and the Founding of the Adäl Dynasty

The defeat almost a century later in 1415 of Sultan Sä'd ad-Din of Ifat, and the resultant disappearance of the Ifat state, was, as we have

---

[20] Marco Polo (1931), pp. 348-9; Tedeschi (1981), pp. 361-89.
[21] Trimingham (1952), p. 70.
[22] Cerulli (1943a), p. 280.

seen, a major turning-point in the region's history. The chief's sons, who had sought refuge in Arabia, subsequently returned to Africa, as Maqrizi reports. Abandoning any interest in their old capital, which had come under imperial rule, they established themselves in lower land to the east at a place called Däkär. They likewise renounced the name of Ifat, and called themselves kings of Adäl. They thus gave recognition to a state of that name, which became thereafter the most important Muslim power east of the Christian empire.

The first ruler of the newly named Adäl dynasty was Sä'd ad-Din's eldest son, Sultan Säbr ad-Din III. He returned from Arabia with ten Arab horsemen, as well as military supplies provided by his family's Arab patron Näsir Ahmäd. Säbr ad-Din and his brothers made their way to a place called Sayara, where they were joined by a number of their father's former followers. Though outnumbered by the soldiers of the Christian state, they fought several successful battles, one at a place called Zikr Amhara, or Memory of the Amhara, and another in the district of Serjan. Scattering their enemies, they burnt many houses and churches, and took a large amount of booty in gold and other valuables.

Such opposition on the eastern borders doubtless angered the Christian rulers of the empire. An unnamed commander, with ten chiefs, each in charge of 20,000 men, moved into the area for a year, thereby restoring it, Maqrizi asserts, to "Amhara rule". Säbr ad-Din and his followers were once more obliged to flee, and endured hunger, thirst and other privations.

The Muslims, however, later regained their strength. Säbr ad-Din was able to send his brother Muhammäd, with Harb Jaush, a defector from the Christian side, to attack the imperial forces in Retwa. The Emperor's commander and many other Christian leaders fell in battle, and their soldiers were killed, except for a few who escaped. Säbr ad-Din seized a considerable amount of booty, after which he ruled the district for some time. He later proceeded towards the Emperor's headquarters in Adäl, where a fierce battle was fought in which many Christian nobles fell, after which Säbr ad-Din put their headquarters to the flames.

The victorious chief then returned to his capital, but gave orders to his followers to continue, and extend, the war. He entrusted his brother Muhammäd with the task of capturing a fort at Barut, and subsequently instructed one of his commanders, Omar, to raid the land of Jab. This was so well defended, by imperial soldiers "as numerous as locusts", that Omar's men were all killed by the former's spears, which Maqrizi likens to rain falling from heaven. Säbr ad-Din was almost captured, and escaped thanks only to the speed of his horse. He soon afterwards died a natural death, in 1422-3.[23]

Mänsur, Dawit and Yeshaq

Säbr ad-Din was succeeded by his brother Sultan Mänsur, who enjoyed the support of his brother Muhammäd. Early in his reign he launched an expedition against an Ethiopian Christian monarch, apparently Emperor Dawit, and drove him to Yedaya, described as his royal seat, where, according to Maqrizi, he was captured and killed. His death, an event of presumably major importance, is not confirmed by the Ethiopian chronicles. This, Taddesse Tamrat argues, is, however, not sufficient reason to reject the statement, for Ethiopian royal chroniclers often deliberately attempted to suppress the violent deaths of the kings whose reigns they extol.[24]

Mänsur later surrounded a considerable imperial force of 30,000 soldiers on the Moha mountain. He besieged them for two months, by the end of which they were suffering from hunger and thirst. He then offered them the choice of embracing Islam or returning to their homes. Some 10,000 accepted the new faith; the remainder went home.

Very soon after this the fortunes of war again changed. In 1424 another Christian monarch, Emperor Yeshaq, set forth with an immense army, which Maqrizi likens to a swarm of locusts. Mänsur and his brother Muhammäd were captured, and Adäl, like Ifat before it, came once more under the "rule of the Christian Amhara".

Jämal ad-Din Muhammäd and Yeshaq

Mänsur was succeeded around 1424 by his youngest brother, Sultan Jämal ad-Din Muhammäd. He had the support of the afore-mentioned defector Harb Jaush who had by then proved himself an outstanding commander. Jamal ad-Din II, a wise and able ruler, dispatched this chief to Emperor Yeshaq in an attempt to arrange a compromise peace, but negotiations failed. A battle ensued, in which Harb Jaush fought with the Emperor's men, who reportedly included 7,000 archers and swordsmen. Despite their number they were put to

---

[23] Rinck (1790), pp. 28-31.
[24] Taddesse Tamrat (1972a), p. 153

flight. Many others on the other hand submitted, accepted Jämal ad-Din's rule, and agreed to pay him tribute.

Yeshaq, disturbed by continuing insurgency in and around Adäl, collected a larger army than before, and occupied Yedaya, but Jämal ad-Din again repulsed him. The Emperor then attacked, and captured, the district of Jazja, but Jämal ad-Din successfully counter-attacked, forcing the imperial soldiers to flee. They were pursued for three days, and suffered so many casualties that the land was reportedly strewn with their corpses. The victorious Adäl troops then burnt the houses, and churches, of the Christians, and carried off numerous women and children, besides much booty. In the course of this expedition, which lasted three months, the victors also captured a hundred saddled horses, besides numerous beasts without saddles.

The Adäl ruler, having reportedly collected a larger force than any of his predecessors, subsequently launched a major attack on the Emperor's army. Making use of a thousand horsemen he killed large numbers of Yeshaq's soldiers, took innumerable prisoners, and seized extensive loot. The Emperor and the remainder of his men fled to the Blue Nile area, with Jämal ad-Din's troops in hot pursuit for five months, after which their commander returned home with so much loot that it was said to have been impossible to describe. He then sent his brother Ahmäd, with Harb Jaush, on an expedition to Däwaro, before returning home in triumph.

Jämal ad-Din later undertook a further expedition in which, it is claimed, he killed, or took prisoner, everyone within twenty days' journey of his frontier. The Emperor's forces countered by attacking three different parts of Adäl, and threatened its capital, where its ruler's family resided. Jämal ad-Din rushed home, traversing a distance of twenty days' journey in only three. He met the imperial army at Harjah, where his army, though exhausted, fought well, but was eventually defeated. The Emperor's soldiers in their turn captured much booty, but Yeshaq, according to Maqrizi, was killed in battle. His death, like that of Dawit, and perhaps for the same reason, is not recorded in the royal chronicles.

The Adäl ruler's victory was short-lived. Weakened by constant fighting he was soon afterwards challenged by envious cousins, who attacked and killed him, around 1432.

The Justice of Jämal ad-Din

Jämal ad-Din was reportedly one of the most remarkable rulers of Ethiopia's eastern provinces. Though pious, he was, according to Maqrizi, terrible to his enemies. During his seven year reign he killed countless numbers of them, and took many more as slaves, who were then exported abroad. India, Arabia, Hormuz, Hejaz, Egypt, Syria, Greece, Iraq and Persia, as a result, became "full of Abyssinian slaves". He likewise captured many lands, "increased the splendour" of Adäl, and enriched himself with "much booty", while "a great multitude" of Amhara Christians at his exhortation embraced Islam.[25]

Jämal ad-Din, according to Maqrizi, also enjoyed a considerable reputation for justice. On one occasion when his children were small, one of them while playing is said to have struck a child smaller than himself, and broke his hand. The sultan did not hear of this until some time afterwards. When he did he was furious that his courtiers had concealed the matter from him. He summoned the injured child's family, and, calling together his subjects, ordered his son to be brought before him, as someone deserving punishment on the Biblical principle of "an eye for an eye, a tooth for a tooth". The leading courtiers begged him to show mercy, and the child's family declared that it had no desire for revenge.

The stern ruler, however, was not to be moved to clemency. When his son came forward to suffer the penalty, all the bystanders bewailed loudly, and the injured child's family reiterated that they were in favour of mercy. Jämal ad-Din, however, seized his son's hand, and broke it with the blow of an iron bar. The boy cried out in pain, and all present lamented his hard lot, but the sultan merely said to his son, "Feel now yourself what you made the other boy feel!".

Perhaps not surprisingly after acts of such severity Jämal ad-Din's subjects are said to have adhered strictly to the law. Maqrizi claims that they dared not touch the possessions of others, and that no one, whether noble or of common birth, did ill to others. Everyone feared their ruler so much that no one was indifferent to his commands or prohibitions. Jämal ad-Din, we are told, was thus respected for the severity of his rule, the force of his punishments, and the excellence of his virtues.[26]

---

[25] Rinck (1790), pp. 32-40.
[26] Rinck (1790), pp. 38-9.

Sultan Bädlay

Jämal ad-Din was succeeded by his brother Sultan Bädlay ibn Sä'd ad-Din, sometimes referred to as Shihab ad-Din Ahmäd Bädlay, who had his capital at Däkär. Continuing his predecessor's policy of confrontation with the Christian empire, he carried out several successful expeditions. He brought numerous Christian lands under his rule, and burnt many of their towns, together, Maqrizi says, with at least six churches. He also killed many Christian leaders, and seized their inhabitants, together with much booty. He and his men likewise collected "great wealth", in gold, silver, clothes, and armour, besides many slaves.[27]

---

[27] Rinck (1790), pp. 40-1.

Chapter 7
THE NORTH-EAST: THE AFAR COUNTRY

Early Contacts with Arabia, and the Coming of Islam

In addition to age-old contacts with the Ethiopian interior, referred to in Chapter 2, the Afar country had important relations across the Red Sea with Arabia.

These links led in early medieval times to an Arab awareness of the Afar people. The latter were first mentioned in the thirteenth century by the Arab writer Ibn Sa'id, whose account was preserved by his compatriot Abu'l Fida. It reveals the vast extent of territory inhabited by the Afar people. Described as "a kind of negroes called *Dankal*", they were reported to have extended from around the Sudanese port of Suakin to as far south-east as Mandeb, near the port of Zäylä'.[1]

Afar contacts with the Arabs resulted in the gradual penetration of Islam, which is said to have been spread by merchants from Arabia who intermarried with local women. According to Trimingham by the early fourteenth century the new religion was well entrenched in the area.[2] Muslim influence, was, however, probably for a long time limited to the towns, for later reports suggest that among the nomads Islam was not deeply rooted.[3]

The Campaigns of 'Amdä Seyon

The Afars came into contact with the Christian empire during the reign of 'Amdä Seyon when they chose, as earlier noted, to involve themselves in the struggle between that ruler and Amir Säbr ad-Din II of Ifat. The ensuing fighting is described in the Emperor's chronicle, which throws interesting light on Afar government, military prowess, and modes of warfare.

The Afar country, it is apparent from the text, was known to the Ethiopian court at this time as "Adäl". The word, was thus applied, in Huntingford's opinion, to the area of the lower Awash River, and to

---

[1] Guyard (1883), II, 128.
[2] Trimingham (1952), pp. 34, 60, 62-4.
[3] A. d'Abbadie (1868), I, 92, 595; Rochet d'Héricourt (1841), p. 111; Munzinger, (1869), p. 219. See also Isenberg and Krapf (1843), p. 20.

the country north of Lake Abbé, that is to "a Danakil state in a heavily forested region with permanent water and swamps".[4]

The Afar lands, it will be perceived, were thus located at a considerable distance from the Christian empire. The Afars for this reason were relatively protected from the religious conflicts in which the more southerly territory of Ifat was so sadly often involved.

This isolation was temporarily brought to an end around 1329. The insurrection by Sultan Säbr ad-Din caused 'Amdä Seyon, as we have seen, to embark on a major expedition to the Muslim lowlands. In the course of the fighting the people of "Adäl", i.e. the Afar, and those of nearby Mora, decided to support the Ifat ruler. They planned a pre-emptive strike while the Emperor was in the Ifat area. The royal chronicle quotes them as saying, "Let us march against the king of the Christians before he reaches our country; if we attack him where he is, he will be afraid and will return to his capital; but if we leave him alone he will come to our capital and destroy us".[5]

The "Adäl"-Mora army accordingly surrounded 'Amdä Seyon and his men. It attacked them for three nights in succession, but he beat off each assault. He then pursued his enemies over a vast stretch of territory. Säbr ad-Din's brother Jämal ad-Din, whom the Emperor had appointed ruler of Ifat, then, as we have seen, urged the latter to return to his own country in peace, and leave the Muslims alone. The victorious monarch, however, proudly refused, declaring, "If I return before I have ravaged the land of Adäl may I not be called a man, but a woman".[6]

'Amdä Seyon thereupon advanced further and further into the lowlands. He was again attacked, this time by a coalition of warriors from many Muslim territories, including both "Adäl", i.e. Afar, and Mora. These soldiers, according to the Christian chronicler, were "as numerous as the sands of the sea". They decided to kill the Emperor in the night, while he and his army were asleep. They undertook three further night attacks, but 'Amdä Seyon successfully repulsed them, after which he continued his expedition virtually unopposed. Crossing a "great river" called Yas, perhaps a local name for the Awash, he advanced to the "city of Mora". Fighting night and day, almost without intermission, he is said to have neither unfastened his belt nor

---

[4] Huntingford (1989), p. 91.
[5] Huntingford (1989), p 91.
[6] Huntingford (1965a), pp. 66-7.

gone to sleep until he entered "the vast land called Adäl", which, the chronicle claims, "no other kings [of Ethiopia] had reached".

Once there he camped by a place named Das, at a water called Fur. The former possibly owed its name to the presence of a *das*, the Afar word for a stone memorial, while the latter was perhaps Fursi or Furzi, about 35 miles north of Lake Abbé, and site of a small lake near the Awash. The chronicler's description of the area is reminiscent of Afarland, for it states that even "in the middle of the wet season" there was "a great heat which burned man and beast", and "no grass was to be found". The Emperor's soldiers had to drink water in "small measures", for there were "no springs of water", only "wells foul and putrid dug by the hands of men". The stones were "like thorns" - possibly an allusion to volcanic chips common in some Afar areas.[7]

Shortly after this the "king of Adäl", who was presumably an Afar, received messages from Jämal ad-Din and from a local charismatic leader called Qazi Seleh, who was "feared and honoured as a god", asking him to join a new Muslim coalition against the Emperor. Jämal ad-Din reportedly declared that "the king of the Christians" had "come to a narrow straight" from which he could not escape. The ruler of "Adäl", he wrote, had therefore to choose between two courses of action: either to pay the Emperor tribute and gifts, and thereby deliver his family and descendants into "perpetual slavery", or show his "wisdom" by summoning his army, "to fight with the sword, the bow, the shield, the spear, the spear of wood, and the rod of iron". If he chose the latter option the Ifat ruler promised to join him, and declared that they could between them surround and destroy the Emperor and his men. Not one would survive.[8]

On receipt of this message the "Adäl" ruler summoned his kings and governors, with their troops, who took four months to assemble. He then addressed them, and, referring to the Emperor, proudly declared, "I will kill [him] with my sword, and I will satiate myself with the spoil". He is said to have boasted, in the same vein as Säbr ad-Din, that he would turn the sanctuary of Christ into a mosque, and seize its gold and silver treasures and costly vestments. He supposedly added that he would destroy 'Amdä Seyon and all the Christians, and take their possessions, including camels and other beasts, and divide them among his soldiers. As for 'Amdä Seyon's consort Jan

---

[7] Huntingford (1965a), pp.36, 67-73.
[8] Huntingford (1965), pp. 73-80.

Mängäsha, her women and the king's concubines and daughters, he would set them to work at the mill.

The "Adäl" leader, it is claimed, was, however, unwilling to share the anticipated spoils. He gave orders to his chiefs and governors, saying, "Let us go forth and attack the Christian king by ourselves before the king of Ifat arrives, because the possessions of the Christians are not enough for us and for him".[9]

The "Adäl" ruler and his men then surrounded the Emperor. The latter was at that time vulnerable. He had despatched many of his troops elsewhere, and was moreover very ill. He was confined to bed, and had not touched food or drink for seven days. The people of "Adäl" by contrast were fully prepared for battle, and were reportedly as numerous as locusts, the stars of heaven, or the sands of the seashore. Faced with this vast horde most of 'Amdä Seyon's multi-ethic army, which included men from Damot in the south-west as well as from Shäwa, Gojjam, Tegray, Bugna and Amhara, lost heart, and fled.[10]

The chronicler, who was impressed by the military prowess of the "Adäls", states that they were "great fighters". When they went into battle, they "tied the ends of their garments, one man with the next, that they might not flee". As for their physical appearance they were "tall", but had "ugly faces". Their hair was plaited like that of women, so that it "reached to their waists". This hair-style is reminiscent of that of the Afars of later times, and thus tends to confirm the assumption that 'Amdä Seyon was in the Afar area.[11]

The Emperor, who had by then recovered from his illness, rallied his few remaining followers, and, though hopelessly outnumbered, attacked the "Adäl" army. The latter reportedly showered arrows on him like rain, and iron and wooden spears like hail. Undeterred by these missiles 'Amdä Seyon charged against the enemy's left wing. He transfixed two men with a single blow from his spear, whereupon many of his enemies "scattered and took flight". Those of his men who had earlier fled then returned to the fray, and helped their master put his foes to flight. He ordered his men to "take no trophies from the dead", but to "pursue the living", leaving it to the women to gather the

---

[9] Huntingford (1965a), pp. 80-1
[10] Huntingford (1965a), pp. 82-90.
[11] Huntingford (1965a), p. 91.

spoils. This the latter did with such gusto that they collected a large number of swords, bows, spears and shields.[12]

Afar warriors in council: an early nineteenth century engraving. From Rochet d'Hericourt, *Voyage sur la côte orientale de la Mer Rouge*.

The "Adäls" suffered immense casualties. The bodies of the dead, the chronicler claims, were strewn around the battlefield like heaps of grain, or even hills, and "no one but God could count their number". Among those who perished was Qazi Seleh, who had helped begin the insurrection, and an old, white-haired woman described as "a maker of poisons", who "took omens from the sand and dust".[13]

Despite his victory the relentless monarch was still not satisfied. His soldiers' only desire was to return home, but he persuaded them to make their way across the "Adäl" country, as far as its capital Täläg, which has been identified as the Afar settlement of Datalg 'Ali. There he ordered them to attack the remaining rebels, before dreaming of returning to Shäwa by another route.[14]

The Emperor and his men accordingly continued their advance into the Afar country. They attacked several settlements, including

---
12   Huntingford (1965a), p. 91.
13   Huntingford (1965a), pp. 66-5. See also Taddesse Tamrat (1972a), p. 106.
14   Huntingford (1965a), pp. 36-7, 100.

Tä'aräk, Zäsäy, and Abälgi, in each of which they killed or captured many people, and seized a large amount of livestock. The dead included 'Abd Allah, the ruler of Zäsäy, who was regarded, the chronicle says, as a kind of Patriarch, i.e. a major Muslim religious leader.[15]

'Amdä Seyon and his army then made their way to the Afar capital, where they fought and killed the "King of Adäl" and many of his men, and laid waste his country. Three of his sons and a brother thereupon came to surrender. They took off their shoes and placed them on their heads as a sign of submission. The Emperor then reproved them for attacking his kingdom. He threatened, if they continued the war, to destroy all their friends and associates, as well as their villages and livestock, and continue the struggle until he had turned their country into a desert. The chiefs begged him to desist, and promised that they would send word to the neighbouring kings and governors urging them to submit.

The four chiefs duly sent messages advising their friends to make peace. One of the Muslim leaders, the king of Hagära, a locality near Awssa, nevertheless refused. A chief of importance, as evident from the fact that he had ninety-nine governors under him, he summoned his people, and told them to "make themselves strong and courageous", so as to destroy 'Amdä Seyon. "If the Christians kill us", he fanatically declared, "we shall be martyrs, and if we kill them we shall gain paradise".[16]

When the Emperor heard of the Hagära leader's stand he too "set out in wrath", crossed the "great Ekua river" - presumably a stretch of the Awash, and ordered his troops to search out the chief. They found him ready for battle. A fierce engagement ensued. The "rebels" were strong, the chronicle reports. They included archers, and other soldiers who protected them with shields, as well as women who fought with sticks, "like brave youths", and threw stones with great force. 'Amdä Seyon, however, was not deterred. He drew his bow, and with an arrow hit the Hagära ruler in the neck. He fell to the ground, whereupon his men fled. The Emperor's soldiers then surrounded and destroyed the Hagära army. Only three soldiers are said to have survived.[17]

---

[15] Huntingford (1965a) 100.
[16] Huntingford (1965a), pp.100-2.
[17] Huntingford (1965a), pp. 37, 103.

'Amdä Seyon then proceeded to Säsogi, where, we are told, he ordered his men to burn towns, demolish mosques, and destroy food supplies. His soldiers killed many of the enemy soldiers, and took much livestock. Crossing the Zär'ät river, they came to the settlement of Araté, where the people reportedly castrated and cut off the ears of their captives. On seeing the victims the Emperor "grieved exceedingly". To punish the "wrong-doers" he pretended to be about to leave the territory, whereupon his soldiers, who were in hiding, surprised and killed many of them. This stratagem was carried out twice in or around Araté, and again at a place called Hajäya.[18]

At the close of this campaign, which, the chronicler claims, was unprecedented in the country's history, Amdä Seyon returned to the highlands, never again to set foot in the Afar country. Its inhabitants apparently reverted to their isolation from the religious conflicts of the area, and do not reappear in the Ethiopian royal chronicles for over a century.

---

[18] Huntingford (1965a), pp. 104-5.

Chapter 8

THE SOUTH-EAST and SOUTH: FATAGAR, DAWARO, ARABABNI, BALI, SHARKA, DARHA and HARÄR

FATAGAR

Fätägar, which was situated south-east of Shäwa, between the Awash and Wäbi Shabellé Rivers, was already part of the Ethiopian Christian empire in the early medieval period. The *Gädl*, or Acts, of Abunä Zéna Marqos claims that the territory was governed, probably in the late twelfth century, by a certain Mädhanina Egzi, the grandfather of the Christian religious leader Saint Täklä Haymanot.[1]

Imperial control of the province is later evident from a soldiers' song of the reign of Emperor 'Amdä Seyon, and from the latter's chronicle, which quotes Säbr ad-Din II of Ifat as recalling that it was the Emperor's practice to appoint a *mäsfen*, or governor, of the territory.[2]

The province probably experienced considerable Christian proselytism in this period, as suggested by the fact that the then Ethiopian Patriarch, Abunä Yaq'ob (1337-1344), entrusted the area for purposes of conversion to Abba Mateyas, one of Saint Täklä Haymanot's leading disciples.[3]

Dawit and Yeshaq

Fätägar, unlike provinces further to the south-east, was little affected by Säbr ad-Din's rebellion, for it remained firmly under imperial rule. Emperor Dawit I took a keen interest in the territory. He endowed two churches, Märtula Mika'él and Asädä Mika'él, at a place called Yäläbasha, and also established fruit plantations in the area.

After Dawit's death, in 1409, there was a succession of short-lived emperors, during whose reigns imperial control probably declined.

---

[1] Getatchew Haile (!987), IX, 268.
[2] Huntingford (1965a), pp. 17, 54, 129, 132.
[3] Taddesse Tamrat (1972a), p. 176; Huntingford (1989), p. 176; Getatchew Haile and Macomber (1981), V, 444. For a discussion of the reasons why Täklä Haymanot's disciples spearheaded the proselytism see Kaplan (1984), pp. 92-5.

Perhaps for that reason Fätägar does not appear in a list of provinces subject to Emperor Yeshaq. The area, Huntingford believes, may therefore have ceased to be a tributary territory. Be that as it may, it was still regarded as within the empire's general orbit, the more so as it was in Fätägar, at a place called Telq, that Yeshaq's famous brother and successor, Zär'a Ya'qob was born.[4]

DAWARO

'Amdä Seyon and Haydära

Däwaro, which lay to the south of Fätägar, had, like it, become part of the Christian empire in early medieval times. Saint Täklä Haymanot reputedly had some influence in the area. His *Gädl*, or Acts, tells of a Muslim from the province who came to Fätägar to be baptised as a Saint. There is later mention of a poor woman of Däwaro who sought to prepare a feast for Täklä Haymanot, but was frustrated by a monkey who stole some of her grain.[5]

Emperor 'Amdä Seyon, after occupying Ifat as seen in the previous chapter, proceeded to garrison Däwaro. The province was accordingly mentioned in a soldiers' song of his reign.[6]

'Amdä Seyon's rule was, however, challenged, in the late 1320s, when Haydära, referred to in the royal chronicle as the province's local *seyum*, or governor, rebelled. Probably influenced by the rebellion of Sultan Säbr ad-Din II of Ifat he is said to have "professed love" for his master "in his words", but "in secret" to have had "evil designs" against him. He therefore approached Säbr ad-Din, and proposed an alliance, saying, "If he [the Emperor] comes against you I will come with my soldiers [to help you]; and if he comes against me, come with your soldiers [to help me]; we will fight together and destroy him utterly with his army". Haydära and his associates then proceeded to take what the chronicle describes as "evil" action against the Emperor. They "treacherously" captured, and killed, some of his messengers, and seized his possessions, and those of his consort, including "much gold and fine clothing".

---

4 Perruchon (1893), p. 67; Guidi (1889), Huntingford (1989), pp. 101-3
5 Getatchew and Macomber (1982), VI, 236, 243, (1983), VII, 241.
6 Cerulli (1936), pp. 7-14; Huntingford (1965a), p. 129; Merid Wolde Aregay (1974), p. 624.

'Amdä Seyon, incensed by this act of rebellion, at once set out with his troops. On reaching Däwaro, he captured Haydära, and, in accordance with the practice of the time, "laid waste the country from one end to the other". He killed young men, took prisoner women and children, seized livestock "without number", and "destroyed the crops of their country". The "wicked" designs of Haydära and his allies were thus "checked" and "brought to nothing".[7]

Ibn Fadl Allah al-'Umäri's Report

Valuable information on Däwaro in this period is provided in the Egyptian courtier al-'Umäri's sympathetic report on Ethiopia's eastern Muslim provinces.

The territory, he states, measured five days' journey by two, i.e. perhaps 100 kilometres by 40. It was thus much smaller than Ifat, but resembled it in that it produced cereals and fruit, and reared horses and beasts of burden. Trade, however, was less developed. It was not carried out with Egyptian money, as in Ifat, but with pieces of iron, a type of "primitive money" called *hakunas*. They were the length of a needle but three times as thick. Five thousand were needed to purchase a cow, and three thousand for a goat.

The social customs of Däwaro were not very different from those of Ifat. The ruler did not, however, have an umbrella carried over his head, and he and his *amir*s when walking were not supported by attendants. The Däwaro army, about the size of that of Ifat, consisted of around 20,000 cavalry and 15,000 infantry.[8]

Missionary Activity

Christian missionary activity in the province was reportedly later carried out by one of Täklä Haymanot's disciples, Täsfa Hezan, who was ordered to do so by the redoubtable patriarch Abunä Ya'qob.[9]

ARABABNI

The Muslim province of Aräbabni was adjacent to Däwaro, but slightly larger, measuring, al-'Umäri says, four day's journey by four, i.e. maybe 80 kilometres square. The province's agricultural production, which included cereals, legumes and fruits, was likewise

---

[7] Huntingford (1965a), pp. 2, 65, 107-8.
[8] Gaudefroy-Demomboynes (1927), pp. 14-15, 26.
[9] Getatchew Haile and Macomber (1981), V, 444.

similar to that of Däwaro. Trade, as in Däwaro, was based on *hakunas*. The province had on the other hand a smaller army, comprising a little less than 10,000 foot soldiers, though its cavalry was described as "very numerous".[10]

BALI

Bali, in the far south of the empire, was separated from Däwaro by the Wäbi Shabellé River, and extended southwards to the Ganale Doria River. The province was inhabited by an animist Sidama people, some of whom had by the fourteenth century at least adopted Islam. The territory was ruled by a Muslim whom 'Amdä Seyon's soldiers' songs refer to as 'Ali.[11]

Ibn Fadl al-'Umäri's Report

Bali, according to al-'Umäri, was one of the largest of Ethiopia's Muslim provinces. It measured twenty days' journey by six, i.e. perhaps about 400 kilometres by 120. Situated in the southern highlands it had greater rainfall, and was hence more fertile, than the neighbouring territories, and enjoyed a fresher climate. Agricultural production, food, dress and social customs nevertheless resembled those of other nearby Muslim lands.

Because of its location to the far south Bali's trade was less developed than that of neighbouring territories. Coins were not in circulation, as in Ifat, nor *hakuna* as in the lands immediately to the north. Trade was therefore mainly based on barter, and largely took the form of the exchange of cattle, sheep and cloth.

Bali also differed from nearby Muslim provinces in that its government was not in the hands of a hereditary dynasty, but of a man of humble origin - possibly the said 'Ali. He had won the favour of 'Amdä Seyon, from whom he obtained investiture as ruler. The province's army consisted of eighteen thousand cavalry, besides "many" infantry.[12]

---

[10] Gaudefroy-Demomboynes (1927), pp.15, 26.
[11] Huntingford (1965a),129. See also Taddesse Tamrat (1972a), p. 155; Merid Wolde Aregay (1974), pp. 625-6.
[12] Gaudefroy-Demombynes (1927), p. 18

Sayfä Ar'ad, Dawit and Yeshaq

Bali was unaffected by Sultan Säbr ad-Din II's rebellion, and therefore remained under Christian control throughout the fourteenth century. During the reign of Emperor Sayfä Ar'ad (1342-1370) the province was ruled by a governor with the title of *gärad*.

Fierce fighting subsequently took place during the time of Emperor Dawit. One of the most powerful rulers of Ifat, Sultan Sä'd ad-Din I, made his way south with fifty horsemen to raid Bali, which, according to Maqrizi, was situated twelve days' distance away. The province was then garrisoned by ten commanders, each with ten thousand soldiers. Sä'd ad-Din, however, easily defeated them. He inflicted such heavy casualties that the corpses of the dead are said to have entirely covered the ground, and people could only move about by trampling over them. The Ifat ruler subsequently ordered a second raid on Bali. It was carried out by an officer called Asad, and led to further grim fighting after which the Ifat warriors returned with rich spoils.

Later, during the reign of Emperor Yeshaq, Sä'd ad-Din's grandson, Sultan Jämal ad-Din, the ruler of Adäl, despatched his commander, Harb Jaush, on an expedition to the province whose Christian governor, according to Maqrizi, had raised a large army. In the ensuing battle both sides fought strenuously, but Harb Jaush was victorious. He subsequently undertook a second expedition, in the course of which he once more killed many inhabitants, and seized "a great many prisoners". So much booty reportedly fell into his hands that every poor man was given three slaves. They were so plentiful that their price dropped heavily. After each of these expeditions, however, the Emperor's forces reasserted their authority.

A subsequent attack on Bali by Sultan Shihab ad-Din Ahmäd Bädlay of Adäl had more long term consequences. Having gained control of the province, he settled it with 1,000 Muslim families, thereby changing its religious, and ethnic, composition.[13]

Despite this development Bali for much of Emperor Yeshaq's reign remained part of the Christian empire, as indicated by a soldiers' song of the time.[14]

---

[13] Rinck (1790), pp. 33-4, 40. See also Budge (1928b), I, 300, 303.
[14] Huntingford (1965a), p. 129.

SHARKHA

Shärkha, one of the smaller Muslim provinces in the region, was situated west of Däwaro, and north of Bali. The territory came under the control of the Ethiopian Christian empire in the early medieval period, and at about the same time was converted to Islam.

The territory was ruled in the early fourteenth century by a governor called Yoséf, who joined the above-mentioned conspiracy of Haydära, governor of Däwaro, against Emperor 'Amdä Seyon. The plot was, however, foiled by the Christian monarch, who, according to his chronicler, broke up the conspiracy. Yoséf was apprehended at the town of Bähela, and bound as a prisoner. The Emperor thereupon sent his troops to Shärkha, where they laid waste the country and seized cattle, sheep, goats, horses, mules, and donkeys in "great numbers", as well as much fine clothing. They then returned to the king their master.[15]

Shärkha was later briefly referred to in al-'Umäri's report. It states that the province measured five days' journey by three, i.e. around 100 kilometres by 60. It was thus about the size of Däwaro or Aräbabni, with both of which it had much in common. Its produce, cereals, legumes and fruit were similar, and it likewise made use as currency of small pieces of iron called *hakunas*. The Shärkha army was, however, substantially smaller than that of either neighbouring state, for it comprised little more than 6,000 infantry and around 3,000 horsemen.[16]

DARHA

Därha was even smaller than Shärkha, and, perhaps for that reason, the least well documented of Ethiopia's Muslim provinces. Its exact location is also far from certain, for a territory of this name was variously described as being in the neighbourhood of Däwaro, on the borders of Bali, and between Bägémder and Gojjam, south-east of Lake Tana.[17]

---

[15] Huntingford (1965a), pp. 2, 65, 107-8.
[16] Rinck (1790), p. 17.
[17] Beckingham and Huntingford (1954), pp. 17, 18, 133; Bruce (1790), III, 253; Taddesse Tamrat (1972a), pp. 142, 188.

The first account of the province was given by al-'Umäri, who states that it measured only three days' journey by three, i.e. perhaps 60 kilometres square, and had a smaller population than any of the territories in the region. Commerce was based only on barter. The local ruler, the weakest in the region, had no more than two thousand cavalry, and about as many infantry.

The province, because of its weakness, was probably later absorbed by one or more of its neighbours, and disappears from view for the next two centuries.

RELATIONSHIP WITH THE ETHIOPIAN EMPIRE, AND IFAT
The Muslim sultanates above discussed, according to al-Umäri, were all subordinate to the Ethiopian Emperor, whom he terms the "King of Amhara". He writes:
"Although all the sovereigns of these [Muslim] kingdoms transmit their power on a hereditary basis, none of them have their own authority except that invested by the sovereign of Amhara. When one of these kings passes away and there are male [heir]s in his family, they all go to the sovereign of Amhara, and use all their means to gain his favour, because it is he who will chose the one to whom he will confer power. Once he has been invested with power he has supreme authority over them, and in front of him they are only his lieutenants."

Al-Umäri, however, makes one significant additional point: The Muslim chiefs, though subject to the "King of Amhara", also afforded special "respect" to the ruler of Ifat, and in certain circumstances gave him their support.[18]

HARAR
Little is known in this period of any settlement called Harär. The name, however, appears in passing in 'Amdä Seyon's chronicle, thus suggesting that the town mentioned in later chapters seems to have dated back to at least the early fourteenth century, if not earlier.[19]

---

[18] Gaudefroy-Demombynes (1927), pp. 18-19.
[19] Huntingford (1965a), pp. 31, 78/

Chapter 9
THE SOUTH-WEST and WEST: GURAGE, WAJ, KAMBATA and WALAMO, GAMO, HADEYA, GANZ, ENARYA, BOSHA, DAMOT, GAFAT, JANJERO, KAFA, and THE COUNTRIES of THE BAREYAS and "SHANQELLAS"

GURAGE

Amdä Seyon, Säbr ad-Din II and Yeshaq

The Guragés lived to the south of Shäwa, and spoke a Semitic language, or cluster of languages, related to those of the nearby Gafats and Argobbas and the Adarés of Harär. One of several contradictory traditions holds that the Guragés in fact originally came from the Harär region.[1]

The area inhabited by the Guragés, which was doubtless considerably larger than that at present, seems to have come under the sovereignty of the Ethiopian empire in early medieval times. Some oral traditions claim that this occurred during the reign of 'Amdä Seyon or shortly afterwards. One of the imperial commanders, a certain Azmach Säbhat from the town of Gura'é in Akälä Guzay, is supposed to have settled at Aymälläl in northern Guragéland. Folk etymology also claims that the name Guragé meant the *Gé*, or "country", of Gura'é. Other authorities have, however, asserted, that the country owed its name to the fact it was on the *Gra*, or "left", when viewed from Entotto or some such early Shäwan capital.[2]

Another tradition linking Guragéland with 'Amdä Seyon is preserved by members of the monastery of Gädamä Iyäsus in the Muhär area. The monarch's forces making their way into the region, were accompanied, it is claimed, by one of Saint Täklä Haymanot's followers, a monk called Zéna Marqos. He is said to have remained in the district for forty years. During this time he reportedly converted even the most committed of traditional leaders, among them one Awa Gyät, and established 157 churches. Forty-four were supposedly in Muhär, which is to this day the Guragé area in which the Ethiopian

---

[1] Mondon-Vidailhet (1900), p. 169, (1901), p. 402; Cohen (1931), pp. 14-37, 42-4; Leslau (1944), pp. 57, 65.

[2] Krapf (1867); Bairu Tafla (1987), pp. 209, 219; Lebel (1974), pp. 101-2.

Orthodox Church is strongest.³ The figure forty-four, in this and most other Ethiopian contexts, should not be taken literally, for it is traditionally used to signify a large number.

Firmer evidence that Guragé was under imperial rule during the reign of 'Amdä Seyon is found in that ruler's chronicle. It claims that Sultan Säbr ad-Din II spoke of his intention of nominating a *mäsfen*, or prince, of Alamalé, i.e. Aymälläl, as 'Amdä Seyon had done.⁴

Säbr ad-Din seems in fact to have obtained some Guragé support. Those joining him, according to the chronicle, included 12 "Geragi", presumably Guragé, chiefs, three Seltogi, possibly Silté leaders, and several other chiefs, among them those of Gito, Wäri and Wäta, whose Guragé identity is debatable.⁵

Imperial rule over the Guragé area was subsequently indicated in a soldiers' song of Emperor Yeshaq's reign, which records that the Ennämor district paid that monarch tribute in horses.⁶

The Guragé area was later the site of considerable missionary activity organised by the renowned Patriarch, Abunä Ya'qob. It was carried out by two of Täklä Haymanot's disciples, Iyosyas, who also preached in nearby Wäj, and Adhani Egzi', who operated in the Selti area and also further west in Damot.⁷

WAJ

The small province of Wäj, about which little is known at this time, was situated around Lake Zway and occupied the area west of Fätägar and east of Hadeya. The province became part of the Ethiopian empire in early medieval times, as evident from the fact that it reportedly supported King Yekuno Amlak's assumption of power in 1270.⁸

The territory was still under imperial sovereignty during 'Amdä Seyon's reign. A soldiers' song of his time indicates that it was ruled for him by a governor called Zebédär.⁹

---

3 Lebel (1974), p. 101.
4 Huntingford (1965a), p. 54.
5 Huntingford (1965a), p. 78; Merid Wolde Aregay (1974), pp. 272-3.
6 Guidi (1889), line 44.
7 Getatchew Haile and Macomber (1981), V, 444.
8 Conti Rossini (1922), p. 297.
9 Huntingford (1965a), pp. 23, 129. Perruchon (1893), p. 15.

This was also a period of Christian missionary work. The Patriarch, Abunä Ya'qob, appointed Abba Iyosyas, to supervise such activity in the area as well as in Guragé.[10]

KAMBATA AND WALAMO

Two other tributary territories deserve mention. Kämbat, or Kämbata, and Wälamo, or Wolyata. The former lay to the west of Lake Abaya; the latter between Lake Awäsa and the Omo River. Both, according to a soldier's song of Yeshaq's reign, paid tribute in horses.[11]

GAMO

Gämo, another small province probably situated to the west of Lake Chamo, was at this time also under imperial rule. The territory seems to have consisted of two separate political entities, Bahr Gämo (doubtless so named because of its proximity to a *bahr*, or stretch of water, in fact Lake Abbaya) and Suf Gämo. Both areas, to judge by a soldiers' song of the time of Yeshaq, paid the latter tribute, also mainly in horses.[12]

HADEYA

Hadeya, one of the best documented territories in the area, was situated in the highlands to the far south-west of the Christian empire, and further west than Shärkha. The province was inhabited by animist Sidama people, some of whom were converted to Islam.

The territory probably became an integral, tax-paying, part of the Ethiopian empire early in the fourteenth century, during the reign of 'Amdä Seyon. In a manuscript written on the island monastery of Hayq, the monarch states that, after conquering Damot around 1316-7, he proceeded to Hadeya, and adds: "God gave me all the people of Hadeya, men and women without number, whom I exiled into another area". Having thus gained control of the territory he recruited many of its inhabitants into his army.

'Amdä Seyon also made at least one land grant to a courtier from Hadeya. It states that the man, surprised at the expense the Emperor incurred in purchasing mules, proposed that they be bred in the royal

---

[10] Taddesse Tamrat (1972a), p. 176; Huntingford (1989), p. 73; Getatchew Haile (1981), V, 444.
[11] Guidi (1989), pp. 43-56; Huntingford (1989), p. 94.
[12] Guidi (1889), pp. 53-66; Huntingford (1989), pp. 94, 118.

stables. The monarch was so pleased that he allowed him to choose whatever *gult*, or estates, he desired. He was accordingly given several outside the Hadeya area, in Enarya, Wäräb and Amhara.[13]

Hadeya was then apparently well known to the Ethiopian body politic. This is suggested by Ethiopia's medieval epic the *Kebrä Nägäst*, or Glory of Kings, which, though written at Aksum, in the far north of the empire, makes reference to the province. The passage claims that Menilek I, son of the Queen of Sheba, on one occasion made war on the Hadeya people.[14] Though not to be taken historically, the passage provides interesting evidence of a northern Ethiopian awareness of the Hadeya identity.

King Amäno, the Prophet Bäl'am and Emperor Amdä Seyon

Hadeya's incorporation into the empire was not without difficulties. 'Amdä Seyon's chronicle reports that Sultan Säbr ad-Din's rebellion spread from Ifat to Hadeya. The local governor, who is referred to as King Amäno (though the name was probably a local generic term for a ruler), was advised by Bäl'am, a "prophet of darkness", to rebel. "Go not to the king of Seyon", i.e. to the Emperor, he is said to have declared, "Do not give him gifts: if he comes against you, be not afraid of him, for he will be delivered into your hands and you will cause him to perish with his army".[15]

The Hadeya ruler, who. we may assume from his name, was almost certainly a local man, hearkened, it is said, to the "the counsel of this lying prophet", and rebelled. The Emperor then "rose up in anger", and set forth for Hadeya, where he "slew the inhabitants of the country with the point of the sword". Describing the vengeance wrought by the warlike Emperor on the people of Hadeya the chronicler declares: "Some he destroyed, and those who survived he took into captivity together with their king; their old ones and young ones, men, women and children, he led them away to the capital of his kingdom". The "false prophet" Bäl'am then "took himself off and fled to the land of Ifat".[16]

---

13 Taddesse Tamrat (1970), p. 96. See also Taddesse Tamrat (1972a), pp. 73, 76, 135, 173; Merid Wolde Aregay (1974), pp. 626; Huntingford (1965a), pp. 9, 60, 99.
14 Budge (1922), p. 165.
15 Huntingford (1965a) p. 58.
16 Huntingford (1965a) pp. 38-9. See also Taddesse Tamrat (1972a), p. 106, 136.

Despite such punishment many men from Hadeya served in 'Amdä Seyon's army, which also contained soldiers from neighbouring Damot, as well as from such central provinces as Shäwa, Amhara, and Gojjam. This is well documented in his chronicle, which tells of him despatching a Hadeya contingent, together with soldiers from Damot, on an expedition in 1329 against the people of Sämén, Wägära, Sälämt and Sägädé, who had been converted to the faith of the Fälashas.[17] Evidence of the province's participation in the army is also found in a soldiers' song of the time.[18]

The Reports of Ibn Fädl Allah al-Omäri and Maqrizi

Valuable glimpses of Hadeya towards the close of 'Amdä Seyon's reign are embodied in al-Umäri's report. It suggests that the province, though small, measuring only eight days' journey by nine, i.e. maybe 160 kilometres by 180, was one of the most important of the territories there discussed. Well favoured by nature, it produced cereals and fruit, raised horses and beasts of burden, and, like Däwaro and Shärkha, used pieces of iron as "primitive money".

Hadeya was much involved in the slave trade, for it imported slaves from the "country of the infidels", presumably nearby Christian or "pagan" lands. The castration of slaves, al-'Umäri learnt from a merchant who had visited the territory, had been forbidden by the Emperor (perhaps in fact 'Amdä Seyon). The operation was, however, often carried out illegally, at the nearby town of Waslu, whither traders took their slaves for castration, which greatly increased their value. Eunuchs were then conveyed to Hadeya, where they remained until they recovered. The province's inhabitants were reputedly skilled in curing the victims of such operations, but the number of slaves who died were said to have been greater than those who survived.

Hadeya, though small, was powerful. Conceivably densely populated, it could, we are told, raise a large army of no less than 40,000 cavalry, and at least twice as many foot soldiers.[19]

The province throughout this time remained firmly under imperial suzerainty. A provincial ruler, whom Maqrizi referred to by the old name or title of Amäno, fought on the Christian side against Sultan

---

[17] Huntingford (1965a), p. 61.
[18] Huntingford (1965a), p. 129. See also Taddesse Tamrat (1972a), p. 91.
[19] Gaudefroy-Demombynes, (Paris, 1927), pp. 15-17. This account was subsequently repeated by Maqrizi. See Rinck (1790), pp. 3, 9. See also pp. 86-7.

Sä'd ad-Din of Ifat, but was defeated. The Amäno was put to flight, and a large number of his men were captured.[20]

GANZ

Gänz was a small tributary state located to the west of Wäj and north of Hadeya. Little documentation on it is available for this period. The territory is, however, known to have been ruled by a local chief with the title of Tata, as evident from a soldiers' song of the reign of Yeshaq.[21]

ENARYA

A Gold-Yielding Tributary State

Enarya, a gold-yielding territory north-west of Hadeya, also known as Inar'it, came under northern Ethiopian influence in the late Aksumite or early medieval period. King Degna Jan, or Anbässa Wedem, an Aksumite ruler of around the first half of the ninth century, is reported in an early Ethiopian text to have travelled to the province.[22]

Christian missionary work was later undertaken during the reign of 'Amdä Seyon. His Patriarch, Abunä Ya'qob, appointed one of Saint Täklä Haymanot's numerous disciples, a monk called Yoséf, to supervise such activity.[23]

A subsequent soldiers' song of Yeshaq's reign indicates that the province was tributary to the Ethiopian empire, paying its tax in gold, for which it was long famous.[24]

BOSHA

Bosha, situated between the Omo and Gojeb rivers, south of Enarya, was another territory about which little is known at this time. The province seems to have had become part of the Ethiopian empire in the early medieval period. A soldiers' song of the reign of Yeshaq indicates that the area, like Enarya, paid tribute, mainly in gold.[25]

---

[20] Rinck (1790), p.23.
[21] Guidi (1889), pp. 53-66; Huntingford (1965a), p. 86.
[22] Taddesse Tamrat (1972a), p. 35.
[23] Taddesse Tamrat (1972a), p. 177; Getatchew Haile (1981), V, 444.
[24] Guidi (1889), line 38. See also Huntingford (1989), pp. 94-5.
[25] Guidi (1989), line 41.

DAMOT

Damot, a province for which relatively abundant documentation is available, was the name given to a territory at this time situated south of the Blue Nile, between it and the Gibé River. The area was probably inhabited by a Sidama people related to those of Enarya and Janjero.[26] Animist by religion they lived on the south-western borders of the empire, and are thought for a time to have had women rulers. A suggestion to this effect is found in the earliest reference to the area, the medieval Egyptian *History of the Patriarchs of Alexandria*. It states that the country of Bani al-Hamwiyah, which the notable Italian scholar Conti Rossini believed to have been a mis-reading of al-Damutah, i.e. Damot, was ruled by a queen. She is said to have rebelled and led her people against the Christians of Ethiopia.[27]

Contacts with the north seem to have developed in early medieval times. A fifteenth century Ethiopian Christian religious text, the *Gädlä Yaréd*, states that one of the Zagwé rulers sent an expedition from his capital at Roha, later Lalibäla, in Lasta all the way to Damot.[28]

Saint Täklä Haymanot and Motä Lamé

Damot is well known in the traditions of the Ethiopian Orthodox Church. A supposedly "pagan" country, it was reportedly the site of some of the most important missionary efforts, and alleged miraculous doings, of Saint Täklä Haymanot. The territory is said to have been ruled, some time in the first half of the thirteenth century, by a "pagan" chief referred to as Motä Lamé (or Motalami). The name, or more precisely, the title was probably derived from the Amharic *méta*, or "guard", and *lam*, or "cattle", and was thus synonymous with the office of *sähafä lahm*, or "writer or recorder of cattle", used in many other areas of Ethiopia.[29]

---

[26] Merid Wolde Aregay (1974), pp. 628-9.
[27] Conti Rossini (1928), p. 286.
[28] Conti Rossini (1904), pp. 22-4. See also Sergew Hable Sellassie (1972), p. 230; Taddesse Tamrat (1972a), p. 65; Taddesse Tamrat (1988), p. 133.. Sergew, p, 281, observes: "the arch enemy of the Zagwé Emperors was Motelomé.. who refused to pay tribute".
[29] Huntingford (1965a), pp. 129, 133; Taddesse Tamrat (1972a), p. 121.

The late thirteenth century Ethiopian Christian missionary Saint Täklä Haymanot in the wilderness, where he travelled to preach to magicians and "idolators": a much later imaginary manuscript illustration of Gondarine times depicting the supposed process of conversion on the southern periphery of the empire.
From E.A. Wallis Budge, *The Life of Takla Haymanot in the Version of Dabra Libanos*.

Täklä Haymanot smiting the king-magician of Bilat, and about to hurl him from his throne: a much later manuscript illustration depicting the advance of Christianity in the south of the empire. From E.A. Wallis Budge, *The Life of Takla Haymanot in the Version of Dabra Libanos*.

Täklä Haymanot conversing with magicians of the pre-Christian faith: another much later manuscript illustration depicting the advance of Christianity in the south of the empire.
From E.A. Wallis Budge, *The Life of Takla Haymanot in the Version of Dabra Libanos.*

Täklä Haymanot baptising a local governor, his wife and son: a further Gondarine manuscript illustration depicting the process on conversion.
From E.A. Wallis Budge, *The Life of Takla Haymanot in the Version of Dabra Libanos.*

King Motälamè of Damot takes up his spears to kill Täklä Haymanot: a much later Gondarine manuscript illustration.
From E.A. Wallis Budge, *The Life of Takla Haymanot in the Version of Dabra Libanos.*

Motälamè, after his conversion to Christianity, gives Täklä Haymanot a gift of one thousand pounds of gold, in gratitude for being allowed to adopt the Saint's own Christian name, Fesseha Seyon.
From E.A. Wallis Budge, *The Life of Takla Haymanot in the Version of Dabra Libanos.*

Motä Lamé, whose capital was said to have been at a place called Malbärdé reportedly in Damot, also held the title of *mäkwännen* or *seyum. He* was thus considered an officer of an Ethiopian monarch, presumably one of the Zagwé dynasty. His *bétä mängesteya,* or palace, was at Malbärdé, or Malbäredé, where he reputedly kept his personal idols.[30]

Motä Lamé and Täklä Haymanot are mentioned in the Ethiopian Synaxary, as well as in the Saint's *Gädl,* or Acts. The former claims that Satan had made Motä Lamé governor of Damot, while the latter describes him as cunning, exceedingly skilful in war, and possessed of magical powers, for which reason he became ruler over the other governors. The Synaxary asserts that he laid waste the whole of Shäwa; the *Gädl* that he tore down all the churches of the Christians, worshipped idols, and "destroyed all the Laws of God". Both texts, which are based on legend, claim that the nobles of the territories he occupied, one after another, gave him their women. The *Gädl* states that the chiefs did this because they were afraid that he would otherwise kill them. The result, it claims, was that there were no more virgins. If any were found they were brought to him, after which he "straightaway abated their virginity". Beautiful women, according to the Synaxary, were all turned into his concubines.

On one occasion his soldiers reportedly arrived at Selalesh, perhaps the modern Sälälé, in Shäwa, where they seized an exceedingly beautiful woman called Egzi'é Kharäya. She was, it is claimed, the future mother of Saint Täklä Haymanot, and was brought to the lustful Motä Lamé. When he saw her he "rejoiced exceedingly", had her adorned with fine clothing, and took her with him to Damot. There his nobles began preparing a feast for his marriage with her - but she was saved, the *Gädl* asserts, by the intervention of the Archangel Mika'él, who carried her on his wings to her husband.

Täklä Haymanot was born shortly afterwards, and, helped by the Holy Spirit, soon devoted his life to good works. He undertook a number of missionary journeys, mainly in Shäwa and lands further south and west. He thus travelled to Kätäta, where he uprooted a tree formerly worshipped, by the "pagans", and reportedly converted six hundred thousand of the latter to Christianity. He then went to Wifat, i.e. Ifat, where he scattered devils; Bilat (probably some 60 kilometres north-north-east of modern Addis Ababa), where he thrust a magician-king from his throne; and Adamo, where he preached and

---

[30] Huntingford (1989), pp. 69-70.

healed the sick.[31] His third missionary journey is said to have brought him to Zeba Fätän, a mountain in Damot, the site of "many idols of stone and wood", which he overthrew.

Motä Lamé, on learning of these remarkable events, ordered his soldiers to bring him the holy man, bound with strong fetters. The chief, it is claimed, then reportedly asked him, "Why dost thou destroy my country?", after which he ordered his men to kill Täklä Haymanot, by throwing him down a great precipice called Tomä Gera. The saint was, however, miraculously saved several times, for God gave him the "strength to endure", and raised him up unharmed.

After this and other fabulous events Täklä Haymanot cured Motä Lamé from a painful disease, from which he had long suffered, and converted him to Christianity. The chief thereupon asked to be given the holy man's own baptismal name, Fesseha Seyon, and in return supposedly presented Täklä Haymanot with no less than one thousand pounds weight of gold. (The rare metal, we may assume, had probably come from the nearby gold-producing province of Enarya). Motä Lamé at the same time ordered his subjects to abandon their idols, and instead to worship the Christian God. He decreed that anyone found with an idol in his house should be hurled down from the rocks.

Täklä Haymanot is meanwhile said to have taught Motä Lamé and his chiefs the Books of the Prophets and Apostles. He subsequently interrogated a group of priests, whom the chief had captured in Shäwa and had abjured their faith. They admitted that they worshipped idols, but declared that they did so against their will. A *tabot,* or representation of the Ark of the Covenant, which had been seized with them, and taken to Damot, was re-consecrated. Motä Lamé inquired as to the number of magicians and such like persons in his country, and was reportedly told that there were 400 magicians, 200 diviners, 300 sorcerers, and 100 enchanters.

The Saint carried out many conversions, "one hundred and two thousand and ninety souls" on a single day, according to the *Gädl,* or "twelve thousand and ninety-nine" according to the Synaxary. He then commanded Motä Lamé to build churches throughout the territory, and the chief consented to do so. He then ordered his governors to build additional churches in their own districts. Places of Christian worship were thus erected throughout the whole country. The soothsayers asked Täklä Haymanot about his teachings, after which

---

[31] Budge (1906), pp. 75-110.

he appointed twelve of them priests "so that they might preach the Gospel in all the country of Damot till the day of their death". The leaders of the old religion, it is interestingly suggested, thus emerged as the leaders of the new.

Täklä Haymanot, it is said, remained in the province twelve years. During this time he "filled the area with his teachings", and his message was heard in a vast area as far as "the land of Bareya", i.e. the country occupied by the "Shanqellas", or black population on the borders of Sudan, and the river Geyon, or Blue Nile.[32]

Emperor 'Amdä Seyon

'Amdä Seyon subsequently incorporated Damot into the Christian empire. A manuscript in the monastery in Lake Hayq, describing events in 1316-17, quotes him as claiming, "God gave me all the people of Damot into my hands: its king, its princes, its rulers and its people, men and women without number". It was after this that he proceeded, as already noted, to seize control of nearby Hadeya.[33]

The Emperor's rule over Damot is also mentioned in 'Amdä Seyon's chronicle. It claims that Sultan Säbr ad-Din II, during his rebellion, appointed a *mäsfen*, or governor, for the province, as the Emperor had earlier done. One of the units in 'Amdä Seyon's army, commanded by a certain Markäsäwäy, was called after the province. Damot warriors likewise played an important military role, and were engaged fighting in the north in Sämén, Wägära, Sälämt and Sägärdé, as well as against the Muslims of Adäl who had invaded Shäwa from the east.

Further Christian missionary activity in Damot also took place at this time. Abunä Ya'qob, the Patriarch, appointed one of Täklä Haymanot's followers, Abba Adhani Egzi', to take charge of this work. The province's local ruler at this time was a chief bearing the old title of Motä Lamé. Doubtless a successor of the king with whom

---

[32] Budge (1906), pp. 109-46, and Plates X and XI, and XLV to LIX; Budge (1928a), IV, 1241-3; Conti Rossini (1896), pp. 102-6. On Saint Täklä Haymanot's activities see also Kinafe-Rigb Zelleke (1975), pp. 92-3, Huntingford (1966), p. 38, (1979), pp. 271, 296, (1989), pp. 69-77; and, on Matä Lomé, see also Sergew Hable Sellassie (1972), p. 281; Huntingford (1979), p. 247; Huntingford (1989), p. 71.For a modern analysis of the Damot ruler see also Kaplan (1984), pp. 10-12.

[33] Taddesse Tamrat (1972a), p. 135.

Täklä Haymanot had contended he is mentioned in a soldiers' song of 'Amdä Seyon's reign. Another Ethiopian missionary, the aforesaid Abba Iyosyas, is reported to have founded a monastery in the area, by name Däbrä Me'raf.[34]

Damot throughout this time played an important role in the Horn of Africa gold trade. Evidence of this is found in al-'Umäri, who asserts that rare metal from the province was despatched as far as Ifat, doubtless for export via Zäylä' or other Gulf of Aden port.[35]

Damot at this time, as later, was probably also a source of slaves. This is suggested by a Ge'ez text of the reign of Emperor Eskender (1478-1494), which tells of a slave from the province, who was taken to the town of Bärara in Shäwa, where he escaped. His owner reportedly prayed to the Virgin Mary for his return. She is said to have responded to his prayer, but so shamed him that he gave the slave to a local church in her name.[36]

Additional information on Damot is provided by local tradition, recorded by the Arab writer Ibn Khaldun (1332-1406). Evidently impressed by the province's importance he states that it had been governed by a "great king" (Motä Lamé?), who reputedly had a "large empire". His authority was reportedly recognised by the distant Wälashma', or ruler, of Ifat, who, we may assume, was probably interested in the territory as a source of gold.[37]

The Damot over which Motä Lamé reigned, and in which Täklä Haymanot wrought his miracles, is sometimes identified with the Wälamo, or Wälayta, or later times.[38] Some traditions suggest that the Saint lived near the present-day town of Soddo, where there is a hill known as Damot. One oral tradition voiced by local Amhara settlers was recorded by the modern Ethiopian scholar Tsehai Berhane Sellasie. It claims that a waterfall, 10 kilometres from Soddo, today known as Tosa Asfo, or God's Precipice, was the Tomä Gera of the hagiography. The local Wolayta people recall that they were once

---

[34] Taddesse Tamrat (1972a), pp. 176-7; Huntingford (1989), p. 73; Getatchew Haile (1981), V, 444, (1993), X, 214.
[35] Gaudefroy-Demombynes (1927), p. 13.
[36] Getatchew Haile (!981), pp. 174-80.
[37] De Slane (1927), II, 108; Cerulli (1943a), p. 284.
[38] Guèbrè Sellassié (1930-1), I, 360-1,

ruled by a king called Motä Lamé, but, interestingly enough, know nothing of Täklä Haymanot.[39]

GAFAT

Gafat, on the south-western periphery of the Christian empire, was inhabited by a population speaking a Semitic language related to Adaré and the Guragé tongues.[40]

The province, or at least parts of it, became tributary to the empire in early medieval times. Like nearby Damot it is reported, in the *Gädlä Yaréd*, to have come under Zagwé rule in the twelfth or thirteenth century. Men from Gafat seem to have later played a major part in helping Emperor Yekuno Amlak's rise to power around 1270, as Taddesse Tamrat has argued. Saint Täklä Haymanot reportedly operated in the province, notably at Bilat, which is described in a hagiography as the site of a palace of a pre-Christian traditional religious leader.[41]

Reference to Gafat as part of the empire is found in a subsequent soldiers' song of the reign of 'Amdä Seyon, which indicates that the province was ruled by a functionary with the title of Awälamo.[42]

Gafat was later the site of missionary activity by several of Täklä Haymanot's followers. They included Abba Qäwestos (d.1340's), who reportedly baptised many "pagans", and erected churches, at Bilat and elsewhere, and Abba Anoréwos (d. 1374). Despite their efforts the Gafat people seem to have remained largely animist.

The assimilation of the Gafats, if Taddesse Tamrat's identification is correct, was also carried out by Zäkaryas, a Shäwan chief from Märrhabeté. Acting on instructions from his superior, the district governor, he carried out an expedition against a "very strong" and "uncircumcised", i.e. "pagan", people (the Gafats?) who were "not accustomed to paying the [king's] tribute, nor to being ruled [by others]". To subjugate them he was ordered "not to spare any of the men, nor any of their cattle", but to burn down their houses.

Gafat by the fifteenth century was firmly under imperial rule. A soldiers' song of Yeshaq's reign tells of the province paying tribute, mainly in cattle, which came from six districts in the region, among

---

[39] Tsehai Berhane Selassie (1975), pp.37-8.
[40] Beke (1845), p. 92; Leslau (1944), pp.56-65; Leslau (1966), 189-98.
[41] Conti Rossini (1904), p.24; Taddesse Tamrat (1988a), pp.123, 125-7.
[42] Huntingford (1965a), p. 129.

them Gämbo and Shat, identified by Taddesse Tamrat as Gafat clan names.[43]

JANJERO

The small kingdom of Janjero, situated between the Omo and Gibé Rivers, was largely isolated throughout this, as well as later times. The territory nevertheless paid tribute, in horses, to Emperor Yeshaq, as indicated by a soldiers' song in his honour, which refers to it as Zenjäro.[44]

KAFA

To the west of Janjero, beyond the confines of the Christian empire, lay the medieval kingdom of Käfa. It is thought to have been founded by a people called the Minjo, who established a dynasty toward the end of the fourteenth century. Oral traditions collected in the late nineteenth century by the Italian Geographical Mission, and in the early twentieth by the Austrian scholar Friedrich Bieber, refer to the first Käfa ruler as the "Minjo *Tato*", or King. He reportedly came to the throne around 1390, and was succeeded by Tato Girra, who was succeeded in turn by the "Addio king", who reigned until about 1495.[45]

Though by this time largely independent there are indications that Käfa, or its immediate environs to the west, had once been under at least partial imperial control. An early medieval Ethiopic text, the *Heggä wäsera'atä mängest*, or Law and Institutions of the Kingdom, notes that the Emperor's tributaries included the inhabitants of Wächära and Kont, doubtless Chära and Konch, or Konta, in or near eastern Käfa. The seventeenth century Jesuit traveller Manoel de Almeida likewise states that the Emperor's rule had formerly extended to Gamaro, the name by which the people of Käfa were generally known by their Gimira neighbours.[46]

---

[43] Taddesse Tamrat (1988a), pp. 127-8, 130-2.
[44] Guidi (1889), line 42.
[45] Cecchi (1885-7), II, 490; Bieber (1920-3), 494-533. See also Beckingham and Huntingford (1954), pp. lvii-lix; Huntingford (1955), p. 104.
[46] Varenbergh (1915-16), p. 12; Beccari (1903-17), II, 272; Huntingford (1955), p. 10.

THE COUNTRIES OF THE BAREYAS and "SHANQELLAS"

Contacts between the Christian empire and the Bareyas and other "black" peoples in the far west date back, as we have seen in Chapter 3, to ancient times, and resulted in the capture of many slaves. Bareyas also played a notable role in the medieval period. 'Amdä Seyon, according to his chronicler, thus made use of Bareya troops, but whether they were slave or free is not specified. They were commanded in 1329 by a certain Angotäy. Some of them, in view of their known use of bows and arrows, may well have been among the monarch's archers referred to elsewhere in the text.[47]

Almost a century later, when the holy monk Saint Marqorewos died in 1419, his followers at Däbrä Marqorewos near Demah north of the Märäb River feared, according to the *Mäshaf Nay 'Alitat*, that the Bareyas would advance upwards from the Särayé lowlands. To prevent this the monks established themselves at Kwedo Fälassi.

Knowledge of the Bareyas duly reached the outside world. The Famous *Egyptus Novelo* map, published in Florence in 1454, indicates the presence of "Baria silaus", or Flat-nosed Bareyas, north of the Märäb River.[48]

The Ethiopian Christian state at around this time was also in contact with another "black" people, the so-called "Shanqellas", who lived around the lower stretches of the Blue Nile. Like the Bareyas they are reputed to have been among the older inhabitants of the region. An Agäw tradition recorded by Charles Beke in the nineteenth century asserts that the "Shanqellas" were in fact the "previous occupiers" of Agäwmeder, but had been "displaced" by the Agäw. Some "Shanqellas", according to a fifteenth century soldier's song of the reign of Yeshaq, paid this monarch tribute in goats.[49]

---

[47] Huntingford (1955), pp. 60, 82.
[48] Conti Rossini (1942) p.213; Crawford (1958), p. 13, figs, 1 and 2.
[49] Beke (1845), II, 95; Guidi (1889), V, 55.

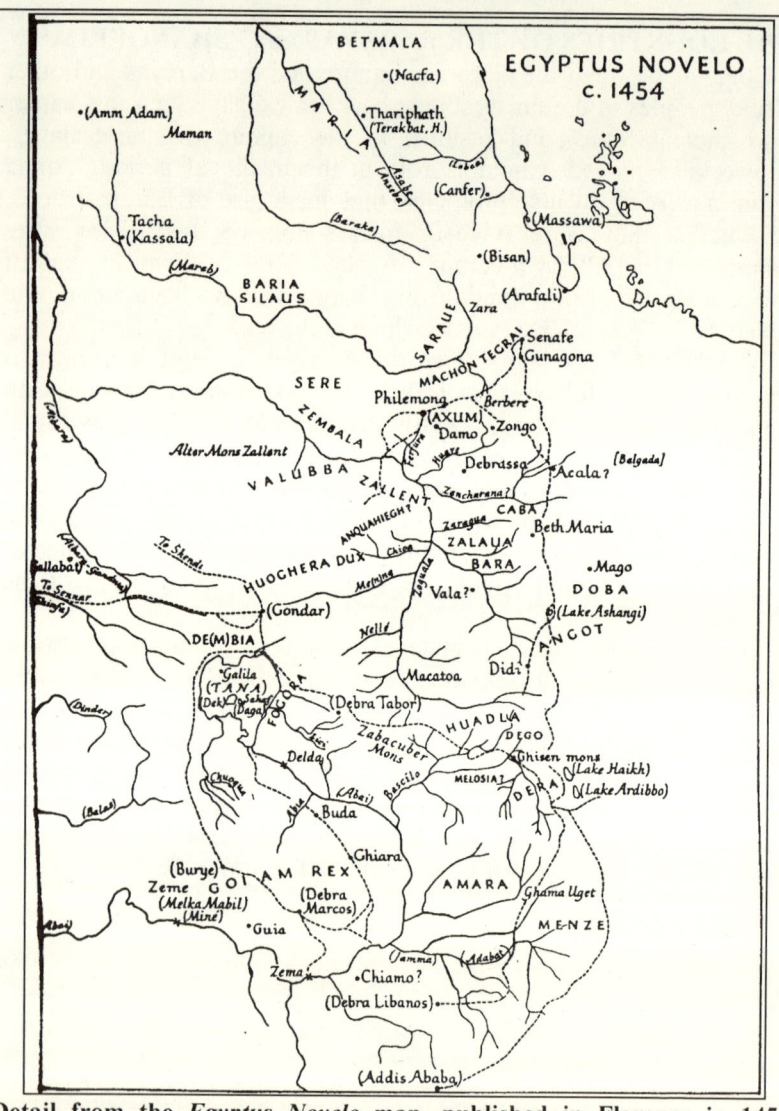

Detail from the *Egyptus Novelo* map, published in Florence in 1454, redrawn on a modern basis.
Note location of the Bareyas (Baria), north of the Märäb River.
From O.G.S. Crawford, *Ethiopian Itineraries ca. 1400-1524.*

Chapter 10
THE BORDERLANDS and THE INTERIOR

This period witnessed three major developments and shifts in imperial Ethiopian power: the decline of the Aksumite kingdom, the rise and fall of the Zagwé dynasty in Lasta, and the emergence of the "Solomonic" dynasty based on Shäwa. One of the greatest monarchs of this latter dynasty, Emperor 'Amdä Seyon, reportedly carried out an expedition to the northern periphery, and undertook major campaigns in the eastern, southern and south-western borderlands. Such operations, and others by several of his successors, did much to integrate, or reintegrate, the peripheral areas into the Christian realm.

The North

The northern periphery was relatively little affected by political changes in the interior. The hinterland's foreign trade continued to pass by way of the Red Sea or Gulf of Aden coasts, which remained of essential importance to the entire region. The Aksumite port of Adulis declined and eventually disappeared, but was replaced in early medieval times by two nearby twin ports: the island port of Massawa and the adjacent mainland port of Hergigo, generally referred to by foreign writers as Arkiko. These two ports, together with others to the east on the Gulf of Aden coast, handled the greater part of the Ethiopian region's commerce. Exports and imports, making due allowance for international advances in technology, were not too different from those in former, Aksumite, days. Ivory, gold and slaves, were thus exported in return for textiles and manufactured goods.

The Afar lowlands in the medieval period continued to yield rock salt. The mineral was transported, as in earlier and later times, to a vast hinterland, where it was used, it may be assumed, for both human and animal consumption, and for exchange as "primitive money".

Significant developments took place during the period in the religious sphere. The northern highlands, like those further south, maintained their Christian identity, and spiritual allegiance to the old capital Aksum. This was symbolised by the erection at Asmära in Hamasén of a church in typically Aksumite style. Two important monasteries were also established on the northern periphery: Däbrä Bizän in Hamasén and Däbrä Maryam in Säraye.

The Afar lowlands, and a wide stretch of territory along the eastern coast, were on the other hand steadily adopting an entirely new religion: Islam.

Politically the link between the Christian empire and the northern borderlands over the centuries remained surprisingly intact. Hamasén and Särayé thus passed rapidly first under Zagwé, and subsequently Shäwan suzerainty. 'Amdä Seyon later reportedly carried out an expedition to the Red Sea coast, and at least four Ethiopian monarchs, 'Amdä Seyon, Säyfä Ar'ad, Dawit and Yeshaq, made land grants to major religious establishments in the northern periphery. Yeshaq is said to have also established a garrison at Massawa.

The East

The eastern borderlands, notably the Muslim sultanates of Ifat and Adäl, played a major role in the on-going trade between the interior and the Gulf of Aden port of Zäylä'. The latter place, which dated back to early medieval times, and was known to early Arab geographers, was frequented by many merchants, as well as by pilgrims bound for Mecca. Zäylä' was a notable emporium, whence gold and slaves were exported, and textiles and other manufactured goods imported. The eastern trade route was of considerable interest to Shäwa-based Christian Emperors, such as 'Amdä Seyon, who at times helped to finance its commerce.

The trade route to Zäylä' competed to some extent with that to Hergigo and Massawa. Though the latter route handled the export-import trade of the north, and the Zäylä' route that of the east, both were involved in the commerce of the central and especially the western provinces. This trade was based on the export of gold, ivory and slaves, and the import of manufactured goods. The articles transported along both routes were in fact largely similar, though the Zäylä' route dealt to a greater extent in the exports of the arid eastern lowlands, notably myrrh and resins. The importance of Ifat's foreign trade is evident from the fact that it was the only territory in the whole region in which currency seems to have circulated, as noted by al-'Umäri.

A significant difference between the two routes to the coast deserves to be mentioned. It sprang from the fact that the edge of the highlands was much further from the coast in the east than in the north. The lowland stretch of the Zäylä' route was thus occupied by two relatively powerful provinces: Ifat, on the edge of the highlands, and Adäl, towards the coast. The area they covered was the scene of a long drawn out political and religious conflict. The lowland area on the Massawa route by contrast consisted of only a narrow strip of land, which was easily dominated either from the highlands or the port.

Ifat and Adäl were both directly affected by the southward move of the imperial state and capital.

Ifat in the late thirteenth century was a fiefdom of Emperor Yekuno Amlak. The latter's reign coincided with the establishment of the local Wälashma' dynasty. Its founder, Sultan 'Umar, rebelled against Ethiopian rule, but, finding the insurrection unpopular, abandoned it. His son 'Ali and five of his successors, Haqq ad-Din I, Säbr ad-Din II, Jämal ad-Din I, Haqq ad-Din II and Sä'd ad-Din, nevertheless resumed what was to be a seemingly intermidable, indeed almost monotonous, war of Muslim against Christian. This conflict reached a climax during the rule of Sultan Säbr ad-Din, whose objective, as stated in 'Amdä Seyon's chronicle, was no less than to make himself "King of all the land of Ethiopia", and to appoint governors over the hitherto Christian empire as the Emperor had done. The ruler of the eastern periphery, if we can believe the chronicler, was thus attempting to reconstitute the traditional Ethiopian state by making himself master of the interior, while substituting Christianity by Islam.

The struggle in Ifat, like other fighting of the time, received warm encouragement from religious leaders on both sides. The conflict led not only to innumerable casualties, but also to the extensive capture of slaves, male and female. Most were probably assimilated by the victors, thereby producing a great mixing of peoples and cultures. Other slaves were, however, exported to Arabia and the East, thus helping to pay for the region's imports, largely of textiles and other manufactured goods.

Though mainly confined to Ifat the conflicts of this period at times extended to neighbouring provinces. Säbr ad-Din's rebellion thus spread from Ifat to Däwaro and the Afar country, and resulted in 'Amdä Seyon's intervention in these areas, while Sä'd ad-Din later fought against the Emperor's Amano, or local ruler, of Hadeya.

Despite many twists of fortune the Ifat leaders were eventually defeated by those of the Christian interior, albeit at the cost of immense bloodshed on both sides. In 1415 Emperor Dawit finally drove Sä'd ad-Din to the coast at Zäylä', where he died in battle, after which his sons fled to Arabia. The independent Ifat state thus came to an end, and was largely assimilated into the Shäwa-based Christian empire.

The situation in Adäl, located in the torrid lowlands to the east, was significantly different. The seizure in the late thirteenth century of an Ethiopian prelate returning from Jerusalem led, Marco Polo claims, to a punitive expedition, probably by Emperor Yagbe'a Seyon. The campaign was reportedly successful, but the monarch soon abandoned the territory. It then became virtually independent, though some measure of imperial sovereignty was subsequently re-asserted.

The sons of Sä'd as-Din, who had found refuge in Arabia, later returned to the Horn of Africa, and, with the help of their father's former supporters and their Arab patron Näsir Ahmäd, fought their way to power. The old ruler's son Sultan Säbr ad-Din established a new Adäl dynasty, and a new capital, Däkär, east of the old town of Ifat. He and his successors, notably his brothers Mänsur, Jämal ad-Din II and Shihab ad-Din, later waged many fierce, and often successful, battles which took them into the eastern highlands.

The Afar country to the north-east was the source of rock salt which was in great demand in the interior. The territory, however, remained largely isolated from the rest of the region, both Christian and Muslim. 'Amdä Seyon, when campaigning against Ifat, nevertheless advanced far into the Afar country. He captured its capital, Täläg, and defeated, and killed, the Afar ruler and many of his chiefs, before finally withdrawing once more into the highlands.

The South-West and West

The south-western borderlands, as in the past, contributed greatly to the wealth of the region as a whole. Political links between these areas and the empire came into existence at an early period. The Christian state's contact with Enarya apparently dated back to the reign of the Aksumite ruler Degna Jan, and that with Damot and Gafat to the Zagwé dynasty. Ties with Wäj came into existence during the reign of Emperor Yekuno Amlak, while those with Hadeya and Guragé were forged by 'Amdä Seyon.

Several south-westerly areas constituted important sources of wealth. Hadeya was reportedly much involved in the slave trade from neighbouring provinces, as well as in the profitable, albeit often fatal, castration of slaves. Enarya, or Inar'it, Bosha and Damot supplied large quantities of gold. The rare metal remained one of the region's principal exports. Damot was probably also a source of slaves. Kämbata, Wälamo, and Gämo contributed horses to the Shäwa-based monarchy, while Janjero, though largely isolated, and the "Shanqellas", both on occasion provided it with horses.

Contacts with the empire led in the south-west to a considerable amount of Christian proselytism. Damot was much influenced in the late thirteenth or early fourteenth centuries by the teachings of Saint Täklä Haymanot. This led to the legendary, and apparently spectacular, conversion of the "pagan" magician-ruler Motä Lamé and his court. Missionary activity in the province, as well as in neighbouring Wäj and Enarya, was resumed during 'Amdä Seyon's reign by the holy man's followers. Gafat was influenced by the teachings of several other disciples, among them Abba Qäwestos and Abba Anoréwos, and by the campaigning of a Märhabeté chief called Zäkaryas. Guragé was the site of missionary activity by several of the Saint's other followers, among them Abba Zéna Marqos, who reportedly lived in Muhär for forty years, and established over a hundred and fifty churches. Two other disciples, Iyosyas and Adhani Ezgi', also played an important missionary role in the province. Yoséf, yet another follower of Täklä Haymanot, was active in Enarya, while the afore-said Adhani Egzi' also operated in Damot.

The south-western region was also much affected by the rise of 'Amdä Seyon. Early in his reign he conquered Damot and Hadeya. Both provided a sizeable number of soldiers for the imperial army, which over the centuries was largely multi-ethnic in character. Men from these provinces fought in distant Sämén, Wägära and other northern provinces, as well as against the Muslims to the east.

Most of the south-west remained aloof from the struggle between the Christian empire and Ifat. The Amäno, or local ruler, of Hadeya, and at least some of the Guragés, nevertheless joined in Säbr ad-Din's rebellion, while one of his successors fought against that of Sä'd ad-Din. The Hadeya ruler on both occasions seems to have misjudged his chances, for each time the province's army was defeated.

Contacts with the western borders, which date back to ancient times, continued throughout this period. Some Bareyas were recruited into 'Amdä Seyon's army, and served under the command of a chief called Angotäy. "Shanqellas", another "black" people further to the south, now for the first time appear in the records. Both groups were a source of slaves.

Käfa, which lay beyond the borders of the empire, and about which no contemporary information is available, became a monarchy in the late fourteenth century, and was ruled by its own local Tato, or King. There are, however, some indications to suggest that the territory, or its eastern environs, were for a time perhaps loosely under imperial sovereignty.

The South and South-East

The southern provinces were economically the least important of the Ethiopian borderlands. Unlike the provinces to the north and east they were not on any major export-import route. Southern commerce was noticeably less advanced than that for example of Ifat. Däwaro, Aräbabni and Shärkha nevertheless made use of small pieces of iron called *hakuna*, which served as "primitive money". The southern provinces were not, however, the source of any item of wealth comparable to those of the south-west, and thus contributed little to imperial tribute.

Contacts between several southern or south-easterly provinces and the empire were, however, not insignificant. Most of the Muslim sultans, according to al-Umäri, received their investiture from the Ethiopian Emperor, though they also held the ruler of Ifat, he says, in special respect. Christian churches meanwhile were built in several areas, notably at Yäläbasha in Däwaro. Considerable Christian activity also took place, mainly by Täklä Haymanot's disciples. One of them, Täsfa Hezan, played a prominent role in Däwaro, and another, Mateyas, in Fätägar.

Two southern provinces were likewise caught up in Säbr ad-Din's rebellion. Haydära, the ruler of Däwaro, and Yoséf, that of Shärkha, both supported the insurrection, but were defeated by 'Amdä Seyon. Bali was subsequently attacked by two successive Ifat rulers, Sä'd ad-Din and Jämal ad-Din, and later by the Adäl ruler Shihab ad-Din. The latter settled a thousand Muslim families in the province, thereby significantly changing its ethnic and religious composition.

PART III
THE ERA OF ZAR'A YA'QOB
and
LEBNA DENGEL
(1433-1540)

Chapter 11
THE NORTH and NORTH-EAST: THE LAND OF THE BAHR NAGASH, THE AFAR COUNTRY and THE COUNTRY OF THE DOBE'AS

THE LAND OF THE BAHR NAGASH

Zär'a Ya'qob and the Bahr Nägash

The northern highlands, as we have seen in Chapter 1, had formed part of the Ethiopian empire since ancient times. They were administered in the middle ages by a functionary known as the Bahr Nägash, literally ruler of the sea, or coastal region. This official appears in written records during the reign of Emperor Zär'a Ya'qob (1433-1468), who may in fact have established the title.

Zär'a Ya'qob, it may be recalled, devoted much of his efforts to the reorganisation of Ethiopian government. As part of his reforms he "increased the power of the Bahr Nägash", his chronicle explains, and raised him "much above" all the *shum*s, or chiefs, of the region. The Bahr Nägash was thus given authority over the rulers of Shiré, south of the Märäb river, as well as over three areas to its north. He was thus accorded control over the *shum* of Särayé, the two *käntiba*s, or local chiefs, of Hamasén, and the *shum* of Bur, a semi-coastal district further to the east.[1]

Zär'a Ya'qob continued the earlier royal practice of issuing charters in favour of the northern monasteries. He thus allotted sizeable lands to those of Däbrä Bizän and Däbrä Maryam, situated in Hamasén and Särayé respectively.[2]

To strengthen his control of the region, as we shall see in Chapter 13, he also settled a group of Mayas, or skilled archers, in Hamasén as military colonists. These men, who were apparently brought from the Shäwa area, arrived in 1448-9, and were believed to have terrified the local population. The earth, it is said, "trembled on their arrival", and the inhabitants were so distressed that they "fled the country in fear".[3]

---

[1] Perruchon (1893), pp. 47-8. See also Taddesse Tamrat (1972a), p. 261; Huntingford (1989), p. 95.
[2] Huntingford (1965b), p. 36; Taddesse Tamrat (1972a), p. 236.
[3] Kolmodin (1914), p. 32; Conti Rossini (1903), pp. 181-3. See also Taddesse Tamrat (1972a), p. 260.

Emperor Zär'a Ya'qob (reigned 1443-1468), a much later manuscript illustration in traditional style. Note ceremonial use of fly-whisk held over monarch's head.
From E.A. Wallis Budge, *The Lives of Maba Seyon and Gabra Krestos*.

Local tradition has it that he also fortified the Gerar peninsula opposite the offshore port of Massawa.[4]

Lebnä Dengel, and the Tribute from the North: The Testimony of Francisco Alvares

The Portuguese diplomatic mission which arrived in Ethiopia in 1520, provides testimony to the power of the Bahr Nägash. Their chaplain, Francisco Alvares, whose detailed writings are so important for any understanding of this period, reports that this official's authority extended from the Hamasén highlands right down to Hergigo, and northwards along the coast almost as far as the port of Suakin, in what is now Sudan. Dafella and Canfella, two chiefs in the neighbourhood of the port, were both his subjects.

Officials holding the rank of Bahr Nägash had their capital, or "chief place" of residence as Alvares calls it, at the town of Debarwa, 30 kilometres south of Asmära. It was situated on the edge of the

---

[4] Kolmodin (1914), p. 32.

highlands. Such functionaries enjoyed the rare privilege of wearing diadems.

The then Bahr Nägash, a man named Dori, had considerable power and influence. He was the uncle of Emperor Lebnä Dengel (1508-1540), the brother of the latter's mother. Dori demonstrated his wealth when, on separating from his wife, he paid her a compensation of 100 ounces of gold. He was also a generous supporter of churches in his governorate, and had given them "everything" they needed, including ornaments, wax, and butter.[5]

The importance of the country of the Bahr Nägash is apparent from the fact that it contributed substantially to Lebnä-Dengel's revenues. Alvares, who witnessed the arrival of the annual *geber*, or tax, from the Bahr Nägash's domains, as well as from three other regions, Tegray, Gojjam and Hadeya, has left a vivid account of the ceremony. The Queen of Hadeya appeared first; the Tegré Mäkonnen, or governor, of Tegray, came fourteen days later, and, on the following day, the Bahr Nägash himself arrived. The two latter rulers came with many lords, and *chäwa*, or troops, stationed in their lands. When all were assembled the Emperor commanded his Behtwädäd, i.e. his "beloved", or principal, courtier, to present the Gojjam *geber*. This was done in the presence of both the Bahr Nägash and the Tegré Mäkonnen.

On the following morning it was the turn of the Bahr Nägash. He began by handing over 150 "very handsome" horses, and "what with running and making them jump, he passed the day without anything else being done". On the morrow he and his men presented the remainder of the tribute. Alvares was unable, on account of illness, to witness this part of the ceremony, and therefore does not describe it in any detail. He nevertheless gives the impression that this *geber* was considerable, and included "many silks and much thin cloth from India".[6]

The Emperor's control of the country of the Bahr Nägash, which stretched from the highlands towards the sea at Bur, is also demonstrated in two of Lebnä-Dengel's land charters. In the first, of around 1529, he granted lands in the Halay and Degsa areas of Hamasén to Zemal, the *seyum*, or ruler, of Bur, to the latter's wife Ad

---

[5] Beckingham and Huntingford (1961), I, 108, 119, 122, 127-8, 171, II, 469.
[6] Beckingham and Huntingford (1961), II, 427-8.

Kamu, and to their son Sebhat Lä'äb. In the second he gave an estate in Särayé to a certain Habtä Ab, whose function is not recorded.[7]

The status of the territory was later specified by Lebnä Dengel in a letter to King Manoel I of Portugal. In it he described himself as Emperor not only of "the high (and vast) Ethiopia", but also of several "great kingdoms, lordships and lands". One of them was that of the Bahr Nägash, to whom he refers, with perhaps some exaggeration, as "lord as far as Egypt".[8]

One of the consequences of imperial control was the recruitment of chiefs and troops from the area to serve in other parts of the empire. One such official, a Bäläw called Awra'i 'Uthman ibn Dar 'Ali, became Lebnä Dengel's governor of Ifat and Fätägar. He subsequently played a major role in the conflict with the Muslim conqueror Imam Ahmäd ibn Ibrahim al-Ghazi, better known as Ahmäd Grañ.[9] Other warriors from the Land of the Bahr Nägäsh were, as we shall see, also later engaged in that struggle.

Hergigo and Massawa

Most of northern Ethiopia's foreign trade at this time continued to pass through the mainland port of Hergigo, also known as Dehono, and the nearby island port of Massawa. Exports in the early sixteenth century consisted, the Portuguese state, of gold and ivory, as well as honey, wax, and slaves.[10] An indication of the ivory trade's importance may be gathered from the name Dehono, which was a rendering of *dakano*, the Saho, or perhaps Afar, word for elephant. Slaves, on arriving in Arabia, were for the most part converted to Islam.[11]

One of our earliest glimpses of Hergigo, the port of the Bahr Nägash, is provided by members of the Portuguese mission. They record that the port's two thousand inhabitants on learning that their visitors, like them, were Christians, rushed down to the water's edge,

---

[7] Huntingford (1965b), pp. 47, 53, 92.
[8] Beckingham and Huntingford (1961) II, 496.
[9] Basset (1897), pp. 76-7.
[10] Beckingham and Huntingford (1961), I, 55.
[11] The Afar word is *dakanu*. Reinisch (1889), p. 408; Parker and Hayward (1985), p. 79.

and with "great delight", all jumped into the sea, attempting to drag the vessel ashore.[12]

As for Massawa the Portuguese recall that the port, which enjoyed local autonomy, was situated on an offshore island. It had "a very fine harbour, quite shut in". Said to be better than Carthage, it possessed "a very good anchorage", and numerous cisterns in which fresh water was stored.[13]

The exports of Massawa consisted at this time, according to Alvares, of gold, slaves and agricultural produce. The first two, we may assume, came from the interior, while the latter were probably grown on the northerly plateau. The Debarwa area thus produced "numerous grain crops of every kind and nature". They were carried to the coast for sale at Mecca, Zabid, Jeddah, Toro (Mount Sinai) and other places in Arabia.[14]

Imported articles disembarked at Massawa were mostly transported to the mainland port of Hergigo, upon which the island relied for most of its victuals, as well as almost all its drinking water. The Portuguese reported that Hergigo, which was at that time under the rule of the Bahr Nägäsh, lay only two cross-bow shots from Massawa, and was well supplied with foodstuffs. Provisions were "countless and very cheap". There were also large numbers of cows, sheep and goats, as well as numerous gazelles and hares, which could easily be killed, even by people on foot. Meat was therefore very cheap. The largest cow cost only four or five pieces of cloth, and a sheep or goat could be obtained for a single piece.[15]

Trade with the West and North

The country of the Bahr Nägash was to some extent also linked to Egypt, North Africa, and conceivably even Europe, by an overland route, which ran westwards through Sudan. Little is known of the trade passing by this route. Early in the sixteenth century the Portuguese commander Afonso d'Albuquerque was told that it was possible to reach Portugal from Prester John's dominions, i.e. Ethiopia, between his kingdom and the Christian empire, by way of Timbuctoo, while an Ethiopian ecclesiastic, Brother Thomas,

---

[12] Thomas and Cortesão (1938), p. 9.
[13] Thomas and Cortesão (1938), p. 88.
[14] Beckingham and Huntingford (1961), I, 117-18.
[15] Thomas (1938), p. 88.

informed the Venetian scholar Alessandro Zorzi that a trade route from his country led via Qwara and Sennar to Tunis. Support for this statement was provided by Alvares, who reported that "Moors" from Tunis travelled via Cairo to Ethiopia bringing with them "white burnouses, but not very good ones, and many other different kinds of merchandise". Tomé Pires, another Portuguese author of this time, believed on the other hand that "very little" produce went to Cairo in this way.[16]

Suakin

Suakin, an island port off the Red Sea coast north of Massawa, was described by Alvares as "at the end of the countries" of Prester John, but in fact lay beyond the area of Ethiopian rule. The port was nevertheless often frequented by Ethiopian Christian pilgrims, many of whom used it on their way to or from Jerusalem, either by sea or land. Those travelling via Suakin included several of Zorzi's Ethiopian informants.[17]

THE AFAR COUNTRY

Contacts with the Christian Highlands in the 15th and 16th Centuries

Despite the fierce conflicts which waged during the reign of 'Amdä Seyon, and the ever-present differences of religion, relations between the Afar people and the Christian empire in the early 15th century were apparently cordial. This was evident during the time of Emperor Bä'edä Maryam (1468-1478). Early in his reign he conducted an expedition against the Dobe'a, a people of "blacks" who were neighbours of the Afar, and inhabited the area between Endärta and Lake Ashangé. According to an Ethiopian royal chronicle the "Dankalé", or ruler of the Danakil, on that occasion offered him military support. He did so, the Scottish traveller and historian James Bruce later declared, because he was "constant in his attachment" to

---

[16] Birch (1875-84), I, 202-3; Crawford (1958), p. 187; Beckingham and Huntingford (1961), I, 252; Pires (1944), p.17.

[17] Crawford (1958), pp. 28, 30-1, 46-7, 61, 78, 129, 137, 145-7, 155, 157, 167; Beckingham and Huntingford (1961), I, 144, II, 449-51. Pilgrims seem to have travelled by way of a monastery in the Bäqla area, See Crowfoot (1911), pp. 104-05.

the Ethiopian state. In pledging his help against the Dobe'a, he sent the Emperor a horse and a mule laden with dates, together with a shield and two spears, and a message which read: "I have set up my camp, O my master, with the intention of stopping these people. If they are your enemies, I will not let them pass, and will seize them". Bä'edä Maryam replied, with warm appreciation, saying, "You have done well; do not let them enter your territory".[18]

Notwithstanding their religious differences the Christian Emperors and the Muslim Afar rulers are said to have been linked from time to time by dynastic marriages. Such alliances were then as much a feature of Ethiopian as of European statecraft. Alvares, whose testimony cannot easily be dismissed, claims that it was customary prior to the reign of Emperor Na'od (1494-1508) for Ethiopian Emperors to have "five or six wives", including daughters of "neighbouring Moorish Kings", among them those of the Danakil. Such marriages contravened the Christian law of monogamy, and perhaps for that reason are not recorded in the royal chronicles. The Afar leaders for their part recognised the need for good relations with their more powerful Christian neighbours, and, as we shall see, later accepted some measure of imperial paramountcy.[19]

Eskender and the Mayas

Difficulties between the Afar rulers and those of the interior nevertheless arose during the reign of Emperor Eskender (1478-1494). An incident occurred at a place called Arho whose inhabitants are reported in a royal chronicle to have killed one of the monarch's favourite servants or officials, by name Täklaye. The exact location of Arho cannot be established with certainty. Though frequently applied to the great Afar salt depression, the word means in the Afar language a "camel caravan", and may have been applied to any place along the Afar trade route.[20] Eskender at all events was much angered, and marched against the killers.

The Arhos, it is claimed, were unaware that it was the Emperor who had come to chastise them, and therefore offered strong

---

[18] Perruchon(1893), pp. 138-9. For James Bruce's interpretation of these events see Bruce (1790), II, 82-3, and, for the geography of the operation, Huntingford (1989) p. 106. See also Budge (1928b), I, 315.

[19] Beckingham and Huntingford (1961), I, 193.

[20] Parker and Hayward (1985), p. 44.

resistance. They made use in particular of Maya archers, who during the night shot many arrows. The monarch was hit by one, which was doubtless poisoned, for he died almost immediately. His infuriated soldiers retaliated by wreaking fierce punishment on the attackers, and reportedly spared neither women nor children.[21]

The clash between the Christian state and the Afars was overshadowed, in the early sixteenth century, by conflicts between the latter and the neighbouring highland Christian peasantry. Alvares, travelling in the Bugna district of Tegray, learnt that inhabitants of the nearby "kingdom of Dancali" were "constantly at war", presumably with the highlanders. Further evidence of conflict was provided by Bä'algada Robél, a notable ruler of Tegray. His governorate included the principal highland markets for Afar salt. This mineral, as earlier noted, had since time immemorial been taken all over the highlands, where it served both as "primitive money" and as an article of consumption. Robél claimed that his domains extended "towards the Red Sea", and included the Afar salt mines. He added that there were frequent battles with the people "towards the sea", presumably the Afar inhabitants of the coastline, against whom "he never ceased making war".[22]

The Salt Trade

Such conflicts notwithstanding the lowlands and highlands were commercially and ecologically linked. Afar rock salt continued to be one of the most important items in the region's economic life. Alvares, who was not prone to exaggeration, went so far as to describe it as "the best thing" in Ethiopia, for it was "current as money, both in the kingdoms and dominions of the Prester [i.e. Emperor] and in the kingdoms of the Moors [i.e. Muslims] and pagans". Bars of Afar salt, measuring a span and a half in length, four fingers thick and three across, were carried all over the country. The mineral, he says, was "very cheap where it was got", but "very dear" at the far-off court in Shäwa. By the time it reached Damot, on the south-west borders of the empire, it was so expensive that "a good slave" could be purchased for only three or four blocks. On reaching the slave-producing countries, on the far borders of the empire, a slave could reportedly be purchased for one block, and "almost for a block its weight in gold".[23]

---

[21] Perruchon (1894), pp. 358-9. See also Huntingford (1989), p. 109.
[22] Beckingham and Huntingford (1961), I, 179-80.
[23] Beckingham and Huntingford (1961), I, 181.

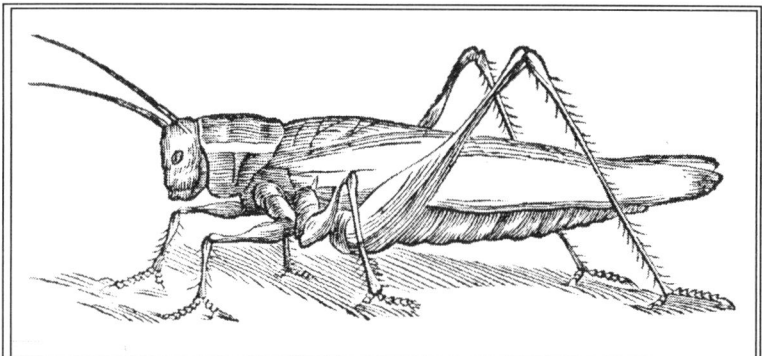

The locust, which bred in the Afar coastal belt, and flew into the fertile highlands, where for many centuries it constituted a serious damage.
From H. Ludolf, *Commentarius ad suam Historiam Aethiopica.*

Large numbers of people all over the country in Tegray and elsewhere were involved in the transportation of Afar salt. Alvares reports on one occasion meeting on the road no less than "300 or 400 animals, in herds, laden with salt", as well as others coming empty to fetch it. Some of this salt belonged to "great lords", who sent north each year to obtain the bars required to meet their expenses at court, while others were the property of smaller men, who travelled with twenty or thirty beasts. Others again carried salt for themselves, or to "make profit from market to market".

The Afar area was at the same time the breeding ground of great swarms of locusts, which often flew up into the highlands. There, as for many centuries to come, they devastated the countryside.[24] Not until after World War II did chemical spraying begin to overcome this age-old scourge.

Alvares's account of the Dankali area is also of interest for its mention of the port of "Belie". This was an early reference to Baylul, some 40 kilometres north-west of 'Asäb. The port, though small, handled the bulk of the Afars' modest foreign trade, and was later, as we shall see, a place of no small historical significance and potential.[25]

---

[24] Beckingham and Huntingford (1961), I, 137
[25] Beckingham and Huntingford (1961), I, 137, II, 452-3.

THE COUNTRY OF THE DOBE'AS

Bä'edä Maryam's Expeditions, and Converts to Christianity

The Dobe'as, whom the nineteenth century British traveller Henry Salt described as an isolated group of "negroes", lived to the west of the Afars on the edge of the northern Ethiopian plateau. Emperor Bä'edä Maryam had, as we have seen, on one occasion despatched an expedition against their country, but failed to trace any of them. He then rode to the area in person, but the Dobe'as recognised him from a distance, and, having previously evacuated their cattle, camels and donkeys, fled. It was then that the Afars offered to intervene on the Emperor's behalf. He once more despatched his soldiers against the Dobe'as, but they defeated his men, inflicting heavy casualties on them.

The Emperor, infuriated at this defeat, criticised his soldiers for attacking without orders, and, determined on revenge, declared that he would remain in the area until he had sown grain there, and his horses had eaten the crop. He then despatched Jan Zeg, the Gärad, or local ruler, of Bali, into the nearby country of Gam, but he too was killed, and his army routed. Depressed at news of this, as well as by an outbreak of cholera or other epidemic among his men, the monarch withdraw to Tegray, where he called for assistance from one of his best fighting regiments, the Jan Amora. The latter at once expressed its willingness to fight and defeat their master's enemies.

The Dobe'a leaders, learning of this new threat, decided to fly into the Adäl lowlands. They accordingly once more gathered their camels and cattle, as well as their women and children, after which their elders, twelve in number, had all their property loaded on beasts of burden, and then dispersed in different directions.

The monarch, on hearing of this, again attacked the Dobe'as, and ordered the governors of Tegray, Qeda and Damot to pursue them. This strategem proved successful. Many of the Dobe'as were killed, and not a few of those who escaped were intercepted by the Tegray and Damot soldiers. A large number of Dobe'a cattle were captured, and given by the Emperor to his men.

The Dobe'as, realising the extent of their defeat, begged the Emperor's pardon, and many were reportedly converted to Christianity, after which Bä'edä Maryam returned their cattle, and gave them many others which he had obtained from the southern provinces of Wäj and Gänz. He then stationed soldiers in the Dobe'a country, and erected a church there in honour of the Virgin Mary. He also planted orange trees, lemon trees, and vines, and thus kept his vow that he would remain in the area until his horses had eaten of the grain he had sown.

Not long after this he returned to the Dobe'a country, where he appointed governors, "regulated the social condition of the people", and urged them to celebrate the festival of the Virgin's death every January. On that occasion he distributed large quantities of bread, beer, and mead. When the celebration was over he ordered the Dobe'as to cultivate the land, instead of taking up arms, after which he and his army left their country for good.[26]

The Report of Alvares

Alvares, who visited the region half a century later, estimated that the Dobe'a country was five days' journey, i.e. about a hundred kilometres, in length, and extended far into Muslim, presumably Afar, lands. The Dobe'a territory had "very fine cows", which, he claimed, were the largest in the world, and so numerous that they could not be counted. The area at the time of his visit was, however, suffering from a serious drought, with the result that the people were losing their flocks, and were unable to sow grain of any kind.

Situated on the edge of the massif, above the Afar lowlands, the Dobe'a country had an important market town, Manadeley, which dealt with the coast, and was a place of "very great trade, like a great city or seaport". It was possible to find there "every kind of merchandise", as well as merchants from many different commercial centres and countries, including Jeddah, Morocco, Fez, Tunis, Greece, Ormuz, Cairo and India. The local market, held on Tuesdays, was likewise attended by an "infinite number" of people from the neighbourhood.

The merchants of Manadeley at the time of Alvares's visit were complaining of inordinately high taxation. They asserted that Emperor Lebnä Dengel had lent them one thousand ounces of gold, but expected them to pay the same amount as interest each year. The ruler of Tegray, they declared, also practised "further extortion".

The Dobe'as, according to Alvares, had twenty-four captaincies, twelve of which were usually at peace, and the other twelve at war.

---

[26] Salt (1814), p. 275; Perruchon (1893), pp. 138-51.

The former had recently rebelled, but had subsequently made peace. Each of the former rebel captains therefore carried a stone on his head, and held it with both his hands. They had also each brought the Emperor over a hundred men, and many "very good" horses and mules. Lebnä Dengel received the chiefs with honour, and for the two months that they stayed at his court provided them daily with beef, mutton, honey and butter. Later, however, he banished the chiefs a distance of over four hundred kilometres, and exiled their followers with numerous guards to far off Damot.

The Dobe'as, the Portuguese priest reports, were "great warriors". It was one of their customs, he claims, that no Dobe'a could marry without first proving that he had killed twelve Christians. The result was that travellers making the two-day journey through the Dobe'a country, an area of "very large woods" and "very high and dense thickets of thorn bushes", were obliged to move in large caravans a thousand or more strong. One group set forth once a week, one from the interior and the other from the coast. Notwithstanding their number "many" merchants were often killed, twelve at the time of his visit.

The Dobe'as then, as earlier, were in conflict with the neighbouring Tegray Christians who were led by the *shum,* or chief, of Jan Amora, a district south of Antalo, apparently named after the regiment of Bä'edä Maryam's day. Many Christians of the area, Alvares says, always "kept an eye over their shoulders" in fear of the "Moors", presumably the Dobe'as or Afars, who came to seize their cattle and burn their houses and churches. One priest he saw went so far as to carry poisoned arrows for use against attacking lowlanders. When the Portuguese cleric criticised him for this, he replied, "Look that way, and you will see the church burnt by the Moors, and close to it they carried off from me fifty cows, and also they burnt my beehives, which were my livelihood; for that reason I carry this poison, to kill him who has killed me".[27]

Such small-time banditry, however, does not seem to have interfered unduly with the course of trade.

---

[27] Beckingham and Huntingford (1961), I, 187-96.

Chapter 12
THE EAST: IFAT and ADAL

Ifat and Adäl, both to the east of the central highlands, lay, as in the past, on a major trade route, which linked much of the interior, including Shawa, with Zäylä' and the Gulf of Aden.

IFAT

Zär'a Ya'qob

Ifat, situated to the immediate east of Shäwa, was, by the middle of the fifteenth century, effectively under imperial rule. The province was affected, like many other parts of the empire, by Zär'a Yaq'ob's attempts to reorganise its administration. To ensure his control over the territory he entrusted it to his daughter, 'Amäta Giyorgis. Later, however, he took personal charge of the whole country, and placed the province under a governor, with the rank of Raq Masäré, a title then widely used at his court.

Because of its strategic importance on the empire's periphery, Ifat was one of a dozen or so in which Zär'a Ya'qob also stationed *chäwa*, or imperial troops. Evidence that the province was an integral part of the empire is also provided by the fact that it was later one of the provinces which supplied building materials for the Emperor's great palace at Däbrä Berhan.[1]

Bä'edä Maryam

Continued imperial control over Ifat was apparent during the reign of Zär'a Ya'qob's son and successor Bä'edä Maryam (1468-1478). Reversing his father's centralising policies, he returned the province's administration to a functionary with the title of Wälashma', who, to judge from this word, was, as in earlier times, apparently a native of the area.

Bä'edä Maryam subsequently visited the province. While residing at a place called Qächeho, or Qacheno, he enquired, according to his chronicle, into the names of the towns of the area. These included Mäkré, described as a "place of transit", Gende Belo, an important market town, and Fälägä Agat, in the district of Gadawi, where he

---

[1] Perruchon (1893), pp. 13-14, 16, 47, 93.

resided for some time. On that occasion he learned that the people of Adäl not only travelled to the area, but also resided there.

Emperor Bäe'dä Maryam (reigned 1468-1478): an imaginary fifteenth century Ethiopian painting in traditional style.
Photo: Bibliothèque Nationale, Paris.

During his visit "all the inhabitants" of Shäwa and Ifat came to visit him. Seeing their number from afar, he requested them to return to their homes. He did so, his chronicle reports, because he feared that they were so numerous that they might create a famine and cause the inhabitants to die of hunger. He subsequently made his way to the town of Tobeya, where his grandfather Emperor Dawit had earlier resided.[2]

---

[2] Perruchon (1893), pp. 112, 151-2.

The reintegration of Ifat into the empire by the early 16th century, as Merid Wolde Aregay has suggested, probably had significant ethnic, as well as religious consequences. Many regiments from other parts of the empire over the years had settled in the area, and large sections of the local Amhara, Argobba and Afar population embraced Christianity. The inhabitants of the lowlands adjoining the Awash River on the other hand remained predominantly Afar Muslims.[3]

The Towns of Gende Belo and Tobeya

Two Ifat towns, Gende Belo and Tobeya, both mentioned in the chronicle, were of particular importance in this period.

Gende Belo, doubtless a meeting place of many cultures, was probably located on the eastern edge of the Ethiopian plateau, and according to the British historical geographer O.G.S. Crawford at the foot of the Shäwan escarpment, perhaps as little as 30 kilometres from Ankobär. The town was referred to by one of Zorzi's Ethiopian informants, Brother Anthony of Lalibäla, as "a great mercantile city", whither camel caravans passing through Adäl from the coast unloaded their merchandise in warehouses. This trade was based on the "excellent port" of Zäylä', then under Adäl rule, and was brought from "the whole of India", and especially from Cambay. Imports included spices of all kinds, except ginger, which was grown locally.

Gende Belo's commerce was well developed. Brother Anthony reported that use was made there not only of barter, but also of "Hungarian and Venetian ducats" and Muslim "silver coins". The circulation of foreign money in Ifat, rare in the region as a whole, had earlier been mentioned, it will be recalled, by al-'Umäri who had reported the use of Egyptian *dinar*s and *dirhem*s, while Maqrizi had quoted local prices in the latter currency.[4]

Tobeya, the second important Ifat settlement, was a place where Emperors Dawit and Bä'edä Maryam had both resided. Brother Anthony describes it as only one day's journey inland from Gende Belo. This statement, taken with the fact that it had been the residence of emperors, who almost invariably camped on elevated ground, would suggest that it too was at the edge of the highlands, overlooking the Adäl, or eastern, depression.[5]

---

[3] Merid Wolde Aregay (1974), p. 23.
[4] Crawford (1958), pp. 172-5. See also pp. 66, 96.
[5] Crawford (1958), pp. 97, 172.

ADAL

Zär'a Ya'qob and Bädlay ibn Sä'd ad-Din

Adäl, it will be recalled, lay to the east of Ifat. Because of its low elevation, and aridity, it was unsuitable for occupation, let alone settlement, by highland troops.[6] As a result of the fighting described in Chapter 6 the province by the fifteenth century was no longer under imperial rule, and perhaps for that reason is noticeable for its absence in the list of territories whose administration Zär'a Ya'qob reorganised.[7]

Adäl early in the Emperor's reign was nearly caught up in the attempted rebellion of Mähiko, governor of Hadeya, considered in Chapter 14. This chief, according to the royal chronicle, asked the territory's inhabitants to help him by attacking the nearby provinces of Däwaro and Bali. The plot was, however, foiled. Zär'a Ya'qob, on learning of it, at once replaced Mähiko by the latter's uncle Bamo, who had remained loyal to him and then despatched an army against the rebel. He also sent messages to the people of Däwaro and Bali, ordering them to prevent Mähiko from escaping into Adäl. He attempted to do so, but was apprehended, and executed.[8]

Emperor Zär'a Yaq'ob's rule in Adäl was challenged, in 1445, by Sultan Bädlay ibn Sä'd ad-Din, a local amir who is disparagingly referred to in the chronicle as the Arwé, or Beast, Bädlay. The text, which goes into some detail, states that the Emperor was building the church of Däbrä Metmaq at Tägulät in northern Shäwa when he learnt that the Adäl ruler was advancing to attack him. Zär'a Ya'qob at that moment had only a very small force, the Hasab Bäwäsän, but immediately marched south to confront the invader in Däwaro.

Zär'a Ya'qob, a fanatical Christian, sent messengers to the monks of Däbrä Libanos and other monasteries, informing them of his determination to confront the enemy. His emissaries returned with the assurance of the clergy that God had heard their prayers, and that he would surely be victorious. The ruler of Hadeya, Gärad Mehmäd, sent him a friendly message, offering, as we shall see in Chapter 14, to

---

[6] Merid Wolde Aregay (1974), p. 623.
[7] Perruchon (1893), pp. 13-14.
[8] Perruchon (1893), pp. 16-20.

provide him with assistance. However, he also made similar protestations of friendship to Bädlay.

When Zär'a Ya'qob reached the place where the Adäl ruler was encamped, and saw the immense size of the latter's army, he was much alarmed. He nevertheless invoked the help of God and the Holy Spirit, and prepared himself and his small contingent for a trial of strength. Aqabé Sä'at Amha Seyon, a high ecclesiastic at his court, warned him against engaging in battle before the rest of his army arrived, but he proudly dismissed such fears. He quoted the Psalms of David, stating that "A king is not saved by reason of a great host",[9] and declared that he placed his trust in God. He then ordered his men to carry out all the customary ceremonies prior to a battle. This involved putting up the royal umbrellas, blowing the *meserqana*, a trumpet played only in the king's presence, beating the *deb anbäsa*, or imperial drums, and unfurling the royal standards.

At the sight of this imposing display the Amir, who is said to have had many magical scrolls, was reportedly seized with fear. Turning to his followers he recalled that they had assured him that he would be confronting only the Hasab Bäwäsän contingent, but that it was evident that they were facing a large army, led by none other than the Emperor himself. While Bädlay was voicing such fears Zär'a Ya'qob moved rapidly forwards, and routed some of the former's army. One of the Emperor's soldiers shot an arrow at the Adäl leader's face, but the latter broke it with his hand, and advanced towards Zär'a Ya'qob in an attempt to seize him. This act of bravado was, however, his undoing, for the monarch struck him in the neck with his spear, and cut his throat. The Adäl soldiers thereupon took flight. They were pursued by the Emperor's men, who killed many of them with their spears and swords, and hurled others down precipices. This battle occurred at a place called 'Ayn Färäs, literally the Eye, or Spring, of the Horse, which was abbreviated as 'Ayfärs. The number of Adäl dead was so great, the chronicle claims, no doubt with exaggeration, that not one of their soldiers survived.

---

[9] Psalms XXXII, 16.

The Ethiopian Borderlands

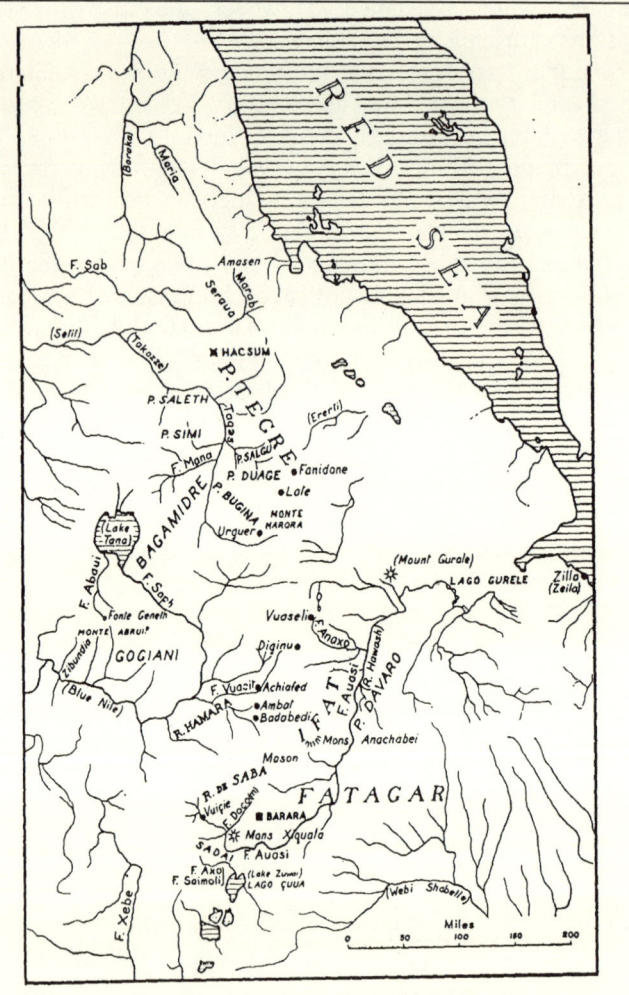

Detail from Fra Mauro's Venetian map of 1460, redrawn, and replotted on a modern basis.
Note the location of Aksum (Hacsum), Lake Zway (Lago Çuua), and of the two peripheral provinces of Ifat, east of the Awash River, and Fätägar, on both sides of that river.
From O.G.S. Crawford, *Ethiopian Itineraries ca. 1400-1524.*

To the Emperor's chagrin Bädlay's brother Karadin succeeded in escaping to the Awash River. He was pursued by one of Zär'a Ya'qob's units, called the Jan Sägäna. They caught him, cut off his head, and brought it to their master. The latter then counted the vast number of enemy dead, after which the priests, celebrating the victory, came singing canticles of joy, while the women in the Emperor's army danced and gave thanks to God.

Zär'a Ya'qob then summoned the Gärad, or ruler, of Hadeya to witness the great victory. Responding to the chief's earlier expressions of support he decorated him in traditional manner with rich clothes. Bädlay's body was then cut into pieces, and despatched to various parts of the country. His weapons and his wife's jewellery were divided among various churches and monasteries.[10]

Mehmäd or Muhammäd ibn Bädlay and a Mission to Cairo

Despite Adäl's temporary re-integration into the empire, the local provincial dynasty remained in office. Bädlay was thus succeeded by his son 'Sultan Mehmäd, or Muhammäd (1445-1471), who is said to have reigned for twenty-six years. According to the Arab writer al-Tägrebirdi he despatched an embassy to Cairo in 1452. This mission doubtless reported on Adäl's defeat, and, in Cerulli's opinion, may well have unsuccessfully appealed for Egyptian help.[11]

Adäl, as a trouble spot on the periphery of the realm, was sometimes used as a place of exile. When Zär'a Ya'qob was confronted with insubordination on the part of his troops in Däwaro, he thus despatched them to Adäl.[12]

Bä'edä Maryam and Mehmäd

During the ensuing reign of Bä'edä Maryam the province was virtually independent, but, according to Spencer Trimingham, "worn out" by the long and "wearisome" round of raids and counter-raids. Early in the reign Bädlay's son and successor Sultan Mehmäd, or Muhammäd, sent Bä'edä Maryam a deputation, which brought him gifts of many pieces of cloth, and a message proposing a compromise peace. The envoys, according to the chronicle, declared that the ruler

---

[10] Perruchon (1893), pp.57-65, 75, 88; Getatchew Haile (1980), p. 225. See also Cerulli (1934), pp. 105-9.
[11] Cerulli (1943a), pp. 293-4.
[12] Perruchon (1893), p. 45.

of Adäl would send Bä'edä Maryam all the tribute due to him, if he for his part would order his troops to cease their incursions. The Emperor accepted this proposal, gave the envoys plentiful food and drink, and provided them with fine clothes. He then sent them back with one of his messengers, Gädäb Hamid, a Muslim from Däwaro, with a message for Mehmäd accepting the latter's demands, but warning him to "stick to his word".[13]

Bä'edä Maryam later chose a consort, Dawit Era, and ordered the governor and chiefs of Tegray to go to Aksum to prepare for his coronation. He learnt shortly afterwards that the governor of Zäylä', Läda'e 'Uthman, had, however, repudiated the agreement made by his predecessor Mehmäd, and was marching against him. He thereupon cancelled the proposed coronation celebrations, and summoned the leaders of Tegray. On their arrival he proceeded with them to Ifat, but did not advance eastward into Adäl.[14]

Later in the reign the *gärad,* or governor, of Bali, Gäbrä Iyäsus, and that province's *chäwa,* or imperial troops, were involved in a plot to defect. They planned to make their way to Adäl, because it was outside the Emperor's control, but their intentions were frustrated. Bä'edä Maryam summoned them to his court, supposedly to receive gifts, but exiled them instead to Gojjam. He then despatched the rebellious *chäwa,* and soldiers from nearby Däwaro and Damot, to make war in Adäl, while he himself proceeded to Däwaro. Nothing more about this expedition is reported in the chronicle, which gives rise to the suspicion that it probably petered out.[15]

Towards the end of his reign Bä'edä Maryam decided on a further expedition to Adäl. He entrusted it once more to Gäbrä Iyäsus, who by then held the title of Behtwädäd, besides that of governor of Bali. With soldiers from his province and others from Däwaro he proceeded eastwards, into the Adäl lowlands. On arriving there they found that the chiefs of the area had all gathered to prepare for an incursion into the Christian empire. A battle was immediately fought. Gäbrä Iyäsus was victorious. Many Adäl chiefs were killed, and others taken prisoner.

Gäbrä Iyäsus and his men did not dally in the torrid Adäl lowlands in which highlanders found it virtually impossible to reside for any

---

[13] Perruchon (1893), pp. 131-3; Trimingham (1852), p. 8; Cerulli (1931), p. 48.
[14] Perruchon (1893), pp. 149-51; Huntingford (1989), p. 106.
[15] Perruchon, (1893), pp. 157-9.

length of time. They almost immediately returned to Bali, whence they sent a message to their master stating that they had reached the province safe and sound. The Emperor gave orders for great rejoicing at the palace, and the saying of prayers.[16]

Not long afterwards Bä'edä Maryam decided upon a further expedition to Adäl. He entrusted it to his oldest and most loyal follower, Mähari Krestos, and to the experienced Gäbrä Iyäsus. The monarch presented them and other soldiers with fine clothes, and ordered his palace troops with much pomp to join the expedition. The men went to war, however, with little enthusiasm, for which reason, the chronicle says, God did not favour them.

The Adäl soldiers immediately seized the offensive. Mähari Krestos and his men soon took flight, and Gäbrä Iyäsus and his followers shortly afterwards did the same. This was their undoing, for they are said to have "perished to the last man".

Bä'edä Maryam was deeply distressed by this debacle. He reportedly loved both generals, and in particular Mähari Krestos, who had "no equal in his sight". The monarch prayed for the souls of all who had died in the battle, and made gifts to numerous holy persons. He sent two thousand ounces of gold for distribution in Tegray, and five hundred to Abunä Yemerehannä Krestos at Däbrä Libanos. Grieving greatly at the defeat he died shortly afterwards.[17]

Despite the conflicts detailed above there were also attempts at coexistence between the Emperors and the Adäl rulers. Alvares claims moreover that dynastic marriages with the latter were forged,[18] but no details of any such arrangements have been preserved.

Eskender and Shäms ad-Din

Bä'edä Maryam's young son Eskender (1478-1494) later took the field against Adäl, which was then ruled by Amir Shäms ad-Din ibn Muhammäd (1472-1487). Imperial forces sacked the Adäl capital, Däkär, but were surprised and defeated.

The story of this defeat is graphically related in Eskender's chronicle. It states that the monarch around 1478 assembled all his troops so as to march down into the Adäl country, but was warned

---

[16] Perruchon (1893), pp.165-8.
[17] Perruchon (1893), pp. 180-2. See also Cerulli (1936), I, 27; Trimingham (1952), pp. 82-3.
[18] Beckingham and Huntingford (1961), I, 193.

against doing so by his holy men, who declared that there was no purpose in embarking on so dangerous an enterprise. He ignored their words, and advanced as far as the Adäl capital, Däkär, which he completely destroyed. On his return march he was, however, pursued by a much larger Adäl army, which killed or took prisoner many of his men. The Emperor only escaped, it is said, through the help of the angels, after which he built a church called Däbrä Meshwa'e, or Place of Sacrifice.[19]

The next ruler of Adäl, Muhammäd ibn Azhar ad-Din (1488-1518), realising the heavy cost of so much fighting, reportedly tried to establish peace with the Christians of the interior, but was outmaneuvered by Mahfuz, a charismatic Amir of Zäylä', who was determined to embark upon a more warlike policy.[20]

The Campaigns of Mähfuz

The last years of Eskender's reign witnessed the opening of a protracted struggle between the rulers of Adäl and those of the interior. Mähfuz, the principal commander of Amir Muhammäd, began a series of annual military incursions into the highlands. By this time he held the religious title of Imam. His adoption of the title, as Trimingham explains, signified a growth of religious fanaticism, and that Mähfuz was engaged in a *jihad*, or Holy War. Information on his campaigns was obtained by Alvares a generation or so later from contemporary observers. They told him that Mähfuz's operations had begun during the reign of Eskender, and continued throughout that of his successor Na'od (1494-1508) and the first five years of that of young Emperor Lebnä Dengel (1508-1540). The Imam, about whom people of the latter monarch's court still sang, had invaded the Christian highlands "every Lent for twenty-five years". He did so, Alvares thought, because the great fast broke the people's strength, and rendered them less able to fight. It was the time moreover when Christians were preparing for the great Easter feast.

Be that as it may, Mähfuz, as Alvares puts it, one year invaded Amhara or Shäwa, and another Fätägar. Sometimes attacking at one place, sometimes at another, the Adäl soldiers had on occasion penetrated more than eighty-five kilometres into Christian territory. In one foray they reportedly captured no less than nineteen thousand

---

[19] Perruchon (1894), pp. 357-8.
[20] Cerulli (1936), I, 27; Trimingham (1952), p. 82.

highlanders, whom their victorious leader sent as slaves to the Muslim rulers of Arabia. The captives were, as usual, subsequently converted to Islam. The invaders also carried off "a very great multitude" of cattle.

On his twenty-fourth expedition Mähfuz made his way to Fätägar. Its inhabitants took refuge in the hills, but he pursued them, burning churches and monasteries. He was so successful, as we shall see in Chapter 13, that he gained control of the territory, after which he put to death all the soldiers who had fought against him.

Lebnä Dengel, Mähfuz, and the Monk Abba Gäbrä Endreyas

Emperor Lebnä Dengel, then only seventeen years old, was much angered by these raids, and especially, Alvares asserts, by the burning of churches and monasteries. Determined on resolute action he sent spies into Adäl to ascertain which territory Mähfuz next intended to invade. It transpired that the chief, who was with his overlord, the Amir of Adäl, was planning to raid Fätägar, when the crops were ripe. He intended to destroy these crops, and attack another territory at Lent. Lebnä Dengel, thus forewarned, decided to await the enemy on the road. He insisted on doing so in person, though many of his courtiers argued that he was too young, and should leave the operation to his senior commanders and their men.

Lebnä Dengel and his soldiers set forth, and, travelling day and night, pitched their camp, in July 1517, in the vicinity of the nearest Adäl market. They found the Adäl army encamped a few miles within the Emperor's domains. At dawn the two sides faced each other, whereupon Mähfuz, a man of great courage, who, as the Emperor's men later sang, never knew what it was to flee, recognised Lebnä Dengel's tents. Shocked by the size of the imperial army he at once reported the Emperor's presence to his master, and warned him that the day would be fatal for Adäl.

Emperor Lebnä Dengel (reigned 1508-1540), a semi-authentic Venetian portrait.
From S. Tedeschi "Le portrait inédit du negus Lebnä-Dengel ayant appartenu à l' historien Paolo Giovio".

The Amir, he declared, should try to save himself, because he, Mähfuz, for his part, was resolved to die there. Amir Muhammäd, who was reputedly a coward, followed this advice, and escaped with four horsemen. One, interestingly enough, was the son of one of Lebnä Dengel's principal courtiers, who, according to Alvares, held the rank of Behtwädäd. He had become a Muslim, but later joined the Emperor and reverted to Christianity. The Portuguese writer, commenting on this apostasy, which was far from rare, observes that Ethiopian Christians at that time thought "nothing of joining the Moors", i.e. Muslims, and "becoming Moors", but, if they wished to return to the faith, were "baptized again" and, once pardoned, become "Christians as before".

The Emperor meanwhile ordered his men to take Communion, and then prepare to attack. Mähfuz at that point approached Lebnä Dengel's men, and enquired if any of them was willing to fight a duel with him unto death. A monk called Gäbrä Endreyas at once offered to do so. The ensuing contest, which was extremely fierce, ended in the victory of Gäbrä Endreyas, who killed Mähfuz, and cut off his head. This could be seen, Alvares reports, over three years later. The monk for his part was still alive, and "much honoured at the Court".

Gäbrä Endreyas's victory is also recorded in an Ethiopian chronicle, which states that after the death of Mähfuz his soldiers fled. The Emperor's troops pursued and killed many of them, including numerous horsemen, as well as foot soldiers.

These events are confirmed by Alvares, who reports that Lebnä Dengel launched a fierce attack on the Adäl army. It had no means of escape, for the passes through which it might have fled had all been occupied by the Emperor's men who routed and killed them. The victorious monarch thereupon advanced into Adäl, and reached the deserted palace of its king. Lebnä Dengel went up to its doors, and struck them with his spear three times, but refrained from entering, as he did not want it said that he had gone there for plunder. Instead he and his followers returned to the highlands whence they had come.

Notwithstanding this show of rectitude Lebnä Dengel captured a considerable amount of booty, including the King of Adäl's tent, which Alvares later saw. It was made of fine brocade and Mecca velvet, lined inside with Chaul cloth. He also seized many short swords, with silver hilts, which, the Portuguese author states, were, however, not well made.[21]

The Emperor's victory constituted a major defeat for Adäl. It was the more serious in that it coincided with Portuguese intervention at the coast. A powerful fleet, led by Lopo Suarez, burnt Zäylä' to the ground in 1517. Sultan Muhammäd, returning from the expedition against Lebnä Dengel in the following year, was murdered. His territory was then torn apart by intestinal struggles, five sultans succeeding one another within two years.[22]

---

[21] Beckingham and Huntingford (1961), II, 413-14; Trimingham (1952), p. 80.
[22] Trimingham (1952), p. 84.

Al-Järad Abun, Sultan Abu Bäkr and the Move to Harär

An attempt to reorganise the Adäl state after this period of chaos was made by a reforming leader called al-Järad Abun ibn Adash. His policy was later described by Shihab ed-Din Ahmäd 'Abd el-Qader, the chronicler of Ahmäd ibn Ibrahim, now better known as Ahmäd Grañ. He says Al-Järad "loved the *ashraf* [descendants of the Prophet], the jurisconsults, the dervishes and the *shaikhs*", and "did good for his subjects". He "affirmed the divine law, governed with justice, and forbade things prohibited [by the law]. He exterminated highway robbers, forbade [the drinking of] wine, and dancing carousals". The country as a result is said to have prospered.[23] One of al-Järad's followers, it is interesting to recall, was none other than the warrior Ahmäd ibn Ibrahim himself.

The then Sultan of Adäl, Abu Bäkr ibn Muhammäd, had meanwhile, in 1520, transferred his capital north-westwards from Däkär to Harär. He is said to have recruited a number of Somali "rogues and highwaymen", with whom he defeated and killed al-Järad at Zäylä'. This ushered in a further period of disorder. Abu Bäkr, if we can believe Shihab ed-Din, "ruined his country". The number of highwaymen and robberies increased, drunkenness and other vices reappeared, and "no one could obtain restitution for injustices".[24]

Despite such difficulties the Amir of Adäl remained, in the words of Alvares, "great and powerful", and continued to rule a considerable territory. This, according to the Portuguese author, included not only the port of Zäylä', but also that of Berbera to the east, and a stretch of land extending towards Cape Guardafui and beyond. Because of his frequent battles with the Christians the neighbouring Muslim rulers are said to have respected him, and "looked upon him as a saint". Significantly, he received considerable support from the ruler of Arabia, the Shaikh of Mecca and "other Moorish kings and lords". They supplied him with many horses and weapons in order to "help in his wars", in return for which he sent to Mecca and Cairo every year "large offerings" of slaves captured in his wars.[25]

Lebnä Dengel, for his part, was only too well aware of the continued strength of Adäl. During his talks with the visiting Portuguese mission he proposed a joint Christian initiative against

---

[23] Basset (1897), p. 13.
[24] Basset (1897), p. 15.
[25] Beckingham and Huntingford (1961), I, 16, 295-6, II, 402, 408, 410-15, 453.

Zäylä, Adäl and "all the countries of the infidels".[26] Nothing came of the idea, but it reveals the Emperor's realisation of the importance of Adäl, and of its potential power.

Zäylä'

Though attacked, and largely destroyed, by the Portuguese in 1517, Zäylä' soon regained its former importance as the emporium of Adäl and of the eastern territories in general, as apparent from the writings of several visiting Europeans. The Portuguese naval commander Afonso de Albuquerque, who sailed in the Gulf of Aden area between 1480 and 1524, reported seeing many ships from Zäylä as well as Berbera off the Arabian coast. He states that these vessels carried provisions and slaves to Mecca and Jeddah, and that the latter town imported all its supplies by sea, mainly from Zäylä', Berbera and Massawa.[27]

Detailed accounts of Zäylä' are also provided by three early sixteenth century travellers: the Italians Ludovico di Varthema and Andrea Corsali, and the Portuguese Duarte Barbosa. Varthema states that the port was a "bad" one, with "poor walls", but Barbosa describes the town as "well-built", with "right good houses, many of them built of stone and mortar, with flat roofs".

All three authors agree that Zäylä' was abundantly supplied with provisions. Varthema reports that it possessed grain, meat, oil, honey and wax. Barbosa goes further, stating that its citizens had "many horses and reared much cattle of all kinds", with the result that they had "butter in plenty, milk and flesh", besides a "great store of millet, barley and fruits", all of which they carried to Aden. Corsali agrees that Zäylä' had plenty of wheat, cattle and many kinds of fruit.

The port is said to have done a flourishing trade. Varthema described it as a place of "immense traffic", while Barbosa says it was visited by "many ships". Some, according to Corsali, came from Aden; others from India. The principal exports, according to Varthema, were gold, ivory and slaves. A "great number" of the latter, captured from the Country of Prester John, were exported by way of Zäylä' to Persia, Arabia, Egypt and India.

---

[26] Beckingham and Huntingford (1961), II, 481.
[27] Birch (1875-1884), I, 58, IV, 27, 28, 35, 58.

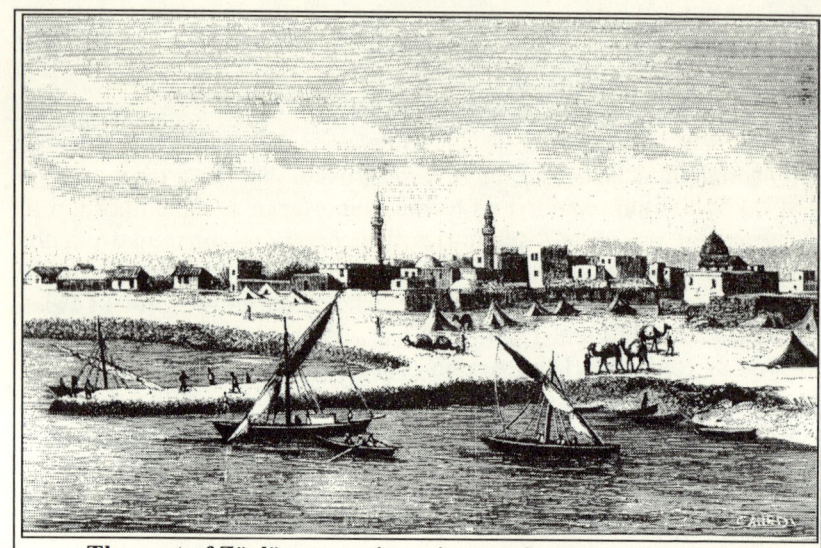

The port of Zäylä, as seen in a nineteenth century engraving. From G. Massaia, *I miei trentacinque anni di missione nell' alta Etiopia*.

Imports are said by Corsali to have consisted mainly of cloth, pepper, and incense from Dufar in Arabia. A large amount of these articles were subsequently transported by camel caravans as far as Ethiopia, the "land of Christian churches".

As a result of this trade the citizens of Zäylä' lived, according to Varthema, "extremely well". They had "many soldiers, both foot and horse", which made their rulers a power to be reckoned with, as we have seen, even in the interior. The town, he believed, also enjoyed "excellent justice".[28]

Lebnä Dengel, talking to the visiting Portuguese mission a few years later, drew a similar picture. He stated that the port was "well supplied" with victuals, which were exported to Aden, Jeddah, Mecca, and "all Arabia". He subsequently emphasised these points in a letter to the Portuguese. In it he declared that Zäylä' was "a port of much provisions for Aden, and all parts of Arabia and many countries and kingdoms". They had "no favour" except what came from the

---

28 Varthema (1863), pp. 86-8; Dames (1918), pp. 35-6; *Historiale Description* (1558), pp. 32-3.

port, and which originated "from our kingdoms and the kingdoms of the Moors".[29]

Genasere: an Awssa Market Town?

A further glimpse of Adäl's commerce is provided by Zorzi's Ethiopian informant Brother Anthony. He states that his country's trade with the East was largely based on the "excellent" port of Zäylä', whence supplies from "the whole of India" were taken to "the city" of Genasere. This settlement was 25 days' journey inland, and 40 days from the Ifat town of Gende Belo. Crawford, assuming a day's journey to be around sixteen kilometres, estimates that these two distances were about 255 and 425 kilometres respectively, which would place Genasere near Lake Abbé, then part of Adäl.[30]

---

[29] Beckingham and Huntingford (1961),I, 305 , II, 479.
[30] Crawford (1958), pp. 95-6, 172-5.

Chapter 13

THE SOUTH-EAST and SOUTH: FATAGAR, THE COUNTRY OF THE MAYAS, DAWARO, BALI, and GALLA"

FATAGAR

Zär'a Ya'qob and Bä'eda Maryam

Fätägar, south-east of Shäwa, was one of the provinces affected by Zär'a Ya'qob's reorganisation of the Ethiopian state. The monarch, who had been born in the territory, placed it under an Azzaj. He also appointed a certain 'Amdä Mika'él as its *mälkäñña*, or governor, with the title of Färäglä Ademnät, and stationed *chäwa*, or troops, in it. Probably located near the frontier, their main purpose was to prevent encroachments by the ruler of Adäl. The presence of these soldiers doubtless resulted there as elsewhere in further ethnic and cultural fusion.

Zär'a Ya'qob, who had close relations with the Prior of Yäläbasha in Fätägar, on one occasion visited the area, and proceeded to Enzoraja where he erected the church of Däbrä Sahin. On subsequently building his fine palace at Däbrä Berhan he made use of supplies obtained from Fätägar, as well as from neighbouring Ifat.[1]

Imperial control over Fätägar continued throughout the ensuing reign of Bä'edä Maryam. Almost immediately after acceding to the throne he appointed an *asgwa*, or governor, for the province, and employed troops stationed there. He later travelled to Yäläbasha and camped near the church of Märtulä Mika'él, a locality where his grandfather Emperor Dawit and his father Zär'a Ya'qob had both resided. Bä'edä Maryam's son Emperor Eskender also lived for a time in Fätägar, and was in fact crowned at Yäläbasha.[2]

Confirmation that the province was under the Emperor's control is provided by Ahmäd ibn Ibrahim's chronicler Shihab ed-Din. He states

---

[1] Perruchon (1893), pp. 15, 28, 30, 47, 57, 67, 93. See also Huntingford (1989), pp. 95, 102.

[2] Perruchon (1893), pp. 112, 137, 155; Perruchon (1894), p. 354. See also Huntingford (1989), p. 107.

that Fätägar had been entrusted by Bä'edä Maryam to a single governor, whereas his grandson Lebnä Dengel later had seven Christian chiefs under him. They are said to have competed among each other in fighting against the neighbouring Muslims.³

Incursions by Imam Mähfuz

Conflict between Fätägar and nearby Adäl erupted at the close of the fifteenth century. This took place, as we have seen in Chapter 12, when Sultan Muhammäd of Adäl and his commander Mähfuz, began a series of annual incursions into the Christian highlands.

Mähfuz's twenty-fourth, and last, foray took him, as already mentioned, into Fätägar which he attacked while the wheat and barley was ripe. The inhabitants fled, taking refuge in the mountains, but were pursued by the Adäl commander. He burnt the province's churches and monasteries, and subsequently made himself master of the territory. Its male population, like that of most parts of the region, comprised, according to Alvares, two main categories: peasants, who did not go to war, and *chäwa*, or soldiers, who did. After taking both groups prisoner the victorious chief ordered them to be separated. He told the peasants to "go in peace", and sow as much wheat and barley as they could, so that the next time he and his followers came they might find "enough to eat for themselves and their horses". He then ordered the execution of the soldiers, some fifteen thousand in number, declaring: "Scoundrels who eat the King's bread and guard his lands so badly, all of you to the sword!". He then returned to Adäl, Alvares says, "with great booty".

It was after this, as we have seen, that Lebnä Dengel mobilised, and marched against Adäl. The ensuing confrontation was followed, as already noted, by the historic duel between Amir Mähfuz and the monk Gäbrä Endreyas, and the ensuing rout of the Adäl army.⁴

The Evidence of Brother Thomas of Angot, and Francisco Alvares

Glimpses of early sixteenth century Fätägar are preserved in the observations of Zorzi's Ethiopian informant Brother Thomas, and in Alvares's memoirs. The province, according to the former, was twenty days' journey, i.e. perhaps almost 400 kilometres, wide, and the

---

3   Basset (1897), p. 83.
4   Beckingham and Huntingford and Huntingford (1961), II, 410-15.

location of a city called Sogra. This settlement had "the best, most temperate and perfect air" in the whole of Ethiopia, and could be "seen from every point in the boundless plains". The Venetian painter Hieronimo Bicini had an estate there, which had been given to him by Emperor Lebnä Dengel.[5]

Alvares, who travelled to Fätägar shortly afterwards, recalls that it was "more plain than mountain", and consisted of "small and low hills". It thus resembled "a great hill", rather than a land of mountains or rocky cliffs. The province seemed "very rich", for it consisted almost entirely of woods and farm land. It was occupied by "big fields" of wheat, barley and other seed crops, and many "very big cultivated fields and meadows". It had "great herds" of cattle, sheep and goats, besides small mares and "hinnies", i.e. the offspring of stallions and she-asses.

The Fätägar highlands were the site also of a large but unidentified lake, from which the Emperor's court, when in the area, obtained "an infinite quantity" of good fish. Many neighbouring streams also contained fish, while the surrounding country yielded "vast quantities" of oranges, lemons, limes, and wild, and presumably inedible, figs.

Fätägar at this time was a Christian province, and the site, Alvares says, of many churches and monasteries. Because of its distance from the capital it was also used as a place of exile. One of the monarch's principal courtiers, a Behtwädäd fallen from favour, had thus been sent to a "very high" mountain, on the borders of Adäl, where there was a deep crater accessible only through a single entrance. The place was apparently well endowed, with herds of cows, but anyone who attempted to leave fell victim to fever, presumably malaria, rampant in the surrounding lowlands, and did not "last more than four or five days".[6]

Lebnä Dengel, like his forebears, considered Fätägar an integral part of his empire. In 1525 he camped at Yäläbasha, the place of residence of Emperors Dawit, Zär'a Ya'qob, Bä'edä Maryam, and Eskender, and in a letter to King Manoel I of Portugal proudly listed the province as one of those under his sovereignty.[7]

---

5 Crawford (1958), pp. 162-3.
6 Beckingham and Huntingford (1961), II, 407-9, 432.
7 Huntingford (1989), p. 112; Beckingham and Huntingford (1961), II, 495. See also Huntingford (1989), 119.

THE COUNTRY OF THE MAYAS

The Maya, a pastoral people renowned, as previously noted, for their archery, had been incorporated in the Christian empire in the medieval period. In the early fifteenth century many of them lived in the vicinity of Wäj, within sight of the great mountain of Zeqwala. Their presence in that area is indicated in the Florentine *Egyptus Novelo* map of 1454, which describes them as "fortes gentes", i.e. "powerful people". Doubtless because of their skill Emperor Zär'a Ya'qob enrolled a number of them into his army, and settled some, as mentioned in Chapter 11, as military colonists in Hamasén on the northern plateau.[8]

Another, possibly related, group of people known as Mayas apparently lived in the Afar country. There they came into conflict, as we have seen, with Emperor Eskender, during his disastrous expedition to Arho in 1498. Fighting by night with bows and poisoned arrows they offered strong resistance, and hit, and fatally wounded, the monarch.[9]

DAWARO

Zär'a Ya'qob and Bä'edä Maryam

Däwaro, a largely Christian province south of Fätägar, was still under imperial rule in this period as evident from the fact that Zär'a Ya'qob appointed a governor for the province. He was known as an *arari bäjer*. He, or a successor, later supported the rebellion of Mähiko, *gärad* of Hadeya, whose story will be told in the following chapter.

Zär'a Ya'qob, angered by Däwaro complicity in the rebellion, ordered the people of Adäl to ravage the province, together with nearby Bali. Mähiko's army was defeated, after which the monarch summoned the people of both territories, and ordered them to prevent the rebel from escaping into Adäl.

To strengthen his control over Däwaro the Emperor stationed *chäwa* in the province. They were, however, later guilty of

---

[8] Kolmodin (1914), p. 32; Conti Rossini (1903), pp. 181-3; Crawford (1958), p. 14. See also Taddesse Tamrat (1972a), p. 260.
[9] Perruchon (1894), pp. 358-9. See also Huntingford (1989), p. 109.

insubordination, on which account Zär'a Ya'qob placed many additional soldiers in the area.

Not long after this the *Amir* Bädlay of Adäl, rebelled as we have seen in Chapter 12. Zär'a Ya'qob had therefore once again to concern himself with Däwaro, which, he feared, might support the rebels. He marched into the territory with a small force of troops, known as the Hasab Bäwäsän, and defeated the rebel army.[10]

Däwaro remained under imperial rule during the ensuing reign of Bä'edä Maryam. On acceding to the throne he appointed a governor for the province, and gave him the prestigious title of Ras. During a further revolt he ordered the *chäwa* in both Bali and Däwaro to march into Adäl while he himself made his way to Däwaro.

Missionary Activity and Apostasy

Däwaro in the late fifteenth century was the scene of considerable religious disputations between adherents of Christianity and Islam. Missionaries of the Ethiopian Orthodox Church were particularly active during the reign of Eskender. The principal proselytiser was one of Saint Täklä Haymanot's many disciples, a monk called Täsfa Hezan, who became known as Zä-Däwaro.

The province figures in the story of one of Täklä Haymanot's miracles. This tells of nine Christians who were captured in "the land of the *arämi*", i.e. heathen, a term here used for the Muslims, and prayed to the Saint to take them from Däwaro to their Christian homeland. On their journey they encountered another forty-one Christians, who had likewise been captured, and planned to murder them. The Saint, however, protected the original nine men who had placed their faith in him. The would-be killers received their deserts: they were devoured by lions, leopards and serpents. The nine men survived, and were later re-christened.

Such re-christenings were probably often carried out on Christians who were captured by Muslims, but later escaped. The rationale for this has been explained by the eminent Ethiopian scholar Getatchew Haile. Christians living in non-Christian areas, and perhaps consorting with non-Christian women, often had little option, he argues, but to abandon Christian customs, such as the observance of holy days, fasting, and eating only ritually approved food. Such Christians, even though they had not actually "denied Christ", were considered as

---

10 Perruchon (1893), pp. 15, 17, 19, 45, 58, 88, 91.

apostates. Having been "stripped of their Christianity", they had to be re-christened. Christians became Christian through the act of Baptism, but since, according to the Bible, this could only take place once, a special Penitential Baptism was performed over ex-captives and others thus considered "unclean".[11]

Zorzi's Informants

The importance of Däwaro was recognised by several of Zorzi's informants. Brother Thomas of Angot reported that the province was forty days' journey, i.e. maybe almost 800 kilometres, in circumference. Another observer, Brother Zorzi, noted that the territory was linked by trade routes to both Shäwa to the north and Bali to the south.[12]

BALI

Zär'a Ya'qob, Bä'edä Maryam and Na'od

Bali, the most southerly territory under review, was at this time still under imperial control. During Zär'a Ya'qob's reign the province was, however, seriously affected by the rebellion of Mähiko, chief of nearby Hadeya. He urged the Muslim leaders of Adäl to attack the Christians of Bali, as well as Däwaro. The people of both provinces held their own, and the Emperor, as we have seen, later summoned their help in preventing Mähiko from escaping into Adäl.

Zär'a Ya'qob's successor Bä'edä Maryam later recruited soldiers from Bali, as well as various other provinces. He sent the *gärad* of Bali, a certain Jan Zeg, with many troops, on an expedition to Gam, but the chief perished in battle with all his men. Jan Zeg, we may assume from his name and title, i.e. *gärad*, was probably a native of the area.

Gäbrä Iyäsus, a subsequent *gärad* of Bali, and the province's *chäwa*, were later involved in a plot. Planning to defect they made their way to Adäl where an insurrection was in progress. Their move was, however, foiled. Bä'edä Maryam, learning of their intentions, summoned them, as we have seen, to his court. They came in the belief that they were to receive gifts, but the Emperor instead exiled many of

---

[11] Getatchew Haile (1984), pp. 113-19.
[12] Crawford (1958), pp.133-5, 163.

them to Gojjam. The remainder were then despatched on an expedition to nearby Däwaro.[13]

Despite such difficulties imperial control of Bali continued into the early sixteenth century when Emperor Na'od (1494-1508) repulsed an attack by an Adäl Muslim chief called 'Adruh.[14]

This or other fighting of the period is recalled in Shihab ed-Din's chronicle which states that Wänag Jan, a prominent nobleman of Bali, made his way to Adäl. There in the presence of its ruler, Sultan Muhammäd, he embraced Islam. The latter appointed him a local chief, and placed him in charge of a military expedition to Bali, in the course of which he "pillaged and ruined" the province, but was later defeated, captured, and taken as a prisoner to Emperor Na'od. The rebel's brother, Wäsän Sägäd, a prominent Christian nobleman, interceded on his behalf. Wänag Jan was accordingly released, and given great honour. He declared his return to the Christian fold, but did so, we are told, with repugnance.

Determined on revenge he some time afterwards invited the Christian nobles to a party, and plied them with drink. When they were intoxicated, he had his servants strangle them, and seize their weapons and horses. He then ordered the people of Bali to embrace Islam, and eat the flesh of animals killed according to Muslim rites. He threatened that if they failed to do so they would share their chief's fate. All, great and small, are said to have converted. To consolidate his position he called on the Adäl sultan to join him, but the latter failed to respond. Wänag Jan accordingly wrote a second message, and later sent his son Simu to beg the chief for urgent military assistance.

Na'od meanwhile despatched a powerful force to Bali. It was commanded by a nobleman called Gäbrä Endreyas, conceivably the monk of that name who had killed Mähfuz. For two or three days a battle raged. Wänag Jan was defeated, and fled towards Adäl. He succeeded in reaching the Wäbi River, but died there. The tardy sultan arrived shortly afterwards, whereupon Gäbrä Endreyas wisely withdrew. The Adäl ruler then declared the country to be under

---

[13] Perruchon (1893), pp. 17, 19, 137, 140-1, 157, 165, 167. See also Taddesse Tamrat (1972a), p. 295; Huntingford (1989), pp. 95, 102, 106; Budge (1928b), I, 316.

[14] Basset (1897), p. 68.

Muslim authority, and spent two months in the territory, nominating Muslim governors.[15]

Adäl control appears, however, to have been short-lived, for by the reign of Lebnä Dengel, Bali was once again integrated in the empire. This is apparent from the fact that the monarch listed the province as one of his domains.[16]

As part of the realm Bali had close contacts with Christians from the north. This doubtless led to the founding of many churches, including a notable rock-hewn church, near Goba, which can be seen to this day.[17]

The Report of Brother Thomas of Angot

A description of Bali at this time is presented by Brother Thomas of Angot, who shows that the province was economically integrated in the region as a whole. Bali, he says, measured thirty days' journey, i.e. perhaps almost six hundred kilometres in circumference, and was in commercial contact with a great emporium at Durbit, which was probably as far north as present-day Wällo. Evidently a place of considerable importance which reportedly held a market on three great occasions a year, it was visited by merchants from as far afield as Damot, Gojjam, Agäw, and Tegray. They handled a wide range of merchandise, including gold, silver, jewels, pearls and silk, besides horses and mules, and many medicinal herbs and roots.[18]

"GALLA"

A neighbouring territory to the south or east of Bali was at this time probably inhabited by the Gallas, more recently referered to as Oromos, a Cushitic people. Their name first appears in Fra Mauro's famous *Mappomondo*, or map of the world, completed in Venice in 1460. It indicates a "Galla" River south of the Awash River.

This reference would seem to indicate that Oromos inhabited this area of southern Ethiopia at least a century and a quarter before the composition of Abba Bahrey's renowned History of the Gallas, which will be examined in Chapter 24.[19]

---

[15] Basset (1897), pp. 164-8.
[16] Beckingham and Huntingford (1961), II, 495.
[17] Zeltner (1904), pp. 189-94. See also Sauter (1963), pp. 138-9. 251.
[18] Crawford (1958), pp. 151-2, 163.
[19] Crawford 919580, map op. p. 21, and p. 198.

Chapter 14

THE SOUTH-WEST and WEST: GURAGE, WAJ, GANZ, GAMO, HADEYA, DAMOT, ENARYA, GAFAT, BIZAMO, THE COUNTRY OF THE GAMBOS, KAFA, and THE COUNTRY OF THE BAREYAS

GURAGE

Zär'a Ya'qob and Bä'edä Maryam

By the fifteenth century the Guragé country had become an established part of the empire. One of the first emperors to visit the area was Bä'edä Maryam, who made his way to Aymälläl. There, in the district of Dägu Dägumäñ, he planted vines, sugar-cane, lime- and orange-trees and "all kinds of sweet-smelling plants". His chronicle states that he loved the area, and it was there that on one occasion he received the provincial tribute from Gojjam.[1]

The Testimony of Alvares

The first written mention of the Guragés by name was in the early sixteenth century narrative of Alvares. He was, however, familiar only with that people's northernmost branch, who lived in the vicinity of the Awash River, south of today's Addis Ababa.

Those whom the Portuguese saw were for the most part troglodytes, or cave-dwellers. Many of their caves were excavated in cliffs by the Awash, where there were "innumerable" such excavations, "one above the other, and some of them very high". Most had doors, or cavities in the rock, no larger than "the mouth of a large vat, through which a man could easily pass". Above these doors there was often a piece of iron fixed in the stone, to which "they fastened cords so as by them to know the house".

Such caves - which can be seen to this day[2] - were situated in the vicinity of Lebnä Dengel's camp, or moving capital. This was located in the neighbourhood of what Alvares describes as the palace of the Guragé kingdom - a structure which has thus far not been located. Because of the camp's proximity to these caves "many of the lower people of the Court" chose to lodge in them. Some caves were so

---

[1] Crawford (1958), pp. 148, 157, 159-61, 182.
[2] Pankhurst (1973), pp.15-35.

large that "twenty or thirty persons could find room inside with their baggage".³

Caves by the River Awash, described by Francisco Alvares in the early sixteenth century.
Photo: Georges Fonteret.

The Guragé area to the south, as well as other neighbouring regions, were the site of numerous stone megaliths, smaller but no

---

3 Beckingham and Huntingford (1961), I, 398-400, 452.

less interesting than the famous obelisks of Aksum. Though not mentioned by Alvares these megaliths must have been there in his day. Now believed to date from possibly the time of Christ many are popularly thought to have been knocked down during the religious turmoil of the early sixteenth century.[4]

Early megalith from Silte, Guragé, decorated with a decorative motif of swords.
From L. de Castro, L *Nella terra dei negus*.

The Guragés struck Alvares as a freedom-loving people. "None of them", he was told, were slaves, for they declared they would "let themselves die, or kill themselves, sooner than serve the Christians", i.e. the men of Lebnä Dengel's court.[5] The Guragés had a reputation of being "very bad", as some of them attacked persons attached to the court. This was particularly serious for those belonging to the camp of the Behtwädäd, the monarch's favourite courtier, whose quarters were

---

[4] Joussaume (1974), pp. 104-5
[5] Beckingham and Huntingford (1961) II, 398.

situated on the left of the Emperor's camp, nearest to the Guragés. Attacks were so common that "there were few days when it was not said: 'Last night the Gorages killed fifteen to twenty persons of the people of the great Betudede'".[6]

Notwithstanding such incidents Lebnä Dengel's power extended throughout much of the Guragé area. Alvares states that the monarch when on an expedition to Hadeya left his wife and children at "Orgabeja", conceivably his rendering of Werbarag, south-west of Lake Zway. The Emperor's sovereignty was also apparent around the lake, on one of the islands of which an earlier sovereign had founded a monastery. The Portuguese writer reports that it had many monks, though the neighbouring mainland was a "Moorish", i.e. Muslim, country.[7]

Evidence of a significant Christian presence south of the Awash is likewise evident from the fact that it was evidently an area of several rock-hewn churches, one of which, Adadi Maryam, is still currently a place of worship.[8]

WAJ

Zär'a Ya'qob and Bä'edä Maryam

The small territory of Wäj, situated south of Shäwa and north of the Guragé country, was also under imperial rule. Emperor Zär'a Ya'qob nominated a governor over the area, with the title of *hegäno*, while his son Bä'edä Maryam subsequently appointed one with that of *qas*.[9]

Bä'edä Maryam had particularly close contacts with Wäj. The territory supplied him with cattle, and was later chosen by him as the site for a palace and church. The former was so beautiful that persons wishing to inspect it actually paid to do so - a practice reported on no other occasion in Ethiopia. The Emperor subsequently visited two other localities in the area, Arari and Abasi, the latter sometimes also referred to as Abäsi Wéra Gäbäya. It was the place where he died.[10]

---

[6] Beckingham and Huntingford (1961) II, 401.
[7] Beckingham and Huntingford (1961)II, 435; Henze (1977), p. 109.
[8] Guèbrè Sellassié (1930-1), II, 568; Pankhurst (1974a), 222-5; Pankhurst (1974b), pp. 226-7. See also Krapf (1867), p. 45.
[9] Huntingford (1965a), pp. 23, 129. Perruchon (1893), pp. 15, 112.
[10] Perruchon (1893), pp. 148, 165, 180, 182.

Lebnä Dengel and Gebergé

Wäj, though small, was of major political and commercial importance. It was easily accessible from Shäwa, and lay on the trade route between Hadeya and Däwaro. Alvares describes Wäj as a "kingdom" within Lebnä Dengel's empire, while Brother Thomas asserts that it was traditionally ruled by a woman, for its inhabitants "would have none but a queen to govern them".[11]

The principal settlement in the area was Gebergé, which lay on the aforesaid trade route, and was the site of a palace belonging to the Emperor. It was one of the seven places in the empire whither Zär'a Ya'qob despatched pieces of the body of the Adäl rebel "Arwé Bädlay.[12]

The town's importance was later noted by Brother Thomas, who described it as a "city" six days journey from the Shäwan capital Bärära. Gebergé resembled Venice, he claimed, in having many "warehouses". One of them belonged to the Florentine trader Andrea Corsali, who was planning to print books in the Ethiopian language.[13]

GANZ

Gänz, a tributary territory to the west of Wäj, was ruled during Bä'edä Maryam's reign by a local chief with the title of *gärad*. The province, like Wäj, supplied the monarch with cattle, but, because of its remoteness, was also a place of detention for the Emperor's sons. They were placed, according to the royal chronicle, in the custody of its governor Matéwos, who held the title of *gärad*.[14]

The territory was well known to Alvares, who states that it was inhabited by "a mixture" of "Pagans" and Christians. The latter were "gradually" coming into the area, presumably from Christian areas to the north.

Lebnä Dengel evidently considered Gänz of some importance, for it was one of the provinces which he listed in his letter to King Manoel of Portugal as part of his empire.[15]

---

[11] Beckingham and Huntingford (1961), II, 432, 454; Crawford (1958), pp. 160-1.
[12] Basset (1897), p. 221.
[13] Perruchon (1893), p. 65; Crawford (1958,) pp.82-5, 161, 177, 183, 191.
[14] Perruchon (1893), pp.112, 148; Perruchon (1894), p.362. See also Taddesse Tamrat (1972a), p. 277.
[15] Beckingham and Huntingford (1961) II, 454, 495.

GAMO

Gämo, or Gamu as Alvares called it, lay to the west of Lake Chamo. The Portuguese writer asserts, on the basis of hearsay, that it was "almost a kingdom in size", but had "no king, only chiefs" who ruled "separately". It was inhabited by "pagans little valued as slaves".[16]

HADEYA

Zär'a Ya'qob, and the Attempted Rebellion of Gärad Mähiko

Hadeya, one of the most important provinces in the south-west, and the site of rebellion a century or so earlier, faced further political problems during Zär'a Ya'qob's reign. They began, according to his chronicle, when the monarch summoned Mähiko, his *gärad*, or governor, to come to pay his taxes. The chief refused, saying, "No, I will not go to your door, and I will not leave my country". He accordingly dismissed the royal envoy.

Almost immediately after this one of Mähiko's functionaries, the Gädayto *gärad,* rushed to the monarch, who was at his capital, Däbrä Berhan. He informed the latter that the Hadeya ruler was preparing for war, and had appealed for help from the rulers of neighbouring Däwaro and Bali. Zär'a Ya'qob asked him who were Mähiko's allies, whether the rebellion was supported by the entire population or only by a part, and what was his advice as to what should be done. The chief replied that Mähiko had the support of only nine *gärad*s, those of Gudola, Diho, Hadäbo, Gänäzo, Saga, Gäb, Qäb'én, Gogälä and Haläb, and advised that he be deposed in favour of his uncle, Gärad Bamo, who would reverse his nephew's policies and destroy his power.

Gärad Bamo

Zär'a Ya'qob accepted this advice. He accordingly summoned Bamo, named him principal *gärad*, presented him and Gärad Gädayto with rich clothes, and sent the two men back to their country with a

---

16 Beckingham and Huntingford (1961) II, 454. See also Crawford (1958), pp. 186, 188.

large army from nearby Damot. The monarch also summoned people from Däwaro and Bali, and ordered them, as we have seen, to ensure that the rebel did not escape into Adäl. Trumpets were then blown, and a large number of priests and monks assembled, after which the Emperor commanded them to pray in their churches for victory.

Gärad Bamo returned to his province, with the support of the forces Zär'a Ya'qob had given him. On seeing them the nine rebel chiefs made their submission. Mähiko, abandoned by his supporters, fled eastwards towards Adäl, pursued by the men of Damot. In his attempt to escape he abandoned many valuables, hoping that this would tempt his enemies to remain behind to collect them. The loyalists, however, did not tarry. They pushed on vigorously, and entered the governor's *amba*, or mountain fortress. Mähiko was killed, and his head, hands and feet cut off. When the Emperor heard the news of the victory he rejoiced greatly. He and his courtiers celebrated with much singing and dancing.

Not long after this Bamo arrived at Zär'a Ya'eqob's capital with Mähiko's severed head and limbs, which he presented to the monarch. The latter thereupon thanked Bamo and Gädayto, and the Damot soldiers for their help, and gave the latter a great feast. The rebel's limbs were hung at the palace gate, to the satisfaction of dogs and hyenas. Gärad Gädayto and his descendants were then exempted from taxation to the third generation, and the soldiers who had killed Mähiko were granted land in his province.[17]

Zär'a Ya'qob and Gärad Mehmäd

Further difficulties in Hadeya arose during the subsequent rebellion of the Adäl ruler Sultan Bädlay ibn Sä'd ad-Din. Though the main focus of activity was far away in the east, Mehmäd, the *gärad* of Hadeya, decided to take advantage of the situation. As we have seen in Chapter 12 he sent a message to the Emperor, inquiring if the latter needed his help, and at the same time gave the rebel leader assurances of his friendship though these, the chronicler later claimed, were in fact false.

Zär'a Ya'qob responded cautiously by ordering Mehmäd to establish his camp, but to remain at Ayfärs until summoned. At the same time he despatched a *mälkäñña*, or officer, to the province, to ensure that these orders were obeyed. He did so, the chronicle explains, because Mehmäd was of the same faith as Bädlay, and his allegiance therefore suspect. After the rebel's defeat, Zär'a Ya'qob summoned Mehmäd to the capital to witness his victory, and gave

---

17 Perruchon (1893), pp. 16-23.

him rich clothes, for he had shown, we are told, that his intentions had after all been good.[18]

Imperial control, which had thus been consolidated by Zär'a Ya'qob, was firmly established during the reign of Bä'edä Maryam, whose chronicle records that he too appointed a *gärad* for the province.[19]

Eléni Mehmäd

Relations between Hadeya and the Christian empire underwent a notable development during the reign of Bä'edä Maryam, who effected a dynastic marriage with Gärad Mehmäd's daughter Ité Jan Zela, later better known as Eléni. She was the sister of the former rebel Gärad Mähiko. The union linked the two ruling houses, one Christian, the other Muslim, and put an end to Hadeya's earlier potential alliance with Ifat.

Eléni, a woman of rare virtues, became the Emperor's senior queen, i.e. Qäñ Bältehät, or Queen of the Right, and is said to have been affectionately regarded by Bä'edä Maryam as his mother.

Later, after the death of Emperor Na'od in 1508, Eléni was instrumental in putting her twelve-year-old step-grandson Emperor Lebnä Dengel on the throne, and served for several years as his Regent. She was, according to a chronicle, "skilled in the laws of the kingdom, having been in the palaces of three illustrious kings", presumably Bä'edä Maryam, Na'od and Lebnä Dengel. Though a woman from the periphery she played a major role in central Ethiopian statecraft, and laboured hard to weld together the imperial and Hadeya dynasties, as well as to ward off impending incursions by the Ottoman Turks.[20]

Alvares, during his stay in the country, had the opportunity to learn much about this distinguished daughter of Hadeya, whom he describes as "an able and popular ruler". He recalls that the then patriarch, Abunä Marqos, once told him that Eléni and himself had together been responsible for choosing Lebnä Dengel as Emperor,

---

[18] Perruchon (1893) pp. 59, 65.
[19] Perruchon (1893) p. 112.
[20] Perruchon (1893), pp. 16, 59, 176-7; Basset (1981), p. 247; Beckingham and Huntingford (1961), II, 425, 458, 603; Budge (1928b), I, 308, 318; Merid Wolde Aragay (1977), I, 63.

"because they had all the great men (and all the treasure) in their hands".

Another megalith from the Guragé area.
From R.P. Azais and R. Chambard, R., *Cinq annés de recherches archéologiques en Ethiopie.*

As well as being a skilled politician Eléni was a woman of great devotion, who stuck to all the Orthodox fasts, and, we are told, only ate meat three times a week, on Tuesdays, Thursdays and Saturdays. She was also reputedly a consummate theologian, and the author of two Ge'ez texts, one on the Trinity and the Purity of the Virgin, and the other on the Laws of God. The owner of many fiefs in Gojjam she had a fine church built there at Märtulä Maryam. It was constructed with the assistance of craftsmen brought specially from Egypt. It was in this place of worship that she was later buried.

Eléni's death, which took place during the Portuguese visit, deeply shocked everyone at the royal court. People said that "since she had died all of them had died great and small, and that while she lived, all lived and were defended and protected; and she was the father and mother of all". For months after her death droves of people were still coming from Gojjam to weep in her tent.[21]

The Testimony of Alvares; Dynastic and Other Ties

At the time of Alvares's visit in the 1520s the Hadeya ruler, whose name is not recorded, wished to consolidate the close alliance between his kingdom and the Christian empire earlier initiated by Bä'edä Maryam. He sent his wife's sister as a prospective bride for the young Emperor Lebnä Dengel. The latter, however, found her displeasing, for she had "two big front teeth, that is to say long ones". Though rejected by the pleasure-loving monarch she was soon married off to an important courtier, Bahr Nägash Ras Näbiyat, who was later elevated to the prestigious position of Behtwädäd.[22]

Somewhat later the Hadeya queen herself arrived at Lebnä Dengel's court, and spent a fortnight there. She came to ask the monarch for help, according to Alvares, because her husband's brother had "risen up against her and was taking the kingdom from her". She arrived "quite like a queen, and brought with her fully fifty honourable (well-dressed) Moors [i.e. Muslims] on mules and 100 men on foot, and six women on good mules". Describing the pomp and circumstance that accompanied her visit, the Portuguese observer continues: "She was received with great honour, and the third day of her arrival was called and came before the tent of the Prester". She had a black canopy, and was "robed twice that day, once at the hour of Prime, and the other at the hour of Vespers; both robes were of brocade and velvet and Moorish dresses from India".

Young Lebnä Dengel, faced with the dynastic struggle in Hadeya, urged the queen to "rest and not be troubled". He declared that he would himself march to her country, as she wished, and that he was only awaiting the arrival of the Bahr Nägash and the ruler of Tegray - "as soon as they arrived he would set out".[23]

---

[21] Beckingaham and Huntingford, (1961), I, 243, 307, II, 395, 425, 434, 458-9; Huntingford (1989), p. 156.
[22] Beckingham and Huntingford (1961), II, 427; Rey (1929), pp. 28-30.
[23] Beckingham and Huntingford (1961), II, 427-8.

The two chiefs, and their followers, duly arrived three weeks later, whereupon the Emperor despatched some 15,000 men, with instructions to go to Hadeya "immediately", and establish the queen's husband "in peace in his kingdom". She herself was "to go more at leisure". She and the Hedug Ras, or Behtwädäd's deputy, nevertheless at once set out, though it was said that it would take her "more than a month's journey" to reach home.[24]

Some time later a message arrived from the Hedug Ras, stating that he and his companions had gone with the queen to help her husband. The Hadeya people, however, had refused to obey him, and "wherever he went they all ran away and took refuge in the mountains". He therefore requested Lebnä Dengel to send more men. On receipt of this news the young monarch determined to go to Hadeya in person. His expedition, it appears, was entirely successful. The Portuguese who accompanied it told Alvares that as soon as Lebnä Dengel entered Hadeya "all the people came in, obeying him as their lord".

The province, Alvares learnt, was "very fruitful". It was "very wooded", so much so that one "could not travel without cutting trees and making roads". It also had "plenty of provisions" of "every kind", "many very big animals", and great herds of cattle".

Further to consolidate his influence Lebnä Dengel ordered "many monasteries and churches" to be built, and left "many priests and monks", and "many laymen" to dwell in the territory until it was pacified, after which they duly returned to Shäwa.[25]

Hadeya, with the assistance of the Church was thus re-established as a tributary state. Though inhabited by Muslims, its population, according to Alvares, was "peaceful" and subject to the Emperor. They paid "tribute of cows in great number", many of which he had seen at the court. Some were "as large as big horses, and white as snow and without horns, with big hanging ears".[26]

Lebnä Dengel for his part was proud of his rule over Hadeya, and lists it in his letter to King Manoel of Portugal, as one of his domains.[27]

---

[24] Beckingham and Huntingford (1961), II, 430.
[25] Beckingham and Huntingford (1961), II, 434-6. See also 453-4.
[26] Beckingham and Huntingford (1961), II 434-6, 453.
[27] Beckingham and Huntingford (1961), II, 495.

DAMOT

Zär'a Ya'qob and Bä'edä Maryam

Damot, another major province in the south-west, traditionally much involved in the gold trade, was one of the territories affected by Zär'a Ya'qob's governmental reforms. Early in his reign he placed the territory under the supervision of one of his daughters, Mädhen Zämäda. Later, however, he assumed personal control of the entire empire, and entrusted Damot to a chief with the title of 'Eraq Masäré.

During the rebellion of Mähiko, governor of Hadeya, Damot remained loyal to the Emperor, and, as earlier noted. soldiers from it helped to defeat the insurrection. They later brought Zär'a Ya'qob the head of the defeated rebel, after which he provided them with a great feast, at which they were allowed to eat and drink as much as they desired. The army of Zär'a Ya'qob, it should be emphasised, was largely multi-ethnic, as evident from his chronicler, who on one occasion revealingly tells of the monarch's palace guards in Shäwa uttering cries in their respective tongues.

Christianity may well have spread in the province at this time. Legend claims that the people of Enselal, in Damot, failed to honour the festival of Maryam, whereupon a violent wind arose, and blew down a huge tree, which, we may suppose, was perhaps worshipped by the animist population. Not long after this a local man broke the law by trying to cut the tree to pieces on another day dedicated to the Virgin, but the tree, and several others which had also fallen, then stood up as before. Zär'a Ya'qob, impressed by this assumed miracle, thereupon erected a church in the Virgin's honour.[28]

On the subsequent accession of Bä'edä Maryam the empire's administration was decentralised. Damot was placed under an official with the title of Sähafä Lahm, i.e. Writer, or Recorder, of Cattle. Soldiers from the territory, as we have seen, later collaborated with troops from Tegray in the Emperor's expedition against the Dobe'a in the north, and served in a campaign in the east against the ruler of Adäl.[29]

The local monastery of Däbrä Me'raf continued to flourish at this time. Mälkä Sédéq, a grandson of Emperor 'Amdä Seyon, travelled

---

[28] Perruchon (1893), pp. 14-15, 21-2, 36; Cerulli (1943b), p. 123.
[29] Perruchon (1893), pp. 112, 145-6, 159, 14. See also Budge (1928b), I, 316.

there to receive his monastic garb, and, after visiting holy places in various parts of Ethiopia, returned to become its abbot.[30]

The Testimony of Alvares and Zorzi's Informants

Damot in the early sixteenth century was by all accounts a vast territory. Alvares described it as "very big", and one of Zorzi's informants, Brother Anthony, who was born in the province, as "very great". Brother Thomas claimed that it took sixty days to cross, which would suggest that it was almost 120 kilometres wide. The weather was for the most part tropical: Brother Thomas called it "very hot and torrid", while Brother Anthony agreed that it was "very hot". This climate made possible a flourishing agriculture. Alvares understood that the area produced "plenty of fresh provisions". When he and his companions kept Lent in nearby Guragé they thus received from Damot much green ginger, grapes, and peaches, and, presumably for consumption after Easter, "many fat sheep, and cows of great size".

The territory was also reputedly an important source of gold. Brother Anthony asserted that a "great quantity" of the precious metal was dug there, and was "perfect" in quality, while Alvares went so far as to declare that "most" of Ethiopia's gold came from Damot, and was "very fine".

The province was likewise renowned for its slaves, who were much esteemed, Alvares says, "by the Moors", i.e. Muslims or Arabs, who would "not let them go at any price". Arabia, Persia, India, Egypt, and Greece were in consequence "full of slaves" from Damot, who, on being converted to Islam, made "very good Moors and great warriors". The story of one such Damot slave found its way into a contemporary Ge'ez work, the *Miracles of Jesus*. It tells of a man who purchased a slave from the province, but lost him before he could re-sell him at the Shäwan capital, Bärara.

Though renowned for both gold and slaves neither originated exclusively in the territory. The gold came mainly from Enarya, while the slaves were brought from many areas, including both Enarya and Bizamo. The importance of Damot thus lay less in its own resources than in its strategic and commercial position.[31]

---

30 Getachew Haile (1993), X, 214-15.
31 Beckingham and Huntingford (1961), II, 455; Getatchew Haile ans Macomber (1982), VI, 352; Merid Wolde Aregay (1974), p. 628; Huntingford (1989), p. 95.

The province had trade links with the northern and central parts of the empire, and at times supplied the court with large quantities of provisions and livestock. Merchants from Damot are said by Brother Thomas to have travelled to Durbit market, in northern Shäwa or southern Wällo. Among the articles brought to Damot was rock salt, which, on account of the long distance from the Afar depression, was so costly that as few as three or four *amolés* could, as we have seen, purchase a good slave. Damot was probably also in contact with one or more of the Gulf of Aden ports, as suggested by the fact that Lebnä Dengel remarked to the Portuguese that the route between the province and these ports was shorter than to Massawa.

Despite its long relationship with the Christian empire Damot in the early sixteenth century was still mainly inhabited by "pagans". Alvares states that there were, however, also "many" Damot Christians, some of whom he had seen at Lebnä Dengel's court. The province was moreover the site of many monasteries and churches, as a result of which its population included a sizeable number of priests, monks and nuns.

Damot, because of its distance from Shäwa, was also a place of detention for political prisoners. Mutineers, after a rebellion in Tegray in the early 1520s, were imprisoned in Damot, under the supervision of numerous guards. A governor of Tegray was likewise exiled to the province, where there was "a very high mountain", with only one man-made entrance. The summit was so exposed to the wind that persons despatched there soon, sad to say, died of cold and hunger.[32]

Though isolated Damot figures in many a Ge'ez *Tä'ämera Maryam*, or Miracles of Mary. These tell of a great storm which hit the province, allegedly because its inhabitants failed to observe her celebration day. Many trees were blown over, and the rainy season lasted for no less than 153 days, from 24 Genbot, at the beginning of May, to 21 Teqemt, at the end of November.[33]

ENARYA

The great gold-producing territory of Enarya, though conceivably still to some extent a tributary state, was in this period probably

---

[32] Beckingham and Huntingford (1961), I, 181, 192, 297, II, 434, 455; Crawford (1958), pp. 95, 148-51, 156-7, 160-1, 172-3, 176-7.
[33] Getatchew Haile and Macomber (1982), VI, 92, 106, 114; Getatchew Haile (1987), IX, 198.

beyond the sway of imperial rule. The only significant reference to it at this time was by Zorzi's informant Brother Anthony of Lalibäla, who spoke of it as a province on the frontier of Damot.[34]

GAFAT

Zär'a Ya'qob, Mäb'a Seyon and Attempts at Conversion

Gafat, as we have seen in Chapter 9, had long been inhabited by animists. Some conversions to Christianity, however, took place during Zär'a Ya'qob's reign. A glimpse of how this was effected is found in the *Gädl*, or Acts, of Mäb'a Seyon, a holy man of the time, which claims that God had promised him the honour of converting the province. The Saint was wandering around it, we are told, when he was met by multitudes of people marching out to meet the monarch "to receive gifts from him because they had been baptized, and had believed in the name of the Trinity". When they saw the monk they pressed forwards to meet him, saying, "Give us thy blessing". He asked, "Do ye believe in Christ my God, so that I may bless you?". They replied, "Yes, we believe". He accordingly blessed each one of them. They then said, "Give us a name, and we want you to set a priest over us; baptize us also, and be you to us as a father".

Mäb'a Seyon said to them, "Christ shall be a father unto you. Behold now that I have blessed you with my own hand ye have become children unto me". Then the Gafats said to him, "Show us your city so that we may come unto you frequently, and that the love of you may come back into our hearts". He accordingly "showed them the name of his city, and they went on their way rejoicing exceedingly".[35]

This conversion was apparently only partial or temporary. Taddesse Tamrat is doubtless correct in stating that "very few" Gafats in fact adopted Christianity.[36] Later evidence indicates indeed that the population continued to be largely "pagan" for several centuries thereafter.

---

[34] Crawford (1958), pp. 97-8, 103, 177, 185, 187.
[35] Budge (1898), pp. 79-80. See also Getatchew Haile (1985), V, 255.
[36] Taddesse Tamrat (1972a), p. 238.

The missionary Saint Mäb'a Seyon, who reputedly converted Gafat to Christianity: a much later manuscript illustration in Gondarine style. From E.A. Wallis Budge, *The Lives of Maba Seyon and Gabra Krestos*.

The Testimony of Alvares and Brother Thomas

Information on Gafat and its people during Lebnä Dengel's reign is preserved in the writings of Alvares. He reports that the territory bordered Shäwa and Gojjam, from which it may be assumed that it was then situated south of the Blue Nile. The Gafats, he declares, were "pagans and great warriors" constantly at war with the Emperor. Some of the Portuguese, who had visited the area, reported that Lebnä Dengel and his Behtwädäd had encountered many problems with the Gafats, who came by night "to kill and plunder", while by day "they took refuge in the mountains and jungle".

These mountains caught the imagination of the Portuguese author, who states that they consisted of "depths rather than heights", thus suggesting that the province was broken up by deep river valleys. Brother Thomas, on the other hand, described it as the site of "great mountains", in which the Awash River had its source.

Despite some banditry Damot was still part of the empire. Lebnä Dengel, when listing the provinces under his rule to King Manoel, placed it immediately after Shäwa.[37]

BIZAMO

Bizamo, which lay between the Abbay and Didessa Rivers, was a small territory on the western borders of the empire. According to an early fifteenth century soldiers' song of Yeshaq's reign it paid tribute in cotton cloth. The Portuguese Jesuit Almeida later confirmed that the province had once formed part of the empire.[38]

THE COUNTRY OF THE GAMBOS

The country of the Gämbos, west of the Chomän swamp, seems also to have paid tribute of some kind to Yeshaq, as the soldiers' songs suggest. Contact with the area is also suggested by its mention in the medieval *Hegga Wäser'atä Mängest*, or Laws and Institutions of the Kingdom.[39]

KAFA

Käfa, largely if not fully beyond the confines of the empire, was in this period still under the rule of an independent local dynasty. The most important Käfa monarch at this time, according to oral tradition, was the "Shadda king", who ruled between around 1495 and 1530.[40]

THE COUNTRY OF THE BAREYAS

By the early sixteenth century there were fairly close, though often inimical, relations between the countries inhabited by the "blacks" and the highland Christian empire. The highlanders, whose point of view alone is reflected in the literature, were on the whole hostile to their "black" neighbours with whom they often fought and took slaves. Brother Thomas, speaking to Zorzi, thus dismissed the Bareyas as "blacks with curly hair", while Brother Anthony complained that the Nubi, or Nubians, were "bad people, robbers and murderers". Alvares was likewise told by highland Christians that the Nubians were a "very vile people, very black and very bad". One of

---

[37] Beckingham and Huntingford (1961), II, 458, 495; Crawford (1958), pp. 149, 161.
[38] Guidi (1889), pp. 55-7; Beckingham and Huntingford (1954), pp. 18-19.
[39] Guidi (1889), pp. 55-7; Huntingford (1989), p. 247.
[40] Bieber (1920-3), II, 494-533.

those who no doubt shared this view was Bahr Nägash Dori, whose son had been killed by them, after which the father proclaimed his intention of making war on them.

"Black" slaves, presumably captured in such warfare, were then a not uncommon sight in many parts of the country. At the port of Hergigo the Portuguese mission's supplies were carried, according to Alvares, "on the backs of negroes", and on reaching Shäwa he notes that the tribute from Tegray was accompanied by "two little negroes dressed in red and yellow livery, each upon a camel covered in the same livery". Where precisely such "negroes" came from is not, however, recorded. Most slaves, then as in other periods, doubtless intermarried with the majority population by whom they were assimilated; others, however, were exported, to Arabia and elsewhere.[41]

---

[41] Crawford (1958), pp. 94, 99, 166, 181; Beckingham and Huntingford, (1961), I, 71, 96, 129, 187, 191-4, II, 429.

Chapter 15
THE BORDERLANDS and THE INTERIOR

The North

The northern highlands in this period as in earlier times represented the empire's principal access to the sea, and thus continued to play a major role in the economy of the region as a whole. The trade of much of the hinterland was still based on the twin ports of Massawa and Hergigo. Their exports as before consisted largely of gold, ivory, and slaves, as well as honey and wax. The significance of the ivory trade would seem reflected in the fact that Hergigo was also known as Dehono, apparently a rendering of the local name for elephant. The more northerly port of Suakin, by this period at least, also served the area, for it was used by Christian pilgrims and others making their way to and from Jerusalem. Some traders likewise took the overland route by way of Sudan to Cairo and Tunis.

The northern highlands, and part of the neighbouring coast, were administered on the Emperor's behalf by a functionary with the rank of Bahr Nägash, or ruler of the sea province, a title which may have been instituted by Emperor Zär'a Ya'qob. The official holding this post had his capital at Debarwa. The position was considered an important one as can be deduced from the fact that one of those occupying it was Lebnä Dengel's uncle. Zär'a Yaq'ob's control over the area was also symbolised by the continued granting of imperial land charters in Hamasén and Säraye, as well as by the stationing in the former district of a contingent of Maya archers from the south. Local tradition has it that he also fortified the Gerar peninsula opposite Massawa.

The country of the Bahr Nägash, as testified by Alvares in the early sixteenth century, paid considerable taxes to the Emperor, mainly in fine horses and imported textiles.

The Afar country's trade with the interior meanwhile continued to be important. Rock salt, a valuable commodity from the Dankali depression, circulated, Alvares states, throughout the empire and beyond.

Relations between the Afar rulers and the emperors of the interior fluctuated. In the fifteenth century an Afar chief gave his support to Emperor Bä'edä Maryam, who was undertaking an expedition against the Dobe'a people. Later in the century, however, conflict erupted when the people of Arho, who were probably located in the Afar country, killed one of Emperor Eskender's servants. The incensed monarch responded by leading an expedition into the area, but was killed by a Maya arrow, whereupon his infuriated soldiers wrought punishment on the Arho people.

The East

Ifat, which lay on the main eastern trade route to the port of Zäylä', was by this time entirely under imperial control. One of the province's principal settlements was the emporium of Gende Belo, on the edge of the plateau, where camels from the coast unloaded their merchandise. The town handled much of the foreign trade of the region, including the import of textiles and other commodities from India, and was a place where many peoples and cultures mixed.

The province was entrusted by Zär'a Ya'qob to one of his daughters, 'Amatä Giyorgis, and later, after a change of policy, to a centrally appointed official with the rank of Raq Masäré. The territory later contributed supplies for the construction of Zär'a Ya'qob's great palace at Däbrä Berhan. Bä'edä Maryam, who adopted a less centralising policy, subsequently appointed as governor a local chief with the title of Wälashma'.

Adäl, situated much further off in the eastern lowlands, was not easily accessible to highland troops who for climatic reasons would have found it virtually impossible to settle there as they had done in Ifat. Zäylä', the province's principal port, meanwhile maintained its economic importance for the lands of the interior. The port handled much of the entire region's foreign trade, including that of Shäwa.

Zär'a Ya'qob's rule was challenged by a local *amir*, Bädlay ibn Sä'd ad-Din, whose rebellion was easily crushed. Adäl was, however, at this time largely outside the sphere of imperial government, though Zär'a Ya'qob used part at least of the territory as a place of exile for some of his troops.

Mehmäd, a subsequent governor of Adäl, offered to provide Bä'edä Maryam with tribute if he refrained from making any incursions into the Shäwan highlands. The monarch agreed, but the pact was later repudiated by a subsequent ruler of Adäl, Läda'e 'Uthman. Fierce fighting resulted. Bä'edä Maryam despatched two expeditions to the territory. In the first his men were reportedly successful, but soon withdrew. The second ended in disaster, with the monarch's two favourite commanders, Mähari Krestos and Gäbrä Iyäsus, among the dead.

Emperor Eskender subsequently attacked Sultan Shäms ad-Din of Adäl, and sacked Däkär, but his forces on their return journey were attacked by a much larger enemy force, and ignominiously defeated. Adäl thus preserved its importance, albeit at a considerable cost of blood, on both sides.

Later in the century Mähfuz, the *amir* of Zäylä, no doubt taking advantage of the wealth and power of the port, began a series of annual incursions, into Amhara, Shäwa and Fätägar. He assumed the religious title of Imam, symbolising the fact that he was engaged in a *jihad,* or Holy War. His expeditions were accompanied by extensive looting and seizure of slaves, many of whom were assimilated in Adäl, while others were exported. Mähfuz sent not a few as gifts to the rulers of Arabia, who in return gave him considerable military support.

Lebnä Dengel, angered by these raids, mobilised his army to confront the invader. Mähfuz, realising the size of the Christian army, and the difficulty of defeating it, offered to fight a duel with one of his enemies. The challenge was taken up by a monk, Abba Gäbrä Endreyas, who won the contest, after which Lebnä Dengel's men routed the Adäl army. Notwithstanding this victory Adäl remained the most powerful, and extensive, of the Muslim states in the region, as Lebnä Dengel himself recognised when he proposed that the Portuguese should help him conquer it.

A nearby stretch of country, to the south or east of Bali, was at this time probably inhabited by Gallas, or Oromos, as suggested by Fra Mauro's well-known map of 1460 which refers to a "Galla" River.

The South and South-East

The southern and south-easterly provinces, notably Fätägar, Däwaro and Bali, were to a greater or lesser extent affected by the political-cum-religious struggles in the east.

Fätägar, the most northerly of these territories, was an integral part of the Ethiopian empire. Zär'a Ya'qob appointed a governor over the province with the titles of *mälkäñña* and *färägla ademnät,* while Bä'edä Maryam later nominated one with the rank of *asgwa.* The latter, or another governor of this reign, was engaged in fighting with the nearby Muslims. Both monarchs stationed *chäwa,* or troops, in the territory, an act which led to ethnic and cultural assimilation. Both rulers likewise lived for a time at the Fätägar town of Yäläbasha, where Emperor Dawit had earlier resided. The territory also provided supplies for the erection of Zär'a Ya'qob's palace at Däbrä Berhan.

The province later suffered from the annual incursions of Mähfuz, who on one occasion executed no less than 15,000 of its Christian soldiers. His attacks were checked by Lebnä Dengel who eventually routed the Adäl armies. He also used the province as a place of detention for politically unreliable persons, and later recognised its importance when he listed it as part of his dominions.

Däwaro, further south, was likewise part of the empire. Zär'a Ya'qob appointed a governor, called an *arari bäjer*, over it. The latter, or a successor, later joined the rebellion of the Hadeya ruler Mähiko, but was easily defeated by Zär'a Ya'qob's forces in Adäl and Bali. To strengthen his position in the province the monarch stationed *chäwa* there.

Imperial control of Däwaro was thus preserved. Bä'edä Maryam subsequently appointed a governor with the prestigious title of Ras. The territory was the site of considerable Ethiopian Christian missionary activity, notably by one of Saint Täklä Haymanot's disciples, the monk Täsfa Hezan, who was aptly given the name of Zä-Däwaro.

Bali, in the far south, was also part of the empire, but at times under strong pressure from Adäl, which afforded access to the Gulf of Aden ports, as well as from Hadeya in the west. During the reign of Zär'a Ya'qob, Mähiko, the rebel ruler of Hadeya, urged the Muslims of Adäl to attack the province, but the Bali leaders held their own. 'Adruh, a chief from Adäl, subsequently launched an attack on Bali during the reign of Emperor Na'od, but was repulsed. This reign likewise witnessed a rebellion by a chief called Wänag Jan, who converted to Islam, and killed many Christian chiefs by a stratagem, but was eventually defeated. The province thus remained part of the empire, and testimony to its Christian affiliation is provided by the remains of a rock-church near Goba.

The South-West and West

The south-western provinces, among them Guragé, Wäj, Hadeya, Damot, Gafat and Enarya, continued to play an important role in the empire's economic and state affairs, as well as in those of the wider region as a whole.

Bä'edä Maryam, the first emperor to visit Guragé, made his way to Aymälläl, and established fruit plantations in the nearby district of Dägu Dägumäñ. Many of the province's inhabitants are said to have been troglodytes, living in caves by the Awash River. Described as a freedom-loving people, some of them reportedly lived by looting Lebnä Dengel's camps.

The small province of Wäj had long been under imperial control. Zär'a Ya'qob nominated a governor of the territory, with the title of *hegäbo*, and Bä'edä Maryam one with that of *qas*. The area supplied the latter monarch with a considerable number of cattle. He established a palace and church there, and visited two neighbouring localities, Arari and Abasi, in the second of which he died. Another nearby settlement, Gebergé, was a renowned commercial centre, and the site of Zär'a Ya'qob's palace.

Hadeya, the most north-easterly of the provinces in this area, was growing rapidly in importance. During the reign of Zär'a Ya'qob, Mähiko, the province's *gärad*, or local ruler, refused to pay his taxes, and urged the rulers of Däwaro and Bali to join him in rebellion. Nine of his chiefs supported his action, but the rest remained loyal to the Emperor. The latter reacted promptly. On the advice of a local chief, Gärad Gädayto, he replaced Mähiko by the latter's uncle Gärad Bamo, and then intervened militarily on Bamo's behalf. The Hadeya chiefs thereupon submitted to the Emperor. Mähiko was defeated and killed.

Mehmäd, a subsequent *gärad* of Hadeya, offered to help Zär'a Ya'qob during the rebellion of Sultan Bädlay of Adäl. The Emperor was, however, unsure of the Hadeya chieftain's loyalty, and did not take up his offer. After crushing the insurrection he nevertheless rewarded Mehmäd by adorning him with fine clothes.

Bä'edä Maryam recognised the importance of the province by marrying Mehmäd's daughter Ité Jan Zela, later better known as Eléni. This dynastic alliance was probably designed by the Emperor to break the potential Hadeya-Adäl axis, which had earlier been a threat to the empire, but was to have even wider implications. Eléni, a clever stateswoman, and an able Christian theologian, was, it is said, an important influence in chosing the infant Lebnä Dengel as Emperor. She later served as Regent during his infancy, appealed for Portuguese help against an anticipated invasion by the Ottoman Turks, and for many years played a major role in imperial state affairs. A woman from the periphery was in effect shaping the policy, and destiny, of the central state.

The Hadeya ruler, seeking to consolidate his alliance with the young Emperor shortly afterwards sent his sister-in-law as a prospective wife. The monarch found her displeasing, and refused to marry her, but she was soon wedded, influentially, to one of the principal courtiers, Ras Behtwädäd Näbiyat.

Hadeya ties with the empire were later threatened by rivalries within the province's ruling family. Lebnä Dengel was obliged to despatch an expedition to keep the reigning chief in power. With a view to strengthening relations he had churches and monasteries built, and despatched many priests, monks, and lay persons to the area. Their presence doubtless led to some cultural as well as religious assimilation.

Ties with Hadeya were of major importance, for the territory became the empire's most loyal ally in the west, and thus helped to maintain imperial power in that region. The territory was also a source of wealth, for it supplied Lebnä Dengel's court with large numbers of cattle and fine horses. For all these reasons the monarch was proud to list the province as one of his principal domains.

Damot, further to the west, was of even greater economic importance. It lay on the trade route from Enarya which, though probably beyond the sway of direct imperial rule, was the source of large quantities of gold and numerous slaves. Many of the latter were exported, via Damot, to Arabia and other parts of the Middle East, where they were almost invariably converted to Islam.

The province at this time was firmly under imperial control. Zär'a Ya'qob entrusted its government to his daughter, Mädhen Zämäda, and later to a chief with the title of 'Eraq Masäré. Troops from Damot served in the monarch's multi-ethnic army, and were used in campaigns against the Dobe'a, near Wäjerät east of the highlands, as well as in Adäl. During the rebellion of Mähiko the territory remained loyal to the Emperor, and its soldiers helped to defeat the rebel. Later, during Bä'edä Maryam's reign, it was placed under an official with the title of Sähatä Lahm. The literal meaning of this title suggests that he was responsible for "writing down", or recording, the numbers of *lahm*, or cattle, paid in taxes. The appellation would seem appropriate, for Damot supplied Lebnä Dengel's court with large quantities of cattle, sheep and other provisions, as well as soldiers.

Gafat was situated north of Damot, though south of the Blue Nile. The province was essentially animist, but during Zär'a Ya'qob's reign was the site of considerable Christian proselytism. Many conversions were carried out by a holy man called Mäb'a Seyon, but failed to have very long-term consequences. The territory was regarded as a place of some importance, and was listed by Lebnä Dengel as one of his domains.

Bizamo, a small territory between the Abbay and Didessa rivers, was likewise a tributary state which provided Emperor Yeshaq with cotton cloth, while the Gämbos, west of the Choman swamp, also contributed tribute.

The provinces in the south-west were thus major sources of wealth. Control over them was important for they had access to gold, ivory and other valuables, and at times also supplied the imperial court with large quantities of cattle and other provisions.

The period witnessed continuing conflicts between the empire and the "blacks" in the west, as well as with the Dobe'a to the north. Fear of the latter caused Zär'a Ya'qob to station a garrison in the area, and his son Bä'edä Maryam subsequently despatched an expedition against them. Further fighting with "blacks" took place in the early sixteenth century, and resulted, as in the past, in the capture of many slaves, whose presence was reported by Alvares both in the interior and on the northern periphery. Their presence contributed to the region's increasing diversity, as well as no doubt to further ethnic and cultural fusion.

Many slaves from the empire's western periphery were also exported.

PART IV
THE ERA OF IMAM AHMAD

(c.1526-1545)

Chapter 16

THE SOUTH and SOUTH-EAST: ADAL, DAWARO, FATAGAR, THE COUNTRIES OF THE MAYAS and DOBE'AS, IFAT, BALI, SHARKHA, and DARHA

ADAL

Early Life of Imam Ahmäd ibn Ibrahim al-Ghazi

The most important figure in the Muslim territory of Adäl and its surroundings in the first decades of the sixteenth century was Ahmäd Ibrahim al-Ghazi (lived 1506-1543), today better known as Ahmäd Grañ, in Amharic the Left-Handed. The story of his rise to power, and of his subsequent campaigns is told in considerable detail in the *Futuh al-Habasha*, or Conquest of Abyssinia, written in Arabic by his able Yamani chronicler Shihab ed-Din Ahmäd ibn 'Abd al-Qadir, surnamed 'Arab-Faqih.

Ahmäd lived in Harär during the rule of Sultan Abu Bäkr, a time, as we have seen in Chapter 12, when corruption is said to have been rife. The story of the relations between the two men is told in the *Futuh*, which having been written, it should be emphasised, by one of Ahmäd's supporters, doubtless presents a partisan account. Ahmäd, we are told, saw that the sultan and his soldiers, who included many Somalis, were violating Holy Law and permitting illicit behaviour. He therefore left the town, together with a number of men who had served under the previous Adäl leader Gärad Abun. They established themselves at Hubat, 30 kilometres to the north-west, where their numbers soon rose to over a hundred. They chose a certain Gärad 'Umar Din as their leader.

At about this time they learnt, according to the *Futuh*, that one of Emperor Lebnä Dengel's governors, Fanil, or Fanu'él, of Däwaro, had undertaken a pillaging expedition. Advancing to the vicinity of Hubat, he is said to have captured many Muslim women and children. On learning of this Ahmäd and his companions rushed against the "infidels", i.e. the Christians, inciting each other to participate in a Holy War in the service of Allah.

Imam Ahmäd ibn Ibrahim al-Ghazi, better known as Ahmäd Grañ, a twentieth century popular Ethiopian painting at the Institute of Ethiopian Studies, Addis Ababa.

A fierce engagement followed in which "nothing was heard but the noise of swords beating against shields". Ahmäd charged the enemy who were soon put to flight. Many Christian lords and soldiers were killed, and the captured Muslim women and children were freed. Ahmäd and his party then returned to a place called Zifah, in the neigbourhood of Harär, without the loss, it is claimed, of a single man. Sultan Abu Bäkr and his Somali supporters learnt of the rebels' victory with dismay. Fearing a possible attack, they abandoned Harär, and withdrew into Somali territory. Ahmäd and his friends pursued them, and a mighty battle followed. The Sultan and his Somali soldiers were once more obliged to flee, after which the victors established themselves in Harär. However, Abu Bäkr and his men later regrouped, and rode back to the city, whereupon Ahmäd and his party again withdrew to Hubat. They established themselves on a high mountain, which the Sultan besieged for ten days, after which Ahmäd and his companions escaped in the night, but their leader, 'Umar Din, was killed.

Ahmäd and his comrades subsequently made peace with the Sultan, and entered his service. The chief, however, soon violated the peace agreement. He seized the erstwhile rebels' horses, and killed one of Ahmäd's companions, 'Uthman ibn Yassein. Ahmäd, fearing for his own life, once more fled by night, and returned to Hubat. Several further engagements followed, after which the Sultan's followers were defeated. Ahmäd returned to Harär, where he appointed himself ruler, and governed, according to the *Futuh*, with justice, putting an end to oppression.

Undeterred the Sultan collected a new army, once more largely composed of Somalis. Further fighting seemed imminent, but a new agreement was made. At about this time a swarm of bees alighted on Ahmäd's head. This incident, which recalls the story of the swarming of bees around the infant prince, later King, Lalibala three centuries earlier, was considered so miraculous that people gave him the title of Imam, by which Mähfuz, it will be recalled, had earlier been known.

For a time Ahmäd and the Sultan lived together in harmony, but the latter, according to the *Futuh*, subsequently "changed his behaviour". He became "unjust to his people", and planned to kill the Imam. The learned people tried once more to establish co-existence between them, but Abu Bäkr refused and went to war against the Imam. The latter succeeded in killing the Sultan, thus delivering the country, we are told, from his tyranny. Ahmäd is said to have made travelling more secure by killing highwaymen, and to have proclaimed that anyone attacking a Muslim would have his goods confiscated.

After establishing peace Ahmäd placed the old Sultan's brother 'Umär Din on the throne, and detailed his own brother Muhammäd ibn Ibrahim to keep an eye on the situation in Harär. Having thus attained effective control over the city he was free to devote himself to his ambition of emulating Mähfuz by undertaking a *jihad*, or Holy War, against the Christians and "Pagans" of the interior. The conflict began, according to the *Futuh*, when the Imam ordered the Muslim towns of Adäl to cease paying Emperor Lebnä Dengel their customary tribute. The monarch responded by despatching to the province his brother-in-law, Azmach Degälhan, governor of Bali, but the Imam defeated the latter decisively at Eddir.

Ahmäd, who had married the late Imam Mähfuz's daughter Bati Del Wänbära, enjoyed considerable popular support, particularly among her father's relatives and followers, who wished to continue their late master's policies. He thus had strong support when he embarked on a series of expeditions against the empire's eastern provinces.[1]

The Imam, situated as he was in the east of the region, was in a good position to undertake these operations, for, as ruler of Adäl, he had easy access to fire-arms, which at this time began to be imported in sizeable numbers. They came from Arabia through the great trading port of Zäylä'. Before carrying out one early expedition he is reported to have obtained seven cannon, as well as seventy well-armed soldiers from Mahra in South Arabia. His army then and later almost invariably enjoyed far greater fire-power than that of Emperor Lebnä Dengel, let alone those of the territories to the west or south.

Military superiority, coupled with able leadership and religious fanaticism, enabled the Imam to embark on a series of generally successful campaigns. They took him and his followers to the east, south, west and north of the region, and will be considered on a regional, rather than chronological, basis in the following pages.

Ahmäd's military superiority was however brought to an end, in 1541, when the Portuguese, coming to the assistance of Emperor Gälawdéwos, landed a well armed expeditionary force at Massawa. This party consisted of over 400 soldiers, and were equipped with six cannon, and no less than a hundred swivel guns and over 600 matchlocks.[2]

The Acquisition of Loot

Though the Imam's motivation, like that of Mähfuz a generation earlier, was doubtless largely religious, his expeditions were immensely profitable to his followers and supporters. Shihab ed-Din, describing his master's earliest skirmishes, recalls that Lebnä Dengel had sent down to the Muslim lands merchants with gold, *wars*, or

---

[1] Basset (1897), pp. 15-33.
[2] Basset (1897), pp. 4, 9, 15, 19-21, 26, 30, 32, 35, 40, 51-2, 54-5. See also Pankhurst(1967), pp. 203-4; Dombrowski (1985), pp. 18-20..

safflower, ivory, civet and slaves, which they sold in Arabia, and brought back in return considerable riches. This wealth, the *Futuh* explains, "became the prey of the Muslims", and, when divided among the tribes participating in the *jihad*, "fortified the believers against the infidels".[3]

Ahmäd, though the recipient of much loot, also made considerable financial sacrifices for his cause. After completing a series of raids on the borders of the Christian highlands for example he sold his wives' jewellery, and his household property, to purchase weapons.[4] Having thus built up his arsenal he left his homeland in 1530-1 to launch his Holy War against Lebnä Dengel's empire. This was a revolutionary step not favoured by all his co-religionaries, and caused the people of Amajäh in eastern Shäwa to warn him against "bringing ruin upon the Muslims".[5]

Later expeditions, which took Ahmäd and his comrades into the Christian interior, involved extensive looting of churches, palaces and markets. This resulted in the arrival in Harär of large quantities of gold and valuable cloth, as well as cattle, pack animals and slaves. Booty brought to the city early in the campaign, according to Shihab ed-Din, included 5,000 head of cattle and 2,500 slaves. Vast amounts of gold were also seized. On one occasion some of the victorious chiefs "obtained 2,000 ounces, others 1,500 and others 500", while on another expedition, if we can believe the *Futuh*, they seized 909,990 ounces of gold, "without counting cattle, vases, plates and ewers". After looting one of the more wealthy churches each of Ahmäd's followers was said to have acquired 300 ounces of gold. The rare metal was at one point so plentiful, it is claimed, that transactions were carried out by the handful. The price of a mule rose to forty ounces. Friends offered each other presents of one or two hundred ounces, and when a man gave only fifty the proposed donee was allegedly so angry that he refused to receive it.[6]

---

[3] Basset (1897), p. 71.
[4] Basset (1897), p. 73.
[5] Basset (1897), p. 87.
[6] Basset (1897), pp. 47, 67, 131, 147-8, 170, 316, 330, 337, 353.

From the Periphery to the Interior

By the summer of 1532 the Imam's exceedingly well-armed forces had overrun almost all the southern and eastern provinces, notably Däwaro, Bali, Hadeya, Gänz, Wäj, Fätägar and Ifat. Having advanced inland from the periphery his men had in fact become the masters of much of the interior. The *Futuh* goes so far as to claim that only a third or a quarter of Abyssinia remained unconquered. Ahmäd at this point called together his principal followers. After thanking God for his successes, he told them that they should summon their wives and children, so as to establish themselves permanently in the highlands. Sultan Säbr ad-Din II of Ifat, it will be recalled, had reportedly tried to do the same thing two centuries earlier. It was "no longer possible", the Imam is quoted as declaring, for his soldiers to return to their own country, or to abandon the territories they had occupied. He then asked his commanders for their comments. They dutifully replied that it was for him to command, and that whatever he ordered they would do.

Having thus gained their acquiescence to the idea of advancing into the interior he despatched letters to Sultan 'Umar Din, the ruler of Harär, and to his own brother Muhammäd ibn Ibrahim, who, it will be recalled, was also in that city. He sent them precious objects captured during his last campaign, and asked them to despatch to him his soldiers' women and children. Every one of the Imam's men, *amir* or simple soldier, likewise wrote to his wife, instructing her to come to join him. Each man sent his spouse what she needed for her journey, as well as for those she left behind. Some men sent thirty ounces of gold, others twenty, others ten. Each gave according to his means. The soldiers also sent mules to transport their womenfolk and their baggage.[7]

The Imam's military operations, a major turning-point in the history of the region, affected the peripheral territories, as we shall now see area by area, no less than its heartlands.

---

[7] Basset (1897), pp. 394-5.

DAWARO

The Imam's Initial Forays

The Christian province of Däwaro, because of its location in the east and its relative proximity to Adäl was one of the first to feel the weight of Ahmäd's campaigns.

After an initial raid into Fätägar in 1526-7 the Imam carried out several forays into Däwaro. In one of the first his men, according to the *Futuh*, took "considerable booty" in horses, slaves, sheep, and beasts of burden. The raiders planned to return to their country, but were obliged to fight a further battle, as the "infidels of Däwaro", i.e. its Christian leaders, assembled a massed army against them. This force was subsequently defeated.

In a later expedition Ahmäd ordered his men to advance as far as Wämbärya, which they reached without a battle. Here again they seized a large amount of loot, before returning to their own country. On their journey home they were attacked by the Däwaro chiefs and soldiers, but these were later beaten at a place called Zämit. The Imam's men then proceeded to Kahalberi, where they defeated a force of Däwaro infantry, and burnt down the church of Zahraq, which a former Ethiopian monarch had erected.[8]

Not long after this the Emperor, who was then at the royal town of Badeqè in eastern Shäwa, received news of an impending, and far larger, invasion of Däwaro. Realising the danger to his realm, he set forth for Amhara, to mobilise his army. He left his forces in charge of one of his principal commanders, Awra'i 'Uthman ibn Dar 'Ali. The latter was a Muslim Bäläw from the far north of Ethiopia, who had been converted to Christianity. The two leaders then devoted their efforts to recruiting further soldiers. Lebnä Dengel rallied men from the northern parts of the empire, including Tegray, Angot and "the sea coast", i.e. the country of the Bahr Nägash in the north, and Agäw, Gojjam, and Bägémder in the north-west. Awra'i assembled troops from the southern provinces, among them Däwaro, as well as Bali,

---

8 Basset (1897), pp. 30-53; Huntingford (1989), pp. 122-3. See also Merid Wolde Aregay (1974), p. 624.

Fätägar, Gänz, and Damot.[9] The imperial army of this time, like that of Zär'ä Ya'qob in the previous century, thus came from virtually all parts of the empire.

Imam Ahmäd was also active. He achieved a notable, but extremely costly, victory at Shembera Koré, literally the Swamp of Chick-Peas (situated between Mojjo and the Awash River, i.e. about 80 kilometres east of modern Addis Ababa) on 7 March 1529. Despite this success he withdrew to his own country, but later crossed the Wäbi River once more into Däwaro. Encountering no armed resistance, he seized many prisoners, and extensive loot. He did this at Jawatir, on the eastern borders of the province, and, further west, at Adäl Mäbräq, which he burnt to the ground. Its Christian governor, Abél, offered stiff resistance, but was soon captured. The provincial governor, Ras Näbiyat (or Bänyat), learning of the ravages committed by Ahmäd's forces, assembled a large army to block their advance. A truce, the first of several in the campaign, was, however, arranged by Abél. It allowed the invaders to pass through the province unmolested, in return for a promise that they would spare its royal churches.[10] Notwithstanding this agreement Näbiyat and a number of Däwaro chiefs continued the fight against Ahmäd's forces.[11]

The Beginning of Occupation

After these first raids and skirmishes the Imam decided, in 1530, to embark on the more permanent occupation of Däwaro. Early in the ensuing campaign he again advanced into the area, and reached the province's northern districts. Lebnä Dengel, on learning of this development, ordered Bahr Sägäd, the son of one of the territory's chiefs, and his commander Wäsän Sägäd, who was away in Damot, to dig a defensive trench at nearby Del Méda. When these earthworks were completed Bahr Sägäd stationed an army to guard them. He died, however, shortly afterwards, whereupon a nobleman called 'Addalu, also known as 'Adälih, who was then in Bali, took over the defence.

---

[9] Basset (1897), pp. 76-84; Huntingford (1989), p. 123.
[10] Basset (1897), pp. 131-7; Huntingford (1989) p. 124.
[11] Basset (1897), pp. 144-6.

'Addalu ordered a large number of soldiers from Bali, as well as others from Däwaro, to guard the trench. Ahmäd, however, was not to be foiled. He made inquiries, and interrogated the prisoners in his possession, and through them learnt a way of circumventing the trench. This enabled his men to reach Del Méda without difficulty. The defenders, obliged to abandon their fortification, massed instead at Bäb Sari. They sent a message to the Emperor, warning him that the Adäl soldiers were advancing on his church, and that, since the truce was no longer in force, they would probably burn it.[12]

The Imam, however, turned northwards, and, leaving Däwaro, proceeded to Antokya in Ifat. There in February 1531 he achieved a decisive victory over Lebnä Dengel's army. Many of the latter, as we shall see, dispersed to their own country, leaving behind only their chiefs. Most of the Däwaro soldiers were among those who went home.[13]

Not long after this Ahmäd set out from 'Andurah, and attacked the Emperor's men at 'Ayn Färäs, or 'Ayfärs, where he defeated them decisively on 31 March, inflicting heavy losses. He proceeded to Qanburah, situated above the principal Däwaro market. Its inhabitants were Muslims, subject to the Däwaro governor, to whom they paid tribute. They received the Imam, as their co-religionary, with respect and honour.

Ahmäd's men remained at Qanburah for a week, at the end of which the Somalis, who had by then captured much booty, assembled their horses, mules, cattle, donkeys and clothes, and said to each other in secret, "We have acquired plenty of loot; let us find the Imam, and ask permission to return to our own country. If he agrees, good; if he refuses, let us depart without permission". The Maläsäy, a name applied to local Muslims, also wanted to defect. The Somalis therefore declared with confidence, "When we return the greater part of the Maläsäy will follow us, and only a few people will remain with the Imam". Ahmäd, appraised of this plot, ordered his spies to keep a watchful eye on the situation.[14]

---

[12] Basset (1897), pp. 174-7; Huntingford (1989), p. 125.
[13] Basset (1897), p. 198.
[14] Huntingford (1989), p. 126. See also Basset (1897), pp. 84, 206.

Around this time the Imam and his companions arrived at 'Andurah. There they found an imposing church built by Wäsän Sägäd, which, it is said, had taken no less than eleven years to erect. A structure the like of which, according to the *Futuh*, had never been seen in Däwaro it was an immense, and splendidly ornamented, building on raised columns. It was guarded by a thousand Duba'ah foot soldiers, armed with poisoned spears called *jato*, but these defenders fled on the enemy's approach. Ahmäd then entered the edifice in wonder, admiring both its construction and its paintings. His men seized a large number of carpets, pieces of cloth, silks and other valuables. After taking everything that could be found, they burnt the church to the ground.

Ahmäd and his men stayed in 'Andurah for six days, during which time they also made a number of expeditions into various parts of Däwaro, on foot and on horseback. They once more seized much booty and captives. Two of the Imam's leaders, Amir Zaharbuy Muhammäd and Gärad Ahmushuh, heard that Wäsän Sägäd had a treasury in the district of Gatur. They set off to loot it, but found only half its contents, for at the news of their approach the defenders had fled with the other half. The treasure consisted of huge quantities of fabrics, silks and other goods, but, unfortunately for the Imam's men, no gold. They then returned to their leader at 'Andurah.

Lebnä Dengel meanwhile, on learning of Ahmäd's advance, and of its destructive consequences, including the burning of Wäsän Sägäd's church, was reportedly much infuriated. He gathered his chiefs and officers, and, recalling the ravages committed in Däwaro and the defeat of his army, summoned the soldiers from Tegray to come to his aid. Large numbers of the latter responded. He called one of his most trusted followers, Täklä Iyäsus, the ruler of Tegray and of the port of Dehono, or Hergigo, appointed him to the additional post of governor of Däwaro, and ordered him to rush to his new fiefdom to fight against the soldiers from Adäl.

Täklä Iyäsus duly set forth for Däwaro, taking with him many chiefs great and small, among them the governor of Särayé in the country of the Bahr Nägash. Despite the size of this army Ahmäd easily outmaneuvered and defeated it, inflicting heavy casualties. Täklä Iyäsus was among the many killed.¹⁵

Reconciliation Manoeuvres

After this victory the Imam decided to bring Däwaro under permanent occupation. The province's Christian inhabitants, on learning this, were much alarmed, for the Imam's well-armed men, as we have seen, had already wrought extensive destruction. This is recognised by the *Futuh* which claims that Ahmäd's soldiers had "looted left and right", and thus "ruined the country".¹⁶

Conditions were so serious that one of Ahmäd's Christian captives, a man called 'Amdu, attempted an interesting peace initiative on the province's behalf. Given the intensity of conflict, and the religious antagonisms engendered, this was no easy task. It involved tact, lengthy negotiation, and diplomatic resourcefulness, which the *Futuh* describes in revealing detail.

'Amdu began his initiative by asking to be granted an audience with the Imam to discuss a plan he had conceived. Ahmäd agreed to receive him, and inquired, "What is your idea? What have you to say?" "Promise me, if I speak", 'Amdu replied, "that you will not kill me". The Imam gave his word, whereupon the prisoner declared that Ahmäd could "ruin the whole country", if he wished, but should not destroy Däwaro. He added that the invaders had already ravaged the area, and made its inhabitants perish in battle or by taking them away as captives - but he repeated, once more, that he "had a plan". The Imam asked him to speak up, and explain.

'Amdu then asked to be freed, and despatched to his former companions, the Christian chiefs of Däwaro. He would tell them, he declared, that, if they agreed to pay the obligatory poll tax, Ahmuad and his men would withdraw from their territory, and the province's Christians would be allowed to remain in their posts, and continue to practice their religion.

On hearing these words the Imam at first declared that the plan was merely a trick to enable 'Amdu to escape, and that if the latter

---

¹⁵ Basset (1897), pp. 194- 204; Huntingford (1989), p. 194.
¹⁶ Basset (1897), p. 207.

spoke as he proposed his companions would not listen to him. He went on to observe, however, that if 'Amdu was really sincere, and confident that his friends would accept his ideas, he was free to go. He nevertheless warned him that if he played false he was "nothing but a dog, the son of a dog" (and would presumably be punished accordingly). If, on the other hand, he was sincere, he would receive his reward.

The captive was duly released, and set forth to meet his former comrades, who had gathered at the settlement of Jan Zedrah, the site of another church built by the province's governor Wäsän Sägäd. There he found a number of the principal southern Christian chiefs. They included 'Addalu, governor of Bali, and one of the commanders, a cousin of 'Amdu's called Giyorgis. On seeing 'Amdu they greeted him warmly, and asked him where he had been. "I was a prisoner of the Muslims", he answered, "but have been released by the Imam to come and find you". At this point he singled out Giyorgis, and asked him to order the other nobles to move some distance away, as he had something to say to him in private.

When they were alone 'Amdu told him that he had come to bring "good advice" on the part of the Muslims. Hitherto, he declared, the latter had carried out only minor incursions before returning to their own country. Ahmäd's present expedition, he explained, was, however, very different, for the Imam had ravaged the country, killed its soldiers, and was determined not leave it. 'Amdu went on to recall the invaders' earlier victories, how at the battle of Shembera Koré the Emperor had been put to flight, and how at the battle of Antokya the Christian army had been routed, and all the nobles killed. "We no longer have the power", 'Amdu concluded, "to fight the Muslims. If the Imam establishes himself in our country he will ravage and ruin it". Finally, he reminded Giyorgis that Wäsän Sägäd, their governor, was away in Damot (and presumably could therefore not help them).

Giyorgis, impressed by these arguments, asked who could negotiate peace, and persuade the Imam to leave. 'Amdu replied that he had a scheme which would do just that. Asked to explain he declared that the Christians should make peace with Ahmäd by paying him the poll tax, and that they should provide his soldiers with hospitality and presents. These should include three good mules, together with sugar, *chat*, and coffee - which would not constitute a "great burden" for Däwaro.

Giyorgis then called the other chiefs, and told them what his kinsman had said. They willingly accepted the plan, declaring that the proposed burden was indeed small. They added that, if the Imam was satisfied with it, they were confident that neither the Emperor nor Wäsän Sägäd would punish them. Emphasising their desire to preserve their province's security they declared that they would willingly give the Muslims the proposed presents and provide hospitality.

The Däwaro chiefs, perhaps not wishing to rely solely on a single envoy, summoned one of their number, by name Zin, who had been a Muslim prisoner, but had later been ransomed and returned to the Christian fold. They ordered him to go with 'Amdu. Declaring that Zin knew Muslim customs in relation to hospitality and the making of gifts, they instructed him to tell Ahmäd that if their governor learnt that they had given him [i.e. Ahmäd] presents he would not leave them in peace, and the Emperor would kill them. They said this, Shihab ed-Din suggests, as an excuse for making only a small gift. They went on to promise, however, that if the Imam crossed the Awash River into Shäwa, defeated the Emperor, and arrived at the nearby town of Gebergé, thus conquering the whole area, they would surrender all their horses and arms. Those among them who wanted to become Muslims would then convert, while those who wished to maintain their religion would pay the required poll tax. They added the additional assurance that "If the Emperor asks us to help him against the Imam we will not join him", and concluded by promising that if Ahmäd would withdraw from Däwaro they would remain in their homes, refrain from making any incursions into Muslim territory, and avoid causing him any kind of trouble.

Zin, on hearing this, declared his willingness to go to the Imam to obtain a "guarantee of peace" for the nobles and their province. He was convinced, he added, that if they stuck to the proposed terms the Muslim leader would do nothing against them - but otherwise they would be in deep trouble. The nobles gave him their oath to abide by their word, and ordered him to depart.

The two envoys then went to the Imam, whom they found encamped on the high land above Däwaro. There Zin presented the gifts of *chat*, coffee and sugar, and Ahmäd politely asked after his vistior's health. These formalities completed the envoy explained that he had been charged by the Däwaro leaders to intercede on their behalf. "How is that?", the Imam enquired. Zin replied that he had instructions to bring presents from the Däwaro leaders. He went on to relate how the negotiations had proceeded, the conditions his comrades had proposed, and what they had sworn.

On hearing this report Ahmäd at first rejected the gifts. Adopting a grumbling stance he exclaimed, "What are these presents you have brought? Leaves of *chat*, coffee and sugar! I will not accept them! God has delivered us your riches and has allowed us to ravage your land!". He accordingly ordered the envoy to take back the presents, and return home. Zin had no option but to recover the gifts. He then went to one of the Muslim leaders, Vizier Addolé, and sadly reported what the Imam had said.

This was, however, not the end of the story, for Addolé and his companions saw a clear advantage in the proposed agreement. They therefore went to their master to discuss the matter afresh. He asked them whether they did not see that the Däwaro leaders, by sending trifling gifts, were playing with them, and reminded his followers that they could easily remain in the province and ruin its inhabitants.

The vizier and chiefs replied, however, that they saw no real advantage in staying in Däwaro. They felt it was better to accept the presents, give the Däwaro leaders clothes of honour,[17] and send them back to their companions. They argued that by agreeing to the truce they would be free to cross the Awash River and march against Lebnä Dengel. Speaking of Däwaro they declared, "If God gives us victory this country will be at our command, and, when we want it, it will be ours". The Imam accepted this advice, and changing his position, declared, "What excellent counsel you have given me!".

---

[17] The gift of ceremonial clothes as part of the peace-making process can be traced back to early Aksumite times. See for example their use byKing Ezana in the early fourth century. Budge (1928b), I, 24.

He therefore accepted the gifts, and, turning to Zin, said to him, "We accept your presents. When we march against the King, do not make any incursions into our territory, and do not help the King. If you are faithful to what you have promised, all will be well". Zin replied that he willingly agreed to Ahmäd's conditions. His colleagues, he added, had sworn their sincerity, and he and 'Amdu would do so the same. The two envoys accordingly pledged their word, after which the Imam dressed them in clothes of honour. They then returned to Däwaro, to report the successful outcome of their mission.[18]

Such, according to Shihab ed-Din, were the negotiations between his victorious master and the defeated Däwaro leaders. The pact was advantageous both to the Imam, whose advance into the interior was facilitated, and to the province's population which, for the time being at least, was spared further destruction. Many of the inhabitants chose to retain their religion by declaring their neutrality and paying the poll tax, though many others agreed to be converted.

Further Looting

Notwithstanding the agreement Ahmäd and his men were far from confident about their occupation of Däwaro. They realised that they had not yet brought the territory under effective control. The Imam, who was then at Däbrä Berhan in Shäwa, asked his chiefs in 1532 whether he should despatch a further expedition to Däwaro. One of his principal advisers, Färäshäham Din, advised against this. He explained that the country between the Awash and Wäbi Rivers, as well as the provinces of Bali, Gänz and Wäj, had not yet been converted to Islam. He therefore urged Ahmäd not to send an army to Däwaro, but rather to go to the province in person, while they remained at Gebergé or Zeqwala (60 kilometres south of Addis Ababa). The Imam accepted this advice, but asked what they should do about territories, such as Ifat to the east, which had been converted, but which, if left without garrisons, would speedily revert to their earlier religion. Färäshäham Din frankly replied that the countries which had embraced Islam had done so only in appearance.

---

[18] Basset (1897), pp. 207-11.

He nevertheless declared that if the Imam went to Däwaro, even for a day, a thousand horsemen from Bali and Hadeya would rally to his support, but that there was little point at that stage in the Muslims establishing themselves in those provinces.

At the end of this council Ahmäd proposed that his follower Awra'i Abun, and his own nephew Abbas Abun, should join Färäshäham, and that they should be reinforced with 400 horsemen. He reckoned that this force would be sufficient to establish itself in Ifat, which had by then accepted Islam. He accordingly summoned the two men, and told them to remain in the province with the reinforcements he would send them, while he himself proceeded to Däwaro. Awra'i replied, however, that it was not possible for him to stay in Ifat, for with the onset of the rains the Awash would become swollen, and he would be isolated from his leader. If the Emperor then attacked he would be unable to resist. The Imam, however, was not to be moved. He insisted that Awra'i should return to Ifat as instructed. The chief thereupon called upon the latter's inhabitants, and others who had embraced Islam, to follow him there. Fifty cavalrymen and 2,000 foot soldiers with their women and children did so.[19]

The Imam subsequently despatched another commander, Amir Hosayn, and twelve chiefs to Däwaro. They were accompanied by 600 horsemen and numerous foot soldiers, who were well equipped, some of them wearing coats of mail. This force proceeded to the country of the Mayas, where a contingent of local people joined them. They then advanced into the territory of Watmät, where they learnt that three Christian nobles, Safu, son of Wäsän Sägäd, Fanu'él, and Amha, had established themselves in Däwaro. Ahmad's soldiers without further ado rushed forward to confront them, whereupon the terrified Däwaro nobles fled to Sari-bär, and the Imam's men occupied the abandoned Christian camp. A Muslim force under Absama-Nur then made its way to the nearby land of Zämit, ravaged it, and seized many women and children.

Ahmäd's forces proceeded to Joraji, and camped above Suq-Däwaro, the principal Däwaro market. One of their commanders, Amir Abu Bäkr, made his way thence to the afore-said Jan Zajora,

---

[19] Basset (1897), pp 360-2.

devastated it, and burnt its church. He then advanced into the country of Jirirawrari, with the intention of forcing its inhabitants either to become Muslims or to pay the poll tax.

This was the turning point of the expedition. Faced by Abu Bäkr's advance the Däwaro people, who were governed by fifty Christian nobles, finally agreed to adopt Islam. The Imam, much pleased with their conversion, appointed one of his followers, Gärad Jushu, as governor of the province. The "affair of Däwaro", as Amir Hosayn claimed, was thus brought to an end, for "all the inhabitants" had, at least temporarily, become Muslims. The province had a revered Qadi, by name Adam ibn Abi Bäkr.[20]

Nasradin Ahmäd and Gälawdéwos

The importance which the Imam attached to Däwaro is apparent from the fact that he entrusted its government, around 1540, to his son Nasradin. The latter, according to an Ethiopian royal chronicle, had a sizeable army of about a thousand cavalrymen and ten thousand infantry.

Despite the Adäl army's strength in Däwaro and elsewhere Lebnä Dengel's son, Gälawdéwos, who succeeded to the throne in 1540, was determined to resume the struggle. According to his chronicle he then had only sixty or seventy horsemen, and an equally small number of foot soldiers. Because of his "great zeal for the Church" he nevertheless resolved to fight on against his father's enemies, and, if necessary, seek death in battle. "A glorious death", he declared, was "preferable to a life of shame".

Many men of Däwaro took a similar view, and fled the province to continue the war. One such was the province's Azmach, or governor, whom the Portuguese adventurer Bermudes later claimed to have met in the north-west of the empire. This chief, and another exiled nobleman who accompanied him, sported two banners, and had a force of a hundred and fifty horsemen and a thousand foot. The two men proudly declared that they were vassals of Gälawdéwos, and that they had come to assist his resistance to the invader.[21]

---

[20] Basset (1897), pp. 169, 367-71, 380, 382.
[21] Whiteway (1902), p.176.

Meanwhile in Däwaro itself the two armies, though unequal in numbers, fought fiercely. The Imam's soldiers were at first victorious, and killed several of Gälawdéwos's chiefs. The young monarch, however, did not lose hope, but, particularly after the coming of military assistance from the Portuguese, determined to seek his revenge. He accordingly re-entered Däwaro, spent the rainy season in the area, and constructed a winter, as well as a summer palace, there.

During this period the Christian Church and its cause is said to have waxed stronger. Several Muslim chiefs, and their followers, were defeated by Gälawdéwos's soldiers. The latter, according to his chronicle, had rebelled against Muslim rule and had become refugees on one of the high Ifat mountains. Nasradin attacked them, but was defeated. Thousands of his warriors perished, after which his power speedily declined.[22]

Control of the area later passed to Ahmäd's nephew Vizier 'Abbas, who ruled for a short time over Däwaro, as well as neighbouring Fätägar and Bali. After the Imam's defeat and death in battle in 1543 he launched a fierce attack on a number of Christian towns, but Gälawdéwos made his way to Wäj to confront him. 'Abbas rushed with his army to meet him. Gälawdéwos awaited him with the eagerness, his chronicle claims, of a young man awaiting his fiancée, and was entirely victorious. 'Abbas, with all his captains, perished by the sword, and the birds of prey, we are told, feasted on their flesh. Those of his followers who escaped became the prey of the local Däwaro populace, who killed all those they could find - just as "the part left by the lion becomes the prey of foxes and other small animals".[23]

FATAGAR

Lebnä Dengel, Awra'i 'Uthman and Robél

Fätägar, another Christian province, which lay immediately north of Däwaro, and had been the site of one of Mähfuz's most famous forays, was another province to feel the early impact of Imam

---

[22] Conzelman (1895), pp. 128-9.
[23] Conzlman (1895), pp. 138-9.

Ahmäd's power. In 1526 or 1527 the Muslim warrior led his army into the territory, and advanced as far as Waduh Mecheg, only a day and a half's journey from where Lebnä Dengel was encamped. The Imam and his men at this point held a council of war to decide what to do. He and some of his *amirs* proposed that they should at once hurl themselves on Lebnä Dengel. This would give them the choice, they declared, of victory, with the reward of immense loot, or martyrdom and consequent entry into Paradise.

Most of the soldiers were, however, opposed to an immediate assault. They urged that they should content themselves instead with the loot they had already taken, and return home. The Imam conceded to this majority view, but shed so many tears of frustration, according to the *Futuh*, that his eyes became red.[24]

After two more such raids, the second into nearby Däwaro, he collected a large and well-equipped army for a much more extensive expedition. Lebnä Dengel, who was at Badeqé, north of the Awash River, decided, as we have seen in the section on Däwaro, to withdraw to Amhara, leaving the converted Bäläw, Awra'i 'Uthman, in charge. The latter collected the Emperor's loyal forces, which included contingents from Fätägar, as well as Däwaro, Bali and Damot. The Imam meanwhile advanced towards Shäwa. He learnt *en route* that Awra'i had stationed himself near the Dukham River some 30 kilometres east of modern Addis Ababa. The Imam and his men responded by making their way to the nearby Maju, or Mojo, River, which was situated in Fätägar. They then halted at a place called Masin, where they burnt one of the Emperor's churches. After this they occupied Badeqé, the site of Lebnä Dengel's palace and treasure, and, as Shihab ed-Din enthusiastically reports, did not pass through an "infidel", i.e. Christian, village "without destroying all trace of it".

Ahmäd's forces then advanced on the royal palace at Badeqé. Told by the local inhabitants that there were no troops to defend it they approached without precaution. They were, however, suddenly confronted by a Christian army which the *Futuh* likens to a swarm of locusts. The Emperor had told his soldiers not to fight until his enemies set fire to the building. His officers, however, disagreed

---

24   Basset (1897), pp. 46-7. See also Huntingford (1989), p. 122.

about these orders. There was therefore some inaction until the army's commander, Robél, governor of Tegray, decided to attack. A fierce battle ensued. The Imam's men were beaten back, and were obliged to retreat across the Dukham River.

The Adäl soldiers later reassembled at Ajamojay, another locality in Fätägar, near the mountain of Zeqwala, where they encountered a force of over 3,000 Maya soldiers armed with bows and poisoned arrows. These warriors came unsuspectingly to the Imam's camp, which they mistakenly assumed to be one of Lebnä Dengel's. On discovering their error they fled in terror, but were pursued by Ahmäd's men, who killed many Mayas, and took the remainder as captives.[25]

Lebnä Dengel later arrived at Badeqé, and congratulated his men on successfully defending the town. He then sought out the Adäl army which he found at the Maju River. Here the battle of Shembera Koré was fought, and the Emperor's army, as we have seen in the previous section, was soundly defeated, incurring heavy losses. The Imam's men, also suffered so many casualties that they withdrew to their own country.[26]

Ahmäd's forces returned to the area, however, later in the year. They made their way to the foot of Zeqwala mountain, and camped by the Dukham River as a preliminary to marching on Badeqé. They supposed that Lebnä Dengel would come forward to resist their entry. While at Dukham they saw a fire in the town, and on enquiring as to its cause, learnt that it had been started by a nobleman who had set his home alight as he did not wish it to fall into their hands.

The Imam later gave orders that the church at Badeqé should also be put to the flames. On that occasion his followers, according to the *Futuh*, seized an immense quantity of gold and precious cloth. They also burnt down the Emperor's palace, which was reportedly decorated with many paintings. No sign of any of its treasures was, however, to be found.[27]

---

[25] Basset (1897), pp. 83-4, 100-1. See also Huntingford (1989), p. 123.
[26] Basset (1897), pp. 113-14. See also Huntingford (1989), p. 123.
[27] Basset (1897), pp. 214-15. See also Huntingford (1989), p. 128.

Not long after this the Imam, who was then at Bärarä, was informed by some collaborators that they knew where the Badeqé treasure had been hidden. He ordered Vizier 'Addolé to proceed there with his army. The chief seized the hoard, and then spent eight days looting Fätägar and nearby Masin, before returning to Bärarä. He and his men brought their leader an immense quantity of loot, including gold and silver plate, and precious silks of many colours.[28]

Interesting light on the thinking in the Imam's army at this juncture is provided by the *Futuh*. It quotes one of the Imam's leaders, Gärad Ahmushuh, as declaring that if his comrades succeeded in killing the Emperor the latter's people would immediately embrace Islam. As for the Imam's own soldiers he declared that once the Awash was full there would be "no way" for them to return to their country. They would therefore have nothing to think of except pillage. If, on the other hand, the rainy season passed without any engagement there would be no way to retain them, for all would want to go home. There was, he insisted, "not an *amir*, great or small, who did not wish to return to his country".[29]

Lebnä Dengel, angered by the destruction in Fätägar, meanwhile decided to seize the military initiative. He ordered his commander Wäsän Sägäd to march against the Imam's forces, and allotted him a considerable army, which included Christians from Fätägar, as well as Däwaro, Ifat and Gojjam. The Emperor ordered this force to cross the Awash to attack the enemy, and had a group of Europeans in his service construct boats for the operation.[30]

Because it was the rainy season the Adäl soldiers were reluctant to fight. The Imam and his men nevertheless held their own, and soon consolidated their control of Fätägar. They recruited men from the province into their army, as well as Somalis and Shäwans converted to Islam. The result was that Fätägar troops later fought in the Imam's service, and were despatched for example to Menz.[31]

---

[28] Basset (1897), pp. 250-1. See also Huntingford, (1989) p. 130.
[29] Basset (1897), p. 253.
[30] Basset (1897), pp. 251-2. See also Huntingford (1989), p. 128.
[31] Basset (1897), pp. 269, 271, 278-80, 287, 294, 298, 325, 337, 339-40, 347, 349-50, 353, 357, 362, 394, 398, 402.

The Collapse of the Occupation

After Portuguese intervention and Ahmäd's death in 1543 Fätägar, like Däwaro and nearby Bali, came under the rule of the Imam's nephew Vizier 'Abbas. He later attacked a number of towns then controlled by Gälawdéwos. The young Emperor responded by marching into Wäj. 'Abbas attacked them, and a fierce engagement followed, in which he, and his soldiers, as we have seen in the section on Däwaro, almost all perished, and the populace reportedly finished off those who had survived.[32] Adäl power in Fätägar, as in Däwaro, then rapidly declined.

THE COUNTRY OF THE MAYAS

The Mayas, because of their location on the eastern borders of Shäwa, and use of poisoned arrows, played an important role in the fighting of the 1520s and early 1530s.

At the beginning of the war the Mayas were Lebnä Dengel's subjects. Many were under the command of the Bäläw warrior Awra'i 'Uthman, who, planning the defence against the Imam's onslaught, collected them at Badeqé, as we have seen, together with men from other southern regions.[33]

In the ensuing fighting the Imam's soldiers found the Mayas a formidable foe. The poison used on their arrows is described in interesting detail by Shihab ed-Din. It was taken, he says, from a tree which grew in the Maya country and that of the Somalis. The poison was produced by burning the branches and roots of this tree, and collecting its essence, which was the colour of tar. This the archers put on the tips of their arrows. It was so powerful that anyone hit by a poisoned arrow died on the spot, and his hair fell out.

The Imam was not to be deterred from a confrontation with so redoubtable an enemy. To minimise the danger from the arrows he ordered his men to pick up all that fell near them, and thus prevent from being used again. So many weapons were collected that his men

---

[32] Conzelman, pp. 138-9.
[33] Basset (1897), p. 82. See also Huntingford, (1989), p. 123.

made a bonfire of them, on which, the *Futuh* claims, they roasted an entire cow.

The Imam's forces near Zeqwala shortly afterwards encountered over three thousand Maya soldiers in the Emperor's service. They were, as usual, armed with bows and arrows. These archers proved of little military use, for they mistakenly assumed, as we have seen in our section on Fätägar, that Ahmäd's camp was a Christian one. On realising their error they were so surprised that they turned round and fled. The Imam's well-armed men at once pursued them, and killed or captured them, to the last man. "God humiliated them so much", the *Futuh* claims, "that one of our cavalry took twenty prisoners, another eighteen, and another ten". The prisoners were brought to Ahmäd, who had them executed. The land around was reportedly entirely covered with their corpses. Their chief offered to pay two hundred ounces of gold for his ransom, but the Imam brushed the offer aside, declaring, "We have no need of your gold. Kill the dog, the son of a dog!". The man was immediately put to death.

Notwithstanding the annihilation of this force other Mayas remained in the Lebnä Dengel's army. They included a sizeable contingent in the service of one of the Emperor's commanders Behtwädäd Eslamo, whom Ahmäd's men defeated near Antokya in February 1531.[34]

After this victory, and the defeat and death of Eslamo at 'Ayfars in March, the Imam decided to advance into the Maya country. Before doing so he summoned his followers, and warned them against looting cattle. The Mayas, he explained, possessed nothing but their livestock, and could be expected to react forcibly if anyone attempted to seize their animals. Confrontation would moreover be dangerous, he added, because the Maya country was rugged, and full of thickets, while the Maya warriors were armed with spears as well as their deadly poisoned arrows. The soldiers hearkened to this advice.[35]

---

[34] Basset (1897), pp. 94, 108-9, 113, 180. See also Huntingford (1989), pp. 124, 126.
[35] Basset (1897), pp. 212-14. See also Huntingford (1989), p. 127.

Despite the Imam's attempt to avoid conflict with the Mayas many of the latter continued to serve in Lebnä Dengel's army. Ahmäd's forces, on reaching the Awash River, were thus confronted by a large defensive army which included numerous Maya warriors armed with arrows. The Imam's men nevertheless decided to swim across the river, and, despite a hail of arrows, succeeded in reaching the other bank. The horse of one of them, Sam'un, was reportedly hit by no less than thirty-five arrows, but miraculously survived. Some of the Mayas later succeeded in penetrating Ahmäd's camp, but were beaten off and routed, with heavy losses.[36]

The Imam's commander, 'Addolé, then despatched one of his followers, Zaharbuy 'Uthman, into Mayaland with a hundred horsemen. They ravaged the district of 'Aram (or 'Azam), and seized many horses and other booty. 'Addolé's men were, however, soon confronted by Yonädab, Lebnä Dengel's governor of Wäj, and a party of Maya archers whom the Emperor had despatched to the area. A fierce battle ensued, in which Zahabuy's horse was felled. Despite this setback his men were victorious, and captured a sizeable amount of booty. While they were carrying it back to their camp, a Maya hiding in a tree shot an arrow at Zahahbuy, who almost immediately fell dead.[37]

Notwithstanding this act of defiance numerous Mayas had by this time gone over to the winning side. The Adäl occupation of a large part of their country enabled Ahmäd to enrol into his army a significant number of Mayas. Many of those who surrendered, and remained in their own country, suffered, however, from counter-attacks by forces loyal to Lebnä Dengel. A Maya delegation accordingly made its way to the Imam to declare that after he had "ruined" their country, Christians from nearby Wäj and Gänz were raiding it night and day. The Mayas appealed to him to send them an Amir and a force of soldiers to protect them. Ahmäd appointed one of his followers, Gärad 'Uthman, as their governor, and despatched him with a hundred soldiers to Jan Zäläq, with orders to guard the area.[38]

---

[36] Basset (1897), pp. 340-3.
[37] Basset (1897), pp. 345-6. See also Huntingford (1989), p. 130.
[38] Basset (1897), pp. 353, 357.

A sizeable portion of Mayas on the other hand remained steadfast in their allegiance to the Emperor. Ahmäd therefore sent his commander Färäshäham Din on a further expedition to Maya territory. It found five thousand Mayas entrenched in the mountains and wooded valleys. The Imam's men camped near the 'Aram River in the centre of the Maya country, after which his officer Besaräh, making his way towards the forest, met a Maya detachment armed with poisoned arrows. An engagement immediately took place. Färäshäham Din sent orders to Besaräh warning him to avoid the woodlands which, he declared, were unsuitable for cavalry. The young man, however, took no notice. He was hit by a Maya arrow, and died almost at once. His fleeing companions were pursued by the Mayas shooting arrows at them.

Another force of the Imam's men, led by Gärad Sam'un, intervened to avenge Besaräh's death. They attacked with such ferocity that they soon routed the Maya warriors, and pursued them to the forest and rocky part of their territory. At the end of the fighting it was found that Sam'un had been hit by no less than fifty arrows, but had been saved by his armour.

On the following day the Imam's men prepared for yet another engagement, only to find that the Mayas had all fled. Shihab ed-Din comments that the archers, seeing the multitude of their dead, had each taken his wife and children, and disappeared to Fätägar in the night. The invading commander then sent his cavalry into Mayaland, where they spent many days looting and taking prisoners.

This pillage marked the end of the struggle. The Mayas then at last submitted, and embraced Islam. Their proud leader Zärji declared that he would do so only in the Imam's presence. On Ahmäd's arrival shortly afterwards he was therefore officially converted. The Imam thereupon appointed Färäshäham Din, the conqueror of the Mayas, as their governor.[39]

THE COUNTRY OF THE DOBE'AS

One of the Imam's early expeditions, led by Vizier 'Addolé in 1530, was to what the *Futuh* describes as the "country of the

---

[39] Basset (1897), pp. 361-3, 367, 390.

Duba'ahs", probably the southern-most section of the Dobe'as mentioned in Chapter 11. They were described as Christians, perhaps, if this identification is correct, having become so as a result of the conversion earlier carried out, as we have seen, by Emperor Bä'edä Maryam. The Adäl soldiers seized many cattle, for which the Dobe'as had long been renowned, and took them to the Imam. The Duba'ahs seem to have been actively engaged in the empire's defence, for one thousand of them armed with poisoned arrows had reportedly been detailed to guard a church in Däwaro.[40]

IFAT
Early Battles

Ifat, which lay to the north of Fätägar, and had by then been an integral part of the Christian empire for over a century, was another of the provinces affected at an early stage by the Imam's invasion. In 1527, a dispute broke out among Ahmäd's followers about the presence in their midst of his wife Bati Del Wänbära. Many felt she should return home to Harär, but she refused to travel alone, with the result that she accompanied her husband as far as Ifat.[41]

To capture the territory the Imam divided his army into three units. One, under Vizier 'Addolé, was detailed to advance to the right of the territory, the second, under Vizier Nur ibn Ibrahim, was to proceed to the left, while Ahmäd himself was to lead the central force, into the heart of Ifat.[42]

The Imam's force duly reached the town of Antokya, which had been one of the Emperor's capitals in the province. Ahmäd destroyed its church, and was joined at about the same time by the other two units. His soldiers then carried out a major raiding expedition throughout much of the province, in the course of which they captured "considerable booty of slaves and objects". They then made their way to Bazmeli, another Ifat town, which was described by the *Futuh* as a "strong place" belonging to the "infidels", i.e. Christians.

---

[40] Basset (1897), pp. 174-5, 194; Huntingford (1989), p. 125.
[41] Basset (1897), pp.51-2; Huntingford (1989), p. 122.
[42] Basset (1897), pp. 56; Huntingford (1989), p. 122.

On the following day Ahmäd's men entered the old market town of Gende Belo, which was inhabited by Muslims who paid Lebnä Dengel a head tax. The citizens and inhabitants of the neighbouring countryside came to the Imam and his men, treated them with great honour, and presented them with twenty ounces of gold. The soldiers, knowing that their leader was then still poor, took part of this gold, and told him that they wanted to give it to his wife Bati Del Wänbära. Ahmäd, however, refused to accept it as a personal gift, for he declared that such wealth should be used only for the Holy War. He accordingly spent the gold in the purchase of a hundred swords, which his men later used most effectively at the battle of Shembera Koré.

While at Gende Belo the Imam found a number of Christian merchants who were in possession of rich articles belonging to the Emperor. He ordered that they be killed, after which he confiscated their property and beasts of burden. He and his men then returned to their own country.[43]

The Invasion

Three years later the Imam began his invasion of the highlands by marching, as we have seen, into Däwaro. The Christian soldiers of Ifat thereupon assembled at Antokya. They did so because they were informed that the invading army was advancing into the area to burn down an important church there. The defending army was joined shortly afterwards by Behtwädäd Eslamo, who arrived with a large force of Maya archers. While they were there Ahmäd's men attempted to occupy the town, but were ambushed and routed. They speedily regrouped, and defeated the Ifat army, in February or March 1531, after which they duly burnt the town.[44]

The Imam subsequently gave orders to his commander Shamsu to march against Ifat, and make himself master of the province. The terrain was so rugged, the *Futuh* states, that it "did not offer any paths for camels". Shamsu, fighting on foot, nevertheless succeeded in

---

[43] Basset (1897), p. 65; Huntingford (1989), p. 122.
[44] Basset (1897), pp. 172-95. See also p. 230; Huntingford (1989), pp. 125-6.

conquering the inhabitants, who fled into the mountains where he besieged them until they agreed to embrace Islam.

At about this time Shamsu came upon a church built by Emperor Eskender, who had presented it with many gold and silver objects. One of them, it is claimed, was a copy of the Gospels written on gold pages and bound in gold. The chief entered the building, seized all its riches, and set fire to it. The loot taken included a fine *burnus*, formerly belonging to Eskender, with a hood containing fifty ounces of gold. Shamsu gave his master all the captured loot. Ahmäd and his followers marvelled at it, and especially at the golden book and beautiful illustrations.

The Muslim conquest of Ifat was, however, still far from complete. The Imam therefore despatched his son Ahmushuh to the province, telling him to continue the struggle until he had forced its inhabitants to submit. Ahmushuh and Ahmäd's Somali brother-in-law Gärad Mattan ibn 'Uthman accordingly made their way to Ifat to bring it under their control.[45]

Awra'i 'Uthman

The occupation of Ifat was much facilitated, as the *Futuh* explains in interesting detail, by the Emperor's southern commander, the Muslim Bäläw convert Awra'i 'Uthman, who was also the province's governor. He had been left, as we have seen, in charge of recruiting soldiers from the southern provinces while the Emperor was in Amhara mobilising those from the north to defend Däwaro.

While the Imam was at Abunah on the borders of Ifat, Awra'i assured his soldiers that he would fight to prevent the invading army from entering the province. He had, however, decided on doing the exact opposite. Doubtless much impressed by the strength of the army with which he was supposed to contend, and doubtless recalling his earlier faith from which he had been weaned, we know not by what means, he sent a secret letter to the Imam, through the local Muslims. In it he wrote, "I was once a Muslim, and the son of a Muslim; the infidels seized me, and made me embrace Christianity, but my heart has always remained with the true faith". That said he declared that if

---

[45] Basset (1897), p. 272.

Ahmäd would accept his repentance, and refrain from punishing him for his past deeds, he would "return to God". He also promised, more practically, to devise a stratagem to bring the Christian troops over to the Imam's side, and make them adopt Islam.

On receipt of this message Ahmäd secretly wrote back to the would-be defector, pardoning him for his past apostasy, and declaring that Awra'i had nothing to fear. He added that they should meet at the Ifat town of Tobeya, which, it will be recalled, was where Emperors Dawit and Bä'eda Maryam had earlier resided. As a sign of good faith the Imam sent him his prayer beads.

Awra'i, though assured of the Imam's support, felt extremely anxious. "I am alone", he said to himself, "and after what I have done to the Muslims I have everything to fear [from them]. If I tell the polytheists [i.e. Christians] to embrace Islam with me they will kill me or make me prisoner". He had with him, however, two of the Imam's former pages. Both had interesting histories, which may well have been not untypical of the times. The first, Shoker, had been imprisoned for killing one of Ahmäd's companions, but had escaped. Fleeing to Lebnä Dengel he had become a Christian, after which the monarch had appointed him a governor of a town in Ifat. The other defector, Ya'qim, had incurred a debt in the Muslim country, and, unable to repay it, had likewise gone over to the Emperor, and been made a district chief.

The commander approached these two men, and told them that the Imam was poised to ravage the country. He asked their advice: should they flee, or fight and die for the Emperor? Both men dutifully replied that they were the commander's loyal followers: they would obediently do as they were told. They were willing to flee, die, or embrace Islam - whatever he wished. Awra'i, gaining confidence, then declared that since they had spoken of adopting Islam he felt that this was in fact the best solution. He then told them of his exchange of letters with the Imam, but asked them how they could handle his large army, which was composed exclusively of Christians.

The two men replied that Awra'i's personal commander, a certain 'Ananya, was so loyal to his master that if the latter walked into a fire he would unflinchingly follow. Awra'i, reassured by these words, called 'Ananya, explained the difficulty faced by the army, and asked for his advice. The man replied that he would willingly do whatever his master commanded. Awra'i commanded him to swear this on oath, which done he revealed his decision once more to become a Muslim. 'Ananya then admitted that he had long had the same intention. He added that he too had actually corresponded with the Imam, and had only refrained from embracing Islam on account of his loyalty to his master.

Awra'i, on hearing this reply, was very happy, but once more asked how they should deal with the soldiers. 'Ananya replied that he would make himself responsible for this: he would talk with the commander's more intimate followers, and the other soldiers. Awra'i, he added, might have to fight the more recalcitrant of them, but he was confident that they would be unable to resist.

'Ananya accordingly approached Awra'i's personal followers, who amounted to 50 horsemen and 2,000 infantry. They declared, "If our master enters the fire, we will enter it with him. Our duty is to follow his orders".

Awra'i, well pleased with this development, then decided to leave the mountain where they were encamped, for the neighbouring plain, which could more easily be defended. Together with his supporters he accordingly moved down, and was joined by eight Ifat noblemen and the entire Gafat army. A thousand of his elite troops, however, refused to follow him. When he sent a message to them asking the reason they replied that they remained loyal to the Emperor, knew of Awra'i's treachery, and would, if necessary, fight him for the faith. They then withdrew to Amhara.

Awra'i, accompanied by the Imam's two former pages and by several shaikhs, who came to intercede on his behalf, then made his way to Tobeya to pay homage to the Imam as instructed. On meeting Ahmäd he kissed his hand. The Muslim leader received him kindly, told him to have no fear, and ordered his soldiers to embrace Islam. Some 20,000, with their women and children, reportedly did so.

Ifat was thus at last brought under Muslim rule, after which the Imam spent ten days in the province before continuing his military operations elsewhere.[46]

---

[46] Basset (1897), pp. 213, 272-80. see also p. 288; ; Huntingford (1989), pp. 128-9.

Awra'i Abun

Ahmäd subsequently entrusted the government of Ifat to another of his followers, Awra'i Abun. The latter, however, was in no position to hold the province against a possible counter-attack by the Emperor's soldiers. He accordingly wrote to his leader, declaring that the area had only just been converted, and that he was in urgent need of reinforcements. Ahmäd responded by despatching his nephew 'Abbas there with fifty cavalrymen, who established themselves at the old capital, Tobeya.

Lebnä Dengel meanwhile ordered one of his most renowned commanders, Ras Näbiyat, to march into Ifat and capture Awra'i. The monarch was, however, sadly unaware that the latter had been reinforced. On arriving in the province he therefore encountered a much stronger force than anticipated. His men were easily defeated. Obliged to flee, they suffered heavy casualties.[47]

Despite Awra'i's victory the occupation of Ifat was still not fully secure. The Imam later admitted as much when he declared that if his forces left the territory without a garrison its population would soon abandon the Muslim faith.

Before leaving for Däwaro, he therefore took steps, as we have seen when considering events in that province, to consolidate his position. He summoned Awra'i, and his own nephew 'Abbas, and ordered them to join his commander Färäshäham Din. All three, he declared, should remain in Ifat, and he promised to supply them with a reinforcement of 400 cavalrymen. Awra'i, however, was not mollified. He replied that he could not stay in the province if the Imam left for Däwaro, for with the onset of the rains he would be cut off from his master. If the Emperor at that point launched another attack he would be unable to resist.

The Imam, however, rejected these arguments. He declared that he had given his orders, and that Awra'i should obey them. He added angrily that the latter had enjoyed the benefit of the taxes of Ifat, and could not therefore abandon the province. At the same time he

---

[47] Basset (1897), pp. 339-40, 356-9.

ordered Amir Abu Bäkr and 'Abbas to go to Ifat with a force of 300 cavalry.

Awra'i Abun had no option but to return to Ifat. On reaching Tobeya he told its inhabitants and those of the province who had become Muslims that the Imam planned to march to Däwaro, and requested them to join in the expedition. The Ifat people were, however, reluctant. They at first refused to leave the province, but after much discussion some consented to go with Awra'i to join the Imam in Däwaro. The chief was therefore accompanied by fifty Ifat cavalrymen and 2,000 infantry, together with their women and children.[48]

The End of the Occupation

The occupation of Ifat, like that of the neighbouring provinces, proved, however, unexpectedly short-lived. After the Imam's death in 1543 a rebellion against his government soon erupted on one of the province's mountains. The insurgents, who were joined by a group of Gälawdéwos's soldiers, took the field against the Muslim leadership. Ahmäd's son Nasradin, the ruler of Däwaro, attacked them, but they defeated him, as we have seen, and killed many of his soldiers, after which Adäl rule rapidly collapsed.[49]

BALI
Early Fighting

Bali, a largely Christian province, situated in the far south of the empire, had, as we have seen in Chapter 13, been invaded by Adäl forces on several occasions. Soldiers from the territory were later mobilised as part of the great southern army which Lebnä Dengel placed under Awra'i 'Uthman's command.[50]

The province, which was then, as we have seen, under the governorship of the Emperor's brother-in-law Azmach Degälhan was affected by the Imam's campaigns at an early stage. Prior to his main drive into the highlands one of his first expeditions took his men

---

[48] Basset (1897), p. 361.
[49] Conzelman (1895), pp. 128-9.
[50] Basset (1897), p. 82.

southwards as far as the territory. The Harāri sultan 'Umär-Din and several of Ahmäd's commanders criticised this expedition. They argued that the army was tired, and short of provisions. Ahmäd, however, insisted on advancing to the province. His journey, as it turned out, was not too arduous, for he was provided by the population *en route* with plenty of supplies. On reaching Bali his soldiers nevertheless suffered from an acute shortage of provisions, so that each man was allowed only one handful of grain a day. Many of the Christians they encountered, however, told them of their willingness to transfer their allegiance to Islam.

Pillage, Resistance and Collaboration

While in Bali the Imam and his men "pillaged to the right and the left", as the *Futuh* says, and took considerable booty. Ahmäd sent his cousin Zaherbuy Muhammäd to Malawa in the centre of the province, where he seized many valuables, burnt the country, and "reduced it to cinders". He also captured many slaves, horses and beasts of burden.[51]

Sanhur, Lebnä Dengel's governor of Bali, on learning how the province was being ravaged, collected his cavalry and foot-soldiers, and assembled all the Christians of the territory to fight the intruders. Muslim sherifs, or descendants of the Prophet, and a number of local Arabs on the other hand welcomed the Imam, who received them cordially, and presented them, in the traditional manner, with clothes of honour.

Further fighting ensued, in which the well armed soldiers of Adäl were as so often victorious. After their triumph Ahmäd left the province, taking with him a concubine called Hajirah whom he had seized there. Formerly the wife of Täklä Haymanot, a minor Muslim functionary turned Christian, she accompanied her new husband on his conquest of the highlands.

Despite the Imam's victory most of the Bali people continued to support the Christian cause. During the fighting in Däwaro the nobleman 'Addalu, also known as 'Adälih, and many other men of Bali were involved, as we have seen, in resistance in the province.

---

[51] Basset (1897), pp. 153-61; Huntingford (1989), p. 125.

They later also participated in the defence of Antokya in Ifat, and ambushed a Muslim force intending to destroy its church. Not long after this the Bali soldiers launched a fierce assault on Ahmäd's forces whom they attacked from two sides, inflicting heavy casualties.

The Bali army likewise took a prominent part in the battle of Antokya. On that occasion the Imam made use of a cannon and a number of Arabs, including two skilled archers from Rif in Egypt. One of the Arabs' canon-balls struck down an olive tree in the middle of the Christian soldiers who were in consequence greatly terrified. When the Muslims charged against them the Bali force was therefore easily put to flight. The *Futuh* was, however, very critical of the people of Bali, who, it claims, were well known for their "cunning and double-dealing".[52]

Notwithstanding this victory 'Addalu, who had been appointed the province's governor, did not abandon the struggle. Learning of Ahmäd's advance to the Awash, and of the Christian retreat, he sent his spies to investigate. They advanced as far as 'Ayfars but, on being discovered, fled. They were pursued by the Imam's men, but succeeded in reaching their master the Emperor.[53]

Bali by the end of 1531 was thus still unconquered, and its inhabitants remained largely unconverted. One of the province's Christian rulers, a man by the name of Abreham, was in particular still active in the field.[54]

Not long after this, however, two notable Bali leaders sent messages to the Imam telling him that they had decided to collaborate in his occupation. One of them was Simu, the son of Wänag Jan, who, as we have seen in Chapter 13, had rebelled against imperial rule a generation earlier during the reign of Na'od. The other was a certain Säbbäru. They declared that they were the Imam's secret supporters, and promised that if Ahmäd sent an army to the province they would be the first to fight on his behalf. Simu, recalling his father's rebellion, which had resulted, it will be recalled, in the killing of many of the

---

[52] Basset (1897), pp. 172, 181, 184-6.
[53] Basset (1897), pp. 342-4.
[54] Basset (1897), pp.325, 349. See also pp. 379-80.

province's Christian lords, proudly added, "I will treat the Bali people as my father treated them, and even worse".

The Imam, rejoicing in this development, summoned Säbbäru, but told Simu to wait until the arrival of the Muslim army. Säbbäru duly arrived, and embraced Islam. Ahmäd meanwhile had sent instructions to Hosayn, his governor of Däwaro, and to another of his chiefs, Vizier 'Addolé, ordering them, if they had finally conquered the latter province, to join him. Hosayn, it transpired, still had military commitments, but 'Addolé came, whereupon the Imam despatched him to Bali, and appointed him its governor.

Ahmäd, learning that 'Addalu, the Christian ruler of the province, had a considerable army, sent 'Addolé reinforcements. They were led, as we shall see in later pages, by 'Abd en-Nasir, his ruler of Gänz, the latter's brother-in-law the governor of Hadeya, and Gärad Siddiq, his chief of Shärkha. Assisted by the newly converted Säbbäru, whose familiarity with the country was of great assistance, the Imam's army was then joined also by Simu. He at once underwent the ceremony of conversion, and informed Vizier 'Addolé of 'Addalu's whereabouts.

Simu, with the vizier's approval, later sent a messenger to 'Addalu, demanding the latter's cooperation. He told him that it was hopeless to suppose it possible to fight against the Muslims, for he must have heard of their victories, and how they had made themselves masters of many provinces, which had obtained security in return for obedience. Many of the people of Abyssinia, he added, had become Muslims, while their Emperor and his army had been put to flight. He concluded by telling the chief that, if he wished to convert, he should not delay, but, if he wished to retain his religion, he could do so by paying the poll tax, and by providing the Imam's men with provisions and horses. If, on the other hand, he refused either of these propositions he should prepare to fight!

After hearing these demands 'Addalu asked the messenger the size of the Imam's army. The man informed him that its core consisted of 500 Muslim horsemen, but that they had been joined by an "immense" number of new converts, mainly from Yäjju, Däwaro and Wäj, i.e. the east and the south of the empire. The governor, unimpressed by these figures, proudly declared that they were small in his eyes, and that he would neither convert nor pay the tax, but would die fighting.

Faced with this defiance Ahmäd's men prepared to attack. 'Addalu also assembled his troops for battle. He ordered them to take their women and children with them. The men were at first reluctant. They said that they would prefer to place their dependants on nearby mountains where they could watch the fight from afar. Their master was, however, adamant. He declared that if the women and children were placed anywhere else, and the men were obliged to flee, their dependants would in any case be left unprotected. He then urged his men to fight bravely "for your country, your wives and your children". His men accordingly took their families with them, and prepared for an imminent clash of arms. The Muslims likewise rallied for what they regarded as a Holy War. They expressed "disdain for life in this world", and affirmed their hopes through battle to "find their Lord".

One of the bloodiest battles of the whole war was then waged, in July or August 1532. The two armies fought fiercely, and bravely, until 'Addalu fell and was promptly beheaded by the Adäl soldiers. His men thereupon fled, pursued by the Imam's forces, who killed many Christians, and, as so often, took many others captive. The wives of Ahmäd's soldiers rode behind their menfolk, and helped to capture prisoners. One woman said, "I took four Christian women!"; others said, "Five, six or seven". That day thousands of Bali's Christian soldiers, including innumerable nobles and 3,000 cavalrymen, were killed, and some 200 nobles were seized. The land, the *Futuh* claims, was covered with corpses, and blood ran like streams. The victors captured a vast number of women and children, besides many horses, mules, tents, gold, silk, brocade and other riches.

Ahmäd, on learning of the death of 'Addalu, prayed, making two genuflections to thank Allah. He wrote to his victorious commander, telling him to take a fifth of the captured nobles, their wives and children for himself; the remainder were to be divided among those who had fought for the faith. As for 'Addalu's widow he declared that Addolé should take her as his concubine. Captured nobles who had embraced Islam should live with the vizier, but those who refused conversion should be killed. "All the inhabitants of Bali, great and small", the *Futuh* reports, thereupon embraced Islam, after which the Imam appointed a certain 'Umar as the province's governor.[55]

Vizier 'Abbas

After the death of the Imam in 1543, the latter's nephew Vizier 'Abbas established himself as ruler of Bali, as well as of neighbouring Fätägar and Däwaro. His rule was, however, short-lived, for Gälawdéwos defeated him, as we have seen, towards the end of the following year. This victory marked the end of Adäl paramountcy in the entire southern region.[56]

SHARKHA

Shärkha, a largely Christian province, was still part of the empire at the opening of the Imam's campaigns when it was governed, on behalf of Lebnä Dengel, by a nobleman called Limu.[57]

Vizier 'Addolé

The territory, because of its location west of Däwaro, became involved in the war a little later than that province. However, in the Spring of 1531, the Imam summoned Vizier 'Addolé, and ordered him to march to Janbah, an area below Shärkha. The chief and his men were instructed, according to the *Futuh*, to kill any of the enemy they encountered, to seize their riches, and to reduce their women to slavery. Ahmäd added that 'Addolé should march ahead of him, for, if he remained in the rear, he would be unable to share in either the battle or the loot.

'Addolé duly set forth and arrived at Janbah, after which his horsemen, many of them musketeers, rode to the right and to the left, ravaging the country, killing unbelievers, and taking booty. The chief himself camped below the town, whither most of his cavalry returned with booty and slaves, while other soldiers looted the countryside.

'Addolé and his followers then advanced into Shärkha. There they discovered one of Lebnä Dengel's principal courtiers, Behtwädäd

---

[55] Basset (1897), pp. 379-90, 396.
[56] Basset (1897), p. 318; Conzelman (1895) pp. 127, 138-9, 26-33; Béguinot (1901), p. 30. See also Budge (1928b), II, 340-1, 347.
[57] Basset (1897), p. 92.

Bädlay, who had fifty horsemen and five hundred foot-soldiers, all equipped for war. Some had stationed themselves on a hill inaccessible to cavalry. 'Addolé's men differed as to how to proceed. Some declared that they should withdraw to obtain reinforcements, but others replied that they had no other aim than the Holy War, and no choice but death or victory.

This latter view soon triumphed. Shouting with a single voice that God was Great, the Imam's men scaled the hill, charged, and began a fierce hand-to-hand battle. Bädlay, realising that defeat was inevitable, fled, whereupon his men followed his example. Many were killed, though others escaped. The victors, who reportedly suffered not a single casualty, then returned to Janbah where they presented the Imam with many prisoners. Several offered to pay him ransom. One man proposed two hundred ounces of gold, and another one hundred, but the victorious chief sternly replied, "We have no need of your gold", and had them all killed. He and his soldiers then remained six days at Janbah.

The Imam's chronicler, describing the loot from Shärkha, notes that it included the wives and children of the Christian nobles, considerable booty in cloth and a large quantity of gold. One of the women was the wife of a nobleman Azmach Arkyah, who, on learning that she and their children had been seized, promptly embraced Islam. Many other chiefs followed his example.[58]

After his victory the Imam appointed Gärad Siddiq as governor of Shärkha. The province's inhabitants then submitted to his authority. He and Limu, Lebnä Dengel's former governor, later participated, on opposite sides, in the struggle further south for Bali. Siddiq was rewarded with a share of the women captured in the expedition, while Limu fell in battle.[59]

DARHA

The small Muslim province of Därha, mentioned two centuries earlier by al-'Umari, still existed at this time. Now extending from Bägémder to Gojjam, it is mentioned in the *Futuh*, which states that the Imam appointed Färäshäham 'Ali as its governor in 1535.[60]

---

[58] Basset (1897), pp. 141,191-4, 198; Huntingford (1989), pp.126-7.
[59] Basset (1897), pp. 92, 141, 240, 325, 344, 373, 377, 380-1, 385, 389-90, 395.
[60] Basset (1897), p. 460. See also Huntingford (1989), p.133.

After the Imam's death the province was probably merged in a neighbouring territory, for it disappears from view. Vestiges of a Muslim presence in the area may, however, possibly be seen in the notable Islamic emporium of Emfraz.[61]

---

[61] Pankhurst (1982), pp. 94-101.

Chapter 17

THE SOUTH-WEST AND WEST: WAJ, GURAGE, HADEYA, GAMO, GANZ, WALAMO (or WOLAITA), KAMBATA, ENARYA, DAMOT, GAFAT, KAFA, MAZAGA and THE COUNTRY OF THE HAMAJS and BAREYAS

After invading the south-eastern and southern provinces the Imam, whose soldiers included many matchlockmen, proceeded to the countries of the west, notably Wäj, Guragé, Hadeya, Gänz, Wälamo, Kämbata, Enarya, Damot and Gafat. Several of these, it will be recalled, were rich territories which had for centuries provided the Christian empire and its rulers with gold and slaves, as well as provisions of all kinds. These westerly territories were also an important source of military man-power, and from them many soldiers were recruited into Lebnä Dengel's armies.

WAJ

Because of its relatively easterly location, Wäj, a primarily Christian territory, was one of the first of the above provinces to became embroiled in the Imam's invasion of the highlands. Lebnä Dengel was at his palace at Gebergé in Wäj when he learnt that soldiers from Adäl had overrun neighbouring Däwaro. He at first imagined that they had come, as they had done since the time of Mähfuz, merely on a raiding expedition. On realising his error, however, he withdrew to Damot while his commander Wäsän Sägäd took his place in Wäj.[1]

Ahmäd's forces subsequently marched to nearby Wis. Shihab ed-Din describes it as "a large town", and the site of a "considerable market without equal in Abyssinia". It was one in which transactions were - unusually - carried out only in gold.[2]

The Imam's men pursued, and defeated, the monarch, who, however, subsequently re-established himself in Wäj, where he spent an entire rainy season. He sent his governor Eslam Dähar to Wis, but was soon obliged to withdraw from the province.[3]

---

[1] Basset (1897), pp. 212, 234. See also Huntingford (1989), p. 128.
[2] Basset (1897), p. 235. On Wis see also Crawford (1958), p. 183.
[3] Basset (1897), pp. 242-3, 281, 351. See also Huntingford (1989), p. 128.

The people of Wäj meanwhile refused to embrace Islam. Two of the province's leading nobles, Azmach Fan'il and Yonädab, played an active role in opposition to the Imam.[4] The men of Wäj and nearby Gänz also launched a number of raids by day and by night against some of the neighbouring Mayas, who, as we have seen, had by then converted to Islam.[5]

Later in the campaign Ahmäd despatched Vizier Mojahid to Wäj, with orders to fight its inhabitants until they surrendered. The chief proceeded to the province, but its population offered no resistance, and at once gave him their allegiance. He then established the poll tax in the region. Eslam Dähar, however, refused to embrace Islam, and made his way to the nearby high Guragé country, while the Imam followed Mojahid to Wäj, and established himself at a place called Jug.

The Christian nobles then separated. Yonädab withdrew to Damot, while Eslam Dähar, fearing the destruction of his country and the burning of its churches, sent his son and Asébo, another noble, to Ahmäd in an effort to make peace. When the Muslim leader asked them why they had come, Asébo replied that they had done so to save their country and its churches, and were willing to pay the poll tax in order to retain their religion. Ahmäd enquired why Eslam Dähar had not come with them. Asébo answered that the chief could not do so as he would be dishonoured in the Emperor's eyes, but that his son was willing to become a Muslim. As for the father he would pay the required tax.

The Imam consulted his companions. They declared that there was no need for the father to be converted, and that he should be allowed to pay the poll tax, and retain his religion. His son, on the other hand, should embrace Islam and join them. Ahmäd accepted this advice, and told his Christian visitors to repeat the words, "We testify that God is God and that Muhammäd is his Apostle." Asébo repeated the time-honoured formula, and became a Muslim, but Eslam Dähar's son at first refused, saying he would not do this unless the Imam accepted him as a son. The conqueror laughingly agreed, saying, "Embrace Islam, and I will do everything you wish". The young man uttered the required words, and became a Muslim. Many inhabitants of the

---

[4] Basset, (1897), pp. 325, 340, 345.
[5] Basset (1897), p. 357.

province followed his example. Ahmäd, much satisfied, then spent the fasting month of Ramadan, i.e. April-May 1532, in the area.[6]

Some while later, when the Imam was firmly established in Däwaro, he sent Vizier Mojahid back to Wäj. Half the inhabitants, we are told, welcomed him, but the other half supported Eslam Dähar, who had decided to continue the struggle. His adherents, led by thirty nobles, took refuge in the high mountains. Mojahid set forth to attack them. Eslam Dähar, seeing the latter's advance, ordered his men to abandon their horses, and fight on foot, for the country, he declared, was not suitable for the use of cavalry. He then took up his sword and shield, and the other chiefs and their men followed his example. The two armies fought hand to hand, for the Imam's cavalry could not climb the mountain.

One of Ahmäd's horsemen, however, secretly found a way up. He was followed by four others who were not noticed by the defenders until loud cries resounded from the top of the hill. When the Christians heard this they fled, pursued by the Imam's men, who killed many lords and soldiers. Eslam Dähar was captured, and put to death, together with virtually all his companions. Only one of the thirty Christian nobles and a few of their followers escaped to tell the tale. The *Futuh* claims that not a single Muslim died.

This battle resulted in the Imam's occupation of Wäj, after which all its inhabitants finally made their submission.[7]

GURAGE

Despite its considerable Muslim population, and the difficulties with Guragé marauders earlier reported by Alvares, many Christian soldiers from the province served in Lebnä Dengel's army during its struggle against the Imam. Their presence was referred to in a message of defiance by one of the Emperor's courtiers addressed to the Imam's men after the Muslim victory at Antokya in 1531. He claimed that the imperial army had been restored to its former strength, through the arrival of contingents from Guragé, as well as other south-westerly provinces, notably Damot, Gafat, Enarya and Jemma.[8] A Muslim chief, Bälaw 'Abdu, ridiculed the very existence of such troops. He declared that these peoples were "slaves", and that

---

[6] Basset (1897), pp. 363-4, 366.
[7] Basset (1897), pp. 390-2.
[8] Basset (1897), p. 222.

he knew how little they were capable of. Reflecting a contemporary attitude to the Guragés, who apparently served as migrant labourers in or around Harär, he exclaimed: "Their sole occupation in our country is to till the fields, to cut trees and to carry wood; they do not know what a battle is, and have never seen one. We are not afraid of slaves because we know them for what they are".[9]

Though despised by the Imam's men not a few Guragés, who included many Muslims, were hostile to Lebnä Dengel's rule. They were therefore sympathetic to Ahmäd, who was able to take over their country with little difficulty or opposition.[10]

The islands of Lake Zway, on the other hand, seem to have remained under Christian control, and were a place where Lebnä Dengel is said to have sent many valuable manuscripts for safe-keeping. [11]

The Adäl occupation of Guragé, as of other provinces, was short-lived, and scarcely survived the Imam's death in 1543.

HADEYA

The Imam's campaigns were destined to have a major impact on Hadeya, an essentially Muslim province, whose rulers, as we have seen, had earlier been dynastically allied to the Christian state.

The province, situated far to the west, did not attract Ahmäd's attention until the end of 1531. During discussions with his followers at that time he pointed out that Hadeya was controlled by enemy, presumably Christian, nobles, who had not yet submitted to his army. He therefore postponed any idea of an immediate occupation of the area.[12]

Not long after this, however, one of the Muslim commanders, 'Abd en-Nasir, occupied Jitu on the province's borders, while the Imam camped above Lake Zway, with a view to seizing its islands, the site of richly endowed churches.[13] Ahmäd learnt that many of the inhabitants of the mainland had embraced Islam, and that they would be sufficient to fight against the islanders. He therefore decided to set forth himself for Hadeya.

---

9   Basset (1897), pp. 222-8.
10 Basset (1897), pp .243, 363, 366.
11 Krapf (1867), p. 45.
12 Basset (1897), pp. 325, 359.
13 Basset (1897), p. 366.

Before arriving in the province he was met by its tributary ruler, whose name is not recorded. He was a Muslim, whose province, the *Futuh* claims, had traditionally been obliged to provide each year a young woman for baptism. The imposition of this bizarre tribute, it should be noted, is not confirmed by any other source, and Shihab ed-Din's report should therefore perhaps be treated with caution. Be that as it may, the Hadeya leader, addressing the Imam reportedly declared, "I am a Muslim, like you; I will obey your orders". Ahmäd afforded him a friendly welcome, and the chief's followers responded by providing the Imam's army with hospitality. Ahmäd then presented the chief with fine clothing, and ceremonially dressed the latter's nobles.

Ahmäd, we are told, then interrogated the Hadeya people on the annual gift of one of their daughters, allegedly chosen for her beauty, grace and nobility. They replied that the Emperor had imposed this tax on their parents, and commented:

"He was stronger than us; he forbade us carry defensive arms, hold swords, ride on saddled horses, allowing us only to ride bare-back; he imposed on us the obligation of giving him each year a young girl, which we do for fear that he will kill us and destroy our mosques. When he sends the envoy who has to receive the girl and the money [i.e. the tribute for the Emperor] we make her leave on a stretcher, we wash her, we cover her in a piece of cloth, and we say a prayer over her and consider her as dead; then we hand her over to the envoy. Our parents and forebears did this, but at last God has led Muslims to us; you have caused our master to flee, you have exterminated his troops; we will make war side by side with you in the path of God; after this they will not torment us any more, treated as they have been by you who have weakened their power".

The Imam, according to the *Futuh*, told the Hadeya people to have no more fear, and called on them to join their efforts to his. After staying five days in their territory he left, taking with him the chief, and the latter's brother, possibly as hostages.[14]

To cement the newly established relationship the Hadeya ruler, following his predecessors' tradition of establishing dynastic ties with the area's dominant family, gave his daughter Mureyas to the Imam as

---

[14] Basset (1897), pp. 371-2. See also p. 190.

a wife. The marriage was of short duration, for the bride unfortunately died only three months later.[15]

Not long afterwards, the Hadeya chief, learning that the Imam's secretary and commander 'Abd en-Nasir had been stationed in nearby Gänz, sent a message to Ahmäd, asking the latter to summon the governor of Gänz to "establish an alliance" with him. Explaining the need for such a union he declared, "When we are united no one can do anything against us". Ahmäd accordingly summoned 'Abd en-Nasir, who came with a considerable number of mules, large cattle, and other gifts from Gänz. He subsequently married the Hadeya ruler's sister. Both men later collaborated in the Imam's occupation of Bali. As a reward for their services the Imam presented them with a share of the horses captured in previous fighting.[16]

Adäl control was, however, still far from secure. Christian forces attacked the province in the Spring of 1532. Ahmäd was obliged to order his faithful 'Abd en-Nasir to remain in the territory, but later sent him to reinforce his forces fighting against 'Addalu, the governor of Bali, as described above in the section of that province.[17]

Gälawdéwos's Reconquest

The Imam's defeat and death in 1543 resulted in another turn of Hadeya fortune. Early in his reign Gälawdéwos, who had by then obtained the support of the Portuguese, launched a successful expedition to the territory which was thus brought once more under imperial control. The province then apparently paid taxes to the Emperor who appointed its governors.[18]

GAMO

The Imam's commander Vizier Mojahid, who had conquered Wäj, later extended his rule westwards. He thus gained control of the nearby "pagan", or animist, territory of Gamo which consisted, as previously, of two districts, known respectively as Suf Gämo and Bahr Gämo. These, the *Futuh* claims, had been under imperial domination only "by convention". Their inhabitants Shihab ed-Din

---

15 Basset (1897), p. 377.
16 Basset (1897), p. 377-8.
17 Basset (1897), pp. 380-1. See also pp. 389-90, 392, 394.
18 Conzelman (1895) p. 141.

refers to deprecatingly as "brutes without religion" or "books of revelation".

Mojahid entered the country, and killed many of its inhabitants. The survivors submitted, and agreed to pay the poll tax. The chief then entrusted the area to his equerry Salih, to whom he allotted a small occupying force of ten cavalrymen and a hundred infantry.[19]

GANZ

Despite its location in the far west, Gänz, a largely animist province, was enmeshed in the Imam's war at an early stage. Well before the Adäl army advanced into the province soldiers from it had been recruited, as earlier noted, into the Emperor's great southern army commanded by Awra'i 'Uthman.[20]

Later, after its defeat, warriors from the area continued the struggle. Some of the Mayas reported to the Imam, as we have seen, that they were being attacked by Christian forces from Gänz, as well as Wäj, and appealed for Muslim soldiers to protect them. Men from Gänz also fought against the Muslim army in Kämbata.

In the Spring of 1532, Ahmäd ordered his secretary 'Abd en-Nasir to go to Gänz, and fight the inhabitants until they became Muslims or agreed to pay the poll tax. The chief at once marched to the area, and established himself there, after which, it is reported, the inhabitants began to obey him. His presence prompted the ruler of neighbouring Hadeya to ask the Imam, as noted above, to arrange an alliance.

Muslim control of the region was, however, far from complete. Christian forces were soon on the offensive in Gänz as well as in Hadeya. The Imam was obliged to order 'Abd en-Nasir and the latter's brother-in-law, the ruler of Hadeya, to remain in their respective provinces to resist enemy pressure.

'Abd en-Nasir was later involved in fierce fighting with 'Addalu, the Christian governor of Bali, who, as earlier related, was killed in battle, and later beheaded. After this victory 'Abd en-Nasir made his way to Hadeya, only to learn that Lebnä Dengel had ordered Ayker, one of his chiefs, to attack. The latter advanced as far as Gänz. The province's Muslim governor, riding day and night for five days, quickly reached the territory. Ayker, unprepared for this speedy return, fled, whereupon, it is claimed, all his men embraced Islam.

---

[19] Basset (1897), p. 396. See als Huntingford (1989), p. 131.
[20] Basset (1897), p. 83.

'Abd en-Nasir then remained in the province, where he "reduced the inhabitants to obedience", and sent word to the Imam of the final conquest of Gänz.[21]

WALAMO (or WOLAITA)

After his occupation of Gämo, Mojahid's aide Salih proceeded to Wälamo, another animist territory, now better known as Wolaita, which the *Futuh* characterises as exceedingly muddy. Its inhabitants agreed to the tribute asked of them, but said that they needed time to collect it, and begged Salih to wait. This was, however, only a trick, for, having assembled, they suddenly attacked him, and his companions were unable to make use of their cavalry, for their horses' feet sank in the mud, and were all killed.

Mojahid was determined to take his revenge on the Wälamo people, and accordingly entered their territory. His followers, however, pleaded with him against staying in it. They argued that the land was unsuitable for the use of cavalry, that it lacked provisions for the troops, and that if they remained there they could easily be cut off by their enemies. Mojahid refused to listen. He stubbornly remained in the area for a month, during which its inhabitants took refuge on a mountain. His army meanwhile suffered, as he had been warned, from an acute shortage of food, and its retreat was blocked by a Christian army. Mojahid and his men were eventually rescued - but the occupation of Wälamo came to an abrupt end.[22]

KAMBATA

Kämbata at this time was an animist territory, with, however, apparently some Christian inhabitants. The area was invaded, in the early 1530s, by the Imam's commander and secretary, 'Abd en-Nasir. He was attracted by treasures left in the province by Lebnä Dengel before his northward retreat. The Kämbata people, and those of nearby Gafat, joined together to resist, but were easily routed. The Adäl army killed many of the inhabitants of Kämbata, and then imposed the usual poll tax. 'Abd en-Nasir found the monarch's hoard of wealth, which had been deposited on Mount Kämbat, and handed it over to the Imam. It consisted, according to the *Futuh*, of all sorts of

---

[21] Basset (1897), pp. 91, 015, 201, 325, 357, 359, 363, 365-6, 378, 80, 383, 392, 394, 389.

[22] Basset (1897), pp. 396-9.

riches, including gold vases, paintings, and rich carpets from "Rome", i.e. Constantinople.[23]

During the ensuing period of Muslim domination the Christians of Kämbata, according to the subsequent chronicle of Emperor Särsä Dengel, are said to have been much persecuted. In the course of this oppression a *tabot* which Lebnä Dengel carried around the country was lost, but was found, as we shall see, in the Guragé country almost half a century later.[24]

ENARYA

Enarya, then another largely animist territory, was much affected by the Imam's conflict with the Emperor. Early in the fighting many soldiers from the province, as well as the neighbouring territories of Guragé, Damot and Gafat, were recruited, as we have seen, into Lebnä Dengel's army.

The province, which Shihab ed-Din described as a "gold mine", was then controlled, he asserts, by a slave from Damot. The chief was most anxious to collaborate with Imam Ahmäd's forces. Hearing that Bäläw Sägäd, a Christian chief of Damot, wished to flee into Enarya, he promised him asylum, but on his arrival immediately seized him and his companions. He then sent them, together with 1,000 ounces of gold and many presents, to the Adäl leader Vizier Addolé, who thereupon fixed the tribute of Enarya. Thus the territory without a fight accepted Muslim suzerainty, and saved itself from Adäl occupation.[25]

DAMOT

Lebnä Dengel, Awra'i 'Uthman and Wäsän Sägäd

At the opening of the war Damot, a mainly animist province, though one probably also inhabited by some Christians, was part of the empire, and soldiers from it served in Emperor Lebnä Dengel's army, as they had done in that of Zär'ä Yaq'ob a century earlier. After Ahmäd's first raids into the highlands troops from Damot, as well as many other territories, were collected by Awra'i 'Uthman, who had been entrusted by Lebnä Dengel with the defence of the south. The

---

[23] Basset (1897), pp. 365-6, 378. See also Huntingford (1989), p. 131.
[24] Conti Rossini (1907), pp. 75-6.
[25] Basset (1897), pp. 224, 400; Huntingford (1955), p. 22.

monarch's principal courtier, Wäsän Sägäd, was for a time established in the province, which was temporarily used by Lebnä Dengel as a place of imprisonment for the Imam's cousin Zaharbuy.

The Emperor's armies were subsequently strengthened by the arrival of further troops from Damot, and several other south-western territories. The Muslim leader Bäläw 'Abdu, when informed of their presence, as we have seen in our section on Guragé, sneeringly dismissed the participation of Damot soldiers. He declared that they were no more than slaves capable of tilling the land, cutting trees and carrying wood, but entirely ignorant of warfare.[26]

Not long afterwards, in 1531, Lebnä Dengel made his way towards Damot. The Imam, learning this, decided to proceed in the same direction. When he discussed the matter with his followers, however, they observed that the province was far away, and none of them knew the route to it. These arguments failed to persuade their master, who declared them merely excuses from soldiers wanting to return to their homes. He accordingly summoned a recent convert, who declared that he "knew all Abyssinia", including the route to Damot, and would willingly show the way. Ahmäd and his companions thereupon set forth to Damot as planned.

The Emperor and Wäsän Sägäd consulted as to what to do. The chief argued that it would be unwise to establish themselves in Damot, for it was a narrow land, in which the Imam's forces could easily pursue them. He therefore proposed that they should divide forces: Lebnä Dengel should proceed at once to the Damot mountains, while he himself would pretend to push forward into the Muslim country, but, on reaching Däwaro, would disengage himself, and turn back to join his master. The Emperor accepted this stratagem, and the two men set forth.

Ahmäd, learning of the scheme through his spies, decided to ignore Wäsän Sägäd, and to confine his attack on the Emperor, that "dog of Christianity" as he called him. He accordingly ordered his men to march on Damot. Lebnä Dengel responded by installing himself in one of the province's inaccessible mountains, which had only a single entrance, at a place called Joraji. He entrusted its gate to Awra'i 'Uthman, while he himself set up his camp on the mountain slope at Dähondur, literally "Elephants' Wood".

---

[26] Basset (1897), pp. 83-4, 90-1, 175, 177, 181, 213-14, 221-8.

The Imam's men, pursuing the Emperor, reached the lowlands just below the mountain, but were uncertain how to proceed. Some suggested that they spend the night where they were, and bring up their artillery to attack on the morrow. Others warned that this would give Wäsän Sägäd time to cut them off in the rear, and therefore advised an immediate assault. Ahmäd, always one for speedy action if at all possible, accepted this latter view, and prepared for battle. His troops approached the gate guarded by Awra'i, but the Imam, considering it impregnable, withdrew, and made his way towards Dähondur. Lebnä Dengel took no notice of this, for the passage there was narrow, and no one, he believed, knew the road. He was therefore confident that the enemy could not break into his defences.

The Imam on approaching Lebnä Dengel's redoubt found three gates which seemed impregnable, for they had been blocked with thorns and branches. Undeterred he ordered his foot-soldiers to place their shields on these defences and climb over them. The men did so, and soon found themselves in an open space, from which they could turn back and easily open the gates, enabling their victorious leader and his army to enter.

Too late, the Emperor realised the danger. He ordered his Tegray soldiers to rush to the gate, but when they reached it they found the Imam's men already in occupation. The latter's cavalry, about fifty in number, immediately charged the Tegray warriors. Fierce hand to hand fighting followed, in which eight Tegray chiefs were killed, and two others, including Täklay the governor of Säräyé, were captured. The Tegray soldiers thereupon fled, and reported to Lebnä Dengel what had happened. He was forced to abandon his palace, and hastily withdrew from Damot, together with Awra'i.[27]

Despite Lebnä Dengel's evacuation Damot had up to that point neither submitted nor embraced Islam. This was recognised by the Imam's chiefs, who told their master that the Emperor's nobles, with their cavalry and other troops, were still in control of much of the region.[28]

The Imam subsequently ordered Vizier 'Addolé to march to Damot, to conquer the province. The chief was accompanied by Sidi Muhammäd, whom Ahmäd had appointed as its governor. On his arrival he found that one of the Emperor's kinsmen, Daharagot, was

---

[27] Basset (1897), pp. 231-41.
[28] Basset (1897), pp. 325. See also p. 34.

camped there with his army. On hearing of 'Addolé's arrival, however, he fled to Gafat, where he was to suffer an ignominious defeat.[29]

GAFAT

Gafat, another animist territory, was pejoratively referred to by Shihab ed-Din as a place inhabited by a nomadic people, who did not know the *Qur'an,* and "had no religion".

The province was affected by the Imam's invasion at the same time as neighbouring Damot. At the beginning of hostilities soldiers from Gafat, together with others from Damot and neighbouring provinces, formed part of Lebnä Dengel's great southern army, and other men from the province were later enlisted. After the monarch's defeat in Shäwa, property from at least one Christian church was taken to Damot for safe-keeping. This was fortunate, for the Imam's forces soon afterwards put the building to the flames.

The Emperor's commander, Awra'i 'Uthman, subsequently made use of a substantial Damot army. When 'Abd en-Nasir later marched into Kämbata the people of Gafat, as well as those of Gänz, joined in the resistance, but were defeated, and suffered heavy casualties. Lebnä Dengel's son, and future successor, Gälawdéwos, according to Bermudes, later found refuge in the Gafat country.

The Gafats, though willing to fight against the Imam's invasion, were reluctant to receive the Emperor's retreating army. They doubtless feared that to do so would result in the customary looting by the soldiers, and would also probably incur Adäl wrath. When Vizier 'Addolé reached Damot, and Lebnä Dengel's kinsman Daharagot fled into Gafat, the inhabitants of the latter territory ordered the chief not to enter their country, but he forcibly did so. The Gafats thereupon gathered to oppose him. Taking up their positions in a muddy area, in which the feet of their opponents' horses would sink, they hid in the nearby trees. Daharagot had no idea of their presence until they suddenly attacked with their spears, which they did on foot (as they did not know how to ride on horseback). He had with him two hundred cavalrymen, who fought desperately, but their horses sank into the mire, and fell victim to the Gafats' spears, in just the same

---

[29] Basset (1897), pp. 398, 405. See also Huntingford (1989), pp. 123, 127-8, 130-1, 133.

way as the Imam's cavalry under Salih had sunk into the mud in Walamo. Daharagot and only a few of his followers escaped. The remainder, including three of his sons and fifteen Damot chiefs, perished. The Gafats involved in this fighting, according to Taddesse Tamrat, were probably of the Gämbo clan, and the fighting doubtless took place in the marshy land of what is now the Choman swamps of north-eastern Wälläga.[30]

The Gafat action not surprisingly won the approval of 'Addolé. On learning of Daharagot's defeat he despatched to the province several Gafat converts to Islam, and instructed them to invite their compatriots to come to him. They did so, bringing with them horses, drums and other captured loot. 'Addolé joyously decorated the Gafat nobles with clothes, and later reported all this to his master Ahmäd who, the *Futuh* recalls, was also well pleased.[31]

KAFA

Käfa, to the south-west, was apparently too far away to be invaded by the Imam's forces, and does not therefore feature in the *Futuh*. The kingdom was ruled, as previously, by a local *tato*, or king. The incumbent of this office at the time was Madi Gafo, who reigned between about 1530 and 1565.[32]

MAZAGA and THE COUNTRY OF THE HAMAJ and BALAYA

The Imam reached the country of the "blacks" in the far west at a relatively late stage of his campaign, around 1535. After advancing into Tegray, as related in Chapter 18, he made his way to Mazäga, a Muslim territory to the west of Wälqayt. The local ruler, Makattér, who had a force of 15,000 Nubians, appealed for Ahmäd's help against his Christian neighbours. The Imam visited him, stayed six days in the territory, and, perhaps for dynastic reasons, married the chief's daughter. Her father died, however, only three days later. His sister Ga'éwah kept the news secret from her soldiers for three days, but sent a message to inform the Imam of what had happened. Ahmäd thereupon appointed the deceased's young son Nafi as ruler, made the

---

[30] Taddesse Tamrat, (1988a), p. 136.
[31] Basset (1897), pp. 224-5, 273, 277, 366, 399-401. See also Whiteway (1902), pp. 216, 235.
[32] Cecchi (1885-7), II, 490; Bieber (1920-3), I, 78, II, 494-533.

latter's aunt regent, and sent back the old chief's nephew Hasän, who was with him, to act as the child's foster parent.

Not long after this the Imam and his men encountered a force of the Hamaj people, whom Bruce describes as "black Pagans", and some Nubians. Both groups were apparently attached to the Emperor's forces, and joined in opposing the Adäl advance, but were vanquished after a day's fierce fighting.

Later, while in Dämbeya, Ahmäd arrived at a major market for gold. The metal was reportedly brought there by "Nubians", and doubtless came from Bäni, or Bela, Shangul, which, as we have seen in Chapter 3, had long been famed for its gold. He ordered the construction of mosques, and gave the Taka area bordering Sudan as a fiefdom to his nephew Vizier 'Abbas.[33]

The Imam, according to the subsequent chronicle of Särsä Dengel, also carried out an abortive raid on the Bäläyas, an animist group west of Agäwmeder. The inhabitants denied Ahmäd's followers access to water, and, hiding in the forests, discharged arrows at any of his men attempting to cut wood or draw water, as well as at their horses and mules. After many of his animals died the Imam prudently withdrew from the area.[34]

---

[33] Basset (1897), pp. 426-31, 452, 461, 465; Bruce (1790), II, 438.
[34] Conti Rossini (1907), p. 174.

Chapter 18

THE NORTH:
THE COUNTRY OF THE BAHR NAGASH

The country of the Bahr Nägash, because of its location in the far north, was one of the last parts of the empire to be confronted by the Imam's advancing forces. Soldiers from Säraye, as we have seen in the section on Däwaro, nevertheless marched with Azzaj Täklä Iyäsus's Tegray army to encounter Ahmäd in that province. In the ensuing fighting Bahr Nägash Zä-Wängel, described as the lord of the port of Dehono, and the *shum* of Hamasén were both killed, while the ruler of Säraye was captured while doing battle against the Adäl army in Damot.[1]

Täsfa Le'ul, Tédros and Täsfawi

After conquering the southern and central provinces, the Imam turned his attention to the north which had long constituted the empire's religious heartland as well as its main place of access to the sea. In 1535 he marched into Tegray and captured Aksum. Some of his forces then crossed the Märäb River into Säraye. There, aware of the advantage of keeping a member of the local ruling family in power, they appointed Tédros, a cousin of a local Christian nobleman called Täsfa Le'ul, as governor under Ahmäd's nephew Vizier 'Abbas. The Adäl occupation was bitterly resisted, notably by Täsfa Le'ul, who killed first Tédros, and later the Imam's general, Vizier 'Addolé. The latter's' head was sent as a trophy to the Emperor, who on receiving it had drums beaten and flutes played, optimistically declaring that it signified that the fortunes of war were at last turning.

The Imam, greatly angered by the death of 'Addolé, made his way towards Säraye, where the district's soldiers, armed with bows and arrows, spears and shields, hastened to oppose him. Supported by men from Dämbeya they attacked the advancing Muslim force, but were defeated, and fled. They were relentlessly pursued by Ahmäd's men, who, according to the *Futuh*, killed all of them, not a single one escaping.

The people of Säraye, crushed like many of their compatriots to the south, agreed to pay the Imam the poll tax. Täsfa Le'ul and his

---

[1] Basset (1897), pp. 127-8, 196, 203.

sons, however, refused to co-operate. They were in consequence killed and their heads despatched to Ahmäd. Recognising once more the importance of the local ruling family he nevertheless appointed Tédros's brother Täsfawi as governor of Särayé, and another local man, 'Afra, as Bahr Nägash. Control of the port of Hergigo was given to one of the Imam's followers, Sherif Nur ibn Ibrahim. All three officials were placed under the command of Vizier 'Abbas who assumed the time-honoured title of Bahr Nägash.

The Imam's Departure

The Imam's occupation of Tegray, which lasted a year, was a difficult one. His forces suffered from an acute shortage of provisions, and in Särayé from the outbreak of an unidentified epidemic. Conditions were so serious that not a few Muslims in Ahmäd's army, converted, as the *Futuh* says, to Christianity. Realising the impossibility of his position Ahmäd decided to abandon the province, and withdrew south-westwards to more fertile Bägémder.

Before leaving he confirmed the appointment of Täsfawi as ruler of Särayé and 'Afra as Bahr Nägash, and appointed a certain Zär Sänay governor of Hamasén. Sherif Nur, who left with the Imam, was on the other hand replaced as chief of Hergigo by a Red Sea dignitary, Ahmäd ibn Isma'il of Dahlak. The port thus fell under the influence of the rulers of the island of that name.[2]

As in other areas the Imam's occupation of the coastal highlands resulted in considerable destruction. The Portuguese warrior Miguel de Castanhoso, who arrived in 1541, found, on climbing the plateau, that a large church within sight of the sea had been destroyed, and that the surrounding countryside had been laid waste. Villages around the Bahr Nägash's capital, Debarwa, were all "depopulated, through fear". Their inhabitants had "taken refuge with their herds on a mountain", thereby "abandoning their husbandry". Many monks, on seeing the Portuguese, came out of hiding "with crosses in their hands, in solemn procession, praying God for pity".

These clerics on meeting the Portuguese commander Christovão da Gama declared that God had brought him to their country in a time of "great trouble", as the enemies of their faith had "lorded it" over them, and had destroyed their churches and monasteries. Christovão,

---

[2] Basset (1897), pp.196, 203, 239-40, 317, 402, 442-50, 454. See also Huntingford (1989), p. 183.

they sweetly added, was an Apostle of God come to deliver them, and they called on him for vengeance against their "evil" enemies. All this they demanded with "such clamour that truly there was none who heard them but was ready to weep a thousand tears".[3]

Notwithstanding this demand for vengeance, uttered by Christian monks when the fortunes of war were turning in their favour, many inhabitants of the country of the Bahr Nägash, as of other parts of the empire, were adept at changing with the times. A case in point was the Bahr Nägash's father, who, according to Castanhoso, had abandoned his allegiance to Lebnä Dengel, because "it appeared to him that the kingdom could never be restored". He converted to Islam, and was "esteemed greatly" by the Imam, who made him an officer in his forces and a tutor to his son. After Ahmäd's' death, the old man, however, escaped with his ward, and sent a message to Emperor Gälawdéwos stating that if the latter pardoned him he would hand over the child. The monarch agreed, largely, Castanhoso believes, in recognition of the services of the Bahr Nägash, who had been one of the first to assist the Portuguese in their struggle against the Imam. Some other turn-coats were less fortunate. They thought, Castanhoso reports, that they too would be pardoned, but when they arrived the Emperor ordered them to be beheaded. Others were, however, granted an amnesty, for there were "so many" in need of it, the Portuguese author slyly comments, that had the monarch ordered all to be killed, he "would have remained alone".[4]

---

[3] Whiteway (1902), pp. 6-7.
[4] Whiteway (1902), pp. 84-6.

Chapter 19
THE BORDERLANDS AND THE INTERIOR
Imam Ahmäd ibn Ibrahim al-Ghazi

The rise of Imam Ahmäd ibn Ibrahim al-Ghazi, a major turning-point in Ethiopian history, had profound consequences on the entire region, and affected the periphery no less than the interior.

Ahmäd gained power in Adäl after a bitter struggle with Sultan Abu Bäkr ibn Muhammäd of Harär, whom he eventually killed in 1525, after which he placed the latter's brother 'Umar Din on the throne as a puppet ruler. He then ordered the Muslim towns of Adäl to stop paying tribute to the Emperor, thus making war with the Christian empire well-nigh inevitable. Ahmad was well prepared for this. Through his marriage to Bati Del Wänbära, daughter of Amir Mähfuz of Zäyla', he enjoyed the support of the latter's family and former followers, and had committed himself to continuing his father-in-law's policy of carrying out a *jihad* against Christian Ethiopia. Making effective use of fire-arms imported from Arabia, which as ruler of Adäl were not difficult for him to acquire, he embarked on a series of expeditions, first in the Somali country and soon afterwards in the empire's eastern provinces. He was so successful that he decided before long, as his chronicle states, on the complete conquest of Abyssinia. and of the "pagan", or animist, lands to the south-west The ruler of the eastern periphery, as in the case of Sultan Säbr ad-Din II of Ifat a century earlier, had thus made up his mind to become the master of the hinterland. Without the conquest of the interior the permanent control of the borderlands could not if fact be achieved.

The East

Ahmäd's early expeditions, like those of Mähfuz before him, were carried out in search of loot as well as in pursuit of a Holy War. Their main thrust roughly coincided with the trade routes running from the Gulf of Aden ports to the interior. These campaigns, the first of which took place mainly in the eastern lowlands, but were later extended into the highlands, involved extensive looting of gold and precious garments, as well as the capture of cattle, pack animals and vast numbers of slaves. Such forays from the east took the Imam and his increasingly powerful forces into the then Christian provinces of

Däwaro, Fätägar, Ifat and Bali, as well as Shärkha, Därha and the country of the Mayas.

Däwaro, because of its proximity to Adäl, was one of the first provinces to be attacked, in 1526 or 1527, when the Imam's men seized considerable booty. In a subsequent expedition they advanced as far as Wämbärya, and captured further loot. On their return journey they were assailed by a substantial force of Däwaro soldiers, but repulsed them. Ahmäd undertook another expedition in 1529, when he ravaged the province. Its Christian governor Ras Näbiyat rallied an army to oppose it. A chief called Abél, who had been one of the Imam's prisoners, nevertheless organised a truce whereby the Adäl army was allowed through Däwaro, and promised in return to spare its churches.

In 1530 the Imam decided to launch an invasion of the highlands, and to replace the old Christian empire by a new Muslim state under his leadership. To this end he again advanced into Däwaro. Lebnä Dengel responded by mobilising forces from many parts of the empire, including the borderland provinces of Bali, Fätägar, Gänz, and Damot, and then confronted the Adäl army at 'Ayfärs in March 1531. In the ensuing fighting the Emperor was overwhelmingly defeated, after which Ahmäd proceeded to Qanburah, which was situated above the principal market of Däwaro. He later carried out a number of *razzias*, in the course of which he destroyed an important church at 'Andurah.

Lebnä Dengel, realising the Imam's strength, gave his governor of Tegray, Täklä Iyäsus, the additional responsibility of ruling Däwaro. The chief marched into the latter province to confront the invader, but was easily defeated, and killed with many of his men.

Ahmäd thereupon decided to bring Däwaro entirely under his control. His occupation was facilitated by one of his prisoners, 'Amdu, who, fearing the consequences of further fighting, succeeded with great perseverance in establishing another truce. By it the province's nobles surrendered their arms, on the understanding that those who insisted on remaining Christians would be allowed to do so by paying a poll tax, while the others would become Muslims.

The Imam subsequently despatched one of his commanders, Amir Hosayn, to Däwaro, whereupon the province's nobles fled. Ahmäd's forces proceeded to Joraji, above the market of Suq-Däwaro, and their general, Amir Abu Bäkr, destroyed a nearby church. The inhabitants agreed to embrace Islam, and the Imam appointed another of his followers, Gärad Jushu, as the province's governor. He was replaced in 1540 by Ahmäd's son Nasradin, who was succeeded in turn by the Imam's nephew Vizier 'Abbas. The latter was, however, soon defeated and killed by Emperor Gälawdéwos, who had by then obtained the support of the Portuguese, after which Muslim power in Däwaro crumbled.

Fätägar, the location a generation earlier of one of Mähfuz's most notable forays, was also attacked early in the campaign. In 1526 or 1527 Ahmäd advanced into the province, as far as Waduh Mecheg in the vicinity of the Emperor's camp. The Adäl leader wanted to attack the monarch immediately, but his men, wishing to make their way home with their loot, to his intense chagrin, refused to do fight.

Ahmäd and his followers later returned to attack Lebnä Dengel's palace at Badeqé, but were forced to retreat across the Dukham River. They soon came back, however, and burnt down the palace, where they captured immense loot, including gold and coloured cloth. Ahmäd's commander Vizier Addolé seized much of the Emperor's treasure. Many people of Fätägar were later recruited into the Imam's army, and on one occasion fought in the Menz highlands.

After the Imam's eventual defeat Fätägar, together with neighbouring Däwaro and Ifat, was placed under Vizier 'Abbas. The latter was, however, subsequently routed, whereupon Adäl power in the province quickly came to an end.

The Mayas, because of their location on the eastern borders of Shäwa, and in the area around Mount Zeqwala, were also caught up in the conflict at an early stage when they served in Lebnä Dengel's army as skilled archers using poisoned arrows. The Imam, well aware of the deadly power of their arrows, ordered his men to pick up the latter to prevent them from being re-used. For this and other reasons the archers were defeated.

Ahmäd later decided to advance into Maya territory. Emphasising that the archers' wealth consisted primarily of cattle he warned his men against seizing any livestock. Vizier 'Addolé, however, indulged in extensive looting, including the seizure of cattle, which provoked the Mayas into battle. One the vizier's officers, Zahahbuy, was felled by a poisoned arrow. Many Mayas nevertheless soon abandoned their allegiance to the Emperor, and were recruited into Ahmäd's forces.

Fierce fighting with other Mayas took place under Ahmäd's commander Färäshäham Din. One of the latter's men, Besaräh, was killed by an arrow after which Ahmäd's men sought to inflict retribution, only to find that the Mayas had disappeared during the night. The Adäl army spent many days pillaging the Maya country. Its inhabitants, led by their proud chief Zärji, had no option but to submit to the Imam, who appointed Färäshäham Din as their governor.

The struggle also reached a people called the Duba'ah, perhaps the Dobe'a, from whom the Imam's men seized many of the cattle for which they had long been renowned.

Ifat was also affected by the Imam's early expeditions. In his first raid, in 1527, Ahmäd divided his army into three forces, commanded respectively by Vizier Addolé, Vizier Nur ibn Ibrahim, and himself. His men advanced to the settlement of Antokya, where they burnt a notable church. They proceeded next to the old market town of Gende Belo, whose Muslim population afforded him a warm welcome. The hapless Christian merchants were on the other hand killed on Ahmäd's orders.

When the Imam subsequently began his main drive into the highlands the Ifat soldiers assembled at Antokya to defend another of its churches, but this too was also soon burnt down. Ahmäd ordered his commander Shamsu to make himself master of the province. Its inhabitants fled, after which the chief destroyed a church built half a century earlier by Emperor Eskender. To consolidate his control of the territory the Imam ordered his son Ahmushuh and his Somali brother-in-law Gärad Mattan to continue operations in Ifat.

Faced with the Imam's growing power Lebnä Dengel's southern commander Awra'i 'Uthman, a converted Bäläw from the northern periphery, secretly subverted his army, which was composed entirely of Christians, and then announced his reversion to the Muslim faith. His change of allegiance enabled the Imam to advance unopposed to the old town of Tobeya, where he received Awra'i's submission. Some 20,000 Christians reportedly also embraced Islam.

Ahmäd entrusted the government of Ifat to another of his followers, Awra'i Abun. The latter, with the Imam's nephew 'Abbas, consolidated Adäl control of the province, but this, however, scarcely survived the Imam's death. A rebellion soon broke out in the Ifat mountains, Ahmäd's son Nasradin was defeated, and Adäl power in the province as elsewhere disintegrated.

The South

Bali, which had earlier been attacked by Muslim foes from Adäl, was another of the targets of one of the Imam's first expeditions. The province, which was ruled by Lebnä Dengel's brother-in-law Azmach Degälhan, witnessed much fighting. Ahmäd's initial foray was criticised by the Haräri sultan 'Umar Din, who argued that the army was exhausted. It nevertheless obtained provisions *en route*, and later engaged in extensive looting.

Sanhur, Lebnä Dengel's governor, assembled his men to fight against the Imam, but the local Muslims and resident Arabs rallied to the Imam's cause. Two local chiefs, Simu and Sabbaru, secretly embraced Islam, and gave the Muslim occupation important tactical support.

Lebnä Dengel despatched a large army in an attempt to regain control of the territory, but one of the Imam's kinsmen, Sultan Muhammäd, defeated it. He then declared the province under his authority, and appointed governors. Numerous Bali soldiers nevertheless continued to support the Emperor, but many of them were later defeated at the battle of Antokya. The province, however, was still not conquered, and many of its inhabitants remained unconverted to Islam.

Ahmäd's forces had therefore to launch a further massive attack. The Emperor's governor 'Addalu attempted to resist, but was defeated and killed. Thousands died in the struggle, and Ahmäd's soldiers took countless women and children as slaves. The population as a whole then at last embraced the Muslim faith.

After the Imam's death in 1543 his nephew 'Abbas established himself as ruler of Bali, but was soon defeated, whereupon Adäl power, as in other areas, quickly came to an end.

Sharkha, on account of its location to the west of Däwaro, was not conquered until somewhat later. In 1531, however, the Imam ordered his commander 'Addolé to attack the province, kill any men who resisted, and seize their wives as slaves. The chief, after some fighting, accomplished this mission. He captured considerable loot, after which most of the population became Muslim.

Därha at about the same time also came under the rule of the Imam, who appointed his commander Färäshäham 'Ali as its governor.

The South-West and West

After gaining control of the eastern provinces the Imam's well-armed forces overran, or attempted to overrun, much of the south-west, including Wäj, Gämo, Gänz, Guragé, Wälamo, Kämbata, Enarya, Damot, Gafat, Hadeya, and later the country of the "blacks" in the west. Ahmäd and his followers thus drove into the rich, largely animist, lands from which Ethiopian Christian rulers had long received considerable quantities of gold, ivory and slaves, as well as not a few of their soldiers.

Lebnä Dengel was at his palace at Gebergé in Wäj when the Imam began his main campaign in the highlands. The monarch withdraw to Damot, leaving his commander Wäsän Sägäd in charge. The Imam's forces, subsequently advanced into the province, and occupied the important market town of Wis.

Later in the struggle Ahmäd ordered Vizier Mojahid to Wäj, and commanded him to fight until its inhabitants surrendered. The latter, however, offered no resistance, and gave Mojahid their allegiance, agreeing to pay the poll tax.

One of the principal Christian nobles of Wäj, Eslam Dähar, an apparently peace-loving man who feared the destruction of his country and the burning of its churches, sent his son and a noble called Asébo, to Ahmäd. They told him that they were willing to pay the poll tax if he would allow them to retain their religion. The Imam declared that Eslam Dähar could do so, but that the latter's son should embrace Islam and join the Muslim army.

Mojahid was later sent back to Wäj where he found the population divided. Half welcomed him, but the other half professed themselves loyal to Eslam Dähar, who had decided to continue the struggle. The Vizier attacked, and defeated the recalcitrant chief, after which the latter's supporters all submitted.

Marching westwards from Wäj, Mohajid soon gained control over Gämo. He killed many of its inhabitants, who are condemned in the *Futuh* as "brutes without religion". The survivors submitted, and agreed to pay the poll tax.

Guragé was also much affected by the war. Soldiers from the province, doubtless Christians, participated in Lebnä Dengel's initial resistance to the Imam's army. Others joined after Ahmäd's victory at Antokya, but were ridiculed by the Muslim commander Bälaw 'Abdu. He declared that they, and the people of Damot, were "slaves" who served as migrant labourers, but were unused to war, and incapable of fighting. Despite such Adäl prejudice many Guragés, for the most part Muslims, were hostile to Lebnä Dengel's rule, and therefore sympathetic to the Imam, whose forces gained control of the province with little difficulty.

Wälamo, now better known as Wolaita, meanwhile was occupied by Mojahid's aide Salih who was however shortly afterwards killed with all his men. Because of the province's remoteness and inaccessibility an attempt to avenge his death failed. The territory therefore remained independent of Adäl rule.

Kämbata was invaded in the early 1530s by the Imam's commander 'Abd en-Nasir, who was attracted by treasure Lebnä Dengel had left there before his defeat. The inhabitants endeavoured to resist, but were easily defeated, and obliged to pay the poll tax. Subsequent report claims that the Christians of the area were persecuted.

Enarya, which at the beginning of the war had contributed troops to the Emperor's army - and had for many centuries been a major source of gold, was reportedly ruled by a slave from Damot. He decided to collaborate with Ahmäd's forces, to whom he supplied a thousand ounces of gold, and apparently became a tributary, thus avoiding an Adäl occupation.

Damot was another territory from which Lebnä Dengel recruited many of his soldiers, and where he had himself resided. Ahmäd advanced into the province to confront the monarch who was encamped at a mountainous place called Dähondur. Though guarded by a large force of Tegray troops it was successfully invested by the Imam's men, after which the Emperor was obliged to evacuate the territory. Ahmäd ordered Vizier 'Addolé and Sidi Muhammäd to march into it, and appointed the latter as its governor.

Gafat also provided soldiers for Lebnä Dengel's army. The province was a place to which Christian property from Shäwa was taken for safe-keeping, and where the Emperor's son, the future monarch Gälawdéwos, found refuge. After Lebnä Dengel's defeat the people of Gafat were, however, reluctant to receive the fugitives. When the Emperor's kinsman Daharagot attempted to take refuge there they resisted him fiercely, and inflicted heavy casualties on his men. This won the approval of Vizier 'Addolé, who invited the Gafat people to visit his headquarters.

Hadeya differed from the above-mentioned territories in that its local ruler, a Muslim, following the province's earlier practice of dynastic alliances with a powerful neighbour, the Christian empire, sought to establish close ties with the Imam. The local chief complained of previous imperial taxation, and alleged that his territory had formerly been obliged to supply every year a young girl chosen for her beauty, who was then converted to Christianity.

Ahmäd responded by offering the Hadeya ruler his friendship. The chief gave his daughter Mureyas to be the Imam's wife, but she died shortly afterwards. Undeterred by this sad event he urged Ahmäd to renew the alliance, and declared that if they were united no one could oppose them. A marriage was arranged between the chief's sister and Ahmäd's secretary and commander 'Abd en-Nasir, ruler of Gänz, but this alliance collapsed as a result of the Imam's subsequent defeat. Gälawdéwos then undertook a successful expedition to the territory, and Hadeya was once more brought under imperial control.

The country of the "blacks" in the west came under Ahmäd's sway only at a late stage, and then but partially. After reaching Tegray the Imam proceeded to the Muslim district of Mazäga, west of Wälqayt, where he was welcomed by the local ruler Makattér, and, doubtless for dynastic reasons, married the latter's daughter. The chief died, however, immediately afterwards, whereupon Ahmäd made the deceased's young son Nafi ruler of the territory, appointing his aunt as regent.

Ahmäd later defeated a force of Hamaj and Nubians, who were apparently in the Emperor's service. In the course of his stay in the region he came upon a market where gold, probably from Bani Shangul, was brought by Nubians. He ordered the construction of mosques, and gave the Taka area as a fiefdom to his nephew Vizier Abbas.

The Imam also tried to subjugate the "pagan" Bäläya. The latter, who, like the Mayas, possessed poisoned arrows, could not, however, be dislodged from their forests, and because of their control of the area's water supply, obliged the invaders to withdraw from the province in humiliation.

Käfa, ruled by its local monarch, Tato Madi Gafo, likewise maintained its old independence of outside control.

The North

The impact of hostilities was first felt on the northern periphery, a staunchly Christian area, early in the conflict when soldiers from the area participated in the fighting in Däwaro. Bahr Nägash Zä-Wängel and the ruler of Hamäsén were both killed, and the ruler of Säraye captured.

The war came closer in 1535 when the Imam's forces arrived in Tegray, and crossed the Märäb River into Säraye. Ahmäd, well aware of the convenience of gaining the allegiance of the local gentry, appointed Tédros, a nobleman of the area, as governor under his nephew Vizier 'Abbas. The occupation was, however, fiercely resisted. Tédros and Vizier 'Addolé, were both killed. The Imam, deeply angered, marched into Säraye, where the local populace, armed with bows and arrows, spears and shields, hastened to resist him. They were, however, defeated. Obliged to flee they are reported to have perished one and all. The local population thereupon, as in the south, agreed to pay the poll tax. Ahmäd appointed Tédros's brother Täsfawi as ruler of the district, and another local man, 'Afra, as Bahr Nägash. Realising the significance of the port of Hergigo he gave it at the same time to one of his own chiefs, Sherif Nur ibn Ibrahim.

The Imam's occupation of the north was, however, short-lived. Only a year later faced with famine, and an epidemic in Säraye, he abandoned Tegray for Bägémder. Before leaving he confirmed his previous appointments in the northern frontier districts, except at Hergigo, which he placed under the ruler of Dahlak, Ahmäd ibn Isma'il.

This political disposition, like that in other peripheral areas, was of short duration. With the coming of the Portuguese, and the restoration of imperial rule under Emperor Gälawdéwos, most of the inhabitants who had defected to Islam speedily reverted to the Christian faith. Hergigo, however, remained under Dahlak control.

Throughout most of these territories, east, south, west and north, this period witnessed innumerable conversions, at first, during the time of the Imam's victories, to Islam; and later, after Ahmäd's defeat, to Christianity, and doubtless also to traditional "animist" faiths.

PART V

THE ERA OF GALAWDEWOS and SARSA DENGEL

(1540-1606)

Chapter 20

THE NORTH:
THE COUNTRY OF THE BAHR NAGASH
and THE LAND OF THE AFARS

The region-wide collapse of the Adäl Muslim regime forged by Imam Ahmäd was followed throughout much of the country by Emperor Gälawdéwos's rapid re-establishment of imperial Christian rule. The consequences were felt not only in the interior of the empire, but also on the periphery: in the Christian north, where the Turks seized the port of Massawa, and began to penetrate into the interior; in the strategically important Muslim east, around Harär, where Gälawdéwos was to die in battle; and in the rich animist provinces of the south-west, which, as in the past, yielded valuable tribute.

Further attempts to consolidate the empire were made by Gälawdéwos's nephew and successor Emperor Särsä Dengel (1563-1597), who, abandoning his predecessor's preoccupation with the east, travelled south, to convert "pagan" populations, and north to confront the Turkish intruders. His battles with the latter were important in that he captured a considerable quantity of fire-arms, including both cannons and rifles, and obtained the services of many Turkish riflemen. This left him far better armed than any forces with which he was to contend, particularly in the militarily weak south and west.[1]

THE COUNTRY OF THE BAHR NAGASH

Gälawdéwos, and the Reassertion of Ethiopian Sovereignty

After the death of Imam Ahmäd in 1543 the government he had established in the northern periphery, as further south, rapidly disintegrated. Gälawdéwos soon established control over the country of the Bahr Nägash, where, significantly enough, he renewed Emperor Zär'a Ya'qob's land charter in favour of the monastery of Däbrä Bizän.[2]

---

[1] Conti Rossini (1907), pp. 3-4, 9. 15-16, 18, 24 *et passim*.
[2] Huntingford (1965b), p. 54.

The old monastery of Däbrä Bizän in Hamasén: a late nineteenth century sketch.
From J.T. Bent, *The Sacred City of Ethiopians*.

The Bahr Nägash meanwhile entrenched himself as the Emperor's vassal. To his capital at Debarwa, Gälawdéwos exiled several of the Portuguese, who had assisted in the Imam's defeat but were beginning to intrigue against him, and trying to convert the country to Catholicism.[3]

The Struggle with the Ottoman Turks

Gälawdéwos's initial success in the north was short-lived, for in 1557 the Ottoman Turks seized the port of Massawa. Within little more than a year a Turkish expeditionary force, led by Ozdemür Pasha, began advancing into the interior. They destroyed, or seriously damaged, a number of Christian places of worship, including the important monastery of Däbrä Damo. The invaders, ravaging parts of Tegray and the semi-coastal district of Bur, also travelled far and wide in search of slaves and cattle. These incursions were resisted by

---

[3] Whiteway (1902), pp. 247-53.

the local populace, who, having acquired a sizeable number of firearms, succeeded in defeating the occupying force. In the course of the fighting the peasants reportedly killed a Turkish general, cut off his head, and despatched it to the Emperor in triumph.

The port of Massawa: an early nineteenth century engraving, depicting vessels of the period.
From T. Lefebvre, *Voyage en Abyssinie. Atlas.*

The Turks for their part occupied the Bahr Nägash's capital, Debarwa. There, Ozdemür Pasha erected a strong fort, with what a royal chronicler describes as "a long wall and a very high tower". This building contained vases of gold and silver, precious stones, rich vestments, and other valuables, from Istanbul, Egypt, Zabid, Jäbal, and other parts of Arabia. The goods had been obtained, the chronicle says, by looting, extractions on trade, and the imposition of a poll tax on the local population.

After establishing themselves at Debarwa the Turks determined to advance into the interior. They entrusted the town to the soldiers of one of their local allies, Gä'ewah, Queen of Säläwa. She was the sister of Makattér, whose daughter Imam Ahmäd ibn Ibrahim had married a generation earlier, and had served as regent for Makattér's young son. They then advanced into the Mäzäga lowlands, where many of them succumbed to malaria or other fever raging in the area. Ozdemür himself was so seriously ill that he had to be carried on a litter, and almost died. At about this time Queen Gä'ewah arrived, asking for assistance against one of the Emperor's commanders.

The Turks at Debarwa, whose leader's return was thus unduly delayed - and who were still facing opposition from the local population, were then in a difficult position. Their provisions were exhausted, and the water cisterns they had dug had dried up. Suffering from hunger and thirst they abandoned their forts in an attempt to seize supplies from the local population by force of arms. Apparently finding this impracticable, they attempted to make their way to the coast, but were attacked, and annihilated, by the populace. The latter captured all the riches of the Turks, including, the chronicler proudly claims, a portrait of their monarch, Sultan Soliman II, besides the belongings of the pro-Turkish Queen Gä'ewah. This loot was duly handed over to the Emperor.[4]

Bahr Nägash Yeshaq, Minas, and Särsä Dengel

The reigns of Emperor Minas (1559-1563) and Särsä Dengel (1563-1597) witnessed the emergence of a powerful and ambitious Bahr Nägash called Yeshaq. He owed much of his strength to the increasing number of fire-arms imported through the Red Sea coast.

Though a ruler of the periphery, Yeshaq attempted to play a major role in Ethiopian imperial politics. Described by Bruce as "an old and tried servant" of Gälawdéwos, he was in fact the latter's kinsman, for his son Täklä Mika'el was married to the daughter of the Emperor's brother and possible heir, Yaq'ob.[5] Yeshaq, according to the Scotsman, had been "treated ill" by Särsä Dengel's successor Minas. Perhaps for this reason the disgruntled chief launched a palace conspiracy, and attempted to place the new emperor's nephew Täzkäro on the throne.

Minas, on learning of the plot, made his way to the Lalibala area to investigate the situation, whereupon Yeshaq retreated northwards to Dambaguina. There a battle was fought, in which the Bahr Nägash was defeated. He fled to the coast, threw himself on the mercy of the Turks, and proclaimed a new emperor, Täzkäro's younger brother Marqos. As the price of Turkish help Yeshaq ceded Debarwa to the Turkish commander, Ozdemür, and recognised Turkish control of the lowlands between it and Massawa. The importance of the Turkish

---

[4] Conzelman (1895), pp. 164-8; Basset (1897), p. 431.
[5] De Barros and de Couto (1877-88), dec. VII, liv. X, cap. VI. pp. 489-90.

reoccupation of the town was later emphasised by Bruce. He describes it as "a large trading town", situated in an area which abounded in "provisions of all kinds", including those on which Massawa depended. Debarwa, he adds, was moreover "the key" to Tegray, as well as to the adjacent "high land of Abyssinia".

Minas, who was doubtless no less conscious of the town's importance, fought against Yeshaq and the Turks in Endärta in 1562, but was defeated. The Bahr Nägash's rebellion, Bruce says, thus "still continued".[6]

Minas's son and successor Särsä Dengel subsequently forgave, and made peace, with the rebel. The latter presented him in return with a number of prize horses, for which his territory had long been renowned, as well as various imported articles, among them many luxurious clothes, each of a different colour, and several exquisite carpets. The reconciliation was, however, short-lived. The Turks chose at that point to withdraw from Debarwa, whereupon Yeshaq hastened to reoccupy it. He seems at first to have contemplated making war on the invaders, but later resumed his alliance with them, and allowed them once more to become masters of the town.[7]

Särsä Dengel, angered by what he considered his vassal's arrogance and treachery, marched against him in 1576, and a year or so later attacked, and defeated, Yeshaq's forces and those of the Turks. This was a signal success, for the latter were well supplied with fire-arms of all kinds, including cannon. Yeshaq was among those who died in the fray. His rebellion, as Merid Wolde Aregay has insisted, did not spring from "separatist motives", but from a "strong desire to influence national policies".[8]

The victorious Emperor advanced on Debarwa, whereupon the Turkish garrison surrendered with all its fire-arms. While doing so it fired a ceremonial cannon salute. This caught the imagination of the Emperor's followers, who emulated it, and thereby established a custom of firing fusilades on notable occasions which has continued in Ethiopia to the present time. Särsä Dengel meanwhile seized the vast riches stored by the Turks, and on the following day celebrated Ethiopian Christmas. He then ordered the destruction of the fort, as well as of a mosque erected during the Turkish occupation. Many

---

[6] Bruce (1790), II, 207-211. See also Huntingford (1989), pp. 136-7.
[7] Conti Rossini (1907), pp. 43, 46, 50-1, 54-7, 60-1, 68-74.
[8] Merid Wolde Aregai (1971), p. 262.

Turks entered the victorious monarch's service, thereby further strengthening his military might.[9]

After Yeshaq's death the Emperor accorded another local chief the title of Bahr Nägash, but the post lost much of its former prestige. The office was temporarily merged with that of governor of Tegray, and, significantly, does not figure in the *Nägärä Wäg*, an account of traditional government compiled at this time. The decline in the Bahr Nägash's position was later noted by Bruce. He claims that, because of Yeshaq's treachery, the post of Bahr Nägash "fell into disrepute", and that in consequence "the sendick [i.e. standard] and nagareet [i.e. drum], the marks of supreme power, were taken from him, and he never was allowed a place in council, unless specially called on by the king". The official continued to have:

"the privilege of being crowned with gold; but, when appointed, has a cloak thrown over him, the one side white, the other a dark blue, and the officer who crowns him admonishes him of what will befall him if he preserves in his allegiance, which is signified by the white side of the cloak; and the disgrace and punishment that is to attend his treason, and which has fallen upon his predecessors, which he figures to him by turning up the colour of mourning".

Bruce's picturesque account is not corroborated by other sources. There would seem, however, no gainsaying Conti Rossini's statement that after Yeshaq's revolt the position of the Bahr Nägash noticeably declined.

After the rains of 1587 the Turks, leaving the port of Dehono, again advanced inland to Debarwa. They then attacked the Emperor's governor, Däjazmach Daharagot, who was likened by the chronicle to a king as he held the position of Bahr Nägash as well as governor of Tegray. He was, however, put to flight, and his men suffered heavy casualties, the *aqäsän*, or chief, of Säraye and the *käntiba*, or district chief, of Hamäsén being among the dead.[10]

'Aquba Mika'él

Särsä Dengel later responded by mobilising his forces to repulse the Turkish invaders, who were looting the neighbouring countryside. They also encountered fierce resistance from the local peasantry.

---

[9] Conti Rossini (1907), pp. 74-6, 83-7, 93. See also Huntingford (1989), pp. 144-5.
[10] Conti Rossini (1907), pp. 113-14, 145-6; Guidi (1903), pp. 151-2; Bruce (1790), III. 249.

While crossing the Märäb River they were ambushed by a local leader by name 'Aquba Mika'él. The monarch, greatly pleased by this deed, awarded him the title of Bahr Nägash, and sent him a bracelet of gold, and other gifts, including a richly caparisoned mule reportedly as fine as his own.

Särsä Dengel advanced to Debarwa, after which he launched a *razzia* to the coast at Hergigo, where the Turkish commander, Kädawred Pasha, was struck to the ground. The monarch returned in triumph to Debarwa, where he received a peace offering from the Turks. He subsequently launched an attack on a rebel called Wäd Ezum, to whom the Turks had given the title of Bahr Nägash. He was killed in battle by 'Aquba Mika'él, whom Särsä Dengel rewarded royally, with further gifts, including a golden collar. He had his herald proclaim that the chief should "henceforth be called not only Bahr Nägash", but also "Son of the King".[11]

The Turks, realising the impossibility of achieving their ambition of gaining control of the northern Ethiopian highlands, then at last abandoned the port of Hergigo. They handed it over to a local Beja chieftain, whom they accorded the title of *Na'ib*, or Deputy.[12] This title was destined to remain in use for over two centuries.

THE LAND OF THE AFARS

The Afars and the Awssa Imamate in the 16th Century

The Afars in the sixteenth century were in contact not only, as in the past, with the Christian highlands, but also with the Muslims at Awssa. The latter, a settlement in the Awash basin, had long been within easy reach of the Afars, but, forming part of the Harär-based Amirate of Adäl, was outside their influence.

The status of Awssa changed radically in 1577. Imam Muhammäd ibn Ibrahim Gasa of Adäl, hoping to escape from the pressure of the Oromos, or Gallas, who had by then appeared in the area in considerable strength, abandoned Harär, as we shall see, and moved his government northward to Awssa. He did so because it was situated in a more isolated, and, as he hoped, safer, location. In this he was mistaken, for he was killed only six years later while fighting with an advancing Oromo force.

---

[11] Conti Rossini (1907), pp. 146-54.
[12] Trimingham (1952), p. 98.

A group of Saho nomads, a population related to the Afars living inland from Massawa, near the main trade route to Adwa and Gondär: a nineteenth century engraving.
From T. Lefebvre, *Voyage en Abyssinie. Atlas.*

The Afars, who were then entirely independent of Awssa, were doubtless opposed to the transfer there of the Adäl capital. An Arabic chronicle, which refers to the Afars by the old term Ada'il, reports that only eight years later they were intercepting one of principal roads out of the town - no doubt that to the coast, and robbing caravans. These depredations resulted in fierce fighting, in the course of which ten Awssa notables were killed.[13]

---

[13] Cerulli (1931), pp. 76-7.

Chapter 21
THE SOUTH-EAST and SOUTH: DAWARO and FATAGAR, WAJ, ADAL, HARAR, and BALI

DAWARO and FATAGAR

Gälawdéwos, Bermudes and Khalid

After Imam Ahmäd's defeat Emperor Gälawdéwos faced problems with the Portuguese, some of whom, as we have seen, he banished to Debarwa. At about the same time he exiled the Portuguese adventurer-cum-prelate João Bermudes and a number of his companions to Däwaro. The Emperor chose this province, the prelate claims, because of its strategic position, near lands then occupied by the advancing Gallas, or Oromos, and on the borders of the hostile kingdom of Zäylä'. The Emperor's banished allies were thus turned in effect into a frontier garrison.

The Portuguese were accompanied by an Indian, Ayres Dias, or Diz, whom Bermudes refers to as a "mulatto" from Coimbra. Known in Ethiopia as Marqos he had accompanied the earlier Portuguese diplomatic expedition of the 1520s, and had learnt Amharic. Described by Bermudes - not always a reliable observer - as "a discreet man and a good cavalier", he had gained the favour of Gälawdéwos, who had pressed the Portuguese to appoint him as their commander. The Emperor was so favourably disposed to him that he reportedly gave him Deneya Ambära, the widow of a prominent Adäl chief, and later appointed him as governor of Däwaro and Bali.[1]

The presence of the Portuguese, if we can believe Bermudes, displeased the Emperor's provincial governor, Khalid. The latter, a cousin of the Bahr Nägash, was a former Christian, who, after the Imam's victory, had embraced Islam, but, after the Muslim defeat, had reverted to his earlier faith. He was displeased by the arrival of the Portuguese, allegedly because some of his income had to be diverted for their upkeep. He therefore ordered that they be killed, or expelled from the province.

Khalid, according to Bermudes, was "a great and powerful lord". He was the ruler not only of Däwaro, but also of Bali, and was allied to the chief of nearby Hadeya. From these three territories he

---
[1] Whiteway (1902), pp.54, 137, 184.

reportedly collected a large force of horsemen, infantry and archers, with whom he attempted to surprise the Portuguese, who were, however, "always vigilant". As soon as the assault began, they shot and killed Khalid, after which most of his supporters became their vassals. The Emperor, Bermudes claims, was very pleased with this outcome, as he had "always feared" the chief.[2]

Gälawdéwos's chronicle makes no mention of these events. It merely states that after the Muslim defeat the monarch proceeded to Däwaro, where he constructed a palace at a place called Agräro. His stay in the area was not, however, peaceful. Some of the neighbouring Muslims soon rebelled, and advanced into the province's lowlands. The Emperor's governor fought and defeated them, killing a large number of their soldiers. He captured the king of Adäl's brother, Wäraba Got, and 'Ali Gärad, the son of Imam Ahmäd's widow Bati Del Wänbärä. They were both taken to the Emperor, together with much booty, including many horses and mules. Not long afterwards, around 1547-8, Gälawdéwos named Fanu'él, one of his principal commanders, as governor of Däwaro and the areas dependent on it.[3]

The peace thus established was only temporary. A decade or so later, in 1559, Gälawdéwos learnt that the Imam's nephew, Amir Nur ibn al-Wazir Mujahid, who married Bati Del Wänbärä on condition that he would avenge her late husband's death, had invaded Fätägar with a huge, and exceedingly well equipped, army. It consisted of thousands of foot soldiers armed with swords, spears and shields, as well as one thousand eight hundred cavalry, "innumerable" archers, five hundred musketeers, and five to seven cannoneers. On receiving this information the Emperor rushed to face the invader. He had with him reportedly no more than seven hundred infantry, two hundred and seventy cavalry, five hundred archers, and a hundred musketeers. His followers, seeing that this force was far too small to confront the huge enemy army, urged him to await reinforcements. This he rashly refused to do.[4] He accordingly marched on Harär, as we shall see in a later section.

---

[2] Whiteway (1902), pp. 225-7.
[3] Conzelman (1895), pp. 141-2, 144,
[4] Conzelman (1895), pp. 175-6.

WAJ

Gälawdéwos, His Palace and Garden

In the aftermath of Imam Ahmäd's defeat Gälawdéwos marched into Wäj. Vizier 'Abbas, learning of his coming, rushed to attack him. A fierce battle was fought, in which the Emperor was entirely victorious. 'Abbas and all his captains perished in the battle, providing a great banquet, the chronicle claims, for the birds of prey. Those of 'Abbas's men who escaped were reportedly killed by the nearby populace.

The Emperor later established a capital in one of the districts of Wäj, thereby, the chronicle claims, abandoning the practice of his ancestors, the kings of Ethiopia, who travelled from place to place until their last resting-place, i.e. where they were buried. There he constructed a tall tower, its interior decorated with the finest marble and gold and silver figures. Nearby he built a palace ornamented inside and out with gold, silver, and precious stones, and surrounded with a high wall. The building is said to have been the work of *Färäng*, i.e. Catholic, or European, and Egyptian craftsmen and Syrian and Indian artists. Two buildings for the church were also erected.

Not far from these structure the Emperor built a house in which he placed white doves from Adäl, and entrusted them to one of his principal chiefs. Near it he planted a beautiful garden, which was well irrigated for it was set, as the chronicle recalls, like Mesopotamia, in the midst of rivers.[5]

Wäj in Särsä Dengel's day remained a province of some importance. The Emperor visited it at least twice, establishing his camp once at Serka, and at another time at Sef Bär. He appointed a prominent nobleman, Daharagot, as *qas*, or governor, of Wäj, and used it as a place of detention for the Fälasha leader Rädét captured in Samén.[6]

ADAL
Bermudes's Report

Imam Ahmäd's death did not lead to an end of the struggle between Adäl and the interior. Bermudes, whose reports, as already

---

[5] Conzelman (1895), pp. 139, 149-50.
[6] Conti Rossini (1907), pp. 49, 114; Basset (1881), XVIII, 111.

mentioned, require to be taken with caution, states that a "king of Adem", by which he presumably means Adäl, soon arose to continue the war. Emperor Gälawdéwos and the Portuguese commander Ayres Dias, alias Marqos, thereupon marched against him, and killed him in battle. It was then, as we have seen, that the chief's widow, Deneya Anbära, was given by Gälawdéwos to be the latter's wife.[7]

Fanu'él and Hasgwa Din

This or later fighting is reported in Gälawdéwos's chronicle. It states that around 1548, Adäl soldiers advanced into the Christian highlands. The Emperor was then in the west of the country, but his commander Fanu'él succeeded in repulsing them. Most of the invaders perished in the fray, but their leader Hasgwa Din and several other soldiers, among them Ahmäd ibn Ibrahim's nephew Nur ibn Mujahid, the ruler of Harar, made good their escape. Gälawdéwos, returning from the west, then in his turn took the offensive, and marched into Adäl, where he fought for six months. He captured much booty, including slaves, cattle, gold and silver, which he is said to have distributed most generously among his subjects.

Determined to continue the struggle the Emperor ordered Fanu'él to advance into what the chronicle terms the country of Bär Sä'd ed-Din, so-called after the earlier Adäl sultan of that name, i.e. the country towards Zäyla'. In the course of the ensuing fighting the Emperor's commander reportedly killed one of the region's two principal chiefs, but the other fled, leaving behind all his possessions.

Later, in 1549, Gälawdéwos resolved to drive further into the country of Bär Sä'd ed-Din, and, as the chronicle claims, to ravage it as its soldiers had ravaged the Christian highlands. He spent five months in this operation, during which he freed Christian slaves who had been taken by Adäl soldiers, and in his turn took many Adäl slaves. He also captured 'Abbas, one of the principal Adäl chiefs, but the other, Amir Nur ibn Mujahid of Harär, again escaped.[8]

---

[7] Whiteway (1902), pp. 199-202.

[8] Conzelman (1895), pp. 144-8. Nur was apparently the son of Mujahid, an earlier ruler of Harär, who, according to Bruce, had attacked Shäwa during the reign of Emperor Dawit III (1508-1540), on which ocasion he had advanced to Amba Geshen, the place of detention of the Christian princes, and "put them all to the sword".. This statement does not seem substantiated by other sources. Bruce (1790), II, 169.

HARAR
Nur ibn al-Wazir Mujahid

The aforesaid Imam Nur had become ruler of the city of Harär and its environs in 1551-2. Known as the "second conqueror" - the first being his uncle Imam Ahmäd - he revived the earlier struggle against the Christian empire. It was symbolic that he was by then married to Imam Mähfuz's daughter, Bati Del Wänbärä, whose remarkable life linked him with her father's raids into the highlands which had begun at the close of the previous century, as well as with her first husband's long to be remembered *jihad* against the empire of Lebnä Dengel and Gälawdéwos.

A late nineteenth century engraving of Harär showing part of the wall believed to have been erected in the late sixteenth century by Amir Nur ibn al-Wazir Mujahid. The picture also features a flag and gate of much later times.
From P. Paulischke, *Harar - Forschungreise nach den Somal und Galla-Ländern Ost-Afrikas.*

Nur's warlike ambitions led to further fierce fighting. In 1559, imperial troops, as we have just seen, marched on Harär. One of the Emperor's chiefs, Fanu'él, succeeded, according to a Haräri chronicle, in entering the city by surprise, but was repulsed. No confirmation of this found in the Ethiopian royal chronicles - but this may only be because their authors in the service of the monarch were reluctant to elaborate on his defeats.

The al-Jami mosque at Harär, a late nineteenth century engraving.
From P. Paulitschke, *Harar - Forschungreise nach den Somal und Galla-Ländern Ost-Afrikas.*

Not long after this the troops of Gälawdéwos's general, Hamälmäl, are said by a Haräri chronicle to have again broken into the city, though this is once more unsubstantiated from the imperial side. Later in the year it seems to have been the Emperor's time to attack the city. A fierce battle ensued, in which there was so much firing that smoke, according to the Harär chronicler, obscured the sky like a cloud. Early in the engagement Gälawdéwos was hit by a bullet, but continued to fight until surrounded by a score of Harari cavalry, who struck him fatally to the ground with their spears.[9] With his death Christian military power in the area crumbled. Nur then despatched the monarch's severed head to the "country of Sä'd ad-Din", and then "devastated the country of Abyssinia" before duly returning to his own country.[10]

---

[9] Conzelman (1895), pp. 175-8. See also Merid Wolde Aregay (1974), p. 624.
[10] Cerulli (1931), pp. 56, 90-1.

Despite this victory the years which followed were difficult for Harär. The city and its environs suffered from a serious famine. Grain and salt prices soared to unprecedented levels. Hunger became so intense, according to the chronicle, that people resorted to eating their children, and in some cases even their spouses. A terrible famine followed, in which Amir Nur himself perished.[11]

ADAL

Amir Muhammäd and Särsä Dengel

The old conflict between Adäl and the Christian empire erupted once more during the reign of Särsä Dengel. The latter learnt in 1576, according to his chronicle, that the provincial ruler, Amir Muhammäd, had killed the leaders of all Muslim groups friendly to the Christian empire, and had advanced beyond the borders of his territory. The Emperor responded by making his way to Wäj, and established himself at Shärkha, whence he despatched thirty horsemen to report on the whereabouts of the Amir. The latter had entered the Hadeya area, where he had been joined by an army led by its ruler, Jafer, and by Asma' ad-Din, a chief of Wäj.

Särsä Dengel's spies discovered that Amir Muhammäd had established his camp above the Wäbi river, perhaps near its source in Guragé. The Emperor marched to the area, and placed his camp within sight of the enemy. The two armies then fought a series of inconclusive battles. During the first few engagements thirty of the Amir's cavalry defected to Särsä Dengel's side. Four or five horsemen, and many foot soldiers, later did so daily, but their defections were not decisive. The fighting grew increasingly fierce, and the Emperor had a defensive rampart erected.

The Amir, seeing that it was impossible to advance any further, decided to return to his country. On learning this the Emperor, who wanted to lure his adversary into battle, pretended to be afraid, and about to flee. The stratagem succeeded, and a month later a major engagement was fought. Jafer was killed, but neither side was victorious. The Wäj chief Asma' ad-Din, who, the chronicle claims, was the Emperor's secret supporter, and had discouraged the Amir's men from fighting properly, thereupon defected to Särsä Dengel, with sixty of his horsemen. His example was followed by other soldiers, including a certain Jebra'él.

---

[11] Cerulli (1931), pp. 57-8; Pankhurst (1982), pp. 51-2.

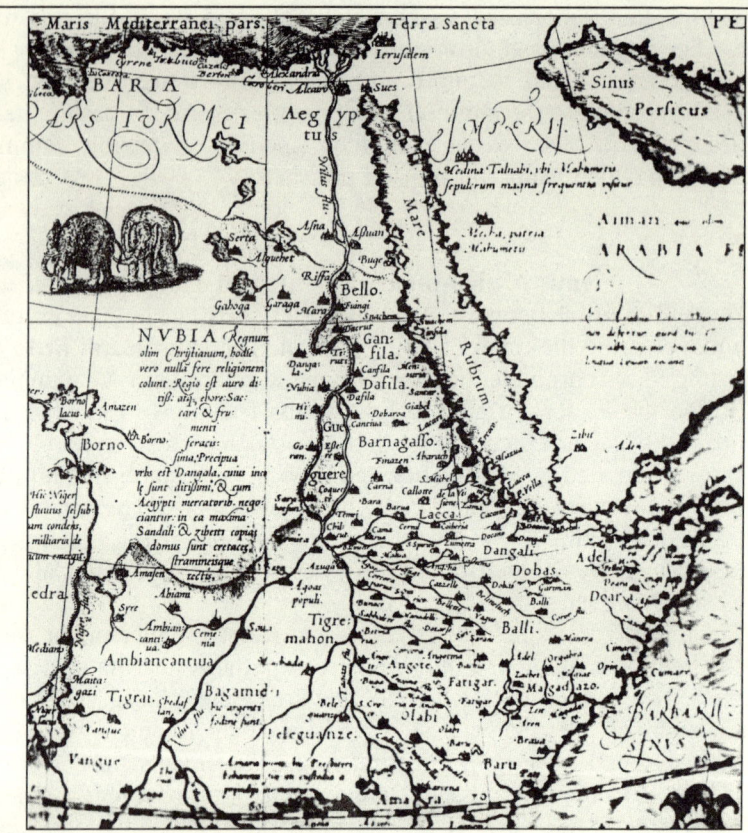

Detail from a late sixteenth century map entitled *Presbiteri Iohannis sive Abissinorvm Imperii Descriptio,* published by Abraham Ortelius at Antwerp in 1570.

Note location of the main provinces of the interior, i.e. Tegray (Tigremahon, a rendering of Tegré Mäkonnen, or ruler of Tegray), Bägémder (Bagamidra), Amhara (Amara), Gojjam (Goiame), and Shäwa (Xoa) all five placed much too far to the south and west. See also the various peripheral provinces indicated, notably Adäl (Adel), Däwaro (Doara), Fätägar (Fatigar) located too far to the south, the Country of the Bahr Nägash (Barnagasso), partially too far to the west, Damot (Damute), identified as a gold-producing province, the lands of the Dobe'as (Dobas), Dänakil (Dangali), and Gafats (Cafates), as well as the ports of Massawa (Mazua), Baylul (Belul), and Zäylä (Zeila).

Amir Muhammäd, realising the impossibility of his position, finally decided to return home, and rode off with fifty horsemen. They made the mistake, however, of looting oxen belonging to the Hadeya peasants. The latter, much angered, responded by blockading the Adäl ruler's escape route. They captured the Amir, and took him to the Emperor. Särsä Dengel reportedly wanted to spare his life, but his chiefs were less merciful. The prisoner was therefore executed, together with several prominant *gärads,* among them Wäbäz Muhammäd, Jebra'él and Wäqär Muhammäd, and three sons of the late Amir Nur.[12]

BALI

After Imam Ahmäd's death Bali was reportedly under the control, as we have seen, first of an Indian "mulatto", Ayres Dias, and, after the latter's death, of a Muslim called Khalid, a former Christian who later embraced Islam, but later reverted to his earlier faith. According to Bermudes, he rebelled against the Emperor's rule, but was later killed by the Portuguese.[13]

Troops from Bali subsequently served in the army of Särsä Dengel, who also appointed *gärads*, or governors, of the province. One, a Muslim by name 'Ali, served for a time in the northern Ethiopian highlands, where he apparently sided with the Turks, and was in consequence executed by the emperor.[14]

---

[12] Conti Rossini (1907), pp. 56-60, 67, 78, 80, 141. See also Basset (1881), XVIII, 111.
[13] Whiteway 1902, pp.225-7.
[14] Conti Rossini (1907), pp. 62, 95, 148-50.

Chapter 22

THE SOUTH-WEST and WEST: GURAGE, ENARYA, WAGAM, GUMAR and BOSHA, DAMOT, GAFAT, HADEYA, BIZAMO, THE COUNTRY OF THE GAMBOS, KONCH or KONTA, KAFA, and THE COUNTRIES OF THE DOBE'AS, SHINASHAS, and BALAYAS

GURAGE

The Report of João Bermudes

After Imam Ahmäd's defeat and death Emperor Gälawdéwos soon brought Guragé once more under imperial suzerainty. The province became a tributary state, and paid the monarch taxes, mainly in livestock, skins, and perhaps some gold. Data on these dues in the late 1540s is provided by Bermudes. He states, plausibly enough, that the annual tax from what he terms the "heathen province" of Guragé consisted of "one thousand live cows, and many skins of lions, leopards, and antelopes". Less credence can, however, be placed on the remainder of his account. He claims that the Guragés paid "every year two golden lions, three golden dogs, an ounce of gold, and some golden fowls with their chickens also of gold". The rare metal, he asserts, was "fine and good", and weighed as much as eight men could lift. His report of a tax of "six buffalo loads of impure silver" would also seem improbable, for the metal, as far as we know, was never mined in the area.

Bermudes goes on to observe that the Guragé country contained "much civet, sandal-wood, black wood, and amber". The population, he adds, included a number of "great wizards" who professed to foretell the future by studying the heart, liver, lungs and entrails of the animals they slaughtered. By their sorcery they made it appear that they were unaffected by fire. After ceremonially killing an ox they would anoint themselves with its fat, light a great fire, enter it, and seat themselves on a chair within it. Apparently sitting at ease they reportedly made prophecies and answered questions, without being burned.[1]

---

[1] Whiteway, (1902), pp. 231-2.

Särsä Dengel

Continued imperial control over Guragé was asserted during the reign of Särsä Dengel, who paid two visits to the area. The first was in 1570 on his return from an expedition to Hadeya, when he spent the rainy season in nearby Wäj. "All the men of Guragé", according to his chronicler, then prostrated themselves before him, and presented their tribute. Differing somewhat from that enumerated by Bermudes it consisted of mules, horses and agricultural produce, as well as wheat and honey. The second visit took place around 1578 when the Emperor waged war on and pillaged the area because its inhabitants were in rebellion. One of the clergy on that occasion is said to have found a *tabot* which Lebnä Dengel had abandoned in Kämbata during Imam Ahmäd's invasion two generations earlier.[2]

ENARYA

Enarya, doubtless because of its wealth, attracted the attention of Gälawdéwos early in his reign. Soon after the Imam's death he reasserted imperial power in nearby Hadeya, as well as in the neighbouring country then recently occupied by the Gallas, or Oromos. At the same time he despatched an army to Enarya where it encountered strong opposition. The expedition was most probably a failure. It is not mentioned in the chronicle of the time, whereas that of Särsä Dengel later admitted that many men died in the fighting.[3]

Gälawdéwos, angered by the intrigues and arrogance of his former Portuguese allies, is said to have despatched some of them to Enarya. Oral tradition collected in the late nineteenth century by the Italian Geographical Society suggests that two Portuguese soldiers, exiled by the monarch, established themselves there. One of them, by name Sigaro, reportedly settled in the north, near the town of Sakka; the other, Sapera, moved to the south, in an area later allegedly known after him as Sappa. The tradition, which can in no way be verified,

---

[2] Conti Rossini (1907), pp. 49, 76. For the Emperor's movements at this time see also Huntingford (1989), pp. 140-1.

[3] Conzelman (1895), p. 141; Conti Rossini (1907), p. 44.

claims that he was the founder of a dynasty from which subsequent rulers of Enarya were descended.[4]

Särsä Dengel, Sepenhi, Lä'äsonhi, and Bädancho's Conversion to Christianity

By Särsä Dengel's time Enarya had become an important tributary, which was ruled by a *shum*, or chief, called Sepenhi. The Emperor's chronicle states that the province had been paying taxes since the inception of his reign. A few years later, while on a journey to Damot in 1567-8, Särsä Dengel summoned Sepenhi, and ordered him to bring the expected tax. The chief complied, and arrived at a place called Däbänawi, in Damot, together with an army "as numerous as the sands of the sea". His tribute reportedly consisted of "a large quantity of gold" such as had never been paid by any of his predecessors. The Jesuits were informed that it amounted to 5,000 *wäqéts*, or ounces, though the normal tribute, according to Almeida, was not more than 1,500.[5]

Sepenhi's successor, Lä'äsonhi, reportedly wished to adopt Christianity, the religion of the empire, but the Emperor's Azzaj, or finance officer, it is claimed, refused to permit this. He did so, according to the chronicle, in the fear that the chief, if he became a Christian, would be allowed to pay less tribute. The tax officers were likewise reportedly afraid that if the country were converted they would be unable to purloin as much revenue as before. Their attitude shocked the chronicler. He complains that their love of riches had led them from the path of righteousness, and concludes that many of them, through their love of gold, had lost their souls.

Reluctance to convert peoples such as those of Enarya may have arisen also from a desire to retain them as "pagans", from whom it was considered permissible to take slaves. Such at least was the assertion of one of the Jesuits of the time, Gonçalo Rodrigues. Writing in 1556 about the unwillingness of Ethiopian Christians to convert animists, he observes in a letter (for the existence and translation of which we are indebted to Dr. Merid Wolde Aregay) that "persons who should well know" had "several times" told him that: "many of those pagans who border upon them [the Christians] and pay them tribute begged them many times that they make them

---

[4] Cecchi (1885-7), II, 157.
[5] Conti Rossini (1907), pp. 44, 180; Beckingham and Huntingford (1954), p. 85.

Christians and that, thus, they would happily continue to pay them their taxes. And they did not want to do so that they may continuously make their raids on them, which they do, and they take from them their children and wives and possessions. And they send them to the sea to be sold to the Turks and Moors, to whom those of this kingdom sell every year more than 10 or 12 thousand slaves, of whom they would not have been one person who would not have willingly become a Christian".

Särsä Dengel, was, however, now at last determined on converting the people of Enarya. Seeing no doubt the urgency of resisting the Oromo advance in the area, and having by then acquired a large number of Turkish fire-arms as well as many Turkish musketeers, he travelled to the territory in 1587, with the aim of introducing Lä'äsonhi's successor Bädancho to Christianity. Making his way towards Damot, the Emperor reached the country of the Mawas, where Bädancho prepared to receive him. On approaching the province the monarch sent the latter a message, saying, "If you become a Christian and renounce idolatry, which the Lord has forbidden, we will reduce your tribute". The chief replied that he would willingly convert, and rejoiced "because the Holy Spirit had inspired him with the desire to become a Christian".

The Emperor accordingly remitted half the annual tax. On that occasion he reminded Bädancho that the latter's father Lä'äsonhi had "loved the Christian religion", and had only refrained from Baptism because the time, as he put it diplomatically, had "not yet arrived". He then called on the Enarya ruler to be baptised, and thereby "show in action" what his father had "meditated in his heart". Further to persuade him he sent him scholars to preach the faith. Bädancho discussed the matter of conversion with his family and chiefs. They are said to have all agreed to change their religion. Speaking with one voice, they reportedly said to him, "Let it be as you have said to us!". They then informed the Emperor of their decision, declaring, "Let the wish of Our Saviour, and not our own will, be done!"

Särsä Dengel, who, as we shall see, had earlier attempted to convert the Gafat people of Shat, thereupon carried out the mass conversion of Enarya. His action in Enarya, the chronicle claims, was far more successful than in Shat. Whereas the inhabitants of the latter continued to flirt with their old idols, and despised their Baptism, those of Enarya accepted conversion with "all their hearts", and remained true to the Orthodox faith.

Detail of the map entitled *Les Pays de l'Ocean Indien,* published by Hughes de Linschoten at the Hague in 1599.
Note the omission of the highland provinces of Tegray and Bägémder, the location of Angot too far to the south, and the listing of peripheral provinces, notably Adäl (Adel), Däwaro (Doara), Fätägar (Fatigar) placed too far to the south-west, and the land of the Dobe'as (Dobas) and Dänakil (Dangali). See also the ports of Massawa (Mazuam), Hergigo (Arquiqo) and Zäyl'ä (Zeyla).

Bädancho, who is described in the royal chronicle as wise, prudent and intelligent, was the first of his people to be baptised. Särsä Dengel became his godfather, saying to him, in accordance with age-old Christian tradition, "You are my son, and I am your father". The chief was renamed Zä-Maryam, after which the Emperor dressed him in magnificent clothes, one of the finest of which was a red robe decorated with gold. He placed a diadem on his head and a cross with a golden chain round his neck. He then ordered his principal churchmen to baptise Bädancho's chiefs. The nobles in his entourage were told to become the spiritual fathers of the chiefs, and to present them with fine tunics, shirts and other costumes. The remainder of the population, old and young - men, women and children - were then baptised. No one, the chronicler says, knew their total number.

The converts were so numerous, we are told, that the priests were unable to baptise them all in the usual manner by putting their hands on the heads of the converts. Instead many people rushed into the water, and baptised themselves, without the aid of any priest. Bädancho's concubine became the godchild of one of the principal women of Särsä Dengel's court, Ité Wälätto. Referred to as the Emperor's mother, she gave the royal Enarya lady a piece of beautiful jewellery.

After everyone present had been converted, another chief arrived with seven thousand more men. Särsä Dengel ordered that he, too, should be baptised. The chief and the men, women and children accompanying him, thereupon accepted the new faith.

Conversions continued for two full days, after which Särsä Dengel gave a great banquet for Bädancho and his chiefs. On that occasion the Emperor had tables prepared for the ruler of Enarya and all the chiefs dependent on him, each with their special, or local, dishes. Calves and bulls were slaughtered, and the people of Enarya spent the day in great joy, eating and drinking to their hearts' content. On the morrow the Emperor called Bädancho, and gave him instructions for the observance of the Sabbath and other festivals, as well as for the implementation of all the laws of Christianity. He gave the chief a scholar to guide him in matters of the faith, and priests and deacons to conduct church services. He also ordered the Baptism of anyone not yet converted, among them those, who, on account of illness or weakness, had not reached the capital.

Särsä Dengel, as expected, then remitted half the province's tribute, amounting to three thousand ounces of gold, and commanded Bädancho to build a church. Not content with obeying this order the latter instructed his subjects to erect Christian places of worship in all their villages.

After this Särsä Dengel ordered Bädancho to stop all "pagan" practices. Foremost among these, according to the chronicle, was sacrifice to the *erawya*, or vulture. Hitherto the chief, it is said, had gone into the countryside every week to slaughter a calf or fattened ox, which he would cut into pieces, and offer with outstretched hands to the birds. Bädancho was likewise told to abandon the custom of fortune-telling by *martänas*, or soothsayers, as well as other forms of idolatry.[6]

Despite the enthusiasm reported in the text the act of conversion does not seem to have been fully successful. Another chronicle states that in 1596, almost at the end of his reign, Särsä Dengel made his way again to Enarya to "introduce Christianity". He never returned from this expedition: for he died shortly afterwards.[7]

Enarya remained, as of old, an essentially animist territory.

WAGAM, GUMAR and BOSHA

After the rains of 1549 Emperor Gälawdéwos, according to his chronicle, undertook an expedition to the districts of Wägäm and Gumär, which were situated to the north-west of Guragé. The inhabitants of the two territories were allies. Wägäm was speedily occupied by the monarch's men, but Gümar is said to have succumbed only after three months' fighting.

Gälawdéwos was also reported, in the subsequent chronicle of Särsä Dengel, to have undertaken an expedition to Bosha. The modern scholar W.J. Lange believes that this operation was in fact the same as that earlier referred to as the Gümar expedition. Be that as it may the campaign, to judge from the subsequent chronicle, seems to have been a failure.[8]

A later, and more successful, expedition to Bosha was carried out by Särsä Dengel shortly after his assumption of power. He evidently established imperial control in the province, for his chronicle states that he received taxes from the territory, as well as from nearby Enarya, from the beginning of his reign. Later, when travelling to Guragé in 1565, he invited the ruler of Bosha to visit him there, and converted him to Christianity. On that occasion he presented him with magnificent jewels, and baptised him with the name of Giyorgis. He

---

[6] Conti Rossini (1907), pp. 136-44, 180-3; Merid Wolde Aregay (1971), p. 104.. See also Basset (1881), p. 111. See also Budge (1828b), II, 368-9.
[7] Béguinot (1901), p. 39; Huntingford (1989), p. 149.
[8] Conzelman (1895), pp. 154-5; Conti Rossini (1907), pp. 45, 177; Lange (1982), p.54.

also gave him a spiritual father, Abba Abib, to instruct him in the faith, and convert his people. The chief then returned to his country.[9] How successful this conversion was is not recorded.

DAMOT

Report of João Bermudes

After Imam Ahmäd's defeat Emperor Gälawdéwos, angered, as we have seen, by the arrogant behaviour of this former allies, the Portuguese, banished Bermudes for a time to Gafat. There the prelate had the opportunity to gather information on nearby Damot.

The province, he says, lay on the bank of the Blue Nile, and was "surrounded" by it rather than "on either side of it", for the river made "many and considerable bends" throughout the area. The approach to Damot was thus "most difficult", on account of its "rugged crags". The area, he claimed, was well fortified by passes "made artificially in rocks bored by a crowbar, and closed by gates guarded by armed men". Even a small force could thus prevent the entry of armies attempting to pass without permission, though on the Emperor's arrival these gates were opened to all who desired to enter.

Damot, according to Bermudes, was a large kingdom, with several subordinate provinces. The entire territory was "well supplied" by nature. The area near the Nile, which had many hills and streams, was particularly fertile. The territory as a whole had "great stores" of gold, and was the abode of numerous animals, They included elephant, lion, leopard, and other wild beasts unknown in Europe, besides "a kind of unicorn" (perhaps an okapi?), which was "wild and timid, of the shape of a horse and the size of an ass". There were also "strange and poisonous serpents". As for livestock, the inhabitants bred cattle, horses, buffaloes, mules, asses, and sheep. The cattle were larger than those of Portugal, some indeed "almost as large as elephants". They had "huge horns", which were used to make jars for the transportation and storage of both water and wine. Though the inhabitants of some provinces were still "pagans" Bermudes claimed, probably with exaggeration, that the "chief part" of the population was by then Christian.[10]

---

[9] Conti Rossini (1907), pp. 44, 145, 180. See also Beckingham and Huntingford (1954), p. 124.
[10] Whiteway (1902), pp. 234-8

Gälawdéwos's Re-assertion of Sovereignty

In Damot, as in many other parts of the country, imperial authority had been destroyed by the Imam, but was speedily re-asserted by Gälawdéwos. He undertook a six-month expedition to the frontiers of the province in 1548. The campaign, according to the chronicle, was directed against "peoples who did not worship God", and had not submitted to the monarch. Fighting resulted in the capture of many slaves. The object, as Wallis Budge sees it, was not so much conquest, as to punish "pagans".[11]

Gälawdéwos returned to Damot a decade or so later, and it was there, in 1555, that he issued perhaps the most important religious document of his reign. This was his famous *Confession of Faith*, which defined the main principles of Ethiopian Orthodox Christianity, and sought to defend it from the attacks of the Catholics.[12]

Särsä Dengel's Expeditions to the South

Later in the century Särsä Dengel also enjoyed close ties with Damot, where he resided on several occasions. Early in his reign the province was ruled by a governor called Azmach Täklo, who was involved in a plot, but later helped to strengthen his master's authority in the area.

The Emperor returned to the province a few years later, after the rainy season of 1567, when he received Sepenhi, ruler of Enarya, before proceeding to Bädel Neb where he spent the ensuing rains.[13]

Learning in 1572 that the Oromos had gained possession of Wäj, the Emperor sent messages to Täklä Giyorgis, a later governor of Damot, and other provincial rulers, ordering them to confront the intruders. In the following year he returned to Damot, where he passed the rains of 1574. He received a considerable amount of gold as tribute, but his soldiers also seized cattle, and reduced men and women to slavery. Later, in 1577, he again travelled towards Damot, and spent the rainy season at Abäjägay or Zähon Dur, conceivably the Dähondur where Lebnä Dengel had earlier been attacked by Imam Ahmäd.[14]

---

[11] Conzelman (1895), pp. 144-5; Budge (1928b), II, 342.
[12] Budge (1928b), II, 356.
[13] Conti Rossini (1907), pp. 14, 19, 21, 25-7, 34-6, 43-4.
[14] Conti Rossini (1907), pp. 51-2, 60; Huntingford (1989), pp 140-3, 149.

The South-West and West

Detail form Gérard Mercator's map *Abyssinoum sive Preciosi Johannis Imperium,* published in 1607.
Note the location of the provinces of the interior, Tegray (Tigremaon), Amhara (Amara) and Shäwa (Xoa), all three much too far to the south and west, also "Beliguanze", a confusion between Bali and Gänz. See also indication of various peripheral provinces, notably the Country of the Bahr Nagash (Bahrnagas) placed too far to the west, Adäl (Adel), Bali (Balli), Fätägar (Fatagar) and the country of the Danakil (Dangali), both placed too far south, also the countries of the Dobe'as (Dobas), and Agäws (Agoas populi), and the ports of Massawa (Masuam P.), Hergigo (Arquiqo), and Zäylä' (Zeila).

Damot, which continued to be administered for the monarch by a governor with the title of Sähafä Lahm, also provided troops for Särsä Dengel's army. Soldiers from the province thus participated in the

1588 campaign against the Turks at Massawa, who were then, as we have seen in Chapter 20, making inroads in the northern coastal areas.[15]

After his second expedition to Enarya, which took place almost a decade later, the Emperor planned a further visit to Medra Damot 'Abiy, i.e. the Land of Great Damot, in 1597. The monks advised him against entering the country of the Mächa Oromos, who were by then in occupation of the area, but he insisted on going. He was reportedly warned not to eat fish, but forgetting this advice, ate some, and at once fell ill. He had to be carried on a litter, but died without returning home.[16]

GAFAT

Gälawdéwos

Gafat was well known to Gälawdéwos, who had found refuge in the province during Imam Ahmäd's ascendancy, and later returned there in 1548-9. He proceeded to the borders of Damot, and made war, according to Bermudes, on "the people who did not worship God" and had "not submitted to his anointed", i.e. himself. This campaign was carried out because the Gafats had been in rebellion since Lebnä Dengel's death, and had refused to pay Gälawdéwos their tribute, or to recognise him as their master.

On the arrival of his army the Gafats gathered together, and one morning at dawn suddenly attacked the imperial camp, inflicting many casualties. A group of Portuguese near the monarch's tent heard the noise, and, being well armed, easily drove the Gafats away, killing several of them. The Portuguese then pursued the fugitives to their villages, where they found "much booty", with which they returned "rich and content". The loot included *basutos*, or "very fine quilts", and cotton cloths so delicate that "a piece of thirty or forty ells could be held between the hands". The visitors also seized "much gold", which was stored in pots and vessels, and buried for secrecy under the heaths of the huts. The Gafats showed it to the Portuguese "to escape death" .

Gälawdéwos did not remain long in the province, Bermudes reports, because he did not want to do the Gafats "great damage", but

---

[15] Conti Rossini (1907), pp. 51, 67, 95, 150.
[16] Huntingford (1989), p. 149.

wished "merely to frighten them". The rainy season was moreover drawing near, and he felt it necessary to return home before the flooding of the rivers brought travel to a halt. This was an important consideration, for the "winter" there was "very rainy", and the lands so mountainous that the rivers collected much water, and swelled exceedingly.[17]

The Detention, and Evidence, of Bermudes

The Emperor, irritated, as we have seen, with Bermudes also temporarily banished him to Gafat, which the prelate was therefore able to describe in some detail. The territory, he reports, was "tributary and subordinate to the Ethiopian empire", and consisted more or less, as Alvares had earlier suggested, of "lofty and precipitous mountains".

Bermudes, who was conducted to Gafat by one of the Emperor's officers, recalls that after crossing mountain ranges they descended into a large valley, "so deep that it seemed as if we were going into hell". The hills by contrast were so high that they appeared to "touch the heavens".

On banishing Bermudes to the province, Gälawdéwos had ordered him to live on its income, which, he said, he had himself done during his earlier exile there. The official accompanying the prelate accordingly instructed the country's "chief people" to assemble and ordered them to consider the visitor as their lord, and to pay him their rents, but at the same time to guard him strictly, and prevent him from leaving that place or returning to the court of the King.

The Gafats struck Bermudes as a "very barbarous" and "evil" people, who were both "rebellious and turbulent", and "commonly" thought to be Jews. Many Gafats, he says, were reputedly "scattered" over "other provinces". They were everywhere "considered strangers", who were "different" from, and "abhorred" by, the rest of the population. In their own province they were, however, lords of the country, for it was inhabited by no other people. The only exception were "a few" Ethiopian Christians who had become Catholics, and, evidently exiled there like him, declared themselves still adherents of the Church of Rome.

Despite his first trepidation at entering a valley resembling his image of Hell, Bermudes recognised that Gafat was favoured by

---

[17] Conzelman (1895), p. 144; Whiteway (1902), pp. 233-4.

nature. It had "much land", and "wide and fertile plains", was "rich with gold", and had some "good articles of merchandise, especially fine cotton cloths".[18]

Gälawdéwos returned to Gafat in 1551-2. There he fought against what his chronicle describes as the "pagan" peoples of the Gämbo area. These, as we have seen, were probably the people who had outwitted his father Lebnä Dengel's kinsman Dahragot. Gälawdéwos reportedly, as we shall see, won a great victory, whereupon the Gämbos and their neighbours submitted. He reduced some to slavery, and imposed taxes on others.[19]

Särsä Dengel's Attempt at Conversion

The Gafats are later mentioned in Särsä Dengel's chronicle, which records that their principal diet was the *hensät*, or *ensete*, i.e. false banana. The text recalls that in 1563, at the beginning of the reign, the monarch's brothers, when crossing the Blue Nile (or, according to Huntingford, one of its tributaries), were guided by people of the province. This was "surprising", the chronicler felt, as many of the inhabitants were "thieves", accustomed to "kill all travellers, sparing neither the old nor the young".

In the following year one of the Emperor's chiefs, a sometime rebel called Azmach Täklo who was then in Damot, sent the monarch a Gafat notable to welcome him, and conduct him to the province. Not long afterwards, in 1566 or 1567, Särsä Dengel came into conflict, however, with the Gafats of Béräbabo, who had supported another rebel called Fasilo. Särsä Dengel made war on them, killed many of their soldiers, after which, as was customary, he destroyed the grain of the defeated populace, and reduced their women and children to slavery.[20]

Särsä Dengel's main contact with the Gafats took place, however, two decades later, in 1585, when he attempted the large-scale conversion of much of the south-west. Before undertaking his already mentioned expedition to convert Enarya, he made his way to the Gafat territory of Shat. Its people tried to resist, but were defeated. The survivors, who showed no desire to be converted, prostrated themselves before the Emperor, and submitted, crying, according to

---

[18] Whiteway (1902), pp. lxxiv, 216-18, 232-3.
[19] Conzelman (1895), pp. 151, 154.
[20] Conti Rossini (1907), pp. 14, 26, 43, 160. See also Budge (1928b), II, 362.

the chronicle, "Master, forgive us our sins and our crimes!". The "long-suffering and merciful" monarch, as the text describes him, thereupon "pardoned their crimes", on condition that they accepted Christian Baptism. The Gafats hastened to agree, because they were "terrified" of the monarch, and knew that conflict with him had already led to the death of many of their most powerful warriors.

After this enforced Baptism the Emperor allocated the Gafats a bishop, priests and deacons. The conversion was not, however, successful. The "wickedness" of the Gafats, as the chronicle puts it, had not left them. They therefore soon returned to their old ways, "lusting after their idols", and "despising" their Holy Baptism". The priests, seeing that their congregation had abandoned the Orthodox faith, and wanted to return to "paganism", feared for their safety, and accordingly fled Gafat by stealth. They made their way to Damot, where they found a town in which their faith was established, and installed themselves there. The conversion of Shat, based on force, thus proved abortive.[21]

A few years later, around 1591, Särsä Dengel, angered by his failure with the Shat, carried out a further expedition to Gafat. This took him to Wämbärya, whose population, according to the chronicle, "did not know the Lord", and "did not pay tribute to the king". After a seven day march his army reached the territory, without the knowledge of the Gafats, and immediately attacked them, and burnt down many of their houses.

Särsä Dengel announced that he would spend the rainy season in the area. This alarmed many of his men whose only desire was to return to their wives and children. Other soldiers, however, preferred to remain in the area in the hope of obtaining booty. On the following day the monarch ordered his commanders with their troops to loot the country from one end to the other. They seized so much that each man is said to have rejoiced for a week. The Emperor then chose a nearby open space, where he and his men set up their camp for the rainy season.

A month or so later, however, his advisers, who because of their investigation of royal affairs were known as the King's Thousand Ears and Thousand Eyes, held a meeting at which they decided after much deliberation that it was inadvisable to spend the rains in either Gafat or Damot. They accordingly advised their master against remaining in

---

[21] Conti Rossini (1907), pp. 136-7. See also Budge (1928b), II, 369.

Wämbärya. The Emperor, who was accustomed, as his chronicler claims, to follow good advice, readily agreed.

The Gafats, obviously much pleased at the army's imminent departure, paid nominal homage to the monarch, and declared that the looting he had carried out would be their punishment. They reportedly begged him to pardon them. Särsä Dengel, we are told, graciously did so, warning them not to "sin" again, lest they receive worse punishment. He then left, never to return.[22]

HADEYA
Gälawdéwos

After Imam Ahmäd's death Emperor Gälawdéwos carried out an expedition to Hadeya, where he overcame local opposition. He then appointed a governor over the territory, which was thus once more brought under imperial sovereignty.[23]

Azé and Särsä Dengel

Later in the century the Hadeya ruler, a chief called Azé, joined, together with several other nobles, in a conspiracy against Emperor Särsä Dengel. The monarch bided his time, until 1568 when he marched to Wäj to prepare an expedition to Hadeya. On entering the territory he waited for two weeks, in the hope that Azé would bring the province's traditional tribute. The wily governor, however, kept on making promises, but had, the chronicle says, no intention of carrying them out for he had decided to rebel. He was reportedly in confident mood, as he had 5,000 well-armed Maläsäy, or Muslim, cavalry, possibly a legacy of Imam Ahmäd's time, besides 1,700 other horsemen and "innumerable" infantry.

Särsä Dengel, realising Azé's intentions, marched against the Hadeya army. A fierce engagement followed, in which, it is claimed, none of the Emperor's soldiers killed less than two or three of the rebel chief's soldiers. The battlefield was soon covered with corpses. Azé and his soldiers thereupon fled "like smoke before the wind". They were pursued by Särsä Dengel's forces, who killed many of them, and captured no less than three hundred horses.

Undeterred, Azé and the survivors of his army regrouped, whereupon Särsä Dengel ordered his soldiers, under the command of

---

[22] Conti Rossini (1907), pp. 176-8.
[23] Conzelman (1895), p. 141.

the governor of Damot, Sähafä Te'ezaz Täklä Giyorgis, to launch a further attack. This resulted in a second battle in which the chief's army was reportedly all killed, whereas the Emperor's men, it is claimed, suffered not a single casualty. Azé, however, once more escaped. The Hadeya nobles then made their submission, and brought Särsä Dengel many presents. He spent the rainy season of 1569 in the territory. During this time Azé, too, finally surrendered, and received royal pardon.

Before leaving, Särsä Dengel appointed Täklä Giyorgis as Däjazmach and governor of Hadeya, and entrusted him with collecting the province's tribute. A conflict, however, between him and Azé soon arose. The latter, who allegedly persevered in his wickedness, was killed, and his severed head sent to the monarch.[24]

In the following decade Muhammäd, the Amir of Adäl, rebelled, as we have seen in Chapter 21, against imperial rule. He marched to Hadeya, where he received the support of the province's ruler, Gärad Jafer, who was however killed in the ensuing fighting. The Amir remained for some time in Hadeya, during which his men engaged in considerable looting. They thereby incurred the wrath of the local peasantry, who harassed them, and later captured him. He was handed over to the Emperor, whose nobles had him executed, together with a number of his chiefs. Resistance to Muhammäd was led by the aforesaid Täklä Giyorgis, who, the chronicle claims, thereby won much glory.[25]

After the conflict with Adäl an attempt was made to re-establish the earlier dynastic alliance between the Hadeya and imperial rulers. Emperor Ya'qob (1597-1604, 1604-1606) took the daughter of Hadeya king as his wife, but he died, according to Almeida, before the wedding ceremony.[26]

BIZAMO

Särsä Dengel's southern expeditions took him twice to Bizamo, which, as we have seen, had been part of the empire in medieval times. He spent the rainy season of 1573 there, and later passed through the territory on his last fatal journey to the south.[27]

---

[24] Conti Rossini (1907), pp. 28-9, 46-9.
[25] Conti Rossini (1907), pp. 57-9, 67.
[26] Beckingham and Huntingford, (1954), p. 69.
[27] Conti Rossini (1907), pp. 52, 64, 160; Huntingford (1989), pp. 141, 143, 149-50.

THE COUNTRY OF THE GAMBOS

Särsä Dengel travelled to the country of the Gämbos, in 1590. He marched there, according to his chronicle, to avenge the blood of Christians whom the Gämbos had killed. He established his camp in the area, after which his soldiers looted the countryside, as was their custom, and captured a large booty of slaves. Much fighting followed, but the Gämbos, as the chronicle claims, soon learnt that an attack by them on Särsä Dengel's army was like an attack by a cow on a lion, or that of a sheep against a wolf. They then retired to an *amba*, or flat-topped mountain, from which they hurled rocks on the Emperor's men below.

Not long afterwards the defenders determined to make peace. They sent a messenger to Abba Abreham, head of Däbrä Libanos monastery, asking him to help them to do so. The prelate duly accomplished this task, after which the Emperor informed the Gämbos that they could come down in safety. This they did, men, women and children, only to be attacked by the Emperor's camp soldiers, who seized them all as slaves. Särsä Dengel, furious at what the chronicle calls this act of "treason", sent his cavalry against the rebellious soldiers, and obliged them to release all the Gämbo slaves they had taken.[28]

KONCH or KONTA

Koncha, or Konta, lay immediately to the east of Käfa. The territory, according to Bermudes, was normally "subordinate" to nearby Damot, but in his day was "in rebellion". The population was "pagan", and ruled by a chief called the "Ax Gagce" (?), who had on one occasion brought Emperor GälawdÈwos "a large amount of gold" and "many slaves, mules, and asses for transport". This chief, he says, could put into the field ten thousand cavalry and twenty thousand foot soldiers. His army would then be serviced by a thousand hand mills worked by women.

Gälawdéwos, according to Bermudes, had converted the local ruler to Christianity, the Abbot of Däbrä Libanos baptising him as André, presumably Endreyas.[29]

---

[28] Conti Rossini (1907), pp. 157-9.
[29] Whiteway (1902), pp. 236-40.

Särsä Dengel later marched towards the province. On reaching the Zibé, or Gibé, River in 1566 he received a loyal welcome from the *Qas*, or local ruler, who seated him on a fine carpeted bed, and presented his men with large quantities of cattle and *täj*, or honey wine, and their horses with abundant fodder.[30]

KAFA

Käfa, west of Konch, remained an independent state throughout this period, but was not entirely isolated from outside contacts. Oral traditions, first collected by Bruce, suggest that Särsä Dengel's expedition to nearby Bosha led to the limited penetration of Christianity into the province. Local rulers of this time included the "Bonga king", presumably a monarch at Bonga, who reigned between about 1565 and 1605. He was in turn succeeded by Tato Giba Nechocho, who was succeeded around 1640 by Tato Gali Gafocho.

Bonga is said to have been the capital for many years, and maintained its importance even after the later establishment of a new capital at nearby Andaracha.[31]

THE COUNTRIES OF THE DOBE'AS, SHINASHAS, and BALAYAS

Fighting between the empire and the "blacks" on its western and northern borderlands was resumed by Emperor Minas, who raided the Dobe'as in 1562, as his chronicle notes, to seize the cattle for which they had long been famous.[32]

His successor Särsa Dengel, who was better armed than his predecessors, later undertook an expedition against several peoples of the western border. One of them the Shinashas, according to the Jesuit patriarch André de Oviedo, begged a relation of the Emperor to stop raiding their country, and instead to give them priests, so that they could adopt Christianity. Särsä Dengel and his friends seem, however,

---

30 Conti Rossini (1907), pp. 38-9.
31 Cecchi (1885-7), II, 490; Bieber (1920-3), II, 494-533; Grühl (1932), pp. 178, 224; Beckingham and Huntingford (1954), pp. lviii-lix; Huntingford (1955), p. 105. Bruce (1790), II, 313, believed, incorrectly, that Käfa had been entirely converted to Christianity by Särsä Dengel.
32 Basset (1881), II, 110; Esteves Pereira (1888), p. 51; Bruce (1790), II, 211.

to have failed to do so, apparently because they preferred to continue with their slave raiding expeditions.[33]

The Emperor later carried out an expedition against the Bäläyas in 1587. They are referred to in his chronicle as *agbert* (singular *gäber*), the Ge'ez term for slave, implying that they were a people from whom slaves were being taken, or from whom it was considered permissible to seize them. The text, which reveals the prejudice with which they then were regarded by their neighbours, claims that they were "entirely different from other men". They were, it adds, large and strong, went around "entirely naked, like animals, anointed their face and body with mud", and, avoiding combat at close quarters, made use of bows and arrows.

As for the campaign itself the chronicle, our sole source of information on it, states that the Emperor wished to attack the Bäläyas, who had never been successfully raided by either kings or governors. Learning from the old men of Dämbeya how Imam Ahmäd's attempt to occupy the area half a century earlier had failed he is said to have placed his faith in his Saviour, which was all the easier in that he had a strong and well equipped army. Camping by a great river, perhaps the Täkkäzé, he advanced into the torrid lowlands, where he captured a certain amount of booty, though this, according to the chronicle, included only a small number of slaves, and neither horses nor mules.

The defeated Agberts then came, carrying stones on their heads as a sign of submission, after which he fixed their annual tax, before making his way to Achäfär to supervise the distribution of the booty he had taken.[34]

---

[33] Beccari (1903-17), V, 437.
[34] Conti Rossini (1907), pp. 174-5.

Chapter 23
THE BORDERLANDS AND THE INTERIOR

The period after the death of Imam Ahmäd in 1543 witnessed Emperor Gälawdéwos's rapid re-establishment of imperial rule throughout much of the country. The consequences were felt in the militarily much contested east and north, as well as in the rich south-west. Control of several of these territories was later consolidated by Gälawdéwos's nephew Särsä Dengel. Both monarchs enjoyed considerable military strength: the former on account of Portuguese assistance despatched during his struggle against the Imam; the latter as a result of his defeat of the Turks, from whom he captured many cannon and rifles, and obtained musketeers to fight in his army.

The North

Important changes took place in the far north. After Ahmäd's death Gälawdéwos rapidly re-established control over the country of the Bahr Nägash, where he renewed Zär'a Ya'qob's old land charter to Däbrä Bizän monastery, and banished some of his former Portuguese allies to the provincial capital, Debarwa.

The situation on the coast was transformed, to the Emperor's disadvantage, when the Ottoman Turks seized the port of Massawa in 1557. Turkish troops later forced their way inland as far as Däbrä Damo, but were resisted by the local highland peasantry. Many of the latter had by then access to fire-arms, and, it is said, killed one of the invaders' generals. The peasants' participation in the struggle is recognised in Särsä Dengel's chronicle, and is the more interesting in that historical works of this genre normally attribute successes almost exclusively to the reigning monarch.

The Turks later occupied the Bahr Nägash's capital, Debarwa, where their commander, Ozdemür Pasha, erected a fort. Having advanced further into the interior, and, enjoying the support of Gä'ewah, Queen of Säläwa, he proceeded to the Mäzäga lowlands, only to succumb to fever. The Turkish expeditionary force, faced with strong local opposition, was obliged to retreat, after which its garrison at Debarwa surrendered to the local population.

Yeshaq, one of Gälawdéwos's courtiers who served as Bahr Nägash, became so powerful, largely on account of the import of fire-arms through the coast, that, though a ruler of the periphery, he involved himself actively in central state affairs. After Emperor Minas's accession he conspired to place first one of the monarch's nephews, Täzkäro, and then another, Marqos, on the throne. Frustrated in these efforts, and defeated by the Emperor in battle, he threw in his lot with the Turks to whom he surrendered the fort of Debarwa. This enabled him to continue his rebellion.

Särsä Dengel attempted to make peace with Yeshaq, who presented him with prize horses, fine imported cloth, and carpets, the traditional taxes of his fiefdom. Conflict between the two men, however, soon erupted, and Yeshaq was eventually killed in battle in 1576. Särsä Dengel proceeded to capture Debarwa, where he seized a large quantity of Turkish fire-arms, obtained the services of many Turkish riflemen, and destroyed the fort. This victory was of major importance, for as a result of it the warlike emperor gained military superiority over almost everyone with whom he did battle, and made his power felt virtually throughout the region.

Angered by what he considered Yeshaq's treachery Särsä Dengel reduced the Bahr Nägash's status, which was never thereafter fully reinstated. 'Aquba Mika'él, a local leader who had fought valiantly against the Turks, was nevertheless accorded the rank of Bahr Nägash, and, because of his loyalty, was given the special additional title of Son of the King. The Turks, realising the impossibility of conquering the area, entrusted the port of Hergigo to a local Beja chief.

Imam Muhammäd ibn Gasa of Adäl, wishing to escape from Oromo pressure, which was beginning to be felt in the area, meanwhile abandoned Harär. He established himself at a new capital, Awssa, in the Afar desert in 1577. This move was regarded with disfavour by the neighbouring Afars, who began attacking Adäl caravans travelling between the new capital and the coast.

The East and South

After Imam Ahmäd's death Gälawdéwos attempted to regain control over the eastern provinces, but, largely because of their strength in fire-arms, was far from successful. He established his presence for a time in Däwaro, but failed in the territories further east, notably in Adäl, where he was later to die in battle.

Däwaro, because of its south-easterly location, was of considerable strategic importance *vis-à-vis* both Adäl to the east and the Oromos, who were then beginning to advance from the south.

Probably for this reason Gälawdéwos chose the province as a place of banishment for the Portuguese prelate Bermudes and a number of the latter's military companions, who, though exiled, served as a kind of frontier garrison. The Indian "mulatto" Ayres Dias, alias Marqos, was reportedly made governor of the province and nearby Bali. He was succeeded by Khalid, a Muslim convert from Christianity. Khalid, who was also ruler of Bali, staged a rebellion, but was defeated and killed by these Portuguese.

At around this time Gälawdéwos travelled to Däwaro where he built a palace. The territory was, however, later invaded by forces from Adäl. They were defeated by the local governor, whose soldiers captured the Adäl ruler's brother Wäraba Got, and Bati Del Wänbärä's son Ali Gärad. The Emperor then appointed Fanu'él, one of his commanders, as governor of the province.

The peace thus established turned out to be only temporary. Imam Ahmäd's nephew Amir Nur ibn al-Wazir Mujahid, now married to the late Imam Mähfuz's symbolically important daughter Bati Del Wänbärä, shortly afterwards invaded Fätägar with a remarkably well-armed force. Gälawdéwos rushed to confront him, but was shortly afterwards killed in battle.

Wäj was the site of a major battle between Gälawdéwos and Vizier Abbas. The latter was killed in battle, after which the Emperor established an exceedingly fine palace and irrigated garden in the area. The province maintained its importance under Särsä Dengel, who visited it twice, and used it as a place of detention for the Fälasha leader Rädét.

In Harär, meanwhile, Ahmäd's defeat had led to momentous developments. The city's records, which are not confirmed from imperial sources, state that shortly after the Imam's death Christian troops led by Fanu'él succeeded in entering the city, but were repulsed. They are said to have again broken in during the time of the afore-said Nur who revived the earlier struggle against the Christian empire. Gälawdéwos's troops, under the command of Hamälmäl reportedly entered the city in 1559, where the Emperor, who broke into it shortly afterwards, died, as we have seen, in battle. His death put an end to the war. There followed, however, a famine of unparalleled proportions which devastated the town's inhabitants.

The death of Gälawdéwos was a turning point in Ethiopia's overall history. His brother and successor, Minas, abandoned the Shäwan state's centuries old interest in the trade routes to the east, and established his capital at Emfraz, north-east of Lake Tana, after which the Christian empire looked north and west for its all-important import-export trade.

Adäl, too, was involved in a major conflict with the Christian empire. It is said to have begun by an unnamed ruler, whom Gälawdéwos killed in battle, but later erupted during Särsä Dengel's reign, when the territory's ruler, Amir Muhammäd, killed the leaders of all Muslim groups friendly to the empire. He then advanced to Hadeya, where he gained the support of its ruler Jafer. Emperor and Amir fought inconclusively, but Jafer was killed. Muhammäd subsequently pillaged the territory, and the inhabitants responded by seizing him, and handing him over to the Emperor for execution.

In the south Bali was placed under the rule of Gälawdéwos's "mulatto" protegé Ayres Dias, and was later controlled by the aforesaid Muslim convert Khalid. The province later contributed soldiers for Särsä Dengel's army, but 'Ali, one of its rulers, while serving in the north, supported the Turks, and was executed.

The South-West and West

Gälawdéwos's accession to power had considerable repercussions in the south-west, in Guragé, Enarya, Wägäm, Gumär, Bosha, Gafat, Damot, Hadeya and elsewhere. Most of these territories were poorly armed, and therefore no match for the well equipped soldiers of the empire. They were, however, still major sources of tribute, which in some areas was very largely paid in gold.

Guragé, which was reportedly still largely "pagan", or animist, became once more a tributary province. According to Bermudes it provided Gälawdéwos with a thousand cattle a year, as well as many lion, leopard and other animal skins. Contacts with the central state were strengthened by Särsä Dengel, who paid the province two visits. In the first, in 1570, he collected the taxes, which included mules, horses, wheat and honey. The second visit, in 1578, was prompted by a rebellion, and was followed by looting on the part of the Emperor's soldiers.

Enarya, because of its wealth in gold, was of major interest to Gälawdéwos. Early in his reign he despatched an expedition to the province, but his forces were repulsed. His sovereignty was later restored, and he used the territory as a place of exile for Portuguese troops who had earlier served in the struggle against Imam Ahmäd.

Tradition holds that one of them, by name Sapera, founded a provincial dynasty.

Within only a decade the province had become an important tributary ruled by a governor called Sepenhi, whom Särsä Dengel summoned to his presence in 1567-8. The chief came with a vast amount of gold said to comprise no less than 5,000 *wäqét,* or ounces, whereas the area's usual tribute was only 1,500.

Sepenhi's successor, Lä'äsonhi, apparently wished to adopt Christianity, but was discouraged by the Emperor's courtiers. They reportedly feared that conversion would lead to a remission of taxes. The presumption was that adherents of other faiths, as under Imam Ahmäd's rule, had to pay a substantially higher tax than that applied to members of the dominant religion. There are, however, indications that conversion was opposed by some who feared that it would have brought an end to slave-raiding.

Särsä Dengel, armed with weapons captured from the Turks, and aware of the growing Oromo pressure in the area, travelled to Enarya in 1587 to encourage the conversion of Lä'äsonhi's successor Bädancho. The latter accepted the new religion enthusiastically, and was baptised with the name Zä-Maryam. His people followed suit, churches were constructed, and "pagan" practices outlawed. Särsä Dengel, as anticipated, then reduced Enarya's tribute. Despite this concession the introduction of Christianity was not as successful as the Emperor had hoped. He had to undertake a second expedition in 1597, but died immediately afterwards, apparently of food poisoning.

Wägäm, Gumär and Bosha likewise attracted the attention of Emperor Gälawdéwos. He despatched an unsuccessful expedition to the area. Särsä Dengel also subsequently travelled to Bosha, and later gained control of it, after which it paid him taxes. He subsequently summoned its ruler to Guragé, where he was baptised with the name of Giyorgis.

Damot was also brought under imperial control by Gälawdéwos, who carried out an expedition to its frontier in 1548, and returned to the province in 1555. It was on that occasion that he issued his famous religious testimony, the *Confession of Faith* to rebut Catholic criticism of the Orthodox faith.

Särsä Dengel also visited Damot on several occasions. Soldiers from the province served in his army, and were engaged for example in fighting against the Oromos in Wäj in 1572. On a subsequent visit to Damot in 1574 he received a large amount of gold as tribute, but also seized many cattle and slaves. The province was then ruled on his behalf by a governor with the title of *Sähafä Lahm*, or Writer of Cattle, i.e. livestock paid as tribute. He planned a further expedition to Damot in 1597, but died before he could accomplish it.

Gafat, too, was restored to imperial rule by Gälawdéwos. He conducted a major expedition to the Gämbo area, whose inhabitants submitted to him, and agreed to pay him taxes. He also used the province as a place of exile for Bermudes, who reported that the territory was rich in gold and cotton cloths. The monarch, irritated by the inhabitants' refusal to pay their taxes, carried out an expedition to the area in 1548-9 when his troops seized a large amount of gold and many pieces of cloth.

Relations between Gafat and the central state were particularly close during Särsä Dengel's reign. The provincial ruler, Azmach Täklo, sent the Emperor a courtier to conduct him to the territory in 1566 or 1567. A conflict, however, later arose which led the Emperor to carry out a *razzia* against the Béräbabo area. Subsequently, in 1585, he led an expedition to Shat, where he attempted to convert the inhabitants. He sent them a bishop and priests, but the Gafats, to the chronicler's chagrin, soon reverted to their "pagan" faith, and the ecclesiastics he had settled in the area were obliged to flee. Särsä Dengel, angered by the failure of his mission, undertook a second expedition in 1591, to Wämbärya. where his soldiers captured much loot.

Hadeya, which was no longer dynastically allied to the empire, was ruled at the beginning of Särsä Dengel's reign by a Muslim chief called Azé, who joined in a rebellion by several of the nobles, and withheld the province's tribute. The Emperor marched against him. Fierce fighting ensued, and resulted in heavy casualties. The Hadeya chiefs surrendered, after which Azé made his submission. Särsä Dengel appointed one of his courtiers, Täklä Giyorgis, as provincial governor. The latter came into conflict with Azé, who was shortly afterwards killed.

The province was attacked by Muhammäd, Amir of Adäl, who marched into the territory. He gained the support of the provincial ruler, Gärad Jafer, who was however killed by Särsä Dengel's forces. The Amir and his men indulged in considerable looting, and thereby incurred the wrath of the peasantry, who captured him, and handed him over to the Emperor.

The Hadeya rulers then attempted to revert to their long-established policy of allying themselves matrimonially with the imperial dynasty. A marriage was effected between the daughter of the local ruler and Emperor Ya'qob, but it was of short duration as the latter passed away shortly afterwards.

Bizamo was likewise temporarily brought under imperial control by Särsä Dengel, whose expedition to Bosha is said to have led to the limited introduction of Christianity into Käfa.

Särsä Dengel also marched to the country of the Gämbos, reputedly to punish those among them who had "shed Christian blood". His men captured many slaves. The survivors, however, arranged a peace treaty with the help of the Abbot of Däbrä Libanos. The Emperor's troops treacherously violated the agreement, but Särsä Dengel, infuriated by this action, attacked them, and made them free the slaves they had taken.

Gälawdéwos and Särsä Dengel likewise both on occasion made their way to Konch, or Konta, where they were warmly received by the local governor.

Raids on the "blacks" on the western and northern borderlands continued throughout the period. Emperor Minas attacked the Dobe'a, and seized some of the cattle for which they had long been famous. Särsä Dengel in his turn subsequently raided the Shinashas, who are said to have appealed in vain for conversion to Christianity, as the Emperor preferred to keep them as a source of slaves. After some fighting they surrendered, after which Särsä Dengel looted the Bäläya, who were condescendingly referred to in his chronicle as *agber*t, or slaves, and described as entirely different from ordinary people. He nevertheless incorporated them into his empire and fixed the annual tax they had to pay.

PART VI

OROMO MIGRATION and THE GONDARINE MONARCHY

(1520-1800)

Chapter 24
THE GREAT OROMO MIGRATION

Prior to the early sixteenth century the Oromos, who were until recently better known as Gallas, a term used by both their Amhara neighbours to the north and by the Bantu Africans to the south, lived for the most part to the south of present day Ethiopia. They then began a remarkably rapid migration from the southern borderlands to the very core of the region, and thence to lands on the eastern, western and almost northern periphery. This northward movement constituted a major turning-point in the history of the entire region.

**The Testimony of Abba Bahrey:
Oromo Migrations, Government, and Soldiery**

The earliest detailed account of the Oromos, the *Zenahu la Galla*, or History of the Gallas, was composed in 1593 by Abba Bahrey, an Ethiopian monk from the southern province of Gamo. His account may be supplemented by information in a number of other important contemporary works, notably Shihab ed-Din's *Futuh al-Habasha*, the autobiography of the sixteenth century Ethiopian monk Abba Pawlos, the memoirs of João Bermudes, the writings of the Jesuits, most notably Almeida and Jerórimo Lobo, the chronicles of Emperors Gälawdéwos, Särsä Dengel (probably written by Bahrey himself), and Susneyos, and the shorter chronicles of the time. The latter, though often referred to as "abbreviated", sometimes contain information not included in the longer texts.

Bahrey, who wrote, over a century and a quarter after Fra Mauro's apparent reference to the Gallas in his *mappamondo* of 1460, suggests that they were a pastoral people, consisting of two main groups, the Bäräytuma and the Borän, both of whom began to migrate because their herds were expanding so fast that they no longer had enough grazing land. Writing in Biblical vein he asserts that the original Oromo custom, when going to war, was to stay together. When their herds became too numerous, however, they "quarrelled among themselves", and separated, as Abraham did with Lot, saying, "Let us separate, so that thou goest to the right and I go to the left; or I go to the right and thou to the left". The reason why the Oromos later spread over wide areas, Bahrey claims, was that, unlike the subjects of the Emperor, they had "no ruler" to "enforce his orders". Each man therefore did what seemed "best to him". When they left their country they therefore did not all leave; those who wished to depart, departed, while those who preferred to remain, remained.

Notwithstanding this fissaperous tendency two historically important Oromo confederations were established. One, consisting of four clans, the Hoko, Chaliya, Gudru and Libän, known corporately as the Afré, from *afur*, the Afan Oromo for "four", came into existence during the Robalé *luba*-ship (1570-1579); the other group, composed of three clans, the Obbo, Suba and Hakako, known together as the Sädäqa, derived from *sadi*, the Afan Oromo for "three", was established during the Birmaji *luba*-ship (1578-1586).[1]

Oromo society was uncoordinated, Bahrey felt, because it was based on the *gada* system of government by age groups rather than on hierarchy such as that in the Christian empire. The Gallas, he insisted, had "neither king nor master", but they obeyed *lubas,* or elected leaders. These exercised power for a period of eight years, at the end of which a new *luba* was chosen, whereupon the first gave up office. The term *luba* literally meant "those who are circumcised at the same time".[2]

This type of government had a direct bearing, Bahrey insists, on Oromo migration, for each *luba,* on coming to power, tended to attack a country which none of its predecessors had penetrated. Raids were therefore usually directed into areas which had never previously been attacked.[3] The author wrote from bitter experience - for the Oromos of the Dawé, or Jawi, a branch of the Boran tribe had then recently overrun his own native land, Gamo, and "looted all that he possessed". Dawé warriors, he adds, also at around this time also "devastated" two other nearby southern areas, Bätera Amora and Wäj.[4]

Despite this obvious grudge Bahrey tries to be dispassionate. He recognises that the Oromos were good warriors, and had one great advantage over the Ethiopian Christians. He asserts that the latter had a number of different professions, and consisted of monks, *däbtäras*, or clerics, judges, elders, artisans, minstrels, etc., with the result that there were relatively few soldiers. Among the Oromos by contrast "all

---

[1] Beckingham and Huntingford (1954), pp. 112-14.
[2] Beckingham and Huntingford (1954), p. 115.
[3] Beckingham and Huntingford (1954), p. 122.
[4] Beckingham and Huntingford (1954), p. 114.

men, from small to great" were "instructed in warfare", and it was for this reason, Bahrey complains, that the Oromos "ruin and kill us".

Among the Oromos prowess in war and hunting, he insists, carried great prestige. A warrior who had killed men or large animals would thus distinguish himself by shaving the whole of his head, leaving only a little tuft of hair in the middle of his skull. Those who had not achieved any such exploit had to leave their heads unshaven, and were in consequence "tormented with lice".[5]

Bahrey's report of Oromo prowess, though probably not without foundation, fails to take account of two other important factors in the contemporary military equasion. Firstly, that the Christian empire and the Muslim state of Adäl had by then both been much weakened by the destructive fighting associated with the campaigns of Ahmäd ibn Ibrahim. Secondly, that the Oromos had the apparent ability to assimilate the populations of the areas they occupied, and thereby to consolidate control over them.[6]

Chronology of Migration

Bahrey's history recalls a succession of *lubas*, and the main events of their eight year periods of rule, thus providing a useful chronology, which may be supplemented by the writings of several of the other above-mentioned sources.[7]

Melbah, Mudäna and Kilolé

Bahrey, who seems to have been unable to probe into early Oromo history, and therefore lacks any long-term perspective, begins his account little more than two generations before his own time. He claims that the earliest Oromo migration started during the rule of what he terms the first *luba*, Mélbah (1522-1530), when Galla forces began, as he says, to "invade" Bali. This happened, it would thus appear, immediately before or just at the time of the first incursions of Imam Ahmäd ibn Ibrahim. The advance of the Oromos at that time was, however, limited, for after each *razzia,* he asserts, they returned

---

[5] Beckingham and Huntingford (1954), pp. 122, 125-6.

[6] For an early nineteenth centuy account of Oromo adoption practices see Isenberg and Krapf (1844), p. 256, and for an historical analysis of the mechanics of adoption see Mohammed Hassen (1990), pp. 6-17, 20-2.

[7] This account was accepted, summarised and reproduced, in some cases word by word, by Almeida. See Beckingham and Huntingford (1954), pp. 138-9.

to their base near the Wäbi Shabellé river. Later, during the time of Bahrey's second *luba*, Mudäna (1530-1538), they crossed the Wäbi Shabellé, and carried out further raids, but, according to author, again returned home. The period of office of his third *luba*, Kilolé (1538-1546), coincided, he claims, with Imam Ahmäd's death in 1543 and the resultant collapse of Adäl power. The Oromos then advanced further, towards the Däwaro plains, but at the end of each raid still returned whence they had come. Bahrey's dating is here open to question. Shihab ad-din, writing during the Imam's lifetime, refers to a locality in Däwaro known as Wärrä Qallu, which presumably owed its name to the presence of the Oromo clan of that name, at least a decade before Ahmäd's death.

Oromo advances in this period were probably halted by the military prowess of Emperor Gälawdéwos. His chronicle claims that he was victorious against the Gallas, and, echoing the Scriptures, declares that he captured their sons and daughters, and obliged them to cut wood and draw water for him. It is further asserted that he spent three years in their country, during which time he appointed a governor over at least some Gallas, and made them pay tribute.[8] This may have been the time when a special cattle tax was instituted, as Almeida reports, perhaps, as the modern Ethiopian historian Mohommed Hasen has suggested, in order to tax Oromo pastoralists.[9]

Bahrey's chronology was accepted by Almeida. He observed that the Gallas, whom he calls a "plague and scourge of God", arrived in the Ethiopian empire during the reign of Emperor Lebnä Dengel (1508-1540), or, more precisely, at the time of Ahmäd ibn Ibrahim's invasion of the Ethiopian highlands, which began in 1527. He follows Bahrey in asserting that they made their first appearance in Bali, with which they had a "common frontier", as well as in neighbouring Adäl, where, he says, they were also a "scourge".[10]

Bifolé and Gälawdéwos

A notable turning-point in the Oromo migration took place, according to Bahrey, during the time of his fourth *luba* Bifolé (1546-1554), i.e. after Imam Ahmäd's death. It was then, he says, that the Oromos, advancing further, "devastated" all Däwaro, and began to

---

[8] Conzelman (1895), p. 141.
[9] Beckingham and Huntingford (1954), p. 88; Mohommed Hassen (1990), p. 207.
[10] Beckingham and Huntingford (1954), p. 134.

make war on Fätägar. Bahrey claims that they then began to "enslave" the inhabitants of the areas they occupied. The conquered populations were thus turned into "slaves called *gäbr*", probably tax-paying serfs, in some ways reminiscent of the pre-Oromo tenant class of imperial Ethiopia.

Gälawdéwos, according to his chronicle, later made his way to the "camp of the Gallas". He fought with them, killed many, and placed the survivors under his rule. This victory, it is claimed, checked the Oromo incursions, at least for a time. Those who continued to advance did so only "like thieves who broke into a house while the master was absent". Describing this period the chronicler states that his master was "troubled" by incursions of Gallas inhabiting the frontier areas, and was therefore obliged, around 1550-1, to settle refugees in a town in Wäj, north of Lake Zway.[11]

Meslé, Gälawdéwos, and Nur ibn Mujahid

A new phase of the Oromo advance took place, according to Bahrey, during the rule of his fifth *luba*, Meslé, also known as Michelle (1554-1562). It was at this time, we are told, that the Oromos defeated Gälawdéwos's Jan Amora corps, and "devastated" many towns, after which they remained in the area they had occupied. This was a new development, for the Oromos, "invading" from the Wäbi River, had, as we have seen, previously always returned at the end of each campaign. They now began a permanent occupation. Resistance to the advancing Oromos was offered by Gälawdéwos at an unidentified place called 'Asa Zänäb. The Emperor's chronicle confirms that this was a time of fierce fighting, and recalls that Gälawdéwos continued to build a town for refugees driven from their lands in the fighting.[12]

The Oromos later fought against the Amir of Harär, Nur ibn Mujahid (1551/2-1567/8), whose soldiers reportedly suffered heavy losses. There had been "no such slaughter", Bahrey claims, "since the Galla first invaded".

This was an important stage in the Oromo migration, for one other reason: it was at this time, if we can believe Bahrey, that the Gallas "began the custom of riding horses and mules". This development, we may assume, must have increased the Oromo warriors' mobility and

---

[11] Conzelman (1985), pp. 149, 157; Beckingham and Huntingford (1954), p. 149.
[12] Conzelman (1895), p. 173.

placed them on a par with soldiers from the central provinces, who had used cavalry in battle since time immemorial.

Bermudes's Report

Testimony to the prowess of the Oromos, and to some of their victories over Emperor Gälawdéwos, is provided by Bermudes. He records that the monarch, after one battle against the Oromos, returned to his camp "wearied and almost defeated, without having accomplished anything of value". Not long after this he reports that the Emperor had been "defeated by the Gallas", who had actually entered his camp, and "slain men close to the royal tent, where there was none to oppose them". Gälawdéwos had been obliged to flee "with great indignity".

Shortly after this the Portuguese, then stationed in Däwaro, were informed by the monarch that the Gallas were going to attack them suddenly. Bermudes states that his compatriots were determined to destroy them "in any possible way". This, he suggests, was scarcely surprising, for he claimed that the Portuguese, who were well armed with rifles, constituted the greatest single hindrance to any Oromo advance.

Turning to the military power of the Oromos, he declared: "they are a fierce and cruel people, who make war on their neighbours, and on all, only to destroy and depopulate their countries. In the places they conquer they slay all the men, cut off the privy parts of the boys, kill the old women, and keep the young for their own use and service".

Describing his first sight of a force of Oromo soldiers he states that they were "innumerable", but "did not come on without order like barbarians, but advanced collected in bodies, like squadrons". Gälawdéwos, he claims, was "amazed" to hear of their advance, and was so shocked that he "did not regain command of himself for a long time". He later "wept like a child", and said "My sin is great that such evil has befallen me". The Emperor, concludes Bermudes, had by then lost three large provinces, Bali, Däwaro and Hadeya.[13]

Resistance to the Oromos was further shattered by Emperor Gälawdéwos's death in battle against the Hararis in 1559.

---

[13] Whiteway (1902), pp. 218, 224, 226, 229.

Minas

The considerable advance achieved by the Oromos in this period became apparent during the reign of Gälawdéwos's brother and successor Emperor Minas (1559-1563). Faced with the Turkish occupation of Massawa, which had taken place in 1557, and the ceaseless Oromo expansion in the south, he made no use of his ancestors' capitals in Ifat and Fätägar, or of his predecessor's in Wäj, both in the south-east of the country, but established his residence at Guba'é, later known as Guzara, a settlement overlooking Lake Tana in the north-west of the empire.

Harmufa and Robalé

Oromo migration gained further momentum, Bahrey suggests, during the time of his sixth *luba*, Harmufa (1562-1570), which coincided roughly with the first part of the reign of Emperor Särsä Dengel (1563-1597). It was then, perhaps due to their use of horses, that the Oromos made their first appearance in Amhara, and, thrusting rapidly northward, advanced as far as Bägémder and Angot.

Robalé, Bahrey's seventh *luba* (1570-1578), broadened the Oromo occupation to the east and west, "devastated" Shäwa, and began to make war in Gojjam. This advance, we are told, was strongly resisted by Emperor Särsä Dengel, who fought a force of Oromos near Lake Zway in 1573. He killed many of them, and captured many of their cattle, as a result of which not a few of his subjects are said to have "became rich".

Särsä Dengel

Confirmation of the Oromo advance into Shäwa at this time is provided in the shorter royal chronicle. It recalls that Särsä Dengel marched to Lake Zway where he attacked a force of Boran Gallas, whose *luba* was called Ambisa.

Further details of this confrontation are afforded in Särsä Dengel's own chronicle. It states that after the rains of 1572 the monarch learnt that the Gallas had made themselves the masters of Wäj. He accordingly summoned troops from all parts of the realm to join him at Gend Bärät, and then made his way towards Wäj. There he found that the Galla warriors, accompanied by their women, children and cattle, had occupied the entire area of Maya and Wäj. The cattle were so numerous, it is claimed, that people could scarcely walk about, and had to drive the animals out of their way to open a path through them.

Despite the size of his army the arrival of the Emperor took the Oromos by surprise. He was therefore able to marshal his men in three separate units: The first attacked the Oromo encampment, while the other two entered the fray one after the other. All three units did battle, and killed "innumerable" Gallas, including women and children. The survivors were chased back towards Fätägar and Däwaro. In their advance the king's soldiers had no time to capture any cattle, but took many on their return. Some seized five hundred, others a thousand, "each one what he could". The local non-Oromo peasantry also seized as many as they were able to care of, and left many they did not want. Since the coming of the Gallas, the chronicler claims, no one, whether Christian or Muslim, had done so much as Särsä Dengel to uproot them.

Not long afterwards, in 1574, the Emperor learnt that the Oromos were once more in Shäwa, and had pillaged cattle in the lowlands of Zéma. He at once despatched fifty cavalry under the command of a courtier, Azzaj Halibo, who came upon the Oromos just as they were leaving with their booty. On seeing him they fled, but he pursued, and killed, many of them, and sent the heads of eighty of them as trophies to his master.[14]

Särsä Dengel, like Minas before him, faced an almost insuperable difficulty in ruling a far-flung empire, and in fighting on both its northern and southern peripheries at the same time. This is vividly revealed in his chronicle. It states that the Emperor, confronted with Bahr Nägash Yeshaq's rebellion in the north, planned to march against the latter. The royal advisers, however, declared, "How can the Emperor march forth, abandoning the country to the Gallas?" Särsä Dengel, consumed with anger against the northern rebel, refused to listen. He accordingly set forth, whereupon his mother came to him, saying, "O my son, why have you decided to do this thing against me and your brothers? Do you really want to deliver us to the Gallas? Does not our loss cause you any sadness?" With such and other words, we are told, she "touched his heart", after which he returned once more to Wäj, in 1577-8, to fight against the Oromos, who had again occupied the area. He found them in the country of the Mayas, where there was fierce fighting, as a result of which the countryside was left covered with corpses. This engagement, according to the

---

[14] Conti Rossini (1907), pp. 51-3; Basset (1881), XVIII, 111.

shorter chronicle, took place against the Boran Gallas in the Mojjo valley, a little to the east of modern Addis Ababa.

The Emperor, according to Bahrey, later learnt that the Abati Oromos had penetrated Dämbeya, north of Lake Tana. He made his way to the area, and attacked them at a place called Wäynä Däg'a, where he killed many. "Not more than ten", it is said, survived to carry back the news. The battle is also reported in Särsä Dengel's chronicle, which declares that the Gallas, on arriving in Dämbeya, began pillaging, and killed many people and cattle. The Emperor thereupon marched to Wäynä Däg'a where he fought victoriously, striking down many of the intruders.[15]

Birmajé and Mul'äta

Notwithstanding Särsä Dengel's supposed victories the Oromos increased their control over several parts of the country during the time of Bahrey's eighth *luba*, Birmajé (1578-1586). This was another important period because it was then, according to Bahrey, that the Oromos adopted the use of body-length shields made of stiff ox-hide. This enabled them to attack, and beat, the Mayas. The latter, it will be recalled, were skilled archers, whose resistance probably delayed Oromo expansion in the Wäj area for a decade.

The Birmajé *lubaship* also witnessed much fighting with one of Särsä Dengel's commanders, Daharagot, who, it is claimed, "many times" defeated them. They nevertheless later "devastated" the Ar'enä area in Wäj, where they killed many prominent courtiers. Taking advantage of the monarch's absence elsewhere they also advanced into the Lake Tana area, and once more penetrated into Dämbeya. They likewise surrounded Damot in the west, where they are reported to have enslaved the people, and carried off much live-stock.

Bahrey's ninth *luba*, Mul'äta (1586-1594) later made a *dulaguto*, or large-scale raid, into Gojjam. Särsä Dengel, however, later regained the initiative, and once more proceeded to Wäj to attack the Dawé, or Jawé, Oromos, who saved themselves by flight. Bahrey, no doubt wishing to flatter his master, the ruling monarch, waxes eloquent about the latter's valour in fighting in person. Särsä Dengel, he declares, "did not act according to the custom of the kings his ancestors, who, when making war were in the habit of sending their

---

[15] Basset (1881), XVIII, 111-12; Conti Rossini (1907), pp. 61-2; Huntingford (1989), pp. 141-12.

troops ahead, remaining themselves in the rear with the pick of their cavalry and infantry, praising those who went forward bravely, and punishing those who lagged behind". Despite his supposedly braver approach he succeeded, like so many rulers in history, only through the use of coercion. One of his decrees, quoted in his chronicle, declared that should any of his subjects fail to respond to the call to arms his house would be pillaged, his property be confiscated, and anyone abetting him would be brought to justice.

Notwithstanding Särsä Dengel's efforts the Oromos soon regained the offensive. The Borans in particular are said to have attacked the Christians of Damot, and to have "scattered them, and devastated their country". Shäwa and Damot, were thus both subjected to strong Oromo pressure, and were, it is claimed, "turned into deserts". The queen mother was obliged to seek refuge at Däbrä Abreham, later known as Addis Zämän, in the vicinity of Guba'é or Guzara.[16]

The fighting of this period is also mentioned in Särsä Dengel's chronicle, which indicates that the fiercest battles in Gojjam took place in 1586 when the Emperor, learning that the Oromos had pillaged numerous cattle, rushed to the area. At the sight of his tent the Wäränsha Oromos were reportedly so terrified that they "shuddered like women about to give birth", but later rallied for a fight. Särsä Dengel, who by then possessed numerous fire-arms, was victorious. He killed a huge number of Wäränsha warriors, including many who tried to hide in ditches or forests, while those who climbed into trees were shot down by rifle-fire. Others fled to the Blue Nile, but were pursued. None, it is claimed, were spared.[17]

Not long after this, however, the Oromos again poured into Wäj. Särsä Dengel once more made his way there, but as soon as they heard of his arrival they fled with their women, children and cattle, and disappeared in all directions, the chronicle claims, like smoke before the wind. The victorious monarch then attacked the Jawi Bätera Amora, and marched as far as Séf Bär. The Jawi, apparently terrified by Särsä Dengel's attack, disappeared, the chronicle claims, without leaving even a trace as to where they had been.

The nobles, who had no desire to follow the Oromos across the Blue Nile, never an easy undertaking, are quoted in the chronicle as asking, "Where shall we search for them. All traces of the Gallas have

---

[16] Conti Rossini (1907), p. 134; Beckingham and Huntingford (1954), pp. 111-29.

[17] Conti Rossini (1907) p.135, Huntingford (1989), p. 147.

disappeared. We do not know where they have gone". Emphasising the difficulty of continuing the campaign they offered an even more compelling argument, namely that the army was in danger of imminent famine. They therefore urged that they should at once return to Guba'é. Särsä Dengel agreed. Not long afterwards, in 1589, he built a fortress, the location of which seemed a recognition that he, like Minas before him, had accepted the loss of much of the territory to the south.[18]

The Oromo Social Scene

Though largely concerned, like so many writers of the past, with fighting, killing, and the taking of prisoners, Bahrey also provides a refreshing, and very graphic, account of late sixteenth century Oromo society.

Small children, he reports, were known as *mucha*, those a little older as *ilman*, and those older still as *gurba*, or youths. These latter, as they grew up, began to take part in warfare like adults. Young men who were not yet circumcised were called *qondala*, and, like soldiers, dressed their hair with wreaths of leaves, a hair style known as *kalala*.

All unmarried Oromos, whether circumcised (*luba*) or uncircumcised (*qondala*) were spoken of as *qéro*. From the point of view of status, circumcision was more important than marriage. This is evident from the fact that men were grouped according to whether they were or were not circumcised, rather than whether they were or were not married. Circumcised youths were known as *qéro luba*, and lived in the same house as circumcised married men. Uncircumcised men, whether married or unmarried, likewise lived together, while unmarried *gäbars,* or tenants, lived with married *gäbars*.

Prior to circumcision men were not supposed to marry, or beget infants. The uncircumcised, if they did so, abandoned their offspring. The circumcised, on the other hand, reared boys and girls, though the latter might be abandoned in the first two or three years after their fathers' circumcision. Such practices, perhaps poorly reported by contemporary observers, may originally have been conceived as a means of controlling population growth.[19]

The Oromo occupational division of labour is also described by Bahrey. He states that the average community would contain a score

---

[18] Conti Rossini (1907), p. 144; Huntingford (1989), p. 144-8, 156.
[19] Merid Wolde Aregai (1971), p. 156.

of *ijartu*, or builders, responsible for the construction of houses and tents, as well as an undefined number of people called *qältu*, or butchers, whose duty was the slaughtering of oxen. Two men, spoken of as *wajo*, or roasters, were supposed to roast meat, cut it into pieces, and distribute it equally to all. Five others, called *halabdo*, or milkers, had to milk the cows, while the *tehito*, or herdsmen, carried the milk in containers and gave everyone their entitlement. Ten other men, known as *täwtu*, or inspectors, herded the cattle, while seven, called *bärbado*, or searchers, brought the herd home at night, and looked for any animals that had strayed. Two other men, called *gorsa*, or warners, were responsible for reprimanding and punishing any men who had illicit relations with women. Such relations were prohibited, Bahrey says, "not from love of virtue", but so that the men might be "always alert and ready for war", for "he who is married strives to please his wife". Men who wished to marry, were referred to as *jelhika*. They would separate themselves from their companions, and stay at home, though, unless they were too feeble, they did not altogether abstain from fighting. Old men were called *melguddo*.[20]

Changes in Social and Other Customs

The Oromos were not surprisingly much influenced by their great migration, which led to several notable developments The first, in the medical field, occurred, if we can believe Bahrey, when *luba* Bifolé (1546-1554) started taking the famous Ethiopian taenicide *kosso* (*Hagenia abyssinica*). This medicine came from the flowers of a tree growing in areas of considerable elevation. Its adoption at this time suggests that the Oromos had by then made their way into the southern Ethiopian highlands, in fact Däwaro and Fätägar, as Bahrey elsewhere reports. The use of *kosso* was a valuable innovation, for until that time the Gallas, as he unkindly puts it, had been able to kill people and animals, but had no means of killing the tapeworm in their own intestines.[21]

---

[20] Beckingham and Huntingford (1954), pp. 127-9.
[21] Beckingham and Huntingford (1954), p. 116.

Leaves and flowers of the Ethiopian highland tree the *kosso (Hagenia abyssinica)* widely used as taenicide. The Oromos are reported by Abba Bahrey to have adopted its use in the mid-sixteenth century.
From J. Bruce, *Travels to Discover the Source of the Nile.*

A perhaps even more important development took place during the time of *luba* Meslé (1554-1562), when the custom was initiated, as we have seen, of riding horses and mules. This *luba* is supposed to have declared, "Those who travel on two or three legs, I have made to travel on four". He said "three legs", Bahrey explains, "because they leant on their spears, as men would on their staffs when they were tired".[22] The innovation of riding was of major significance, for it substantially increased the mobility of the Oromos, and gave them, as already suggested, equality with inhabitants of the northern provinces who had long been renowned horsemen. It was at this very time,

---

[22] Beckingham and Huntingford (1954), p. 117.

Bahrey indicates, that the Oromos began their permanent occupation of the territories into which they advanced.

Not long after this the practice of circumcision, possibly also resulting from contact with peoples the Oromos encountered in the course of their migration, is said by Bahrey to have became common. Though the first *luba*, Mélbah (1522-1530) was circumcised, the children of the first five *lubas* were reportedly uncircumcised. Circumcision, however, thereafter become general in Oromo society.[23]

Another development occurred during the time of *luba* Birmajé (1578-1586), who, as we have seen, introduced the use of body-length ox-hide shields. This enabled the Oromos to attack the Mayas, who had for centuries been feared on account of their deadly poisoned arrows, and were subsequently defeated, Bahrey says, "because there was no place for their arrows to strike".

Later again, at the time of *luba* Mul'äta (1586-1594), the Oromos began eating buffalo, which become an item of ordinary diet, rather than an object of hunting prowess. Some Oromos accordingly declared, "Since we eat it, it is like an ox, and we ought not to shave our heads when we kill it".[24]

Ya'qob and Susneyos:
Fighting, Internal Stresses, and Assimilation

Fighting between the Oromos and the Christian empire, mainly in Gojjam and Bägémder, continued during the reign of Emperor Ya'qob (1597-1606), who embarked on at least one major expedition against the Boran Oromos. His kinsman Prince Susneyos, the future Emperor, wished to participate, but was dissuaded from doing so. Despite this conflict Ya'qob was later accused of having adopted the Oromo custom of consulting the fat of animals for purposes of prophecy.[25]

Susneyos likewise took a keen interest in the Oromos. During his youth a group of Boran Oromos had carried out a raid into Gojjam, and his father, Prince Fasilädäs, had been killed. Susneyos himself had survived, and was brought up by a kindly Oromo as his son. Later, while still a youth, he encountered a group of Kono Oromos, led by a certain Buko, on their way to attack Wäläqa. They at first

---

[23] Beckingham and Huntingford (1954), pp. 115, 118.
[24] Beckingham and Huntingford (1954), p. 127.
[25] Esteves Pereira (1900), pp. 7, 39.

appeared hostile, but, on discovering that the prince was of royal descent, rushed forward to prostrate themselves in honour, and kiss his feet. This reception was so warm that on learning that the half-Fälasha Emperor Ya'qob was planning to arrest him he fled, and joined the Oromos. He met them again in 1602, and found them so friendly that when the people of Mägäz later rebelled he used the Tuläma Oromos to fight against them.[26]

Young Susneyos learnt more than Ya'qob from his Oromo contacts. He probably acquired a good knowledge the Galla, or Afan Oromo, language, and we find his chronicler, Täklä Sellasé, being nicknamed in that tongue as Tinno, or the Small. The prince also gained a knowledge of the Oromo mode of warfare, for his chronicle on one occasion tells of him arranging his soldiers in the "Galla style". He also acquired numerous Oromo supporters. His army included many Bärtuma Oromos, and in 1604 he had the help of the Mächa Oromos in attacking Gwemcho, the ruler of Enarya.[27]

Despite his early friendship with the Oromos, Susneyos, like his predecessors, was disturbed by their rapid advance into hitherto Christian-inhabited territories. Shortly prior to his accession to the throne in 1606 he made his way to the Lake Hayq area, where he expelled a group of Oromos who had infiltrated into the vicinity of the monastery of Iyäsus Mo'a. Later, after his coronation, he learnt of an incursion by the Bäränta Oromos, and rode to confront them. He subsequently defeated three further Oromo groups. They were the Wäränshas, one of the sub-groups of the Bärtumas; the Libäns, whom his chronicle describes as the largest and most powerful of the Oromos; and the Digalus, of whom relatively little is known. All three groups suffered heavy casualties, with the result that the neighbouring countryside was reportedly covered with blood.[28]

Notwithstanding this victory the Emperor, like other Ethiopian sovereigns before and since, found it difficult to persuade his soldiers to follow his orders. When he tried to march south of the Blue Nile his troops murmured so insistently that he was obliged, according to the chronicle, to abandon his plans.[29]

---

[26] Esteves Pereira (1900), pp. 9, 30-1, 286.
[27] Esteves Pereira (1900), pp. 160, 34-5, 39.
[28] Esteves Pereira (1900), pp.65-6, 81-5.
[29] Esteves Pereira (1900), pp. 82, 84.

Shortly after this, in 1609-10, Susneyos learnt that three other Oromo groups, the Anas, Urus, and Abatis, jointly known as the Märäwas, had occupied Weqro in the north of the country, and were advancing on Bägémder. He rushed to confront them, with only a small part of his army, and was soundly defeated. The victors then reportedly ravaged the entire land of Emfraz, and burnt down the royal capital at Qoga by Lake Tana, before crossing the Täkkäzé River. Susneyos, having obtained reinforcements, attacked this Oromo force, and defeated it at Hamus Wänz, a tributary of the Reb, near Ebenat, as well as at Darago. After this victory he returned to their owners all the cattle which the intruders had seized.[30]

In 1611 Susneyos again clashed with the Wäränshas, with whom he appears however to have earlier come to terms, for the chronicle states that he had given them land in Wäläqa. He also fought against the Wärdaya or Wärrä Daya, who had land in Jämma and Amonat in Wäläqa. The Wäränshas were supported by the Ittu Oromos, who had come up from Adäl, and threatened both Wäläqa and Gojjam. Susneyos fought against them, and defeated them at Shäbäl, in Gojjam. Evidently wishing for a reconciliation, however, he returned to the Wäränshas an old woman whom he had captured, and told her to negotiate a peace agreement with her people. This was duly effected.[31]

Fighting broke out again not far from Gorgora on the northern shore of Lake Tana in 1614. In the course of this struggle the Emperor killed many Oromo soldiers, and captured not a few women, children and cattle. He also went on a campaign against the Oromos in Geraya, between the Jämma and Mugär Rivers.[32]

The Oromos, however, took the offensive again in 1616. Report had it that large numbers of Käräyus were advancing into Tegray, that the Märäwas were moving into Bägémder, and that the Ittus and Boräns were about to attack Gojjam. Susneyos, shocked by the destruction already wrought by the Käräyus in Tegray, decided to proceed to that province, and summoned his officers to advise on the route he should follow. They told him that because of lack of grass

---

[30] Esteves Pereira (1900), pp. 90-5. See also Basset (1881), XVIII, 121; Huntingford (1989), pp. 161-2.
[31] Esteves Pereira (1900), pp. 108-11. See also Basset (1881), XVIII, 121-2; Huntingford (1989), p. 165.
[32] Esteves Pereira (1900), p. 115; Huntingford (1989). p. 166.

the pack animals would be unable to undertake the journey to the north, and proposed that he should instead ride westwards to protect Gojjam. He acted on their advice, only to discover that the Oromos threatening that province had already been defeated by an officer of his brother Ras Se'elä Krestos. Recognising the victor's prowess he despatched him against a force of Ittus in the Mugär area of Shäwa, but they immediately fled, thus enabling the officer to capture many women, children, and cattle.[33]

The Oromos, who for over a century had been advancing, but were now largely contained by the imperial armies, were around this time weakened by internal conflict. This largely arose from the fact that the assimilation of people who had been overrun, or captured as slaves, was far from complete. Despite extensive intermarriage much of the population of the occupied lands was still in fact unassimilated, or only partially assimilated, and many of the Oromos' newly acquired subjects do not seem to have been inducted into the *gada* system. Not a few doubtless resented the subject status imposed on them, which had relegated them, as Bahrey had noted, to the position of *gäbars*, or tenants. Many likewise seem to have identified themselves with the old empire, and hankered after the Christian religion in which they had been reared.

The size and precise character of this disaffected population is difficult to determine. The chronicles, particularly that of Susneyos, nevertheless suggest that it was numerous. Three unassimilated immigrant, and potentially rebel, groups, mentioned in the text, can be identified. 1) The Yähabäta, or Yabäta, literally in Afan Oromo "those who are mounted", a term used for cavalry and other soldiers of non-Oromo origin in the service Oromos. 2) Ilma gwozit, or originally it seems i*lma gossa*, in Afan Oromo "sons of the *gossa"*, or clan, into which such non-Oromos had been adopted. 3) Tälata, apparently an Amharic or Ge'ez corruption of the Afan Oromo word *dhalatta*, "he who is born", a term also used to signify non-Oromos in Oromo service.[34]

The first signs of discontent within the hitherto apparently solid ranks of the Oromos became evident in 1618 when, as related in Susneyos's chronicle, a fierce dispute broke out in Bizamo, where two

---

[33] Esteves Pereira (1900), pp. 121-3. See also Basset (1881), XVIII, 122.
[34] Tutschek (1844), I, 109; Pereira (1900), pp. 467; Bairu Tafla (!987), pp 155, 930, 974, 990; Tilahun Gamta (1989), p, 142-3; Mohamed Hassan (1990), p. 64.

apparently non-Oromo, or only semi-assimilated Oromo groups, the Yahabätas and Ilmägwäzit Borans, quarrelled with the Cheleha Obos, and appealed for assistance to Ras Se'elä Krestos, and to Däjazmach Buko, the Sähafä Lahm of Damot. "Behold", the two groups wrote, "we have quarrelled with our masters the Gallas. We have fought them until we have both shed blood. Come quickly and receive us, for from olden times our origin and descent was from you. and not from the Gallas!".

Ras Se'elä Krestos thereupon sent his men across the Blue Nile to join the two rebel groups, who, according to the chronicle, welcomed them with "great joy". Together they defeated their Oromo enemies, from whom they captured numerous women, children and cattle. The victory owed much to the fact that the Yähabätas knew the topography of the land, as well as the secret dwelling places of their Oromo enemies, and led Ras Se'elä Krestos's men to them. The two victorious rebel groups then concluded an alliance with Se'elä Krestos, who waged several further victorious battles against the Obbos. Bénaro, the local ruler of Enarya, seized this opportunity, as will be seen in the ensuing chapters, to attack the latter, who suffered more heavy losses.

At the end of the fighting the Yähabätas, satisfied with the assistance they had received from Susneyos, and reportedly amazed by the number of his soldiers and the quantity and quality of their weapons, came to him, and, prostrating themselves, offered him their submission. He thanked God for liberating them from their servitude to their masters, the Gallas, and declared them henceforth free from such suzereinty. He also gave them many gifts, including fine horses, mules and cattle, and decorations. The Emperor, who under Jesuit influence, had become a fanatical Catholic, also pressed them to embrace Christianity, so that they would, as he declared, become his "equals in the sight of God". Some of the Yähabätas willingly agreed, saying, "Yes, O King, let it be as you say!". Others, however, prevaricated, and, apparently still loyal to Oromo values, or reluctant to incur Oromo wrath, asked to be left alone until the next *gueta*, or Oromo clan ceremony, so that their customs should "not be violated before the time". He settled them in several probably strategically selected areas, including Mächakäl between Dämbacha and Däbrä

Marqos, Fesé Bädin, west of Dämbacha, and Arbuq and Yämäbal in Gojjam.³⁵

Hiob Ludolf's beautiful, and very detailed, map *Habessinia Seu Abassia*, designed by the scholar's son from an original manuscript, and published in Frankfurt in 1683.

Note the more or less correct location of Lake Tana and the Blue Nile, as well as of the interior provinces of Sämèn (Samen), Gojjam (Gojam), Bägémder (Bagemder), Amhara (Amara), and Upper and Lower Shäwa (Shoa superior, Shoa inferior). See also the location of many peripheral provinces, notably, to the north and east, the Country of the Bahr Nägash (Midra Bahr "cujus Pro Rex vocatur Bahr Nagash", i.e. ruled by a Viceroy called Bahr Nagash), Upper and Lower Bur (Bur superior, Bur inferior), the "kingdom" of the Danakil (Dancale R.), Adäl (Adel R.), Bali (Bali R.), Ifat (Ifat. "Proregis titulus est Ifat Walasma",

---

35 Esteves Pereira (1900), pp. 146-7; Huntingford (1989), p. 169.

i.e. territory ruled by an official called *Ifat Walasma*), Fätägar (Fatagar R.) Wäj (Wed R. "Lus. Oge", i.e. called Oge by the Portuguese), Gamo (Bahargam, probably a confusion with the nearby Lake Chamo), and Alaba. Also, to the west, Hadeya Chad-ya malé Adea), Shat, Kämbata (Cambat), Ganz (Gänz R.), Guragé (Guraghe R. Proregis Titulus *Gurague shum*), Mugar (Mugär) and Aymällal (Alamalé), Damot (Damot R.), Bizamo (Bizamo R.), and the Countries of the Gongas (Gonga) and "Shanqellas" (Shankala. "Aethiops Nomades incertis sedibus per deserta vigantes", i.e. Ethiopian nomads dwelling throughout desert areas in unknown habitations, both located east and west of the river.

Note also the ports, Massawa (Mazua, "Portus, quem nunc Turcae tenente", i.e. now held by the Turks), Hergigo (Arkiko), and Baylul (Baylur. "Portus R. Dancale", i.e. the port of the Danakil kingdom). Note also the location of the Oromos (Gallas) south, north-east and east of Lake Zway (Zawaja), Damot and Gafat south of the Blue Nile, and the "Shanqellas" and Gongas to the east and west of that river.

Susneyos later attempted to convert other Oromo groups to Christianity. In 1620 he urged his old enemies, the Wäränshas, to accept this faith, once again declaring that their baptism would make them equal to him in God's eyes. He likewise invited the Wäytos, the hunting community around Lake Tana, to adopt the Christian religion. The latter tribesmen asked how they could do so as it was their custom to eat hippopotamus flesh, which was traditionally rejected by Orthodox Christians. In reply he quoted St. Paul's statement that whatever went into the mouth could not defile, and assured them that they were free to eat whatever they wished. The Wäränshas and Wäytos then both reportedly accepted the Christian faith.[36]

Fierce fighting with the Oromos erupted again shortly afterwards. It began when the Mächa Oromos, who had earlier been defeated by the Hadeyas and Guragés, and by two other Oromo groups, the Bärtumas and Tulämas, launched a two-pronged attack on Gojjam and Enarya. Susneyos, once more assisted by his new friends, the Yähabäta Borans, immediately marched to Gojjam, where he learnt that the Mächas had killed a chief whom he had appointed over them. Ras Se'elä Krestos and the Yähabätas duly fought together against the Mächas, who were defeated, and driven back as far as the Blue Nile.

Susneyos, though victorious, found it difficult to win the support of his own subjects. This is graphically illustrated in the chronicle. Describing the monarch's attempts to defend Gojjam against the

---

[36] Esteves Pereira (1900), pp. 165-6.

Oromo advance, it recalls that the Emperor asked the province's inhabitants to chose a village by lot on which he could quarter his troops. The people of the province, perhaps more afraid of the monarch's army than of the Oromos, ignored his request, whereupon he withdrew from the area, after which the Tuläma Oromos, we are told, came, and "devastated half Gojjam", as far as Däbrä Wärq. In the course of their advance they reportedly killed countless people, including one of the Emperor's uncles. Susneyos and his brother Se'elä Krestos responded by attacking the advancing Tulämas, and put them to flight. A large number were killed in the fighting, while others were castrated. Another group, the Talätas, who, it will be recalled, had only partially been assimilated to the Oromos, sided with the Emperor in this fight, and were later generously rewarded by him.[37]

Notwithstanding this victory further fighting broke out shortly afterwards, when Susneyos fought at Mäshälämya, not far from Näfas Mäwcha, against five other Oromo groups, the Wällos, Jelés, Märäwas, Bäräytumas and Käräyus. He was once more victorious.[38]

Despite the result of this battle the Mächas soon afterwards again advanced into western Gojjam. They occupied a wide stretch of territory, including Dangela, Hankasha, Chära, Mätäkäl and the country of the Gongas, and seized many of the local inhabitants and their cattle. The people of these areas appealed to Ras Se'elä Krestos for help. He asked them what they would do for him if he defeated their enemies. They offered him extensive tribute, but he declared that he had no desire for their worldly goods, and wished only that they should accept Jesus Christ, and abandon their old idols. This they agreed to do, after which the Ras, who, like his brother, was a staunch Catholic, defeated their enemies in two successive battles. He then told them to take back their women, children and cattle seized by the Oromos, but the grateful inhabitants declared that the captured livestock should be retained for the Ras's soldiers, after which they embraced Christianity. Se'elä Krestos personally baptised the new converts, and had their names recorded.[39]

In 1620 the Emperor learnt of an Oromo attack in Bägémder. He again rapidly descended to Mäsalämya, where he inflicted

---

[37] Esteves Pereira (1900), pp. 167-81.
[38] Esteves Pereira (1900), p. 189.
[39] Esteves Pereira (1900), pp. 192-5.

considerable casualties on the advancing force. Fighting also took place, in 1621-22, with the Wechalés who killed an important nobleman, Däjazmach Wäldä Hawaryat. Before long, however, Susneyos, obtained his revenge. He fought against the Wällos and Wechalés in 1624, defeated and killed a large number of them, seized their cattle, and led away their women as slaves.[40]

Susneyos at about this time marched eastwards to attack the Wällo Oromos. The latter, who were also known as the Sädäqa, consisted of three main groups, the Wärrä Kuryas, the Wärrä Nolés and the Wärrä Illus. The Emperor defeated them, killed many of them, and captured not a few of their women, children and cattle. While campaigning at Wäsäl, in the neighbourhood of modern Däsé, he was, however, assailed by seven contingents of Wällos and Märäwas, who carried out a surprise attack, but failed to break into his camp, and were soon repulsed. They then reportedly fled, and abandoned all their spears and shields.[41]

Fighting with the Oromos erupted in Gojjam again around 1627, on which occasion Susneyos once more proceeded to the province, where he succeeded in putting the intruders to flight. Before fleeing, however, they succeeded in killing one of his principal governors, Däjazmach Buko.[42]

Despite such repeated conflicts many Oromos, as well as only partially assimilated Oromos, responded to Susneyos's efforts at reconciliation, and joined the imperial service. One of them, known as Arka-Negus, or Friend of the King, killed the rebel Yona'él, and took the latter's sexual organs as a trophy to the monarch. Yähabäta and Wäränsha troops likewise served the Emperor in numerous campaigns, notably at Atbara in the north and Damot and Achäfar in the west.[43]

Ras Se'elä Krestos also recruited many Yähabätas, comprising Chäleha Obbos, Gallans and Jawis. With their help he fought for example in 1622 against five Oromo groups, the Käräyus, Abus, Subas, Jelés and Balaes.[44]

---

[40] Basset (1881), XVIII, 123.
[41] Esteves Pereira (1900), pp. 202-3.
[42] Basset (1881), XVIII, 119, 121-4; Esteves Pereira (1900), pp. 90-5, 109, 114-15, 122-3; Huntingford (1989), pp. 161-2, 165, 167.
[43] Basset (1881), XVIII, 124; Esteves Pereira (1900), pp. 113, 151-2, 158, 196, 198.
[44] Esteves Pereira (1900), pp. 198, 200, 202.

Azzaj Täklä Sellasé, or Tinno

Susneyos's chronicle, like other works of its genre, was primarily written to record the exploits of the monarch. Its principal author, Azzaj Täklä Sellasé, alias Tinno, a learned cleric and member of the imperial court, is nevertheless exceptional in that he included in his work several tantalisingly brief, but exceptionally interesting references to Oromo life.

He devotes some attention to the division of Oromo society into age groups. In a passage reminiscent of Bahrey he explains that each Oromo clan was divided into five groups which were every eight years "appointed" to public office. Those so elevated were called *luba*, and were uncircumcised until the time of their *lubenät*, or appointment.

Members of the various age groups, he explains, often operated separately. In one battle with the Emperor an Oromo army was thus divided into three separate units: one made up exclusively of *luba*, or circumcised, another of *qondala*, or not yet circumcised, and the third of *qéro*, or young unmarried men.[45] This confirms Bahrey's statement that Oromo group members tended to associate with their peers.

The rituals connected with military or other prowess are also mentioned in the chronicle, and add significantly to the information gathered by Bahrey. *Lubas* who killed an enemy during their term of office, we are told, cut the hair of their head. The ceremony of shaving, known as *gutu*, was thus a sign of warlike success, and those who failed to achieve it "remained sad, weeping as someone against whom a death sentence had been passed".

Oromo religious ideas are also briefly outlined. The Gallas, Täklä Sellasé reports, regarded the sky as their God. The latter was, they believed, the Creator, who killed and kept alive those whom he wished, and was the holder of all power and authority. They also paid great honour to one of their number, the Abba Muda, or Father of Annointing,[46] and visited him, "to be blessed by him with the blessings of victory and the blessings of trophies". As part of the ceremony he would reportedly spit out some of his saliva, mixed with

---

[45] The *qéro*, according to Tutschek, were young unmarried men, generally under twenty-five years of age. Tutschek (1844), p. 46.
[46] Huntingford (1955), p. 83. For a discussion of the term *gutu* see Bairu Tafla (1987), p. 163.

myrrh, which would then be carried around by the warriors, and served them as a talisman.

Oromo traditional worship of nature found expression in the festooning of large trees with cloth and various votive offerings, as illustrated in this much later, nineteenth century, engraving.
From G. Massaia, *I miei trentacinque anni di missione nell' alta Etiopia.*

The Oromos, Täklä Sellasé reports, also attached considerable importance to their soothsayers or prophets, who, as we have already noted in relation to the above-cited accusation against Emperor Ya'qob, consulted the fat or skin of a cow to look into the future.[47]

The Reports of Lobo and Almeida

The Oromo migration was still at its height in the late sixteenth and early seventeenth centuries, during the presence in the area of the Jesuits. Their writings, particularly those of Jerónimo Lobo and Manoel de Almeida, also provide valuable, if at times biased, information on the subject.

The Oromos, the Jesuits believed, were entirely pastoralists. Lobo, who had seen them in Jubaland, as well as near Lake Ashanghi, south of Tegray, i.e. two relatively arid areas where agricultural activity

---

[47] Esteves Pereira (1900), pp.39, 82, 165, 167.

would have been virtually impossible, claimed that they neither sowed nor cultivated the land, but subsisted only on meat and milk. Almeida, who accepted this view, likewise wrote of the Oromos: "They never cultivate land and sow nothing at all. They live on the cattle which they pasture on wide expanses of country; they drink their milk and eat their flesh". That, he asserts, was all they normally consumed, though he concedes that during their expeditions they also ate whatever food they found.

As for the prohibition on soldiers' marriages, and the abandonment of illicitly born children, which Bahrey had earlier mentioned, the Jesuits drew attention mainly to the children's fate. Lobo claimed that the Gallas did not look after children born to soldiers, but had them "thrown into the forest to the wild beasts", and that no one could rescue them "without undergoing the death penalty". He recognised, however, that soldiers who had laid down their arms, reared their children like other parents. Almeida, on the other hand, sensationalised the story. Ignoring the fact that children were apparently abandoned only when born to soldiers illicitly he writes as though abandonment was a general practice. He thus asserts, evidently incorrectly, that "for the first six or seven years after they marry they cast away in the open country all the sons and daughters born to them and leave them to die of sheer neglect". Anyone trying to take care of them, he adds, was considered "not merely as an enemy but as an accursed and devilish person".

The Jesuits were impressed, and indeed alarmed, by Oromo military power. Almeida declared that the Gallas were "much feared" because they went to war "determined and firmly resolved to conquer or die". They had moreover, he believed, "increased greatly" in numbers, because "each man had many wives". Turning to their remarkable military successes he claims that the "first thing" a new *luba* did on coming to power was to assemble the "best people" they could find, and make "several raids into the territories of the empire", in the course of which the Oromo soldiers won fame and enriched themselves with much booty. This they called *Dela Guto*, or "general muster". They had the custom, he confirms, of "not cutting the hair of their heads" until they had killed an enemy in war, or some fierce wild animal, such as a lion. As soon as they killed one they shaved their heads, leaving the top long.[48]

---

[48] Lockhart (1984), p. 61; Beckingham and Huntingford (1954), pp. 50, 136-7.

Lobo took a similar view. He declared that the Gallas, though often small in number, owed their military success primarily to "the fear they inspired" on account of their "cruelty and ferocity". They were, he insists, "a barbarous and exceedingly ferocious people", who sometimes came in "countless numbers, destroying kingdoms and provinces through which they passed", and leaving them deserted, for they "put to the sword every living thing they found". Elsewhere, describing an Oromo "squadron" he had encountered, he says that they "came in great numbers" armed with "javelins and bucklers, making great shouts and threatening noises to strike fear into our hearts and show themselves at their fiercest".[49]

Emperor Susneyos, according to Almeida, was also much impressed by the courage and determination of the Oromos, to which he attributed both their victories, and the "defeats and routs" of his own forces. These occurred even though the latter were "usually much more numerous". The Oromos, he reports, seldom came in bands of more than six to eight thousand, but these were "mostly picked young men", and therefore almost invincible. The Emperor's soldiers, he says, "could not possibly withstand" the first onslaught of the Oromos, for which reason the monarch would generally "let them invade the country and steal the cattle and whatever else they found". He and his soldiers would then wait for them on their return, by which time their "first fury" had been broken, and they were thinking of reaching their country and securing and preserving their booty. It was by this stratagem that he often defeated them.

Another reason for the successful advance of the Oromos was, Almeida thought, that they were essentially pastoralists, rather than agriculturalists. Since they did not sow, and were therefore without grain, the Emperor's armies, who took no food supplies with them, could not "penetrate far into their country". When it was known that the latter were advancing against them the Oromos would therefore retire "many days' journey into the interior". The monarch's soldiers, unable to find any supplies in the Oromo lands, were unable to follow them for any distance, and were therefore soon "compelled to withdraw", often with "heavy losses of men from sheer hunger".[50]

A further, and no less important, geographical factor for the Oromo advance was that it took place, Almeida insists, in eastern or

---

[49] Lockhart (1984), pp. 61-2, 159, 212.
[50] Lockhart (1984) p. 159: Beckingham and Huntingford (1954), p. 136.

southern provinces, such as Wäj, Fätägar, Däwaro and Bali, which consisted "mostly" of "level country with wide open plains" in which Galla horsemen could easily penetrate. Most of the northern provinces held by the Emperor, notably Tegray, Bägémder, Gojjam, Amhara, Sämén, Wägära, Sägädé, Wälqayt, Shäwa and Wäläqa, were by contrast "nearly all amazingly mountainous". Explaining the strategic importance of this he argued that the Oromos would have taken possession of the entire empire if it had not been for the mountains, and in particular for the country's *ambas*, or flat-topped mountains. These were "very lofty" and had "perpendicular sides" which could only be "climbed with difficulty by one or two paths". Their tops comprised level and well-watered land on which the inhabitants lived "as in a fortress or a city established by God". There were "many" such *ambas,* but most of those in Amhara would have fallen to the Gallas, if God had not given it "natural frontiers" which were held to be "impregnable".[51]

Other geographical factors were also of importance, Almeida explains, in arresting the Oromo expansion. Gojjam was thus protected by the Blue Nile and Dämbeya by Lake Tana, while Enarya, lacking such natural defences, relied on the "great bravery" and intelligence of its inhabitants.[52]

By the time of Susneyos's succession the Oromos had made themselves masters, Almeida reiterates, of "most" of the empire. They had "surrounded" the "greater part" of the lands subject to the Emperor, from Angot in the north-east southwards through Däwaro, Ifat, Bali, Fätägar, Wäj, part of Shäwa, Bizamo and Damot, to the country of the Gongas. Elaborating on this movement, as well as on the growing disunity of the Oromos - and introducing a somewhat naive theological argument for good measure - he concluded:

"If God had not blinded them [the Gallas] and willed that certain families or tribes among them should be at war with one another constantly, there would not have been an inch of land in the empire, of which they were not masters. To this end God ordained also that the kingdoms which are today subject should be very mountainous and consist of very steep ranges where the Gallas' cavalry cannot readily make raids, which is the kind of fighting they practise".[53]

---

[51] Beckingham and Huntingford (1954), pp. 37-8, 56, 83, 97.
[52] Beckingham and Huntingford (1954), pp. 19, 150.
[53] Beckingham and Huntingford (1954), pp. 135-6, 146.

The victories of the Oromos, which were by then drawing to a close, were, it should be emphasised, unlike those of many peoples in history, not based on either superior numbers or better weapons. The Emperor's forces, according to Almeida, were in fact "usually much more numerous" than those of the Oromos, and had better horses, as well as "muskets, helmets, and coats of mail in plenty". Almeida states that the only offensive weapons of the Oromos were spears and clubs, and their defensive ones shields, mostly made of double ox-hide, though the tougher ones were of buffalo hide. The horses of the Oromos were moreover not as good as those of their adversaries. Almeida reports that the former rode nags, which were, however, capable of enduring the "great fatigue" to which their riders accustomed them, "making them trot at half speed for whole days at a time". Oromo saddles were likewise not particularly noteworthy, for they were "very light and very simply made". Oromo stirrups were made of iron, thin and narrow, for they did not hold the foot, but, like those of the people to the north, held only the big toe.[54]

Consequences of the Oromo Migration

The contraction of the empire resulting from the Oromo conquests led to a significant fall, Almeida notes, in imperial revenues. The Emperors of earlier times thus had "a great advantage" over those of his day, for they had formerly possessed many more and "much bigger" kingdoms. Some by his time had been occupied by the Oromos, while others had been isolated by them, and had therefore become "partly independent". Enarya, the empire's principal gold-producing province, in particular had been "hard pressed", with the result that its tax revenue had dropped from one thousand ounces to only five hundred.[55] Difficulties were also reported in the nearby district of Guman. Its inhabitants, according to Susneyos's chronicle, in 1609 had taken advantage of the situation to withhold their gold tribute. The monarch, much irritated, had the defaulters bound, and later despatched an expedition, which ravaged their country before he eventually forgave them.[56]

The Oromo advance also had interesting ethnic consequences. In his efforts to resist Oromo advances, Susneyos, Almeida reports, had

---

[54] Beckingham and Huntingford (1954), p. 137.
[55] Beckingham and Huntingford (1954), pp. 86-7.
[56] Esteves Pereira (1900), p. 105.

allocated "much land" in Gojjam and Dämbeya to various other non-Oromo groups, among them Agäws, Gongas, and Gafats, whom he hoped would help him resist Oromo pressure. Land had also been given, as indicated by Täklä Sellasé, to "loyal" Oromos, who had allied themselves with the monarch.[57]

In other parts of the country the coming of the Oromos had on the other hand led to the assimilation, or in some instances only partial assimilation, of various ethnic groups, notably in the case of Bizamo and Damot, where there had been extensive Oromo intermarriage with Gafats.[58]

Religious Ideas, and Dress

The Jesuits, as Catholic missionaries, were hostile to Oromo religious ideas. Lobo complained that the Gallas were "all pagan", for, though they adored no idols, they followed what he terms "superstitious practices". Though they acknowledged a "superior being" called Wak, their ideas, he claimed, were so "confused" that it could not be equated with either Heaven or God. Almeida took a similar, though not identical, view. Most Oromos, he believed, were "heathens", though not fully so, for though they worshipped no idols, they took "very little account of God". A few Oromos, he was happy to report, had, however, been converted to Catholicism. They had taken it "so much to heart" that after Fasilädäs's re-introduction of the Orthodox faith they suffered much persecution.[59]

One of the most interesting accounts of Oromo dress at this time was penned by Lobo. Describing a group of Oromo soldiers, and the women accompanying them, he stated that both sexes were dressed in leather, rather than cotton which was more common in the north. They anointed themselves with blood, painted signs on their faces, chests and arms, and used the entrails of slaughtered livestock to make small ribbons which they wore around their necks. These decorations, first worn by the men, were subsequently passed on to the women, by which time, he sneers, they were "not very fragrant".[60]

---

[57] Beckingham and Huntingford (1954), p. 54.
[58] Beckingham and Huntingford (1954), p. 136.
[59] Lockhart (1984), p.159; Beckingham and Huntingford (1954), pp. 136-7.
[60] Lockhart (1984), p. 61.

Fasilädäs and Yohannes I

Fighting between Oromos and the empire continued during the Gondär monarchy, whose rulers were becoming steadily better equipped with fire-arms. Power during the reigns of Emperor Fasilädäs (1632-1667) and his son Yohannes I (1667-1681) was for that reason shifting significantly against any and all enemies of the central Ethiopian state.

Fasilädäs, as evident from the shorter chronicle for the period, was much involved, like his father Susneyos, in resistance to Oromo incursions. This resulted in further heavy fighting, mainly in Gojjam and Bägémder. Learning in 1639-40 that Oromos were advancing in the region he established himself at Jara, near the Blue Nile. The following year he was informed of renewed Oromo penetration in Gojjam, and fought a fierce battle in the area. He waged war against the Akäbo Oromos in the Sabé country in 1649-50. Five years later he went once more to Gojjam, and advanced to Addis Aläm, but this time the Oromos fled at the news of his arrival.

Later, while in Bägémder in 1652, he despatched one of his officers, Ras Wäldä Giyorgis, on an expedition against the Wako Oromos. The chief defeated them, and in 1658-9 was sent on a further mission, to Jara, which was again successful.

Fasilädäs returned to Gojjam in 1661-2 to fight against the Oromos, but, hearing of his coming, they once again retreated. Another Oromo army appeared in Bägémder shortly afterwards, whereupon he sent one of his officers, Däjazmach Mahdärä Maryam, to defend the province. He marched against the Wärrä Himanus, defeated them, and, it is claimed, exterminated them to the last man.[61]

Further fierce fighting took place during the reign of Yohannes I. An Oromo force made an incursion into Bägémder in 1668, and reached Asgwagwa near the source of the Täkkäzé River. The Oromos comprised no less than twelve groups, namely the Wechalés, Rätayas, Räminus, Régus, Abätis, Anas, Guras, Sabas, Rébkos, Rejus, Arsus and Urukalas, but were defeated by the Emperor's commander, Mälka Krestos. Another confrontation took place in 1672, when Yohannes marched against the Tulämas, who, realising their inability to resist, fled and could not be found.[62]

---

[61] Basset (1881), XVIII, 287-90; Huntingford (1989), pp. 183-5.
[62] Guidi, (1903-5), pp. 9, 16.

Notwithstanding such conflicts the Ethiopian empire and the more northerly Oromos were becoming inextricably involved in each others' affairs. Dramatic evidence of this was seen in 1680 when Yohannes's son Iyasu, the future Emperor, came into conflict with his father - and, according to the chronicle, crossed the Blue Nile, and found refuge for a short while among the "pagan" Gallas. Several dissatisfied young nobles, and, interestingly enough, three monks of Dima, followed his example, and allied themselves with their former Oromo enemies.

While at a place called Bétä Wäläto, in Oromo-occupied territory, Iyasu met a large number of his father's former subjects, the Kordidas, some of whom had joined the Oromos voluntarily, while others had been captured by the latter. The Kordidas for one reason or another had abandoned Christianity, and adopted the religion of their Oromo masters, but wished to return to their former faith. They accordingly made Iyasu promise that if and when he came to the throne he would help them to achieve this ambition.

Not long after this the Emperor and his son were reconciled, and Yohannes agreed, on pain of excommunication, to forgive his son and to give him back a provincial governorship.[63]

Iyasu I: Conflict and Reconciliation

Emperor Iyasu I (1681-1706), though a sometime refugee among the Oromos, continued his father's policy of resistance to the latter. He marshalled considerably greater strength, and many more firearms, than his predecessors. He was therefore militarily in a much better position than the Oromos, many of whom he sought to assimilate or bring under his control. Increasing numbers of Oromos were moreover by this time coming to accept imperial sovereignty, and even those who did not were by then reluctant to do battle with the well-armed imperial forces.

Confrontation with the Oromos took place in 1684, when the Emperor despatched scouts to the country of both the Tulämas and Wällos. His emissaries to the Tulämas reported, according to his chronicle, that because of drought there was no grass in the area. Messengers from the Guratis and other Tulämas arrived at about the same time. They urged him not to advance into their country, for they declared that they were his subjects, and had given proof of their

---

[63] Guidi (1903-5), pp. 50-3, 132.

affection. The scouts returning from the Wällos on the other hand stated that the latter had plenty of grass, and, being unaware of his presence, could easily be taken by surprise. The Emperor, after consulting his advisers, decided to proceed to Wällo. Before doing so, however, he sent his commander, Ras Anestayos, to confront another nearby Oromo group, the Wechalés, who lived west of Wällo. His forces killed a considerable number of Wechalé warriors, burnt their houses and fields, seized many women as slaves, and carried off numerous cattle.

Iyasu then carried out his main assault on the Wällos, who were so terrified by the fate of the Wechalés, and so afraid of passing through the latter's burning fields, that they were unable to offer any resistance. The Emperor pillaged their country, killed many of their soldiers, and seized many women, and large herds of cattle. The victory was so complete that the Wechalés appealed for Iyasu's clemency. They declared that they were his subjects, and would serve him in any way he wished. He undertook an expedition to another Galla country in the following year, but the inhabitants, aware of his earlier victory, either hid or fled.[64]

A few years later, in 1689, Iyasu redeemed the promise he had made while still a prince to the Oromos' subjects, the Kordidas, who had begged him assist their return to the Christian fold. This happened when he marched south to Dära, where he took many of the Tuläma Oromos prisoner. He then freed the Kordidas, no less than 100,000 of whom, accompanied by their women and children, are reported to have entered his camp singing and dancing with joy. This figure, if true, was truly immense in view of the country's small population at the time.[65]

Despite the defeat of the Tulämas, another Oromo group, the Libäns took the offensive in 1691. They crossed the Blue Nile, and were reportedly bent on occupying all Gojjam. Iyasu responded by riding to the province, whereupon the Oromos once again fled. The Emperor's presence is said to have also stopped the depredations of other Oromo groups, among them the Afächalas, Tulämas and Mächas. Peace and tranquility was thus re-established in the Blue

---

[64] Basset (1881), XVIII, pp. 244, 287, 294; Guidi (1903-5) pp. 69-79.
[65] Guidi (1903-5), pp. 132-8.

Nile area, with the result, the chronicle claims, that woodcutters and water-carriers were once again able to travel there in safety.[66]

Another Oromo group, the Qäla Gändas, shortly afterwards gave their support to Iyasu. They came to him in 1693 declaring that they were his subjects. Unlike the Kordidas, an apparently largely Amhara group who had wished to free themselves from Oromo rule, these were actual Oromos whose objective was to support the Emperor against incursions by other Oromos. These Qäla Gändas reported that they had driven away his Tuläma and Libän enemies, and had eliminated the former from a wide stretch of country from Halqa to Gend Bärät and Kilolé. The Emperor rewarded these new allies royally, giving them a thousand (in another text 10,000) *shämmas* and a thousand (or 10,000) *chan*, or containers, of grain.[67]

Oromo pressure was nevertheless re-asserted in 1695 when Iyasu was informed that Galla armies were expected to advance along five routes into Gojjam, Damot, Buré, Wämbarma and Agäwmeder. Alarmed at this report, he rode secretly to Damot with a small band, but the Oromos again fled as soon as they heard of his arrival.[68]

In the following year he made his way southwards to Shäwa. There he was angered to see that the Oromos had advanced to the vicinity of several important towns, and he declared his intention to drive them as far as the Awash River. His Amhara and Shäwa subjects, perhaps unwilling to see their country ravaged by the coming of imperial troops, or perhaps reluctant to incur Oromo enmity, advised him, however, against embarking on a campaign against the neighbouring Oromos that year. His presence in the area is nevertheless said to have terrorised the Käräyu and Qäla Gända Oromos, as well as some unspecified group in Adäl.[69]

Iyasu then proceeded to nearby Mörat. Report has it that its inhabitants and those of nearby Märhabété when coming to pay their respects were attacked by Oromo marauders, but the latter, on learning of his presence, were also so terrified that they too disappeared, leaving most of their horses and weapons behind.[70]

---

[66] Basset (1881), XVIII, 297-8; Guidi (1903-5), p. 161.
[67] Guidi, 174; Basset (1881), XVIII, 303-4; Bruce (1790), II, 959.
[68] Guidi (1903-5), pp. 183-5; Basset (1881), XVIII, 307.
[69] Guidi (1903-5), pp. 189-90.
[70] Basset (1881), XVIII, 308; Guidi (1903-5), p. 190.

Some months later the Emperor took steps to defend Damot and Gojjam against another Oromo force reportedly crossing the Blue Nile. There he received a message from the Tälätä Oromos, who, it will be recalled, were part of the subject non-Oromo population under Oromo rule, saying that they were in conflict with the Wälädäñña Oromos, and needed his help against the latter. He accordingly called upon his soldiers to proceed across the Blue Nile, but the greater part of them refused to leave their estates. They argued that they were free men, obliged only to pay tribute on their land. He nevertheless made his way with a small force to the country of the Wälädaññas, who, learning of his arrival, made peace with their erstwhile enemies, the Tälätas, and, together with them, fled with their wives, children, cattle and household goods. He was reputedly very sad at the behaviour of the Tälätas, and sent them a message, reminding them that it was at their request that he had come, and summoning them to join him. This, however, they failed to do so, and after waiting three days, he withdrew from the area, and returned to Gondär.[71]

On a subsequent expedition, in 1697, he made his way to Bibuñ in central Gojjam to confront an expected Oromo incursion, but this threat also failed to materialise.[72]

Returning to Shäwa in 1699 Iyasu proceeded to the site of the old Däbra Libanos monastery, which he learnt, to his chagrin, had earlier been "devastated" by the Ahmäd ibn Ibrahim, or Grañ, and later by the Oromos. Not far away at a place called Zéga Wädäb he found another group of Kordidas, possibly prisoners of the Oromos, or defectors thereto, and arranged for them to join him. He then deployed his troops over a wide area, and gave the orders that, if any Gallas attacked, his soldiers should discharge their guns, so that he, thus warned, could rush to their aid. Nothing, however, came of the plan, for the Oromos once again failed to appear. He therefore advanced towards the country of the Wällos, who, learning of his coming, immediately fled. The same happened in 1697 when he rode to the country of the Libäns, who, hearing of his arrival, were "seized by a great fear, and fled before him". When he shortly afterwards went to the country of the Machakal Oromos they likewise on two occasions are said to have immediately disappeared.[73]

---

[71] Basset (1881), XVIII, 310; Guidi (1903-5), pp. 199-201.
[72] Basset (1881), XVIII, 310; Guidi (1903-5), pp. 201-3.
[73] Guidi (1903-5), pp. 211-12, 218-19.

Interesting testimony to Oromo acceptance of Iyasu's rule came in 1700 when his commander Ras Farés was approached by some of the Christians of Lasta, who were then under strong Oromo pressure. They asked him to cut down, or burn, a forest at nearby Däbrä Gärza, which, they claimed, was used as a hiding place by the Abäti, Wäro, Qoré and Ana Gallas, who were encircling them. The chief did as he was bid, but the Oromos at once came to him to complain. Declaring that the forest was their shelter from both cold and heat, as well as a fortress in time of war, they begged him to desist from destroying the trees, and warned him that if he did not do so they would fight against him, as Iyasu's loyal subjects, and, after castrating him, would throw his private parts in front of the monarch, for they were, they claimed, Iyasu's guards no less than he. The Emperor apparently accepted this view, for he sent a message to the Ras to stop the wood-cutting, on the ground that the Oromos were guards in his service.[74]

A major clash of arms between Iyasu and another Oromo group, the Gudrus, nevertheless took place later that year when he carried out an expedition south of the Blue Nile. The operation started inauspiciously, for some of his men were attacked by the Gudrus when camping at night. On crossing the river, however, they retaliated by killing numerous Gudru warriors, took many women as slaves, and seized numerous cattle. In the ensuing fighting Iyasu was confronted by a renowned Oromo warrior, who tried to strike him with his spear, but, before he could do so, the monarch shot him with his rifle. The Gudru chiefs thereupon withdrew, after which the Emperor's men took many prisoners, and set fire to the Gudru countryside.[75]

Iyasu prepared to return home, but the Gudrus, regrouping, attacked his baggage train, killed many soldiers, and seized not a few horses and mules. His army was thrown into complete disarray. He at one point was surrounded by his assailants, but succeeded in disengaging himself, though many of his chiefs perished in the fray.

Notwithstanding this debacle Iyasu reached home safely. He subsequently made peace, in 1702, with some of the more friendly Bässo Gudrus, whose nobles entered his camp, and danced ceremonially in his honour. He nevertheless determined to avenge himself on those Gudrus who had earlier killed many of his Oromo friends, the Bursas and the Chäfäntas. He accordingly attacked and

---

[74] Guidi (1903-5), pp. 219-20.
[75] Basset (1881), XVIII, 314-15; Guidi (1903-5), pp. 222-6.

defeated their army, after which he led its women into captivity, and took away many cattle. When he advanced further the inhabitants, seeing him from afar, fled into the mountains and caves, and are reported to have "disappeared like smoke before the wind". Many defeated Gudrus made their way to the country of the Libäns, who, siding with Iyasu, attacked them with spears, and killed many of them. The Bässo Oromos in the Emperor's service then joined in the attack, leaving the Gudrus no escape. This, the chronicler angrily declares, was no more than they deserved, for they had, he complains, spilt the blood of old and young, as well as priests, deacons and monks.[76]

Despite such conflicts increasing numbers of Oromos were by this time accepting imperial sovereignty. Not long after the above fighting five Mächa groups came to pay homage to Iyasu. Later when travelling southwards from Gondär to Qäbäro Méda near Yebaba in Gojjam in 1704 he was greeted by many Tälätas, Häros and Libäns, who declared that God had delivered their country over to him, and asked him to swear that he would treat them with mercy. Iyasu swore by his crown that he would do so, and proceeded to decorate all the Tälätas, great and small. Some of the Tent Oromos, who had presumably not joined in the agreement, were on the other hand placed in chains.[77]

Iyasu, setting forth on another campaign, ordered his men to prepare for four months' service. Some of his followers did so obediently, but others grumbled, saying, "Four months. We cannot stay even four days in the land of the Machas!"[78]

After crossing the Blue Nile, Iyasu gave the Bässo Oromos some land he had captured at a place called Yägefo. He was later visited by two other Oromo groups, the Täläta Horos and the Jemmas, both of whom came dancing ceremonially before him. They spoke flatteringly of his greatness, and declared their desire to prostrate themselves before him. They later pleaded with the Bässos to make peace. The Tents, however, remained recalcitrant. Iyasu therefore ordered his men to attack, whereupon the Tents, terrified, sent him a message saying that they had sinned by rebelling, and begged him to forgive them. This he agreed to do, after which the Tents gave him seven hostages as an assurance of their good faith. He then issued orders to

---

[76] Basset (1881), XVIII, 315; Guidi (1903-5), pp. 246, 232-6.
[77] Basset (1881), XVIII, 318-19; Guidi, pp. 250-1.
[78] Guidi (1903-5), pp. 251-4.

his men to the sound of trumpets, saying, "Do not pillage the habitations of the Jemmas because they are my subjects".[79]

Despite these initiatives several Oromo groups rejected the Emperor's attempts at reconciliation, and decided to continue the fight. They included a number of Gudrus, Libäns, Jemmas, Chälehas, Wäbos, and Amoru Horos, and related clans. They were commanded by a warrior called Dilamo, who was the Abba Gada, or clan leader, of the Libäns. He reportedly told his men, the Mächa Oromos, not to take trophies or loot individually, but instead to wait for him to destroy Iyasu's army, after which he would himself divide among them all the treasures they captured. He declared, interestingly enough, that he would then place Iyasu's crown on his head, sit on Iyasu's throne, and become a king like him.

The Oromo army, the chronicle claims, was at this time as numerous as the clouds, and had as many foot soldiers as the sand, besides countless cavalry. Iyasu's men, though apparently fewer in number, were in possession of fire-arms, and used them to full advantage. The Máchas, faced with these weapons, rapidly succumbed. Dilamo fell from his horse, and was seriously crushed, after which a certain Zämbeté, a Bässo Oromo warrior, castrated him. The Abba Gada of the Wäbos also died in battle, and large numbers of Oromo soldiers were wounded. The survivors fled.

After this victory Iyasu ordered his men to live off the country of the Chälehas, but, wishing to win the hearts of the vanquished, declared that the soldiers should spare the latters' houses, and not touch even a single blade of grass in their thatch. His armies then swept southwards as far as Enarya.

The defeated Oromos then accepted Iyasu's rule. The Täläta Libäns came to the Emperor dancing ceremonially, and brought him much tribute consisting of clothes, wheat and donkeys, while the Täläta Wäbos brought fattened cattle, honey and butter. A great Oromo chief and *qallecha*, or religious leader, called Abeko likewise sent his sons with tribute in cattle, honey, and innumerable male and female slaves. Iyasu responded by presenting him and his offspring with many fine gifts, including a golden saddle.[80]

Iyasu meanwhile had taken many captives, whom he baptised as Christians. He also established Täläta Jawi troops to guard the

---

[79] Guidi (1903-5), pp. 253-4.
[80] Basset (1881), XVIII, 318-19; Guidi (1903-5), pp. 254-8, 262-3.

frontiers against incursions by Oromo groups from the country south of the Blue Nile.[81]

Travelling southwards he proceeded to the Gibé River, where he ordered his men to discharge all their rifles, with the result that the entire area reportedly trembled. The hymns of the clergy then also resounded, and, as the chronicle puts it, the worship of God replaced that of fat, i.e. the traditional Oromo method of using ritually slaughtered animals as a basis for prophecies.[82]

Iyasu, who was accompanied by a cohort of Bursa, Chäfänta, Qalä Gända and Libän Oromos, planned to continue his journey even further southwards to attack the remainder of the opposition Tents. He was, however, prevented by the coming of the rains. His advisers urged him to return home, but he replied that he could not do so without the consent of his Täläta allies. The latter duly agreed that he should withdraw, but begged him to take them with him, and thus free them from slavery to the Oromos. Iyasu concurred, on condition that they abandoned their traditional cult, and worship instead the Christian God. He then ordered them to proceed in front of him so that he could defend them against attacks from the rear.[83]

An epidemic broke out at about this time, whereupon the paternalistic Emperor commanded everyone to look after those infected, and take them to their homes. Anyone failing to do so, he declared, would have his property seized, and handed over to the sick. One Oromo group, the Lénchas, whose custom was possibly to isolate the infected so as to prevent the spread of the disease, ignored the royal order. Iyasu was furious with them, but shortly afterwards pardoned them. He later fought successful engagements with three other Oromo groups, the Léqa and Sibu Tälätas, the Bässos, and some of the Mächas, after which he returned home.[84]

Iyasu's numerous expeditions and political initiatives described above were important in that they resulted in many Oromos entering into imperial service. One of the most important was Awadi Näto, a Täläta from the Jemma area, whom the Emperor, according to the chronicle, loved and trusted more than any of his courtiers, but who, like so many nobles later rebelled. Another Oromo functionary was

---

[81] Guidi (1903-5), pp. 261, 268, 294.
[82] Guidi (1903-5), p. 264.
[83] Guidi (1903-5), pp. 267-70.
[84] Guidi (1903-5), pp. 266-7, 270-6.

Tigé, a Libän leader, whom Iyasu elevated to the rank of Däjazmach. He was put in charge of the Horo and Dewise Tälätas and the Mächas, all three of whom had by then allied themselves to the royal cause. Iyasu told him also to guard the Libän country, and establish a town in Gend Bärät. To assist him in this task he provided him, significantly, with men who knew how to handle rifles. Tigé, as a loyal courtier, was later promoted to the prestigious rank of Behtwädäd, or "Beloved" of the King, apparently the first Oromo to enjoy that highly esteemed status.[85]

Téwoflos, Dawit III and Bäkäffa: Integration

The period after Iyasu's death, and the accession of Emperor Téwoflos in 1708, witnessed a further integration of Oromos in imperial affairs. The aforesaid courtier Tigé played a major role in a palace conspiracy, and was arrested, and imprisoned in far away Hamasén. He soon escaped, however, and induced many Libän, Qäla Gänd and Bässo Oromos to give their support to a usurping Amhara emperor. Fierce fighting ensued in the course of which the Bässos and Libäns suffered heavy casualties, and Tigé was killed.[86]

Contacts between Oromos and the empire developed further after the death of Emperor Yostos in 1716. Fifty royal princes, who had been imprisoned on the mountain of Wähni, the place of detention for members of the royal family, made their way to Gondär to claim the throne. The choice fell on Iyasu's eldest son, who was crowned as Emperor Dawit III (1716-1721). His younger brother Bäkäffa thereupon fled, like Susneyos and Iyasu before him, to the nearby Oromos, and sought hospitality with Amizo, the leader of the Yäjju Gallas. This Oromo chief received him warmly, and it was his clansmen, according to Bruce, who first gave their guest the nickname Bäkäffa, i.e. the Inexorable, by which he was thereafter generally known. After residing some time with them he made his way to Bägémder, but was soon captured, and again incarcerated at Wähni. He nevertheless remained grateful to Amizo for the kindness shown to him during his short spell of freedom.[87]

Dawit meanwhile had also developed Oromo contacts. Like his father Iyasu he employed a contingent of Jawi Galla troops, whom he

---

[85] Guidi (1903-5), pp. 275, 278; Basset (1881), III, 329.
[86] Basset (1881), XVIII, 329, 331-2; Bruce (1790), II, 533-5.
[87] Bruce (1790), II, 574, 585, 593, 659; Guidi (1903-5), pp. 275, 278.

used in 1717 to suppress a rebellious gathering of monks. In the ensuing fracas over a hundred persons were reportedly killed.[88]

On Dawit's death in 1721 Bäkäffa once more came down from Wähni, and by popular demand was proclaimed emperor. "Resolute, active and politic", as Bruce describes him, he was said, like Yaq'ob and Susneyos before him, to have been much influenced by his stay among the Oromos. In particular, according to the Scotsman, he had adopted their belief in "divinations, dreams and prophecies".[89]

Bäkäffa continued the by then well established use of Oromo Jawi cavalry. Early in his reign he is stated by Bruce to have employed a thousand of them to crush a rebellion by one of the royal princesses. The Jawi were on that and other occasions commanded by an Oromo warrior called Wäräñña. Bruce claims that the latter was a convert to Christianity, and had originally been a merchant, but, because of his bravery, had been promoted to high rank. He served Bäkäffa throughout his reign, and at various times held the titles of Bajerond, or Treasurer, Shaläqa, or Commander of a Thousand Men, and Qäññazmach, governor of Damot and Agäw. He defended both provinces against Oromo incursions from south of the Blue Nile, but did so, Bruce claims, more through friendship than by the use of force.[90]

Despite Wäräñña's personal loyalty the Jawi, like other imperial forces, were often in a state of rebellion. A group of Täläta Jawi, whom Iyasu had stationed by the Blue Nile, revolted in 1723, but were easily defeated by Damot troops in Bäkäffa's service. Difficulties with other Jawis erupted in the following year when those in Damot rebelled, but were likewise easily crushed, largely by Bäkäffa's Libän and Bässo Oromo troops. They seized the Jawi women and children, and innumerable cattle and sheep. Surrendering the Jawis reminded the Emperor that they had been freed from slavery by his father, and begged for his pardon. This he granted, reportedly giving rise to much rejoicing in the land.[91]

Notwithstanding such insurrections Oromo soldiers were constantly active in the Emperor's service. Bässos thus fought against

---

[88] Basset (1881), XVIII, 342; Bruce (1790), II, 590.
[89] Bruce (1790), II, 593, 597.
[90] Bruce (1790), II, 600, 605-6, 613; Bruce (1813), VII, 91; Guidi (1912), p. 28.
[91] Guidi (1903-5), pp. 294-5, 297-301; Basset (1881), XVIII, 350.

Bäkäffa's enemies in Gojjam in 1724, and Jawis and Bässos against a Lasta rebel in 1725.[92]

Wärañña once more came to the fore after the death of Bakäffa in 1730. The latter's widow the redoubtable Dowager Queen, Mentewwäb, who with her kinsmen was then taking over the government, despatched Wärañña, together with a force of Tuläma Oromo wariors and some Muslim riflemen, to guard Mount Wähni. She did this, as the chronicle says, to prevent the imprisoned princes from conspiring for the throne as her husband had done nine years earlier. Her young son was thereupon proclaimed Iyasu II. The Mächa Oromos, interestingly enough, were the first to pay hommage to the new monarch, who thereupon decorated them with *kabba*s, or cermonial cloaks.[93]

Iyasu II

Imperial dependence on Oromo support was by this time so considerable that when a rebellion broke out in Damot shortly after young Emperor Iyasu's coronation in 1730 Mentewwäb turned to her late husband's old Oromo courtier Wärañña, and appointed him to the post of governor of the province which he had held in her husband's time. The nobleman, who made use of Jawi, Däräbi and Mächa Oromo troops, later crushed an insurrection by the nearby Agäws. Realising, Bruce says, that Gondär was heavily dependent on them for its provisions he nevertheless refrained from any punitive action, but merely used the threat of Oromo intervention to ensure the enforcement of the peace he had established. Iyasu's chronicler goes out of his way to praise the "devotion of the Gallas", and particularly of the Mächa and Wariho clans. Jawi and Tuläma troops in Iyasu's service were also highly honoured, and later played a major role in resisting a rebellion in Gondär. It was finally crushed by Wärañña, who mobilised many Oromos of the Mächa, Yelmana and Densa clans in support of the crown.[94]

Wärañña, by then a highly trusted courtier, was later given the rank of Fitawrari, or Commander of the Advance Guard, and subsequently served successively as Däjazmach, or governor, of the southern frontier districts, and later of Damot, Gojjam, and eventually

---

[92] Basset, 354, 357; Guidi (1903-5), pp. 310, 320.
[93] Guidi (1912), pp. 31, 40, 59; Bruce (1790), II, 614.
[94] Bruce (1790), II, 616-17; Guidi (1912) pp.39- 40, 58, 77, 79.

Bägémder, the strategically all-important province in which the imperial capital was situated. He was described in the royal chronicle as being as sharp as a sword and as fast as a bird, and served in 1744 as the Fitawrari, or commander, in a campaign which Iyasu carried out disasterously, as we shall see, against the kingdom of Sennar on the western frontier.

Iyasu's soldiers, often commanded by Wärañäa, throughout this time included many Mächa, Yelmäna, Densa and Bässo Oromos. They fought for the monarchy not only in the south, but also in many areas of the north, including the Atbara River area, Tegray, and Lasta.[95]

Wobit and Iyo'as

The political importance the Oromos had acquired was later recognised by Empress Mentewwäb. Determined, according to Bruce, to reduce the influence of her son's first wife, an Amhara woman, she banished her with her children to Mount Wähni, and arranged for Iyasu to marry an Oromo princess called Wobit. She was the daughter of Amizo, the Yäjju leader who had earlier afforded refuge to Bäkäffa. A member of the Tuläma clan she was thereupon christened Bersabesh, and duly gave birth to a son by name Iyo'as, who on Iyasu's death in 1755 succeeded to the throne as a child. The first courtier to arrive at the palace to proclaim Iyo'as's accession was, significantly, none other than Wärañña, then governor of Damot.[96]

Wärañña's power, and that of Queen Wobit and of her half-Oromo son Iyo'as, was strengthened shortly afterwards by the arrival in Gondär of no less than 1,200 Oromo horsemen. They were accompanied by many other Oromos, not a few of whom were enrolled in an infantry force of 600 men, commanded, according to Bruce, by a Galla officer called Woshéka, who was a relative of the queen.[97]

Wärañña, by this time one of the most important men in the realm, fought a successful campaign against Näna Giyorgis, chief of an Agäw clan in Damot. The old Oromo courtier died, however, in 1763, "full of years and glory", as Bruce puts it, for he had "preserved his

---

[95] Guidi (1912), pp. 46-7, 53-4, 74-6, 122-5, 137, 163, 165; Bruce (1790), II, 619, 624-7, 636.

[96] Bruce (1790), II, 659-660; Guidi (1912), 180.

[97] Bruce (1790), II, 665, 716.

allegiance to the last, and more than once saved the state by his wisdom, bravery, and activity".[98]

Despite Wäräñña's death Oromo influence at Gondär rapidly increased. The great favour shown to the Oromos, according to Bruce, encouraged many of their countrymen to follow them to the imperial capital. Young Iyo'as later summoned two of his Oromo uncles, Biralé and Lubo, who came with a thousand Oromo horsemen, and were given high titles and placed in charge of the king's person. "In an instant", writes Bruce, "nothing was heard in the palace but Galla", and Iyo'as himself "affected to speak nothing else".[99]

The upshot was that the Oromos, who had two centuries earlier been fighting to establish themselves on the country's periphery, had by now become a major influence in the very centre of imperial power. Young Emperor Iyo'as and his advisers attempted to appoint Oromo noblemen to high provincial office throughout much of the empire. One of his Oromo uncles, Lubo, was made governor of Amhara, while Wäräñña's son Fasil succeeded his father as ruler of Damot. Iyo'as's other Oromo uncle, Biralé, was appointed governor of Bägémder, but was killed before he could take up this important office.[100]

Many Oromos of lesser rank also rose to prominence. One of them was Gwangwél, described by Bruce as chief of the eastern Gallas, or Oromos, of Angot. On one occasion he arrived in Gondär, the Scotsman recalls, riding a cow. Carrying a short spear with a simple iron head and a hide skin shield, he was accompanied by forty horsemen and 500 foot soldiers. He it was who came to the aid of the Gondar monarchy by recovering Emperor Iyasu II's crown, which had been lost during the afore-mentioned disasterous expedition to Sennar, though this appears to have been kept secret, and was not recorded in the royal chronicle at the time.[101] Other Oromos in imperial service included Gobäna, chief of the Mächas, who played a notable role in several contemporary struggles; Toma Gondé, the Abba Gada, or chief, of the Tuläma; two Shaläqas, or officers, Turi, a Tuläma from Wäläqa, who was given the title of Aggafari, or Royal

---

[98] Bruce (1790), II, 664.
[99] Bruce (1790), II, 662; Guidi (1912), p. 234, 237.
[100] Guidi (1912), pp. 237-42, 250, 253, 256.
[101] Guidi (1912), pp. 214, 219-20. For a representation of this crown see Leroy (1964), plate xlix, and discusstion on p. 58

Attendant, and a certain Shäläqa Léncho; and Guncha, the commander of the Seda Tulämas.[102]

Ras Mika'él Sehul, the "astute" (1688-1775), ruler of Tegray and sometime master of Gondär, whose rise to power curtailed increasing Oromo influence at the capital.
From J. Bruce, *Travels to Discover the Source of the Nile.*

Oromo influence on the court had, however, by then reached its zenith. This influence later declined as a result of the rise of the Tegray chieftain Ras Mika'él Sehul, who, after bitter conflict with Wobit's extended family, made himself master of Gondär in 1768. In the following year he deposed the unfortunate Iyo'as, who was murdered a week later.[103] Many Oromos had nevertheless by then found their way into the imperial body politic, and continued thereafter to be involved in Gondärine state affairs. Bruce, who knew

---

[102] Guidi (1912), pp. 61, 65, 82, 85, 237, 248; Bruce (1790), IV, 99.
[103] Guidi (1912), pp. 252-6.

a number of them, claims that they were in his day "better Christians and better soldiers" than any in the Emperor's service.[104]

One further important Oromo of this time was a chief whom the Scotsman refers to as "Woodage Asahel", and describes as a would-be king maker, strongly opposed to Ras Mika'él.[105]

"Woodage Asahel" a late eighteenth century Oromo chief, and would-be king-maker: an engraving based on a sketch by James Bruce's Italian draftsman Luigi Balugani.

---

[104] Bruce (1790), II, 226.
[105] Bruce (1790), III, 421, IV, 32, 200-1.

Chapter 25

THE SOUTH: BALI, DAWARO, FATAGAR, WAJ, IFAT, and the COUNTRY of the MAYAS

The great Oromo migration had a major impact on the southern and eastern provinces, notably Bali, Däwaro, Fätägar, Ifat, and the country of the Mayas, which were the first to be affected.

BALI

Oromo Expansion and Särsä Dengel

The Oromos, according to Bahrey, began their northern migration, as we have seen, during the reign of Lebnä Dengel (1508-1540). They crossed the Gäläna river, the location of which cannot exactly be identified, and "began to invade" Bali during the *lubaship* of Mélbah (1522-1530).[1] Subsequent Oromo penetration was probably curtailed by Imam Ahmäd's conquest of the province, but was later facilitated by the collapse of Muslim power in the area.

Bali at the end of the sixteenth century was, however, still part of the empire. Emperor Särsä Dengel (1563-1597), like his predecessors, appointed a *gärad*, or provincial ruler, for the territory, and employed *chäwa*, or troops, from it to oppose the Oromo advance.[2] This chief or his successor, by name Dägano, later brought tribute, including horses and mules, to Emperor Ya'qob (1597-1604, 1605-1606).[3]

Oromo pressure in the area was later again intensified. The territory was then occupied by the Oromos with little difficulty, for, as Almeida notes, it was "mostly level" with "wide open plains", presenting no obstacles for a semi-nomadic people to overrun.[4]

DAWARO

The latter phase of Imam Ahmäd's rule of Däwaro, described in Chapter 16, coincided with the beginning of Oromo expansion in the province. The occupation was accomplished easily for, as Almeida

---

[1] Beckingham and Huntingford (1954), pp. 111, 115.
[2] Conti Rossini (1912), pp. 62, 95. See also Huntingford (1989), p. 142.
[3] Esteves Pereira (1900), p. 12.
[4] Conti Rossini (1907), p. 195; Huntingford (1989), p. 137; Beckingham and Huntingford (1954), pp. 37. See also Budge (1928), II, 341.

observed, the territory, like Bali, was generally flat with "wide open plains". The Oromo *luba* Kilolé, is said by Bahrey to have thus "made war in the lowlands of Däwaro" in the late 1530s or early 1540s. The Oromos fought at this time with the Adäl Mäbräq, perhaps one of the Emperor's best contingents, as well as with the inhabitants of the region. The Oromo assault was continued by the next *luba*, Bifolé (1546-1554), when all Däwaro was reportedly "devastated ".[5]

After the rains of 1579 Särsä Dengel planned to repulse the Oromos in Däwaro, as well as in neighbouring Fätägar and Ifat, but failed to do so. His chronicle explains this delicately, stating that he discussed the scheme with his chiefs, but that it was not God's will that it should be realised. The proposed campaign was thus abandoned. Instead of marching against the Oromos in the south-east of the empire he therefore launched an expedition against the Fälashas in the north-west.[6]

The Oromo occupation of Däwaro was thus no longer much contested. Many people from the province fled northwards. One such refugee was apparently Yona'él, a rebel during the reign of Susneyos, who "sometimes declared that he was from Däwaro, at other times that he was from Gafat or Angot". Another prominent chief of Däwaro origin at that time was a noble called Keflo, who was reportedly the son of one of the province's *chäwa*..[7]

FATAGAR and WAJ

The Oromo occupation of Fätägar was also easy, for the province, like Bali and Däwaro, consisted, Almeida says, largely of "level country" with "wide open plains". The Oromo occupation began, according to Bahrey, in the time of *luba* Bifolé (1546-1554), when its inhabitants were forced into slavery, and turned into *gäbar*, or tax-paying serfs.[8]

The Oromos, taking with them vast herds of cattle, later advanced into Wäj. The herds, as we have seen, were said, no doubt with much exaggeration, to be so extensive that they seemed to occupy the whole province, rendering it difficult for people to walk anywhere.

---

[5] Conti Rossini (1907), p. 198; Beckingham and Huntingford (1954), pp. 37, 115.
[6] Conti Rossini (1907), pp. 96-7.
[7] Esteves Pereira (1900), pp. 143, 205.
[8] Conti Rossini (1907), p. 198; Beckingham and Huntingford (1954), pp. lxxv, 37, 56, 116, 135.

Särsä Dengel responded, in 1574, by marching south. His men launched an immediate assault, killing a vast number of Oromo warriors, but sparing their women and children. The soldiers then drove the invaders back into Fätägar and Däwaro, and took little interest in the cattle, until their return journey when each man, as noted in the previous chapter, seized as many as five hundred or a thousand head. The peasantry took as many animals as they wished, but still left not a few behind.

After the rains of 1579, Särsä Dengel decided to launch a major campaign against the Oromos in Fätägar, as well as Däwaro and Ifat, but the plan, as earlier noted, was later abandoned.[9]

Fätägar accordingly remained part of the expanding Oromo domain. Some of its population, as of other areas in the south, nevertheless withdrew, Almeida reports, and settled in provinces to the north.[10]

IFAT

Ifat, the scene in previous centuries of much bitter fighting between Christians and Muslims, was by this time regarded as an appendage of nearby Shäwa. Emperor Susneyos for example appointed Yolyos, one of his chiefs, as governor of both provinces. He was accorded the traditional Ifat title of Wälashma', and had his Ifat headquarters on an *amba*, or natural mountain fortress, called Gäfägäf, which he defended against the Muslims of nearby Qächeno.

The province was later largely occupied by the Oromos, but was on at least one occasion in the eighteenth century raided by Shäwan highlanders in search of crops.[11]

THE COUNTRY OF THE MAYAS

The Mayas, hitherto virtually invincible on account of their use of poisoned arrows, succumbed to the Oromos, as we have seen, when the latter during the *luba*ship of Birmajé (1578-1586) adopted body length shields. The result, Bahrey affirms, was that there was nowhere for the Mayas' arrows to strike.[12]

---

[9] Conti Rossini (1907), pp. 52, 96.
[10] Beckingham and Huntingford (1954), p. 56.
[11] Esteves Pereira (1900), pp. 36, 130, 215, 219.
[12] Beckingham and Huntingford (1954), p. 120.

Chapter 26

THE SOUTH-WEST and WEST: GAMO, GURAGE and WAJ, HADEYA, KAMBATA, ENARYA, DAMOT, GAFAT, BIZAMO, THE COUNTRY OF THE GAMBOS, JANJERO, KAFA, and THE COUNTRIES OF THE "SHANQELLAS", GONGAS and DOBE'AS, and the SENNAR FRONTIER

The provinces of the south-west, among them Gämo, Guragé, Hadeya, Enarya, Damot, Gafat, Bizamo, and the country of the Gämbos, were affected by the Oromo advance somewhat later than the territories to the south.

GAMO

Gämo, on account of its southerly location near the south-western shore of Lake Abaya, was one of the first territories in this area to be occupied by the Oromos. This happened, as we have seen, during the life-time of Bahrey, prior to 1593, when, he complains, they "laid waste his country", and "looted all that he possessed".[1]

GURAGE

Because of its south-central location Guragé came under Oromo pressure at a relatively early stage, though later than provinces further south. The first contact was probably during the reign of Emperor Susneyos, whose favourite brother Ras Se'elä Krestos reported that the Mächa Oromos had defeated the Guragés as well as several neighbouring peoples.[2]

The country for the most part survived the Oromo incursion. Local tradition, which is apparently unfamiliar with the above-mentioned conflict, contends that the continued independence of the Guragés owed much to their reliance on the *enset*, or false banana (*Ensete ventricosum*), a staple crop which the Oromos reputedly disliked.[3]

---

[1] Beckingham and Huntingford (1954), p. 114.
[2] Esteves Pereira (1900), pp. 26, 167.
[3] Lebel (1974), pp. 104-5.

Detail from the map *Cate de l'Ethiopie Orientale,* published in M. Legrand's *Voyage historique d'Abissinie,* Paris 1628.

Note indication of the provinces of the interiour, Gojjam (Gojam Rme), Amhara, Angot, and Upper and Lower Shäwa (Haute Shoa, Bas Shoa), and those on the periphery, among them Ifat, Däwaro (Dawaro), Bali, Adäl (Adel), Fätägar (Fatagar), Gamo (Bahargamo, or Lake Gamo), Wäj (Wed), the two Guragé districts of Mugär (Mugar) and Aymällal (Alamalé), Guragé (Gurague R.), Kämbata (Cambat), Alaba (Roy.me d'Alaba), Gänz (Ganz), Janjero (Royamume de Zendero ou Gengiro "qui est un Etat puissant", i.e. which is a powerful kingdom), Enarya (Enaria "ou il y a des mines d'or", i.e. where there gold mines), Shat, Bizamo (Bizamo rme.), Agäw (Agaw), and the country of the Shanqellas (Shankala. "C'est ainsi que les Abyssins noment les Peuples qui n'ont point de demeure fixe", i.e. what the Abyssinians call peoples who have no fixed abode).

Note also location of the Western and Eastern Oromos ("Boren-Galla ou Galles Occidentaux" and "Bertuma-Galla ou Galles Orientaux"), and of the Gafats

(Gafat R.) and Damots (Damot Rm.), both then inhabiting lands south of the Blue Nile.

Susneyos

Guragé contacts with the imperial state, dating back to medieval times, were once more apparent during the reign of Emperor Ya'qob (1597-1603, 1604-7), who chose, or accepted, Ras Zä-Sellasé, a man from the area, as his principal courtier. The chief, whom Bruce describes as "esteemed for bravery and conduct" and "beloved by the soldiers", later overthrew the monarch, and, according to the royal chronicle, for a time "held the realm in his hands".[4]

Relations with the Guragé area likewise came to the fore in 1600 when Prince Susneyos, the future Emperor, undertook an expedition against Sidi, the ruler of Hadeya. Crossing the Gudär River to Wäräb, the prince was received, according to his chronicle, by a number of presumably Christian Guragés. He proceeded to Hazo, where representatives of forty-four Guragé clans came, and showed him that they were men of military prowess. Bowing before him, they offered him their homage, in a manner befitting a son of a king. They urged him to attack the neighbouring Muslims, with whom they were in conflict. This he agreed to do.

After further consultation Susneyos joined with the Christian Guragés in attacking a Muslim army of at least a thousand cavalry and countless foot soldiers. Despite their number the Muslims were reluctant to fight, and remained at a distance, near the Wäri River. Susneyos, who reportedly had only thirty horsemen, was, not surprisingly, soon defeated. His Guragé allies then fled the field, and his own men followed suit. He himself fought heroically, but was obliged to escape to Yäbso.

The Muslims then launched an attack on the Christian Guragés. Many of the latter, allegedly out of fear, afforded the Muslims a welcome, and concluded a peace treaty with them. Other Christian Guragés, on the other hand, sent an envoy to Susneyos, informing him that their Muslim enemies had attacked them. They appealed to him for help, recalling that they had earlier afforded him assistance.

Susneyos left Yäbso, and, making his way into Guragé, advanced to Ennämor, and thence to Mugär. There, however, the Ennämor people deserted him, and allied themselves with the Muslims. A

---

[4] Béguinot (1901), pp. 40-2; Bruce (1790), II, 241.

number of Susneyos's followers also deserted, and went over to the enemy, to whom they revealed which of the elders had supported the Christian cause. Many Christians were in consequence arrested. The prince, saddened by these desertions, was at Mugär when the Muslims, encouraged by their newly found friends, decided to attack. A fierce, but inconclusive battle was waged for seven days, after which Susneyos withdrew to Yäbso, and later to Shäwa.[5]

Dämä Krestos

Not long after this Dämä Krestos, the Christian chief of nearby Wäj, decided to make peace with the Muslims, and secretly offered to capture Susneyos for them. The prince discovered the plot, and arrested the chief before he could carry out his plan. The arrest of Dämä Krestos, however, greatly incensed the presumably "pagan" or pro-Muslim Guragés, who rallied in vast numbers to fight for him. Susneyos, realising that they would almost certainly overpower him, attempted a rapid departure. Dämä Krestos's followers, who were well equipped with spears, as well as bows and arrows, launched an attack. A fierce battle resulted. Susneyos, hopelessly outnumbered, but holding Dämä Krestos as a prisoner, succeeded in escaping to the Hazo River. The Guragés abandoned the chase, and returned home grieving for the captured leader. Susneyos, having assured his safety, released Dämä Krestos, but only after seizing fifty of his horses and three hundred cattle.[6]

Susneyos subsequently embarked on an expedition to Enarya, but while he was returning home, laden with booty, the Ennämor people again attacked him. A bloody battle ensued, in which the Ennämors killed many of his soldiers, and seized five or six hundred of his horses, and many mules. Despite these losses the prince later attempted to advance on the Guragé country, but his army was seriously depleted by further desertions. He nevertheless made his way to Ennämor, where the entire population, which the chronicler described as "pagan", came out to resist him. This caused the bulk of his men to flee. Only two cavalrymen are said to have remained with their master.

---

[5] Esteves Pereira (1900), pp. 25-9. For the geography of these and the ensuing events see Huntingford (1989), pp.155-6.
[6] Esteves Pereira (1900), pp. 29-30.

Susneyos and his two companions rallied his soldiers, who, we are told, consisted of both Oromos and Amharas. They returned to face the Ennämor people, with whom the prince once more did battle. His soldiers are said to have been "amazed" at the Ennämors' strength and skill in fighting, and concluded that they were "superior in arms" to either Galla or Amhara warriors. Susneyos's men, however, eventually succeeded in breaking into the Ennämor camp. They killed many of its defenders and captured much booty. Just as they were coming out of the camp, however, they heard a great shout from the Ennämors, whereupon the prince's men fled. Susneyos himself reportedly escaped only with difficulty.[7]

For the remainder of Susneyos's reign little more is heard of the Guragés, who with the northward movement of the capital and empire, had become independent of imperial rule.

The Reports of Almeida and Bruce

The Guragés were, however, well known to the Jesuits. Almeida described them as "heathens and Moors", who did not often obey the Emperor. Their country was situated, he says, on the important trade route between Gojjam and Enarya, and their warriors included horsemen, as well as men skilled in the use of bows and arrows.[8]

The Scottish traveller James Bruce, who learnt of the Guragé country only at second hand, insisted that its inhabitants lived "mostly in caves and holes in the ground". In his report on the battle of Sarbakusa, fought near Gondär in 1772 in the civil war of his time, he also provides intriguing evidence of what may have been a long tradition of Guragé migration to royal camps. Describing the attempted assassination of the favourite servant of the Tegray ruler Ras Mika'él Sehul, he states that the culprit, apparently mistaking the servant for his master, was a Guragé, a member of what Bruce calls a "very barbarous" people of "troglodytes", i.e. cave-dwellers, and "robbers". Their "constant occupation", he claims, was attending Ethiopian military camps, and stealing from them horses and mules, or whatever they could find. This was done in a "very singular manner", which he describes in interesting detail as follows:

"They all wear their hair very short, strip themselves stark-naked and besmear themselves from head to foot with butter, or some sort of

---

[7] Esteves Pereira (!900), pp. 36-9.
[8] Beckingham and Huntingford (1954), pp. 19, 162-3.

grease, whilst, along the outer side of their arm, they tie a long, straight, two-edged, sharp-pointed knife, the handle reaching the palm of their hand, and about four inches of the blade above the knob of their elbow, so that the whole blade is safe and inoffensive when the arm is extended, but when it is bent, about four inches projects, and is bare beyond the elbow joint; this being all prepared, they take a leafy faggot, such as the gatherers of fuel bring to the camp, which they fasten to their middle by string or withy, spreading it over to conceal or cover all their back, and then drawing in their legs, they lie down, in all appearance, as a faggot, and in the part of the camp they intend to rob, crawling slowly in the dark when they think they are unperceived, and lying still when there is any noise or movement near them. In case they find themselves discovered, they slip the faggot and run; and whatever part of them you seize escapes your fingers by reason of the grease. If you endeavour to clasp them, however, which is the only way left, the Gurague bends his elbow and strikes you with his knife, and you are mortally wounded".

Returning to the question of the would-be assassin, Bruce recalls that the man, when interrogated, "at first refused to speak, but, being threatened with torture, answered in his own language", presumably Guragé. A search of the camp was then carried out, "but no stranger found", excepting another Guragé who had "planted himself and his faggot near the tent of the Abuna; and who being seized, examined, and promised pardon, declared himself absolutely ignorant of any scheme but robbing, for which purpose, three of them, he said, had come to the camp together; one of them had stolen two mules the night before, and gone off, and that he supposed his companion had the same intention".

After torture the man persisted in this statement, and when further interrogated, declared, that they all three had come from their country with Amha Iyäsus, the prince of Shäwa, to load and unload his baggage, and take care of his beasts.[9]

This evidence of Guragés serving as baggage attendants, and camp-robbers, may be considered in conjunction with the earlier report by Alvares that Guragés, likewise described by him as troglodytes, were raiding Emperor Lebnä Dengel's camp a quarter of a millennium earlier. The two accounts seem to suggest an enduring Guragé tradition of troglodytism, possibly centred around the Awash

---

[9] Bruce (1790), II, 325, IV, 148-50.

River,[10] as well as perhaps a long-established practice of camp-robbing. This may have originated in Shäwa, albeit later carried out further north by Guragés accompanying the visiting Shäwan prince, as Bruce suggests. Guragés, it may be recalled, were subsequently renowned, as migrants, who in the late nineteenth and early twentieth centuries, made their way to the Shäwan capitals, Ankobär and later Addis Ababa, and, as in Bruce's account, seem to suggest, were often closely shaven.

HADEYA

Hadeya, like most other territories in the south-west, was much affected by the migration of the Oromos, who seem to have approached the province in the late sixteenth century. Särsä Dengel's governor, Sähafä Lahm Täklä Giyorgis, reportedly won "much glory" in defending the territory against the Gallas.[11]

The territory was later ruled, in the early seventeenth century, by a Muslim chief called Sidi against whom Susneyos, as we have seen above, undertook a largely unsuccessful expedition. The prince was later confronted by a powerful Oromo drive on the province. In 1620 he learnt from his brother, Ras Se'elä Krestos, that the Mächa Oromos had defeated the Hadeyas, as well as the Guragés and other groups, and were expected to advance further into Gojjam and Enarya.[12]

Oromo pressure on Hadeya was, however, contained. The province therefore maintained its distinct identity. Memories of imperial suzerainty were, however, still alive almost a century later. Emperor Iyasu I's Armenian trade agent Khodja Murad told the Dutch in Batavia, in 1689, that the "king or monarch" of Hadeya had "submitted of his own free will to the rule of Abyssinia". The chief, "together with his entire people" had furthermore "embraced the Christian religion", and married "a certain princess from the dynasty of the Abyssinian emperors".[13] Hadeya was thereafter largely independent of both the Oromos and the Christian empire.

---

[10] On these caves see *inter alia* Pankhurst (1973), pp.15-35.
[11] Conti Rossini (1907), p. 67.
[12] Esteves Pereira (1900), pp. 26, 167.
[13] Donzel (1979), p. 72.

Confirmation of the province's continuing contact with the empire is found in the chronicle of Iyasu I, which records that this monarch received tribute from Hadeya as late as 1704 in clothes, wheat and donkeys.[14]

KAMBATA

Kämbata, which was at that time part of the empire, was governed for Emperor Susneyos by an important noblemen, by name Hamälmal. The Jesuit traveller Antonio Fernandez, who had a lengthy talk with him, affirms that the chief paid tribute to the Emperor.[15]

ENARYA

Ya'qob and Susneyos

Enarya, which had long possessed a considerable amount of gold, and whose inhabitants Särsä Dengel had attempted to convert to Christianity, now attracted the interest of Susneyos. Prior to his accession to the throne he travelled to the province with a large army, composed of both infantry and cavalry, as well as many Mächa Oromo warriors. After three days' fighting against the local ruler, Gwemcho, the prince was victorious and entered the area. Gwemcho, and countless men, women and children, were killed in the fighting, and his bracelet of office and gold-decorated sword fell into Susneyos's possession, and were given to the soldier who had killed him. While returning home at night with their booty, Susneyos and his men were ambushed by a force of Enaryans, who defeated them, killing many, and capturing numerous horses and mules. Some said that six hundred animals were taken, others said five hundred, but "only God", the chronicler declares, "in truth knew their number".[16]

Imperial control over Enarya was apparently soon re-established. The province was chosen, around 1606, as a place of detention for the deposed half-Fälasha Emperor Ya'qob, and for two nobles Ras Anatéwos and Zä-Sellasé.[17]

---

[14] Guidi (1903-5), pp. 246, 258.
[15] Beckingham and Huntingford (1954), pp. 162-6.
[16] Esteves Pereira (1900), pp. 36-7.
[17] Esteves Pereira (1900), pp. 39-40, 42-3, 87, 127, 133, 137, 144.

Power in Enarya was later assumed, in 1611, by a chief called Bênäro, who fought vigorously against the Oromos. Their advance may have caused him to feel a need for the support of the Christian empire. He developed close relations with Susneyos, and was friendly to the latter's supporters the Jesuits. When Fernandez visited him in 1616 the chief generously gave him 50 crusados of gold "to help him on his way and made many excuses for giving so little, because it was the time when he had to send his customary annual tribute to the emperor, which is a thousand ounces".[18]

Reference to such tribute is also found in Susneyos's chronicle. It states that the Emperor around 1617 despatched envoys to the province to collect its tribute. They were accompanied by the Emperor's brother, Ras Se'elä Krestos, and the ruler of Gojjam, Nägash Keflo, both of whom were on an expedition against the Oromos in Bizamo.[19]

Benaro's ties with the Emperor were so cordial, or important, that the monarch arranged for the chief's son, Yämanä Krestos, who evidently was, or had become, a Christian, to marry one of his nieces, a daughter of his favourite brother, Ras Se'elä Krestos.[20]

Almeida's Testimony

The first detailed account of Enarya in this period was written by Almeida in the early 1620s. He cites information collected by Fernandez, who stated that the military chief of Enarya, presumably a functionary of Bênäro, was a man called Abekan, who lived on the steep, strategically located, and "fully inhabited" mountain of Ganqa. This was situated near the frontier facing the "many enemies" with which his people were at war.

Enarya, Almeida indicates, was then the most southerly part of the empire, and a "subject kingdom", whose inhabitants, he claims, were "the best in the whole of Ethiopia". The province was rich in foodstuffs, as well as cattle, mules and horses. The staple diet of the people, like that of their neighbours, was the *enset*, or false banana. The territory lay on a major trade route, through which caravans travelled northwards to Gojjam. Enarya had relations also with gold-producing lands to the west from which it acquired the precious

---

[18] Beckingham and Huntingford (1954), p. 152.
[19] Esteves Pereira (1900), p. 120.
[20] Esteves Pereira (1900), p. 150.

metal, Fernandez says, in exchange for clothing, cows, salt, and other goods. Enarya's commerce was based partially, as in many other parts of the country, on the use of gold, but small pieces of iron also circulated as money. Considerably larger than the *hakunas* of fourteenth century Däwaro they were "light and flat, two inches wide and three long".[21]

Bénäro, Sisgayo, and Yämanä Krestos

Bénäro, whose son had married into the imperial family, was a loyal tributary of the Christian empire. He fought in support of the Emperor against Oromo incursions, and struggled particularly hard, according to Susneyos's chronicle, against the Akako Gallas. In 1619, he "killed many" of the latter, captured their women and children, seized their cattle, and "left them nothing". In the following year he also did battle against the Borans, killing many of their soldiers, and capturing numerous women and children. In these victories he was assisted by the fact that the Yähabätas, who consisted of both cavalry and infantry, abandoned their Oromo leaders, and joined him.[22]

He subsequently came with his son, Yämanä Krestos, in 1620, to bring Susneyos the gold tribute which their province traditionally paid. Greeting the monarch on that occasion he is quoted in the chronicle as loyally declaring, "O my lord, here is your gold, and my son, your servant, the son of your servant!".[23]

Despite Bénäro's efforts the Oromos maintained the military initiative. Ras Se'elä Krestos reported a few months later that the Mächa Gallas had advanced to Bizamo, whence they apparently sought to "attack and destroy" Enarya as well as Gojjam. He accordingly called on the Emperor, his brother, to come quickly with all his troops, so that they might jointly attack and repulse the intruders. Susneyos, as we have seen in a previous chapter, responded to this appeal, and fierce, but inconclusive fighting ensued.

Bénäro, though the friend of the Emperor, was accused of being a cruel tyrant, and, perhaps for that reason, was killed in 1620 by his own people, some of whom may have resented the taxation he presumably levied to provide his tribute to the Emperor. Almeida, on the other hand, took an entirely different view. He asserts that Bénäro

---

21 Beckingham and Huntingford (1954), pp. 18-19, 29, 47, 144, 148-50.
22 Esteves Pereira (1900), pp. 149, 161.
23 Esteves Pereira (1900), p. 161.

had been "treacherously" murdered by his enemies, in what could have been a typical palace coup.[24]

Be that as it may, the regicide chiefs at once despatched a letter to Susneyos, setting out their complaints against the governor, and their reasons for killing him. They asserted that Bénäro had committed "unjust massacres", had amputated the hands and legs of his subjects, and had pulled out their eyes, "without discriminating between the young and the old, children and infants." He had, they claimed, also appropriated the Emperor's tribute, "fraudulently amassed goods belonging to others", and was guilty of adultery, greed and all sorts of injustices. "As a woman becomes pregnant for nine months, and gives birth in the tenth", they declared, "so we bore his iniquity in our womb for nine years, and in the tenth conceived his death, and killed him". This remarkable epistle concluded by announcing that the signatories, having executed Bénäro, had in his place appointed Arutano, "a kind and pious person", also known as Sisgayo.

Susneyos was much angered by this letter, as well as, no doubt, by the murder of his kinsman by marriage. He wrote back to the chiefs of Enarya, chiding them for their high-handed behaviour, and declaring, "Even if Bénäro was so evil towards you, and had displeased you by all sorts of iniquities, you should have sent to us, and said, 'Remove him for us, and appoint another man in his place'. Why did you assassinate our *seyum* [i.e. governor] whom we appointed nine years ago? You have not done right. You have shown great arrogance by murdering him, on your own authority and without orders".

With this letter Susneyos sent his chief rifleman, a Turk called Mustapha Basha (or Pasha), and a number of other Turkish musketeers. Susneyos, an able statesman, felt it diplomatic, however, to acquiesce in Sisgayo's appointment. He declared that since the chief had not been involved in Bénäro's assassination, his appointment should be confirmed. The letter ended with a demand for the payment of an indemnity in addition to the customary tribute.[25]

Sisgayo's rule was short lived. The "kind and pious" ruler was soon killed by Bénäro's supporters, whereupon Bénäro's son Yämanä Maryam was appointed in his stead. A "very good Catholic", as Almeida called him, he continued his father's resistance to the Oromos, who, according to the missionary, had by then conquered the

---

[24] Esteves Pereira (1900), p. 167; Beckingham and Huntingford (1954), p. 150.
[25] Esteves Pereira (1900), pp. 184-5.

land between his province and Gojjam, thereby isolating Enarya from the empire. They failed, however, to overcome the Enarya people, who continued to defend themselves successfully, virtually without the Emperor's help.

Almeida, writing after Sisgayo's assassination, declared that Enarya still gave the Emperor "some recognition", and from time to time paid him tribute, though most years it failed to do so. The territory, he explains, was the source from which the Ethiopian emperors obtained most of their gold, though only in limited quantities. Susneyos had never received more than 1,500 ounces, though the tribute was usually only 1,000. The province had subsequently been "hard pressed" by the Oromos, as a result of which the tax had dropped to only about 500 ounces. Some of the rare metal actually originated in Enarya, but the greater part was brought there from the nearby country of the Cafres, i.e. "Shanqellas", or blacks, from whom it was obtained in exchange for clothing, cows, salt and other goods. One of the principal auriferous areas, he was informed, was a large river called the Beber, doubtless the Birbir, River renowned for gold to this day.[26]

Emphasising the importance of Enarya gold he observed that the territory's inhabitants were said to have continued to pay Susneyos their tribute. They did so, Almeida claims, "out of their native loyalty". Had they wanted to free themselves from it, the monarch, he believed, could hardly have waged war against them, for their province was isolated "in the midst of the Gallas", as well as often by rebels near his court.[27]

Enarya, surrounded by Oromos and "Shanqellas", and almost entirely isolated from the empire, was thus without direct contact with any province subject to the Emperor. It nevertheless defended itself well, for its inhabitants, Almeida says, displayed "great bravery" and were "very intelligent". Their *shum,* or governor, was neither "a stranger" from outside the province nor the Emperor's appointee, but "a descendant of their former kings", for sons succeeded fathers, as they had done when they bore the title of kings.[28]

Almeida's praise for the people of Enarya was later echoed by Hiob Ludolf's Ethiopian informant Abba Gorgoreyos, so often a

---

[26] Beccari (1903-1917), II, 347; Beckingham and Huntingford (1954), pp. 85, 149.
[27] Beckingham and Huntingford (1954), pp. lxi, 150-1.
[28] Beckingham and Huntingford (1954), p. 19.

valuable commentator, who "much applauded" its inhabitants for their "probity and integrity", and added that they possessed "a fertile Soile", and one "abounding in Gold".[29]

Susneyos's abdication in 1632, and the subsequent execution of Yämanä Krestos's Roman Catholic father-in-law Ras Se'elä Krestos, later brought an end to the special relationship between Enarya and the Christian empire. The province, according to oral tradition, suffered in the aftermath of these events from increasing internal dissent, which enabled the Oromos to consolidate their power at Enarya expense.[30]

Iyasu I

Contacts with the empire were, however, renewed by Emperor Iyasu I. Crossing the Gibé River around 1705 he travelled to the frontier of the province, apparently also referred to as Ganqa, at a place called Mälka Chera. There two rival chiefs sent him messages, each asking him to confirm them in their office. He later proceeded to the market of Enarya, after which he sent one of the contending chiefs a ceremonial tunic and other fine clothing.[31]

James Bruce

Bruce, three-quarters of a century later, reported that Enarya, though "quite surrounded" by the Oromos, "especially on the south-east and north", was still "governed by its native princes". Their territory stood "like a fortified place in the middle of a plain, and their subjects were "exceedingly brave". Though defeated by the Oromos, and driven from the surrounding low country which they had formerly occupied, they had been overcome only by the "multitude" of their opponents, who had "poured in upon them", and their advance had been assisted by horses, to which the people of Enarya were "perfect strangers". In such fighting, as well as in the course of slave-raiding, many people of Enarya were captured as slaves and taken to Gondär, whence they were exported. Describing the qualities of these slaves from Enarya the Scotsman declares: "At Constantinople, India, or Cairo, the women are more esteemed as slaves than those of any other part of the world, and the men are reckoned faithful, active and

---

[29] Ludolf (1684), p. 15.
[30] Lange (1978), p. 18.
[31] Guidi (1903-5), pp. 246, 262-3.

intelligent. Both sexes are remarkable for a cheerful, kind disposition, and, if properly treated, soon attach themselves inviolably to their masters".

Enarya was well supplied, according to Bruce, with gold, which came from lands to the west. The territory also had a "great abundance" of cattle, grain and "all sorts of provisions", as well as numerous coffee trees. Gold, sold by weight, was the "medium of commerce within the country itself", while trade articles included cotton cloth, stibium, beads and incense.[32]

DAMOT

Damot was even more profoundly affected than Enarya by the coming of the Oromos. The latter reached the area, according to Bahrey, during the Birmajé *luba*ship (1578-1586) when the Boran clan surrounded the province, "enslaved the men, and carried off the livestock". This happened, he claims, because the land was "without a saviour or deliverer".[33]

The Oromo advance in the area was also mentioned in Särsä Dengel's chronicle. It reports that when the Oromos occupied Wäj in 1572 the monarch sent messages to his governor of the district, Täkla Giyorgis, and other provincial rulers, instructing them to confront the intruders. A decade or so later, Särsä Dengel proceeded to Damot, which the Mächa Oromos had occupied, and it was there, as we have seen, that he died.[34]

The Oromo Occupation and the New Damot

Damot, as Almeida says, was thus "conquered" by the Oromos. Part of the local population, like that of other southern areas, was doubtless assimilated by the advancing migrants, but others retreated across the Blue Nile to Gojjam where they settled as a distinct community. The Jesuit, describing how the people of Damot, and some of their neighbours, had "withdrawn" to lands under imperial rule, declares that in Gojjam and nearby areas peoples of "many races and different languages" had settled, establishing villages of Damots, as well as others from Gafat, Shäwa and elsewhere.[35]

---

[32] Bruce (1780), II, 312-14, 318.
[33] Beckingham and Huntingford (1954), pp. 121.
[34] Conti Rossini, (1907), pp. 51-2; Béguinot (1901), p. 39.
[35] Beckingham and Huntingford (1954), pp. 27, 56. See also p. 135.

A consequence of this move was that the term Damot came to be applied to the new area of settlement north of the Blue Nile. The name was used for example to apply to the Däbrä Marqos area of southern Gojjam. It is, however, uncertain when precisely the move, and the change of name, occurred.[36]

The Late 16th and Early 17th Century

The new Damot, like the old, was in close contact with the rest of the empire. At the end of the sixteenth century Emperor Ya'qob marched to the province to resist the Boran Gallas, and on at least one other occasion received visitors from it. Susneyos later appointed a succession of governors for Damot. They were usually persons of importance, such as his brother Ras Se'elä Krestos, who held the long-established Damot title of Sähafä-lahm, or Recorder of Cattle.

Adherents of the Orthodox Church

The people of Damot were vigorous opponents of Susneyos's attempts to introduce Roman Catholicism. Angered by their stubborn adherence to the Orthodox faith, he issued an edict around 1620 ordering them to cease celebrating the traditional Ethiopian Saturday Sabbath. The Damot people, however, refused to obey, and, according to the chronicle, displayed "great arrogance" towards the monarch. Ras Se'elä Krestos later also sent messages urging them to comply with his imperial brother's wish, but they became "even more arrogant". Their rebellious spirit spread to the chief's soldiers, some of whom deserted and joined the insurrection. The Ras launched a fierce attack on the Damots at Haräfa, where he burnt down their houses and captured many of their cattle. Peace negotiations were attempted, but failed. Se'elä Krestos, after praying in front of a picture of the Crucifixion, is said to have then unleashed a further powerful assault. The Damots reportedly fell like dried leaves, and there was not one Amhara or Galla in the chief's army, it is said, who failed to kill Damot soldiers in tens, fives, threes or twos. A vast number of their cattle were also seized.[37]

---

[36] Tsehai Brhane Selassie (1975), p. 39; Huntingford (1989), pp. 138, 143-4.
[37] Esteves Pereira (1900), pp. 195-7.

The Report of Jerónimo Lobo

By the early seventeenth century, when the Jesuits visited the country, Damot was definitely situated to the north of the Blue Nile. Lobo, who resided in the area at a place known as Lej Negus, states that it had an "excellent" climate, and was "extremely healthy and wholesome", and a "delightful" place to look at. It consisted of "fields, valleys, and mountains, all as perfectly proportioned and as beautiful as anything that could be imagined". The province's charm, he says, was "enhanced to no small degree by the coolness and beauty of the woods of excellent trees", probably junipers, which abounded both on the mountains and in the valleys. The climate was "so temperate" that he in some places witnessed sowing, reaping, threshing, and gathering, taking place simultaneously, for the land never tired of the "continual production" of fruits, or "failed in its readiness to produce them".

One of the plants native to the area was the *enset*, or false banana, which Lobo enthusiastically described as "admirably profitable to man", for "no part of it" was not "used advantageously". The branches and stems were made into an "extremely fine, white, pure flour", which, eaten with milk, constituted a "very delicious and delightful food, while the trunk and roots tasted "like turnips or potatoes". The plant was regarded by the wealthy as a delicacy, but was also a "tree against hunger", as any population growing it had no "fear of hunger". Other parts of the plant were scarcely less useful. The leaves, when fresh, served as plates, or carpets for the houses, to which it gave a "sprightly green colour". The dry leaves were made into a type of flax which was woven into rope, and into tapestries of various colours.

Lobo, who elsewhere describes the Damots as "noble and of excellent temper", complains that they were, however, "stubborn in their errors", i.e. adherence to the Orthodox faith, and therefore "great enemies" of the Church of Rome. He reports that when Emperor Susneyos ordered them to accept the latter, more than seventy of their monks committed mass suicide. "Obstinate in their false beliefs and practices", as the Jesuit puts it, rather than "abandon their errors", they preferred to "enter Hell ahead of time". Helping one another to do so they cast themselves from a very high cliff, and were broken to pieces on the steep rocks before reaching the ground at the bottom. More than six hundred Damot monks and nuns also died fighting for the faith.

The *Enset*, or false banana (*Ensete ventricosum*), cultivated by the people of Damot and Enarya, the Guragés, and other peoples in the south and west of the region.
From J. Bruce, *Travels to Discover the Source of the Nile*.

The Damots were eventually defeated by Susneyos's army. The survivors were obliged to accept Catholicism, after which, Lobo claims, there were "no more devout or better instructed Christians". Much pleased with this conversion, he commemorated it by erecting a "beautiful church" of freestone lined with cedar - which thus far has not been traced.[38]

Damot throughout this time provided the empire with a not insignificant amount of tribute. The annual tax, the Spanish Jesuit Pero Paes believed, was no less than two thousand cattle, i.e. about the same as Amhara, or a third of that of Bägémder.[39]

---

[38] Lockhart (1984), pp. 226, 244-6. On the location of Damot in the post-Oromo period see also Bruce (1790), III, 257.
[39] Beccari (1905-17), II, 286.

Supporters of Emperor Fasilädäs

Soldiers from Damot came to the fore again in 1634-5, early in the reign of Emperor Fasilädäs, when a rebel, Mälk'a Krestos, marched on Gondär, and established himself at the palace. The monarch appealed for help from various courtiers, including Ras Zä-Krestos, his governor of Damot. The latter responded to the call, and defeated the rebel, who perished in the fray.[40]

Damot throughout this period was part of the Gondarine empire, and is frequently mentioned in its chronicles. They indicate that Emperors Yohannes I, Iyasu I and Bäkaffa all from time to time visited the province, and appointed governors. One of the most impressive royal visits to the area was carried out by Bäkaffa to nearby Ennamora, where Damots and Agäws came to greet him, and staged very colourful equestrian displays in his honour.

After the decline of the monarchy the rulers of Damot continued to play a major role in state affairs. Bruce believed that they paid an annual tribute in his day of no less than eight hundred ounces of gold, though they had earlier paid a thousand.[41]

GAFAT

Susneyos and the Oromo Advance

Contacts between the Gafats and the Christian empire came to the fore once more during the reign of Susneyos, which also witnessed the advent of the Oromos in the area. This ruler, like his predecessors, carried out several major expeditions to the province, in the course of which he attempted to convert its inhabitants to Christianity. His first encounters with the Gafats were peaceful. During a famine in 1597-8, almost a decade prior to his accession to the throne, he was befriended by a Gafat called Fesen, of the Beräbabo clan. The man saved him and his followers from hunger by presenting them with a herd of cattle, which he had stolen in Gojjam. By this gift he established good relations, for the time being at least, between the prince and Gafats living on the borders of Gojjam and beyond the Blue Nile. Fesen is described in the chronicle as a man of good behaviour in all respects, except for the stealing of cattle.

---

[40] Basset (1881), XVIII, 286. See also Budge (1928b) p. 402.
[41] Guidi (1903-5), pp. 14, 38, 63, 108, 137-8, 210-11, 219, 298; Basset (1881), XVIII, 307, 318, 346, 349; Budge (1928b), II, 450, 471, 477; Bruce (1813), VII, 94.

Later, around 1600, young Susneyos made his way to the land of a Gafat group called Abädray, who welcomed him hospitably. Following Fesen's advice he went to Gojjam, and proceeded to the Gafat area of Yäzämbäl, where, however, his soldiers indulged, as was their wont, in extensive looting. They plundered the area's principal city, banqueted on what they had seized, and carried off clothes, shields, spears and other weapons. On their return to the Abädray the governor of Shat presented the Emperor with a *nägarit*, or drum, and a *santi*, or flute. The prince then set forth for Wämbärma, and, encountering a Gafat group called Yasubli, captured many of its cattle.

Not long after this, in 1600-1, Susneyos attacked another Gafat group, the Ashmän, from whom he seized much livestock. He then made his way to the Wäläqa River, where several Gafat groups, among them the Harb Wash, the Wängé, and the Ashmän, came forward to confront him. They were so numerous, according to his chronicle, that they resembled the leaves of the trees or the grass of the fields. They attacked with great ferocity, "from the left and the right, from the front and the rear", and showered poisoned arrows on him "like rain and hail", but he encouraged his soldiers to fight with determination, and urged them not to leave behind any loot they had taken.

Fighting fiercely his men crossed the river, and were at once faced by another Gafat group, the Harb Akäl, who lived on the other side. One of the prince's chiefs, Sähafä Lahm Seno, then called upon their leader, Jan Bägdem, and asked him why he was fighting against the ruler who had converted him to the Christian faith. The chief, moved, it is claimed, by these words, at once rushed forward, fell at the prince's feet, and kissed his hands. After this all the Harb Akäl received Susneyos in peace, and allowed him to depart with his booty. The Ashmän, and Wängé also abandoned the struggle. Realising that they were unable to wrest away the loot, they dispersed, each to his own territory. Susneyos then left Gafat, but soon returned. He is said to have "destroyed" the Gafat group of Den, as well as "all the Gafats" beyond the Blue Nile.

It was around this time that the Oromos appeared in the locality. One of their first encounters was with the Gafat clan of Den, who as a result abandoned their former country, and fled into Gojjam. Their old area of settlement was left a wilderness, and, the chronicle claims, remained so for a very long time.

Shortly afterwards the Libäns, reportedly the largest of all the Oromo groups, moved forward in 1608-9, and seized many Gafat cattle. They also captured herds from neighbouring groups: the Chomés, Agäws, and Damots, killing many people, and seizing numerous women and children. While returning with their booty they were, however, attacked by Susneyos. A fierce battle was waged, in which the Oromos suffered serious casualties.

Further Oromo attacks on the Gafats were reported around 1621-2. An unidentified clan launched a assault on Gojjam, in the course of which they raided the Gafats and neighbouring peoples. Countless men were killed, and large numbers of livestock seized.[42]

Though the chronicles contain many references to conflicts involving the Gafats, they have little to say about the latter's way of life. Almeida is slightly more forthcoming. He states that the Gafats were "tall, spare and not very black", and lived, he thought, "entirely" on the milk and meat of their cattle.

As for their social life he provided but one piece of information: that on hearing of the death of a relative or master, they did not throw themselves to the ground, like most other inhabitants of their region, but reacting even more forcefully, gave themselves "very large wounds in the head and arms".[43]

Northward Migration as a Result of the Oromo Occupation

By the early seventeenth century a "large part" of the Gafat territories, according to Almeida, had been occupied by the Oromos. This had interesting, but varied, consequences. Many Gafats, particularly in Bizamo, married Oromos, while others lived apart from them within the area of Oromo occupation. Others again fled, and retreated across the Blue Nile to lands under imperial rule, mainly in southern Gojjam, where, like the Damots, they formed distinct communities. Gojjam and nearby territories in this way, as we have seen, became the site of villages of Gafats, as well as other displaced persons from Damot, Shäwa and elsewhere.[44]

As a result of this northward move the term Gafat, which, like that of Damot, had hitherto applied to the area south of the Blue Nile,

---

[42] Esteves Pereira (1900), pp. 10, 19-24, 82-3, 172. See also p. 205; Huntingford (1989), pp. 152, 154-5, 160, 172-3.
[43] Beckingham and Huntingford (1954), pp. 50, 67, 156.
[44] Beckingham and Huntingford (1954), pp. 18, 54, 56, 136.

came to refer to new areas of settlement north of the river. These were for the most part in Gojjam, but to some extent also in Bägémder.[45]

The Evidence of Bruce

Interesting, if superficially brief, information on the Gafats was collected by Bruce. Writing in the late eighteenth century he states that they were "Pagans", and had always been so. He claims that they, like their neighbours the Agäws, worshipped the Nile, but he could not "pretend to explain" what this faith entailed.[46]

The Gafats at that time, as prior to their northward migration, were reputed to possess vast numbers of cattle. The Scotsman went so far as to declare that "nowhere in the world" were there so numerous or such beautiful livestock as those of the Gafats. Large plains, for many days' journey, he claims, were so "filled to the full" with these animals that they seemed to be in a single market.[47]

BIZAMO

Bizamo was another of the south-western provinces "captured", as Almeida notes, by the Oromos. To curb their expansion Susneyos carried out three expeditions in the area. In the first he is said by his chronicler to have devastated the country of the Boran Oromos and laid it waste, but in later ones they fled without doing battle. The territory nevertheless remained firmly under the control of the Oromos, and was entirely inhabited by them as Almeida explains.

Some of the original Bizamo population intermarried with the Oromos, but the remainder, like several other southern peoples, withdrew northwards across the Blue Nile to territories under imperial rule.[48]

THE COUNTRY OF THE GAMBOS

The country of the Gämbos, of which relatively little is known in this period, was visited around 1600 by Emperor Susneyos, who despatched one of his earliest expeditions there.[49]

---

[45] Huntingford (1989), pp. 138, 143.
[46] Bruce (1790), I, 402.
[47] Bruce (1790), II, 384.
[48] Esteves Pereira (1900), pp. 21, 108, 120, 147, 167, 169, 171, 185; Beckingham and Huntingford (1954), pp. 18, 27, 56.
[49] Esteves Pereira (1900), pp. 23-4.

JANJERO

The Testimony of Father Antonio Fernandez

The small kingdom of Janjero, east of Enarya, differed from most of the area under consideration in that it was scarcely affected by the Oromo migration. Largely encircled by the Omo and Gibé Rivers it is said by Almeida to have recognised the Emperor, but not to have been strictly subject to him. The province's population consisted entirely of "heathens", i.e. adherents of traditional religion, who had "never been part of the empire".[50] Their culture moreover differed considerably from that of their neighbours, and it was on that account, he claims, that they were given the name Janjero, in Amharic, "monkey".

On the basis of a report from his fellow-Jesuit, Antonio Fernandez, one of the few visitors to this largely inaccessible territory, he gave an interesting, if over sensationalised, account of the Janjero people. He described them as "heathens much given to sorcery", and declared that their customs were "so barbarous and strange" that none could "be any more so".

One of the most remarkable Janjero practices, which Almeida chose to consider more "ape-like" than human, related to the treatment of comrades wounded in war, who, he claims, were invariably killed by their relatives. If the latter did not do so, a friend of the wounded man would kill him, however much he might cry for mercy. At the beginning of every reign it was also traditional for the monarch to order a search throughout the realm for any man or woman suffering from leprosy or ringworm. Those so affected would be despatched across the Gibé river, and beheaded "so that no such disease should infect other people".[51]

Slavery

The king of Janjero, according to this account, was deeply involved in the institution of slavery. Whenever he purchased foreign cloth from the merchants, the price, Almeida says, would be fixed in slaves. The monarch would instruct his servants to go into one or more of his subjects' houses, take the inmates' sons and daughters, and hand them over to the traders. He did the same when he wanted to make a present to a courtier, neighbouring prince, or king. He would

---

[50] Beckingham and Huntingford (1954), pp. 19, 29, 72.
[51] Beckingham and Huntingford (1954), pp. 158, 162.

order that the handsomest sons and daughters of any of his subjects be taken, provided only that they did not belong to a certain family which had the "dubious distinction" of being slaughtered for ritual purposes. Such was the submissiveness of the Janjero people, and their reverence for their monarch that no one ever murmured at such harsh practices.[52]

Royal Succession

The Janjero system of royal succession is also described in some detail by Almeida. His account, curiously enough, was accepted by James Bruce, usually sceptical of all things Jesuit, but cannot perhaps be taken fully at face value. When the king died his body, Almeida reports, would be dressed in rich cloth, and wrapped in the skin of a cow slaughtered for the purpose. The sons of the deceased, and any other male relatives who hoped to succeed, would then flee from the honour of being chosen, and seek refuge in the forest, as if the honour would pursue them. The electors, whom the Jesuit describes as "very great sorcerers", meanwhile chose the future monarch, and entered the forest to find him. They did this with the help of a bird like an eagle, which, it was said, would rise in the air, and, uttering loud cries, descend in the vicinity of the future ruler. The electors, knowing the chosen heir to be there, would then go and look for him, and perhaps find him surrounded by lions, leopards, or snakes. The prince would fight as hard as he could against being taken, and might even wound or kill some of his assailants. Those seeking him would put up with all this, but would eventually seize him, and drag him away by force, while he, seeing that further resistance was impossible, would accept the honour they wished to bestow on him.

The journey from the forest invariably involved a further skirmish, or even pitched battle. This was because there was a family which had the customary right to seize the king, if they could, from the hands of the electors, so that one of its number should instead be put in control of the kingdom. To this end they would join with their friends and allies, and fight the electors and the latters' supporters. The victors would then carry off and enthrone their king. Those who did so would have earned his favour, and could expect to be given the most honourable positions in the kingdom.

---

[52] Beckingham and Huntingford (1954), p. 162.

After taking the new king to the court the electors, or their rivals, would install him in a tent. On the seventh day after his predecessor's death they would bring a maggot which they claimed had come out of the deceased's mouth, and wrap it in a piece of silk, and make the new king kill it by squeezing its head between his teeth. They would then carry the late ruler's body to the grave, dragging it along the ground, and asking it to bless the fields and lands through which it passed. On reaching the burial place, they would dig a pit and throw the corpse into it, and slaughter many cows nearby so that their blood would fall on the corpse. Thereafter, until another king died, they would daily kill a cow, and arrange that its blood should drop on to the body. The slaughterers, however, were entitled to consume the meat.

Some people taking part in this ritual would remain beside the body of the deceased. Most, however, would accompany the new monarch, and, when he killed the maggot, cheer him loudly and proclaim him king. The celebration would then end with mourning on the part of the greatest in the kingdom. This was because the new king would immediately summon all his predecessor's favourites, and tell them that they were so much part of the late monarch that they could not be separated from him, and must therefore go to the next world to remain in his favour. He would then order their execution, and choose new courtiers to be appointed in their stead.

The houses in which the old king had lived, together with all their furniture and utensils, would meanwhile be ritually burnt. Nothing was allowed to remain. Everything, however valuable, was reduced to ashes. When any private person died, it was the custom likewise for his house, as well as all the nearby trees and plants, to be burnt, allegedly so that he "who was accustomed to the place, should not return".

After the destruction of his predecessor's palace the new monarch would at once have a new one built. This was not difficult, Almeida states, as the materials required cost little. The structure was a round hut, 25 or 30 palms in diameter, its walls made of wooden posts filled in with mud and stones, and its roof of roughly fashioned split logs, resting on a tall pole cut from a straight but not very thick tree.

Before felling this tree, Almeida claims, the Janjeros would cut off the head of a man, the first they found belonging to the family exempt from the tribute of having their children taken as slaves. When the house was built the king would enter it with much festivity, but before he did so another member of the said family would be killed if the house had a single door, or two if it had two. The blood thus shed was then used to daub the house's threshold and door-posts.[53]

How much credence can be placed on these grim stories is open to debate.

KAFA

Käfa, unlike nearby Janjero, was visited by no foreign travellers in this period. Our knowledge of the territory therefore relies solely on local traditions collected at least two centuries later. They indicate that the territory, which was guarded by deep trenches, successfully withstood a number of Oromo onslaughts.

One of the most important Käfa monarchs of this time, Tato Gali Ginocho, who reigned from around 1675 until about 1710, is believed to have incorporated, or reincorporated, the nearby small Gimira states of Shé, Benesho and Masogo or Mashengo.

Käfa expansion was reportedly continued by Tato Shagi Sherocho, who ruled between about 1775 and 1795. He is said to have extended his kingdom as far as the Omo River in the south-east and nearly to the confluence of the Omo and Dincha Rivers in the south.[54]

THE COUNTRY OF THE "SHANQELLAS", GONGAS and DOBE'AS

The country of the "Shanqellas" and Gongas in the west and that of the Dobe'as in the north-east were the site in this period of frequent slave-raids. These were carried out by a succession of relatively well-armed emperors, as their chronicles testify.

---

[53] Beckingham and Huntingford (1954), pp. 158-61; Bruce (1790), II, 324-5. This Jesuit account of Janjero coronation customs was accepted by Bruce (1790), II, 324-5, who claims that he "often" heard similar stories from people coming from the area. The picture is also is partially substantiated by the nineteenth century study of the Italian Geographical Society, which also reports the practice of human sacrifice, on which see Cecchi (1885-7), II, 356-8. See also Huntingford (1955), pp. 137-44.

[54] Cecchi (1885-7), II, 490; Bieber (1920-3), II, 494-533; Beckingham and Huntingford (1954), p. lx; Huntingford (1955), pp. 104-5.

Susneyos

Fighting against the "blacks" on the western borderlands, which had been going on for centuries, was intensified during the reign of Emperor Susneyos, who had a succession of capitals in the Lake Tana area, from which he despatched six expeditions against the nearby north-western lowlands. These raids were directed mainly against two groups, the "Shanqellas" and the Gongas. Like the Bäläyas earlier referred to in Särsä Dengel's chronicle the "Shanqellas" were held by their eastern neighbours in low repute. Susneyos's chronicler indeed deprecatingly observes that their colour was *sälim*, or black, not red, as normal *säba*, or people.[55]

Susneyos's first expedition against the "blacks" took place soon after his coronation in 1606 when, according to Bruce, he sent his cavalry on an expedition against the "Shanqellas" and Gongas. Operations were entrusted to two leading officers, Nägash Keflo, governor of Gojjam, and Azmach Yona'él, master of the royal household. The main attack was against the Jigat people, who, according to the chronicle, were the colour of "nearly ripe grapes". Susneyos's army advanced as far as the Dura River, a tributary of the Blue Nile, where it captured "many slaves, both male and female".

The second expedition, of 1607, was also led by Nägash Keflo, who advanced further west into Wambärya, and "destroyed" numerous "Shanqella" lands. Their inhabitants, however, held their own, and killed many soldiers before fleeing to Serki, a dependency of Sennar. Bruce believed that this fighting was directed against the Gongas, and claims that the latter's "principal village", Sinass, two days' journey beyond Wambärya, was "nearly destroyed, rather than subdued". The magnitude of this expedition is apparent from a subsequent report by Pero Paes, who had seen an extensive procession of the slaves captured on it. He claims that he had remonstrated with Susneyos on the matter, as a result of which some twelve thousand captives had been freed.

The Emperor's third expedition, of 1613, was carried out when Susneyos marched by way of Mätäkäl to attack the Agäw, Gonga and Jigat peoples. He seized "many slaves, male and female, more than ever before", while his commander Yona'él also captured numerous slaves and much livestock.

---

[55] Esteves Pereira (1892), p. 192.

The fourth expedition was launched in 1615 or 1616 when the Emperor ordered Nägash and Yona'él to attack the Bäläyas. Bruce claims that the soldiers had instructions to surprise the Gongas and Gubas, against whom the monarch "every year... made war for the sake of taking slaves for the use of the palace". The campaign resulted in the capture of a number of slaves, but the two chiefs could not complete their objective because of the onset of the rains.

The fifth expedition, in 1618, was led by the Emperor's brother Ras Se'elä Krestos, then governor of Gojjam, who attacked the "Shanqellas" and Gongas. Susneyos, according to the shorter chronicle, went down into the *qolla*, or lowlands, on two successive years to fight against the "Shanqellas". They are in one instance referred to as the Ragreig people, who lived on the present-day Sudan frontier.

The sixth, and last, expedition took place in the following year when another courtier, Abéto Melkä Krestos, proceeded further north to the Atbara area. He fought against a "Shanqella" leader called Nastoy, killed half the latter's army, and took the remainder, as well as many women and children, as slaves.[56]

The result of these raids was that Susneyos, like Särsä Dengel before him, came into possession of numerous "black" slaves. Almeida notes that they were of many different races, among them Agäws, Gongas, and Bäläws. Such slaves, he explains, were often appointed as *shum*s, or chiefs, and the Emperor raised some to the "greatest offices" of the court. Since they were entirely dependent on his whim he is said to have trusted them more than his free-born subjects, above all more than the nobles who had power bases of their own. Speaking of this to his confidant Pero Paes he observed, "Father, those whom I raise and honour serve me with a true heart", whereas among the nobles there were "few who could be trusted". Almeida likewise quotes the Emperor as declaring that men whom he had "created and made from the dust", were the only ones faithful to him, and, if they were not all so, the Jesuit believed that they were more so than others.[57]

Another consequence of Susneyos's expeditions was that the existence of the "Shanqellas" and Gongas began to be known to the

---

[56] Esteves Pereira (1900), pp. 85, 91, 108, 112, 119, 149, 162, 386, 399; Basset (1881), XVII, 121-26; Beccari (1903-17), XI, 267-8..
[57] Beccari (1903-17), II, 55; Beckingham and Huntingford (1954), p. 75.

European scholarly world, and appear on international maps. Lobo placed the "Shanqellas" south of the Blue Nile, near the present Sudan border, but with a misleading caption stating that "the Abyssinians so designate any people who have no fixed abode". Ludolf, on the other hand, indicated that the "Shanqellas" lived on both sides of the river, a little south of Fazughli, but also refers to them as a people of nomads or troglodytes.[58]

The Gongas, too, are first mentioned in the Jesuit writings of this period. Almeida states that they lived on both sides of the Blue Nile, and were among the area's "first inhabitants". Lobo, however, placed them on his map exclusively south of the river. Their importance was likewise recognised by Ludolf, who listed their country as one of the major provinces of the Ethiopian realm.[59]

Reference to the Gongas is also found in Susneyos's chronicle. It describes them as forest dwellers, who were attacked on occasion by the Mächa Oromos, as well as by imperial troops. Though irregular in their tax payments the Gongas are reported to have welcomed the Emperor loyally in 1620, beating drums, playing their musical instruments, and proudly displaying their arrows and spears.[60]

Fasilädäs

Attacks on the "Shanqellas" and Gongas came to an end during the last turbulent years of Susneyos's life, when the Christian empire was torn apart by civil war. They were, however, resumed during the reign of Emperor Fäsiladas, who, after establishing himself at Gondär in 1636, was geographically well situated to follow his father's practice of seizing slaves in the neighbouring western frontier areas.

Fasilädäs undertook three main slave-raiding expeditions against the "Shanqellas" and related groups. The first was in 1641-2 when he marched into Gojjam, and despatched his commander Fitawrari Mammo to attack the "Shanqellas" to the west. Operations, according to the shorter chronicle, were carried out primarily against the Bäläyas.

The second expedition took place in 1651-2, when the Emperor despatched an army under Abéto Be'elä Krestos against another

---

[58] Legrand (1728), op. p. 221; Ludolf (1684), map.
[59] Beckingham and Huntingford (1954), pp. 17, 25, 56, 145-6; Legrand (1728), p. 221; Ludolf (1684), p. 16.
[60] Esteves Pereira (1900), pp. 91, 149, 170, 185, 192.

"Shanqella" group, the Dangesh. The campaign was by no means successful, for it led to the death of two officers, Elä Zogä and Bätro, whom Bruce describes as persons of "great distinction at the palace". The French historian Legrand claims that the Dangesh, learning of Be'elä Krestos's advance, occupied and fortified all the passes, fell on the chief's army from all sides, and effected "so cruel a carnage" that "Abyssinia had not suffered so great a loss" since Gälawdéwos's reign over a century earlier. Bruce states that a "great part" of Be'elä Krestos's troops were slain by the arrows of the enemy. The latter, in their caves in the mountains, were beyond reach of soldiers' spears and swords, but were able to pour their stones and arrows on the troops at such a short distance that "every one reached it target". Other soldiers were overpowered by large bodies of men who fell from the thickets, and fought them in hand to hand combat. Many officers of the Emperor's army were killed.

The third, and last, expedition, was in 1658 or 1659, when Fasilädäs despatched another courtier, Ras Giyorgis, against the Gongas.[61]

Yohannes I

Operations against the "Shanqellas" were resumed by Emperor Yohannes I. Learning in 1609 of a revolt on the western border by a certain Muhammäd, who is referred to as a *gäbar*, or slave, he despatched two courtiers, Blatténgéta Gäbrä Le'ul, and Teqaqen Aygäbaz, to the district. The chronicle claims that they ravaged the area, but that Muhammäd escaped to Sennar. The expedition's importance is, however, discounted by Bruce, who described it as "feeble", and without material consequences.[62]

More serious fighting occurred in 1680, when Yohannes despatched the governor of Mätäkäl and "thousands" of soldiers against the "Shanqellas". The latter suffered 766 casualties, but the number carried into slavery was much greater, and reportedly "could not be counted". The area of fighting is not specified, but reference to Mätäkäl suggests that the raid took place near the southern stretches of the Blue Nile.[63]

---

61 Basset (1881), XVIII, 285-91; Legrand (1728), p. 156; Bruce (1790), II, 416-17.
62 Guidi (1903-5), p. 9; Bruce (1790), II, 423.
63 Guidi (1903-5), p. 47.

Title-page of Hiob Ludolf's Amharic-Latin dictionary *Lexicon Amharico-Latinum*, published in Frankfurt in 1698, with an early citation in it of the Amharic word *bareya*, or slave.

Terminology

Centuries of slave-raiding against the Bareya people on the western borders led to the adoption into the Amharic language of the word *bareya* as a generic name for a slave. This term is first recorded by Ludolf in his *Lexicon Amharico-Latinum* of 1698.[64]

The presence of "black" slaves in the fulness of time had two other interesting linguistic consequences. 1) The term *bareya*, was

---

[64] Ludolf (1698), cols. 11, 40.

incorporated, in the last two-thirds of the eighteenth century, into many Christian names, in such forms as Yä-Sellasé Bareya, i.e. Slave of the Trinity, or Yä-Maryam Bareya, Slave of Mary. 2) The fact that the beliefs and customs of the slaves were so different from those of the societies in which they lived caused the latter to regard them with fear or suspicion. The term *bareya* was often therefore employed as the name of an evil spirit, used for example in a number of Ge'ez prayers by both Christian and Fälasha communities.[65]

Iyasu I and Yostos

Warfare, and slave-raiding, which owed much to Gondär's growing wealth, and demand for servile labour, as well as to the increasing acquisition and utilisation of fire-arms, was intensified during the reign of Emperor Iyasu I (1682-1706). The most powerful of the Gondär rulers, he was militarily far better equipped than his predecessors, and succeeded in capturing an unparalleled number of slaves in the north-western and western borderlands.

Iyasu carried out his first expedition in 1688, when, advancing westwards by way of Mätäkäl he attacked the "Shanqella town" of Gisa. He set fire to it, killed many of its inhabitants, and led away not a few slaves, men and women, besides numerous cattle. He proceeded to Gorsi, another "Shanqella town", where he also captured many male and female slaves. He advanced next to what the chronicle refers to as the "rebel country" of Wämbärya, which, we are told, had defied three previous rulers, Susneyos, Fasilädäs and Yohannes. Killing two of the enemy, one with a rifle and the other with a spear, he reportedly wrought further destruction, killing many of his adversaries, and taking immense loot. He then crossed the Dura River, where the "Shanqellas", on seeing the size of his forces and the number of his fire-arms, fled, and "disappeared like smoke".

Though often the victims of slave hunts the "Shanqellas" were by no means always on the defensive. Taking the offensive in 1689 they reportedly "exterminated" their Christian enemies in the Shiré desert. Iyasu, angered by this event, despatched one of his commanders, Fesseha Krestos, who vented his wrath on the "Shanqellas", and castrated many of them, before returning to Gondär with the trophies for his master's inspection

---

[65] Guidi (1912), passim; Weld Blundell (1922), passim; Aescoly (1932), p. 132; Aescoly (1951), pp. 192-3, 227-8.

Iyasu undertook a second major campaign in 1693. Advancing north-eastwards to Kuana near the Märäb River he personally struck down two "Shanqella" leaders. His followers were no less successful, some, we are told, killing one and others two of the enemy. The imperial forces reportedly suffered but a single casualty, a guard who was killed by an arrow. The monarch then proceeded towards Sä'ada Amba, which Bruce described as the largest and most powerful "Shanqella" settlement between the Märäb and Täkkäzé Rivers. Iyasu attacked the inhabitants of four *amba*s, or flat-topped mountains. The rest of the "Shanqellas", realising that resistance was vain, hid, Bruce says, in "inaccessible caves in the mountains", and in "the thickest parts of the woods, where they lay perfectly concealed in the daytime, and only stole out when thirst obliged them at night". The Emperor, knowing that they had no water save that brought from the Märäb River, placed his troops along its banks, and kept them there until the "Shanqellas" died of thirst or were killed by his army.

Iyasu, planning to attack the nearby Dubäni "Shanqellas", then made his way to the Batkom or Laydä River, the location, according to Bruce, of a "large habitation" of "Shanqellas" east of the Märäb, whose "number, strength and reputation for courage" had hitherto saved them from attack. Having heard of their comrades' fate in other engagements, they refrained, however, from battle, and "dispersed themselves in unknown and desolate places". The monarch nonetheless succeeded in taking a "considerable number of slaves of the younger sort". On his departure, the "Shanqellas" surrounded Fesseha Krestos, but one of the king's riflemen shot two of them, after which their companions fled, suffering heavy losses.

A group of Tegray soldiers, led by one Däjazmach Gälawdéwos Mästäfa, later fought against other "Shanqellas", and pillaged four of their "towns". The situation was at one moment so desperate that the chief, to the monarch's displeasure, fled the field. The army was eventually victorious, and not a single "Shanqella", the chronicle claims, was allowed to escape. Bruce, however, rejects this account. He claims that the "great part" of the Emperor's army "perished in the flight", and that Shiré, for fear of the "Shanqellas", was "half abandoned".

Iyasu, according to the chronicler, later sent another commander, Ras Farés, with "innumerable forces" against eight further Shanqella "towns", where his soldiers overcame all resistance, and carried off many slaves, male and female, as well as numerous cattle. The

Emperor's army reportedly suffered not a single casualty, whereas the Shanqella men and women captured were "as numerous as the sands on the seashore". The neighbouring Bäläw were reportedly filled with terror.

Iyasu later returned to the Märäb area, where the remnant of the "Shanqellas" attempted to attack part of his rearguard, but he ambushed them, and inflicted further heavy casualties. On subsequently reaching Aksum he was joyously welcomed by its priests. There he stripped the cowardly Gälawdéwos of his rank, and punished the people of Adda Dagana in Shiré who had destroyed nearby villages and thereby created a "no man's land" which had enabled the "Shanqellas" to attack the monastery of Wäldebba. To close this access route he settled Tegray soldiers as guards.

Fighting with the "Shanqellas" was resumed early in 1695, when Iyasu marched to Bäläs and the Zelew country, and despatched his soldiers to attack the area. The "Shanqellas", men, women and children, climbed up to Wasi Amba, from which they hurled down large numbers of stones. These reportedly fell like hail on the king's soldiers. The latter, however, soon seized the mountain after which Iyasu captured another *amba*. His men then assailed the "Shanqellas" in the caves by the Kokäl River, as well as the Bäläw, and another group of "Shanqellas", who, however, escaped during the night.

Another round of operations took place in 1696 when Iyasu marched to the "town" of Werki. There he is said by his chronicle to have killed "the elite of the valliant Shanqellas", and captured many slaves and much booty. In the following year he despatched his soldiers against the Tola "Shanqellas". They fled before his troops, who captured further extensive booty, including many slaves.

Yet another campaign occurred in 1698 when Iyasu, assisted, his chronicle claims, by the power of God, made his way against the Dangesh "Shanqellas". He reportedly won a great victory, and thus avenged Abéto Be'elä Krestos's defeat during the reign of Fasilädäs. Iyasu killed many of the Dangesh people, captured innumerable slaves, and put fire to not a few houses, which, we are told, burnt like Sodom and Gomorrah in the time of Lot.[66]

Campaigns against "black" groups loosely known as "Shanqellas" were so common by the turn of the century that the French traveller

---

[66] Guidi (1903-5), pp. 117-21, 128, 142, 158, 160, 166-73, 179-82, 186, 196, 204; Bruce (1790), II, 451-6.

Charles Poncet observed that Iyasu took the field against them immediately after each rainy season. He had, however, by then "struck such horror" into them that as soon as his army appeared they retired to their rugged mountains, where they sold their lives dear whenever attacked.

The power of the "Shanqellas" was in fact by then on the wane. The imperial army, Poncet reports, had recently found an antedote for their opponents' poisoned arrows. It consisted of a urine plaster, which drew out the poison and achieved a rapid cure. Explaining the crucial importance of this discovery from the army's point of view he declares that the struggle with the "Shanqellas" had hitherto been "a most murdering war". The troops had been "at their wits' end", for as soon as they were hit by an arrow their lives were "irrecoverably lost", with the result that "great losses" were "daily sustained". After the discovery of the cure for the poison, however, the "Shanqellas" were forced increasingly on the defensive.[67]

Iyasu's last expedition against the "Shanqellas" took place in 1703, when he proceeded, once more by way of Mätäkäl, to Gesi near the Dura River. There, according to one chronicle, he waged war against the *dagmawi* Gisa, or "second Gisa", and according to another, assailed both the Säliman, or "blacks", and the Gongas. He also attacked the "town" of Degu, where he killed many soldiers, and, as so often, carried off the women as slaves.[68]

Two similar campaigns, accompanied by the extensive capture of slaves, were subsequently carried out during the reign of the usurping Emperor Yostos. In 1709-10 he marched against a group of "Shanqellas", and, according to the chronicles, killed or captured many of them. Bruce describes them as a lowland people called Baasa. The second expedition, which was led by three courtiers, took place against an unidentified "Shanqella" group in 1711-12.[69]

Bäkaffa and the Gondärine Slave Troops

Gondär, and other parts of the Christian empire, had by this time a considerable slave population. A significant proportion consisted of "Shanqellas" and other "blacks" from the far west. Most were too

---

[67] Foster (1949), pp.128-9.
[68] Guidi (1903-5), pp. 239-40. On this and Iyasu's earlier expeditions see also Basset (1881), XVIII, 293-323.
[69] Basset (1881), XVIII, 333-6; Bruce (1790), II, 545, 568.

humble to be noticed by court chroniclers, but a few became palace guards, and occasionally feature in the records. Persons of partial slave descent were then generally known as *welajoch*, literally "relations", and slave troops were often so referred to. Other units were known as Känisa, the precise meaning of which is obscure.

The Welajoch, like other slave troops in history, soon acquired considerable political power. After Emperor Dawit III's death in 1721 the "black servants" at the palace, who served as archers, were involved, according to Bruce, in a palace plot master-minded by one of the princesses. No mention of this is to be found in the chronicle, which merely states that the ensuing monarch, Bäkaffa, banished both the Welajoch and the Känisa from the capital. The Welaloch ignored the royal command, whereupon the Emperor proclaimed that anyone found in one of their houses would receive the severest punishment. The Welajoch thereupon left for their lands in Gazgé, and the Känisa to theirs in Anso. Both groups are bitterly condemned by the chronicler. He claims that they were murderers, who had seized wives in the presence of their husbands, and virgins in that of their mothers, and that their wickedness was "known to all the world".

The Welajoch then held a counsel, and decided to return to Gondär, as the chronicle claims, to shed the blood of its citizens, and to seize the latter's goods. Bäkaffa, learning of this "audacity", despatched a force which took the Welajoch by surprise at Barka, a little south of the capital. They were reportedly exterminated, not one being allowed to escape. The Känisa, still at Anso, were also attacked, allegedly because they had "troubled the world by their insolence". Many were killed, though others, as well as a few Welajoch, were captured. Some were banished, but others were allowed to go free. Bäkaffa's victory was greeted by great rejoicing in the capital, whose citizens, we are told, would all have been victims if the Welajoch had succeeded.

Bruce sets the above events in a different light. Apparently basing himself on what he was told a couple of generations later, he states that after the conspiracy the Emperor ordered all the "black slaves", and some of their ring-leaders, to leave Gondär, and sent them to Barka, where they were to be attacked by a thousand Oromo horsemen. The "black servants", being unarmed and suspecting nothing, were "surrounded and cut to pieces", after which orders were sent to the capital to "extirpate" those there. This execution, the Scotsman comments, laid the foundation for a feud that endured to his day between "the Galla troops and the black horse, who were then abolished".[70]

Be that as it may, there can be no denying that slave troops from the western periphery, like Oromos originally from the southern borderlands, had become important in the very centre of imperial power.

Iyasu II

The subsequent decline of the Gondär monarchy may well have led to a temporary reduction of slave-raiding. Campaigning was, however, resumed by Emperor Iyasu II, who undertook at least seven expeditions to the north-western and northern frontier regions.

In the Spring of 1741 he conducted a first campaign against the Bäläws, who, his chronicle claims, no previous Emperor had dared to attack since the time of Susneyos. Iyasu fought with them at Däbayna, after which he captured numerous camels and pack animals, and "led into slavery many men and women". Bruce, who accepts this account, states that the monarch drove off to Gondär "cattle, women and provisions", and that their arrival at the capital provided an entertainment to which its citizens had "long been strangers".

Iyasu carried out a second expedition in the following year, when he put the Asim Bäläws to flight, and inflicted heavy casualties on them.

In a third expedition, in 1744, the Emperor led his forces northwards across the Atbära river to the Gäbo country, where they killed and captured many men, women and children, as well as numerous horses and camels, and burnt down a large number of houses. He then made his way to Serki, where he defeated the inhabitants, killing some, taking others as slaves, and burning their dwellings. He contemplated advancing to the Bäläw capital, but was dissuaded by his chiefs, though some of his men advanced as far as the Täkkäzé.

Iyasu's fourth expedition took place in December 1747, when he turned his attention eastwards to the Dobe'a people, who, according to his chronicle, had resisted Susneyos, Fasilädäs and Bäkaffa, but now suffered many casualties. The Dobe'as were also attacked around the

---

[70] Guidi (1903-5), pp.132, 164, 218, 303-4; Guidi (1912), pp. 76, 192; Bruce (1790), II, 600.

same time by Ras Mika'él Sehul, the ruler of Tegray, who killed a hundred and fifty of them and took 133 prisoners.

In his fifth expedition, in 1751, Iyasu again made his way northwards to the Atbära River, where, finding that the Bäläws had fled, he destroyed their houses. Further fighting occurred in the following year, when a nobleman, Cherkin Nächo, arrived in Gondär with many Bäläw prisoners and camels.

Iyasu undertook his sixth expedition early in 1754 when he marched once more against the Asim Bäläws, and won a "great victory", in which, it is claimed, there was not one of his nobles and soldiers who did not kill at least one of the enemy. A year later he received the submission of the "Shanqellas" at the "town" of Zenjeris. He then returned to the Bäläw country, where in his seventh, and last, expedition he is said to have destroyed its inhabitants like "straw before the fire or dust in the face of the wind".[71]

These campaigns were accompanied by the building up in Gondär of a powerful contingent of slave troops. They included the Känisa, who, during Iyasu's reign, constituted an important, and highly honoured, force.[72]

Iyo'as

A further campaign against the "Shanqellas" took place in 1758, during the reign of Iyo'as. The forces of one of the principal nobles, Balambaras Eshäté, advanced into the Dangura country near Bäläya, allegedly because the "Shanqellas" had refused to pay their taxes, and were "troubling the country". The chief's forces reputedly achieved a great victory, for not one of the soldiers, according to his chronicle, failed to kill some of the enemy, or lead away prisoners, male and female. This was allegedly an easy victory, for only a "small number" of the soldiers were hit by "Shanqella" arrows.[73]

"Shanqella" Economic and Social Life: Bruce's Testimony

Our first detailed descriptions of the "Shanqellas", and the way in which they were enslaved and entered the Emperor's military service, is provided by Bruce, who saw many of them at Gondär. Though

---

[71] Guidi (1912), pp. 118-20, 122-5, 131-2, 133-7, 157-8, 160, 163, 167, 170-1; Bruce (1790), II, 632. See also Crawford (1951), p. 239.
[72] Guidi (1912), pp. 180, 194, 203, 209, 213.
[73] Guidi (1912), pp.194-5.

patronising his account is substantially fuller than that in the chronicles. He describes them as "flat-nosed and flat-lipped, very black, best shaped in the upper parts, but with bad knees and legs". While single they went about "entirely naked", but the married of both sexes wore "a slender covering about their waist". Most men had several wives, who were "very prolific".

The "Shanqellas", he believed, had once been "very numerous", and had been divided into various "tribes", each living separately under its own chief. The country they occupied was, however, "by no means considerable", for it was "never more" than thirty-five kilometres away from that of their neighbours. The largest and most powerful groups dwelt where the flat lowland belt in the west was "broadest, the trees thickest, and the water in the largest pools". Until not long before his day various "Shanqella" groups had made "constant inroads" on their neighbours, notably in Waldebba, where they had "destroyed" many of its inhabitants. Such attacks, however, had "lately stopped", supposedly on account of the prayers of the monks, though he felt that the real cause had been an outbreak of smallpox which had "greatly reduced" the "strength and number" of the "Shanqellas", and "extinguished, to a man, whole tribes of them".

The traditional armament of the "Shanqellas" included a long shield, which covered the whole body, and five spears, each of which was thrown or used for stabbing, but their principal weapons were bows and arrows. The "Shanqellas", he claims, were "all archers from their infancy". Their bows, which were made of wild fennel, were thicker than those of other communities, about seven feet long, and very elastic. Children used the same bow in their infancy as when they grew up, and because of its length were at first obliged to hold it "parallel, instead of perpendicular to the horizon". Arrows were "full a yard and a half long", and had "large heads of very bad iron rudely shaped".

Some "Shanqellas", as for ages past, were occupied in the gold trade, which was apparently based on private initiative, for "every individual", Bruce claims, was "free to search for it". The rare metal was found in a reddish earth, which was burnt in the fire until the gold ran out in small pieces like shot, after which it was collected, and placed in purses or small bags.

"Shanqella" gold was found in small lumps, which were also put into quills, and taken to market in Damot. By his time the "tribesmen" had acquired scales, and had a good idea of the metal's value. It was purchased from them by Agäws, who adulterated it by mixing one part of silver with ten of gold, thereby giving it a pale colour.[74]

As for housing, the "Shanqellas" lived throughout the dry season under the shade of trees. They cut the lowest branches near the stem, and then bent or broke them down, planting the ends in the earth, after which they removed all the small interior branches. In this manner they fashioned a "spacious pavillion", which at a distance appeared like a tent, the tree serving for the pole in the middle, while the large top overshadowing it gave the whole a "very picturesque appearance". These houses were occupied by "a multitude of inhabitants", who also entrenched their huts against surprise, and burnt large fires.

During the period in which they resided in these dwellings the "Shanqellas" spent much of their time hunting elephant, rhinoceros and other large animals, while those who lived near water killed hippopotamus, which were "exceedingly numerous" in the nearby pools and stagnant rivers.

On the coming of the rains the "Shanqellas" retired to caves in the mountains, where they lived as troglodytes. At the end of the rainy season they left their caves, and, finding the grass high, set fire to it. The flames then ran with "incredible violence", though with "such velocity" as "not to hurt the trees, but to occasion every leaf to fall". Then began the annual hunting of elephants and other wild animals. This seasonal pattern had a direct bearing on slave-raiding, which invariably took place "just before the rains", when the "Shanqellas" were "lodged under trees" preparing their food for the approaching rains prior to retiring into their caves.

Slave-raiding in Bruce's day was still largely based on Gondär, and resulted, he believed in a "prodigious effusion of blood". Whenever a settlement was surprised the men were "all slaughtered". Many of the women were also killed, while others would "throw themselves down precipices, run mad, hang themselves or starve, obstinately refusing food". Such action evoked little or no compassion on the part of the Gondär citizens who still regarded the "Shanqellas" as unworthy of consideration. This is apparent from the Scotsman's statement that a great lady of the city, Wäyzero Astér, proudly told him of a prophecy that there would arise a Saviour-king, called Téwodros during whose reign the "Shanqellas" and other enemies would all be destroyed.

---

[74] Bruce (1813), VIII, 75.

Raiding, the traveller claims, was then still considerable, and "all the countries" bordering the "Shanqella" lands, from the country of the Bahr Nägash in the north to the Blue Nile in the west, were "obliged to pay a certain number of slaves" as taxes to Gondär.

Another group of "blacks" from whom slaves were then being captured, but who were also engaged in raiding of their own, was the Ginjar, near Ras el-Fil, in the far west. Described by Bruce as "a very numerous" group of hunters, consisting of several thousand horse", they had reportedly once lived in Sennar, but had been dispossessed by the Funj government of the Sudan. They had all fled to the districts they then occupied, where they had "greatly increased in numbers". Still independent they were the "natural enemies" of their neighbours at Ras el-Fil, and "much blood" had been shed in conflicts between them, for each people had made inroads upon the other, "murdering the men, and carrying their women into slavery".[75]

The "Shanqella" Slave Troops at Gondär

Slave troops were prominent at Gondär throughout the second half of the eighteenth century. Bruce reported that so many "Shanqellas" had been brought to the capital that "every department" was "full" of them. They were looked after with great care. Boys and girls under the age of seventeen or eighteen, the younger the better, were "taken and educated by the king", and were "servants in all the great houses". Such youngsters were "instructed early in the Christian religion", and "the tallest, handsomest, and best inclined" were the only servants allowed to attend the royal person in the palace.

The most important slaves at Gondär were the Emperor's "black" cavalry, in Bruce's day three hundred in number. They were "all clothed in coats of mail, and mounted on black horses; always commanded by foreigners entirely devoted to the King's will". These slaves were exceedingly well treated. "Strict attention" was paid to their morals, all bad examples were removed from them, and premiums paid to those that read most and best. The king took "great delight and pleasure" in conversing with them. In "firmness and coolness in action" they were "equal perhaps" to any in the world, and the monarch encountered the "greatest difficulty" in keeping them, for "all the great men" wanted to have one of them in charge of his door, a position of "very great trust among the Abyssinians".

---

[75] Bruce (1790), II, 546-69, IV, 327-8, (1813), VII, 91.

St. George and the Dragon: from an Ethiopian manuscript acquired by the British collector Lady Meux: note the two-toe stirrup used by many shoe-less horsemen.
From E.A. Wallis Budge, *Legends of Our Lady Mary, the Perpetual Virgin, and Her Mother Hanna.*

The "black" cavalry's horses were likewise privileged. They were protected with "plates of brass on their cheeks and faces, with a sharp iron spike of above five inches in length, which stuck out of the middle of their forehead". The horses' bridles consisted of iron chains, and their bodies were covered with a thin quilt stuffed with cotton, with two openings above the flaps of the saddle, into which the rider put his thighs and legs, and covered him from his hip, where his coat of mail ended, down to a little below his anklet. The horseman wore thin leather slippers, without heels. Stirrups were of the Turkish or Moorish form, which held the rider's whole foot, rather than of the then Ethiopian type, which held only the big toe. Being hung very short, they enabled the rider to "raise himself, and "stand as firmly as if he was upon plain ground".

Saddles were likewise of the Moorish type, high in front and behind. Each rider carried a small axe and a spear about fourteen feet long, with which he charged. Made of light wood from trees growing on the banks of the Blue Nile, they ended in a long spike of iron, which was kept in a leather case fastened by a thong to the saddle. The horseman's helmet, an impressive affair, was made of copper or block tin, with large crests of black horse tail.

Thus protected, and armed to the teeth, the "black" horsemen from the empire's periphery constituted a powerful force, which, Bruce claims, could "make their way through all the cavalry of Abyssinia". This slave cavalry was well nigh invincible, for each horseman "sat immovable upon his saddle", acted "most powerfully by his weight alone", and was "perfectly master of his person".[76]

THE BORDERS OF SENNAR

The shift of the imperial capital in the early seventeenth century to the Lake Tana area, and the growth of Gondär city, led to increasing contacts between Ethiopia and Sennar, and resultant activity in the Ethiopia's north-western borderlands.

The existence of an overland trade route between Ethiopia and Egypt, which had earlier been referred to by Alvares, was later mentioned by Ludolf. He states that Cairo merchants were accustomed to sail up the Nile as far as Monfalot, after which they travelled by land via Dongola to Chelga on the Ethiopian border. Since they traded all along the way the journey from Egypt to Sennar took as long as three months, and that between Sennar and Ethiopia fourteen days. Hitherto when the intervening country was under "stricter government" the route was "safe enough and more frequented", but by his day it was "difficult and subject to many dangers". These included "the Extortions of the Turks", "Robberies committed by several vagabond Nations", and the "Unwholesomeness of the Climate". Several groups of merchants were nevertheless venturesome enough to travel by this route. Some of them were probably involved in the transport of horses from Sennar to Ethiopia, as suggested by Pero Paes, who on one occasion witnessed the arrival of a no less than 470 animals.[77]

Susneyos

The market town of Chelga, to judge from Susneyos's chronicle was frequented by both Ethiopians from the east and people from the

---

[76] Bruce (1790), II, 551-2, IV, 114, 116-18, 134.
[77] Ludolf (1684), pp. 394-5; Esteves Pereira (1903-18), III, 346.

The South-West and West

borders of Sennar in the west. The Emperor, who was much interested in the Chelga trade route, appointed the deposed king of Sennar, 'Abd al-Qadir, as his governor of the market town. Later, in 1616, Susneyos proceeded to the Tänkäl area on the frontiers of Sudan, where he received the allegiance of a local chief, Nayl Agub, whom he decorated with a bracelet and dagger of gold, and vestments of silver and silk. Nayl later guided the Emperor to Serki, a territory under Fung rule, which Susneyos conquered, after which he burnt it to the ground, and took many women and children as captives.[78]

An Ethiopian local chief, Käntiba Zä-Giyorgis, made his way to the area three years later, when he too captured many slaves. King Erubat of Sennar, who had earlier detained Abba Yeshaq, an Egyptian bishop bound for Ethiopia, responded by intervening with a large army, and killed one of the Emperor's officials, a Muslim called Muhammäd Sayd. Susneyos reacted by marching to the frontier, where he defeated Erubat's men. The King of Fung, 'Abd el-Qader, thereupon came to the Emperor' camp at Dehana, and paid him hommage.[79]

Susneyos subsequently ordered his son-in-law, Abétahun Wäldä Hawaryat, to make war on the Atbara country on the empire's north-western borders, i.e. the Gedaref area, while another official, Däjazmach Täklä Giyorgis, was detailed to attack Taka, or Käsäla. The monarch's troops reportedly ravaged "all the country of Fung and the Arabs", and captured numerous swords, helmets and horses, as well as many rifles and drums. Wäldä Hawaryat later returned for further loot. The Emperor, according to his chronicler, thus made his power felt all the way from the Red Sea port of Suakin to the gold producing country of Fazughli.[80]

Poncet's Evidence

The commercial situation on the western trade route at the end of the seventeenth century was later described by the French physician Poncet. He states that Senaar's imports from Egypt and beyond, much

---

[78] Esteves Pereira (1900), pp. 80-1, 96, 124-5, 133. The chronicle gives five reasons for the quarrel between Susneyos and the rulers of Sennar. One was that the latter had given asylum to Aléb, the ruler of Mäzäga, a Muslim territory which, it will be recalled, had earlier sided with Ahmäd ibn Ibrahim.
[79] Esteves Pereira (1900), pp. 154, 157.
[80] Esteves Pereira (1900), pp. 158-61. See also Bruce (1790), II, 284-5, 288-9; Huntingford (1989), p. 171.

of which were passed on to Gondär and other parts of the Ethiopian empire, included spices, paper, brass, iron, brass wire, iron ware, and Venice goods, among them several sorts of glass beads of all colours. Other imports comprised *kohl*, or antimony, to blacken the eyes, a strongly scented grain known in Arabic as *mahlab*, and various medicines, among them sublimate of mercury used in the treatment of syphilis, and white and yellow arsenic. "All these commodities", he says, had "a good vent in Ethiopia, with this difference that in Sennar large beads of glass are most esteem'd and in Ethiopia the lesser".

Exports from western Ethiopia to Sennar included local produce, above all coffee, as well as slaves, the strongest and most robust of whom are said by Poncet to have fetched as much as ten crowns, or dollars, each.

Chelga at this time was under Ethiopian rule, but the King of Sennar, by consent of the Emperor, had a customs official there, who collected duties on cotton brought from Sennar. These fees were divided equally between the two rulers.[81]

Iyasu II and the Kingdom of Fung

The peaceful situation described by Poncet came to an end during the reign of Iyasu II. He carried out a reportedly successful expedition to Sennar in 1742, and returned with many prisoners and booty of all kinds. This included no less than 300 camels and 20,000 cattle, which were kept for a time within the Gondar palace compound. Bruce states that this provided the citizens with "an entertainment to which they had long been strangers".[82]

Iyasu, stung, according to Bruce, by criticism of being less active than his namesake Iyasu the Great, later embarked in 1744 on a second expedition to Sennar, which he led in person, with the help of his faithful Oromo chief Wäräñña.

The enterprise proved disastrous. The Ethiopian army suffered considerable casualties, and fled in complete disarray. In the course of the fighting Iyasu lost his crown, as well as the effigy of the *Kwer'ata Re'esu*, or representation of Christ with the Crown of Thorns, which Ethiopian monarchs had traditionally taken with them to war. The painting was later repurchased by the Emperor at no small expense, while the crown was restored to the monarchy, as we have seen, by

---

[81] Foster (1949), pp. 105, 109, 113.
[82] Guidi (1912), p. 119; Bruce (1790), II, 632.

the Gondarine Oromo chief Gwangwél. The icon remained thereafter in Ethiopian royal possession until it was looted by the British expedition against Emperor Téwodros II in 1868, and has thus far not returned to Ethiopia.[83]

Bruce's Testimony

With the return of peace the western trade route resumed some, but by no means all, of its importance. Bruce, who travelled along it in 1771-2, reported that Ras-el-Fil constituted a buffer zone between Ethiopia and Sennar. Ras-el-Fil had formerly consisted of thirty-nine villages to which the Arabs of Atbara came to trade in butter, honey, horses, gold, and "many other" commodities. The Shaykhs of Atbara and Ras-el-Fil enjoyed good relations. The former sent his neighbour every year a Dongola horse, two razors and two dogs, and the Ras-el-Fil chief gave him in return a mule and a female slave. The "effect of such intercourse", the Scotsman claims, had been "to keep all the intermediate Arabs in their duty".

Since Iyasu II's abortive expedition there had, however, been "no peace" between the two states. The Arabs who had supported the Emperor, and had been defeated with him, had fled east to live on the Ethiopian side of the frontier, where they enjoyed imperial protection - and no longer paid tribute to Sennar. The chiefs of Ras-el-Fil and Sennar nevertheless understood each other "perfectly", and gave the neighbouring Arabs "no trouble". If the latter paid their tribute to either chief they divided it equally between them. The Emperor in this way received many valuable, and heavy, horses. Ras-el-Fil had formerly paid 400 ounces of gold, and Sancho, sixty miles to the north-east, a further hundred. Since Iyasu's expedition "many people" had, however, gone to Cherkin, twenty miles to the south, though the Emperor's demands had not on that account been reduced. The Cherkin trade had also suffered from molestation by the "Shanqellas", though the latter's ability to interfere had been reduced as a result of the losses they had suffered from smallpox.

Sennar and the neighbouring lands were by then no longer prosperous. "Formerly when the ways were open and merchants went in caravans with safety", Bruce claims, "Indian goods" were brought from Jeddah in considerable quantity, and were dispersed over the

---

[83] Guidi (1912), pp. 124, 126, 219-20; Budge (1928b), II, 453-5; Crawford (1951), pp. 239-43. See also Pankhurst (1977), pp. 169-87.

neighbouring "black country", where exactly he does not specify. The return was made in gold, gold dust, civet, rhinoceros horn, and, above all, slaves. This trade, by the late eighteenth century, was, however, "almost destroyed", though some gold, ivory and slaves were still sold. Trade in gold was in the hands of Muslim and "pagan" merchants from the Sudan, while that in slaves was carried out by Dabayna Arabs, great hunters who crossed into Ethiopia without fear. The slackening of trade also owed much, Bruce felt, to the "violence" of the Arabs, and to the "faithlessness" of the Sennar government, which had closed the country's trade on every side except that of Jeddah, whither caravans went every year by way of Suakin.

Trade on the Gondär-Sennar route was, however, far from entirely dead. Cherkin for example held a market every Saturday, at which raw cotton, cattle, honey and coarse cotton cloths were sold. Fine horses continued to reach the Emperor from Sennar, and Fazugli was still an important source of gold.[84]

The western borderlands, like those to the north and east, thus remained of major economic importance to the central highlands, as well as a source of at least limited prosperity to the region as a whole.[85]

---

[84] Bruce (1790), II, 563, IV, 311, 325, 327, 485-6, (1813), VII, 98. See also Pankhurst (1951), pp.316-21. On the Sennar trade route see also Bruce (1813), VII, 102-4.

[85] Contact with Sennar at this time, it is interesting to note, also led to increased use of Arabic in Ethiopian official letter-writing, and notably to the use of seals with Arabic inscriptions, on which see Pankhurst (1968), pp. 397-417.

Chapter 27
THE EAST: ADAL, HARAR, and AWSSA

ADAL and HARAR

The great famine of 1559 coincided with, but may have been intensified by, the first Oromo advance into the Harär area. Oromo warriors, according to a local Adaré chronicle, devastated the regions of Sim, Shäwa, Nägäb, Gidayä and the old Adäl capital, Däkär, i.e. a wide stretch of country from Adäl to the vicinity of Harär.

Harär: a mid-nineteenth century view of the town. From R.F. Burton, *First Footsteps in East Africa*.

In an attempt to check Oromo incursions the survivors of the famine are said to have dug ditches and built forts. It was at this time, during the reign of Amir Nur ibn Mujahid, according to tradition, that the city's famous walls were erected with the help of two chiefs, Ahu Abadir and Ahu 'Ali. This construction work was hampered, it is said, by an intensification of the famine, which was followed, as so often in Ethiopian history, by an unidentified epidemic. Many people succumbed, including Amir Nur himself. He died around 1567, three months after returning from a battle against the Oromos, who soon occupied much of the surrounding countryside.[1]

---

[1] Cerulli (1931), pp. 57-8; Azais and Chambard (1931), I, 4; Pankhurst (1982), pp. 51-2.

The walls of Harär were of crucial importance, for they helped to preserve the city's independence for the next three centuries, but at the same time prevented any expansion of the settlement which, as time went by, became ever more densely populated.

Amirs 'Uthman, Talha, Nasir, and Muhammäd ibn Nasir

Nur was succeeded by Amir 'Uthman "the Abyssinian", who had been one his slaves, but adopted a much laxer approach to religion than his predecessors. He reportedly permitted wine drinking, which had hitherto been prohibited, and appropriated the considerable wealth which Nur had bequeathed for Muslim orphans, thus reportedly acquiring 35,000 of the city's local coins. 'Uthman, who was apparently a pragmatist, also made peace with the Oromos, on condition that they sold their cotton cloth for fixed prices at markets within his territory. He agreed in return that Oromo refugees who had found asylum in the city should be returned to the groups from whom they had fled. To further trade he placed the Oromo markets under the supervision of his predecessor's son-in-law Jibril.

Jibril, a pious man, however, soon defected, and made his way to Awssa, a remote region, as Cerulli observed, which served as a place of refuge for rebels against the Haräri *amirs*. There Jebril denounced what he considered 'Uthman's transgressions against Qoranic law.

The conflict came to a head shortly afterwards, when a woman of Muslim origin who had been taken by the "pagan" Oromos, arrived as a refugee in Awssa. Though she was the daughter of a Shaykh, 'Uthman ordered Jibril to send her back to her compatriots. Jibril refused, declaring that to do so would be contrary to God's law. Fearing Uthman's wrath, he then fled to Zäylä'.

This act of defiance gained Jibril considerable popularity. 'Uthman was, however, determined to nip the rebellion in the bud. He despatched an army against his insubordinate official, who was soon defeated, and killed. The insurrection, however, was continued by one of Jebril's followers, Talha son of Wazir 'Abbas. A kinsman of the great warrior Ahmäd ibn Ibrahim he defeated a military force sent from Harär in 1569, whereupon the city's religious leaders assembled, and appointed him as their sultan. This won the approval of the Haräri army, and led to much rejoicing in the city.

Talha, a man of peace, soon displeased the militaristic party, for, as a local Muslim chronicle states, he "did not leave on a campaign or for a *jihad*". He was therefore deposed in 1571, and replaced by

'Uthman's son Nasir. The latter was soon succeeded in turn by his son Muhammäd, who, entrusting the government to his brother Wazir Hamid, sought to emulate the action of Imam Ahmäd half a century earlier by embarking in 1572-3 on an expedition against Emperor Särsä Dengel.

The endeavour was a total disaster. While Amir Muhammäd was away on campaign the Oromos devastated the region. They are said to have destroyed a hundred Muslim villages, and, advancing to the city's very walls, besieged Harär. Fierce fighting took place at one of the gates, which was soon "full of corpses". Wazir Hamid was reportedly struck by twenty spears, but, though seriously wounded, succeeded in returning to the city alive. The invaders were later repulsed.

The Amir's campaign in the Christian highlands was meanwhile also running into serious difficulties. A great battle was fought with Särsä Dengel, but God gave the victory, the Muslim chronicler says, to the "infidels", i.e. Christians. Muhammäd was captured, and put to death. One of Muhammäd's chiefs, Asma' ad-Din, then changed sides, and gave his support to Särsä Dengel.

Mänsur ibn Muhammäd and Imam Muhammäd Gasa

Notwithstanding this debacle a new Haräri leader, Mänsur ibn Muhammäd, soon emerged. After establishing himself in the city in 1575 he waged a fierce war against the Oromos, and captured a hundred and fifty horses from the Somalis. He subsequently made his way to Zäylä, and later to Awssa.

He was succeeded, in 1577, by another of Imam Ahmäd's kinsmen, Imam Muhammäd Gasa. The latter was such an able leader that many men, who had previously fought against either the Emperor or the Oromos, rallied to his cause. The number of his followers increased, and before long he had six hundred horsemen, a thousand infantry, and seventy riflemen, with whom in 1579-80 he invaded the highlands, but was duly repulsed by Särsä Dengel.

Muhammäd Gasa, concerned by the Oromo attacks, which were endangering the city's access to the sea, felt obliged to abandon Harär. In the first year of his reign he therefore left his brother in charge of the city, with the title of *wazir*, and established himself in Awssa. He did so in the hope, Trimingham says, that this remote settlement would be "less accessible to Galla raids". In this he was mistaken, for he was killed only a few years later in 1583 while fighting against the Wärdaya (or Wärrä Däya) Oromos.[2]

The transfer of capital to Awssa did little to help the Adäl state, which, Cerulli contends, had already been exhausted by the conflict with the Christian empire. The Oromos renewed their incursions, and obliged the rulers of Adäl to remain on the defensive. The Afar nomads meanwhile, profiting from Adäl weakness, raided caravans travelling to and from the coast, and even attacked Zäylä'. Adäl was at the same time profoundly weakened by internal discord: in the five years between 1585 and 1590 no fewer than eight *amir*s succeeded each other, most of them being overthrown by their rivals. Cerulli's verdict on this "sad condition" of Adäl decadence was that whereas the Christian empire under Särsä Dengel was able to reorganise itself to withstand Oromo expansion the Muslim kingdom of Adäl was too newly established to transcend tribal differences. The result, he claims, was that the nomadic population, deprived of the chiefs who had earlier led them to victory, "instinctively" returned to their "eternal disintegrating struggles" of people against people, and tribe against tribe.[3]

Susneyos

By the early seventeenth century much of Adäl was occupied by the Ittu Oromos. The Adäl state nevertheless had some contacts with Emperor Susneyos, who early in his reign despatched there an envoy called Sutafé Krestos. He returned in 1607 with many precious gifts from the king of Adäl, including fine clothes and many bullets, aptly described by the chronicler as items useful for war.[4]

THE HARAR CITY STATE

The town of Harär, though abandoned for far-off Awssa in 1577, survived as an independent city state. The only polity in the region to issue its own currency, it was destined to survive as a major religious centre and a place of learning.[5]

---

[2] Cerulli (1931), pp. 59-62, 68-9; Cerulli (1942), pp. 3-4; Basset (1881), XVIII, 111; Trimingham (1952), pp 95-7.
[3] Cerulli (1931), p. 80.
[4] Beckingham and Huntingford (1954), p. 196; Esteves Pereira (1900), pp. 78, 109.
[5] Ahmed Zekaria (1991), pp. 23-46.

Harari dress, as seen in the mid-nineteenth century. From R.F. Burton, *First Footsteps in East Africa.*

One of the most important of the city's early rulers was Amir 'Ali ibn Da'ud, who came to power in 1647, and founded a new dynasty. He and his successors, like their predecessors, faced numerous difficulties with the surrounding Oromos. A battle, mentioned in a marginal note to a Harārı manuscript, took place with the Illamo Gallas, at the very end of 'Ali's reign in 1662. The engagement resulted in heavy casualties, doubtless on both sides. Those killed included the Amir's son Säbr ad-Din.[6]

Amir 'Ali was succeeded by another son, Amir 'Abdullah (1671-1700), who, following traditional local practice, had a number of

---

[6] Cerulli (1931), pp. 95-6; Cerulli (1942), p. 7.

wives. Several came from beyond the city walls. One was described as a Geri Somali, and another an Arussi Galla, while two others were referred to merely as Gallas. None of 'Ali's children by these non-Harāri women, however, ascended the throne. This honour was apparently reserved for pure Harāris, who because of their mothers' connections, would naturally have enjoyed stronger family support within the city. The presence of such Oromo and Somali women, and doubtless also others from outside Harär, nevertheless caused Cerulli to comment that the citizens, while fighting the surrounding peoples, were subjected to strong Galla and Somali influences.[7] Influences, we may assume, were, however, reciprocal, with the Harari inhabitants of the walled city, a centre of trade, urban culture and Islamic learning, also influencing the nomads and peasantry of the surrounding lands.

An *ashrafi*, or coin, struck in Harär by Sultan 'Abd al-Shakur in 1197 A.H., i.e. 1783-4.
Photo: Ahmed Zakaria.

AWSSA

The Awssa sultanate, like many lands further to the south, was much affected by the migration of the Oromos, who arrived in the area during the reign of Särsä Dengel. They began to dominate the territory, according to an Awssa chronicle, during the time of Imam Hizanäh Zähl, i.e. around 1583-4, when they besieged two important settlements, Fänfära and Wäräba. Oromo incursions increased after 1589, during the reign of Imam 'Abbas ibn Abun, when the invaders seized many caravans travelling in their vicinity.

---

[7] Cerulli (1942), pp. 5-7.

Fighting was intensified by Amir Ahmäd ibn Asma' ad-Din, who launched an attack in which he killed many Wällo Oromos, presumably on Awssa's western borders. The Oromos, however, soon resumed the military initiative, killing numerous Awssa nobles, while many others, including the Amir, died of thirst in the struggle.

A generation or so later the Awssa rulers sought to revenge themselves on the Wärdaya Gallas for the killing of Muhammäd ibn Ibrahim Gasa. Imam Adräh Tadrus launched an attack on the Oromos in 1621, and a subsequent ruler, Muhammäd Isa, undertook a victorious expedition against them ten years later.[8]

The Jesuits Machado and Pereira

Useful information on Awssa in this period is provided by Jerónimo Lobo and Manoel de Almeida, whose accounts compliment each other. They tell of a mission led by their fellow Jesuits, Francisco Machado and Bernardo Pereira, which reached the area in 1624.

Lobo, telling the first part of the story, claims that Susneyos, who had by then become a Catholic, wanted to invite a group of Jesuits into his country, and informed them that they could enter it by way of the Dankali kingdom His secretary had, however, "erroneously" written Zäylä' instead of Dankali, "little dreaming" how much this word would cost the Jesuit Fathers. The two missionaries landed at Zäylä', i.e. far to the south-east of their expected destination. They were welcomed by the local shaikh, with "words and demonstrations of feigned benevolence". He then sent them inland to the Awssa ruler, who also received them "with good words", but "soon with evil deeds". He ordered them to be stript of their possessions and thrown in a "harsh prison", on the pretext that one of his envoys had been killed by Emperor Susneyos. This charge, Lobo claims, was entirely false, for the man had "died a natural death", and the king's "cruel treatment" was "motivated by greed", and an "inherited hatred of Catholics, particularly the Portuguese", who had killed his famous ancestor Ahmäd ibn Ibrahim.

---

[8] Cerulli (1931), pp. 74, 77-9, 82-4.

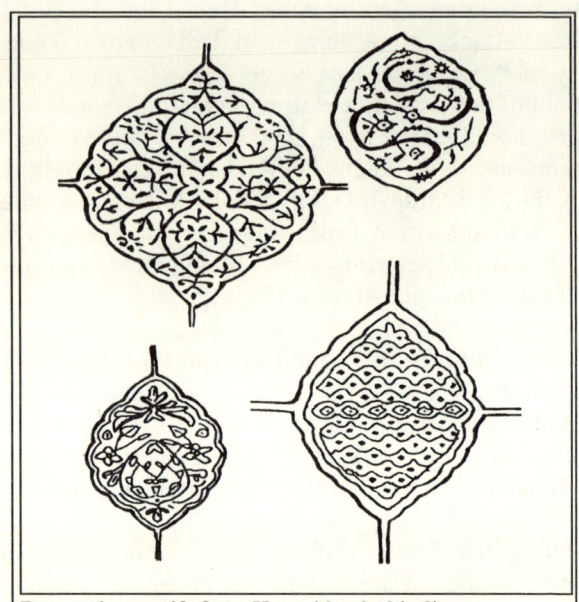
Decorative motifs from Harari book-bindings.
From R. Pankhurst, *The Manuscript Bindings of Harar.*

Susneyos, on learning that the two Jesuits had travelled inland by way of Zäylä', despaired for their lives, but nevertheless "made every effort to save them". He sent the chief many messages and presents" and promised him "great rewards" if he would release his captives. The ruler's "hatred for the Catholic faith and for the very name 'Portuguese' was, however, "too deeply engrained" to permit of clemency, the more so as it was reinforced by "the machinations of a cruel Ethiopian heretic", i.e. Orthodox Christian. The latter "nullified" the Emperor's efforts by advising the chief to kill the visitors so as to "prevent them going to preach the Roman faith". He ensured the success of his scheme by promising the Awssa king "great wealth". The monarch accordingly gave orders for the two Jesuits to be beheaded.[9]

Almeida, whose report dwells mainly on the last phase of the story, makes no mention of the alleged mistake in Susneyos's letter. He merely states that the two Jesuits, "eager to enter Abyssinian

---

[9] Lockhart (1984) pp.48-51.

territory" via Zäylä, travelled for ten days to the inland city of Awssa Gurrelé, which he refers to as the capital of the Kings of Zäylä'.[10]

The ruler of Awssa, according to Almeida, had sent ambassadors to the Emperor with the present of a musket and a "big well-bred donkey", and hoped to receive in exchange gifts of greater value. Concealing the "poison and hatred" he "bore in his depraved heart", he therefore detained the Jesuits for almost two months, promising to despatch them before long wherever they wanted to go, but did not allow them to tell the Emperor of their arrival. On the return of the ambassadors, however, the chief ordered that his captives be put in a dark shed, and fettered. To justify this act, he informed them that the Emperor had "treated his ambassadors very badly". He ordered them to tell Susneyos that, if he wanted to see them again, he should give him gold and valuable cloth, for if he failed to do so they would "not leave that prison alive". Unwilling to follow these orders the captives informed the Emperor that they were "ready to shed their blood for the Lord whose holy faith they came to preach".

The chief also sent Susneyos a letter which "abused him as an apostate", for having "abandoned the faith of his ancestors" for that of Rome.

The Emperor, filled with compassion for the missionaries, as well as anger at the chief's letter, is said to have done all he could to save them. He sent the Awssa ruler a message "full of affability", promising him everything he wanted, in return for the Jesuits' release. Susneyos's brother Ras Se'elä Krestos likewise promised him a fine horse and valuable trappings, as well as jewels and rich pieces of cloth. Such offers were, however, unavailing, for the Awssa chief ordered the priests to be executed. They were secretly killed that very night, and their bodies were the next morning thrown in a nearby courtyard.

The ruler of Awssa, according to Almeida, later sent a message to an Orthodox Christian rebel against Susneyos. It exhorted him to "fight bravely" for the faith of his fathers, and declared that it was to destroy the faith of the Portuguese that he had killed the two Jesuits who had come to preach it. As evidence of what he had done he sent the chief a handsome knife belonging to the deceased missionaries.[11]

Contacts with the Gondärine Monarchy

---

[10] Awssa Gurrelé in Huntingford's opinion was another name for Awwsa, the old term Gurralé perhaps represented by a hill of that name found on the modern British War Office map, NC 37, ninety miles north-west of Lake Abbé.

[11] Beckingham and Huntingford (1954), pp. 195-201, 229. See also Caraman (1985), pp. 135-6.

Contacts between Awssa and the Gondär monarchy continued during the ensuing reign of Emperor Fasilädäs. Evidence of this is found in a report by the Yämäni envoy Hasän ibn Ahmäd al-Haymi that messengers from Awssa visited the Gondär court in 1647.[12] No information on the subject of their discussions has survived, but it may be surmised that the two parties felt an identity of interest as both were then under strong Oromo pressure. No alliance between them as far as is known was, however, concluded.

Renewed Oromo Pressure

The Oromos resumed their military initiative in the Awssa area in 1647-8. A local chronicle states that they at this time raided the Ada'il, in fact the Afars, and plundered them, before returning to their country. Faced with this onslaught the Afars appealed for the help of Imam Adam Isa of Awssa. The latter responded to this appeal, but was soon killed in the fighting. The Awssa leadership, which had formerly considered the Afars as hostile caravan-raiders, had thus come to regard them as natural, and no doubt useful, allies against the common enemy.

A generation or so later Imam Adam's son and successor, Imam 'Umar-Din, gathering a larger force than his predecessors, undertook an expedition to the Afar country, where he fought, on behalf of its inhabitants, against the Basso Oromos. He was reportedly victorious, and seized many Galla children as slaves. He later carried out other successful expeditions against the Oromos, who are said to have accordingly become much dispirited.[13]

Despite these victories the power of the Awssa state was by then seriously weakened by internal disorders. In a period of seventy-three years the territory had no less than ten rulers, four of whom were killed in battle, and two deposed. The Imamate suffered moreover from the fact that its capital had been transferred to a remote area near the Afar country, while the port of Zäylä' and the walled city of Harär had both become virtually independent. Awssa, isolated from its old contacts with these important settlements, could no longer hold its own against the Afars. Amir 'Umar-Din Adam, who assumed office in 1672-3, was the last Adäl ruler of Awssa. Not long after his accession the old Adäl state, over which he had presided, crumbled, and the Afars, as we shall see, gained absolute supremacy over it.

---

[12] Beckingham and Huntingford, p. 193. See also p. 113.
[13] Cerulli (1931), pp. 84-6.

Chapter 28

THE NORTH: THE LAND OF THE AFARS, THE COUNTRY OF THE BAHR NAGASH, and MASSAWA

THE LAND OF THE AFARS

Sahim, Kamil and Susneyos

Despite the conflicts of the past the Afar rulers had by the early seventeenth century, developed peaceful relations with the Christian monarchy, whose capital was by then situated in the Lake Tana area. The need for co-existence between the two polities was grounded on two major developments: Firstly. the advance of the Oromos, which threatened the Afars and their commerce with the interior, and secondly, the Turkish occupation of Massawa, which deprived the Emperors of easy access to that port, and left the Afar territory as perhaps their only safe route to the sea.

The Afar rulers of this time accepted the paramountcy of the Christian empire. The relationship between them and the Christian rulers during the reign of Susneyos was discussed by Almeida. He declares that the Muslim "King of Dancaly", though strictly speaking not a subject of the Ethiopian monarch, recognised the latter as his "superior". The Afar ruler, he adds, was then so "poor in land and power" that he might "rather be called a goatherd than a King", and for that reason paid due respect, and some recognition, to his mighty Christian neighbour.[1]

Further light on the position of the Afar ruler *vis-à-vis* the Christian state is provided by Susneyos's chronicle. It reports that the Dankali king Kamil, who had then recently overthrown his brother Sahim, travelled up to the Emperor's camp at Dehana in 1620. He prostrated himself in front of Susneyos, and appealed for his protection. The monarch thereupon crowned him, "made celebration for him", "confirmed him in his royalty", and established that as his tribute he should pay half the taxes collected in his country.[2] Several members of Kamil's family were later brought up at the Emperor's court.

---

[1] Beckingham, and Huntingford (1954), pp.12, 72.
[2] Esteves Pereira (1900), pp. 156-7.

Susneyos, who like several of his predecessors, was concerned at the Turkish control of Massawa, took a keen interest in the Afar country, which, he believed, could afford an alternative means of access to sea. It was for this reason, as we have seen in the previous chapter, that he had encouraged the Jesuit missionaries Machado and Pereira to proceed on their fatal journey. He informed them in 1624 that they could go through the Dankali kingdom, but they landed instead in Adäl, far to the east of Afarland, and, were executed.[3]

The Afar State and its Port: The Evidence of Lobo

Their fellow Jesuit Jerónimo Lobo was more successful. On the Emperor's advice he disembarked at the Afar port of Baylul, in 1625. Susneyos had informed him by letter that access to Massawa was then difficult, but that he could enter the empire through the Dankali kingdom, whose inhabitants "although Muslim, were his vassals and friends". Lobo, the first foreign writer to visit the area, provides valuable evidence. He states that the Afar ruler, for "reasons of self-preservation" or because of an "historic feudal relationship", recognised "a certain vassalage to the Emperor", and was "always loyal and obedient" to his orders.[4]

Baylul, where the Jesuit traveller spent thirteen days, was "a small town", consisting only of straw houses, and inhabited by "no more than fifty inhabitants". It had "not much in the way of provisions" beyond "a few goats and kids", which the people readily sold, for, like all their people, they were "poor, rough and usually very wretched". Lobo and his party were put up in "a shed", which, because of the heat and need for ventilation, was "open on all sides". There they slept on mats, and had to subsist mainly on their own supplies, though they also found some flour, and goats' meat. Goats were not expensive, and their "only drawback" was that there were "too few of them". The travellers also managed to purchase a small number of camels and donkeys for their subsequent journey inland.[5]

The palace of the king - Kamil? - was situated at an unnamed capital three days' journey inland. The structure, which consisted of a small thatched round hut made of sticks and clay, with a straw roof, could hold fifty people, seated on the ground. The royal throne, a

---

[3] Lockhart (1984), pp. 48-51.
[4] Lockhart (1984), pp. 48, 11.
[5] Lockhart (1984), pp. 117.

platform of stone and earth covered with a carpet and two velvet cushions, occupied one part of the building. The other was allotted to the monarch's horse, together with harnesses and other items "appropriate to the stable", for it was the Afar rulers' custom to keep their horses and mules "right in their homes and in their sight". A similar practice, it is interesting to recall, was reported at Emperor Yohannes IV's palace at Däbrä Tabor two centuries later.[6]

An Ethiopian zebra sent as a gift to the Mughal emperor Jahangir, a miniature painted in 1621 by the Mughal artist Ustad, or "master", Mänsur.
Photo: Victoria and Albert Museum, London.

On entering the palace Lobo and his companions seated themselves on the ground, after which the king's pages appeared, one with a gourd of mead, another with porcelain drinking-cups, probably imported from China, a third with a tobacco pipe. The latter, the likes of which the Jesuit had never previously seen, consisted of a coconut shell, full of water, connected with the bowl of the pipe, and a silver

---

[6] Bianchi (1884), p. 46.

tube through which the smoker inhaled, filtering the smoke through the water to make it "refined and mild".

After the arrival of several more "honoured servants" the monarch himself appeared. He was "well dressed in silken *cabaias*", a turban on his head, with some jewels, in particular two amulets of "finely wrought gold" which came down over his temples. He had a small lance in his hand by way of sceptre, and seated himself on a small velvet covered chair. Behind him came his officers of state. After rising to pay their respects everyone sat down. Lobo and his party then went up to kiss the king's hand before returning to their seats. Describing the ensuing audience he continues:

"Everyone was silent, as is the custom, for about eight minutes... The period of silence was ended by the king, who gave the signal to talk by saying to the interpreter that we were welcome, that he had been expecting us for days because of the information he had received from the Emperor [i.e. Susneyos], his father (a term and name they use to show love and good will with a suggestion of filial devotion to persons to whom they profess obedience)....and, in conclusion, that we should be as unworried and free of fear as if we were in our homelands since his lands belonged to the Emperor, who loved us so much and recommended us so highly".[7]

Despite these kind words, and the affirmation of the king's loyalty to the Emperor, Lobo found that the Afar ruler, who relied heavily on taxes on trade, was extortionate in his demands. This did little to improve his opinion of the Baylul trade route.[8]

The route inland from Baylul proved moreover far less convenient than expected. The Oromos had by this time penetrated into the adjacent hinterland, and carried out several attacks on the Jesuit party. The Baylul route thus seemed far from secure, and proved a great disappointment.[9]

The Reminiscences of Hasän ibn Ahmäd al-Haymi

Despite the difficulties which Lobo had encountered the Afar route was not abandoned. One of those who used it, in 1639-40, was a

---

[7] Lockhart (1984), pp. 124.
[8] Lockhart (1984), pp. 124-31.
[9] Lockhart (1984), pp. 138,140, 146-51.

Coptic bishop from Egypt, Abunä Mika'él, who travelled to Gondär by way of "the country of the Danakil", as a chronicle states.[10]

The port was later visited by the Yämäni ambassador Hasän ibn Ahmäd al-Haymi, who had been advised by Fasilädäs to employ it on his journey to Gondär in 1647. Al-Haymi, who spent almost two months at Baylul, reports that it was under the control of Sultan Shuhaym ibn Kamil al-Dankali. The latter was the son of the aforementioned Kamil, who, as we have seen, had spent some time at the Emperor's court. Shuhaym was a Muslim, the envoy claims, "in name only", for he scarcely followed the prescriptions of Islam. He was said to have been married, perhaps partially for dynastic reasons, to twelve women. Some of his subjects, the ambassador complains, also had more than the number of wives prescribed by Islam.

Shuhaym, like Kamil, had close ties with the ruling Emperor, at this time Fasilädäs. The Dankali ruler, we are told, thus had "relations with the king of al-Habasha", in whose territory he had grown up, and still had relatives and children there. Fasilädäs "reckoned him among his nobles and members of his suite". Shuhaym, however, also had close contacts with Arabia, notably with the Na'ib, or local governor, of Mokha, with whom there were "connections, prosperous business transactions (*al-mu'amala*) and good relations".[11]

Al-Haymi, a proud Yämäni, was no sympathetic observer. He considered the Afars "repulsive in appearance", and complains that they were "all of them naked, not covering their nakedness", and that among them relations between the sexes were "promiscuous". He added, even more arrogantly, that the Afar language was "barbaric". Those who had lived at Mokha, he was pleased to report, nevertheless "often" knew Arabic. The nomads of the interior, on the other hand, were less sophisticated. They were, he claims, "utterly (*ghaya*) astonished at the firing of muskets", and, anticipating the coming of the machine-gun by two centuries, "firmly believed that the marksman, when he had shot, was able to continue shooting without operation and that no time passed between each of the two shots".[12]

Though advised to use Baylul the Yämani envoy concluded, like Lobo, that the route inland was "full of dangers", notably from the Oromos. He therefore observed that the Emperor could not have been

---

[10] Basset (1881) (1881), XVIII, 288. See also Bruce (1790), II, 415.
[11] Donzel (1986), pp. 35, 91, 105.
[12] Donzel (1986), pp. 106-9.

"completely acquainted" with the road, for he would not otherwise have "approved" of it.[13]

Notwithstanding such difficulties the Baylul route was still then the most convenient means of access to the coast. It was doubtless not without reason that Fasilädäs arranged for al-Haymi, at the close of his visit, to return the way he had come, via the Afar port.

The Advent of the Oromos

The Oromos, about whom Lobo and al-Haymi had both complained, made their appearance in the Awssa area, it will be recalled, in the late sixteenth century. As early as 1583 they had killed Amir Muhammäd ibn Ibrahim Gasa in battle. On gaining control in the area, they soon came into conflict with the Afars, who were forced willy-nilly into an alliance with the Awssa state against which they had earlier fought. This new politico-strategic alignment became evident in 1647-8 when the Oromos attacked the Afars. The latter, who had been raiding Awssa caravans little more than half a century earlier, appealed for Awssa help. The Awssa ruler, Imam Adam Isa, responded by attacking the Oromos, but was killed in the ensuing fighting, after which the latter consolidated their position in the area.[14]

The Afar-Awssa alliance continued for several decades. In 1672-3 Imam 'Umar-Din, as noted earlier, undertook an expedition to the Afar country, where he attacked the Basso Gallas, and later carried out other victorious operations in the area.[15]

One of the results of this Awssa victory was that ties between the Afar rulers and the Emperors were preserved, and the trade route to Baylul, though fraught with difficulties, remained open. The situation in the late seventeenth century was summed up by Ludolf who declared that the Dankali king was still "a firm Allie" of the Emperor, but was by then "oblig'd to no sort of Tribute".[16] On this latter point he was soon to be corrected by the well-informed Armenian, Khodja Murad.

---

[13] Donzel (1986), pp.109, 113-27 167.
[14] Cerulli (1931), pp. 84-5. See also Bruce (1790), II, 349.
[15] Cerulli (1931), p. 86.
[16] Ludolf (1684), p. 234.

Khodja Murad's Account of Baylul

Considerable light on the Baylul trade route is afforded by Murad, who served as perhaps the principal trade agent of Emperor Yohannes I and his son Iyasu I.

An Ethiopian rhinoceros presented as a gift to the Emperor of Persia at Isfahan in the late seventeenth or early eighteenth century.
From J. Chardin, *Voyage de Monsieur Le Chevalier Chardin en Perse.*

Murad travelled from Gondär to Baylul in 1663, before sailing to India. He subsequently told the French traveller François Bernier that he had taken this route on account of unspecified problems on the Massawa route, but had been obliged to pass, like earlier travellers, through "very rough country".[17]

Baylul was not extensively used at this time. This was partly due to difficulties encountered on the journey, but also, as the Dutch merchant, Justinus Weijns, reported in 1676, because the Turks in control of Massawa sought to prevent evasion of their toll at that port. They would therefore "not permit sailing" from Baylul, which they regarded as a rival place of access to the sea.[18]

Further information on Baylul was provided by Murad a decade or so later when he answered a questionnaire submitted to him by Ludolf

---

[17] Donzel (1979), p. 20
[18] Donzel (1979), p. 52.

in 1685. Several of the latter's questions concerned the actual situation at the port, "whether any ships sailed there", and, if so, "from what place and of what nation?". The Armenian replied emphatically that the only ships sailing to Baylul were *jalbas*, or large local vessels, that arrived there yearly. They came from Mokha, and "nowhere else", and carried "Arabs and Abyssinians", who came to barter coarse linen for butter, sheep and other "small merchandise".[19]

On a subsequent journey to Batavia, in 1689, Murad supplied his hosts with additional information. He observed that Ethiopia's "shores or seaside places" were "all occupied by the Turks" with the sole exception of Baylul.[20] Elaborating on the status and trade of the port, and on the relations between the Afar ruler and the Emperor, he declares:

"The port of Beilul... in the small kingdom of Dankale, still belongs to the emperor of Ethiopia, but is kept as a fief by a Muslim Kaffir, who leaves his children as a pledge with the emperor and has to pay an annual tribute. But since the inhabitants there and in the surrounding regions are savage Kaffirs and mostly Muslims, no Christians are found there nor as many Muslim merchants from up country as in Matsua [Massawa] because of the bad reception and great extortions. There is however a moderate navigation from Mocha, Aden, etc. whose inhabitants, the Arabs, come there with their ships, taking provisions of corn, butter, honey and also tusks, cow-hides and civet, which together with a few slaves are brought there from the highlands and are exchanged for spices, pepper, broadcloth, etc.".[21]

Reverting to conditions in the Afar country on a later visit to Batavia, in 1697, Murad reiterated, emphatically, that the Afar king continued to be "subject to the emperor of Abyssinia".[22] As for Baylul it was still only a "tiny little town" three or four miles from the sea, and consisted of no more than fifty or sixty small houses. They were inhabited by "wild people", with "a religion of their own", who walked around "completely naked", but who, when sitting, covered their nakedness with a small piece of cloth. They were "subject to the emperor of Abyssinia", this being the "only place" on the coast in his

---

[19] Donzel (1979), p. 58.
[20] Donzel (1979), p. 72.
[21] Donzel (1979), p. 78.
[22] Donzel (1979), p. 101.

possession. Caravans from Baylul had once travelled to and from the interior, but the port by then was "totally desolate". "Good fat sheep and big pigs" could nevertheless to be obtained there cheaply, in exchange for coarse imported cloth.[23]

The Decline of the Awssa Imamate, and its Assimilation by the Afars

The Awssa imamate, torn apart by internal strife, declined, as we have seen, in the late seventeenth century. The state became so enfeebled that it finally succumbed to the Afars, who, Cerulli argues, gained "absolute supremacy" over it. The last of its Adäl rulers, according to local tradition, was a certain Imam Salman.

The collapse of the Adäl sultanate, and the beginnings of Afar rule, for which there are no contemporary records, cannot be dated with any certainty. Cerulli, who took a negative view of the change, considered that Awssa's fate paralleled that of the Ethiopian Christian empire. Just as the latter became a prey to Oromo military chiefs, who reduced the Gondar emperors to the status of puppets, so, he claimed, Muslim Adäl, "which had for two centuries assumed for itself the mission of spreading Islam in Ethiopia, transformed itself into a semi-barbarous state dominated by those Dankali nomads whom the Semitic or Semiticised aristocracy had always regarded only as wild plunderers of caravans".

For the Afars the seizure of Awssa was, however, an important, and highly beneficial, event. The area was the region's only extensively watered, fertile and cultivable area. It was as such a paradise, producing grain, not only for local consumption, but also for visiting caravans. The end of Adäl rule thus marked the beginning of a new, and more sophisticated Afar state, which, despite many serious difficulties, was to survive into the European colonial period.

The first Afar sultan of Awssa, Kedafu, the chief of the Modaito clan, held power for about fifteen years and established an on-going dynasty. He was succeeded by his son Muhammäd Kedafu, who ruled for thirty years, and was succeeded in turn by Kedafu's grandson Ijdahis, who reigned for twenty-two years. These were long reigns by contemporary standards, and suggest an element of political stability. Power at this time was exercised within the Modaito clan by the

---

[23] Donzel (1979), p. 103.

Assimara, or "Red", nobles, who kept their rivals, the Adoimara, or "White" commoners, at bay.[24]

The Term *Amolé*

Bars of rock-salt, mined in the Afar depression, had been used instead of money throughout much of the highlands, as we have seen, since time immemorial. The first mention of these bars by their present Amharic name, i.e. *amolé*, is found, however, only at the close of the seventeenth century, in the memoirs of the French physician Poncet. The term, according to the Italian lexicographer Guidi, was perhaps derived from that of an Afar tribe, but no such group, as far as the present author is aware, has been identified.[25]

Remedius Prutky and James Bruce

Subsequent information on Baylul, and on the Afars, in the late eighteenth century was gleaned by the Czech missionary Remedius Prutky, who visited Ethiopia in 1751, and a decade or so later by James Bruce. Both wrote from hearsay, for neither had actually visited the area.

Prutky described Baylul, in romantic vein, as a large and "beautiful" port, with a "natural" harbour, "excellently endowed by nature", and "safe from storms". He nevertheless admits that it was "completely deserted", except for a "few Arabs", and was no longer visited by ships of any size. Though "little used" he was convinced that it held possibilities for the future, for the basic reason that, unlike Massawa, it was still under Ethiopian rule.[26]

Bruce was also aware of Baylul's potential significance. He was, however, at pains to emphasise the inhospitable character of the country inland. Describing the aridity of the Afar realm, and ignoring the fertile Awssa area, of which he was probably ignorant, he observes that there were "but two small rivers of fresh water in the whole kingdom". Even those were "not visible" in the dry season, for they were "swallowed up in the sand", and their water could only be obtained by digging. The rest of the water was "brackish, and not fit for use, unless in absolute necessity". The country's modest rains

---

[24] Cerulli (1931), p. 87; Abir (1968); 23. On the distinction and differences between the Assimara and the Adoimara see Lewis (1955), pp. 157-9.
[25] Foster (1949), p. 122; Guidi, (1901), p. 419.
[26] Arrowsmith-Brown, (1991), pp. 132-3, 356.

moreover sometimes failed, at which time the inhabitants were obliged to seek, "far off in the rainy frontiers of Abyssinia, water for themselves, and pasture for their miserable goats and sheep".[27]

As for commerce the Scotsman claimed that in earlier times, when trade with India had flourished, the Afar rulers' revenue had come chiefly from furnishing camels for the transportation of merchandise to the interior. Afar trade by his day, however, was in decline. It was largely confined to the age-old carriage of bars of rock salt, which were excavated in the Afar lowlands, and had to be transported through "dry and burning deserts". This entailed "great risk of being murdered by Galla", before being delivered to the nearest highland market, and earned only "a very moderate profit".[28]

Awssa and Yämäni Involvement in Afar Affairs

Awssa, though unknown to Bruce, was by then a settlement of no small importance. This was later recognised by several early nineteenth century foreign travellers, among them the British envoy Captain W.C. Harris. He described it as "a bright spot of beauty in a waste of barrenness", and an "important" town, "the capital and principal seat" of Afar government, and a place of "wisdom and learning".[29]

Awssa's prosperity was coveted by Afars from neighbouring lands, and in particular by the Debene-Wemas, the strongest of the southern Adoimara people. Wishing to capture the settlement they enlisted the support, in the last decade of the eighteenth century, of a number of Yämäni matchlockmen from Aden (or, some said, Zäylä'). These riflemen, according to the German Protestant missionaries Isenberg and Krapf, were no less than four hundred strong, and enjoyed an almost complete monopoly of fire-power. With their help the Debene-Wemas launched a fierce assault on the town.

Accounts of the battle, collected by foreign travellers several decades later and by the modern Israeli historian Mordechai Abir, do not tally. Harris states that the town's defence was organised by its ruler, Yusuf ibn Ijdahis, "a brave and martial sultan", whose armoury boasted several cannon and many matchlocks. Abir's informants, on the other hand, "completely disclaim" the existence of any such

---

[27] Bruce (1790), II, 83.
[28] Bruce (1790), II, 83. See also II, 349.
[29] Lefebvre (1845-9), III: 3; Johnston (1844), I, 237; Harris, (1844), I, 179-80.

figure. Isenberg and Krapf believed that the attackers easily conquered the Modaitos then in control of the town. Harris, however, claims that the defenders caught the would-be attackers off guard, while they were sleeping, and cut the throats of "all save one". The Debene-Wemas, according to this account, were not "intimidated" by this reverse. Joined by fresh allies from the coast, they are said to have rallied, and achieved a "murderous defeat" of the Modaitos.

The Modaito stronghold thus fell into the hands of the Adoimara. Yusuf was then "slain", Harris claims, after which the town was "sacked", and its garrison "put to the sword". The victors, according to Isenberg and Krapf, however, soon "became indignant" at the "licentiousness" of the Yämänis, and "endeavoured to remove them as soon as possible".[30]

Whatever the precise details of the struggle there would seem no denying that the Awssa state suffered greatly from the war. Harris was doubtless correct in declaring that "the sun" of Awssa prosperity "at length set". The Afar capital, once an "important place", for a time lost much of its political significance. It nevertheless remained "an extensive encampment", as well as a "perpetual fair", frequented by innumerable Afars and Somalis.[31]

THE COUNTRY OF THE BAHR NAGASH

The situation on the northern seaboard had been significantly affected, as we have seen, by the Turkish seizure of Massawa in 1557. The ensuing Ottoman occupation, which had earlier been opposed by Särsä Dengel, was resisted by several of his successors, who were, however, in no position to overcome it.

Zä-Dengel

Opposition to the Turkish presence at the coast was voiced by Emperor Zä-Dengel. He wrote to King Felipe III of Spain, in 1604, urging him to seize Massawa, after which, he proposed, they should share its revenues. The Ethiopian monarch went on to argue that his people could easily impose their will in the coastal area, for the Turks on the island port were dependent on food and water from the mainland: without such provisions they would die of hunger and thirst. His subjects, he promised, would not send honey, slaves or

---

[30] Isenberg and Krapf (1843), p. 24; Harris (1844), I.184-5; Abir (1968), pp. 23-4.
[31] Harris (1844), I,179-80.

other merchandise to Massawa until they had wrested it from the Turks.[32] Spanish help was, however, not forthcoming.

Susneyos

Contacts between the Country of the Bahr Nägash and the interior remained close during the reign of Emperor Susneyos, one of whose daughters was married, doubtless for politico-strategic reasons to a Bahr Nägash, by name Amdä Mika'él.[33]

Susneyos, like his forebears, was much concerned about the situation at the coast. Soon after coming to the throne he was visited, his chronicler says, by Keflä Wahid, the governor of Tegray, who brought his tribute, consisting of beautiful horses and many other valuable articles. The chief was accompanied by subordinate officials from a wide area stretching from the Tegray highlands to "the furthest part of Hamasén and Bäqla". The latter was a locality north-west of present-day Asmära.[34]

Not long after this a pretender to the throne appeared, and made such progress in the northern provinces that Susneyos was obliged to carry out a punitive expedition to Tegray. It took him as far as the Red Sea, which the chronicle describes as constituting "the confines of the Ethiopian kingdom", beyond which lay "only the salt sea". In the course of this operation he visited at least six localities in the north: Säraye; Täderär in Akäla Guzay; the semi-coastal peninsula of Bur; the country of the Sahos, who lived immediately inland from Massawa; Därbeta, another place near the coast; and Selma, the district around Debarwa. The chronicler notes, presumably as something unusual, that land on the banks of the Märäb River were "worked my men and not by oxen"[35]

Conflict between the Ethiopians and the Turks came to the fore again in 1615, when the latter seized supplies sent from India to the Emperor's Jesuit protegé, Pero Paes. The invaders claimed that they had taken this action as a reprisal against the Ethiopians, who had attacked, and defeated, a Turkish raiding party. The Turkish Pasha declared that he would hold the property until the Ethiopians restored sixty rifles they had captured. Susneyos indignantly replied that the

---

[32] Pais (1945-6), III, 43-5.
[33] Beccari (1903-17), VII, 19-20, 80, VIII, 217, XII, 336, 363, XV, 32.
[34] Esteves Pereira (1900), pp. 77-8.
[35] Esteves Periera (1900), pp. 99-100; Huntingford (1989), pp. 162-3.

Turks had been at fault in seizing a number of cattle belonging to the local populace. He threatened that unless the articles taken by the invaders were handed over he would not allow any provisions to go down to the port. He accordingly ordered the governor of Tegray to close the trade route to Massawa. The Turks thereupon agreed to parley. The ensuing negotiations were, however, protracted, and apparently inconclusive, for the Pasha left on pilgrimage, and was later recalled to Constantinople without any settlement being effected.[36]

Further difficulties arose in the following decade when the Turks, supported by a force of 400 doubtless well armed Arabs, undertook another raiding expedition, and captured numerous cattle. The invaders were, however, later defeated by the Ethiopians, who retrieved all the booty, as well as over a hundred rifles, and a large number of scimitars, after which they sacked the port of Hergigo. The Jesuit Pero Paes, writing of the situation at this time, declared that Susneyos, "if he wished", could "easily make himself master" of Massawa, but had no wish to hold it. For this reason he had several times told the Jesuits that he would like Portuguese help in running the port. In this connection he had offered them lands in the country of the Bahr Nägash, which "dominated the sea and because of its fertility supplied all the places along the Red Sea". He also discussed the matter with another Jesuit, Manoel Barradas, who spoke to him of the advantage of occupying Hergigo, to which the monarch diffidently replied, "If I wish to retake Hergigo I could do so quickly, but how could I keep it?".[37]

Difficulties with the Turks later became so serious that Susneyos imposed a blockade on caravans going down to the coast. The Turks were obliged to appeal to the Jesuits to negotiate an agreement so that the Emperor would allow the resumption of caravans. A pact was duly concluded whereby the Emperor could import all goods he wanted free of tax, and send his envoys through Massawa without molestation. The Jesuits, it was further agreed, could import church property through the port without payment, and personal goods for only a modest fee. Their servants and slaves were also promised unrestricted freedom to pass through the port.[38]

---

[36] Beccari (1903-17), I, 347-9.
[37] Lettere (1628), pp. 5-7; Histoire (1629), p. 5-8.; Beccari (1903-17), I, 297.
[38] Lettere (1628), pp. 177-8.

Susneyos, Bahr Nägash Gäbrä Maryam, and the Queen of Arom

Susneyos, interested in the coast, continued the old tradition of appointing provincial rulers with the title of Bahr Nägash. One of them, Gäbrä Maryam, he despatched on an expedition to Arom north-west of Käsäla, which had failed to pay its customary tax. The territory was ruled by a queen called Fatima, who hid on his coming, but later submitted. She was taken to the Emperor, who, seeing that she was old and frail, made her sit in his presence. He then asked her why she had ceased paying her tribute. She replied that it was because her territory had fallen under the domination of the state of Fung. Susneyos forgave her, after which he fixed her tax, presented her with costly gifts, and sent her back to her country.[39]

Fasilädas, Massawa and Suakin

Emperor Fasilädäs was later also aware of the importance of the coast. After expelling the Jesuits in 1632 he entered into strategic treaties with the Pashas of Massawa and Suakin. Both agreed to close their ports to Catholics attempting to enter the region. He also sent emissaries to the these ports, with instruction to report the arrival of any ships likely to be bringing in Portuguese.[40]

The Establishment of Gondär

Contacts between the country of the Bahr Nägash and the interior became closer after the establishment of Gondär as the imperial capital in 1636. The city rapidly emerged as a major political, commercial and religious centre, and because of its location in the north-west of the empire, and difficulties of communication with the Sudan, had particularly close ties with the coast.

The metropolis was visited over the years by many personalities from the Land of the Bahr Nägash, as well as by merchants and others who passed through the latter while travelling between the coast and the rich countries south of the Blue Nile. Gondär was at the same time heavily dependent on the trade route via Hamasén to the coast, and it

---

[39] Esteves Periera (1900), pp. 110, 163, 227.
[40] Budge (1928b), II, 401, 403.

was through it that most of the capital's imports, including fire-arms, had to pass.[41]

Hamasén Local Traditions:
Fasilädäs, Emmha and Hab Sellus

Evidence of contacts between the land of the Bahr Nägash and the Gondarine monarchy, that is to say between the northern periphery and the central state, is preserved in the oral traditions of Hamasén, recorded in the early twentieth century by the Swedish scholar Johannes Kolmodin. They represent an amalgam of fact and fantasy, but are nonetheless historically revealing. They show that the Gondär monarchs' sovereignty extended as far as Hamasén, whose local chiefs they appointed, and from whom they received tribute, as well as military, guard or other service. The traditions, though concerned primarily with Hamasén, are of much wider relevance. They illustrate the traditional manner in which local rulers and dynasties of the periphery were often in personal relationship with, as well as dependent on, the central Ethiopian state, as represented by its Emperors and their families. The story applies to the north, but, as evident from the foregoing pages, had many parallels elsewhere, notably in Adäl, Hadeya, Enarya, and on at least one well documented occasion among the Afars.

The earliest Hamasén traditions about Gondär deal with the time of the first of the city's rulers, Emperor Fasilädäs. They tell the story of Gärä Krestos Samson, a Käntiba, or governor, of the town of Sä'äzzäga, who sent his son Emmha to "the country of Amhara" to hand over his tribute. The young man travelled to Gondär, where he presented himself to the monarch, and was given the duty of guarding the royal gate and serving in various other ways, for which he was rewarded with the title of Käntiba. The appointment was unusual in that Emmha's father was still alive, and held the same title. However, the young man, on returning home, dutifully declared that it was improper for him to assume the post during the lifetime of his sire, to whom he accordingly transferred the title.[42]

On Gärä Krestos's death, however, the rank of Käntiba reverted to Emmha, who unfortunately proved an arrogant and harsh ruler. Soon after assuming his office he was visited by his cousin, Gärä Sellasé,

---

[41] Pankhurst (1961), pp. 307-12.
[42] Kolmodin (1916), ch. 59.

and the latter's son Hab Sellus, who came to bring him a gift of a fattened goat and some honey. The proud Emmha refused either to receive the visitors or to accept their presents. Father and son waited three days, after which they left in a dejected mood. On the journey home Hab Sellus declared that he would like to have a *nägarit*, or drum (a traditional symbol of authority), but his father replied that there was little hope of this since those who had the power to appoint him, i.e. Emmha and his clique, obviously hated their sight. Hab Sellus, who was later to emerge as a Hamasén folk hero, replied that it was "better to perish" than to remain with such people. He accordingly left for Gondär, and, to show that he was a knight, took with him a fine iron bridle.

Gondär, the imperial capital, which was visited by many personages from the borderlands, including Hamasén, as seen in a nineteenth century engraving.
From T. Waldmeier, *The Autobiography of Theophilus Waldmeier.*

On arriving at the capital he made his way to the palace, where he reputedly lived a life of poverty and humiliation for seven full years. During this period he spent his days and nights where he could, and was often obliged to sleep in the stables. He was in consequence soon covered with scabs, and became known as Hab Sellus "the mangy".

Emmha meanwhile, having learnt that Hab Sellus was living at the capital, and fearing that he might establish contact with the Emperor, made his way once more to Gondär. As Käntiba he had the freedom of the palace, while the unfortunate Hab Sellus was obliged to sleep outside, and eat only with the servants.

Some time later, however, an incident occurred which brought the young man to the monarch's attention. Fasilädäs had a fierce horse which none of his soldiers dared mount. One day, while talking with Emmha - and perhaps recalling that Hamasén was a renowned source of horses, he asked him whether anyone among the Hamasén people was expert at horse-riding. The wily chief, hoping to bring about Hab Sellus's death, or disgrace, replied that his young cousin could ride admirably. Fasilädäs, who had no idea of the Käntiba's real motive, asked Emmha to summon his relative without delay.

Hab Sellus, dressed in tatters, but carrying his fine bridle concealed under them, appeared before the monarch, who, seeing the young man's rags and scabs, looked on him with contempt. Astonished that such a creature had been brought to him, he asked, "Can you really ride a horse?" "Certainly, my lord", Hab Sellus replied, "and since you have commanded me to do so I will try". The steed was then saddled, and brought to the young man. He jumped on it, released the rope tying it, and immediately disappeared on it.

As soon as he was out of sight he dismounted, removed the horse's bridle, and replaced it with the one he had brought from Hamasén. He then rode the animal all day until, its spirit broken, it trembled with sweat and fatigue, after which, having once more changed bridles, he reappeared at the palace on horseback. The courtiers had spent the day discussing where the young man would be hurled to the ground, and Emmha had observed, in a seemingly disheartened tone, that his cousin had "without doubt been killed". It was then that Hab Sellus, to everyone's amazement, arrived triumphantly at a gallop.[43]

Emmha, we are told, soon afterwards had resort to a further trick against Hab Sellus. Another Hamasén nobleman, Zämat Keflä of 'Ad Täkklé-zan, whom Fasilädäs had invested with the title of Käntiba, was due to return to his village, and the monarch enquired whether there was anyone brave enough to accompany the chief home and then return back. Emmha ingenuously asked the Emperor whether anyone was more capable than Hab Sellus. Fasilädäs had the young

---

[43] Kolmodin (1916), chs. 64 and 65.

man once again summoned, and asked him whether he felt able to carry out the mission. Hab Sellus answered, more or less as before, "Yes, since Your Majesty commands me to do it". The monarch then presented Zämät with a golden ring, and told him that after Hab Sellus had conducted him to his village he should hand it to the latter. "If he returns with the ring", he declared, "I will know you have reached your village; but, if he comes without it, I will not receive him any more".

The crafty Emmha then sent a message to the people of Sä'äzzäga ordering them to kill Hab Sellus. However, the young man, suspecting his cousin's wickedness, avoided the usual route through Säraye and Akälä Guzay where his enemies were lying in wait, and passed instead further south by way of Wälqayt and the country of the Bareya. The two men therefore arrived safely at 'Ad Täklé-Zan. When the people who were to kill him learnt this they planned to catch him on his return journey. They waited for him in the desert passes, but he made his way back by the coastal route, and Agamé, and thus arrived at the court without incident.

On the young man's return Fasilädäs interrogated him closely, asking him if he had really conducted the Käntiba to his village. Hab Sellus replied, "Yes, Sire, I have done as you ordered me". The monarch then inquired whether he had brought proof of this, to which the messenger responded, "I have none". The king, irritated by this response, demanded whether Zämat had not given him anything. He answered, "Nothing, except this ring", which he then handed to Fasilädäs. The Emperor, on hearing this, was much impressed. He presented the young man with many decorations, including a ceremonial shirt, and later gave him his daughter's hand in marriage, nominated him a governor, and gave him permission to return to his country.[44]

Fasilädäs subsequently elevated his son-in-law to the rank of Abéto, a status normally reserved for princes of royal blood, and gave him control of Bambolo-Mellash, a term which covered not only the country of the Bahr Nägash, but also a large stretch of Tegray up to the Bambolo river. On the journey home it transpired that Hab Sellus's wife despised him, and refused to accept him as him as her husband. Deeply angered by this he abused her so violently that she died, after which he made his way back to Gondär. On arriving at the

---

[44] Kolmodin (1916), ch. 66.

palace he paid his respects to the Emperor, and holding in his hand a sword and a rope, two symbols of punishment, addressed him, saying, "Your Majesty, in your great magnanimity, gave me your daughter, and appointed me; but when I wished to approach my wife in accordance with nature and the law, saying, 'She is my wife', she rejected my approach; whereupon I, incited by Satan, raised my hand and struck her; and she died as a result of my blow. Because of this misfortune I stand here before Your Majesty". So saying he threw his sword and the rope before him.

Fasilädäs, having heard all this, questioned one of his daughter's slaves, who spoke up for her late mistress's husband, declaring, "Everything Hab Sellus says is true". The monarch, who, we may assume, had no wish to alienate the people of Hamasén, thereupon asked the opinion of the theologians at his court, inquiring, "If I pardon him would I be guilty?". To this they replied in the negative. He accordingly forgave his son-in-law, saying, "You did to her what she deserved", after which he allowed Hab Sellus to leave. However, he deprived him of the government of Bambolo-Mellash, and left him only with that of Märäb-Mellash, i.e. a smaller fiefdom covering only land north of the Märäb river. Further, declaring that the title of Abéto was appropriate only to members of the royal house, he demoted him from that rank, but declared that he, and his descendants, should bear the rank of Däjazmach.[45]

Hab Sellus then returned to Hamasén. He brought the entire country of Märäb-Mellash under his authority, and exercised his government for forty years. His heirs, it is said, inherited his title, and were thereafter known as members of the Family of the Däjazmach.[46]

Iyasu I and Wälätta Seyon

Emperor Iyasu I, the greatest of the Gondarine rulers, also had close associations with Hamasén, as is evident from his chronicle. In September 1683, a year after assuming the throne, he summoned the Patriarch, and asked him to marry him to Wälätta Seyon, the daughter of Habtä Iyäsus of the Däq Asgädé family from Bäqla, a district of Hamasén. The bride was described as beautiful and gracious, but the monarch, it may be assumed, chose her at least partially because of the desirability of a political alliance with her strategically important

---

[45] Kolmodin (1916), ch. 67.
[46] Kolmodin (1916), p. xvi, ch. 68.

province. The marriage was a long one, and came to an end only with Wälätta Seyon's death in 1693. She was buried with much ceremony on the island of Mesraha in Lake Tana. Her brother Asmä Giyorgis was (or became) a person of consequence: he was accorded the princely title of Abéto, and on his death, in 1700, his royal brother-in-law reportedly "wept bitterly" because he "loved him much".[47]

Murad's Problems with the Na'ib

Hamasén's importance during the reign of Iyasu is evident from the chronicle's reference to an incident which occurred in 1693 when the Emperor's Armenian trade agent Murad returned from a journey to the Dutch East Indies. His property, which consisted largely of presents for the monarch, was seized by the Massawa ruler, Na'ib Musa. Murad at once despatched a message to Iyasu, explaining what had happened. Iyasu, who was "greatly angered", decided, like Susneyos before him, to impose a blockade on the coast. He accordingly sent a message to Hab Sellus, the official who figures so importantly in the above-cited local traditions, and to two other functionaries, Zär'a Beruk and Gäbrä Krestos, and to "all the people of Hamasén". He ordered them to proclaim by herald throughout their domains that no one should go to Massawa with honey, butter, cheese or "anything necessary for life" until he arrived at Massawa to attack it. Anyone transgressing this command, he warned, would forfeit his life, and have his house destroyed.

On receipt of this message Hab Sellus and the Hamasén officials prevented any provisions from being carried to the Na'ib. When the latter realised that he was denied food, and that the monarch was on his way to attack him, he "was terrified", the chronicle reports, and "trembled, not knowing what to do; the size of Massawa was for him [as small as] the hole of a needle. He suffered pains like a woman about to give birth. He reflected, and realised that there was nothing he could do to save himself, except to restore the King's possessions and make peace with him. For this reason Na'ib Musa hastened to restore the King's property which he had seized from Murad, and added to it objects a thousand times more numerous, which he brought to the King".[48]

---

[47] Guidi (1903-5), pp. 179, 222; Basset (1881), XVIII, 306, 314. See also Cheesman (1936), p.190-1.
[48] Guidi (1903-5), p. 171.

This incident, so graphically described in Iyasu's chronicle, is also referred to in the shorter annals. They assert that the Na'ib, seeking to make reparation, gave Iyasu "many slaves" brought from "the country of the Turks". Hab Sellus, who, it will be recalled, is said in the traditions to have ruled for forty years, apparently outlived Emperor Iyasu, for the chronicle suggests that he was still alive around 1710.[49]

Valuable evidence on the tribute paid by the land of the Bahr Nägash in this period is provided by Murad, who travelled to Batavia in 1686-7. He told the Dutch that the Massawa trade was so considerable that Debarwa, the capital of Hamasén, and Särayé further south, each provided Iyasu with five hundred ounces of gold a year, or a total of a thousand ounces.[50]

Charles Poncet's Report

Confirmation of the close relationship between Hamasén and the Gondarine monarchy in this period is provided by the French physician Poncet. He left a poignant account of the mourning ceremonies which took place at Debarwa in 1700, when news arrived of the death of Iyasu's eldest son Fasilädäs. There were at that time two functionaries with the title of Bahr Nägash, who immediately ordered the news to be made public throughout the area, with "sound of trumpet", whereupon, the Frenchman reports:

"Everyone put on mourning, which consists in shaving their heads... The day following, the two Governours, attended by all the militia and an infinite number of people, went to the church dedicated to the Blessed Virgin, where they perform'd a solemn service for the prince; after which they return'd to the palace in the same order. The two *Barnagas* seated themselves in a great hall.... After that the officers and persons of note, both men and women, rang'd themselves round the hall. Certain women with tabors, and men without, plac'd themselves in the middle of the hall and began to sing, as it were in parts, little songs in honour of the prince; but in so doleful a tone that I cou'd not hinder being seiz'd with grief and weeping for a whole hour that the ceremony lasted. There were some who, to testify their sorrow, tore their faces till they were cover'd with blood, or burnt their temples with little wax candles. There were none in this hall but persons of quality. The common people stood without in the courts,

---

[49] Basset (1881), XVIII, 331.
[50] Donzel (1979), p. 93.

where they gave such lamentable cries that it would have moved the hardest hearts".

These remarkable ceremonies for the death of the prince at far-off Gondär lasted, according to local custom, for three whole days.[51]

Oral Traditions of the Reign of Iyasu I: Gära Krestos

Relations with the Gondarine state during the reign of Iyasu I also figure in the Hamasén traditions . They state that Däjazmach Hab Sellus ordered his eldest son and heir, who held the title of Bahr Nägash, to travel to Gondär to introduce himself to the Emperor, and present the customary tribute of the area, as he, Hab Sellus, had done before him. The young man, by name Iyasu, was, however, frightened of the journey. Pleading illness, he declined to travel. His younger brother, Gära Krestos, went in his stead. (He was probably the Gäbrä Krestos mentioned in the chronicle whom the Emperor had addressed over the Murad affair). Speaking of his elder brother he said to himself, "Since he has refused to go it is I who will become the chief".

On reaching the capital Gärä Krestos, like his father a generation earlier, served for a long time as a palace guard. He thereby became well known to the Emperor, and was eventually given the title of Däjazmach. Iyasu, because of his regard for the young man's father Hab Sellus, subsequently gave him the hand of his daughter, Säbänä Gärgesh[52] - significantly enough the third reported marriage between the Hamasén and imperial ruling houses. On the occasion of the wedding the monarch promised his son-in-law that wherever Säbänä Gägesh passed the night would be Gärä Krestos's hereditary fief. At the same time he appointed the young man governor of Bambalo-Mellash, the position earlier held by Hab Sellus.[53]

The appointment of Gärä Krestos while his father was still alive caused considerable disquiet in Hamasén. The elders deliberated on the matter, but dispersed without coming to any decision. Their gathering was therefore likened to the croaking of frogs, and the place where it was held became known as May Mänka'e, i.e. the Water, or River, of Frogs.

---

[51] Foster (1949), pp. 149-50.
[52] Elsewhere in the traditions it is suggested that the princess was not the daughter of Iyasu, but of the latter's brother Yohannes I.
[53] Kolmodin (1916), ch. 70.

News of all this duly reached Gärä Krestos. Anxious to avoid any conflict, he sent messengers to his father and countrymen, telling them he had no intention of opposing their wishes. He placed himself loyally under Hab Sellus, and seated himself at the latter's feet. On his father's death, however, he inherited the government, and ruled for thirty-eight years. He was by then a rich man, for as a result of the Emperor's decree he held many fiefs between Gondär and Hamasén, reportedly wherever his wife had spent the night. These estates were subsequently inherited by his children.[54]

Täsfa Sén and Mammo

Gärä Kestos, like his father, continued to pay taxes to Gondär. On one occasion he sent his son, Täsfa Sén to the capital, instructing him to "bring the tribute, then leave". The young man, however, tarried instead at the palace, where, like his father and grandfather before him, he served as a guard, and won the Emperor's favour. Though his father was still alive, he persuaded the monarch to appoint him as governor. Observing, that Täsfa Sén was the son of his sister, Säbänä Gägesh, the monarch nominated him to the rank of Däjazmach, and gave him Gärä Krestos's father's fiefdom. Täsfa Sén thereupon returned to Sa'azzega, and became governor of Bambolo-Mellash.

Mammo, a second son of Gärä Kestos by Säbänä Gärgesh (and hence Emperor Iyasu's grandson), subsequently embarked, with imperial authorisation, on a campaign to the south against the Oromos, probably in Wällo. He defeated them, baptised them as Christians, and made himself their governor. The monarch rejoiced, gave him many decorations, and elevated him to the rank of Däjazmach.[55]

Relations between Täsfa Sén and his deposed father had meanwhile deteriorated. The young man, so far from behaving in a filial manner, lorded it arrogantly over Gärä Kestos. His father was so bitter that he rejoiced when his son fell ill, for he hoped that by the latter's death he would regain his title. When Täsfa Sén actually died, however, the old man was full of remorse. He passed away shortly afterwards, whereupon his son Mammo succeeded him as governor of Bambolo-Mellash.

---

[54] Kolmodin (1916), p. xvi, chs. 71-3.
[55] Kolmodin (1916), ch. 75.

Mammo subsequently fought once more against the Oromos, during which time his office was temporarily occupied by another brother, Re'esä Haymanot. The latter obtained the Emperor's permission to wage war in Wäjerat, far to the south in Tegray.[56]

Dispute over the Tribute from Bambolo-Mellash and Wälqayt

Mammo, according to the traditions, subsequently resumed his position as ruler of Bambolo-Mellash. He was involved in a long-remembered, and historically interesting, dispute with Däjazmach Nayzgi, the governor of Wälqayt. It concerned the tribute they each paid to the Emperor. Nayzgi, it appears, had sneered at the taxes paid by Mammo, and in front of everyone at court declared by way of a challenge, "Let us see who will pay the largest tribute, you or I!" Mammo replied, "Alright, let us fix the day!" Emperor Iyasu, who was no doubt well pleased with such competition between his liegemen, asked each how long they needed to collect their dues. Nayzgi disdainfully replied, "Six months", but Mammo, more cautiously, answered, "A year". They then both left to collect their respective taxes, to be paid at the times proposed.

After six months Nayzgi arrived with his tribute. It consisted of cooking utensils (presumably made of pottery), cotton cloth, cloaks, guns, and silver coins (probably imported Austrian thalers), three herds of cattle, white, black and brown, and a large number of cotton *shämmas*, or togas. When Mammo saw these magnificent items he feared he might lose the contest, but gave orders that the most precious things, utensils and cattle, in his district be collected and brought to him.[57]

The traditions, which thus far reflected the customary tribute obtained from the northern periphery, at this point begin to take on a fantastic character. They claim that Mammo was riding with some of his companions when his horse's hoof sank into the ground. Jumping off his steed he saw a small hole where his horse had placed its foot, and ordered his men to dig there. They soon came upon a magic

---

[56] Kolmodin (1916), p. xvii, chs. 79-80.
[57] Kolmodin (1916), ch. 82.

house, where they discovered a gold mouse, a gold frog, a gold lizard, a gold snake, a gold royal coach, and many other objects of gold.[58]

Mammo later set forth for Gondär taking with him all the taxes his people had collected. They consisted of ordinary tribute, as well as the fabulous gold objects he had discovered. His gifts all in all were so plentiful that while the first of his mules were being unloaded at May Sa'äda the last was still at far-off Addi Baro.

On eventually reaching the Emperor's court at the appointed time he proudly displayed his presents. The first instalment consisted of nothing but scarlet and striped cloth. Then came pieces of *abugedid*, or cotton cloth, carpets, jars, *berellé*, or glass bottles, lamps, cloaks and rifles. All this was followed by six herds of cattle, white, black, brown, brown speckled, black speckled and grey speckled, and a troop of monkeys. Finally came a herd of mules, carrying glass bowls, glass beads, precious stones, needles, tweezers for removing thorns from the feet, and silver coins, presumably imported.

Seeing all this wealth the monarch exclaimed to Mammo, "You have won!", and all his chiefs agreed. The victor, on hearing his triumph, then made a remarkable display of largesse, by offering gifts to all present. Addressing the nobles he cried out, "Here is a meal for the chiefs!", after which he poured out of a bag some of the golden objects he had so miraculously found. A moment later, he shouted, "And here is a meal for the King's wife!", and proffered her a gold cat and cock. Then, proclaiming, "The meal of the King!", he produced a golden snake, its eyes glittering with fine pearls, and gave it to Iyasu himself. The monarch, we are told, was, not surprisingly, "much astonished" at this profusion of wealth.[59]

Nayzgi, angered by his humiliating defeat, challenged Mammo to a duel. The two men fought, and Mammo was once more victorious, taking Nayzgi prisoner. The latter's domains thereupon passed to Mammo who in consequence assumed the government of Wälqayt for seven years. Emperor Iyasu later interceded on the defeated chief's behalf. A pact was concluded, whereby Mammo gave his daughter in marriage to Nayzgi's son, while Nayzgi was allowed to resume his old government, albeit under Mammo's overall sovereignty.[60]

---

[58] Kolmodin (1916), ch. 83.
[59] Kolmodin (1916), ch. 84.
[60] Kolmodin (1916), p. xvii, ch. 85.

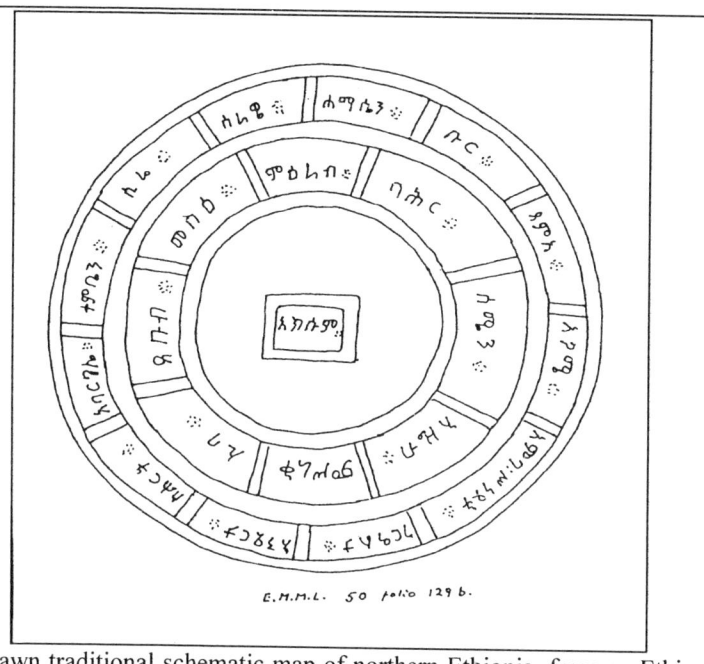

A redrawn traditional schematic map of northern Ethiopia, from an Ethiopic manuscript of the *Mäshafä Aksum*, or Book of Aksum, probably written prior to the eighteenth century. Based on Aksum, indicated in the central box, the outer ring shows the principal provinces of the north, including Saräyé (Särawé), Hamasén and Bur (top and top-right). The central ring depicts the four cardinal points, North (*Samén*) on the right, south (*Däbub*) on the left, West (*Me'rab*) on the top, and East (*Mesraq*) at the bottom, as well as four intermediate positions.
The entire sequence in the outer ring, starting from the left clockwise, reads: "Tämbén, Shiré, Särawé, Hamasén, Bur, Säm'a, Agamé, Amba Senayt, Gär'alta, Endärta, Sähart, Abergälé"
From A. Pankhurst, *An Early Ethiopian Manuscript Map of Tegré*.

Mammo was reputedly a just and able ruler. The traditions relate that on one occasion locusts overran all Hamasén, and that the inhabitants were unable to pay their taxes to Gondär, which the chief accordingly paid on their behalf. The following year, presumably using the age-old trade route from the coast, he brought up a cannon, which was so heavy that four hundred men could not lift it. This piece of artillery was transported by way of Akäla Guzay to Amhara, where Mammo presented it to the Emperor. The chief, taking advantage of the latter's pleasure, asked permission to draw something to his attention. This granted, he told Iyasu that he had transported the cannon only through the help of his people, whose lands had been ravaged by the locusts, and, so far from being able to pay their taxes, had scarcely enough food to eat. He therefore begged the Emperor to have pity on them, which he did, by remitting the customary taxes.[61]

Mammo, the traditions suggest, was a person of substance. His mother Säbänä Gärgesh had received from Iyasu no less than one thousand five hundred slaves. Most of these men, who probably bore arms, were settled in Sä'äzzäga and nearby villages.[62]

Bäkaffa

Mammo, according to the traditions, lived on into the reign of Emperor Bäkaffa. During this time the old Hamasén chief faced a rebellion by Däjazmach Debleyés, a noble who had married one of Emperor Särsä Dengel's kinswomen. Because of this matrimonial lineage he objected to being Mammo's vassal. "Except for the King of Kings", he declared, "I have no one above me!" He subsequently gained support among the people of nearby Särayé, but Mammo, after obtaining Bäkaffa's permission, attacked and defeated him in battle.[63]

The old chief died not long afterwards, the traditions state, at the Emperor's camp at Qaha, just outside Gondär. He was buried with great pomp, drums beating and flags flying, amid a great concourse of people. He had ruled over his home province for twelve years, over Bambolo-Mallesh for nine, and over it and Wälqayt for seven, a total of twenty-eight years.[64]

Confirmation that Mammo was a real personage, and indeed one of importance, is provided in a brief chronicle of Bäkaffa's time. This text, which is reminiscent of the traditions, tersely states that a man called Mammo, with the title of "Däjazmach of Hamasén", died at the king's palace at Qaha in 1730, and was buried with flags and drums.[65]

---

[61] Kolmodin (1916), ch. 86 and 87.
[62] Kolmodin (1916), ch. 88. Another prominent Hamasén nobleman, Bahr Nägash Zä-Krestos, is likewise said to have married a grand-daughter of Emperor Särsä Dengel. Kolmodin, ch. 97.
[63] Kolmodin (1916), ch. 89.
[64] Kolmodin (1916), ch. 90.
[65] Kolmodin (1916), p. 126.

Iyasu II and Ras Mika'él Sehul

With the decline of the Gondarine monarchy in the second half of the eighteenth century relations between Hamasén and the capital weakened. Emperor Iyasu II, according to his chronicle, "made a tour of the provinces" in 1744, which took him to Däbrä Bizän, in Hamasén. This journey is also recalled in the traditions. They state that he arrived to "tax the people" during the time of Bahr Nägash Sälomon Täsfa Sén, a brother of the afore-mentioned Mammo. Iyasu, his chronicle reveals, had at around this time a number of Hamasén riflemen in his army, in addition to many from Tegray.[66]

The on-going importance of Hamasén in national affairs was likewise apparent in 1745 when a deputation of three Christian clerics accompanied by three Muslims left Gondär for Egypt in quest of a new *Abun*, or Patriarch. They spent several months in the district before descending to Massawa, where they encountered considerable obstruction on the part of the *Na'ib*. Iyasu and his redoubtable Regent-mother, Empress Mentewwab ordered the Bahr Nägash to join the powerful ruler of Tegray, Ras Mika'él Sehul, and a certain Däjazmach Baselyos in attacking the port. The *Na'ib*, whom the chronicler refers to as "a devil incarnate", and the port's "wicked inhabitants", responded by seizing and chaining the envoys.[67]

The events which followed were recorded by Bruce, who states that the threat of intervention proved decisive. Before it could be executed, however, the *Na'ib* "called the priests before him", forced them by threats to hand over the money in their possession, and hurried them on board a vessel bound for Egypt. He then artfully informed Ras Mika'él and the Bahr Nägash that his prisoners were "gone in safety, and that he had obeyed the King's orders in all respects". The ecclesiastical party, released after six months' detention, thus proceeded to Egypt, and in due course brought back the *Abun*, by name Abba Yohannes. The latter, on reaching Massawa, was detained for five months. Towards the end of this time two monks from Däbrä Bizän monastery, Abba Ewostatéwos and Abba Gäbrä Maryam, concerned at the detention of the head of their church, made their way to the port. They succeeded in securing the nocturnal escape of the *Abun*, after which they took him secretly to

---

[66] Guidi (1912), pp. 125-6; Kolmodin (1916), ch. 94.Guidi (1912), pp. 145, 204.
[67] Guidi (1912), p. 128.

their monastery, where he remained for two months before resuming his journey to Gondär.[68]

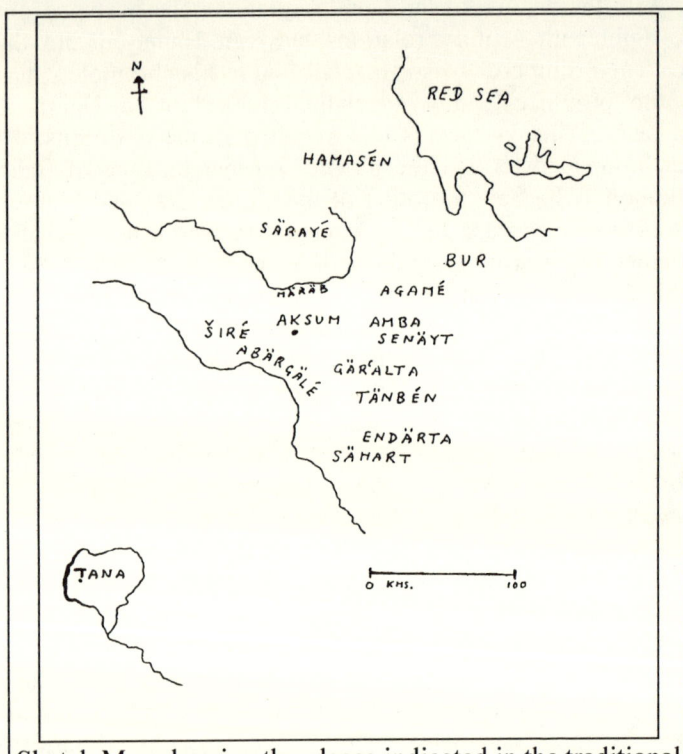

Sketch Map showing the places indicated in the traditional schematic map based on Aksum, on page 409.

The capital's continued importance in Hamasén affairs is also evident in the traditions. They recall that at around this time a local Hamasén functionary, Käntiba Gärä Maryam, was falsely accused of some unstated offence, and asked to pay a fine. He collected two thousand silver coins, doubtless Austrian thalers, but, unwilling to hand them over to his enemies, secretly left his village with the cash, and made his way to the capital. There he appealed to the Emperor for justice. After listening to the case, the monarch declared the Käntiba innocent. The latter then spent his money on purchasing beautiful

---

[68] Bruce (1790), II, 643-4; Guidi (1912), pp. 128-30.

crosses, umbrellas and robes, for which the capital was justly famous, and brought them back to Hamasén to beautify the church of Sä'ada Kestan.[69]

The Decline of the Gondär Monarchy, and the Rise of Ras Mika'él Sehul

The power of the Gondarine monarchy was by then waning. Evidence of this is apparent in the traditions which note that Bahr Nägash Sälomon's son Bäkru held his authority "not from the King, but from his father". His successor, Zewäldä Maryam, on the other hand, was reportedly appointed by the Emperor. A later tradition, however, tells of a monarch, probably Emperor Iyo'as, who attempted to ride into Hamasén, but was prevented from doing so by a local leader, Käntiba Keflä Giyorgis. The latter, shooting with a flint-lock from behind a rock, single-handedly defended his people and their cattle from the monarch's soldiers, who were obliged to withdraw.[70]

The decline of the Gondarine monarchy coincided with the advent of Ras Mika'él Sehul of Tegray. As a ruler of the north, he inherited the old imperial interest in the land of the Bahr Nägash and Massawa. Through these areas he obtained large quantities of fire-arms, which enabled him, as we have seen, to become, for a time, the most powerful leader in the land. On one occasion, in 1766, he crossed the Märäb river, to control Hamasén and Särayé, and resided, a chronicle reports, for a short time at Debarwa. He then made his way to Degsa on the very edge of the plateau, and proceeded to the coast at Hergigo. His occupation of the port, like that of previous rulers of the interior, was, however, temporary, and he soon returned to the highlands.[71]

The rise of Ras Mika'él eroded Hamasén's ties with Gondär, and established new ones with Tegray. Contact with the old capital, however, was by no means totally severed. The trade route between Gondär and the coast remained of crucial importance, and people from the northern provinces continued to travel to the capital. One who did so was the Bahr Nägash of Bruce's day, who fought in one of the battles of Sarbakusa, north of Lake Tana, in 1772, which led to the collapse of Ras Mika'él's power. The Hamasén chief and his son, the Scottish traveller reports, both "died valiantly" in Emperor Täklä

---

[69] Kolmodin (1916), p. xx. chs. 100-1.
[70] Kolmodin (1916), ch. 118.
[71] Guidi (1912), pp. 227-9.

Haymanot's service. A decade or so later, in 1783, a man from Hamasén and Särayé arrived at the capital, bringing gifts for Emperor Täklä Giyorgis and his Queen, as well as for one of the great lords, Ras Ayadar. This event is apparently reflected in the Hamasén traditions, which tell of a monarch decorating Bahr Nägash Täsfa Seyon, doubtless one of the persons bringing these presents, and giving him a "robe of honour".[72]

By the end of the eighteenth century the Ethiopian empire was, however, virtually defunct, and the emperors had become little more than puppets of the great feudal lords. One of the latter, Ras Wäldä Sellasé of Tegray, subsequently took his nominal sovereign, Täklä Giyorgis, to his capital, Antalo, where in 1800 he planned an expedition to Särayé and Hamasén. Before he could do so, however, people from these districts, as well as various parts of Tegray, arrived, the chronicle reports, "bearing tribute beyond count". The projected journey was therefore abandoned, and the monarch and the Ras "bade the envoys farewell in peace".[73]

The country of the Bahr Nägash, economically and strategically one of the most important in the entire region, thus remained as for so long in the past a major tributary territory.

MASSAWA

Despite changing fortunes in the interior, as well as at the coast, Massawa maintained its historic role as the region's principal port. It was described by Almeida, in the early seventeenth century, as a commercial centre of importance. Some of its houses were of wood and matting, but others were made of stone and mud, painted with lime or whitewash. Imports consisted largely of Indian cloth, as well as carpets, silks and Mecca brocades, drugs, pepper, cloves, and "a thousand other things". This list was underscored by Ludolf, who observed that goods brought to the port by sea included "Garments of all sorts, Velvet, Silken, but chiefly Woolen and Fustian", as well as *kohl*, i.e. stibium or antimony, with which the Ethiopians decorated their eyelids in accordance with the "frequent and ancient custom of the Orientals".

---

[72] Bruce (1790), III, 95-6, 99-100, IV, 176; Weld Blundell (1922), p. 299; Kolmodin (1916), ch. 120. On the participation of troops from Särayé see also Bruce, III, 447.
[73] Weld Blundell (1922), 469. On the taxes collected by Ras Wäldä Sellasé see Kolmodin (1916), ch. 143.

Massawa's exports by contrast were, as in the past. few in number. They consisted, according to Ludolf, almost entirely of "Gold, Skins, Hides, Wax, Honey and Ivory", all of them, we may note, produce of the interior.

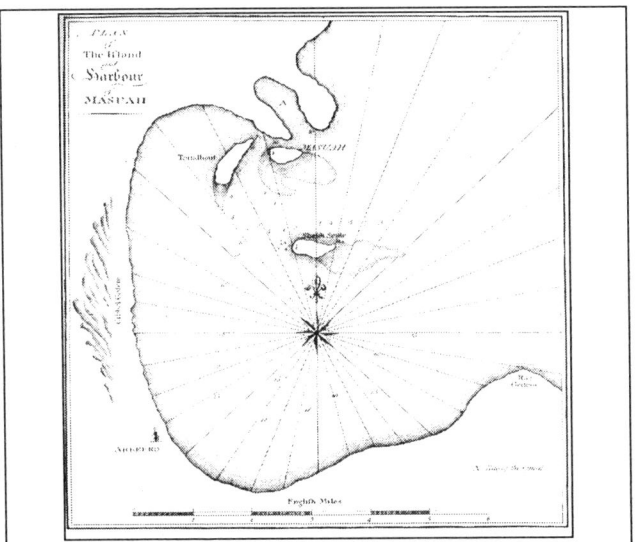

Map of the Bay of Massawa showing the island port of that name, and the mainland port of Hergigo (Arkiko). From J. Bruce, *Travels to Discover the Source of the Nile*.

The port thus handled the trade of both the interior and the outside world, and above all India. Pero Paes, writing at about the same time, declared that there was extensive commerce between India and Ethiopia. A Cypriot Jesuit, Antonius Nacchi, subsequently reported, in 1698, that Massawa was frequented by many Indian and Ethiopian merchants, the former arriving by ships, and the latter every month by caravan.[74]

The situation almost a century later was explained by Bruce, who provides a more detailed account of the port and its trade. Massawa, a small island "immediately off the Abyssinian shore", had, he declared, "an excellent harbour" and was "deep enough for ships of any size to

---

[74] Beckingham and Huntingford (1954), p. 43; Ludolf (1684), pp. 32, 398; Beccari (1903-18), II, 269, XIV, 486.

approach the very edge of the island". They could thus ride in the "utmost security", whatever the direction of the wind.

Most of Massawa's houses then, as in the past, were made of poles and grass, but there were also about twenty stone buildings, six or eight of which were of two storeys, though the second floor seldom consisted of more than one room. The town was a place of extensive commerce. It took a significant share, Bruce says, of India's foreign trade, and served as the export centre for much of the Ethiopian interior. The principal imports arriving by sea, then as previously, were textiles, among them coarse cotton cloth, known as Surat, the Indian port from which they were shipped, as well as blue cotton cloth and cochineal cloth called *kemis*, fine cloth from various parts of India, coarse white cotton cloth, and unspun cotton in balls from Yaman. Other imports consisted of Venetian beads, crystal, drinking-bottles called *bärellé,* looking glasses, and *kohl*, or antimony. The latter came from Egypt, and was taken to Jeddah, whence it was transshipped to Massawa in small barks. Much profit was also obtained from the import of old copper, a "great quantity" of which was despatched into the interior. Bracelets of this metal were worn by Oromos and other people south or west of Gondär, and was said to exchange near the country of the Gongas and Gubas, for equal weight of gold. Shells from the Arabian coast were also in considerable demand in the interior, but others from the waters near the Dahlak islands were less esteemed though they passed as money among the Jawi and other western Gallas.

The main exports of the interior brought down to Massawa consisted, as in the past, mainly of gold and ivory, elephant and buffalo hides, and "above all, slaves". There was also some trade in pearls, "considerable for size, water or colour", which, according to Bruce, were found all along the Red Sea coast. Most of these commodities were shipped to Mecca, where a former Ethiopian slave called Metical Aga, acting on behalf of the Emperor and Ras Mika'él Sehul, sold them and sent back in return fire-arms, which were then, as always, in great demand in the Ethiopian interior.

Merchants of Massawa negotiating with Banyan, or Indian traders, an early nineteenth century engraving.
From T.Lefebvre *Voyage en Abyssinie, Atlas.*

Massawa's trade, according to Bruce, was no longer in the hands of Banyans, or Indians. Once the port's "principal merchants", their number had fallen to only six. Several of them were silversmiths, who weighed gold, and produced ear-rings and other women's jewellery, but, Bruce feared, made but a poor livlihood.[75]

Hergigo

The trade of Massawa throughout this time continued to pass by way of the mainland port of Hergigo. It consisted, according to Almeida, of a few "very flimsy", two-storeyed houses, where the Turkish governor resided. The settlement also had many wells, with good drinking water, which was taken to Massawa daily in three or four small boats. The island's dependence on Hergigo was also noted by another Jesuit, Baltazar Telles. He aptly remarked that since the people of Massawa were unable to "subsist without Water", they had been obliged to make themselves the "masters" of Hergigo, where the Turks had "erected a Fort with four Bastions".[76] Hergigo, as a result of this fort, was thus at this time almost as firmly under Turkish control as the island port of Massawa itself.

---

[75] Bruce (1790), III, 1. 4-5, 52
[76] Beckingham and Huntingford (1954), pp. 181-12; Tellez (1710), p. 255.

Chapter 29

THE BORDERLANDS AND THE INTERIOR

The Oromo Migration

The northward migration of the Oromos, whose presence in the south is first apparently recognised in Fra Mauro's *mappomondo* of 1460, had a major impact on the Ethiopian borderlands and their inhabitants, as well as on the latter's relationship with the central state.

This great movement of population is said to have begun prior to the first incursions of Imam Ahmäd ibn Ibrahim in the early sixteenth century. The advent of the Oromos, we are told, was initially characterised by a number of raids or forays, which took place, according to Abba Bahrey, at the time of *luba* Mélbah (1522-1530), who, he claims, first invaded Bali. Later, during the *luba*ship of Kilolé (1538-1546) the Oromos penetrated into the Däwaro lowlands, and subsequently made their way into Fätägar in the time of the *luba* Bifolé (1546-1554). It was then that the Oromos began to establish themselves in the area on a more permanent basis. This northward movement of the Oromos was strenuously opposed by Emperor Gälawdéwos. His chronicle presents him as a notable military leader, who set up a settlement in Wäj for many persons displaced in the fighting, while Bermudes tells of him suffering significant defeats.

The advance of the Oromos continued during the *luba*ship of Meslé or Michelle (1554-1562) when they came in contact with the Amirate of Härar. This resulted in fierce fighting with Amir Nur ibn al-Wazir Mujahid. At about this time, Bahrey reports, the Oromos developed the custom of riding horses. This skill enhanced their mobility, and possibly assisted their expansion, notably during the time of *luba* Harmufa (1562-1570), when they made their way into Amhara, as far as Bägémder and Angot. The Oromo thrust gained further momentum during the *luba*ship of Robalé (1570-1578) when Oromo warriors reportedly "devastated" Shäwa, and proceeded to Gojjam. The Oromo migration was at this time strongly opposed by Emperor Särsä Dengel, who fought, his chronicle reports, against Galla forces near Lake Zway, drove them south-eastwards towards Fätagar and Däwaro, and seized a vast number of their cattle.

Notwithstanding these engagements, which are presented in the chronicle as great victories, the Oromos before long returned to the areas from which they had been repulsed. Särsä Dengel was soon fighting them in Shäwa, and later again in Wäj, as well as in Dambeya. The military prowess of the Oromos was reportedly enhanced during the *luba*ship of Birmajé (1578-1586) when they are said to have adopted the use of body-length shields. This enabled them to attack, and defeat, the Mayas, a formidable group whose poisoned arrows had hitherto impeded penetration into their area. The Oromo advance was then resumed, and led to the occupation in the *luba*ship of Mul'äta (1586-1594) of much of Shäwa and Damot.

Pressure from the Oromos continued during the ensuing reign of Emperor Susneyos, and, after the establishment of the capital at Gondär, those of Emperors Fasilädäs and Yohannes I. The resultant fighting with imperial armies was concentrated largely in areas further north than previously, notably in Gojjam and Bägémder.

Increasing imports of fire-arms were at the same time strengthening the position of the Gondärine empire *vis-à-vis* the Oromos. When Emperor Iyasu I carried out expeditions against the latter they either accepted his rule or, as the chronicle more than once puts it, "disappeared like smoke before the wind". His declared objective of driving the Gallas back as far as the Awash River was, however, never achieved.

Oromo Integration in the Gondär Monarchy

The early seventeenth witnessed the steady absorption of Oromos into the imperial state. Susneyos, who had been taken a prisoner by the Oromos, and brought up by one of them, was well acquainted with Oromo ways. During his reign three only partially assimilated Oromo groups, the Yähabätas, the Ilma Gwozit, and the Tälätas, allied themselves to the empire. Many pure Oromos, under the pressure of the Emperor and his brother Ras Se'elä Krestos, were also converted to Christianity, or, more specifically, Catholicism.

Later, during the reign of Yohannes I, Iyasu, the heir to the throne, found refuge in the Oromo country, where he befriended the Kordidas, a large group of Amhara defectors or slaves who wished to return to imperial rule and the Christian faith. On subsequently assuming the throne he assisted no less than 100,000 of them achieve their ambition. During his reign many Oromos also allied themselves with the imperial state. This period likewise witnessed the rise of several Oromo leaders to positions of prominence in Gondarine service. The most notable among them was the Libän chief Tigé, who attained the rank of Behtwäddäd, or the King's Beloved courtier. A number of Oromos, among them the Bässos, Jawis and Tälätas, contributed contingents to the Emperor's army.

Oromo involvement in imperial affairs increased during the reigns of Téwoflos, Yostos, and in particular Dawit III, who on one occasion used Jawi troops to suppress dissident monks. His successor Bäkäffa spent part of his youth among the Yäjju Oromos, and received hospitality from their chief Amizo. Bäkäffa also employed Jawi, as well as Libän and Bässo, troops, and showed great favour to an Oromo courtier, Wäräñña, whom he made governor of Damot.

Jawi, Tuläma and other Oromo troops played an even more important role during the reign of Bäkäffa's son Iyasu II. Under the influence of his mother Empress Mentewwäb he promoted Wäräñña to a series of high offices, and married Wabit, the daughter of the Yäjju chief Amizo, who a generation earlier had befriended the old empress's husband Bäkäffa .

Iyasu was succeeded by his half-Oromo son Emperor Iyo'as, who depended heavily on Wäräñña, as well as on his Oromo mother Wobit. Many Oromos, including the young monarch's two uncles Lubo and Biralé, came to Gondär, and rose to important positions. Afan Oromo is said by Bruce to have become overnight the language of the court. The Oromos, who two centuries earlier had been fighting on the periphery, thus gained very considerable influence in the centre of the region, at the empire's very capital.

The result of these developments was that Oromo lands south of the Blue Nile, as well as Wällo to the east, were to a greater or lesser extent integrated into the empire. A total Oromo take-over at Gondär, which for a time seemed likely, was shortly afterward prevented by the rise of the Tegray chieftain Ras Mika'él Sehul, who made himself for a time master of the capital.

The South and East

Oromo migration had a major impact on the southern and eastern territories, most notably Bali, Däwaro, Fätägar, Ifat, and the country of the Mayas. These territories, because of their relative vicinity to the Oromo homelands, were the first to be attacked, and, on account of their flat open country, were easily overrun. Some of the earlier population of the region fled northward, but others were assimilated into Oromo society.

Bali, situated in the far south, came under Oromo pressure as early as the *luba*ship of Mélbah, i.e. before the advent of Imam Ahmäd ibn Ibrahim. The Oromo advance in the area was later contained by Särsä Dengel, who towards the end of the sixteenth century appointed a *gärad*, or ruler, for the province, and also stationed *chäwa*, or troops, there. The chief, or his successor, by name Dägano, subsequently brought tribute to Emperor Ya'qob. The province, which consisted, as Almeida notes, of "wide open plains", nevertheless soon succumbed to the Oromos, and was largely occupied without much difficulty.

Däwaro was overrun during the time of *luba* Kilolé, i.e. in the late 1530s or early 1540s. Local resistance was apparently less successful than in Bali. The Oromo drive on Däwaro, which Almeida describes as another essentially flat province, continued during the ensuing *luba*ship of Bifolé, when the entire province, according to Bahrey, was "devastated".

Fätägar, which was another flat territory easy to occupy, was confronted by the Oromo advance at the time of *luba* Bifolé. The province's inhabitants are said to have been turned into *gäbar*s, or tax-paying serfs. Särsä Dengel, when later fighting the Oromos in Wäj, drove many into Fätägar, but was unable to eject them from the province as he had hoped.

The Mayas, formerly almost indomitable because of their poisoned arrows, succumbed to the Oromos when the latter adopted the use of body-length shields.

The South-West and West

The provinces of the south-west, notably Gämo, Guragé, Hadeya, Enarya, Damot, Gafat, Bizamo, the country of the Gämbos, Janjero, and Käfa, were further from the Oromos' original homeland, and therefore felt the weight of the migration somewhat later than the territories to the south. Several south-westerly peoples succeeded in resisting Oromo pressure, though others were assimilated or forced northward, in some cases across the Blue Nile.

Gämo, because of its southerly position, was one of the first territories in the area to be occupied by the Oromos, as Bahrey, an ex-resident of the area, complained.

The Guragés, who consisted of Christians, Muslims and animists, did not come under Oromo pressure until the early seventeenth century, and their country even then does not appear to have attracted immigrant settlement. One widely canvassed, but by no means fully acceptable, hypothesis claims that this was because the Oromos disliked the province's staple crop, the *ensete*, or false banana.

Emperor Susneyos for his part was much involved in the Guragé country. Prior to his coronation he marched into the province, where the Christians asked him to support them against Sidi, the Muslim ruler of Hadeya. In the course of an ensuing expedition he visited both Ennämor and Mugär.

Dämä Krestos, the ruler of nearby Wäj, later allied himself with the Muslims, and offered to capture the prince for them. Susneyos, however, discovered the plot, and seized the chief. Many "pagan" or pro-Muslim Guragés attempted to secure Dämä Krestos's escape. Susneyos was obliged to flee the area, after which he released his prisoner. Much fighting ensued, in which the people of Ennämor fought so well that Susneyos's chronicler described them as better soldiers than either the Amharas or Gallas. Guragé weapons, according to Almeida, included both bows and arrows.

Hadeya, which was ruled by the afore-mentioned Muslim called Sidi, was likewise confronted by the Oromo advance during the reign of Susneyos. Oromo pressure was largely contained, with the result that the province maintained its separate identity throughout this period. It is, however, known to have on one occasion paid tribute to Iyasu I.

Kämbata, south of Hadeya, was also a sometime tributary state, and paid taxes to Susneyos.

Enarya, being located further to the north-west, came in contact with the Oromos at a later stage than either Guragé or Hadeya. The province, which Särsä Dengel had temporarily converted, and had yielded him a considerable revenue in gold, later attracted the attention of Susneyos. Before his accession he undertook an expedition to the area, and with Oromo help fought against a local ruler called Gwemcho. Imperial control over the territory was later re-imposed. Susneyos on one occasion sent a tax collecting expedition, and arranged for one of his nieces, the daughter of his Ras Se'elä Krestos, to marry Yämanä Krestos, the son of the local ruler Bénäro, a strong opponent of the Oromos.

Bénäro, who had thus become the Emperor's kinsman, joined the Emperor in opposing Oromo incursions. Allegedly a cruel tyrant he was murdered by his own people, who replaced him by a certain Arutano or Sisgayo. Susneyos seems to have had little choice but to concur in this appointment. The new chief was, however, soon killed, whereupon Yämanä Maryam, a Roman Catholic convert, became ruler of Enarya. He continued his father's resistance to the Oromos, who had by then driven a wedge between his province and Gojjam, thus isolating Enarya from the Christian empire.

Susneyos's abdication, and the subsequent execution of Ras Se'elä Krestos, brought an end to close relations between Enarya and the Gondarine empire, and permitted the Oromos to increase their pressure in the area. The people of territory nevertheless continued to pay some tribute to the Emperor, allegedly on a more or less voluntary basis. Iyasu I later marched to Enarya, where two rival chiefs appealed to him to recognise their status, which he did, presenting the ruler of his choice with ceremonial clothes. The continued independence of the area was later noted Bruce, who reported that slaves from Enarya were exported in considerable numbers, and highly regarded in the East.

Damot, too, was affected by the Oromo advance during the reign of Särsä Dengel. Bahrey claims that the Gallas at this time surrounded the province, enslaved its men, and carried off their livestock. The Emperor attempted to check these incursions, but died there, allegedly of food poisoning, in 1597.

Numerous Damots, faced with continuing Oromo incursions, fled northwards across the Blue Nile, and found refuge in Gojjam where many of them, like displaced persons from Shäwa and elsewhere, settled in refugee villages, and, it may be presumed, inter-married with the local population. The term Damot, which had earlier been used for a territory south of the river, was thereafter applied to an area or areas north of it.

Not a few of the inhabitants of Damot had by then been converted to Christianity. Strong adherents of the Orthodox faith they opposed Susneyos's attempts to introduce Catholicism, and stubbornly refused to abandon the traditional Ethiopian Saturday Sabbath. Many were killed fighting for their faith. Defeated in battle they later became once more the Emperor's tributaries, and some were recruited to fight in Fasilädäs's army. Soldiers from the province, it will be recalled, had served in the imperial army since early medieval times.

Gafat was another province with which Susneyos had close contact. Prior to his coronation he carried out several expeditions to the territory, and later fought against the Oromos, who were by then forcing their way into the area.

The Oromo advance was so powerful that many people of Gafat, like those of Damot, fled northwards across the Blue Nile. The name Gafat, hitherto applied to a country south of the river, was thereafter used to refer to areas north of it. Many Gafats on the other hand intermarried with the Oromos, though others, like displaced persons from Damot, Shäwa and elsewhere, settled in refugee villages, mainly in Gojjam.

Bizamo was likewise around this time brought under Oromo occupation. Many of inhabitants of the province fled northwards across the Blue Nile, and were reputed to be in possession of vast numbers of livestock, but others intermarried and were assimilated by the Oromos.

Janjero, though situated to the south of the above-mentioned provinces, was largely encircled by the Omo and Gibé Rivers, and thus isolated from external pressures. The territory therefore maintained its distinctive animist civilisation, and was apparently little affected by outside influences, Christian, Muslim or Oromo. The Janjero state, its clans, monarchical institutions and mode of royal succession, attracted attention from the Jesuits, whose somewhat fanciful accounts constitute the only records of the territory at this time.

Käfa, guarded by deep trenches, also withstood the Oromo advance. This enabled two of its local *tatos*, or kings, Gali Ginocho and Shagi Sherocho, substantially to expand the territory's frontiers.

The western frontier region, the abode of the "Shanqellas" and other "black" peoples, continued to be an area of extensive slave-raiding. This was conducted, as in the past, mainly by the rulers of the Christian highlands. Raiding increased after the north-westward shift of the imperial capital to the Lake Tana area. This brought the monarchs and their chiefs in closer contact with the "black" population on the Sudan border. Susneyos undertook no fewer than six expeditions against the "Shanqellas", Gongas, Bäläyas or other "blacks" in the west. Such operations were accompanied by loss of life, considerable seizure of both slaves and livestock and no small destruction of property. Many captured slaves nevertheless rose to prominent military and other positions at the imperial court. Susneyos reportedly declared that only such men, whom he had created and lifted from the dust, were faithful to him.

Slave-raiding in the west continued during the reign of Fasilädäs, whose capital, Gondär, emerged as a major slave city. Its wealth, and the imperial forces' increasing access to fire-arms, led to extensive raiding, not only in the far west, but also in other areas, notably between the Täkkäzé and Märäb Rivers. Successful campaigns were later carried out by both Yohannes I and Iyasu I. During the latter reign the imperial soldiers, it is said, learnt of an antedote to the poison used by the "Shanqellas" on their arrows, the wounds of which had until then usually been fatal. Further raids were conducted by Emperors Iyasu II and Iyo'as, and later by some of prominent nobles of the period of the Mäsafent, or Judges.

Slave troops meanwhile were becoming increasingly important at Gondär, where many of them married local women. The offspring of such unions were known as Welajoch, or Relations. Involved in a plot after Emperor Dawit III's death in 1721 they were banished by Emperor Bäkaffa. Three hundred "black" horsemen were nonetheless prominent at the palace at Gondär in the last quarter of the century, when Bruce claimed that they were capable of cutting their way through "all the cavalry of Abyssinia". Many of these and other slaves intermarried with the local population, and were assimilated into Gondär life.

Though numerous "Shanqella" and other "black" communities were taken as slaves many continued to live in the western borderlands. They were described by Bruce as a semi-nomadic population of hunters, large numbers of whom were engaged, as since early times, in the collection of gold. Supplies of the rare metal found their way all over the Ethiopian region, where they served as an article of tribute, as well as one of the empire's major exports.

The long history of slave-raiding on the borders had significant linguistic and cultural repercussions in the interior. Capture of Bareya slaves apparently led to the adoption of the term *bareya* to signify "slave". The word also came to be used in many Christian names, such as Yä-Maryam Bareya, or Slave of Mary. Suspicion, or fear, of slaves, on account of their difference of tradition and belief also caused the word to be used for an evil spirit, as evident from Ge'ez prayers of the time.

The shift of the imperial capital to the north-west, and later more specifically to Gondär, led meanwhile to closer commercial and other contacts with Sennar. The western trade route increased in importance, and contributed significantly to the region's overall import-export trade. Susneyos, later consolidated his control in the border area. Subsequent attempts by Iyasu II to make his influence felt there led to two expeditions to Senaar. The first was successful, and led to the capture of many prisoners and much loot, but the second ended in disaster.

The East

The Oromo impact was also felt in the east, in Adäl and the trading city of Harär, and as far north as Awssa.

Adäl, and its capital Harär, were faced in the aftermath of Imam Ahmäd's defeat by rapid Oromo expansion. Fierce fighting took place during the *luba*ship of Meslé, which coincided with the reign of Amir Nur ibn al-Wazir Mujahid. This struggle, which was mentioned by Bahrey, led to the "devastation", according to a local chronicle, of many neighbouring regions. To protect Harar the chief reputedly built the city's encircling wall, which guarded the settlement for several centuries, preserving it as a kind of Adaré Muslim island in an Oromo sea.

Nur's successors were often in conflict with the two main powers of the region: the advancing Oromos and the receding Christian empire. Amir 'Uthman "the Abyssinian", one of Nur's former slaves, relaxed his predecessors' pro-Islamic policy, and sought an accommodation with the Oromos. This angered many Muslims, and led to a rebellion, in which he was overthrown, and replaced by another leader, Talha. The latter was, however, soon denounced by some of his more fanatical subjects, who were intent on a *jihad*, or Holy War, against the Christian state. He was deposed, after which 'Uthman's grand son Muhammäd carried out an expedition against Särsä Dengel in 1572-3. The operation was a fiasco. While the army was away the Oromos ravaged the neighbouring countryside, up to the gates of the city. Muhammäd was at about the same time defeated, and killed by Särsä Dengel's forces.

Muhammäd's successor Mänsur waged a fierce war against the Oromos, but was unable to defeat them. He was succeeded by Muhammäd Gasa, who mounted an unsuccessful campaign in the highlands. Finding the city's position untenable, however, he later transferred his capital to Awssa in 1577, but was killed a few years later, while fighting the Oromos in 1583.

Harär, though abandoned by its rulers, survived as an independent state. The only place in the entire region to issue its own currency, it was throughout this time a notable religious centre and place of Islamic learning, as well as a major centre of commerce handling much of the region's trade. The city doubtless also exerted an important economic and cultural influence on the surrounding countryside.

Awssa, though situated far away in the north-east, was also affected by the coming of the Oromos, who first appeared in the area during the reign of Särsä Dengel. They besieged two settlements in 1583-4, and attacked caravans in the area in 1589. Fighting was intensified in the following year, when Amir Ahmäd ibn Asma' ad-Din undertook a campaign against the Oromos, but was killed in battle. Further Awssa expeditions against the Oromos were undertaken in the 1620s and 1630s.

Despite their conflict with the Oromos the Awssa rulers were strongly opposed to any accommodation with the Jesuits, who had by then won the confidence of Susneyos. Two Portuguese missionaries, Francisco Machado and Bernardo Pereira, whom the Emperor had invited to his country, entered the territory in 1624, but were promptly put to death. Reports of this event indicate that the Awssa chief was in contact with the Christian empire. He had earlier despatched envoys to Susneyos, and after the execution, sent messages to an Orthodox rebel against the Emperor, urging him to fight against the Portuguese for the faith of his fathers. The Awssa leader was thus at least in intermittant contact with both the Catholic monarch and his Orthodox opponents.

Conflicts with the Oromos later resulted in renewed diplomatic relations between Awssa and the Gondärine monarchy. Awssa messangers travelled to Gondär in 1647, but no information on the ensuing talks is extant.

Oromo pressure on Awssa seems to have increased at about this time. A local chronicle speaks of the Gallas raiding the Ada'ils, or Afars, who appealed for help to Imam Adam Isa of Awssa. The latter was killed in the ensuing fighting. His successor, Imam 'Umar-Din, undertook several successful expeditions against the Oromos. and reportedly captured many of their children as slaves. Notwithstanding these victories Awssa was by this time in decline, and the Afars soon afterwards assumed complete control over the territory.

The North

The Afar country was affected at this time not only by the Oromo advance, but also by the continued Turkish occupation of the port of Massawa. These two factors combined to bring the Afars and their rulers into closer contact with the Christian empire.

Relations between the Afars and Susneyos were particularly close. In 1620 the Afar ruler Kamil travelled inland to be crowned by the Emperor at the latter's camp at Dehana. Kamil, who thus gained increased legitimacy for his royal title, agreed to pay Susneyos half the taxes he collected, and left several members of his family with the monarch. Jesuit writings state that the Afar chief, though not strictly speaking a "subject", recognised the Emperor as his "superior".

Susneyos and his successor Fasilädäs both envisaged the Afar port of Baylul as a politically interesting alternative to Massawa, and potentially the empire's more important point of access to the sea. Several notable personages, including the Jesuit Jerónimo Lobo, the Yämani envoy Hasan ibn Ahmäd al-Haymi, the Egyptian bishop Abunä Mika'él, and the Armenian trader-cum-ambassador Khodja Murad, entered the empire by way of Baylul. None, however, found the route fully satisfactory. This was in part because of the difficult and waterless terrain inland from the port, and in part because of frequent Oromo incursions into the interior. Two subsequent eighteenth century writers, the Czech missionary Remedius Prutky and the Scottish traveller James Bruce, nevertheless still thought the port offered interesting possibilities.

Baylul throughout this time constituted the Afars' sole port. It handled the bulk of Afar imports and exports, and was visited on a regular basis by some merchants from the Christian interior, as well as by Arabs from across the Red Sea. The port never, however, achieved anything like the volume of trade passing through the twin ports of Hergigo and Massawa, which maintained the dominant commercial position they had enjoyed since medieval times.

Internal struggles among the Afars, and intervention by Arab riflemen from Yämän, later led to a struggle for control over the Afar capital Awssa. The Modaito Afars, hitherto in control of the settlement, were ousted by their rivals the Adoimara. The settlement, which no foreign author visited, nevertheless retained much of its former commercial importance.

The land of the Bahr Nägash, further north, differed from most of the borderlands in that it was virtually unaffected by the Oromo migration. The continued Turkish occupation of Massawa, against which Emperor Särsä Dengel had earlier fought so fiercely, nevertheless had profound consequences on the area and its political and economic life.

The Turkish presence at the port was bitterly resented by the rulers of the Christian interior. Emperor Zä-Dengel wrote to King Felipe III of Spain in 1604, urging him to seize Massawa. Susneyos, who received tribute from Hamasén and Bäqla, and was a kinsman by marriage of Bahr Nägash 'Amdä Mika'él, later undertook an expedition to the area. Faced with Turkish incursions from the port he subsequently imposed a blocade on the coast, after which the Turkish governor of Massawa agreed that the Emperor's envoys could pass through the port without molestation. Susneyos declared himself easily able to occupy Massawa, but unable to hold it in face of a Turkish attack.

Susneyos also took a keen interest in the country to the north-west of the empire, and in particular in the market town of Chelga on the trade route to Sudan, where he appointed the former ruler of Sennar, 'Abd al-Qadir, as one of his governors. The Ethiopian monarch later despatched expeditions to the Gedaref or Atbara area, and to Taka or Käsäla, both across the borders of what is now Sudan.

Emperor Fasilädäs, after expelling the Jesuits from the interior, entered into agreements with the Pashas of Massawa and Suakin to prevent the entry of Catholics into the region.

The age-old ties between the interior and the coast became possibly even closer after the move of the imperial capital to Gondär in 1636. The country of the Bahr Nägash, which was located within relatively easy access of the city, recognised the sovereignty of the Gondär emperors. Not a few Hamäsén and other chiefs took their tribute to the city, and it was there that they received recognition of their administrative and honorific titles. A large proportion of the capital's foreign trade likewise passed through the northern hinterland to and from Massawa, which also remained of crucial significance for the import of fire-arms.

Contacts between the land of the Bahr Nägash and the Gondarine monarchy, which are vividly reflected in Hamasén traditions collected by the Swedish scholar Kolmodin, were particularly important during the reign of Emperor Iyasu I. This monarch was married, conceivably for political reasons, to Wälätta Seyon, a noblewoman from Bäqla in Hamasén.

Further difficulties at the coast erupted in 1693, when the ruler of Massawa, Na'ib Musa, seized some of Iyasu's imports carried by the Armenian trader Murad. The Emperor responded by instructing Hab Sellus, Zär'a Beruk and Gäbrä Krestos, three functionaries of Hamasén, to blocade the coast. The Turkish governor, according to the Ethiopian chronicle, thereupon "trembled" in fear, and restored all the goods in dispute. Hamasén respect for Iyasu was likewise evident from Poncet's report of a mourning ceremony held at Debarwa, the capital of the Bahr Nägash, for the monarch's son Fasilädäs in 1700.

Yet another clash at the coast occurred in 1745 when the Turks seized a delegation which was travelling to Egypt to bring back an Abun, or Patriarch. This interference was resolved only by the threat of intervention by Empress Mentewwab and Ras Mika'él Sehul, the redoubtable ruler of Tegray.

With the decay of the Gondärine monarchy in the second half of the eighteenth century relations between Hamasén and the capital, however, declined. The land of the Bahr Nägash became a closer appendage of Tegray province, to whose ruler it paid tribute. Most of the north's foreign trade nevertheless continued to pass through its territory, as well as through the ports of Massawa and Hergigo which continued to flourish.

Chapter 30

CONCLUSIONS

The Ethiopian borderlands were spread out over a vast area measuring a thousand kilometres from north to south and almost as much from east to west. These territories were even more difficult to traverse than the central core of land they encompassed. The terrain of the borderlands was in many areas as rugged as that of the empire's heartlands, and included precipitous mountains, deep ravines, inhospitable deserts, impenetrable jungles, and unfordable rivers.

The lands on the periphery, like those of the interior, were characterised by immense variations of altitude, and hence of climate, rainfall and vegetation. The borderlands for this and other reasons were inhabited by a great variety of peoples. They included hunter-gatherers, pastoralists, and agriculturalists, as well as persons practising a combination of two or more of these kinds of activity, not to mention warriors, traders, artisans, and political and religious leaders.

The peoples of the borderlands likewise had very varied customs, and types of political organisation, and spoke a babel of tongues belonging to the region's four main linguistic groups, Nilo-Saharan, Omotic, Cushitic, and Semitic. Many of the inhabitants were animists, or adherents of traditional local faiths, while others were Muslims or Christians. Some, however, subscribed to a blending of two or more faiths.

Despite such immense diversity the borderlands were in many ways linked to the central core, as well as in some cases to each other, and played a major, in some ways indispensable, role in the economic, social and political life of the region as a whole.

Economic Links

Throughout the millennia under review the central core's internal trade was based very largely on *amolé*s, or bars of rock salt, a type of "primitive money" obtained from the salt plains in the north-eastern borderlands. This area was a source of salt for much of the northern and central highlands, the heartlands of the empire, where the mineral was a virtual necessity to man and livestock alike. The internal trade, and taxation, of the central core was also heavily dependent on gold obtained from the western or south-western periphery. The rare metal was taken all over the country, and was also one of the major export items of the region, which paid for much of its imports..

The foreign trade of the interior was heavily dependent on the borderlands. All such commerce passed either through the Red Sea or Gulf of Aden ports, on the northern or eastern periphery, or by way of Sudan, on the western borderland. The ports were of great antiquity, and since ancient times had owed their importance to their location on a major international seaway which had linked the Mediterranean world with the East since time immemorial.

Several of the region's principal exports originated in the borderlands. Gold, ivory and civet came largely from the rich lands on the south-western periphery, while myrrh and other resins originated in the arid lowlands in that of the east.

The borderlands were likewise a major source of slaves. Captured for the most part in the course of raids from the central or northern highlands many came from the western, north-western, or south-western periphery. Slaves from these borderlands were a common sight in many other areas. They played a major role in the domestic economy of the Christian and Muslim realms, and served at Gondär as palace servants and highly respected troops. Slaves constituted one of the region's most valuable exports. They were a source of wealth, and taxes, not only in the central core but also in the northern, eastern and north-western borderlands, for they were either shipped through the Red Sea or Gulf of Aden ports or conveyed by land via Gondär to Sudan.

The region's imports, like its exports, passed exclusively through the northern, eastern or western borderlands. Import articles throughout the period comprised both essential and luxury articles. They included textiles, as well as manufactured goods of all kinds, and most importantly, since the late fifteenth century, fire-arms.

Control of trade routes, and above all of points of access to the sea, not surprisingly played a major role in the history of the entire region. The interior, though largely self-sufficient, and inhabited by subsistence farmers and herdsmen, had long also been heavily dependent on imports. This was particularly apparent in the case of fire-arms, which for almost half a millenium determined the fate of battles, and had a decisive impact on the balance of political power, in the interior and on the periphery alike.

The borderlands and central core, for all their differences of geography, tradition and culture, were thus economically linked. They were heavily dependent on each other, and the prosperity, and paramountcy, of any area was often determined not so much by local events as by ones in distant parts of the region.

Commerce was based very largely on long distance caravans, which travelled regularly between the periphery and the interior, as well as on numerous markets, great and small, at which peoples of different areas exchanged their wares, and doubtless shared some of their experiences good and bad.

Tribute and Taxation

The core-based Christian state, the region's principal centre of political power, was the recipient over the centuries of a considerable amount of tribute from the western and south-western borderlands, as well as from areas on the northern trade route to the coast.

Taxes arriving at the imperial court from the west and south-west included a vast amount of provisions of all kinds. At one period or another these included wheat and honey from Guragé and Hadeya, cattle from Wäj, Guragé, Hadeya, Damot and the country of the Oromos, sheep from Damot, goats from the country of the "Shanqellas", and butter from various Oromo lands. Other taxes consisted of horses from Guragé, Gamo, Kämbata and Wälamo, donkeys from Hadeya, mules from Guragé and Konch, cotton cloth from Bizamo, clothes from Hadeya, lion, leopard and other skins from Guragé, and gold from Enarya, Damot, Bosha, and Konch, as well as slaves from Enarya and the countries of the Bareyas and "Shanqellas".

Much of the tribute from the north came from the country of the Bahr Nägash, on the region's northern periphery, which, because of its position on the great trade route to the north, was of major economic importance. They consisted largely of imported goods, among them fine horses, textiles, and carpets, as well as, above all, fire-arms.

Such articles, whether local or imported, were often brought to the capital or centre of power by local chiefs or governors, who came in person, not only to bring their taxes, but also to build up connections with the reigning Emperor, to gain appointment to office, to have their status recognised, or to petition for justice.

Taxation was important not only for the central state, but also for political entities nearer to the periphery, such as Tegray, the country of the Bahr Nägash and Adäl, which were no less dependent on dues levied on goods from the interior or the coast. The ports similarly owed their importance almost entirely to revenues obtained from inland commerce.

Migration, Political and Religious Alliances and Conflict

The borderlands were linked to the central core, and/or to each other, not only by commerce and taxation, but also, over the centuries, by migration, military expeditions, and political, dynastic and religious alliances.

The countries of the periphery were involved in most of the great migrations of the period. The northern borderlands in which the Aksumite kingdom had its origins, was thus the area from which the Aksumites expanded throughout Tegray, and thence southwards and westwards into much of the region's central core.

Aksumite expansion was also felt in both the north-western and south-western borderlands. Early in the fourth century King Ezana of Aksum despatched an important expedition against the Noba and Tangaitae on the "borders of Egypt", i.e. to the north-west of the Aksumite realm, while King Degna Jan, also of Aksum, later reportedly sent another to Enarya far away in the south-west.

The northern coastlands and adjacent highlands were likewise of crucial importance to the entire region as they constituted the area whence Christianity, which became the Aksumite state religion in the early fourth century, spread southwards into a large stretch of the interior. This began a process of cultural assimilation which was to continue for almost two millennia.

Despite the later decline of the Aksumite realm political contacts between the core and the borderlands were soon resumed by the Lasta-based Zagwé dynasty. The districts of Hamasén and Särayé in the far north were quickly brought under Zagwé rule. Expeditions from Lasta were likewise later despatched to the south-western borderlands of Damot and Gafat.

Contacts between the core and the periphery were further developed by one of the most notable unifying rulers, Emperor 'Amdä Seyon, who conducted major campaigns to the northern periphery, Damot and Hadeya, as well as to Ifat. It was shortly afterwards reported that most of the Muslim sultans of the eastern and southern regions received their investiture from the Ethiopian emperor, though they also owed special respect to the ruler of Ifat.

The eastern borderlands, notably Adäl and Ifat, had meanwhile come under the influence of Islam, which spread far into the region's central core. Though King Armah of Aksum is said to have earlier offered asylum to some of the first followers of the Prophet Muhammäd the existence of two different religions was soon a source of conflict. A late thirteenth century ruler of Adäl reportedly seized an Ethiopian prelate returning from Jerusalem, and thereby provoked a punitive expedition by Emperor Yagbe'a Seyon. Ifat, which had earlier been a fiefdom of Emperor Yekuno Amlak, the first Solomonic ruler of Shäwa, was subsequently the site of a series of rebellions. The most notable of these was organised by Sultan Säbr ad-Din II, whose insurrection in the early fourteenth century had far-reaching consequences. Aimed, according to 'Amdä Seyon's chronicle, at gaining control over the entire Ethiopian state, it spread to the neighbouring territories of Däwaro and Afar, and gained support in both Shärkha in the east and Hadeya in the west.

Säbr ad-Din's rebellion was, however, contained, and crushed, by 'Amdä Seyon. Advancing from the Shäwan highlands into Ifat he proceeded to the Afar country in the east, where he attacked and looted its capital, Täläg. He likewise marched westwards to Damot and Hadeya, asserted his power over Guragé and Gafat, and reportedly made his way as far as the Red Sea in the north . To carry out these and other expeditions he recruited many soldiers from the western periphery, notably Damot, Gafat and the country of the Bareya. Troops from the western borderlands thereafter fought in many distant parts of the empire, including Wägära in the north-west, the Sämén mountains in the north, and several provinces in the east. Such expeditions, like the many which followed, were accompanied by the capture of numerous slaves, both male and female, and resulted in a considerable mixture of peoples, as well as doubtless no small amount of cultural assimilation.

Another important ruler of Ifat, Sultan Sä'd ad-Din, subsequently waged war against the Christian empire, but was eventually defeated by Emperor Dawit I, who drove him as far as the port of Zäylä', where he died in battle in 1415. Sa'd ad-Din's sons sought refuge in Arabia, but later returned to found a new dynasty, situated in Adäl and based at Däkär. From that settlement they waged many, often successful, battles with the imperial forces. Such fighting resulted in considerable casualties on both sides, as well as in the capture of numerous slaves. Many of the latter were as usual appropriated and assimilated by the victors, though others, particularly those taken by the Muslims, were also exported to Arabia.

The Muslim rulers of the eastern borderlands were throughout this time unable to advance far into the region's central core, where the Christian emperors mobilised powerful armies, but made greater headway in the south. Sä'd ad-Din of Ifat and Jämal ad-Din II of Adäl, attacked far-off Bali. Sultan Shihab ad-Din of Adäl later settled a sizeable number of Adäl Muslim families in that province.

The Christian monarchy was meanwhile consolidating its position in the borderlands. In the late thirteenth century Saint Täklä Haymanot is reported to have converted King Motä Lamé of Damot to Christianity. Subsequently, in the late fourteenth and early fifteenth centuries, Emperors Säyfä Ar'ad, Dawit I and Yeshaq granted land charters as far north as Hamäsén and Säraye. Yeshaq also established a garrison at Massawa, while at the same time receiving tribute from Bizamo and the country of the "Shanqellas" far away in the south-west.

The subsequent integration, or in some cases reintegration, of many borderlands into the Christian empire owed much to the notable early fifteenth century state-builder and religious zealot Emperor Zär'a Ya'qob, whose government reorganisation was felt in several peripheral areas. In the north, from which he received valuable taxes, he established a functionary with the title of Bahr Nägash, or ruler of the sea province, a post of considerable importance which was later occupied by one of Emperor Lebnä Dengel's uncles. Zär'a Ya'qob also made his power felt in other areas. In the east he appointed one of his daughters as governor of Ifat, and also chose administrators for Däwaro and Fätägar. In the west he placed Damot under the rule of another of his daughters, and assigned an officer as ruler of Wäj. To strengthen his control of the borderlands he likewise stationed garrisons in Hamäsén in the north, as well as Däwaro and Fätägar in the south-east.

Such efforts at state consolidation on the periphery, based partly on garrisons and partly on settlement, were challenged in this period by both Gärad Mähiko, the ruler of Hadeya, and Sultan Shihab ed-Din Bädlay of Adäl. Both chiefs, and their insurrections, were, however, easily defeated by the imperial armies.

The centralising policies of Zär'a Ya'qob were partially abandoned by his son Bä'edä Maryam, who allowed more power to some of the local rulers, particularly in the east. Ifat thus passed under the administration of a local Muslim ruler with the title of Wälashma', while Adäl became virtually independent. In other areas, however, the

Emperor sought to exert control. He launched expeditions against the Dobe'a, who according to a royal chronicle had shown themselves unruly. Bä'edä Maryam also conducted two campaigns against Adäl, the second of which ended in complete disaster. He was, however, more successful elsewhere, for he stationed troops in Fätägar, and travelled south to Guragé where he established fruit plantations.

Bä'edä Maryam's most remarkable act of statecraft *vis-à-vis* the borderlands was his dynastic alliance in the west with the ruling family of Hadeya. By marrying the local chief's daughter, Ité Jan Zela, later better known as Eléni, he broke the province's earlier ties with Ifat and Adäl, and linked it much more closely with the empire. The alliance with Hadeya, which provided the Christian empire with its most loyal support in the west, long the region's principal source of gold and slaves, continued up to the reign of Lebnä Dengel. The latter monarch declined to marry a Hadeya princess, who failed to attract him, but arranged for her to wed his principal courtier. On the outbreak of a power struggle within her family Lebnä Dengel later sent an expedition to strengthen his position in the province, together with Christian priests and monks who sought its religious assimilation.

This period also witnessed continued Christian missionary activity by Ethiopian clerics, many of them disciples of Saint Täklä Haymanot. They were active in both the eastern and western borderlands, notably in Däwaro, where a monk aptly known as Zä-Däwaro gained great renown, and Damot, where many conversions were carried out by a holy man called Mäba Seyon.

The empire's preponderance in the east meanwhile continued to be challenged from time to time by Muslim rulers, most notably in Adäl. One of its principal rulers, Amir, later Imam, Mähfuz of Zäylä', embarked on a series of raids into Fätägar, Shäwa, and Däwaro. He was assisted by Arabs from across the Gulf of Aden, to whom he gave many slaves captured in his expeditions. Despite this support he was eventually defeated, and killed in a duel with a monk called Gäbrä Endreyas, who was attached to Lebnä Dengel's army.

After the death of Mähfuz the power of the eastern lowlands was reasserted by the latter's famous son-in-law Imam Ahmäd ibn Ibrahim al-Ghazi, also known as Ahmäd Grañ. Making decisive use of firearms obtained from Arabia, and far more readily available in Adäl than elsewhere, he emulated his father-in-law's policies by carrying out a series of raids into the eastern and south-eastern borderlands, as well as some of the central core-lands. This advance, which began in the late 1520s, was resisted, for the most part unsuccessfully, by Lebnä Dengel, whose soldiers, like those of many of his predecessors, came not only from the empire's heartlands, but also from many of the borderlands, including Hamäsén and Särayé in the north, Guragé, Enarya and Gafat in the west, and Bali in the south. As a result of the Imam's victories many Christians on the eastern and southern periphery, as well as in the interior, voluntarily or forcibly embraced Islam. Those who refused to convert were in many cases subjected to a poll tax.

Imam Ahmäd, who sought to make himself the master of the entire Ethiopian region, later overran much of the south-west, including Wäj, Gamo, Guragé, and Wälamo, the latter with great difficulty, as well as Kämbata, Enarya, Damot, Gafat, and Hadeya. In the last mentioned territory the local chief, doubtless recalling earlier dynastic marriages with the Christian rulers of the empire, gave Ahmäd his daughter Mureyas to wed. The Imam's men also penetrated some of the lands of the "blacks" in the far west, but an attempt to occupy Wälamo was frustrated. Despite this setback vast areas of the south-west were converted to Islam.

The Imam, advancing northwards, later gained control of Tegray and fought his way to the northern periphery, including Särayé, Hamäsén, and the port of Hergigo. In all three areas he appointed governors. His occupation was, however, only temporary, for he soon afterwards found it necessary to abandon the area, and left various local chiefs in office. One of them was the ruler of the Dahlak islands to whom he entrusted the mainland port of Hergigo, which thus passed under the influence of people from beyond the sea.

Ahmäd's defeat and death in 1543 led to the rapid collapse of the power structure he had established. Several members of his family attempted to retain control of various areas, including the eastern and southern borderlands of Däwaro, Fätägar, Ifat, and Bali, but were soon defeated by Lebnä Dengel's son and successor Emperor Gälawdéwos, who easily gained control of many areas towards the periphery. In the north he established control over the country of the Bahr Nägash, where he renewed a land charter earlier granted by Zär'a Yaq'ob. Gälawdéwos's position in the area suffered a major reverse, however, when the port of Massawa was seized by the Ottoman Turks in 1557. The victorious monarch nevertheless re-established imperial rule in many other borderlands, among them Gafat, Damot and Bosha to the west, and Däwaro, Fätägar and Ifat to the east. He also advanced further eastwards as far as Harär, but was killed in battle by Imam Ahmäd's renowned nephew Amir Nur ibn al-Wazir Mujahid in 1559. The Emperor's successor, Minas, learning from his brother Gälawdéwos's death, abandoned the centuries old Shäwan interest in the east, and, by establishing his capital at Emfraz, near Lake Tana, shifted the empire's principal commercial interest to the trade routes to the north and east. Attention thus transferred from the eastern borderlands to those of the north and west.

These events coincided with the beginning of the great Oromo, or Galla, migration, which began in the southern borderlands in the early sixteenth century. This started, like the advance of Mähfuz and Imam Ahmäd, with a series of raids carried out in the flat lands of Bali, Däwaro and Fätägar, as well as parts of Adäl. In all these areas the Oromos were able to advance with considerable rapidity. Their initial raids were soon followed by a more permanent occupation, as a result of which most of the earlier inhabitants of the south were assimilated with greater or lesser success, or fled northwards. Report has it that the local population of Fätägar was turned into serfs.

The warlike Emperor Särsä Dengel, whose reign coincided with late sixteenth century Oromo expansion in the south, succeeded in advancing to the country of the Bahr Nägash, where he captured many fire-arms, and riflemen, from the Turks. This enabled him to carry out or despatch a number of major expeditions, including several to the southern and south-western borderlands. These included Enarya, where he converted the local ruler Bädancho and many of his subjects in 1587, and Bosha, whose chief also adopted Christianity, as well as Guragé, Gafat, Damot, Hadeya and Bizamo. As a result of the Emperor's activities Christianity reportedly may even have reached Käfa.

Särsä Dengel had meanwhile organised expeditions to the north, where the Turks, gaining the support of an ambitious local chief, Bahr Nägash Yeshaq, had advanced southwards to occupy Däbrä Damo and Debarwa. With the assistance of the local population, who had by then gained access to fire-arms, the Emperor won victories over both Yeshaq and the Turks. Särsä Dengel captured many of their weapons, and persuaded some of their riflemen to serve in his army. He was, however, unable to expel the Turks from Massawa. Yeshaq's treachery reportedly had long-term consequences, for the status of Bahr Nägash was thereafter greatly reduced, though it was subsequently granted to a local man, 'Aquba Mika'él, who had fought valiantly against the Turks.

The Oromos meanwhile, continuing their northward advance, swept into the region's central core. They made their way to Shäwa, Bägémder, Gojjam, and lands to the east, as far as Harär, where they were opposed by Amir Nur ibn al-Wazir Mujahid.

This remarkable advance was probably facilitated by the use by the Oromos of cavalry, which they are believed to have acquired in this period, as well as by their adoption of body-length shields, which protected them against the poisoned arrows of some of their opponents, among them the hitherto almost invincible Mayas.

The Oromo advance in the west was, however, contained in Guragé and Hadeya, as well as in Enarya, where Emperor Susneyos arranged for a daughter of his favourite brother Ras Se'elä Krestos to marry the son of the local ruler Bénaro. Janjero, though by this time largely isolated by the Oromos, also maintained its separate identity. Käfa protected itself by digging deep ditches, after which two of its rulers, Gali Gafocho and Shagi Sherocho, expanded the realm. Oromo pressure on Damot, Gafat and Bizamo on the other hand caused many of the local inhabitants to flee northwards across the Blue Nile to Gojjam, where not a few settled as refugees, together with persons of other displaced groups. This migration caused the names of Damot and Gafat to be applied thenceforth to areas north of the river rather than as previously to those south of it, and was doubtless also accompanied by considerable cultural assimilation.

The Oromo expansion was also felt far away on the eastern periphery. Adäl was largely overrun. Oromo pressure in the area was, however, so intense that in 1577 a later ruler, Muhammäd Gasa, transferred the seat of Adäl government to Awssa, an oasis far away in the north-eastern desert. The move in the long run proved disastrous to the Adäl leadership, for the area was later taken over by the neighbouring Afar nomads who made Awssa their capital. The city of Harär, on the other hand, preserved its independent identity as a result of strong walls thought to have been built by Amir Nur.

Särsä Dengel, like later imperial rulers, was however unable to fight successfully in two peripheral areas at the same time. His victories in the far north against the Turks were achieved at the cost of abandoning effective resistance to the Oromos in the south.

The advent of the Oromos was of immense importance in the history of the entire region, for it introduced a new, and apparently more egalitarian, type of social organisation based on the *gada*, or age-group, system, a hitherto scarcely known Cushitic language, Afan Oromo, and various "animist" beliefs and practices which were allegedly in varying degrees adopted by several Christian emperors of the period.

The north-westward move of the imperial capital to the Lake Tana area, and the subsequent rise in the early seventeenth century of a Gondär-based monarchy (which in a sense represented an escape from the difficulties associated with Adäl and the eastern borderlands) meanwhile also had a notable impact on the entire region, and one which was felt in all but the most southerly borderlands.

In the north the country of the Bahr Nägash came at this time into even closer contact with the imperial capital than previously. Local chiefs from Hamäsén and its environs often travelled to Gondär to receive titles from the hands of the Emperors, and brought tribute or gifts, including fire-arms and other articles imported from abroad, sometimes with considerable difficulty on account of interference or abuses by the Turkish rulers of Massawa. Such visitors from the land of the Bahr Nägash, in effect courtiers, in many cases apparently remained for months or even years at the capital, where they were to a greater or lesser extent assimilated to Gondärine ways.

The Turkish occupation of Massawa was meanwhile opposed, not only by the local population but also by a succession of imperial rulers. Emperor Zä-Dengel wrote to the King of Spain in 1604, proposing joint intervention to expel the Turks. Nothing came of this diplomatic initiative, but Emperors Susneyos and Iyasu I, following in Särsä Dengel's footsteps, both later despatched expeditions against the Turks in the country of the Bahr Nägash. Apparently to strengthen imperial ties with the area Iyasu also married a Hamäsén noblewoman, by name Wälätta Seyon.

One of the results of the Turkish stranglehold at Massawa was that the imperial rulers of this time developed a keen interest in the port of Baylul, which they conceived as a possible alternative point of access to the sea. Susneyos forged close ties with the Afar rulers, notably with Kamil, who, like several chiefs of the country of the Bahr Nägash, travelled inland to obtain the monarch's recognition. Several members of the Afar ruling family also later resided at Gondär.

Mutual fear of Oromo expansion apparently led to some political contacts between the Christian emperors of Gondär and the Muslim rulers of Adäl, but little actual co-operation resulted.

The Oromos, though originally inhabitants of the southern periphery, soon played a major role not only in the borderlands, but also in the core of the region. Emperor Susneyos, who spent some of his youth with Oromo warriors, acquired a knowledge of their language as well as of their way of life and military organisation. Emperor Iyasu I, who had found refuge among the Oromos prior to his accession to the throne, made an Oromo one of his favourite courtiers, and employed several contingents of Oromo troops. Emperor Bäkäffa, who obtained refuge among the Yäjju Oromos in his youth, and was reportedly also much influenced by his stay among them, likewise had an important Oromo adviser called Wäräñña, who played a major role in Gondarine state affairs. Iyasu II married Wobit, an Oromo princess, daughter of Amizo, the chief who had afforded asylum to his father. Their young half-Oromo son Emperor Iyo'as, influenced by his mother and Wäräñña, brought two of her brothers and other Oromos to Gondär, with the result that Afan Oromo, according to Bruce, was for a time the most important language of the capital.

The territories of the south-west meanwhile, though further than in the past from the centre of imperial power, still had close relations with the empire. Its capital, Gondär, handled most of their external trade, both with the Red Sea and with the Sudan. Several provinces of the south-west also had significant political ties with the Christian state. Damot, which had by then been converted to the Orthodox faith, was strongly involved in the country-wide opposition to Susneyos's attempt at introducing Catholicism. His army, like that of several of his predecessors, nevertheless later included many men from the province. Contacts between Hadeya and the empire were re-asserted when the local ruler's daughter, continuing a tradition dating back to Ba'edä Maryam's reign, married Emperor Ya'qob, whose reign was however but a short one.

The development of the Gondär monarchy, and its acquisition of ever increasing numbers of fire-arms, was followed meanwhile by continued, and expanded, slave raiding in the western borderlands. Susneyos and his successors, notably Fasilädäs and Iyasu I, conducted numerous raids against the "Shanqellas", Gongas and other "blacks". This, like so much other fighting over the centuries, resulted in the capture of numerous male and female slaves, most of whom were probably assimilated by their captors. Many were taken to Gondär, where they were employed in domestic service. Others rose to positions of authority in imperial government, or were recruited into the Emperor's redoubtable black cavalry, which constituted a powerful and respected elite force. Prejudices against persons of slave origin, sometimes referred to as Welajoch, were nonetheless common, and the term Bareya, or slave, was often associated with a magical spirit.

Expeditions were also carried out in the north-west. Susneyos despatched one of his commanders as far as the Atbara-Gedaref area on the Sudanese border, where his men fought against the kingdom of Fung, while Iyasu II and his Oromo general Wäräñña later led a disastrous one to Sennar.

****

The borderlands, we may conclude, were throughout this time far from isolated from the central Ethiopic core. Linked to the latter by major trade routes, which ran between the interior and the coast or Sudan, they formed part of an economically largely inter-dependent region.

The peoples of the periphery were involved moreover in most, if not all, of the great migrations, as well as the major political and religious conflicts of the time. Many inhabitants of the borderlands as of the central core travelled widely, in peace or war, as soldiers on campaign or garrison duty, itinerant merchants, officers of state, tax-collectors, refugees, petitioners, prisoners, priests, monks, wandering students, pilgrims or slaves.

Innumerable social, linguistic, and cultural differences between the various peoples of the region of course remained, but there were also important points of contact, both peaceful and warlike. These resulted in a vast amount of assimilation of populations, both slave and free, very considerable adoption of languages, innumerable conversions from one faith to another (and often back again!), and extensive inter-marriage, often, but by no means only for dynastic reasons. The borderlands therefore deserve a major place in the history of the region as a whole.

```
BC
 |— 3500
 |          FIRST EGYPTIAN CONTANCS WITH THE LAND OF PUNT
 |          PUNTITE SLAVE EMPLOYED BUILDING CHEOPS PYRAMIDS
 |
 |— 3000   FIRST DIRECT SAILINGS FROM EGYPT TO PUNT
 |
 |          EGYPTIAN INVENTION OF A NEW TYPE OF RUDDER
 |
 |— 2500
 |                RISE OF THE EGYPTIAN CITY OF THEBES
 |              FOUNDING OF THE EGYPTIAN PORT OF WADI GASUS
 |                  OPENING OF THE NILE-RED SEA CANAL
 |— 2000
 |
 |
 |— 1500   QUEEN HATSHEPSUT'S GREAT EXPEDITION TO PUNT
 |           FIRST RECORD OF PUNTITE SAILINGS TO EGYPT
 |
 |— 1000        KING SOLOMON'S EXPEDITIONS TO OPHIR
 |
 |              PROBABLE FOUNDING OF THE CITY OF YEHA
 |— 500
 |         PTOLEMAIC EXPEDITIONS TO THE RED SEA COAST OF AFRICA
 |
 |                         RISE OF AKSUM
 |— 0     COMPOSITION OF THE PERIPLUS OF THE ERITHRAEAN SEA
 |             STRIKING OF THE FIRST AKSUMITE COINS
 |
 |— 500         TRAVELS OF KOSMAS INDIKOPLEUSTES
 |
 |                       DECLINE OF AKSUM
 |— 1000
AD
```

Historical Tables

YEAR	KAFA	DAMOT	HADEYA	OROMO	EMPERORS	IFAT	ADAL	HARAR
1250		MOTALÄMÉ			End of Zagwe Rule			
1260								
1270					YEKUNO AMLAK	UMAR		
1280								
1290					YEGB'A SEYON	BAZIYU		
1300								
1310								
1320			AMANO		WENDEM AR'AD	HAQQ AD-DIN		
1330					AMDÄ SEYON	SÄ BR AD-DIN		
1340						JAMAL AD-DIN		
1350					SÄYFÄ AR'AD	ALI		
1360								
1370								
1380					NEWAYÄ MARIAM			
1390	MINJO KING							
1400					DAWIT	HAQQ AD-DIN		
1410						S'AD AD-DIN		
1420								
1430	GIRRA		MAHIKO		YESHAQ		SÄBR AD-DIN	
1440			MEHMÄD				MANSUR	
1450							JAMAL	
1460							BÄDLAY	
1470	ADDIO KING				ZÄRA YA'QOB		MUHAMMÄD IBN BÄDLAY	
1480					BÄ'EDÄ MARIAM		SHÄMS AD-DIN	
1490	SHADDA KING				ESKENDER		MUHAMMÄD IBN AZHAR AD-DIN	
1500								
1510				*Gada*	NA'OD		ABU BÄKR	
1520	MADIGAFO			MELBAH				
1530				MUDÄNA	LIBNÄ DENGEL		AHMÄD IBN IBRAHIM	UMAR AD-DIN
1540				KILOLE			Death of Ahmäd ibn Ibrahim	
1550								

HISTORICAL TABLES

COAST	KAFA	HADEYA	ENARYA	OROMOS	EMPERORS	WAJ	HARAR	ADAL	AFAR
rks Occupy Massawa				Gada MESLE	GÄLAWDË		NUR	HASGWA DIN	
YESHAQ AD EZUM	BONGA KING	AZÉ		HARMUFA	MINAS				
			SEPENHI	ROBALÉ	SÄRSÄ DENGEL		UTHMÄN		
							TALHA		
QUBA MIKA'ËL		JAFER	LÄ'ÄSONNI	BIRMAJÉ			**MUHAMMÄD**		
			BÄDANCHO	MUL'ÄTA			**MUHAMMÄD GASA**		
					YA'QÖB				
	GIBA NECHOCHO				ZÄ-DENGEL	DÄMÄ KRESTOS		AWASSA	SAHIM KAMIL
			BENÄRO		SUSNEYOS			'UMÄR-DIN	
			SIGAYO					ADRÄH	
MMHA			YÄMNÄ KR.						
AB SELUS								MUHAMMÄD	SHUHAYM
A'IB MUSA								ADÄM	
	GALI GAFOCHO				FASILÄDÄS		ALI IBN DAWUD	IBRAHIM	
							HASHIM	SULÄYMAN	
					YOHANNES			ABD AR-RÄ	
							ABDÄLLAH IBN 'ALI		
ÄRA KR	GALI GINOCHO								
ASFA SËN									
MAMMO					IYASU I				
	GAKI GAOCHO				YOSTOS		TÄLBAH		
					DAWIT III				
				AMIZO	BÄKAFFA		ABU BÄKR		
							HAMID		
	GALI GAOCHO				IYASU II		YUSUF		
					IYOAS		AHMÄD IBN YUSUF		
	SHAGI SHEROCHO				TÄKLÄ HAYMANOT				
					TÄKLÄ GIYO		'ABD AS-SHÄKUR		
	HOTTI GINOCHO				HEZQEYAS		AHMÄD		

BIBLIOGRAPHY

Abbadie, Antoine d' (1891a) *Dictionnaire de la langue amariñña,* Paris.
Abbadie, Antoine d' (1891b) *Gégraphie d'Ethiopie,* Paris.
Abbadie, Arnaud d' (1868) *Douze ans de séjour dans la Haute Ethiopie (Abyssinie),* Paris.
Abbink, J. (1991) "Mytho-legendes et histoire: L'énigme de l'ethnogenèse des Beta Esra'el", *Les Cahiers du CEDAF.*
Aberra Gessesse (1980) *A Tentative History of the Raya Azebo,* Addis Ababa University, Senior Essay
Abir, M. (1968) *Ethiopia. The Era of the Princes,* London.
Abir, M. (1980) *Ethiopia and the Red Sea,* London.
Abir, M. (1966) "Salt Trade and Politics in Ethiopia in the 'Zämänä Mäsefent'", *Journal of Ethiopian Studies,* IV, No. 2, pp. 1-10.
Abdurahman Mohamed Korram (1969) "Oromo Proverbs", *Journal of Ethiopian Studies,* VII, No. 1, pp. 65-80.
Aescoly, A.Z. (1928) "Les noms magiques dans les Apocryphes crétiens des Ethiopiens" *Journal Asiatique,* CCXX, 87-137.
Aescoly, A.Z. (1951) *Receuil de textes falachas,* Paris.
Ahmed Zekaria (1991), "Harari Coins; A Preliminary Survey", *Journal of Ethiopian Studies,* XXIV, 23-46.
Aklilu Gizew (1984) *Christianity in Mugar,* Addis Abab University, Senior Essay.
Altaye Alaro (1982) *A Political History of Walayta in the 18th and 19th centuries,* Addis Ababa University, Senior Essay.
Alula Abate (1969) *Studien zur Jüngeren Entwicklung der Kulturland im Hochland von Harar,* Bonn (doctoral thesis).
Anfray, F., Caquot, A. and Nautin, P. (1970) "Une nouvelle inscription greque d'Ezana, roi d'Axium", *Journal des Savants,* I, 252-7.
Arrowsmith-Brown, J.H. (1991) *Prutky's Travels to Ethiopia and Other Countries,* London.
Asmarom Legesse (1973) *Gada. Three Approaches to the Study of African Society,* New York.
Azais, R.P and Chambard, R. (1931) *Cinq années de recherches archéologiques en Ethiopie,* Paris.
Bairu Tafla (1987) *Asma Giyorgis and His Work. History of the Galla and the Kingdom of Sawa,* Stuttgart.

Barros, João de, and Couto, Diego de (1877-88) *Da Asia*, Lisboa.
Bartels, L. (1983) *Oromo Religion. Myths and Rites of the Western Oromo - An Attempt to Understand*, Berlin.
Bartels, L. (1970), "Studies of the Galla in Wälläga", *Journal of Ethiopian Studies*, VIII, No. 1, pp. 135-60.
Basset, R. (1881) "Etudes sur l'histoire d'Ethiopie", *Journal Asiatique*, XVII, 315-434, XVIII, 93-183, 285-389.
Basset, R. (1897) *Histoire de la conquete de l'Abyssinie (XVIe siècle) par Chihab ed-Din Ahmed ben 'Abd el-Qader, surnomé Arab-Faqih*, Paris.
Beccari, C. (1903-17), *Rerum Aethiopicarum Scriptores Occidentales*, Roma.
Beckingham, C.F. (1961) "Notes on an Unpublished Manuscript of Francisco Alvares: *Veradera Informaçam das Terras do Joam das Indias*", *Annales d'Ethiopie*, IV, 139-54.
Beckingham, C.F. and Huntingford, G.W.B. (1961) *The Prester John of the Indies*, Cambridge.
Beckingham, C.F. and Huntingford, G.W.B. (1954) *Some Records of Ethiopia 1593-1646*, London.
Béguinot, F. (1901) *La cronaca abbreviata*, Roma.
Beke, C.T. (1844) "Abyssinia - being a Continuation of Routes in that Country", *Journal of the Royal Geographical Society*, XIV, 1-76.
Beke, C.T. (1845) "On the Languages and Dialects of Abyssinia and the Countries to the South", *Proceedings of the Philological Society*, II, 89-107.
Belaynesh Michael, S. Chojnacki, and R. Pankhurst (1975) *The Dictionary of Ethiopian Biigraphy*, Volume I, Addis Ababa.
Bender, M.L. (1975) *The Ethiopian Nilo-Saharans*, Addis Ababa.
Bender, M.L. (1976) *The Non-Semitic Languages of Ethiopia*, East Lansing, Michigan.
Bent, J.T. (1894) *The Sacred City of the Ethiopians*, 1896.
Bernatz, J.M. (1852) *Scenes in Ethiopia*, London.
Bianchi, G. (1884) *Alla terra dei Galla*, Milano
Bieber, F.J. (1920-23) *Kaffa, ein altkuschitisches Volkstum in Inner-Africa*, Wien.
Birch, W. de G. (1875-84) *The Commentaries of the Great Dalbuquerque*, London.
Borelli, J. (1888) *Ethiopie méridionale*, Paris.

Braukämper, U. (1973) "The Correlation of Oral Traditions and Historical Records in Southern Ethiopia: A Case Study of the Hadiya-Sidamo Past", *Journal of Ethiopian Studies*, VIII, No. 2, pp. 1-20.
Braukämper, U. (1980) *Geschichte der Hadiya Süd-Athiopiens von den Anfängen bis zur Revolution 1974*, Wiesbaden.
Braukämper, U. (1983) *Die Kambata. Geschichte und Gesellschaft eines Südäthiopischen Bauernvolkes*, Wiesbaden.
Breasted, J.H. (1962) *Ancient Records of Egypt*, New York.
Breasted, J.H. (1905) *A History of Egypt*, London.
Brogger, J. (1986) *Belief and Experience among the Sidamo. A Case Study towards an Anthroplogy of Knowledge*, London.
Bruce, J. (1790) *Travels to Discover the Source of the Nile*, Edinburgh.
Bruce, J. (1813) *Travels to Discover the Source of the Nile*, Edinburgh.
Burton, R.F. (1888) *First Footsteps in East Africa*, London.
Bryan, M.A. (1948) *The Distribution of the Semitic and Cushitic Languages of Africa*, London.
Budge, E.A. Wallis (1928a) *The Book of the Saints of the Ethiopian Church*, Cambridge.
Budge, E.A. Wallis (1902) *A History of Egypt,* London.
Budge, E.A. Wallis (1928b) *A History of Ethiopia,* London.
Budge, E.A. Wallis (1933) *Legends of Our Lady Mary the Perpetual Virgin and Her Mother Hanna*, London.
Budge, E.A. Wallis (1906) *The Life of Takla Haymanot in the Version of Dabra Libanos*, London.
Budge, E.A. Wallis (1898) *The Lives of Maba' Seyon and Gabra Krestos*, London.
Budge, E.A.Wallis (1922) *The Queen of Sheba & her only son Menyelek*, London.
Bureau, J. (1980-2) "Comment s'écrit l'Histoire d'une province d'Ethiopie: le Wollaita" *Abbay*, XI, 225-41
Bureau, J. (1990a) "Un fragment de l'histoire du peuple Wollaita d'Afewerk Gebre-Sellassie", *Annales d'Ethiopie*, XV, 47-82.
Bureau, J. (1976) "Notes sur les églises du Gamo", *Annales d'Ethiopie*, X, 295-301.
Bureau, J. (1990b) "The 'Tigre' Chronicle of Wollaita; A pattern of Kingship", in R. Pankhurst, Ahmed Zekaria and Taddese

Beyene, *Proceedings of the First National Conference of Ethiopian Studies*, pp. 49-64.
Bureau, J. (1994) *Le verdict du serpent. Mythes, contes et recits des Gamo d'Ethiopie,* Paris and Addis Ababa.
Burstein, S.M. (1989) *Agartarchides of Cnidus: On the Erythraen Sea,* London.
Burton, R.F. (1856) *First Footsteps in East Africa,* London.
Caquot, A. (1957) "Histoire amharique de Grañ et des Gallas", *Annales d'Ethiopie*,II, 123-43.
Caquot, J. (1955) "L'Homélie en l'honneur de l'archange Ouriel (Dersana Ura'él)", *Annales d'Ethiopie,* I, 61-88.
Caraman, P. (1985) *The Lost Empire. The Story of the Jesuits in Ethiopia 1555-1634,* London.
Casson, L. (1989) *The Periplus Maris Erythraei,* Princeton.
Castro, L. de (1915) *Nella terra dei negus,* Milano.
Cecchi, A. (1885-7) *Da Zeila alle frontiere del Caffa,* Roma.
Cerulli, Enrico (1931) "Documenti arabi per la storia dell'Etiopia", *Memorie della Reale Accademia dei Lincei,* IV, 39-101.
Cerulli, Enrico (1942) "Gli emiri di Harar dal secolo XVI alla conquista egiziana (1875)", *Rassegna di Studi Etiopici,* II, No. 1, pp. 3-20.
Cerulli, Enrico (1943a) "L'Etiopia medievale in alcuni brani di scrittori arabi", *Rassegna di Studi Etiopici,* III, 272-94.
Cerulli, Enrico (1933) *Etiopia occidentale,* Roma.
Cerulli, Enrico (1922) "The folk-literature of the Galla of Southern Abyssinia", *Varia Africana,* III, 9-228.
Cerulli, Enrico (1943b) *Il libro etiopico dei miracoli di Maria,* Roma.
Cerulli, Enrico (1934) "La scofitta del Sultano Badlay ibn Sa'ad ad-Din in due miracoli di S. Giorgio etiopici", *Aethiopica,* II, 105-9.
Cerulli, Enrico (1936) *Studi Etiopici. I. La lingua e la storia di Harar,* Roma.
Cerulli, Enrico (1938) *Studi Etiopici. II. La lingua e la storia dei Sidamo,* Roma.
Cerulli, Enrico (1951) *Studi Etiopici. III. Il linguaggio dei Giangero ed alcune lingue Sidama dell' Omo (Basketo, Ciara, Zaisse),* Roma.
Cerulli, Enrico (1951) *Studi Etiopici. IV. La lingua caffina,* Roma.

Cerulli, Enrico (1941) "It sultanato dello Scioa nel secolo XIII secondo un nuovo documento storico, *Rassegna di Studi Etiopici*,I, 5-14.
Cerulli, Ernesta (1965) *Peoples of South-West Ethiopia and its Borderland*, London.
Chardin, J. (1711) *Voyages de Monsieur Le Chevalier Chardin en Perse, et autres lieux de l'Orient*, Amsterdam.
Cheesman, R.E. (1936) *Lake Tana and the Blue Nile*, London.
Chernetsov, S.B. (1988a) "Medieval Ethiopian Historiographies and their Methods", *Proceedings of the Nineth International Congress of Ethiopian Studies*, Moscow, V, 191-200.
Chernetsov, S.B. (1988b) "Who wrote 'The History of King Sarsa Dengel' - Was it the Monk Bahrey?", in Taddese Beyene, *Proceedings of the Eighth International Conference of Ethiopian Studies*, I, 131-6, Addis Ababa.
Chojnacki, S. (1983) "A Note on the Costumes in 15th. and Early 16th. Century Paintings: Portraits of the Nobles and their Relation to Images of Saints on Horseback", S. Segert and A.J.E. Bodrogligeti, *Ethiopian Studies. Dedicated to Wolf Leslau*, Wiesbaden, pp. 519-53.
Cipriani, L. (n.d.) *Abitazioni indigeni dell'Africa Orientale Italiana*, Naples.
Cohen, M. (1931) *Etudes d'Ethiopien méridional*, Paris.
Conti Rossini, C. (1904) *Acta Yaréd et Pantalewon*, Paris.
Conti Rossini, C. (1903) "Gli atti di Abba Yonas", *Rendiconti della Reale Accademia dei Lincei*, XII, 176-201, 236-62.
Conti Rossini, C. (1918) "L'autobiografia di Pawlos monacco abissino del secolo XVI", *Rendiconti della Reale Accademia dei Lincei*, XXVIII, 279-96.
Conti Rossini, C. (1922) "La caduta della dinastia Zagué e la versione amarica del Be'ela Nagast", *Rendiconti della Reale Accademia Nazionale dei Lincei*, XXXI, 379-314.
Conti Rossini, C. (1901) "L'evangelo d'oro di Dabra Libanos", *Rendiconti della Reale Accademia Nazionale dei Lincei*, X, 177-219.
Conti Rossini, C. (1900) "Il Gadla Filipos e il Gadla Yohannes di Dabra Bizan", *Atti della Reale Accademia dei Lincei*, VIII, 62-170.

Conti Rossini, C. (1896) "Il 'Gadla Takla Haymanot' secondo la relazione Waldebbana", *Memorie della Reale Accademia dei Lincei*, II, 97-143.
Conti Rossini, C. (1907) *Historia Regis Sarsa Dengel (Malak Sagad)*, Paris.
Conti Rossini, C. (1942) *Proverbi, tradizioni, e canzone tigrine*, Verbania.
Conti Rossini, C. (1928) *Storia d' Etiopia*, Bergamo.
Conti Rossini, C. (1914-15) "Studi su popolazione dell' Ethiopia IV", *Rivista degli Studi Orientali*, VI.
Conzelman, W.E. (1895) *Chronique de Galawdewos (Claudius) Roi d'Ethiopie*, Paris.
Cortesão, A.(1944) *The Suma Oriental of Tomé Pires*, London.
Cortesão, A. and Thomas, H. (1938) *Carta das Novas que vierama el Rey Nosso Senhor do descrobrimento do Preste Joam*, Lisbão.
Crawford, O.G.S. (1958) *Ethiopian Itineraries ca. 1400-1524*, Cambridge.
Crawford, O.G.S. (1951) *The Fung Kingdom of Sennar*, Gloucester.
Crowfoot, J.W. (1911) "Some Red Sea Ports", *Geographical Journal*, XXXVII, 523-50.
Cuoq, J. (1981) *L'Islam en Ethiopie des origines au XVIe siecle*, Paris.
Dames, M.L. (1918) *The Book of Duarte Barbosa*, London.
Davies, N. de G. (1935) "The Egyptian Expedition of 1934-1935. Trading with the Land of Punt", *Bulletin of the Metropolitan Museum of Art* (1935), XXX, 46-9.
De Slane, W., MacGuckin (1927) I*bn Khaldun, Histoire des Berbères et des dynasties musulmanes de l'Afrique septentrionale*, Paris.
Devic, M.-L. (1892) *Les pays de Zendjs ou la côte orientale de l'Afrique du moyen-age*, Paris.
Dombrowski, F.A. (1985) *Ethiopia's Access to the Sea*, Leiden.
Dombrowski, F.A. (1984) "Some Ideas about the Historical Role of Ethiopia's Access to the Sea", *Northeast African Studies*, VI, Nos. 1-2, 171-7.
Donham, D. and James, W. (1986) *The Southern Marches of Imperial Ethiopia. Essays in History and Social Anthropology*, Cambridge.
Donzel, E.J. van (1979) *Foreign Relations of Ethiopia 1642-1700. Documents Relating to the Journeys of Khodja Murad*, Istanbul.

Donzel, E.J. van (1994) "Primary and Secondary Sources for Ethiopian Historiography. The Case of the Slave Trade", in C. Lepage, *Etudes éthiopiens*, Paris, I, 183-8.
Donzel, E.J. van (1986) *A Yemenite Embassy to Ethiopia 1647-1649*, Stuttgart.
Dozy, R.P.A. and Goeje. M.J. de (1866) *Descrioption de l'Afrique et de Espagne*, Leyden.
Drewes, A.J. (1962) *Inscriptions d'Ethiopie antique*, Leyden.
Erlich, H. (1994) *Ethiopia and the Middle East*, Boulder, Colorado.
Eshete Kebede (1982) *A History of Kistane (Aymallal Gurage), 1800-1941*, Addis Ababa Unversity, Senior Essay.
Esteves Pereira, F.M. (1892= text, 1900=translation) *Chronica de Susenyos, Rei de Ethiopia*, Lisboa.
Esteves Pereira, F.M. (1888) *Historia de Minàs 'Ademas Sagad Rei de Ethiopia*, Lisboa.
Foster, W. (1949) *The Red Sea and Adjacent Countries at the Close of the Seventeenth Century*, London.
Gamst, F.C. (1969) *The Qemant. A Pagan-Hebraic Peasantry of Ethiopia*, New York.
Gaudefroy-Demombynes, M. (!927) *Ibn Fadl Allah, al 'Umari, Masalik al Absar fi Mamalik el Amsar*, Paris.
Getachew Fulle (1985) *The Kingdom of Janjero: An Historical Survey to 1984*, Addis Ababa University, Senior Essay.
Getachew Haile (1984) "Ethiopian Christian Captives in the Territory of the *Arämi*", *Proceedings of the Seventh International Conference of Ethiopian Studies*, Addis Ababa and Uppsala, pp. 113-119.
Getachew Haile (1981) "From the Markets of Damot to that of Bärara. A Note on Slavery in Medieval Ethiopia", *Paiduma*, XXVII, 174-80.
Getachew Haile (1980) "A Preliminary Investigation of the Tomara Tesbe't of Emperor Zar'a Ya'eqob", *Bulletin of the School of Oriental and African Studies*, XLIII, 207-34.
Getachew Haile and Macomber, W.F. (1981) *A Catalogue of Ethiopian Manuscripts Microfilmed for the Ethiopian Manuscript Microfilm Library, Addis Ababa, and for the Hill Monastic Microfilm Library, Collegeville, Minnesota, Collegeville*, Minn. (and other volumes edited by Getatchew Haile alone).
Gibb, H.A.R. (1929) *Ibn Battuta. Travels in Asia and Africa*, London.

Gragg, G.B. (1982) *Oromo Dictionary*, East Lansing, Michigan.
Grühl, M. (1932) *The Citadel of Ethiopia. The Empire of the Divine Emperor*, London.
Guèbrè Sellassié (1930-1) *Chronique du règne de Ménélik II, rois de rois d'Ethiopie*, Paris.
Guidi, I. (1903-5) *Annales Iohannis I. 'Iyasu I et Bakaffa*, Paris.
Guidi, I. (1912) *Annales Regum 'Iyasu II et 'Iyo'as,* Paris.
Guidi, I. (1907) "Strofe e breve testi amarici", *Mitteilungen des Seminars für Sprachen zu Berlin. Westasische Abteilung*, X, 17-184.
Guidi, I. (1889) "Le canzoni geez-amariñña in onore di re abissini", *Rendiconti della Reale Accademia dei Lincei*, IV, 53-66.
Guidi, I. (1901) *Vocabolario amarico-italiano*, Roma.
Guluma Gemeda (1984) *Gomma and Limmu: The Process of State-formation among the Oromo in the Gibe Region*, Addis Ababa University, M.A. thesis.
Guyard, S. (1883) *Géographie d'Aboulféda*, Paris.
Haberland, E. (1964) "The Influence of the Christian Empire on Southern Ethiopia", *Journal of Semitic Studies*, IX, 255-38.
Haile Bubbamo Arficio (1973) "Some Notes on Traditional Hadiya Women", *Journal of Ethiopian Studies*, XI, No. 2, pp. 131-56.
Haile Meskel Gabre Wold (1990) *The Ethiopian Nationalities. A Bibliography*, Addis Ababa.
Haile-Michael Mesginna (1966) "Salt Mining in Enderta", *Journal of Ethiopian Studies*, IV, No. 2, pp. 127-36.
Hamilton, G.M. (1951) *In the Wake of Da Gama. The Story of Portuguese Pioneers in East Africa 1497-1729,* London.
Harris, W.C. (1844) *The Highlands of Aethiopia,* London.
Hecht, E.-D. (1988) "Ethiopia Threatens to Block the Nile", *Azania*, XXIII, 1-10.
Henze, P.B.(1977) *Ethiopian Journeys. Travels in Ethiopia 1969-72*, London.
Herzog, R. (1968) *Punt*, Cairo.
Hess, R.L. (1969) "An Outline of Falasha History", *Proceedings of the Third International Conference of Ethiopian Studies* , I, 99-112, Addis Ababa.
Historiale Description de l'Abyssinie (1558), Antwerp.
Histoire de ce qui s'est passé au royaume d'Ethiopie, (1629), Paris.
Houtsma, M.T. (1883) *Ibn Wadhih qui dictur Historiae*, Leyden.

Hultin, J. (1982) "The Oromo Expansion Reconsidered", *N.E.A. Journal of Research on North East Africa*, I, No. 3, 188-203.
Huntingford, G.W.B. (1955) *The Galla of Ethiopia. The Kingdoms of Kafa and Janjero*, London.
Huntingford, G.W.B. (1965a) *The Glorious Victories of 'Amda Seyon King of Ethiopia*, Oxford.
Huntingford, G.W.B. (1989) *The Historical Geography of Ethiopia. From the First Century to 1704*, London.
Huntingford, G.W.B. (1965b) *The Land Charters of Northern Ethiopia*, Addis Ababa.
Huntingford, G.W.B. (1966) "The Lives of Takla Haymanot", *Journal of Ethiopian Studies*, IV, No. 2, pp. 35-40.
Huntingford, G.W.B. (1980) *The Periplus of the Erythraean Sea*, London.
Huntingford, G.W.B. (1979) "Saints of Medieval Ethiopia", *Abba Salama*, X, 257-326.
Husein Ahmad (1992) "The Historiography of Islam in Ethiopia", *Journal of Islamic Studies*, III, 15-46.
Ibn Hauqal (1954) *Configuration de la terre (Kitab Surat al-Ard)*, Beyrouth and Paris.
Isenberg, C.W. and Krapf, J.L. (1843), *Journals of the Rev. Messrs Isenberg and Krapf*, London.
Jelenc, D.A. (1966) *Mineral Occurences of Ethiopia*, Addis Ababa.
Jensen, A.E. *Im Landes des Gada*, Stuttgart.
Johnston, C. (1844) *Travels in Southern Abyssinia*, London.
Joussaume, R. (1974) *Le Mégalithisme en Ethiopie. Monuments funéraires protohistoriques du Harar*, Paris.
Kaplan, S. (1992) *The Beta Israel (Falasha) iin Ethiopia from Early Times to the Twentieth Century*, New York.
Kaplan, S. (1984) *The Monastic Holy Man and the Christianization of Early Solomonic Ethiopia*, Wiesbaden.
Kessler, D. (1982) *The Falashas. The Forgotten Jews of Ethiopia*, London.
Kidane Mariam Demlew (1987) *The Shanqilla of Metekel: Some Tentative Notes*, Addis Ababa University, Senior Essay.
Kinafe-Rigb Zelleke (1975) "Bibliography of the Ethiopic Hagiographical Traditions", *Journal of Ethiopian Studies*, XIII, No. 2, pp. 57-102.
Kitchen, K.A. (1971) "Punt and How to Get There' , *Orientalia*, XL, 184-207.

Knutsson, K.E. (1967) *Authority and Change. A Study of the Kallu Institution among the Macha Galla of Ethiopia,* Göteborg.
Kolmodin, J. (1916) *Traditions de Tsazzega et Hazzega,* Uppsala.
Kolmodin, J. (1914) *Traditions de Tsazzega et Hazzega. Annales et documents,* Uppsala.
Kramers, J.H. and Wiet, G. (1964) *Ibn Hauqal, Configuration de la terre,* Beirut.
Krapf, J.L. (1867) *Travels, Researches and Missionary Labours,* London.
Kropp, M. (1981) "Zur 'Kurzen Chronik' der äthiopischen Könige", *Oriens Christianus,* LXV, 137-87.
Lange, W.J. (1978) *Domination and Resistance: Narrative Songs of the Kaffa Highlands,* East Lansing, Michigan.
Lange, W.J. (1982) *History of the Southern Gonga (Southwestern Ethiopia),* Wiesbaden.
Lebel, P. (1974) "Oral Tradition and Chronicles on Guragé Immigration", *Journal of Ethiopian Studies,* XII, No. 2. 95-106.
Lefebvre, T. (1845-9) *Voyage en Abyssinie,* Paris.
Legrand, M. (1728) *Voyage historique d'Abissinie du R.P. Jerome Lobo,* Paris.
Leroy, J. (1964) *Ethiopian Painting. In the Middle Ages and under the Gondar Dynasty,* London.
Leslau, W. (1951) *Falasha Anthology,* New Haven, Connecticut.
Leslau, W. (1955) *Gafat Documents,* New Haven, Connecticut.
Leslau, W. (1944) "The Position of Gafat in Ethiopic", *Language,* XX, No. 2. pp. 56-65.
Leslau, W. (1966) "A Short Chronicle of the Gafat", *Rivista degli Studi Orientali,* XLI, 189-98.
Lettere annue di Ethiopia. Del 1624, 1625, e 1626. (1628), Roma.
Levine, D.L. (1974) *Greater Ethiopia. The Evolution of a Multiethnic Society.* New York.
Lewis, H.S. (1965) *A Galla Monarchy. Jimma Abba Jifar, Ethiopia, 1830-1932,* Madison, Wisconsin.
Lewis, H.S. (1966) "The Origins of the Galla and Somali", *Journal of African History,* VII, 27-46.
Lewis, I.M. (1955) *Peoples of the Horn of Africa. Somali. Afar and Saho,* London.
Littmann, E. (1912) *Deutsche Aksum-Expedition,* Berlin.
Lockhart, D.M. (1984) *The Itinerário of Jerónimo Lobo,* London.

Ludolf, H. (1691) *Commentarius ad suam Historiam Aethiopicam*, Frankfurt.
Ludolf, H. (1684) *A New History of Ethiopia*, London.
Ludolf, H. (1689) *Lexicon Amharico-Latinum*, Frankfurt.
Marco Polo (1931) *The Travels of Marco Polo*, London.
Marrassini, P. (1993) *Lo scettro e la croce. La campagna di 'Amda Seyon I contro l'Ifat* (1332), Napoli.
Martial de Salviac (n.d.) *Les Galla. Un peuple antique. au pays de Ménélik*, Paris.
Martin, B.G. (1974) "Arab Migration to East Africa", *International Journal of African Historical Studies*, VII, 367-90.
Maspero, G. (1889) *Egyptian Archaeology*, London.
Maspero, G. (1879) "De quelques navigations des égyptiens sur les cotes de la mer érythrée", *Revue Historique*, V, 10-26.
Mathew, D. (1947) *Ethiopia. The Study of a Polity*, London.
McCrindle, J.W. (1929) *The Christian Topography of Cosmas, an Egyptian Monk*, London.
Merid Wolde Aregay (1977) "Eléni", *The Encyclopedia Africana Dictionary of African Biography*, London, I, 63.
Merid Wolde Aregay (1974a) "Political Geography of Ethiopia at the Beginning of the Sixteenth Century", Accademia Nazionale dei Lincei, *IV Congresso Internazionale di Studi Etiopici*, Roma, II, 613-31.
Merid Wolde Aregay (1974b) "Population Movements as a Possible Factor in the Christian-Muslim Conflict of Medieval Ethiopia", *Symposium Leo Frobenius*, Köln.
Merid Wolde Aregay (1971) *Southern Ethiopia and the Christian Kingdom, 1508-1708, with Special Reference to the Galla Migrations and their Consequences*, London (doctoral dissertation).
Messing, S.D. (1982) *The Story of the Falashas. ""Black Jews" of Ethiopia*, Hamden, Connecticut.
Meynard, J.B. de and Courteille, P. de (1861-1877) *Maçoudi. Les prairies d'or*, Paris.
Mohammed Hassen (1990) T*he Oromo of Ethiopia: A History 1750-1860*, Cambridge.
Mohammed Hassen (1994) "The Pre-Sixteenth-Century Oromo Psesence within the Medieval Christian Kingdom of Ethiopia", in David Brokensha, *A River of Blessings. Essays in Honour of Paul Baxter*, Syracuse, pp. 43-65.

Mondon-Vidailhet, F.M.C. (1900) "Les dialectes éthiopiens du gouraghe", *Revue Sémitique,* VIII, 168-75, 226-74, 370-7, (1901), IX, 64-70.
Mondon-Vidailhet, F.M.C. (1901) "Etude sur le harari", *Journal Asiatique,* XVIII, 401-29, (1902), XIX, 5-50.
Montandon, G. (1913) *Au pays Ghimmira,* Neuchâtel.
Mordini, A. (1940) "Un'antica porta in legno proviente della Chiesa di Gunaguna (Scimezana, Eritrea)", *Rassegna di Studi Orientali,* XIX, 105-107.
Mordini, A. (1959) "La chiesa di Aramò", *Rassegna di Studi Etiopici,* XV, 39-54.
Mordini, A. (1961) "La chiesa di Baraknaha nello Scimezana", *Annales d'Ethiopie,* IV, 131-8.
Moreno, M.M. (1935) *Favole e rime Galla,* Roma.
Munro-Hay, S. (1991) *Aksum. An African Civilisation of Late Antiquity,* Edinburgh.
Munzinger, W. (1869) "Narrative of a Journey through the Afar Country", *Journal of the Royal Geographical Society,* XXXIX, 188-232.
Negaso Gidada (1984) *History of the Sayyoo Oromoo of Southwestern Wallaga, Ethiopia, from about 1886,* Frankfurt am Main (doctoral thesis).
Neville, E. (1894) *The Temple of Deir-el-Bahari, Introductory Memoir,* London.
Oldfather, C.H. (1935) *Diodorus of Sicily,* Cambridge, Mass. and London.
Olmstead, J. (1974) "The versatile *ensete* plant", *Journal of Ethiopian Studies,* XII, No. 2, pp. 147-58.
Orhonlu, C. (1974) *Osmanli Imperatorlugu'nun güney Siyaseti Habes Eyaleti,* Istanbul.
Ostrogorsky, G. (1968) *History of the Byzantine State,* Oxford.
Pais, P. (1945-6) *Historia da Etiopia,* Porto.
Pankhurst, A. (1989) "An Early Ethiopian Map of Tegré", in Taddese Beyene, *Proceedings of the Eighth International Conference of Ethiopian Studies,* Addis Ababa, II, 73-88.
Pankhurst, R. (1973) "Caves in Ethiopian History, with a Survey of Cave Sites in the Environs of Addis Ababa", *Ethiopia Observer,* XVI, 15-35.
Pankhurst, R. (1968) *Economic History of Ethiopia 1800-1935,* Addis Ababa.

Pankhurst, R. (1984) "Early Pharaonic Contacts with the Land of Punt", *Quaderni di Studi Etiopici*, V, 5-19.

Pankhurst, R. (1986) "Ethiopian Royal Seals of the Seventeenth and Eighteenth Centuries", in G. Goldenberg, *Ethiopian Studies. Proceedings of the Sixth International Conference*, Rotterdam, pp. 397-417.

Pankhurst, R. (1976) "The Golden Age of Graeco-Egyptian Discoveries on the Horn of Africa, the Rise and Fall of the Elephant Trade, and the Introduction of Iron into the Region", *Ekkliastikos Faros [title transliterated from Greek]*, I, No. 2, pp. 119-29.

Pankhurst (1981) "Hamasén and the Gondarine Monarchy", *NEA Journal of Research on North East Africa*, I, No. 1, pp. 32-50.

Pankhurst, R. (1977) "The History of Däbrä Tabor (Ethiopia)", *Bulletin of the School of Oriental and African Studies*, XL, Part 2. pp. 235-66.

Pankhurst, R. (1967) "The History of Fire-arms in Ethiopia prior to the 19th. century", *Ethiopia Observer*, XI, pp. 203-55.

Pankhurst, R. (1982b) *History of Ethiopian Towns. From the Middle Ages to the Early Nineteenth Century,* Wiesbaden.

Pankhurst, R. (1961) *An Introduction to the Economic History of Ethiopia*, London.

Pankhurst, R. (1979) "The Kwer'ata Re'su: The History of an Ethiopian Icon", *Abba Salama*, X, 169-87.

Pankhurst, R. (1987) "The Manuscript Bindings of Harar. A Preliminary Examination", *Azania*, XXII, 47-54.

Pankhurst, R. (1988) "Muslim Commercial Towns, Villages and Markets of Christian Ethiopia", in S. Uhlig and Bairu Tafla, *Collectanea Aethiopica*, Stuttgart, pp. 111-30.

Pankhurst, R. (1974a) "The Rock-hewn Church of Gufti Leman, south of Tulu Bolo", *Ethiopia Observer*, XVI, 222-5.

Pankhurst, R. (1974b) "The Rock-hewn Church of Tulu Gabriel, near Adadi, south of the Awash", *Ethiopia Observer*, XVI, 226-7.

Pankhurst, R. (1990) *A Social History of Ethiopia. The Northern and Central Highlands from Early Medieval Times to the Rise of Emperor Téwodros,* Addis Ababa, Kings Ripton, and Trenton, New Jersey.

Parker, E.M. (1971) "Afar Stories, Riddles and Proverbs", *Journal of Ethiopian Studies*, IX, No. 2, pp. 219-87.

Parker, E.M. (1985) *An Afar-English Dictionary*, London.

Parker, E.M. and Hayward, R.J. (1985) *Afar-English-French Dictionary*, London.
Paulitschke, P. (1893, 1896) *Ethnographie Nordost-Afrikas*, I. *Die materielle Cultur der Danakil, Galla und Somal*; II. *Die geistige Cultur der Danakil, Galla und Somal*, Berlin.
Paulitschke, P. (1888) *Harar - Forchungreise nach den Somal und Ländern Ost-Afrikas*, Leipzig.
Perruchon, J. (1893) *Les chroniques de Zar'a Ya'eqob et de Ba'eda Maryam rois d'Ethiopie de 1434 a 478*, Paris.
Perruchon, J. (1894) "Histoire d'Eskender, d'Amda-Seyon II et de Na'od, rois d'Ethiopie", *Journal Asiatique*, III, 319-66.
Perruchon, J. (1889) "Histoire des guerres d"Amda Syon, roi d'Ethiopie", *Journal Asiatique*, XIV, 271-493.
Pirenne, J. (1961) *Histoire de la civilisation de l'Egypte ancienne*, Paris.
Pires, T. (1944) *The Suma Oriental of Tomé Pires*, London.
Pollera, A. (1912) *I Baria e i Cunama*, Naples.
Quatremère, E. (1837-45) *Histoire des sutans Mamlouks,* Paris.
Querin, J. (1978) "The Beta Israel (Felasha) and the Process of Occupational Caste Formation", *Proceedings of the Fifth International International Conference of Ethiopian Studies*, Evanston, Illinois, pp. 133-43.
Reid, J.M. (1968) *Traveller Extraordinary. The Life of James Bruce of Kinnaird*, London.
Reinisch, L. (1889) *Texte der Saho-Sprache*, Wien.
Rey, C.F. (1929) *The Romance of the Portuguese in Abyssinia*, London.
Rinck, F.T. (1790) *Macrizi Historia Regnum Islamiticorum in Abyssinia*, Leiden.
Rochet d' Héricourt, C.F.X. (1841) *Voyage sur la cote orientale de la Mer Rouge*, Paris.
Rodinson, M. (1964) "Sur la question des 'influences juives' en Ethiopie, *Journal of Semitic Studies*, IX, No. 1, pp. 1-10.
Salt, H. (1814) *A Voyage to Abyssinia*, London.
Sauter, R. (1963) "Ou en est notre connaissance ded églises rupestres d'Ethiopie?", *Annales d'Ethiopie*, V, 237-51.
Savard, G.C. (1965) "War Chants in Praise of Ancient Afar Heroes", *Journal of Ethiopian Studies*, III, No. 1, pp. 105-8.
Säve-Söderberg, T. "The Navy of the Eighteenth Egyptian Dynasty", *Uppsala Universitets Arsskrift* (1946), VI, 1-94.

Schoff, W.H. (1912) *The Periplus of the Erythraean Sea*, New York.
Sergew Hable Sellassie (1972) *Ancient and Medieval History of Ethiopia to 1270,* Addis Ababa.
Shack, W.A. (1966) *The Gurage. A People of the Ensete Culture*, London.
Shack, W.A. and Habte-Mariam Marcos (1974) *Gods and Heroes. Oral Traditions of the Gurage of Ethiopia*, Oxford.
Shehim Kesim (1982) "The Influence of Islam on the Afar", University of Washington Ph.D thesis.
Shelemay, K.K. (1986) *Music, Ritual, and Falasha History*, East Lansing, Michigan.
Stinson, L. (1965) "Folk Tales of the Hadiya", *Journal of Ethiopian Studies*, III, No. 2, pp. 87-124.
Sumner, C. (1995) *Oromo Wisdom. I. Proverbs, Collection and Analysis*, Addis Ababa.
Taddesse Tamrat (1970) "The Abbots of Däbrä Hayq, 1248-1535", *Journal of Ethiopian Studies*, VIII, No. 1, 87-117.
Taddesse Tamrat (1972a) *Church and State in Ethiopia 1270-1527*, Oxford.
Taddesse Tamrat (1994) "Ethiopia in Mineature. The Peopling of Gojam", H.G Marcus and G. Hudson, *New Trends in Ethiopian Studies*, Lawrenceville, New Jersey, I, 951-62.
Taddesse Tamrat (1988a) "Ethnic Interaction and Integration in Ethiopian History: The Case of the Gaffat", *Journal of Ethiopian Studies*, XXI, 121-54.
Taddesse Tamrat (1988b) "Processes of Ethnic Interaction and Integration in Ethiopian History: The Case of the Agaw", *Proceedings of the Nineth International Congress of Ethiopian Studies*, Moscow, V, 192-206.
Taddesse Tamrat (1972b) "A Short Note on the Tradition of Pagan Resistance to the Ethiopian Church", *Journal of Ethiopian Studies*, X, No. 1, pp. 137-50.
Takla Sadeq Makweriya (1966E.C.) *YaGrañ Ahmad Warada*, Addis Ababa.
Tayyä Gäbrä Maryam (1914 E.C.) *Yältyopya Hezb Tarik*, Asmara.
Teclehaimanot G. Selassie (1984) *The Wayto of Lake Tana: An Ethno-history*, Addis Ababa University, M.A. Thesis.
Tedeschi, S. (1981) "L'Abissinia nel libro di Marco Polo", *Africa*, XXXVI, 361-89.

Tedeschi, S. (1974) "L'emirato di Harar secondo un documento inedito", *Problemi Attuali di Scienze e di Cultura*, CXCI, 82-101.
Tedeschi, S. (1967-8) "L'Etiopia nella storia di Patriarchi alessandri", *Rassegna di Studi Etiopici*, XXIII, 133-71.
Tedeschi, S. (1979) "Le gesta di 'Amda-Seyon nella cronologia e nella storia", *Rassegna di Studi Etiopici*, XXVII, 123-46.
Tedeschi, S. (1980) "Ludovico de Varthema nel Corno d"Africa", *Africa*, XXXV, 275-80.
Tedeschi, S. (1966) "Poncet et son voyage en Ethiopie", *Journal of Ethiopian Studies*, IV, No. 2, pp. 99-126.
Tedeschi, S. (1989) "Le portrait inédit du negus Lebnä-Dengel ayant appartenu à l' historien Paolo Giovio", *Proceedings of the First International Conference on the History of Ethiopian Art*, pp. 44-52, London.
Tesema Ta'a (1994) "Oral Historiography on Oromo Studies", H.G. Marcus and G. Hudson, *New Trends in Ethiopian Studies*, Lawrenceville, New Jersey, I, 981-92.
Tesema Ta'a (1986) T*he Political Economy of Western Central Ethiopia from the Mid-16th to the Early 20th Centuries*, East Lansing, Mich (doctoral dissertation).
Tessema Chamiso (1982) *History of the Hadiya People from the Beginning of the 19th c. to the 20th c.*, Addis Ababa University, Senior Essay.
Thesiger, W. (1935) "The Awash River and the Aussa Sultanate", *Geographical Journal*, LXXXV, 1-23.
Thomas, H. and Cortesâo, A. (1938) *The Discovery of Abyssinia by the Portuguese*, London.
Tilahun Gamta (1989) *Oromo-English Dictionary*, Addis Ababa.
Tippett, A.R. (1970) Peoples of Southwest Ethiopia, South Pasadena, California.
Trimingham, J.Spencer (1952) *Islam in Ethiopia*, London.
Triulzi, A. (1981) *Salt, Gold and Legitimacy. Prelude to the History of a No-Man's Land. Bela Shangul, Wallagga, Ethiopia (ca. 1800-1898)*, Napoli.
Tsehai Brhane Selassie (1975) "The Question of Damot and Wälamo", *Journal of Ethiopian Studies*, XIII, No. 1, pp. 37-46.
Tuma Nadamo (1982) *A History of Zay in the 19th and Early 20th Centuries*, Addis Ababa University, Senior Essay.
Tutschek, C. (1844) *Dictionary of the Galla Language*, München.

Ullendorff, E. (1968) *Ethiopia and the Bible. The Schweich Lectures 1967*, London.
Urreta, L. de (1610) *Historia de la sagrada orden de predicatores, en los remotos Reynos de la Etiopia*, Valentia.
Urreta, L. de (1610-11) *Historia ecclesiastica, politica, naturel y moral de los grandes y remotos reynos de la Etiopia, monarchia del emperador, llamado Preste Juan de las Indias*, Valentia.
Usoni, L. (n.d.) *Risorse minerarie del'Africa Orientale*, Roma.
Varenbergh, J. (1915-16) "Studien zur abessinischen Reichsordnung (Ser'ata Mangest)", *Zeitschrift für Assyriologie*, XXX, 1-45.
Varthema, L. di (1863) T*he Travels of Ludovico di Varthema*, London.
Vernaux, R. (1899) "Les migrations des Ethiopiens", *L'Anthropologie*, X, 641-62.
Vycichl, W. (1957) "Notes on the Story of the Shripwrecked Sailor", *Kush*, V. 71-2.
Wagner, E. (1975) "Arabische Heilingenlieder aus Harar", *Zeitschrift der Deutschen Morgenländischen Gesellschaft*, CXXV, 28-65.
Waldmeier, T. (1888) *The Autobiography of Theophilus Waldmeier*, London and Leominster.
Weld Blundell, H. (1906) "Exploration in the Abai Basin", *Geographical Journal*, XXVII, 529-51.
Weld Blundell, H. (1922) *The Royal Chronicle of Abyssinia*, Cambridge.
Wendt, K. (1935) "Amharische Geschichte eines Emirs von Harar im XVI Jahrhundert", *Orientalia*, IV, 484-501.
Whiteway, R.S. (1902) *The Portuguese Expedition to Abyssinia in 1541-1543, as Narrated by Castanhoso*, London.
Wiet, G. (1937) *Ya'kubi. Le pays*, Cairo.
Wilson, N.G. (1994) *Photius: The Biblioteca*, London.
Wright, W. (1877) *Catalogue of the Ethiopic Manuscripts in the British Museum Acquired since the Year 1847*, London.
Yaqob Beyene (1987) *Fesseha Giyorgis. Storia d'Etiopia*, Napoli.
Yelma Deressa (1957EC) *Yältyopya Tarik*, Addis Ababa.
Zeltner, F. de (1904) "Le monastère souterrain de Goba", *L'Anthropogie*, XV, 189-94.

INDEX

Abadir, *ahu*, 373
Abädray Gafat, 345
Abäjägay, 258
Abälgi, 66
Abasi Wéra Gäbäya, 141
Abasi, 141, 160
Abati Oromo, 287, 294, 308, 312
'Abbas, Adäl chief, 244
'Abbas, vizier, 182-3, 186, 195-6, 201, 217-19, 223, 228, 243
'Abbas ibn Abun, *imam*, 378
'Abbas ibn Asma' ad-Din, *amir*, 379
Abbé, lake, 52-3, 62-3, 129
'Abd Allah, of Zäsäy, 66
'Abd Allah, of Zäylä', 45
'Abd el-Qader, king, 369, 429
'Abd en-Nasir, 199-200, 207, 209-211, 215, 227-8
'Abdullah ibn 'Ali, 387
Abekan, 335
Abeko, 315
Abél, 172, 222
Abergälé, 409
abéto, 354, 359, 401
Abib, *abba*, 257
Abib, *abba*, 257
Abir, M., 393
Abreham, *abba*, 260
Abreham, Bali ruler, 198
Absama Nur, 180
Abu Bäkr ibn Muhammäd, sultan, 126, 165-7, 221
Abu Bäkr, *amir*, 181, 196, 222
Abu Oromo, 300
Abu'l Fida, 53, 61
abujedid, 408
Abun, *gärad*, 165
abun, 332, 411
Abunah, 192
Achäfär, 268, 300
Ad Kamu, 103-4
'Ad Täklé-zan, 400-1
Ada Dagana, 359
Ada'il, 240, 382, 427
Adadi Maryam, 141
Adäl Mäbräq, 172, 325
"Adal", 61--6
Adäl, vii, 44-6, 52-60, 72, 87, 94-5, 98, 110, 113, 115-31, 133-6, 144, 149

157-61, 165-71, 174-5, 181, 186, 188, 196-7, 201, 204, 207, 210-12, 215, 217-18, 221-4, 226-7, 233, 239, 241-4, 247-9, 254, 259, 265, 270-2, 281-2, 294, 297, 328, 373-6, 398, 426, 433-7, 439-42
Adälih, 173, 198. See also: 'Addalu
Adam ibn Abi Bäkr, 181
Adam Issa, *imam*, 382, 388, 427
Adamo, 86
Adaré, 75, 89. See also: Harär
'Addalu, 172-33, 198-201, 209-10
Addi Baro, 407
Addio, king, *tato*, 90
Addis Aläm, 308
Addis Baro, 408
Addis Zämän, 288
Addolé, vizier, 178, 185, 188, 190, 199-200, 202, 212, 214-16, 218, 223-4, 227, 228
Adefan, 26, 33
Adem, king, 243
Aden, 4, 54, 56, 127, 390, 393
Aden, gulf of, 3-4, 7, 20, 31, 88, 93, 127, 151, 159, 221, 432, 437
Adhani Egzi', *abba*, 76, 87, 97
Adiabari, 27
Adoimara, 392-3, 428
Adräh Tadrus, *imam*, 379
Adulis, 17-20, 24, 26, 31
Afächala Oromo, 310
Afan, 21
Afar country, people, and language, 3, 17, 25, 33, 61-7, 93-4, 104, 106-12, 115, 133, 151, 156-7, 239-40, 270, 382-94, 398, 427-8, 435, 441
Afré, 280
Afra, *bahr nägäsh*, 219, 229
Agamé, 401, 409, 411
Agäw, Agäwmedr, 28-9, 91, 137, 171, 217, 259, 306, 320, 346-7, 352-3, 365
agbert, 267, 275
Agräro, 242
Ahmäd 'Ali, 49. See also: Harb Arad ibn 'Ali
Ahmäd Grañ. See: Ahmäd ibn Ibrahim al-Ghazi, *Imam*
Ahmäd ibn Asma' ad-Din, 379, 427
Ahmäd ibn Ibrahim al-Ghazi, Imam, vii, 165-229, 233, 235, 241, 243, 245,

249-51, 257-8, 264, 268-72, 281-2, 312, 324, 373, 375, 418, 420, 435-9
Ahmäd ibn Isma'il, 219, 229
Ahmäd, or Harb Arad ibn 'Ali, 49
Ahmushuh, *gärad*, 174, 185, 224
Ajanojay, 184
Akäbo Oromo, 308
Akako Oromo, 336
Akäla Guzay, 75, 395, 401, 410
Aksum, Aksumites, vii, 18-24, 26-9, 32, 37, 78, 93, 118, 120, 140, 218, 409, 434
Al-Damutah, 81
Al-Järad Abun ibn Adash, 126
Al-Mas'udi, 37, 53
Al-Mufäddäl ibn Abi'l'-fada'il
Al-Tägrebirdi, 119
Al-Yaqubi, 24, 37, 53
Alaba, 328
Alamalé, 42, 76. See also: Aymälläl
Albuquerque, Afonso d', 105, 127
algum, 17
Ali Gärad, 242, 271
'Ali ibn Da'ud, *amir*, 377
'Ali ibn Säbr ad-din, 40, 49-50
'Ali, *ahu*, 373
'Ali, of Bali, 14th century, 71
'Ali, of Bali, 16th century, 249, 272
Almeida, Manoel de, 154, 252, 265, 279, 282, 302-7, 324, 326, 331, 335-8, 340, 347-50, 354, 368, 379-81, 383, 414, 421-2
Alvares, Francisco, 102-3, 105, 107-9, 111-12, 121-2, 124-5, 131-2, 138-9, 140-3, 145, 147-8, 150, 154, 162, 206, 261, 332
Amajäh, 169
Amäno, 43, 51, 78, 79, 97
Amäta Giyorgis, princess, 113, 157
Amba Geshen, 244
Amba Senayt, 409, 412
amba, 266, 305
amber, 250
Ambisa, 285
Amda Mika'él, *bahr nägash*, 395, 428
'Amda Seyon, emperor, vii, 38, 40-4, 61-71, 73-8, 80, 89, 90-1, 93-4, 96-8, 106, 149, 434
'Amdä Mika'él, of Fätägar, 130, 153
'Amdu, 175-7, 179
Amenemhet, pharaoh, 6, 16
Amanhotep, pharaoh, 13
Amha Iyäsus, prince, 332

Amha Seyon, *aqabé sä'a*t, 117
Amha, 180
Amhara, 42-3, 56, 64, 74, 78, 115, 122, 158, 171, 194, 248, 259, 279, 285, 297, 305, 310, 328, 320-1, 331, 341, 343, 398, 418, 419, 421, 435
Amizo, 317-18, 320, 420, 442
amolé, 25, 151, 392, 431
Amon, 7-12
Amonat, 294 Amoru Oromos, 315
Amoru, 314
amulets, 294, 386
An-Nasir Muhammad ibn Qala'un, sultan, 40
Ana Oromo, 294, 308, 312
'Ananya, 194-5
Anatéwos, *ras*, 334
Anbässa Wedem, king, 80
Andaracha, 267
André, *abba*, 266
'Andurah, 173-4, 222
Anestayos, *ras*, 309
Angot, 42-3, 171, 254, 285, 325, 328, 418
Angotäy, 91, 97
animists, vi, 81, 85, 89, 149, 210, 212, 221, 226, 228-9, 253, 256, 260, 272, 440
anklets, 19
Ankobär, 333
Anoréwos, *abba*, 89, 97
Anso, 361
Antalo, 414
antelopes, 46, 250
Anthony, brother, 115, 129, 150, 155
antimony, 414-16
Antokya, 173, 176, 187 191-2, 198, 206, 224-5
apostasy, 45, 96, 134-6, 181, 186, 193-4, 197-8, 205, 220, 241, 309. See also: convertions; proselytism,
apricots, 46
aqäsän, 228
Aquba Mika'él, *bahr nägäsh*, 238-9, 270, 439
Ar'enä, 287
Aräbabni, 70-1, 73, 97
Arabs, Arabia, 3, 18, 47, 52-5, 59, 61, 95, 104-5, 123, 126-8, 150, 155, 158, 161, 168, 197, 221, 235, 369, 390, 392, 428, 435, 437
'Aram, 188-9
arämi, 134

Aramo, 23
arari bäjer, 159
Arari, 141, 160
Araté, 67
Arbuq, 296
archers, 48, 58, 66, 91, 101, 107, 156-7, 184, 186-7, 190-1, 198, 223, 242, 287, 364. See also: bows; arrows
Argobba, 75, 115
Arho, 107, 113, 156
Arkiko. See: Hergigo
Arkyah, *azmach*, 202
Armah, king, 434
Armenia, Armenians, 38, 333, 388-9, 403
armour, 60, 190, 306, 367-8. See also: coats of mail
Arom, 397
arrows, 28, 64, 91, 107, 133, 157, 184, 186-9, 217-18, , 223, 228, 268, 292, 331, 345, 354-5, 358, 360, 364, 419, 421-2, 440. See also: archers, bows
arsenic, 370
Arsinoe, 17-18
arson, 41, 57-8, 60, 67, 89, 112, 131, 171-4, 181, 184-5, 190, 197, 215, 218, 224, 263, 294, 310, 313, 326, 341, 357, 359, 362, 369
Arsu Oromo, 308
Arussi Oromo, 378
Arutano, 337, 422. See also: Sisgayo
Arwé, 116. See also: Bädlay ibn Sä'd ad-Din
Asa Zänäb, 283
'Asäb, 109
Asad, 72
Asädä Mika'él, 68
Asbeha, king, 28
Asébo, 205, 226
asgwa, 130, 158
Asgwagwa, 308
Ashangi, lake, 302
Ashmän Gafat, 345
ashraf, 126
ashrafi, 378
Asim Bäläw, 362-2
Asmä Giyorgis, *abéto*, 402
Asma' ad-Din, of Adäl, 375
Asma' ad-Din, of Wäj, 247
Asmära, 23-24, 93, 395
asses, wild, 46, 266. See also: donkeys
Asta, 27
Astaboras, 27

Astér, *wäyzero*, 365
Atbara, place and river, 5, 27, 300, 319, 353, 362-3, 369, 371, 429, 443
aubergines, 46
Aue, 24
Avalites, 21, 31, 53
Awa Gyät, 75
Awadi Näto, 316
Awälamo, 89
Awash river, 46-7, 52-3, 61-3, 66, 68, 115, 118-19, 137-9, 153, 159, 178-9, 185, 188, 198, 239, 311, 333, 419
Awat, See: Ifat
Awra'i 'Uthman ibn Dar 'Ali, 104, 171, 182-4, 186-7, 193-5, 197, 210, 212-15, 224
Awra'i Abun, 180, 195-62, 224
Awssa Gurrelé, 381
Awssa, 44, 52, 66, 239-40, 270, 374-6, 378-82, 388, 391-4, 426-7, 440
Ax Gagce, 266
Ayadar, *ras*, 414
'Ayfärs, 117, 173, 187, 198, 222
Aygäbäz, *teqaqen*, 355
Ayker, 210
Aymälläl, 42, 75-6, 138, 159, 297-8, 328. See also: Alamalé
'Ayn Faräs, 117, 173. See also: 'Ayfärs
'Azam. See also: 'Aram
Azé, 264-5, 274
azmach, 182
azzaj, 130, 252
Bä'edä Maryam, emperor, 106-7, 110, 112-15, 119-20, 131-2, 134-5, 138, 141-2, 145, 156, 158-60, 190, 436-7, 442
Baasa, 360
Bäb Sari, 173
Bädancho, *shum*, 253-6, 273, 439
Bädel Neb, 258
Badeqé, 171, 183-5, 187, 223
Badi. See: Basé
Bädlay ibn Sä'd ad-Din, sultan, of Adäl, 59, 116-17, 119
Bädlay, *behtwädäd*, 202
Bägémder, 42, 171, 203, 229, 248, 285, 292, 294, 297, 299, 305, 308, 317, 319-21, 343, 347, 418-19, 440
Bähela, 73
Bahr Gamo, 77, 209
Bahr Nägash, ruler and country, 21, 37, 101-6, 147, 155-6, 171, 175, 218-20, 228, 233-9, 241, 248, 259, 270, 297,

THE ETHIOPIAN BORDERLANDS 472

366, 394-417, 429-30, 433, 436, 438-9, 441
Bahr Sägäd, 172-3
Bahrey, *abba*, 137, 279-83, 285-6, 289-92, 301, 324-7, 340, 418, 421, 423, 426
Bairu Tafla, 302
Bäkaffa, emperor, 317-20, 344, 361, 410, 420, 425, 442
Bäkru Sälomon, *bahr nägash*, 413
Bäl'am, prophet, 78
Balae Oromo, 300
Bäläs, 359
Bäläw 'Abdu, 206, 213, 226
Bäläw Sägäd, 212
Bäläw, 104, 171, 186, 193, 224, 353, 359, 362-3
Bäläya, 217, 228, 267, 275, 352, 363, 424
Bali, 71-3, 110, 116, 120, 133-7, 143, 158-60, 168, 171, 173, 179-80 182-3, 196-201, 209-10, 222, 224-5, 241, 249, 259, 271-2, 282, 284, 297, 304, 324-5, 328, 418, 420-1, 438-9
Bambolo-Mellash, 401-2, 405-7, 410
Bamo, *gärad*, 116, 143-4, 160
bananas, 46
Bäni Shangul, 329, 217, 228. See also: Bela Shangul
Bankwal, 38
Banyan, 416
Bänyat, *ras*. See: Näbyat, *ras*
Bäqla, 23, 32, 106, 395, 402, 428-30
Bär Sä'd ed-Din, country, 52, 244, 246
Baraka river, 28
Baraknaha, 23
Bärânta Oromo, 293
Bärära, 88, 142, 150, 185
Bäräytuma Oromo, 279, 299, 328
bärbado, 290
Barbaria, 24
Barbosa, Duarte, 127
bärellé, 416
bareya, 356-7, 425
Bareyas, 26-8, 32, 87, 91-2, 97, 154-5, 204, 356, 401, 425, 433, 435, 442
bari, 27
Barka, 361
barley, 127, 131-2
barter, 71, 74. See also: "primitive money"
Bärtuma Oromo, 293, 298
Barut, 57

Barwa, 51
Basé, 37
Baselyos, *däjazmach*, 411
Bässo Oromo, 313-19, 382, 387, 420
basuto, 260
Batavia, 390, 404. See also: Dutch East Indies
Bätera Amora, 280, 288
Bati Del Wänbära, 168, 190, 221, 242, 245, 271
Batkom, 358
Bätro, 354
Baylul, 108, 248, 384-92, 428
Bazén, Bazin, 28
Bäzitu, 40
Bazmeli, 191
Be'elä Krestos, *abéto*, 354-5, 359
beads, 340, 370, 408
beans, 46
Beber river, 338
beer, 9, 26
bees, bee-hives, 112, 167. See also: honey
Béga, 26-7, 32. See also: Béja
behtwädäd, 140-1, 153, 317, 420
Béja, 26, 32, 239, 270
Beke, C.T, 91
Bela Shangul, 217
Bénaro, *shum*, 296, 334-7, 422, 440
Benesho, 351
Bent, J.T., 27
Bequlzar, 41, 46
Bérababo, 262, 274, 344
Berbera, 21, 32, 126-7
berellë, 408
Bermudes, João, 181, 215, 241-4, 249-50, 257, 260-1, 266, 271-2, 274, 279, 284, 418
Bernier, F., 389
Bersabesh, queen, 320
Besaräh, 189, 223
Bétä Wäläto, 309
bétä mängestaya, 85
Bicini, Hieronimo, 132
Bieber, F., 90
Bifolé, *luba*, 282, 290, 325, 418. 421
Bilat, king-magician, 82, 85, 89
Biralé, 320, 420
Birbir river, 338
birds, 243
Birmaji, *luba*, 280, 287, 292, 326, 340, 419
bishops, 54, 263, 274. See also: priests

Bizamo, 151, 154, 162, 265, 275, 295, 297-8, 307, 327-8, 335, 336, 346-7, 421, 424, 433, 436, 439-40
boats, 185, 389-90, 415
"Bonga king", *tato*, 267
Bonga, 267
Bora, 27
Boran Oromo. See also: Boran
Borän, 279-80, 285-8, 292, 294, 336, 340-1, 347
Bosha, 80, 96, 256, 267, 272-3, 275, 433, 438
bows, 28-9, 63, 65-6, 133, 184, 218, 268, 331, 364, 422
bracelets, 18, 239, 334, 339, 416
brass, 18, 369. See also: bronze
bread, 9, 26, 131
Breasted, J.H., 5-6
bridles, 399, 401
British, 370
bronze, 41. See also: brass
Bruce, J., 106-7, 216, 236-8, 244, 267, 317-23, 320, 329, 331-3, 339-40, 344, 347, 349, 351-3, 355, 358, 360-6, 368, 370-2, 392-3, 413, 415-17, 420, 423, 425, 428, 442
Budge, E.A.W., 258
buffaloes, 257, 292, 306
Bugna, 64
Buko, *dajäzmach*, 292, 296, 300
Bur, 101, 103, 234, 297, 395, 409, 412
Buré, 311
burnouses, 106, 192
burnus, 192
Bursa Oromo, 313 316
butter, 46, 103, 112, 332, 371, 390, 403, 433
Cafres, 338
Cairo, 40, 105, 111, 119, 126, 156, 339, 368
Cambay, 115
camels, 47, 53-4, 63, 110, 115, 128, 155, 157, 362-3, 370, 384, 392-3
candles, 404
Canfella, 102
carpets, 174, 211, 237, 267, 270, 384, 408, 414, 433
Castanhoso, Miguel de, 219-20
castration, 67, 79, 96, 284, 299-300, 313, 315, 357
cattle, 10, 13, 25-6, 28-9, 32, 48, 51, 53, 70-1, 73, 81, 89-90, 105, 110, 112, 127, 132, 141, 148, 150, 160-2, 169,

173, 188, 190, 221, 223-4, 234, 244, 250, 255, 257-8, 267, 272, 274, 282, 285, 287-9, 295-6, 299-300, 304, 310, 314-15, 318, 321, 325, 330, 335-6, 338-9, 341, 343-5, 350, 358, 362, 370, 397, 407, 433. See also: livestock; oxen
cauliflowers, 46
cavalry. See: horses, horsemen
caves, 138-9, 159, 314, 331-3, 354, 357-9, 365. See also troglodytes
cereals, 46, 70, 73, 132
Cerulli, E., 119, 374, 376, 391
Ceylon, 12, 24
Chäfänta Oromo, 313, 316
Chäleha Oromo, 300, 314-5
Chaliya Oromo, 280
Chamo, lake, 143
chan, 311
Chära, 90, 292
chat, 42, 46, 177-8
Chaul, 125
chäwa, 103, 113, 120, 130-1, 135, 158-9, 325, 421. See also: soldiers
cheetahs, 15
Chelga, 368-70, 429
Cherkin Nächo, 363
Cherkin, 371
chickens, 46, 250
children, 8-9, 14-15, 43, 58-9, 70, 78, 110, 141, 165-6, 170, 180, 180, 195, 200, 202, 247, 252, 255, 262-3, 266, 285, 288-9, 295-6, 299-300, 303, 312, 318, 320, 334, 336, 346, 351, 362, 369, 382, 427
China, 385
Chomän swamp, 154, 162, 215
Chomé, 346
Christianity, 21, 32, 81-7, 124, 134-5, 141, 171, 193, 229, 241, 252-3, 255-6, 266-7, 271, 273, 275, 298-9, 309, 318, 334, 423, 439
Christians, vi, 51-3, 60, 63, 68, 72, 81, 104, 112, 122, 124, 126, 131, 134-7, 140, 142, 145, 165-6, 175-6, 191, 193, 197, 201, 212, 219, 222, 224, 227, 257, 312, 315, 326, 329, 357, 366, 422
churches, 23-4, 42, 51, 56, 58, 60, 63, 68, 75-6, 86, 88-9, 98, 103, 111-12, 116, 122-3, 130-1, 137, 141, 144, 146, 149, 151, 160-1, 169, 171-2, 174, 176, 181, 184, 191-2, 198, 201, 205, 207, 215, 219-20, 222, 224, 226, 243, 255,

273, 343, 404, 413. See also: monasteries
cinnamon, 12
circumcision, 54, 289, 292
citrons, 46, 93
civet, vii, 169, 250, 371, 390, 432
cloth, 20, 71, 103, 105-6, 125, 154, 162, 169, 185, 202, 223, 262, 270, 302, 340, 346-9, 372, 374, 381, 390, 407, 414, 416, 433
clothes, 18-19, 43-4, 47, 60, 63, 69, 71, 73, 85, 120-1, 123, 143-5, 147, 155, 162, 173, 178, 192, 198, 208, 216, 221, 234-5, 237-8, 255, 260, 270, 274, 307-8, 311, 315, 319, 334-5, 338, 369, 374, 377, 386, 401, 414-15, 423
cloves, 414
coats of mail, 180, 306. See also: armour
coffee, 177-8, 340, 370
Coimbra, 241
coins, 23, 30, 33, 115, 376, 378, 407-8, 412, 426. See also: money
Coloe, 18-20, 32
concubines, 64, 85, 198, 201, 255
Constantinple, 211, 339, 396. See also: Istanbul
Conti Rossini, C., 81, 238
conversions, 115, 124, 149, 162, 179, 193, 199-200, 203, 205, 216, 219-20, 224-6, 228-9, 234, 253-5, 262-3, 266, 271, 316, 334, 343, 345, 438-9. See also apostasy; proselytism
copper, 18-19, 416
Copts, 40, 55, 387
Corsali, Andrea, 127-8, 142
cotton, 19, 47, 307, 340, 370, 374, 407-8, 416. See also: cloth
craftsmenm 146, 165
Crawford, O.G.S., 115, 129
cucumbers, 46
cups, 19
Däbänawi, 252
Däbayna, 362, 372
Däbrä Abbay, 38
Däbrä Abreham, 288
Däbrä Berhan, 113, 130,143, 157-8, 179, 411
Däbrä Bizän, 37-8, 93, 101, 233-4, 269
Däbrä Damo, 234, 269, 439
Däbrä Gärza, 312
Däbrä Krestos, 403, 405, 430
Däbrä Libanos, Shäwa, 116, 121, 266, 275, 312

Däbrä Libanos, Tegray, 22, 37-8
Däbrä Marqoréwos, 91
Däbrä Marqos, 296, 340
Däbrä Maryam, 37, 97, 101
Däbrä Me'raf, 88, 149
Däbrä Meshwa'e, 122
Däbrä Metmaq, 116
Däbrä Sahin, 130
Däbrä Tabor, 385
Däbrä Wärq, 299
däbtära, 280
Dädader Haqq ad-Din, 41
Dafella, 102
Dägano, 324, 421
daggers, 3, 7, 31
Dägu Dägumäñ, 138, 159
Dägwe, 45
Daharagot, *dajazmach*, 214-16, 227, 238, 243, 262, 287
Dahlak islands, 18, 24, 219, 229, 416, 438
Dähondur, 213-14, 227, 258
dakano, dakanu, 104
Däkär, 56, 59, 122, 158, 373
Däma Krestos, *shum*, 330, 422
Dämbächa, 296
Dambaguina, 236
Dämbeya, 217-18, 268, 286, 305, 306, 419
Damot, 42, 47, 64, 76-7, 81-9, 96, 108, 110, 112, 120, 137, 143-4, 149-52, 159, 161, 172, 177, 183, 204-6, 212-15, 222, 226-7, 252-3, 257-60, 263, 264, 272-3, 287-8, 296-8, 300, 307, 311, 318-20, 324, 328, 340-44, 346, 419-20, 423-4, 433-40, 442
dancing, 126, 310
Danél, king, 28
Dangela, 299
Dangesh, 354, 359
Dangura, 363
Dankali area, 25, 32, 62, 106, 156, 248, 254, 259, 297, 379, 383-4, 386-7, 391. See also: Afar
Däq Asgädé, 402
Dar el-Bahri, 7-13
Dära, 310
Däräbi Oromo, 319
Darago, 294
Därbeta, 395
Därha, 73-4, 203, 222
das, 63
Datalg 'Ali, 65

dates, 106
Davis, N. de Garis, 14-15
Däwaro, 43, 58, 69-70, 73, 98, 116, 119 129, 133-6, 142, 144, 158-60, 165, 171-83, 186, 192 196-201, 204, 213, 218, 222-3, 225, 228, 241-2, 249, 254, 270-1, 282-5, 290, 304, 324-6, 328, 335, 418, 420-1, 435-7, 438-9
Dawé, 280, 287. See also: Jawi
Dawit Era, queen, 120
Dawit I, emperor, 38, 51-2, 57-8, 68, 94, 114-15, 132, 158, 435-6
Dawit III, emperor, 244, 317-18, 361, 420, 425
deb anbäsa, 117
Debarwa, 102, 105, 156, 219, 234-7, 239, 269-70, 395, 404, 413, 429, 439
Debene-Wemas, 393-4
Debleyés, *däjazmach*, 410
Degälhan, *azmach*, 168, 197, 224
Degna Jan, king, 80, 96, 434
Degsa, 103, 413
Degu, 360
Dehana, 369, 383, 427
Dehono, 37, 104, 156, 174, 218, 238. See also Hergigo
Del Méda, 173
dela guto, 303
Delhoya, 45
Demah, 28, 91
Den Gafat, 345
Deneya Ambära, 241, 244
Densa Oromo, 319
devils, 85
Dewise Oromo, 317
dhalatta, 295
Dias, Ayres, 241, 243, 249, 271
Diaspolis, 18
Digalus Oromo, 293
Diho, 143
Dilamo, 314
Dima, 309
dinar, 47, 115
Dincha river, 351
Diodorus of Sicily, 17, 27
dirhem, 47, 49, 115,
Dobe'a, 106-7, 110-12, 149, 156, 161-2, 190, 224, 254, 259, 275, 351, 362, 436
dogs, 9, 144, 371,
Dongola, 368, 371
donkeys, 15, 73, 132, 173, 257, 266, 315, 334, 381, 384, 433
Dori, chief, 103, 155

drums, 48, 117, 216, 218, 238, 345, 354, 369, 399, 410
Duba'ah, 174, 190, 224. See also: Dobe'a
Dubani "Shanqellas", 358
Dufar, 128
Dukham river, 183-5, 165, 223
dulaguto, 287
Dura river, 352, 357, 360
Durbit, 137, 150
Dutch East Indies, 403-4. See also: Batavia
Dutch, 389
Ebenat, king, 294
ebony, 9-10, 13-4
Eddir, 168
Egypt, Egyptians, 3-16, 18, 26, 31-2, 40-1, 45-6, 59, 70, 104-5, 119, 127, 146, 150, 198, 235, 243, 368-9, 386, 411, 416, 434
Egyptus Novelo, 91-2, 133
Egzi'e Kharäya, 85
Ekua river, 66
Ela Zogä, 354
electrum, 5, 10-11
Eléni Mehmät, 145-7, 160
elephantegoi, 17
Elephantine, 5-6
elephants, 17-18, 24, 27, 31, 104, 365
Ella Abraha, king, 28
Emfraz, 203, 272, 294, 439
Emmha Gärä Krestos, 398-401
Emu, 9
Emzoraja, 130
Enarya, 78, 80, 86, 96-7, 150-2, 152, 159, 204, 206, 212, 225-7, 251-6, 262, 272-3, 293, 296, 298, 305-6, 315, 327-8, 331, 333-40, 343, 398, 421-3, 433, 438, 438-40
Endärta, 42, 106, 237, 409, 412, 421-2
Endreyas, *abba*, 266
Ennämor, 330-1, 422
Ennamora, 344
Enselal, 149
ensete, 262, 327, 335, 342-3, 422
Entotto, 75
epidemics, 110, 316
eraq masäré, 149
erawya, 256
Erubat, king, 369
Eshäté, *balambaras*, 363
Eskender, king, 88, 107, 121 130, 132-3, 157-8, 192, 224, 245
Eslam Dähar, 204-6, 226

Eslamo, *behtwäddäd*, 187, 191
eunuchs, 79. See also: castration
Europe, Europeans, 105, 185, 243
Ewostatéwos, *abunä*, 411
Ewostatéwos, saint, 38
Ezana, king, 21, 23, 27-8, 32, 434
Fädsé, 41
Fäläga Agat, 113
Fälashas, 79, 243, 271, 293, 325, 334, 357
famines, 246-7, 271, 288, 344, 373
Fan'il. See: Fanu'él
Fänfära, 378
Fanu'él, azmach, 165, 180, 205, 242, 244-5, 271
färäglä ademnät, 130, 158
färäng, 243. See: Europe, Europeans
Färäshäham Ali, 203
Färäshäham Din, 180, 189-90, 196, 223-5
Farés, *ras*, 313, 358
Fasil Wäräñña, 321
Fasilädas Iyasu, prince, 404, 429
Fasilädäs, emperor, 307-8, 344, 354-5, 357, 359, 382, 387-8, 397-8, 400-2, 419, 421, 424, 429, 442
Fasilo, 262
Fätägar, 42, 54, 68-9, 98, 104, 118, 122-3, 130-2, 158-9, 170-2, 182-6, 190, 201, 222-3, 242, 248, 254, 282, 285, 290, 297-8, 304, 324-6, 328, 418, 421, 437-9
Fazughli, 354, 369, 372
feasts, 255
Felepos, *abba*, 37
Felipe III, king, 304, 428
Fernandez, Antonio, 335
Fesé Bädin, 296
Fesen, 344
Fesseha Krestos, 357-8
Fesseha Seyon, 84, 86. See also: Täklä Haymanot, saint
fever, 132, 269
Fez, 111
figs, 46, 132
fire-arms, 168, 198, 214, 221, 233, 236-7, 242, 246, 253, 267, 269-70, 284, 288, 296, 306-9, 313, 315, 316-19, 357-8, 369, 375, 381, 387, 393, 395, 408-11, 413, 416, 419, 424, 428-9, 432-3, 437, 439
fish, 132
flags, 411

flutes, 218, 345
forests, 112, 132, 148, 153, 159, 217, 228, 313, 342, 349, 358. See also: trees
frankincense, 24. See also: incense; myrrh
French, 355, 359, 369, 389, 404
fruit, 9, 46, 68, 70, 73, 111, 127, 132, 150, 342
Fung, 369, 397, 443
Fur, 63
Futuh al-Habasha, 165, 167, 169-71, 174-5, 183-5, 187, 191-3, 199, 200-3, 206, 208-9, 211, 218-19, 226, 279
Ga'éwah, queen, 216, 235-6, 269
Gäb, 143
Gäbal, 41
Gäbala, 44
gäbar, 267, 283, 289, 295, 325, 355, 421
gäber, 267, 283
Gäbo, 362
Gäbrä Endreyas, *abba*, 125, 158, 437
Gäbrä Endreyas, nobleman, 136
Gäbrä Iyäsus, 120, 135, 157
Gäbrä Le'ul, *blatténgéta*, 355
Gäbrä Maryam, *abba*, 411
Gäbrä Maryam, *bahr nägash*, 397
Gäbrä Mäsqäl, king, 22
Gada , Abba, 314, 322
gada, 280, 295
Gädäb Hamid, 120
Gadawi, 113
Gädayto, *gärad*, 144, 160
Gäfägäf, 326
Gafat, 75, 89-90, 96, 152-4, 159, 161, 194, 204, 206, 211-12, 215-16, 225-7, 248, 253, 257, 260-4, 272, 274, 306, 325, 328, 344-7, 421, 423-4, 434-5, 438-40
Gäläna river, 324
Gälawdéwos Mästäfa, *däjazmach*, 358, 359
Gälawdéwos, emperor, vii, 168, 181-2, 186, 196, 209, 215, 223, 228-9, 233-4, 236, 241-3, 245-6, 250-1, 256-8, 260-2, 264, 266, 269-73, 282-6, 327, 355, 358, 418, 438-9
Gali Gafocho, *tato*, 267, 440
Gali Ginocho, *tato*, 351, 424
Galla language, 293, 321, 420, 442
Galla river, 137, 158
Gallan Oromos, 300

Gallas, 137, 158, 239, 141, 251, 279, 281-4, 293, 303-7, 309, 311, 317-20, 329, 333, 336, 338, 362, 378, 362, 393, 416, 418-19, 422-3, 427, 439. See also: Oromos
Gam, 110, 135
Gama, Christovão da, 219-20
Gamaro, 90
Gämbo, 89, 154, 162, 215, 262, 266, 274-5, 327, 347, 421
Gämo, 77, 97, 143, 204, 209-10, 225-6, 279-80, 297-8, 327-8, 421, 433, 438
Gamu. See: Gamo
Ganale Doria river, 71
Ganäzo, 143
Ganqa, 335, 339
Gänz, 80, 110, 142, 170, 172, 179, 189, 199, 204-5, 209-10, 215, 225, 228, 259, 297-8, 328
Gär'alta, 409, 412
Gärä Krestos Hab-Sellus, 405-7
Gärä Krestos Samson, *käntiba*, 398
Gärä Maryam, *käntiba*, 412-13
Gärä Sellasé, 398
gärad, 116, 118, 120, 133, 135, 142-3, 160, 249, 421
gardens, 68, 138, 243, 271, 437
Gatur, 174
gazelles, 46, 105
Gazgé, 361
geber, 103
Gebergé, 142, 160, 179, 204-5
Gedaref, 369, 429, 443
Gedayä, 41
Genasere, 129
Gend Bärät, 285, 311, 316
Gende Belo, 113, 115, 129, 157, 191, 224
Gerar, peninsula, 102, 156
Geraya, 294
Geri Somali, 378
Gesi, 360
Getachew Haile, 134
ghaya, 387
Giba Nechocho, *tato*, 267
Gibé river, 266, 315, 339, 348
Gidäya, 373
Gimira, 90, 351
ginger, 115, 150
Ginjar, 366
giraffe, 12
Gisa, 357, 360
Gito, 76

Giyorgis, 16th century nobleman 176-7,
Giyorgis, Bosha ruler, 256, 273
Giyorgis, *ras*, 355
glass, 18, 416
goats, 53, 70, 73, 81, 105, 132, 384, 393, 398, 433
Goba, 137, 159
Gobäna, 321
Gogälä, 143
Gojjam, 28, 42, 64, 103, 120, 135-8, 146, 186, 248, 287, 294, 297-9, 305, 307-8, 310-11, 314, 319, 328, 331, 333, 335, 340, 344-7, 352-4, 418-19, 423, 440
gold, vii, 5, 9-14, 16, 19, 25, 28-33, 41-3, 47, 53, 56, 60, 63, 80, 84, 86, 88, 93-4, 96, 101, 104-5, 111, 121, 127, 137, 150, 153, 156, 162, 169-71, 174, 185, 191-2, 201-2, 212, 217, 221, 223, 227, 235, 239, 243-4, 250, 252, 255, 257-8, 260, 262, 272-4, 297-8, 306, 311, 318-19, 335-6, 337-40, 344, 364-5, 369, 371-2, 381, 386, 401, 404, 407-8, 415-17, 424-5, 431-3
Gondär, 308, 312, 314, 317, 319-22, 331, 339, 344, 355, 357, 360-3, 365-6, 368-70, 383, 387, 389, 391, 397-401 405-13, 416, 419-20, 425, 427, 429, 441-2
Gonga, 297-8, 306, 352-5, 360-1, 363, 365-6, 401, 404-6, 408, 412-13, 416, 424, 442
Gorgora, 294
Gorgoreyos, *abba*, 338
gorsa, 290
Gorsi, 357
gossa, 295
grain, 105 110-11, 127, 197, 246, 262, 304, 311, 340, 390-1
grapes, 46, 49, 150. See also: vines
Greece, Greeks, 17, 26, 59, 111, 150
grinding-mills, 42, 64, 66, 266
Guba'é, 285, 288. See also: Guzara
Guba, 353, 416
Gudär river, 329
Gudola, 143
Gudru Oromo, 280, 313-5
Guét, 45
gueta, 296
Guidi, I., 392
gult, 78
Guman, 306
Gumär, 256, 272-3

Gunaguna, 23
Gura Oromo, 308
Gura'é, 75
Guragé, 42, 75-7, 89, 96-7, 138-41, 146, 150, 159, 204-7, 211-13, 225-6, 247, 250-1, 256, 272, 297-8, 327-33, 343, 421-2, 433, 435, 437-440
Gurati Tuläma, 309
gurba, 289
gutu, 301-2
Guzara, 285, 288
Gwangwél, 321, 370
Gwemcho, 293, 334, 422
Hab Sellus Gära Sellasé, *däjazmach*, 399-406, 429
Habtä Ab, 104
Habtä Iyäsus, 402
Hadäbo, 143
Hadeya, 43, 51, 71-80, 97, 103, 116, 141-8, 159-61, 170, 199, 204, 207-8, 210, 226-8, 241, 247, 249, 251, 264-5, 272, 274, 284, 297-8, 327, 329, 333-4, 398, 421-2, 433-440, 442
Hägära, 66
hair styles, 64-5, 281, 301, 303-4, 331
Hajäya, 67
Hajirah, 197
Hakako Oromo, 280
hakuna, 70, 73, 98, 336
Haläb, 143
halabdo, 289
Halay, 103
Halibo, *azzaj*, 286
Halqa, 311
Hamaj, 204, 216, 228
Hamälmäl, 245
Hamasén, 21, 37-8, 93-4, 101-3, 133, 156, 218-19, 228, 234, 238, 317, 395, 397-400, 402-6, 409-14, 429-30, 434, 436, 438, 441
Hamid ibn Nasir, *wazir*, 375
Hamus Wänz, 294
Hankasha, 299
Haqq ad-Din [II] ibn Ahmäd, of Ifat, 49-50, 95
Haqq ad-Din [I] ibn Muhammad ibn 'Ali, of Ifat, 41, 95
Haräfa, 341
Harär, 74-5, 165-7, 169-70, 190, 197, 207, 224, 239, 242, 244-7, 271, 283-4, 376-8, 380, 382, 418, 426-7, 438, 440
Harb Akäl Gafat, 345
Harb Arad ibn 'Ali, 49

Harb Jaush, 56-7 72
Harb Wash Gafat, 345
hares, 105
Hargayä, 41
Harjah, 58
Harla, 45
Harmhab, pharaoh, 15
Harmufa, *luba*, 285, 418
Häro Oromo, 314
Harris, W.C., 393-4
Hasab Bäwäsän, 116-17, 134
Hasän ibn Ahmäd, al-Haymi, 382, 387-8, 428
Hasän, 216
Hasgwa Din, 244
hatchets, 3, 7, 31
Hathor, 8
Hatshepsut, queen, 7-13
Haydära, 43, 69-70, 73, 98
Hayq, lake, 87, 293
Hazo, 329-330
hedug ras, 148
hegäno, 141
Heggä wäsera'atä mängest, 90
Hejaz, 53, 59
hensät, 262. See also: *enset*
herbs, 137
Hergigo, 37, 93-4, 102, 104-5, 155-6, 174, 219, 229, 239, 254, 259, 413, 415, 417, 428, 430, 438. See also: Arkiko
hippopotamus, 18, 365
History of the Patriarchs of Alexandria, 81
Hizanäh Zähl, 378
Hoko Oromo 280
Holy War, 166-7, 191, 200-2. See also: *jihad*.
honey, 46, 104, 112, 156, 272, 315, 371, 390, 394, 398, 401, 415, 433. See also: bees, beehives
Hormuz, 59
Horo Oromo, 314, 316
horses, horsemen, 48, 53, 59, 70, 76-7, 90, 97, 103, 107, 110-12, 127, 131, 136-7, 156, 161, 173-4, 180, 182, 188, 194-7, 200-2, 206, 208,-9, 214-15, 217, 237, 242, 246-7, 251, 257, 264, 266, 270, 283, 286, 291, 295, 304-6, 320-21, 329-31, 339, 366-9, 371, 375, 385, 395, 400, 418, 425, 433, 443
Hosayn, 199, 222
Hubat, 166-7

hunting, 281, 292, 298, 365, 425
Huntingford, G.W.B., 29, 39, 41, 61, 69, 262, 381
hutbäh, 55
hyenas, 46 144
Ibn al-Wardi, 53
Ibn Batutta, 53
Ibn Fadl Allah al'Umäri, 45-9, 70-1, 73-4, 79, 88, 94, 98, 115
Ibn Hawqal, 28, 53
Ibn Khaldun, 88
Ibn Sa'id, 61
idols, 85-6, 253, 263, 299
Ifat, vii, 39-52, 56-7, 61-2, 64, 68-72, 74, 78, 80, 94-5, 97-8, 104, 113-16, 118, 129, 157, 170, 173, 178, 185, 190-8, 222-4, 285, 297-8, 305, 324-6, 328, 420, 434-8
ijartu, 289
Illamo Oromo, 377
Ilma Gwozit, 295, 419
ilma gossa, 295
ilman, 289
imam, 122
Inar'it, 80, 96. See also: Enarya
incense, 9, 14, 17, 31, 340. See also: frankincense; myrrh; sandal wood
India, Indians, 3, 12, 18-19, 24, 32, 59, 103, 111, 115, 127, 129, 147, 150, 243, 249, 339, 385, 395, 414-15, 417
Iraq, 59
iron, 18-19, 28, 47, 59, 63, 70, 73, 98, 138, 321, 335, 369, 399
Isenberg, K.W., 393-4
Islam, viii, 57, 59, 61, 71, 73, 77, 94, 134, 136, 150, 159, 161, 180, 186-6, 192-5, 197, 199, 201-2, 205, 214, 216, 220, 224-6, 229, 241, 249, 378, 387, 426, 434, 438. See also: Muslims
Israel, 31
Istanbul, 235. See also: Constantinople
Italian Geographical Society, 90, 251, 351
Italy, Italians, 19, 351
Ittu Oromo, 294-5
ivory, vii, 3, 9-10, 13, 18, 20, 31, 93-4, 127, 156, 162, 169, 372, 390, 415-16, 432
Iyasu Hab-Sellus, 405
Iyasu I, emperor, 308-17, 333-4, 339, 344, 357-60, 370, 389, 402-8, 419, 422-3, 424, 429, 441

Iyasu II, emperor, 319-21, 362, 370-1, 411 420, 425-6, 443
Iyäsus Mo'a monastery, 293
Iyäsus, *gädam*, 75
Iyo'as, emperor, 320-1, 323, 363, 413, 425
Iyosyas, *abba*, 76-7, 88, 97
Jab, 56
Jäbal, 235
Jafer, *gärad*, 247, 265, 271, 274
Jahangir, emperor, 385
Jämal ad-Din [II] Muhammäd, sultan of Adäl, 57-60, 72, 96
Jämal ad-Din [I], sultan of Ifat, 44, 62-7, 98, 436
Jambah, 201-2
Jämma, 46, 294
Jan Amora, 110, 112, 283
Jan Bägdem, 345
Jan Mängäsha, queen, 42-3, 64
Jan Sägäna, 119
Jan Zajora, 181
Jan Zäläq, 189
Jan Zedrah, 176
Jan Zeg, *gärad*, 110, 135
Jan Zela, *ité*, 145, 160, 437. See also: Eléni Mehmäd
Janbah, 203-4
Janjero, 90, 97, 328, 348-51, 421, 424, 440
Jara, 308
Java, 13
Jawatir, p. 172
Jawé, 280, 287. See also: Jawi
Jawi, 280, 288, 300, 315, 318-19, 416, 420. see also: Dawé
Jazja, 58
Jebra'él, 247, 249
Jeddah, 105, 111, 127-8, 372, 416
Jelé Oromo, 299-
jelhika, 290
Jemma, 206, 314, 316
Jerusalem, 54, 96, 106, 156
Jesuits, 154, 252, 267, 279, 302-3, 307, 331, 334-5, 340, 342-3, 349, 351, 353, 379-81, 383-4, 386, 395-6, 415, 417, 424, 427-9
jewellers, jewellery, 30, 33, 43, 103, 119, 137, 239, 255-6, 374, 381, 386, 408, 417
Jibril, 374
Jigat, 352

jihad, 43, 122, 158, 167, 221, 245, 374, 426. See also Holy War
Jirirawrari, 181
Jitu, 207
Joradi, 181, 213, 222
Jubaland, 303
Jushu, *gärad*, 181, 222
justice, 48, 59
kabba, 319
Kädawred, *pasha*, 239
Käfa, 90, 98, 154, 216, 228, 266-7, 275, 351, 421, 424, 439-40
Kahaberi, 169
kalala, 289
Kaléb, king, 26
Kämbat, 211
Kämbata, 77, 96, 204, 210-12, 215, 225, 227, 251, 297-8, 328, 334, 422, 433, 438
Kamil, king, 383-4, 387, 427, 441
kandi, 46
Känisa, 361, 362
käntiba, 101, 238, 398, 400-1, 412-13
Karadin, 119
Käräyu Oromo, 294, 299-300, 311
Karneshim, 38
Käsäla, 28, 369, 397, 429
Kasu, 26-7
Kätäta, 85
Kebra Nägäst, 78
Kedefu, 391
Keflä Giyorgis, *käntiba*, 413
Keflä Wahid, 395
Keflo, 325
kemis, 416
Kesad Da'ro, 22
Khalid, 241-2, 249, 272
Kilolé, *luba*, 282, 325, 418, 421
Kitchen, K.A., 3
Kohaitu, 18-20, 32
kohl, 370, 414-16
Kokäl river, 359
Kolmodin, J., 398, 429
Konch, 90, 266-7, 275, 433
Kono Oromo, 292
Kont, 90
Konta, 90, 266-7, 275
Kordida, 309-312, 419
Kosmas Indikopleustes, 24-26, 28-30, 33
kosso, 290-1
Krapf, J.L. 393-4
Kuana, 358
Kubät, 41

Kuelgorä, 41, 46
kuffiyas, 47
Kunama, 28
Kush, 26
Kwedo Fälassi, 91
Kwer'ata Re'esu, 370
Lä'äsonhi, *shum*, 252-3, 273
Läbäkäla, 44
lac, 19
Läda'e 'Uthman, 120, 157
Lalibala, king and place, 37, 81, 167
lam, 81
land grants, 38, 48, 77, 103-4, 132, 144, 146, 233, 269, 306, 396, 405, 436
Lange, W.J, 256
Läo, 46
Laodicea, 19
Lasta, 81, 93, 312, 318-19, 434
Latakia, 19
Layda river, 358
lead, 41
leather, 307, 368. See also: skins
Lebnä Dengel, emperor, vii, 103-5, 122-6, 128, 131-2, 137, 142, 145-9, 151, 153-4, 156, 158, 160-1, 165, 167-8, 171-3, 181, 183-6, 188-9, 191, 193, 195, 197-9, 202-3, 206-7, 210-15, 220, 222-7, 245, 251, 258, 260, 262, 282, 324, 436-8
Legrand, M., 354
legumes, 70, 73
Lej Negus, 342
lemons, 46, 111
Léncha Oromo, 316
Léncha, *shäläqa*, 322
leopards, 46, 132, 250, 349
leprosy, 348
Léqa Oromo, 316
Lewis, I.M., 392
Liban Oromo 280, 293, 310, 315-17, 346, 419
Libanos, *abba*, 23, 32
limes, 46, 132, 138
Limu, 202-3
lions, 46, 304, 349
livestock, 41, 45, 66-7, 151, 250, 257, 285, 345-7, 423-4
Lobo, J., 279, 302-4, 307, 341-2, 353-4, 379, 384, 386-8
locusts, 109, 409-10
looting, vi, 41-3, 45, 51, 56, 58-60, 66-7, 122-3, 133, 153, 158, 168-76, 183, 185, 188, 190-2, 197, 201-3, 215, 221,

222-3, 225, 234, 239, 244-5, 249, 251-2, 258, 262-8, 272, 280, 284-7, 312, 314, 327, 330, 345, 357, 373, 394, 396, 418
luba, lubenat, 280-1, 291, 301, 303-4, 325, 421
Lubo, 320, 420
Ludolf, H., 338, 353, 356, 368, 388-8, 414
Mä'ätläyla, 40
Mäb'a Seyon, saint, 152-3, 162, 437
Mächa Oromo, 260, 293, 298, 310, 314-16, 319-20, 327, 334, 336, 340, 354
Machado, Francisco, 379, 384, 427
Mächakäl, 296, 312
Mädhanina Egzi', *abba*, 38, 54, 68
Mädhen Zämäda, princess, 149, 161
Madi Gafo, *tato*, 216, 228
Mägäz, 293
magicians, 82-3, 86, 97, 250, 348. See also: prophets
Mähari Krestos, 121, 157
Mahdära Maryam, 308
Mähfuz, *imam*, 122-3, 131, 136, 158-9, 167-8, 183, 204, 221-2, 245, 437, 439
Mähiko, 116, 133, 135, 143-5, 149, 159-60, 436
Mahra, 168
Majo river, 183
Maju river, 183. See also: Majo; Mojjo
Makattér, 216, 228, 235
Mäkré, 113
mäkwännen, 85
Malao, 21, 31
malaria, 132, 235
Maläsäy, 173-4, 264
Malawa, 197
Malbärdé, 85
Mälka Chera, 339
Mälka Krestos, 308, 344, 53
Mälkä Sédék, 149
mälkäñña, 144, 158
Mamluks, 41-2
Mammo Gärä Krestos, 406-11
Mammo, *fitawrari*, 154
Mandeb, 61
Mandeley, 111
Manoel I, king, 104, 132, 142, 148, 154
Mänsur ibn Muhammäd, 375, 426
Mänsur Sä'd ad-Din, 57
Mänsur, Ustad, 385
manuscripts, 192, 207, 380, 409. See also: paintings

Manzeh, 41. See: Menz
Maqrizi, 40, 46-51, 56-7, 58-9, 72, 79, 113
Mär'adé, 42
Märäb river, 21, 28, 91-2, 101, 218, 229, 239, 358, 395, 413
Märäb-Mellash, 402
Märäwa Oromo, 294, 299-300
Marco Polo, 54-5, 96
Märhabeté, 89, 97, 311
Markäsäwäy, 87
markets, and market towns, viii, 53, 111, 113, 115, 123, 129, 137, 151, 157, 160, 169, 173, 181, 191, 204, 222, 224, 226, 237, 364, 369, 372, 374, 393
Marqos, *abun*, 145
Marqos, alias Ayres Dias, 243, 271
Marqos, prince and royal pretender, 236, 270
marriages, dynastic, viii, 107, 121, 147, 168, 208-9, 216, 227, 235, 242, 251, 265, 273-4 333, 335-6, 401-3, 405, 410, 422, 435, 442
marriages, other, 112, 289, 303, 446
marrows, 46
martänas, 256
Märtula Maryam, 146
Märtula Mika'él, 68, 130
mäsafent, era of, 425
Masogo, 351
mäsfen, 68, 87
Mäshaf Nay 'Alitat, 27, 91
Mäshälämya, 299
Mashengo, 351
Masin, 183, 185
Masogo, 351
Massawa, 23, 37, 93-5, 102, 104-5, 127, 151, 156, 168, 233, 235-7, 248, 254, 259, 269, 284, 383 387, 390, 392, 396-7, 403-4, 411, 413-17, 427-30, 436, 439, 441
Mätä'a, *abba*, 23, 32
Mätäkäl, 299, 352, 355, 357, 360, 364-5
Matéwos, 142
Mateyas, *abba*, 68, 98
Matlia, 26, 32
Mattan ibn 'Uthman, *gärad*, 192, 224
Mauro, fra, *Mappamondo* map, 118, 137, 158, 179, 418
Mawa, 253
May Mänka'e, 405
May Sa'äda, 407

Maya, 101, 107, 133, 157, 161, 184, 180, 186-91, 205, 210, 222-4, 228, 285-7, 292, 324, 326, 419-21, 440
Mazäga, 204, 216, 228, 235, 269
mead, 385. See also: wine
meat, 9, 26, 29, 105, 112, 127, 136, 289, 302, 346, 350, 384
Mecca, viii, 53, 94, 105, 125-8, 414
medicine, 137, 414
Medra Damot 'Abiy, 260
Medra Zega, 41
Megabari, 27
Mehmäd, *gärad*, 116, 144-5, 157, 160
Mélbah, *luba*, 281, 292, 324, 418, 420
melguddo, 290
melons, 46
Menilek I, king, 78
Menilek II, emperor, vi
Mentewwäb, empress, 318-20, 411, 420, 430
Mentuhotep IV, pharaoh, 6
Menz, 41, 186, 223
merchants, vii, 23, 29-30, 37, 47, 61, 79, 94, 112, 137, 151, 169, 191, 224, 318, 348, 368, 371, 397, 415, 428
mercury, 370
Merid Wolde Aregay, 39, 114, 237, 252
Meroe, 27
meserqana, 117
Meslé, *luba*, 283, 290, 418, 426
Mesraha island, 402
méta, 81
Metical Aga, 416
Michelle, l*uba*, 283. See also: Meslé
Mika'él Sehul, *ras*, 322-3, 331, 362, 413, 416, 420, 430
Mika'él, *abun*, 386, 428
Mika'él, archangel, 85
milk, 289, 303, 346
millet, 127
Minas, emperor, 236-7, 267, 270-1, 275, 284-6, 289, 438
Minjo, 90
miracles, 86, 134
mirrors, 416
missionaries, Orthodox Christian, viii, 76-7, 80-7, 97, 134, 152, 161. See also: proselytism
Modaito, 391, 428
Moha, mountain, 57
Mohommed Hasan, 282
Mojahid, vizier, 205-6, 209, 226
Mojjo, 287. See also: Majo

Mokha, 387, 390
Mola Asfah 'Ali, 49-50
monache, 20
monasteries, viii, 22-3, 37-8, 75, 116, 123, 131-2, 141, 148-51, 161, 293, 411-12. See also: monks
money, 18-19, 47, 70, 73, 94, 115, 376, 407, 426. See also: coins
monkeys, 9, 14
monks, 220, 280, 309, 314, 318, 342, 364, 420, 443
"Moors", 106, 108, 112, 124, 126, 129, 141, 147, 150, 253, 331
Mora, 44 61
Morät, 311
Morocco, 111
mosques, 42, 51, 55, 63, 67, 208, 217, 237, 246
Mota Lamé, 81-6, 97, 436
Motalami. See: Mota Lamé
mucha, 289
Muda, Abba, 301
Mudäna, *luba*, 281
Mugär, 294-5, 297-8, 328-30, 330, 422
Muhammäd Abu 'Abd Allah, shaikh, 55
Muhammäd Gasa, i*mam*, 375, 379, 426, 440
Muhammäd ibn Azhar ad-Din, 122, 124-5, 131, 136
Muhammäd ibn Bädlay, 119
Muhammäd ibn Ibrahim Gasa, 239, 270, 387
Muhammäd ibn Ibrahim, 170
Muhammäd ibn Nasir, 375
Muhammäd Isa, 379
Muhammäd Kedefu, 391
Muhammäd Sä'd ad-Din, 56-7
Muhammäd Sayd, 369
Muhammäd, the Prophet, 435
Muhammäd, *amir*, late 15th century, 247, 249, 265
Muhammäd, *amir*, mid-16th century, 51
Muhammäd, "*gabar*", 355Muhär, 75, 97
Mul'äta, *luba*, 287, 292, 419
mulberries, 46
mules, 48, 70, 73, 77-8, 106, 109-11 137, 147, 161, 169-71, 173, 191, 197, 200, 217, 221, 239, 242, 251, 257, 266, 272, 283, 295, 331-2, 334-5, 371, 385, 407, 433
Murad, Khoja, 333, 388-91, 401, 404-5, 428-9
Mureyas, 208, 227, 438

murhine, 18
Musa, *na'ib*, 403, 429
musical instruments, 48, 117, 144, 218, 314, 345, 354. See also: drums; flutes; trumpets
Muslims, vi, viii, 40-4, 51-5, 62, 66, 69, 72, 87, 94, 97-8, 115, 120, 124, 126, 131, 135, 141, 145, 148, 150, 158-9, 167, 169, 174, 176-7, 182, 191, 193, 199 207-8, 210, 212, 219, 222, 227, 249, 319, 326, 329-30, 387, 411, 421, 441. See also: Islam
muslin, 19
Mustapha, *basha*, 337
mustard, 46
myrrh, myrrh trees, 3, 5-6, 9-13, 16, 31, 94, 302, 432
na'ib, 239, 411
Na'od, emperor, 107, 122, 136, 145, 159, 199, 245
Näbiyat, *ras*, 147, 161, 172, 195, 222
Nacchi, Antonius, 415
Näfas Mäwcha, 299
Nafi, 216, 228
Nägäb, 373
Nägärä Wäg, 238
nägarit, 399. See also: drums
Nägash Keflo, 335, 352
Nana Giyorgis, 320
Nasé, 37
Nasir Ahmäd ibn Ashraf Ismail, Yämän ruler, 51, 96
Nasir ibn 'Uthman, 375
Näsir ad-Din, 45
Nasradin ibn Ahmäd, 181-2, 196, 222-4
Nastoy, 353
Nayl Agub, 369
Nayzgi, *däjazmach*, 407-8
necklaces, 3, 7, 31
Nehsi, 12
Nile, 368
Nile, Blue, 5-7, 27, 29 32-3, 39-41, 58, 91, 153-4, 160, 257, 262, 288, 293, 296, 298, 305, 308, 310-14, 315, 318, 340-1, 344-7, 352-5, 366, 368, 297, 420-1, 423-4, 440
Nine Saints, 23, 32
Noba, 27, 32. See also: Nubia; Sennar; Sudan
nomads, 215, 240, 282, 324, 354, 391
Nubi, 155. See also: Nubia
Nubia, Nubians, 10-11, 24, 154, 216-17, 228

Nur ibn al-Wazir Mujahid, 242, 244-6, 271, 283, 373-4, 418, 426, 438. 440
Nur ibn Ibrahim, sherif, vizier, 190, 219, 224, 229, 249
'Obbo Oromo, 280, 295, 300
obsidian, 18
oil, olive, etc. 19, 127, 198
Omar, 56
omens, 65, 292, 302
Omo river, 351
Ophir, 16, 31
oranges, 110, 132, 138
Orgabeja. See: Werbarag
Ormuz
Oromos, vii, 137, 158, 239, 241, 258, 273, 279-328, 331, 334, 336, 338-40, 346-7, 361-2, 373-8, 382-3, 386-8, 391, 406, 416, 418-24, 426-9, 433, 439-43. See also: Gallas
ostriches, ostrich feathers, 3, 14, 31, 46
Ottoman Turks, 145, 160, 233-9, 249, 269, 394, 438. See also: Turks
Oviedo, André de, 267
oxen, 13, 28, 249-50, 289, 292, 395. See also: cattle
Ozdemür, *pasha*, 234-6, 269
Paes, Pero., 343, 352-3, 368, 395, 415
"pagans", 85, 89, 97, 142-3, 151, 153, 167, 216, 221, 225, 228, 252, 255, 257-6, 261-3, 272-4, 330, 331, 347, 372, 374, 440. See also: animists
Paguma, 44
paintings, 174, 185, 192, 211, 236, 341, 370-1. See also: manuscripts
panthers, 3, 9-10, 13
paper, 369
Pawlos, *abba*, 279
peaches, 46, 150
pearls, 416. See also: jewellery
peasants, 131, 238-9, 243, 265, 249, 265, 269, 274, 286, 378
pepper, 390,414
Pepy II, pharaoh, 5
Perehu, 7
Pereira, Bernardo, 379, 384, 427
Peripus of the Erythraean Sea, 18-21
Persia, 59, 127, 150, 389
pharaohs, 3-16
pigs, 391
pilgrimage, viii, 53-4, 94,106
Pirenne, J., 6
Pires, Tomé, 106
Pliny, 18, 27

484

poison, 28, 65, 133, 174, 184, 186-90, 228, 292, 326, 345, 360, 419, 421, 440
pomegranates, 46
Poncet, C., 360, 369-70, 404, 429
Portugal, Portuguese, 102, 105, 124-8, 132, 143, 142, 146, 151, 154, 181, 186, 209, 219-20, 222, 229, 234, 241-3, 249, 251, 257, 260, 269-70, 272, 284, 326, 379-81, 396, 427
preachers, Muslim, 51
priests, 86-7, 112, 119, 144, 147-8, 151-3, 155, 158, 161, 255, 257, 267, 274, 314, 315, 359, 411, 463. See also: bishops; monks
"primitive money", vii, 25, 32, 70, 93, 98, 335, 416, 431
prisons, 151
prophets, 63, 65, 76, 87, 250, 256, 292, 302, 316, 318
proselytism, 54, 57, 68-70, 83-4, 91, 98, 124, 134, 152, 161, 192, 195, 255, 257. See also: missionaries
provisions, agricultural, 105, 127-8, 148, 150-1, 161-2, 197, 200, 204, 219, 237, 251, 319, 335, 319, 340, 362, 389-90, 396, 401, 403, 433
Prutky, Remedius, 392, 428
Ptolemy III, Eurgetes, king, 17, 19
Punt, land of, 3-16, 31
Qäb'én, 143
Qäbäro Méda, 314
Qächeho, 113. See also: Qächeno
Qächeno, 113, 326
qadi, 48
Qädsé, 41
Qaha river, 410-11
Qäla Gända Oromo, 310-11, 316-17
qallecha, 315
qältu, 290
qäñ bältehät, 145
Qanburah, 173, 222
qäs, 141, 243, 266
Qäwestos, *abba*, 89, 97
Qeda, 107
qéro, 289, 301
Qoga, 294
qolla, 353
qondala, 289, 301
Qoré Oromo, 312
Qwara, 106
Rädét, 243, 271
Ragreig, 353
Räminu Oromo, 308

Ramses III, pharaoh, 15
raq masäré, 113
Ras el-Fil, 366
Rätaya Oromo, 308
razors, 371
Re'esä Haymanot Täsfa Sén, 406
Rebko Oromo, 308
Red Sea, 3, 5-7, 17, 23, 31, 37-8, 54, 71, 93, 219, 236, 369, 395-6, 428, 432, 435, 442
Régu Oromo, 308
Reju Oromo, 308
Retwa, 56
rhinoceros, 13, 18, 31, 46, 371, 389
Rif, 198
Robalé, 280, 285, 418
robbers, 126, 154, 167. See also: thieves
Robél, 184
Rodrigues, Gonçalo, 252
Roha, 81. See also: Lalibala
Roman Catholics, Roman Catholicism, 234, 243, 258, 261, 296, 307, 337, 339, 341-3, 379-81, 397, 419, 423, 429. See also: Italy; Portugal; Spain
Sä'ada Amba, 358
Sä'ada Kestan, 413
Sä'äzzäga, 398, 401, 410
Sä'd ad-Din Abdul Muhammäd, sultan of Ifat, 50-1, 72, 80, 95, 97, 244, 435-6
Saba Oromo, 308
säba qäyh, 27, 32
Sabaeans, 26
Säbänä Gärgesh Iyasu, princess, 405-6, 410
Säbbäru, 199, 225
Sabé, 308
Sabhat, *azmach*, 75
Säbr ad-Din 'Ali, 377
Säbr ad-Din [III] ibn Sä'd ad-Din, sultan of Adäl, 56, 95
Säbr ad-Din [II] Muhammäd, sultan of Ifat, vi, 42-4, 61-3, 72, 87, 95, 72, 76, 78, 95, 97, 170, 221, 435
Säbr ad-Din [I] Nawi ibn Mänsur ibn 'Umar Walashma', sultan of Ifat, 40
Sädäqa Oromo, 280, 300
Safu Wäsän Sägäd, 180
Saga, 143
Sägädé, 79, 87, 305
sagatogene, 20
sähafä lahm, 81, 149, 161, 259, 273, 296, 333, 341, 345
Sähart, 409, 411

Index

Sahim, king, 383
Saho, 21, 104, 240. 395
Sahure, pharaoh, 5
Saizana, 26, 32
Sakka, 251
Sälälé, 85
Salämt, 79, 87
Säläwa, 235, 269
Salih, 210-11 215, 227
Sälim, 27, 32. See also: *sälim*
sälim, säliman, 152, 360. See also: Sälim
Salman, *imam*, 391
Sälomon Tädfa Sén, 411
Salt, H., 110
salt, vii, 25, 28, 32, 93, 108, 151, 156, 246, 335, 338, 393, 431. See also: *amolé*
Säm'a, 409, 412
Sam'un, 188-9
Sämén, 79, 87, 97, 243, 305, 435
Sancho, 371
sandal wood, 250
Sanhur, 197, 225
santi, 345
Sapera, 251, 272
Sappa, 251
Särawé, 409. See Säräyé
Säräyé, 21-22, 37-8, 91, 93-4, 101, 104, 156, 175, 214, 218, 228-9, 238, 395, 401, 404, 409-10, 412-14, 434, 436, 438
Sarbakusa, 331, 414
Sari-bär, 180
Sarsa Dengel, emperor, 211-12, 217, 233, 236-9, 243, 247, 249, 251-6, 258, 262-75, 279, 285-8, 324-6, 333-4, 340, 352, 375-6, 378, 394, 410, 418-23, 426-7, 428, 439-41
Säsogi, 67
Sasu, 28-30, 32-3
Säve-Söderberg, 1., 13
Sayara, 56
Säyfä Ar'ad, emperor, 38, 49, 72, 94, 436
Scimezana, 23
Se'elä Krestos, *ras*, 295-6, 298-9, 327, 333, 335-6, 339, 341, 353, 381, 419, 422-3, 440
Sebhat Lä'äb, 104
Seda Oromo, 322
Sef Bär, 243, 288
Sefkhet, 11
Seleh, *qazi*, 63, 65
Selma, 395

Seltogi, 76
Sennar, 105, 320, 352, 355, 366, 368-72, 425, 429, 443. See also: Sudan
Seno, *sähafä lahm*, 345
Sepenhi, *shum*, 252, 258, 273
Serjan, 56
Serka, 243
Serki, 352, 362, 369
servants, 48. See also: slaves
Sesostris II, pharaoh, 6
Sesostris III, pharaoh, 6
séwa, 27
seyum, 85, 103, 337
Shäbäl, 294
Shadda king, t*ato*, 154
Shagi Sherocho, *tato*, 351, 420, 440
shämma, 311, 407
Shams ad-Din Abu 'Abdallah Muhammäd, 53
Shams ad-Din ibn Muhammäd, *amir*, 121
Shamsu, 192, 224
"Shanqellas", 30, 87, 91, 97, 297-8, 328, 338, 351-68, 42405, 433, 436, 442
Shärkha, 73, 98, 199, 201-3, 222, 247, 435
Shat, 89, 253, 262-3, 274, 297-8, 328, 345
Shäwa, vii, 38-9, 41, 43, 46, 52-3, 64-5, 75, 85-8, 93-4, 97, 108, 114-16, 122, 135, 142, 150-1, 153-5, 157-8, 171, 177, 179, 183, 186, 227, 244, 248, 271, 285-6, 295, 297, 305, 311-12, 326, 328, 330, 332-3, 340, 346, 373, 418-19, 423-4, 437, 439
Shé, 351
Sheba, queen of, 78
sheep, 26, 46, 71, 73, 105, 132, 150, 161, 257, 318, 390, 393, 433
shells, 416
Shembera Koré, 172, 176, 184, 191
shields, 27-8, 63, 65, 106, 166, 206, 214, 218, 242, 275, 292, 300, 306, 321, 326, 419, 421, 440
Shihab ad-Din Ahmäd al Mujasi, *sheikh*, 48
Shihab ad-Din Ahmäd Bädlay, sultan of Adäl, 59, 72, 98, 436
Shihab ed-Din Ahmäd el-Qader, 126, 130, 136, 165, 169, 179, 183, 186, 189, 204, 208-9, 215, 279, 282
Shimi, 46
Shinashas, 267, 275
Shiré, 101, 357-9. See also: Siré

Shoker, 193
Shuhaym ibn Kamil, king, 387
shum, 101, 112, 252
Sibu Oromo, 316
Sidama, 71, 77, 81
Siddiq, *gärad*, 199, 203
Sidi Muhammäd, 214, 227
Sidi, 329, 333, 422
Sigaro, 251
silk, 47-8, 103, 137, 174, 185, 200, 350, 369, 386, 414=15
Silté, 76, 140
silver, 5, 19, 41-3, 60, 63, 115, 137, 185, 192, 234, 243-4, 250, 365, 369, 384, 386, 407-8. See also: coins; jewellery
Sim, 373
Simu Wänag Jan, 199, 225
Sinai, mount, 105
Sinass, 352
Siré, 409, 412. See also: Shiré
Sisgayo, 337-8, 423
skins, 3, 9-10, 13-14, 19, 31, 20, 27, 390, 415-6, 433
slave raiders, slave raiding, 38, 267, 273, 365-6, 425, 442, 424
slavery, 202, 258, 262, 318-19, 325, 348-9
slaves, vi-vii, 4, 13, 15, 18, 26-7, 31-2, 53, 60, 63, 72, 78-9, 91, 93-4, 96-7, 104-5, 122, 127, 150-1, 155-6, 158, 161-2, 169, 191, 197, 206, 221, 225, 234, 244, 252-3, 258, 266-8, 274-5, 300, 310, 315-16, 339-40, 351-64, 390, 394, 396, 403, 416, 423-4, 427, 432-3, 435, 442
smallpox, 364, 371
snakes, 257, 349
Soddo, 88
Sogra, 113
soldiers, vi, 6, 26, 41, 43-5, 47-8, 50, 55-8, 62-65, 66-7, 69-71, 73-4, 78-9, 87-8, 91, 97, 110, 116-17, 119-20, 122, 125, 130-1, 138, 149, 156-8, 161-2, 168, 171-6, 180, 186, 191-2, 194, 196, 199, 203-4, 205-6, 210, 212, 214-15, 218, 222, 225-7, 233, 242, 249, 252-3, 258, 262-4, 266, 272-3, 280, 284, 288, 299, 303, 310, 312-13, 315, 318-21, 329, 345, 362, 366-8, 370, 421, 438. See also: *chäwa*
Soliman II, sultan, 236
Solomon, king, 16
Somalis, 165-7, 173-4, 186-7, 192, 221, 224, 375, 378, 394
sorghum, 46
Spain, Spanish, 343, 394-5, 428, 441
spears, 18, 28, 48, 56, 63-5, 106, 174, 215, 218, 242, 246, 291, 300, 304, 306, 321, 354-5, 357, 367-8
spices, 115, 369, 390
stibium, 340, 414
stirrups, 306, 367
Strabo, 27
Suakin, 61, 102, 106, 156, 369, 372, 397, 429
Suarez, Lopo, 125
Suba Oromo, 280, 300
Sudan, 28, 61, 102, 105, 156, 217, 353, 366, 369, 424, 429, 432, 442-3
Suf Gamo, 77, 209
sugar, 46, 138, 177-8
Suq-Däwaro, 181, 222
Surat, 416
Susneyos, emperor, 279, 292-4, 296, 298-300, 304-6, 317, 326-7, 329-31, 333-8, 340, 344-7, 352-4, 357, 362, 368, 376, 379-81, 383-4, 386, 395-7, 419, 422-4, 426-9, 441
Sutafé Krestos, 376
swords, 19, 58, 65, 78, 166, 191, 206, 208, 242, 334-5, 369, 379, 396
sycamore, 46
Synaxary, Ethiopian, 85-6
Syria, Syrians, viii, 19, 32, 59, 243
Tä'amera Maryam, 151
Tä'räk, 66
tabot, 86, 251
Taddesse Tamrat, 37, 50, 57, 81, 89, 152, 215
Täderär, 395
Tägulät, 42, 116
täj, 267. See also: wine
Taka, 217, 228, 369, 429
Täkkäzé river, 27, 32, 294, 308, 358, 362, 424
Täklä Giyorgis, *däjazmach*, 258, 264, 274, 333, 340
Täklä Giyorgis, Hamasén chief, 414
Täklä Hawaryat, *dajazmach*, 369
Täklä Haymanot, emperor, 413-14
Täklä Haymanot, functionary, 198
Täklä Haymanot, saint, 54, 68-70, 76, 80-7, 97-8, 134, 436-7
Täklä Iyäsus, 174-5, 218, 222
Täklä Mika'él, 236

Index

Täklä Sellasé, *azzaj*, 293, 300-2, 307
Täklay, 214
Täklay,e 107,
Täklo, *azmach*, 258, 262, 274
Täläg, 65, 434
Täläta, 295, 299, 311, 314-18, 419-20
Talha ibn Wazir 'Abbas, 374, 426
Tämbén, 409, 412
Tana, lake, 285, 287, 284, 298, 305, 352, 368, 383, 402, 413-14, 424, 439, 441
tancharas, 29-30
Tangaitae, 27, 32, 434
Tänkäl, 369
tapeworm, 290
Täsfä Hezan, Zä-Däwaro, *abba*, 70, 98, 134, 159
Täsfä Le'ul, 218
Täsfä Sén Gärä Krestos, 406
Täsfä Seyon, *bahr nägash*, 414
Täsfawi, 219, 229
tata, or Gänz chief, 80
tato, or Käfa king, 90, 98, 216, 228, 267, 351
täwtu, 290
taxation. See: tribute
Täzkäro, prince, 236, 270
Te'eyentäy, 41
Tédros, 218-19, 229
téff, 46
Tegray, 64, 103, 109-10, 120-1, 137, 147, 149-51, 156, 172, 174, 184, 214, 218-19, 222, 227-9, 234-5, 248, 259, 294, 302, 305, 319, 322, 331, 358-8, 363, 395-6, 401, 406, 411, 413-14, 430, 433-4, 438
Tegré Mäkonnen, 103, 248
tehito, 289
Telles, Baltazar, 417
Telq, 69
Tent Oromo, 314-15
tents, 9, 13, 123, 147, 200, 260, 284, 288-9, 350
Téwodros II, emperor, vi, 371
Téwodros, of prophecy, 365
Téwoflos, emperor, 317, 420
textiles, 18-19, 32, 71, 93-5, 103, 125, 147, 157, 174, 200, 260, 372, 414-16, 432-3
thalers, Austrian, 407-8, 412
Thebes, 7-8, 11
thieves, 126, 154-5, 262, 331-2, 344. See also: robbers
Thiutiy, 11
Thomas, brothers, 105, 131, 135, 137, 150-1, 153-4
Thoth, 11
Thutmose II, pharaoh, 13
Tigé, *däjazmach*, 316-17, 419
Timbuctoo, 105
Tinno, 293, 300-1. See also Täklä Sellasé, *azzaj*
Tiqo, 44
tobacco, 385-6
Tobeya, 52, 114-15, 193-5, 224
Tola "Shanqella", 359
Toma Gondé, 322
Tomä Gera, 86, 88
Toro, 105
tortoise, 18
Tosa Asfo, 88
trade, and trade routes, vii-iii, 3-21, 28-32, 39, 42, 47, 53, 70-1, 74, 79, 88, 93-4, 104-109, 111-12, 115, 127-8, 135, 142, 155-7, 161, 169, 235, 271-2, 311, 335-6, 340, 364, 369, 371-2, 384, 386, 415-16, 425-6
trees, 148-9, 151, 189, 198, 207, 213, 215, 217, 228, 342, 350, 365, 368, 389-90, 396-7, 404, 413-17, 426-7, 430-3, 442. See also: forests
tribute, 5, 9-10, 42, 49, 58, 69, 76-7, 80, 89-91, 98, 103, 111, 138, 143, 148, 151, 154, 156, 160-2, 167, 175-7, 181, 191, 196, 200, 205, 209-12, 218, 221-3, 226-7, 229, 235, 250, 252-3, 256, 258, 260, 262-4, 272-5, 282, 306, 311, 315, 334-8, 343-4, 350, 371, 383, 386, 388, 390, 394-5, 397-8, 404, 406-11, 414, 422-3, 428, 430-4, 436, 438
Trimingham, J.S., 51, 61, 119, 122, 375
troglodytes, 138, 159, 331-2, 354, 365
trumpets, 144, 314, 404
Tsarane, 21
Tschai Berhane Sellasé, 88
Tuläma Oromo, 293, 298-9, 308-11, 319-20, 322, 420
Tunis, 105, 111
Turi, *shäläqa*, 322
Turks, 233, 249, 252, 269-70, 272, 284, 368, 383, 390, 394-6, 401, 403, 417, 428-9, 439-41. See also: Ottoman Turks
Tutschek, C., 301
'Umar Din ibn Muhammäd, sultan, 167, 170, 197, 221, 225
'Umar Din, *gärad*, 165, 167

'Umar ibn Dunya-huz, sultan, 40, 95
'Umar-Din ibn Adam, *imam*, 382, 388, 427
umbrellas, 48, 70, 117
Uru Oromo, 294
Urukala Oromo, 308
'Uthman, "the Abyssinian", 374, 426
Uthman ibn Nasir, 375, 426
'Uthman ibn Yassein, 167
'Uthman, gärad, 189
Varthema, Ludovico di, 127, 128
Venetians, 54, 106, 132, 137
vines, 111, 138. See also: grapes
Wäbäz Muhammäd, 249
Wabi river, 136, 179, 247, 281, 283
Wabi Shabellé river, 68, 71, 281
Wäbo Ortomo, 314
Wächär, 90
Wäd Ezum, 239
Wadug Mecheg, 183, 223
Wagam, 256, 272-3
Wägära, 79, 87, 97, 305, 435
Wähni, 317-20
Wäj, 76-7, 96-7, 110, 141-2, 159-60, 170, 179, 186, 188-9, 200, 204, 210, 225-6, 243, 247, 251, 258, 264, 271, 273, 280, 283-4, 286-8, 304, 328, 340, 418-19, 421-2, 433, 436, 438
Wäjerat, 406
wajo, 289
Wak, 307
Wako Oromo, 308
Wälädäñña Oromo, 311
Wälamo, 77, 88, 204, 215, 225, 226-7, 433, 438
Wäläqa, place and river, 292, 294, 305, 322, 345
Wälashma' dynasty and title, 40, 88, 113, 157, 326, 436
Wälätta Seyon, 402- 429, 441
Wälätto, *ité*, 255
Wäldä Giyorgis, *ras*, 308
Wäldä Hawaryat, *däjazmach*, 299, 369
Wäldä Sellasé, *ras*, 414
Wäldebba, 359, 364
Wällo Oromo, 299-300, 310-2, 379
Wällo, 137, 151, 309, 406, 420
Wälqayt, 216, 228, 401, 407-8, 410
Wämbärma, 311, 345
Wämbärya, 29, 222, 264, 271, 274, 352, 357
Wänäg Jan, 136, 159
Wangé Gafat, 345

Wäqär Muhammäd, 249
wäqet, 252, 273
Wäräb, 78, 329
Wäraba Got, 242, 271
Wäräba, 378
Wäräñña, *däjazmach*, 318-21, 370, 420, 442-3
Wäränsha Oromos, 288, 293-4, 298, 300
Wärdaya, 294, 376
Wärgar, 44
Wäri, 76, 329
Wariho Oromo, 319
Wärjeh, 40, 45
Wäro Oromo, 313
Wärrä Däya Oromo, 294, 376
Wärrä Himanu, 308
Wärrä Illu Oromo, 300
Wärrä Kurya Oromo, 300
Wärrä Nolé Oromo, 300
Wärrä Qallu, 282
wars, or safflower, 169
wars, v-vi, 26-7, 32-3, 39-45, 50-2, 55-7, 61-9, 72, 78-9, 97, 104, 106, 111, 117, 119-27, 131, 133-4, 156-8, 162, 236-7, 244-6, 258, 260, 262, 270, 279-89, 292-301, 308-26, 329-31, 333-5, 341. 345-6, 351-63, 370-1, 373-6, 382, 395, 406
Wäsäl, 300
Wäsän Sägäd, 172, 174, 176-7, 180,185, 204, 212-13, 226
Wasi Amba, 359
Waslu, 79
Wata, 76
Watmät, 180
wax, 103-4, 127, 156, 415
Wäynä Däg'a, 286
Wäyto, 298
Wechalé Oromo, 299, 308-10
Weijns, J., 389
Welaloch, 361, 425, 443
wells, 63
Werbarag, 141
Werki, 359
wheat, 46, 127, 131-2, 272, 315, 334, 433
Wifat, 39, 85. See: Ifat
wild life, 18, 148, 257, 281, 304, 365, 385, 389
wine, 9, 19, 26, 126, 257, 374
Wis, 204, 226
Wobit, princess, 320, 322, 420
Wolyata, 77, 88, 204, 226-7

women, 18, 27, 40, 43, 45, 51, 58, 61, 65, 69, 72, 78, 81, 103, 107, 110, 119, 134, 141, 142, 145-7, 160, 165-6, 168, 170, 180-, 189-90, 195, 200-3, 208-9, 216, 225, 228, 235, 241, 244, 252, 255, 258, 262-3, 265-6, 282, 284-5, 288-9, 295-6, 299-300, 307, 310, 312-13, 315, 318-20, 330, 336, 339-40, 346, 351-2, 357-60, 362-3, 365-6, 369, 371, 374, 378, 396, 400, 442
wood, 310, 332, 367, 414. See also: trees
"Woodage Asahel", 323
Woshéka, 320
Ya'qim, 194
Ya'qob Gälawdéwos, 236
Yabäta. See: Yähabäta
Yäbso, 320
Yagbe'a Seyon, emperor, 40, 54, 435
Yägefo, 314
Yähabäta, 295-5, 298, 300, 336, 419
Yäjju, 200, 317, 320, 420, 442
Yäläbasha, 68, 98, 130, 132, 158
Yämäbal, 396
Yämän, Yämänis, 46-7, 53, 55, 382, 387, 393-4, 416, 428
Yämäna Krestos, 335-8, 422-3
Yaq'im, 194
Yaq'ob, abun, 68, 70, 76-7, 80, 87
Yaq'ob, emperor, 236, 265, 275, 292-3, 302, 317, 324, 334, 421, 442
Yas, 62
Yasubli Gafat, 345
Yäzämbäl, 345
Yebaba, 314
Yedaya, 57-8
Yekuno Amlak, emperor, 40, 76, 89, 93, 96, 435
Yelmana Oromo, 319-
Yemerehannä Krestos, *abun*, 121
Yeshaq, *abba*, 369
Yeshaq, *bahr nägash*, vii, 236-8, 269, 286, 439
Yeshaq, emperor, 38, 57-8, 69, 72, 77, 80, 88, 90-1, 94, 154, 162, 270, 436
Yohannes I, emperor, 308-9, 344, 355, 357, 389, 419, 424
Yohannes IV, emperor, 385
Yohannes, *abun*, 411
Yolyos, 326
Yona'él, *azmach*, 300, 325, 352
Yonädab, 188, 205
Yoséf, *abba*, 80, 97-8
Yoséf, of Shärkha, 73

Yostos, emperor, 317, 360
Yusuf ibn Ijdahis, 393
Zä-Däwaro, *abba*, 134
Zä-Dengel, emperor, 394, 428, 441
Zä-Giyorgis, *käntiba*, 369
Zä-Krestos, *bahr nägash*, 410
Zä-Krestos, nobleman, 344
Zä-Maryam, *shum*, 251, 274
Zä-Sellasé, 329, 334
Zä-Wängel, *bahr nägäsh*, 218, 228
Zabid, 105, 235
Zagwé dynasty, 37, 81, 85, 89, 93-4, 96, 434
Zaharbuy 'Uthman, 188-90
Zaharbuy Muhammäd, *amir*, 174, 197, 212, 223
Zähon Dur, 258. See also: Dähondur
Zahraq, 171
Zäkaryas, 89, 97
Zälän, 51
Zämät Keflä, 400-1
Zämbeté, 315
Zamdu, 51
Zämit, 171, 180
Zär Sänay, 219
Zär'a Beruk, 403, 430
Zär'a Ya'qob, emperor, 69, 101-2, 113, 116 -17, 119, 130, 132-5, 141-4, 149, 152, 156-61, 172, 212, 233, 269, 436, 438
Zärji, 189, 224
Zäsäy, 66
Zäylä', 21, 32, 39-40, 47, 51-3, 55, 62, 88, 94-5, 115, 120, 125-9, 157, 168, 241, 246, 248, 254, 259, 374-6, 379-82, 393
Zeba Fätän, 86
Zebédär, 76
zebras, 385
Zéga Wädäb, 312
Zelew, 359
Zema, 286
Zemal, 103
Zéna Marqos, *abba*, 75, 97
Zéna Marqos, *abun*, 54, 68
Zenjeris, 363
Zeqwala, 133, 179, 184, 187, 223
Zewäldä Maryam, *bahr nägash*, 413
Zifah, 166
Zikr Amhara, 56
Zin, 177-9
Zorzi, A., 105, 115, 129, 131, 135
Zorzi, brother, 135
Zway, lake, 76, 141, 207, 283, 285

The Red Sea Press, Inc.
11-D Princess Rd., Lawrenceville, NJ 08648-2319
(609) 844-9583 ◻ FAX: (609) 844-0198
P.O. Box 48, Asmara, ERITREA ◻ Tel/Fax:. 291-1-120707
P.O. Box 40634, Addis Ababa, ETHIOPIA ◻ Tel: 251-1-651073, Fax: 251-1-651100

Legacy of Bitterness
Ethiopia and Fascist Italy, 1935-1941

Alberto Sbacchi

Legacy of Bitterness is a broad description of the Italo Ethiopian war in the global context. The study looks at the response to the war by the emergent Black nationalism in the Diaspora, and Ethiopia's bitter struggle to tip the balance of world opinion in its favor.

Albert Sbacchi is professor of History at Atlantic Union College in Massachussets. The author of three books and numerous articles, Alberto Sbacchi is considered one of the world's leading experts on Italy's involvement in Ethiopia.

0-932415-73-3 *hc* $69.95
0-932415-74-1 *pb* $19.95

A Social History of Ethiopia

Richard Pankhurst

This Volume, dealing with various aspects of Ethiopia's varied social history, is devoted by and large to the northern and central highlands, and covers the period from early medieval times to the reign of Emperor Tewdros II which is considered a turning- point of departure for dramatic changes that were to characterize the late nineteenth and twentieth centuries. The region under review was important in that it constituted the core of the traditional Ethiopian State, and was over centuries to exercise no small influence on the other parts of the country. The area was at the same time distinctive - and formed a cohesive entity - in that it had a unique highland, and predominantly Christian culture. The region is moreover of special interest on account of its indigenous chronicles and hagiographies, and the many descriptions by foreign travelers, which made it, at least until the middle or second half of the nineteenth century, by far best documented part of Ethiopia. It is thus an area that can be studied over a considerable span of time.

0-932415-85-7 *hc* $49.9
0-932415-86-5 *pb* $16.9

Richard Pankhurst, one of the most prolific writers on Ethiopian social hsitory, is the author of *An Introduction to the Medica History of Ethiopia* (RSP 1991) and *The Ethiopian Borderlands* (RSP 1997). He is a former director of the Institute of Ethiopian Studies, Addis Ababa University, Ethiopia.

The Red Sea Press, Inc.
11-D Princess Rd., Lawrenceville, NJ 08648-2319
(609) 844-9583 ◻ FAX: (609) 844-0198
P.O. Box 48, Asmara, ERITREA ◻ Tel/Fax: 291-1-120707
P.O. Box 40634, Addis Ababa, ETHIOPIA ◻ Tel: 251-1-651073, Fax: 251-1-651100

Ras Alula and the Scramble for Africa
A Political Biography: Ethiopia & Eritrea 1875-1897

Haggai Erlich

"Erlich surveys skillfully, and in considerable detail, two of the most eventful decades of Ethiopia's diplomatic history, 1875-97. . . . [He] has unearthed a considerable mass of detail on the Ras's life for which scholars will be grateful."
—*Richard Pankurst*

"[A]n example of a genre comparatively rare in Ethiopian historical studies, . . . [this] work of biography is virtually unique. Erlich's work addresses important questions of contemporary interest."
—*Donald E. Crummey*

The life and times of this great Ethiopian political figure of the 19th century in its vicissitudes reflects some of the major issues in his period. This biography makes a significant contribution in the study of an important chapter in the history of Ethiopia and Eritrea through the experience of a person who was not the head of state. As such it is also an insightful analysis of late 19th-century Ethiopian sociopolitics.

1-56902-028-0 *hc* $59.95
1-56902-029-9 *pb* $18.95

Haggai Erlich, Professor of Middle Eastern and African History at Tel Aviv University, was born in Isreal, and received his Ph.D. from the Uniiversity of London, SOAS, in 1973. He is the author of seven books, and has published extensively on Ethiopian and Middle Eastern history and politics.

Black Lions
The Creative Lives of Modern Ethiopia's Literary Giants and Pioneers

Reidulf K. Molvaer

This is a fascinating portrait of 20th-century Ethiopian writers of fiction and an in-depth analysis of the history of the development of Amharic literature and those who have shaped it, as well as the impact these writers have had on Ethiopian society at large in changing old ideas, contributing towards the modernization of the country and revolutionizing the educational, social and political systems.

Reidulf K. Molvaer is a Norwegian well-versed in Amharic and Ethiopian literature and traditions. He has published several books on Amharic literature, history and social study of modern Ethiopia as well as various development issues relating to Africa.

1-56902-016-7 *hc* $69.95
1-56902-017-5 *pb* $21.95

The Red Sea Press, Inc.

11-D Princess Rd., Lawrenceville, NJ 08648-2319
(609) 844-9583 □ FAX: (609) 844-0198
P.O. Box 48, Asmara, ERITREA □ Tel/Fax:. +291-1-120707
P.O. Box 40634, Addis Ababa, ETHIOPIA □ Tel:. +251-1-651073 Fax: +251-1-651100

TO ORDER:
SEND $4.00 POSTAGE FOR FIRST BOOK, AND $1.00 FOR EACH ADDITIONAL BOOK

		Price	ISBN	Qty.	Amount
Ras Alula and the Scramble for Africa A Political Biography: Ethiopia & Eritrea 1875-1897	Hc	$59.95	1-56902-029-9		
	Pb	$18.95	1-56902-028-0		
Black Lions: The Creative Lives of Modern Ethiopia's Literary Giants and Pioneers	Hc	$69.95	1-56902-016-7		
	Pb	$21.95	1-56902-017-5		
Legacy of Bitterness: Ethiopia and Fascist Italy, 1935-1941	Hc	$69.95	0-932415-73-3		
	Pb	$19.95	0-932415-74-1		
A Social History of Ethiopia	Hc	$49.95	0-932415-85-7		
	Pb	$16.95	0-932415-86-5		

Please make checks or money order payable to: The Red Sea Press, Inc.

Yes, we accept ☐ Discover ☐ Diners Club ☐ Visa ☐ Master Card
☐ American Express (*indicate which card*)

Name _____
Address _____
City _____ State _____ Zip _____
Telephone (___) _____
Credit Card Number _____ Expiration Date _____
X Signature _____

Subtotal
Shipping & Handling
NJ Residents Add 6% Sales Tax
TOTAL

Visit us at our new website at http://www.africanworld.com